HANDBOOK OF ALTERNATIVE THEORIES OF POLITICAL ECONOMY

Handbook of Alternative Theories of Political Economy

Edited by

Frank Stilwell

Professor Emeritus, Department of Political Economy, University of Sydney, Australia

David Primrose

Academic Fellow, Menzies Centre for Health Policy and Economics, University of Sydney, Australia

Tim B. Thornton

Senior Research Fellow, Economics in Context Initiative, Global Development Policy Centre, Boston University, USA

EE Edward Elgar
PUBLISHING

Cheltenham, UK • Northampton, MA, USA

Published by
Edward Elgar Publishing Limited
The Lypiatts
15 Lansdown Road
Cheltenham
Glos GL50 2JA
UK

Edward Elgar Publishing, Inc.
William Pratt House
9 Dewey Court
Northampton
Massachusetts 01060
USA

Paperback edition 2024

A catalogue record for this book
is available from the British Library

Library of Congress Control Number: 2022932634

This book is available electronically in the **Elgar**online
Economics subject collection
http://dx.doi.org/10.4337/9781789909067

ISBN 978 1 78990 905 0 (Hardback)
ISBN 978 1 78990 906 7 (eBook)
ISBN 978 1 0353 3424 7 (Paperback)

Printed and bound by CPI Group (UK) Ltd, Croydon, CR0 4YY

Contents

Contributors

Andreas Bieler, Professor of Political Economy, University of Nottingham. United Kingdom.

Peter J. Boettke, Professor of Economics and Philosophy, George Mason University, United States.

Gavan Butler, Honorary Associate, Department of Political Economy, University of Sydney, Australia.

Jenny Cameron, Conjoint Associate Professor in Geography and Environmental Studies, University of Newcastle, Australia; and Deputy Chair, Community Economies Institute.

Rosolino Candela, Senior Fellow, F. A. Hayek Program for Advanced Study in Philosophy, Politics, and Economics. George Mason University, United States.

Mario Cedrini, Associate Professor, Dipartimento di Economia e Statistica 'Cognetti de Martiis', Università di Torino, Italy.

Robin Chang, PhD Candidate, Department of Politics, York University, Canada.

Brett Christophers, Professor in the Department of Social and Economic Geography at Uppsala University, Sweden.

Jennifer Cohen, Assistant Professor of Global and Intercultural Studies, Miami University, United States; and Joint Researcher with Ezintsha, Wits Reproductive Health and HIV Institute, Faculty of Health Sciences, University of the Witwatersrand, Johannesburg, South Africa.

Joselle Dagnes, Assistant Professor, Dipartimento di Culture, Politica e Società, Università di Torino, Italy.

John B. Davis, Professor Emeritus of Economics, Marquette University, United States; Professor Emeritus of Economics, University of Amsterdam, the Netherlands.

Tim Di Muzio, Associate Professor in International Relations and Critical Political Economy, University of Wollongong, Australia.

Matt Dow, Department of Politics, York University, Canada.

Bill Dunn, Professor of Economics, Kingston University, United Kingdom.

Rinaldo Evangelista, Professor of Economic Policy, University of Camerino, Italy.

Katherine Gibson, Professor, Institute for Culture and Society, Western Sydney University, Australia. She writes her academic contributions under the combined name of J.K. Gibson-Graham.

Penny Griffin, Senior Lecturer in Politics and International Relations, University of New South Wales, Australia.

Heidi Hartmann, Distinguished Economist in Residence, Program on Gender Analysis in Economics, American University; and President Emerita, Institute for Women's Policy Research, United States.

Brett Heino, Lecturer in Law, University of Technology Sydney, Australia.

Arturo Hermann, Senior research fellow at the Italian National Institute of Statistics, Italy.

Bob Jessop, Emeritus Professor of Sociology, Lancaster University, United Kingdom.

Tae-Hee Jo, Associate Professor, Economics and Finance Department, State University of New York, Buffalo State, United States.

Pratistha Joshi Rajkarnikar, Associate Director, Economics in Context Initiative, Global Development Policy Center, Boston University, United States.

John E. King, Emeritus Professor of Economics, La Trobe University, Australia.

David M. Kotz, Emeritus Professor of Economics and Senior Research Fellow in the Political Economy Research Institute, University of Massachusetts Amherst, United States.

Karras J. Lambert, PhD Candidate, Department of Economics, George Mason University, United States.

Nuno Ornelas Martins, Professor of Economics, Católica Porto Business School and CEGE, Universidade Católica Portuguesa, Portugal.

Terrence McDonough, Emeritus Professor of Economics, the National University of Ireland, Galway, Ireland. Sadly, Terry passed away between co-authoring his chapter and this book's publication.

Jamie Morgan, Professor, School of Economics, Analytics and International Business, Leeds Beckett University Business School, United Kingdom.

Adam David Morton, Professor, Department of Political Economy, University of Sydney, Australia.

Franklin Obeng-Odoom, Associate Professor, Global Development Studies, Helsinki Institute of Sustainability Science, University of Helsinki, Finland.

Joy Paton, Senior Lecturer, School of Social Sciences, Western Sydney University, Australia.

Neil Perry, Associate Professor, Corporate Social Responsibility and Sustainability, Western Sydney University, Australia.

Elke Pirgmaier, Postdoctoral researcher, Institute of Geography and Sustainability (IGD), University of Lausanne, Switzerland.

David Primrose, Academic Fellow, Menzies Centre for Health Policy and Economics, University of Sydney, Australia.

Jim Stanford, Director of the Centre for Future Work, Australia and Canada; Honorary Professor, Department of Political Economy, University of Sydney, Australia; Harold Innis Industry Professor of Economics, McMaster University, Canada.

Frank Stilwell, Professor Emeritus, Department of Political Economy, University of Sydney, Australia

Ngai-Ling Sum, Co-director, Cultural Political Economy Research Centre, Lancaster University, United Kingdom.

Dillon Tauzin, PhD Student, Department of Economics, George Mason University, United States.

Tim B. Thornton, Senior Research Fellow, Economics in Context Initiative, Global Development Policy Centre, Boston University, USA.

Phillip Toner, Senior Research Fellow, Department of Political Economy, University of Sydney, Australia.

L. Randall Wray, Professor of Economics, Bard College; Senior Scholar, Levy Economics Institute, United States.

PART I

POLITICAL ECONOMY AS AN
AREA OF KNOWLEDGE

1.   Introduction to the *Handbook of Alternative Theories of Political Economy*

Frank Stilwell, David Primrose and Tim B. Thornton

Political economy is the study of the material basis of human societies. It analyses the process of provisioning, whereby goods and services are produced for profit and/or the satisfaction of human need. It considers the ideas, interests and institutions that shape those processes, the power they exercise and the distributional outcomes that result. Relatedly, it explores the systemic dynamics in which these processes are configured, and their implications for the reproduction of both humanity and the ecological systems we inhabit. As a mode of inquiry, it is inherently complex and controversial because economic issues are entwined with socio-cultural concerns and political judgements.

As a field of knowledge, the subject has fundamental importance and intrinsic interest because people are drawn to understand the forces and processes that shapes their livelihoods and well-being. Anyone who engages in systematic thinking about the opportunities and hazards they face in making a living is taking a first step in political economy, the more so when they also consider the broader social context in which they function. Careful consideration of the inter-related factors that shape the material conditions of our lives, individually and collectively, leads to reflection on how economic, social and environmental aspects inter-relate.

The recurrence of deep problems in the world around us throws these concerns into particularly sharp relief. The global Coronavirus crisis that began in early 2020, for example, made us all more aware of the fragile nexus of socio-ecological preconditions and health on which the prevailing global political order rests. Twelve years earlier, the onset of the global financial crisis had highlighted how a precarious global economic system could impact the livelihoods of ordinary people. History is replete with such examples.

It is not just intermittent crises that create concerns, however. Many political economic problems are persistent, some of steadily mounting intensity. Consider, for example, inequalities in the distribution of income and wealth that result from the stark differences of economic opportunity and power between people in different socio-economic circumstances, particularly those relating to class, race and gender. Think of the entrenched problems of hunger, water insecurity and poverty that persist in different forms across the global South and North. Think too of the problems of economic insecurity, arising from more 'flexible' labour markets that favour employers but make incomes from paid work more precarious and irregular for a growing proportion of workers. Yet other concerns relate to the processes of privatisation and financialisation that have shifted more risks to households and individuals who are often ill-equipped to cope.

Overshadowing all these stresses is the biggest challenge of all – environmental degradation, manifest most acutely as climate change. To probe its political economic roots requires analysing the unsustainably extractivist forms of production on which much modern economic activity is based. Some six decades ago, political economist J.K. Galbraith ([1958] 1999) asserted that the fundamental economic problem of production – producing sufficient goods and services to meet the basic needs of all – had been largely solved in the affluent nations. It was not a complacent statement because it underpinned his call for much more attention to be given to problems of inequality, poverty, and the imbalance between private affluence and public squalor. Galbraith also identified the issue of *how* production occurs – whether by ecologically sustainable process or not – as a growing problem. However, these early alarm bells were insufficiently heeded by mainstream economists and economic policymakers (Galbraith 2020). Global problems of economic insecurity, maldistribution and ecological stress have become increasingly acute. Effective policy responses guided by appropriate political economic analysis are now required more than ever.

FROM TUNNEL VISION TO ALTERNATIVE WAYS OF SEEING

To come to terms with these overlapping and substantial challenges requires correspondingly broad and deep economic analysis. The narrow focus that is characteristic of mainstream economic theory – centred on a neoclassical theory of individuals each seeking their maximum utility and interacting in self-equilibrating markets – cannot suffice. Abstract economic theorising that is devoid of social and historical analysis seriously limits comprehension of the complexity and unpredictability of any real economic system, especially that of capitalism. It produces tunnel vision; and going deeper into that tunnel is unlikely to cast light on the big issues of current political economic concern. Indeed, confining oneself to neoclassical economic theory to confront the complex, existential challenges facing the contemporary global economy suggests that any 'light at the end of the tunnel is probably the headlight of another train approaching us from the opposite direction' (Žižek 2017: xii).

A more comprehensive, critical political economic perspective is needed. This entails more than expanding the terrain to include political as well as economic considerations, as the term 'political economy' might seem to imply to outsiders. Indeed, just bringing in political considerations deepens the problems if the political analysis adopts the methodological individualism of neoclassical economics. Such is the case with 'public choice' theory, as promulgated by the Virginia school and others. Political economy, properly understood, is not about broadening the topics to which neoclassical economic tools are applied: rather it is about constructing an alternative means of understanding the real world. There is a rich and long history of sometimes complementary and sometimes competing theoretical traditions that provide a basis for doing so. Based on these alternatives, political economy adopts a critical and social scientific epistemology, contrasting with the neoclassical attempt to replicate the formalism and universalism of the natural sciences. Political economy adopts a more pluralist approach to economic knowledge, acknowledging the diversity of interpretations that need to be considered when studying social phenomena. This is also reflected in political economy's interdisciplinary character, drawing insights from a range of different disciplines – such as geography, history, sociology, anthropology, political science, psychology, and environmental studies – to inform and extend its study of economic issues.

Of course, such an expansive, diverse project creates its own challenges. Judgements must be made – for instance, about how to select from or combine different, sometimes incommensurable, conceptual toolkits and methods of analysis. Similarly, it is necessary to reflect on how best to balance abstract, conceptual analysis with more empirically grounded inquiries.

Explicitly ethical considerations must also be faced when applying knowledge to inform public policies or the strategies of social movements seeking to challenge the status quo. The attention given to these difficult, yet vital, questions is a hallmark of the political economy approach.

The key characteristics of political economy need careful consideration, recognising that it has been a great, evolving tradition of thought during the last three centuries. Its most salient features have developed in parallel with the emergence, evolution and increasing global dominance of capitalism. Early expressions included foundational works by classical political economists such as Adam Smith, David Ricardo and John Stuart Mill, all of whom would have understood themselves to be practising a unified social science (Milonakis and Fine 2009). Following the classical political economists, key contributors such as Karl Marx, Thorstein Veblen and John Maynard Keynes paved the way for other political economic thinkers whose ideas are also explored in subsequent chapters in this book. Notably too, the very depth and breadth of this field of inquiry means that other disciplines also have legitimate claims to have produced key contributors to political economic knowledge. The concern to transcend neat, abstract formalisations of economic processes is a common theme. Modern political economy, like the earlier classical political economy, can be regarded as seeking to form a unified, if diverse, social science that focuses on the production and distribution of goods and services in all economic spheres while seeking to integrate the study of those economic features into a broader understanding of society.

Following Tabb (1999), we regard this broad social science approach to political economy as representing the *mainline* tradition in understanding economic phenomena. It is a view that directly challenges neoclassical economists' claims to centrality in the analysis of economic matters. As political economists, we regard the neoclassical approach to economic inquiry as a side-line that branched off from the mainline after the 'marginal revolution' in economic thought that occurred in the 1870s (albeit a side-line carrying an enormous volume of traffic). Having branched off in its own peculiar intellectual journey, neoclassical economics has picked up assorted fellow travellers along the way. The characterisation of economic orthodoxy therefore needs to be more nuanced nowadays, acknowledging that some internal diversity has emerged, albeit within a context of striking continuities and constraints (Madra 2017). Thus, it is traditional neoclassical theory, awkwardly augmented with subfields such as new behavioural economics, that currently constitutes the core of mainstream economics. Nevertheless, our general claim remains – that an 'economic *mainstream*' (comprising neoclassical economics and its offshoots) should be distinguished from a longer, richer and broader political economic *mainline*. Figure 1.1 presents a simple schematic image of this relationship.

Of course, depicting and classifying academic disciplines cannot really be quite as tidy as Figure 1.1 portrays; and we certainly do not claim that such matters are simple and agreed upon. Indeed, there are *always* problems with the fuzziness of disciplinary boundaries and in classifying complex objects such as social science disciplines (Mearman 2010, 2011, 2012). Nonetheless, we take the view that political economy is distinct from mainstream economics, which is in turn distinct from all other social sciences – notwithstanding its increasing penetration into the latter during recent decades. Mainstream economics is highly unusual in its methodological and theoretical commitments and in its fundamentally different ontological foundations (Potts 2000), making it an offshoot from political economy and from social science in general.

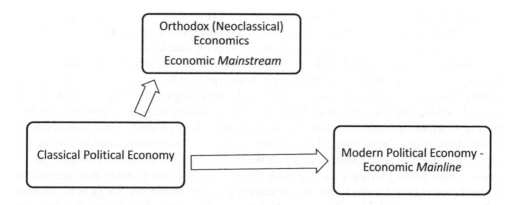

Figure 1.1   Economic mainstream v. economic mainline

POLITICAL ECONOMY AS CONTESTED TERRAIN

How then can political economy provide a penetrating and practical form of analysis of what is happening 'out there' in the world? Not surprisingly, this is a matter of ongoing controversy, reflecting different interpretations of the subject area and alternative analytical approaches. All the major thinkers in both classical and modern political economy have sought to analyse the nature and determinants of economic activity and how the economy might be changed to produce more socially propitious outcomes. Inspired by these big thinkers, many other academics, writers, teachers and activists have contributed to political economic thought. Sometimes this work is undertaken with the designation 'heterodox economics' rather than political economy. This 'heterodox' label covers the concerns of various schools of thought that have a dissident relationship to the orthodoxy.[1] Whether operating under the label of heterodox economics or political economy, the dissident approach enables an optimism of *both* the intellect and the will – as emancipatory social science should (Olin-Wright 2011).

Because political economists seek alternative understandings and strategies, critique of the orthodoxy is a necessary starting point. In the current era, the critique must acknowledge the modicum of internal diversity within orthodox economics, including the contestable idea of an 'internal heterodoxy within orthodoxy' said to be constituted by the development of sub-fields such as game theory, new institutional economics, new growth theory, complexity economics, environmental economics, behavioural economics and neuroeconomics (Colander 2000; Thornton 2015, 2016; Primrose 2017). As noted earlier, this diversity within mainstream economics indicates some points of departure from neoclassical economics. However, we consider it best understood as an 'air and variations' approach to the subject, having significant continuities with the ontological, methodological and theoretical features of the traditional neoclassical approach. The latter still pervades most teaching, applied and policy work understood as 'mainstream' or 'orthodox' economics. Moreover, looking at how the discipline relates to the real world 'out there', it is evident that an implicit and sometimes explicit political bias in favour of the status quo, perhaps with minor modifications, also remains in much of what orthodox economists commonly claim to be objective, value-neutral analysis. In general, the intellectual tools continue to be either inadequate, irrelevant, or counter-productive for the task of building a more stable, equitable and sustainable world.

There is therefore broad agreement among political economists in rejecting the current economic orthodoxy and in seeking an alternative to it. Indeed, this *unity in opposition* provides political economy with its most obvious source of cohesion – the belief that better alternatives to orthodoxy exist and that the broader social interest would be well served if those alternatives gained greater policy influence, research support and space in the curriculum. Contemporary political economists also have – and certainly need – some degree of *unity in diversity*. Their research, writing and teaching is notably non-monolithic in many respects. A pluralist commitment is therefore fundamental to working together and making progress. Some individuals or groups that self-describe as political economists or heterodox economists claim to provide *the* preferred alternative to orthodoxy, calling on the rest of us to file in behind. However, many others, whilst holding strongly to their own views, recognise that plurality can function to extend knowledge and, indeed, that 'real science is pluralist' (Fullbrook 2001). A key reason is that engagement with ideas from other traditions within political economy often helps to complete, clarify or improve aspects of one's own theories (Lavoie 2020).

This concern with pluralism is more than a point of demarcation between political economy and mainstream economics. It also serves to highlight fundamentally different preconceptions of reality – what can be called differences of 'pre-analytical vision' (Schumpeter 1954: 42). In explaining why this is so, we emphasise the difference between political economy's *open-system* reality and orthodoxy's *closed-system* reality (Dow 2007; Thornton, Chapter 28 in this volume). Whilst values of tolerance and open-mindedness support pluralism, it is political economy's ontological foundations that provide the deeper intellectual rationale for co-informing dialogues within the discipline and with other disciplines (Dow 2007).

Pluralism does not mean 'anything goes'; nor is it inconsistent with the quest for synthesis. Modern political economy features a mix of both agreement and disagreement about many matters, including which analytical frameworks are most useful and productive for dealing with specific issues. Complementary and competing ideas coexist. There are lively debates within and between those working in traditions as diverse as Marxism, post-Keynesianism, institutionalism, feminism, ecological and evolutionary political economy. As in other disciplines, a competition of ideas occurs on the terrain of reason and evidence in pursuit of authority, influence and impact, both within and beyond the discipline.

Given this diversity, it is important to consider what points of articulation between the currents of thought within political economy are most promising. For instance, can work at the interface between Marxist and institutional political economy get the 'best of both worlds' by combining an analytical structure centred on the capital–labour relationship and the dynamics of capitalism with 'grounded' study of real institutions wielding economic power in diverse ways? Modern proponents of the 'capital as power', 'social structures of accumulation' and 'regulationist' approaches to political economy, for example, may respond to such a question by claiming that their analyses offer exactly this type of 'fusion cooking', although the nature of the dishes served varies in each case. Other schools of thought would make different claims for their relevance. For example, Georgist political economy, often regarded as having peripheral status, offers analysis focused on the economic processes and social relations associated with landed property, which can be especially salient in dealing with topics such as housing crises and inequality.

The presence of these diverse currents of thought within political economy raises myriad other questions that are pertinent for the direction of the discipline. For instance, can and should competing approaches be combined to comprehend the diverse factors shaping political economic processes? Bringing in considerations of the natural world, what insights can political economy provide for comprehending the direction of ecological reproduction through exploring the contradictions arising from capital–labour–landed property relations? What, too, of gender and race as dimensions of social relations that intersect with class, giving rise to complex patterns of stratification, exploitation, oppression and domination? How should the interrelations between capitalist and non-capitalist economic dynamics be conceptualised? Are there particularly fruitful articulations of these currents in political economy that deserve greater attention and research? Seeking to address such questions pervades the construction of modern political economy and generates much of its intellectual ferment.

What then of the possibilities of theoretical synthesis; and is that search for synthesis compatible with our earlier argument for the necessity of pluralism as an inevitable and desirable response to the complex and ever shifting nature of economic and social reality? We think it is, because pluralism is the precondition for seeking progress through contestation between the various schools of thought. It is the *process* of recognising legitimate diversity while continually seeking elements of (at least partial) synthesis that constitutes the best way forward. To this we would add that inevitable differences of values and purposes will usually lead to different ways of looking and selecting. Accordingly, progress in political economy is about both ongoing diversity and probing the possibility of productive synthesis.

It may be illuminating to consider the following analogy with stage lighting:

> One way of grasping the necessarily paradigmatic nature of academic scholarship in the social sciences is to deploy the image of spotlights beaming down upon a stage. At the core of the image is the notion of the stage lit from different points high above the stage itself. In such a theater, each spotlight throws a particular part of the stage into clearest relief, and leaves slightly darker and unexplored areas caught in the center of the other beams. In such a universe of stages and lights, general intellectual progress comes from the examination of the conceptual and theoretical structures within each spotlight, and from a comparative assessment of their relative strengths and weaknesses [...] we need to understand what is going on within each beam of light (what concepts and theories each contains), what the strengths and weaknesses of each beam turn out to be, and what – if any – illuminates most of the stage on which all of them are at play. (Coates 2005: 2)

To this, we would add that the various 'spotlights' can partly or significantly overlap, further illuminating a particular area of the stage. If the view offered by different spotlights seems largely the same, it can increase our confidence that what we think we see is, in fact, there. Furthermore, it may sometimes be the case that using more than one light at a time – that is, pluralism – might offer the best way to illuminate as much of the stage as possible.

An alternative, and perhaps more familiar, comparison is not with lights but with *lenses*. Seeing different schools of thought in political economy as lenses through which we can look at the world adds a further relevant consideration: that lenses are capable of both clarifying and distorting, sometimes doing so simultaneously. Progress requires careful engagement with the alternatives on offer, paying due attention to both the insights they provide and the problems of incommensurability that may inhibit synthesis.

DEVELOPING THE CONTENTS OF THIS BOOK

Given that political economy is characterised by an ongoing contest of ideas, someone wanting to make informed choices on such matters needs to able to understand and evaluate the principal schools of political economic thought that currently exist.[2] This book is designed to assist its readers to do exactly that. It represents a substantial stocktaking of the current 'state of the art', providing an overview of the most significant currents of thought within political economy, including both canonical and cutting-edge ideas. This should allow the reader to make a more educated choice between schools of thought; and to form judgements as to if and how different approaches may be combined when trying to understand political economic phenomena.

We have adopted a broad, inclusive approach in this volume that is not only pluralist but also, to some extent, interdisciplinary. This latter feature may be regarded as another way in which political economy can be differentiated from 'heterodox economics' as well as from economic orthodoxy. Heterodox economics, whilst internally pluralist, tends (but not always) to focus on the interplay of the more obviously 'economic' variables. We view political economy as having more porous disciplinary boundaries because it seeks to engage with the challenges thrown up in a complex and continuously changing economic, social, political and environmental reality. Indeed, many political economic issues cannot be understood without applying concepts developed within cognate fields of inquiry. In doing so, modern political economy is again illustrating that it is part of a 'mainline' tradition that goes back to classical political economy.

This conception of political economy has led us, as editors, to include chapters on topics where there are shared concerns with other social sciences. There are chapters on cultural political economy, spatial political economy, ecological political economy, social structures of accumulation, and the diverse economies tradition, together with consideration of the legacies of influential figures in the social sciences such as Joseph Schumpeter, Henry George and Karl Polanyi, and modern contributions in fields such as behavioural economics, neuroeconomics, and poststructuralist and postcolonial thought.

In compiling the contents of the book, we have had to consider numerous conceptual and organisational challenges. Can the various schools of thought be clearly distinguished? How many can sensibly be included in a single volume? Are all of them of equal status; or are some more central and others peripheral? How are they defined in relation to each other; and do they benefit from mutual engagement, even vigorous contestation? These are open questions that we encourage you to bear in mind as you read on. You will see that, while we have organised chapters mainly according to conventional categories, we have done so in a way that tends to raise important questions about what is conducive to further progress.

The ethical and normative elements in political economic thought are also clearly present in many of the following chapters. This is as it should be, because making explicit ethical judgements is another of the factors distinguishing political economy from orthodox economics. Of course, the orthodoxy is no more value-free than political economy, much as many economists deny or do not realise it. The values embodied in political economic analysis typically have a reformist or radical orientation, thus tending to occupy the left side of the conventional 'political spectrum', though not exclusively so. However, there is nothing in the intellectual foundations of political economy that dictates any particular ideological or political affiliation. Accordingly, this handbook contains contributions that are drawn from across the ideological spectrum – conservative, liberal, social democratic and radical – all claiming to offer a means to increased understanding and a particular vision of what is viable and desirable. Political economy is not defined by a particular political stance: rather, its common element is the view that all economics is political, whether explicitly or implicitly.

As co-editors, we initially considered the possibility of organising the book's contents according to aspects of the real world that political economists need to analyse and illuminate. That would have meant including sections on topics such as the environmental problems caused by economic activities, the nature of economic inequalities, the drivers of economic growth and crises, the character of globalisation, financialisation, neoliberalism, and so forth. This topic-oriented approach has previously been adopted in other recent political economic volumes (see Jo et al. 2017; Deane and Van Waeyenberge 2020; Dunn 2020; Hermann and Mouatt 2020). Our 'schools of thought' approach complements these existing works by focusing on the analytical frameworks within which those diverse issues are studied. We think this different perspective is essential because how one *decides* to look almost always affects what one sees. Focusing on schools of thought, rather than topics or 'issues', thereby brings the questions of framing and selection of analytical tool-kits to the centre of attention. It highlights *why* and *how* political economists address real-world issues – whether of inequality, globalisation, the socio-economic determinants of health or whatever. In other words, we take the view that the best way to understand what political economists do is by studying the lenses through which they observe the challenges thrown up in a changing world. With this conceptual orientation, we are then better able to systematically engage with those real-world issues.

Following this editorial introduction, the book begins with a chapter that provides the reader with a clear sense of political economy as an area of knowledge. Its focus is the urgent problem of climate change, which is a topic not confined to political economy, of course. However, it is the *way* the topic is approached that is distinctive, particularly when compared with mainstream economics. The analysis is *interdisciplinary* in the way its spans the economic, social and ecological. It is also *pluralist* in that it is the product of deep engagement with both Marxist political economy and ecological economics that has produced a creative synthesis whereby alternative foundations and directions are offered to ecological political economy. The chapter also illustrates that political economic analysis can be bold in both diagnosis and prescription. For example, there is both the willingness and the capacity to look for underlying structural causes (and solutions) to problems as well as an openness to activist, radical and creative strategies of change. This contribution from an exciting young scholar in political economy is thus an appropriate way to start the journey through the book.

Five main sections follow. Part II, 'Identifying Foundational Approaches to Political Economy' comprises six chapters that deal with classical political economy, Marxism, institutional political economy, post-Keynesianism, feminist political economy and the Sraffian school. In our view, these are key, longstanding traditions within political economic thought, each continuing to evolve and develop in important and interesting directions. The proponents of other schools of thought commonly define their approaches to political economy in relation to the features of these foundational traditions. The chapters take stock of their characteristics, achievements and potential for further development.

Part III, 'Analysing the Dynamics of Economic Systems' considers a cluster of other important and distinctive approaches to modern political economy. Their proponents may claim comparable significance to those previously considered. The section begins with consideration of the processes of circular and cumulative causation that shape socio-economic change. It continues with chapters on the contributions to political economy made by proponents of evolutionary political economy, neo-Schumpeterian economics, regulation theory, social structures of accumulation, capital as power, modern monetary theory and the Austrian school. In each case, the reader is presented with an outline of the essential features of the area of knowledge, enabling contemplation of how it sits in relation to other schools of thought within political economy.

In Part IV, 'Exploring Socio-ecological Foundations of Economic Systems' the subject matters are diverse; but they share, as a broadly common theme, concern to understand the economy in terms of its interconnections with society and nature. The differences arise from how the connections are identified and analysed within political economy. Successive chapters explore the influence of Karl Polanyi and Henry George in political economy, ecological economics, social economics, the social property relations approach to studying inequalities of class, gender and race, the systems of provision approach, and the diverse economies approach. In their distinctively different ways, these chapters variously seek to conceptualise political economic issues as inexorably social and/or ecological and to establish analytical approaches that build on, but also challenge, the foundational traditions. Together, these chapters significantly broaden the agenda and ambitions for political economy.

Further broadening comes in Part V, 'Extending Political Economy Through Interdisciplinarity'. The emphasis here is on linking modern political economy with insights derived from other disciplinary perspectives. The chapters explore spatial political economy, cultural political economy, poststructuralism and postcolonialism (the 'posts' in political economy), and behavioural economics and neuroeconomics. The key questions are: what's in, what's out and what, if anything, does political economy gain by expanding its terrain in these various directions?

These first four sections of the book indicate a large and variegated territory. Readers may well find themselves reflecting on whether all these currents within political economic thought are compatible; and which they feel most attracted to, and why. They might also be contemplating how these ideas can create progress in political economy, and ultimately, progress in making a better world. Five chapters that explore principles and paths towards those goals comprise Part VI, 'Making a Difference'. Topics include the nature and role of pluralism in political economic thought; economics imperialism and interdisciplinary social science; different measures and approaches to assessing what constitutes 'progress'; strategies for educational change; and formulating an activist praxis that links academic analyses with economic and political struggles in the broader society. Concluding the volume with these topics invites readers to engage with the complex, yet necessarily normative, question implicitly arising from the conceptual schools explored in preceding chapters: 'what is to be done?'

CONSIDERING CHALLENGES IN POLITICAL ECONOMY

The allocation of chapters between these five main sections of the book is not intended to be hard and fast nor definitive. Indeed, because many chapters' concerns are interconnected, they might well have been organised in a different order or according to different general themes. Rather like offering a smorgasbord lunch, we're happy for diners to sample the various dishes in whatever is their preferred order.

As editors, we are mindful that the menu, although already large, might be considered deficient in particular ways. Indeed, there are other approaches to, or touching upon, political economy that get only brief mention in the present volume. For instance, burgeoning research in *psychoanalytic political economy* asserts that analysis of logics of capital accumulation must be accompanied by consideration of the psychodynamic mechanisms that drive these processes (Özselçuk and Madra 2010; Tomšič 2013). *Social reproduction theory* explores the inexorable interrelation between the production of goods and services and production of life, highlighting how the regeneration of human life (and, thus, labour power) underpins the obstinacy of capitalism (Bhattacharya 2017; Ferguson 2019). *Complexity economics* conceptualises economic systems as complex, non-equilibrating systems, comprising a nexus of dynamically interacting, heterogeneous agents distinguished by evolving behaviours, strategies and social interactions (Elsner 2017; Heise 2017). *Stratification economics* seeks to explain the dynamics of economic inequality based on the separation or stratification of social groups according to relative group status (Davis 2015; Obeng-Odoom 2020). These analytical currents, although not fully explored in dedicated chapters, get some consideration in various chapters of the current volume. They are indicative of ongoing innovations, creating theoretical insights that are potentially complementary, albeit developing them in distinctive directions.

Some other uncertainties about boundary issues also deserve mention. Consider Austrian economics, for example. This has been a distinctive school of thought for more than a century, having its own journals and academic community. However, it is not always regarded as part of political economy or heterodox economics (see, for example, Lee 2009). That this exclusion commonly occurs is not wholly surprising, given the school's commitments to methodological individualism and subjectivism, together with the common observation about its close ties with the genesis of neoliberalism. Whether this exclusionary orientation *should* occur is far less clear, however. The 'Austrian Socialism' of Burczak (2009) or the recent ideological makeover of Hayek undertaken by some evolutionary economists (Sloan Wilson 2015) illustrate the interesting ways in which the ideas of the Austrian school can be related to other traditions in political economy, as well as the openness of various Austrian economists to engage with fellow political economists. Intellectual trade and possible gains from this trade need careful consideration.

Other schools of thought considered in the volume also deal with quite strongly contested territories. Behavioural economics, neuroeconomics and evolutionary economics are prominent examples because they have been proudly proclaimed as illustrations of the 'internal heterodoxy' within contemporary mainstream economics (Colander et al. 2004; Colander 2009). Yet, as indicated by the two chapters on these schools of thought, mainstream economics has a striking ability to absorb new or dissident ideas on its own terms and in a manner that protects its commitments to extant, longstanding techniques, methods and goals. A similar point could be illustrated through examining the differences between the 'new' and 'old' institutional economics (Hodgson 2002), or macroeconomics drawing on new-Keynesian versus post-Keynesian economics (Rotheim 2014).

Whether some of the approaches included in this book constitute distinct schools of political economic thought, rather than branches of other longstanding schools, is also an open question. For example, the capital as power, social structures of accumulation, and systems of provision approaches might be considered primarily as variants of Marxist political economy. Modern Monetary Theory might be seen as essentially post-Keynesian (as argued by Lavoie 2019), rather than the separate school of thought as is implied by at least some of its practitioners (for example, Mitchell 2015). The authors of Chapter 9, 'Circular and Cumulative Causation' even state explicitly that they regard it as a principle rather than a school of thought; and indeed, it is a 'way of seeing' that can be woven into many types of political economic analysis. Is that a strength or weakness? We take the former view but, either way, the very fact that certain concepts are so widely utilised by political economists justifies their prominent presence on the menu here.

Suffice to say that the proponents of all these analytical approaches challenge conventional economic understandings, are heterodox and clearly within the field of political economy. Resolving all questions of categorisation and intellectual lineage, though perhaps a laudable aim, is unlikely to readily occur. Our intention here is to not to try and impose a rigid taxonomy on the field, but to instead facilitate access to the many principal currents and tributaries of political economy. We hope that it offers a productive, interesting and illuminating journey.

SHOWCASING A SCHOLARLY COMMUNITY

Political economists are all engaged in an ongoing process of seeking to understand the world and to contribute knowledge that may help change it for the better. They form a broad, global scholarly community, albeit sometimes seemingly more united in what they are against rather than in developing a common programme. How we, as editors, decided who, from among that community, would be invited to contribute to a book requires some explanation. We tried to select a wide range of authors known for their expertise in the various schools of thought and approaches to political economy, mixing established leaders in their fields with younger contributors known for their innovative contributions. Each author was invited to set out in their chapter what they regard as the general state of political economic thought in the field, to point to problems and variations, and to indicate what could be conducive to further progress.

It is also pertinent to state the editors' own institutional affiliations and experiences, because these have undoubtedly influenced our ways of viewing the territory, as well as possibilities for development and change. Two of us (Frank and David) have been primarily associated with teaching and research in the Department of Political Economy at the University of Sydney. The Department was born out of more than four decades of struggle (documented in Butler et al. 2009) and has since become known for what a US economist described as the 'world's most distinctive undergraduate program in heterodox economics' (Nesiba 2012). Frank played a central role in establishing the Department and designing its curriculum, before becoming the first Professor of Political Economy. David subsequently enjoyed the fruits of these efforts, completing his undergraduate, master's and doctoral degrees within the Department, where he has also worked as a lecturer, tutor, research assistant and project manager. The third editor (Tim) has worked in the Economics Departments at Monash and La Trobe Universities in Melbourne, and directed a Politics, Philosophy and Economics Degree and Master of International Development programme whilst working in the Department of Politics and Philosophy at La Trobe. He has also worked with the Economics in Context Initiative at Boston University, where he retains an ongoing affiliation as a research fellow. He has recently established an independent School of Political Economy, which offers tertiary-level political economic education from outside the confines of the university to a student cohort that has quickly become global. Our collective teaching experiences have made us keenly aware of what students can achieve through the systematic study of political economy, the pedagogic choices political economists need to make, and the ongoing challenges that must be faced if political economic ideas are to have traction beyond the groves of academe. In our different ways, we have grappled with the challenges of making progress in political economy, both within universities and beyond, and this has influenced our work as editors of this collection.

Putting the book together has been a pleasure. For this, as co-editors, we primarily thank each other! We are also deeply grateful to all the chapter authors for their fine contributions, their willingness to work within the imposed constraints of time and space – especially during the difficult conditions imposed by the global Covid-19 crisis – and for their cooperation with the editors during the processes of revision. We welcomed the invitation from Edward Elgar to compile and edit this book, and thank Alexandra O'Connell, our primary contact, for her enthusiasm and all the production team for their excellent work in bringing the project to fruition. Finally, to our families and loved ones, we express warm appreciation for your ongoing support and patience while we completed the volume.

Periodically taking stock is always important, whatever the enterprise or undertaking. The key questions are always: 'what do we have?', 'what do we need?' and 'what strategy will get us from where we are to where we want to be?' This *Handbook of Alternative Theories of Political Economy* offers some responses to those questions and much food for thought that should be helpful in formulating personal assessments. We hope that it will be useful to readers seeking to understand the established and cutting-edge ideas within political economy, providing a powerful means to better understand the world in which we live and offering useful tools for improving it.

NOTES

1. For a discussion on relative merits of the descriptor 'political economy' versus 'heterodox economics', see Stilwell (2016). We see compelling intellectual and strategic reasons for preferring of the term 'political economy', although we acknowledge that some contributors to this volume may prefer the term heterodox economics. The strength of the critiques and the value of the alternative schools of thought on offer are largely unaffected by this terminological preference.
2. The alternative that political economy offers to mainstream economics is a rationale for this book's title. The emphasis throughout is on the plurality of alternatives. Were it not for the publisher's preference for consistent labels across a series of different subject areas, the book might just as readily be titled 'Handbook of Theories of Political Economy'.

REFERENCES

Bhattacharya, T. (2017) *Social Reproduction Theory: Remapping Class, Recentering Oppression*, London: Pluto Press.

Burczak, T. (2009) 'Why Austrian socialism?', *Review of Austrian Economics*, **22**, pp. 297–300.

Butler, G., Jones, E. and Stilwell, F. (2009) *Political Economy Now! The Struggle for Alternative Economics at the University of Sydney*, Sydney: Darlington Press.

Coates, D. (ed.) (2005) *Varieties of Capitalism, Varieties of Approaches*, Basingstoke: Palgrave Macmillan.

Colander, D.C. (2000) 'The death of neoclassical economics', *Journal of the History of Economic Thought*, **22** (June): pp. 127–43.

Colander, D.C. (2009) 'Moving beyond the rhetoric of pluralism: suggestions for an "inside-the-mainstream" heterodoxy', in Garnett, R.F., Olsen, E. and Starr, M. (eds), *Economic Pluralism*, Hoboken, NJ: Taylor and Francis, pp. 36–47.

Colander, D.C., Rosser, B.J. and Holt, R.P.F. (2004) 'The changing face of mainstream economics', *Review of Political Economy*, **16** (4), pp. 485–99.

Davis, J.B. (2015) 'Stratification economics and identity economics', *Cambridge Journal of Economics*, **39** (5), pp. 1215–29.

Deane, K. and van Waeyenberge, E. (eds) (2020) *Recharting the History of Economic Thought*, London: Red Globe Press.

Dow, S.C. (2007) 'Pluralism in economics', in Groenewegen, J. (ed.), *Teaching Pluralism in Economics*, Cheltenham, UK and Northampton, MA, USA: Edward Elgar Publishing, pp. 22–39.

Dunn, B. (ed.) (2020) *A Research Agenda for Critical Political Economy*, Cheltenham, UK and Northampton, MA, USA: Edward Elgar Publishing.

Elsner, W. (2017) 'Economics as heterodoxy: theory and policy', *Journal of Economic Issues*, **51** (4), pp. 939–78.

Ferguson, S. (2019) *Women and Work: Feminism, Labour, and Social Reproduction*, London: Pluto Press.

Fullbrook, E. (2001) 'Real science is pluralist', *Post-Autistic Economics Review*, March, http://www.paecon.net/PAEtexts/Fullbrook1.htm.

Galbraith, J.K. ([1958] 1999) *The Affluent Society*, London: Penguin.

Galbraith, J.K. (2020) 'Economics and the climate catastrophe', *Globalizations*, accessed 1.9.2021 at https://www.tandfonline.com/doi/full/10.1080/14747731.2020.1807858.

Heise, A. (2017) 'Whither economic compleoopsxity? A new heterodox economic paradigm or just another variation within the mainstream?', *International Journal of Pluralism and Economics Education*, **8** (2), pp. 115–29.

Hermann, A. and Mouatt, S. (eds) (2020) *Contemporary Issues in Heterodox Economics: Implications for Theory and Policy Action*, London and New York: Routledge.

Hodgson, G.M. (2002) *How Economics Forgot History: The Problem of Historical Specificity in Social Science*, London and New York: Routledge.

Jo, T.-H., Chester, L. and D'Ippoliti, C. (eds) (2017) *The Routledge Handbook of Heterodox Economics: Theorizing, Analyzing, and Transforming Capitalism*, London and New York: Routledge.

Lavoie, M. (2019) 'Modern monetary theory and post-Keynesian economics', *Real-World Economics Review*, **89**, pp. 97–108.

Lavoie, M. (2020) 'Heterodox economics as seen by Geoffrey Hodgson: an assessment', *European Journal of Economics and Economic Policies: Intervention*, **17** (1), pp. 9–18.

Lee, F.S. (2009) *A History of Heterodox Economics: Challenging the Mainstream in the Twentieth Century*, London: Routledge.

Madra, Y.M. (2017) *Late Neoclassical Economics: The Restoration of Theoretical Humanism in Contemporary Economic Theory*, London and New York: Routledge.

Mearman, A. (2010) 'What is this thing called "heterodox economics"?', Working Paper, Bristol: University of West England.

Mearman, A. (2011) 'Who do Heterodox Economists think they are?', *American Journal of Economics and Sociology*, **70**, pp. 480–510.

Mearman, A. (2012) '"Heterodox economics" and the problems of classification', *Journal of Economic Methodology*, **19** (4), pp. 407–24.

Milonakis, D. and Fine, B. (2009) *From Political Economy to Economics: Method, the Social and the Historical in the Evolution of Economic Theory*, London: Routledge.

Mitchell, W. (2015) 'The roots of MMT do not lie in Keynes', *Bill Mitchell – Modern Monetary Theory*, accessed on 25.7.21 at http://bilbo.economicoutlook.net/blog/?p=31681.

Nesiba, R. (2012) 'What do undergraduates study in heterodox economics programs?', *On the Horizon*, **20** (3), pp. 182–93.

Obeng-Odoom, F. (2020) *Property, Institutions and Social Stratification in Africa*, Cambridge: Cambridge University Press.

Özselçuk, C. and Madra, Y.M. (2010) 'Enjoyment as an economic factor: reading Marx with Lacan', *Subjectivity*, **3**, pp. 323–47.

Potts, J. (2000) *The New Eolutionary Microeconomics: Complexity, Competence, and Adaptive Behaviour*, Cheltenham, UK and Northampton, MA, USA: Edward Elgar Publishing.

Primrose, D. (2017) 'The subjectification of *Homo economicus* in behavioural economics', *Journal of Australian Political Economy*, **80**, pp. 88–128.

Rotheim, R. (ed.) (2014) *New Keynesian Economics/Post Keynesian Alternatives*, London: Routledge.

Schumpeter, J.A. (1954) *History of Economic Analysis*, London: Allen & Unwin.

Sloan Wilson, D. (2015) 'The Libertarian economist Friedrich Hayek gets a makeover: rethinking the concept of laissez-faire and complexity', *Evonomics*, accessed 1.9.20 at https://evonomics.com/the-libertarian-economist-friedrich/.

Stilwell, F. (2016) 'Heterodox economics or political economy?', *World Economics Association Newsletter*, **6**, pp. 1–3.

Tabb, W.K. (1999) *Reconstructing Political Economy: The Great Divide in Economic Thought*, London: Routledge.

Thornton, T.B. (2015) 'The changing face of mainstream economics?', *Journal of Australian Political Economy*, **75**, pp. 11–26.

Thornton, T.B. (2016) 'The "complexity revolution" seen from a historical and heterodox perspective', in Courvisanos, J., Millmow, A. and Doughney, J. (eds), *Reclaiming Pluralism*, London: Routledge.

Tomšič, S. (2013) *The Capitalist Unconscious: Marx and Lacan*, London: Verso.

Olin-Wright, E. (2011) *Envisioning Real Utopias*, London: Verso.

Žižek, S. (2017) *The Courage of Hopelessness: Chronicles of a Year of Acting Dangerously*, London: Allen Lane.

2.   Capitalism, climate change and freedom

Elke Pirgmaier

A few years ago, I sometimes felt ignorant to believe that I live at a time when the destruction of the natural world might become so overwhelming that it could bring human civilisation to its knees. Life on Earth is being wiped out at an accelerating speed and we are approaching irreversible tipping points much faster than anticipated (Steffen et al. 2015). The Amazonian lungs of the Earth are now emitting more carbon than they absorb (Qin et al. 2021) and the gulf stream which brings mild weather to Europe has started to slow down (Caesar et al. 2021), both probably caused by climate breakdown. In 2018, the Intergovernmental Panel on Climate Change (IPCC) announced that there are ten years left to halve global carbon emission if the planet is to stay below 1.5 degrees of global warming (IPCC 2018). We are the first generation in 200,000 years that experiences the climate we have today, and the last generation to do something about it (Burke et al. 2018).[1]

The loss of biodiversity is accelerating too. One in four plant and animal species are threatened by extinction (IPBES 2019). One million species face extinction caused by the actions of one species! Around 70 per cent of all mammals, birds, amphibians and reptiles have vanished in the last 45 years alone (WWF 2020), gone, forever, in the blink of an eye relative to the planet's history. There has not been anything like this before in human history. Forests are dying, oceans are dying, insects and many other beautiful creatures too. As the natural world gets suffocated, people's misery intensifies. Allowing ourselves to feel this suffering all around is hard to bear. Yet it is essential to feel – to soak it into our bodies in deep uncomforting breaths – to be able to detest further destruction, to stand up for life, and to heal what can be saved.

The good news is that it is not too late. Ten billion people could live well by 2050 – using as much energy as we did 60 years ago, with existing technologies and radical demand-side reductions to sufficiency levels. In countries where per capita consumption is currently highest, such as the USA and Australia, energy use could be slashed by 90–95 percent while maintaining decent living standards (Millward-Hopkins et al. 2020; Millward-Hopkins 2020). 'Decent' living here does not mean going back to living in caves. This scenario world is one in which there are laptops, smartphones and washing machines in every home, and where everyone has access to hospitals, schools and mobility. But it means a farewell to unnecessary overconsumption.

The very good news is that, if the global movement of dedicated freedom fighters succeed in radically and rapidly transforming every aspect of society in the 2020s, bringing this vision of a more frugal existence for all to life, the world would unfold into something much more beautiful than it is today. Our future lives could be more social, artistic, intellectual than they are at present – more sparkling and alive. This vision is not a distant utopia, but within reach. The youth climate strikers, extinction rebels and sunrise movement activists have been successful in inviting people to join the global fight for climate and social justice. Many more people are beginning to grasp what climate emergency means and alternatives that have simmered in pockets are bubbling and entering mainstream debates.

But let's be under no illusion that a transformation to a better future is guaranteed. The case for radical and rapid social change this decade, and practical routes towards it, has to be made and escalated at a time when large fractions of mainstream politics are adding to the problems. The rise of fascist leaders in late-stage capitalism signals that ruling powers resort to other means to sustain – rather than change – the status quo. They lie, deceive and blind people to prevent collective visioning and organising. Entrenched alliances between fossil capital, industry and the state highlight the key role of social movements, independent media and critical universities in giving birth to a liveable future.

In this chapter, I focus on aspects of Marxian political economy and ecological economics that can help support the struggle for life this decade. The Marxian tradition provides a systemic explanation of capitalism as a whole and remains key to understanding the reproduction of life in the current provisioning context. Ecological economics, on the other hand, combines a biophysical critique of the economic process with theories of well-being, human needs and justice, to address key questions: How much energy and resources are required to live well? What institutions and deliberations are suited to transform energy and resource use into desirable social outcomes, such as healthy food and decent housing for everyone? Both traditions dare to think big, which is essential for inspiring and legitimising actions consonant with planetary challenges.

RADICAL THEORY FOR RADICAL CHANGE

Theories are tools to make sense of the world. Radical theories are tools that illuminate the root causes of planetary crises (*radical* comes from the Latin radix and means *root*). Helping people to see and feel what is deeply wrong with our imperial mode of living (Brand and Wissen 2017) is one precondition to act more in line with the health of the whole. This is how things could shift. Paulo Freire (1970) argued that radical action and radical theory must go together to instigate social change because activism without reflection lacks direction, and pure verbalism is a dead-end because solutions cannot be achieved in purely idealistic ways. Much theorising is system-stabilising rather than system-challenging though; because ideas matter for sustaining the reproduction of any society, and in our case: the political economy base of capitalism.

> The most important area of domination was the mental universe of the colonised, the control, through culture, of how people perceived themselves and their relationship to the world. Economic and political control can never be complete or effective without mental control. To control a people's culture is to control their tools of self-definition in relationship to others. (Thiong'o 1981: 16)

These words from Ngũgĩ wa Thiong'o remind us that mind control is a more effective and insidious tool of cultural domination than brute force, which often evokes stronger resistance. This means that theories are not innocent tools of reflection, but powerful political instruments. They either illuminate and bring into consciousness what we otherwise do not see, or obscure and camouflage what is important. As such, they offer better or worse shortcuts to learning and guidance for meaningful action.

If we were to adopt theory 'fit for purpose' to advance knowledge and action on planetary crises, what would we look for? It seems clear that multiple crises – people in poverty proliferating, dandelions and dragonflies disappearing, money-making-for-money's sake mushrooming – need to be understood together to strengthen alternatives that identify and remedy root causes. But this is easier said than done. Reality is complex, contradictory and constantly changing; at times it seems impossible to grasp. This holds especially if we are committed to adopting a realist perspective to avoid misleading distortions and fantasy assumptions that are widespread in mainstream economics. It is relatively easy to criticise the mainstream for being dualist, reductionist and incrementalist; but it is not so straightforward what to offer instead. What shall we study, and how, to capture what is important? I suggest combining realism with ambition – that is, a deep and honest confrontation of the world as it is – coupled with imaginaries of the much better future within reach.

BOX 2.1   THEORISING FIT FOR PURPOSE: PRINCIPLES FOR COMBINING REALISM AND AMBITION

1. Explain monetary, biophysical and social interrelations ($\neq$ silo thinking).
2. Capture reality in motion (dynamics, processes, change, history including the future) ($\neq$ equilibrium).
3. Allow for cultural and historical specificities ($\neq$ universalism).
4. Unmask narratives, ideas, and justifications for not changing much ($\neq$ value-neutrality).
5. Uncover root causes of injustice and unsustainability[2] ($\neq$ crude empiricism).
6. Highlight people's power to challenge structures and institutions ($\neq$ atomistic individual change).
7. Envision deep transformations ($\neq$ incremental change).
8. Pay attention to possibilities that align with the good of the whole ($\neq$ criticism).
9. Look for contradictions as leverage points for change and ways to transcend them.
10. Use plain language and concepts to communicate research ($\neq$ academic ivory tower).
11. Beware of prejudices and blind spots (white middle-class privileged academics have many) ($\neq$ elitism).
12. See yourself as a change-maker ($\neq$ information-provider and observer).
13. Stay open, humble, and curious ($\neq$ ideology-trapped).
14. Fight for the conditions within academia that allow and encourage the whole of 1–13 in research, teaching and outreach ($\neq$ neoliberal suppression of academic freedom and creativity).

This list is inspired by systems theorists (Luhmann 1987; Capra 1997; Meadows 2009) and dialecticians in the Marxian tradition (Cornforth 1987; Ollman 1993; Lewontin and Levins 2007). What excites me most about Marxian political economy is the mode of reasoning that underpins it: dialectical logic. Dialectics is a way of seeing processes of becoming. The focus is on uncovering the essences of a system – thus reducing complexity – without losing the flexibility to comprehend the specific and varying cultural, social, geographical and temporal conditions in which a complex system evolves.

A century and a half ago, Marx developed a specific dialectical method to comprehend capitalism as a complex evolving system: systematic dialectics. The method has three steps. It starts with emphasising the whole system, rather than isolated parts. The idea is to dare and comprehend the system as a totality, as an integrated whole, from different vantage points and by adopting what we would today call a mixed-methods approach. This step allows identifying core elements. What then follows is an attempt to order the evidence and find a logic that explains how different elements inter-relate. This second step is about relationships, order and organisation. It aims to grasp the hierarchical structure of the system, which is essential for understanding what elements are more important for sustaining, or changing, the status quo. Finally, the third step describes how capitalism as a complex adaptive system unfolds, starting from the most abstract and simple to ever more concrete and complex realities. This step is reflected in how Marx explains capitalism as a whole in the three volumes of *Das Kapital* – starting from the most abstract (the commodity and value) towards ever more specific categories (money, machinery, the state, etc.) (Smith 1990; Brown 2007).

The Marxian method stands in contrast to what is sometimes understood to be the 'normal' scientific method that prevails in mainstream economics, including environmental economics. In the economic mainstream, analytical reasoning slices up reality into simple and 'manageable' parts, thereby excluding most of what is important – the factors that connect these parts, such as power, politics and values. It is then hoped that isolated building blocks can be glued together in a meaningful way. This is the dominant way in which Western science and institutions have developed since the Enlightenment. This approach has clear merits when the task is to build a bridge or fix a sewing machine, and it may be more relevant in some natural sciences, but it fails to provide a deeper understanding of complex social and economic systems, and how to change them (Capra 1975).

CAPITAL AND THE WEB OF LIFE

From a Marxian perspective, capitalism is a complex system that continually transforms, yet its core has remained the same. What is this core? The essence of capitalism can be summarised as M–C–M', the general circuit of capital that expresses how the goods and services people need – the food we eat, the clothes we wear, the houses we live in – are predominantly provisioned in capitalist society. Money (M) is invested to buy people's capacity to work (labour power LP) and natural resources (means of production MP) to produce commodities (C), that if successfully sold, realise a higher value than was initially spent (M' > M). Part of this surplus value is re-invested to maintain and expand production over time. This is not controversial, but Marxian political economists make it explicit.[3]

M–C–M' is a simple model of the basic dynamics of the capitalist mode of living; but it explains a lot. If we think through what these elements mean, what they entail and how they arise, a whole universe unfolds in front of us. I like to compare M–C–M' to Einstein's formula $E=mc^2$. As Einstein revolutionised physics, Marx revolutionised our way of understanding life under capitalism. What Marx writes in *Kapital* can be understood as a 3,000-page answer to the question: if M–C–M' is the basic structure of the system as a whole, what consequences does it entail for society, its institutions and people? Today, we can ask a similar question: if M–C–M' is the system's core engine, how can we understand climate emergency, i.e. the rise of planetary crises coupled with the social inability to act accordingly (so far)? What does M–C–M' tell us about why humanity has fallen out of alignment with life?

One way to understand planetary emergency is to identify dominant tendencies that arise from the M–C–M' structure. Here, I identify eight endogenous tendencies: overproduction, technological dynamism, appropriation, commodification, overconsumption, acceleration, alienation, and financialisation (Figure 2.1). Taken together, such tendencies form the fabric of capital, the entangled web of the system as a whole. They explain barriers to just sustainability transitions, but also potential ways to break through them.

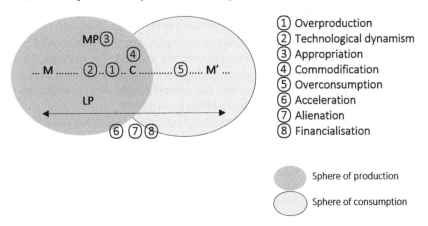

(1) Overproduction
(2) Technological dynamism
(3) Appropriation
(4) Commodification
(5) Overconsumption
(6) Acceleration
(7) Alienation
(8) Financialisation

Sphere of production

Sphere of consumption

Source: Pirgmaier (2018).

Figure 2.1   *Dominant tendencies*

(1)   *Overproduction* means that capitalist businesses are incentivised to produce and sell as much as they can. Mass commodity production goes hand in hand with the misuse of the soil, the rivers, the forests, the animal kingdom – and of people, because the production of too much 'stuff' is exhausting and exceeds natural regeneration cycles. If people work too much, their health suffers. If too much oil is burnt, too much CO_2 emissions are released into the atmosphere.

(2)   *Technological dynamism* is not necessarily a solution to problems caused by overproduction because, under capitalism, technological advance is primarily directed at replacing people with machines to increase capitalist efficiency. This is not the same as increasing energy and resource efficiency, or freeing people from overwork. If machines are designed to run faster for longer, they feed on more resources and human labour, rather than less.

(3)   *Appropriation* tackles where and how resources are extracted. To keep production costs low, materials are accessed as cheaply as possible, based on international trade agreements and/or by exercising brute force (Temper et al. 2015). A long history of colonisation, imperialism and geographical expansion continues today as land grabbing, green grabbing and blue grabbing (Benjaminsen and Bryceson 2012; Fairhead et al. 2012). Communities at the locations of extraction are at the sharp end of the spear of environmentally damaging capitalism (Bookchin 1982).

(4)   *Commodification* relates to how capitalist processes expand the realm of 'the commodity' – a thing produced for sale and exchanged for money (Murray and Schuler 2017) – into new domains that were formerly not subject to the logic of capitalist market exchange. Turning peasants into city labourers, and carbon emissions into tradeable permits, for example, sustains and legitimises the expansion of the capitalist way of living.

(5) *Overconsumption* is the global mirror-image of overproduction. What is produced for profit needs to be sold, otherwise reproduction stumbles. To increase demand, people's willingness to consume is artificially stretched, which is why marketing departments, advertising agencies and planned obsolescence exist. People's ability to consume has also been fuelled by the expansion of credit.

(6) *Acceleration* highlights the in-built short-termism and speeding-up of the rhythm of work and life under capitalism. Capitalist firms try to capture time by reducing turnover times and intensifying labour time. This incentivises a throw-away consumption culture and the intensification of production. Without cheap, fast, and expanding transport and communication systems this would not be possible. Low fossil fuel prices have been crucial to this end.

(7) *Alienation* describes what type of people, and relations between people, capitalism produces. Alienation happens when the essential human traits that characterise us as feeling, thinking and creative social creatures become side-lined (Ollman 1971). Living well means to balance different aspects of our lives, which is not encouraged in a world dominated by private property, capitalist competition and profit because it would mean going slower ($\neq$ acceleration); encouraging people to develop a sense of 'enough' once basic human needs are met ($\neq$ overproduction and overconsumption); being softer with ourselves and our environments ($\neq$ appropriation); developing more meaningful relations with people instead of machines ($\neq$ technological dynamism); and learning to let go of desires to own and possess ($\neq$ commodification).

(8) *Financialisation* is the process by which finance mushrooms and expands into new territories. The transformation of future income streams into tradeable assets is not removed from production. Rather, M–M' arises out of, depends on and shapes M–C–M'. Without the creation of carbon markets, for instance, speculation upon these revenue streams would not be possible.

Such features of capitalist societies are *tendencies*. A tendency is something through which an outcome is likely to come into being. It does not manifest everywhere and all the time. Countertendencies and social struggles are at work that offset, delay or suspend tendencies. And yet, such struggles are difficult to implement and sustain in a system geared towards the production of surplus value, because capitalist tendencies form a network of supporting structures. They reinforce each other in ways that sustain the reproduction of the system. M–C–M' unmasked, is as a planetary problem-generating structure.

This does not mean that we are doomed. Marxian theory is not a one-sided pessimistic 'doomsday' portrayal of society, nor is it just a theory of production or the economy. Above all, it is a theory of dominant power relations of the society in which we live. Knowing what *capital* is, and how it operates as dominant social relation, is emancipatory: it helps to see through the veil of a reality that is deeply destructive and to formulate viable and desirable alternatives. Capital shapes people's way of life, their aspirations, identities, values and beliefs. Barriers to systemic, just sustainability transitions arise because many people are being deceived, blinded and oppressed to sustain the dominant M–C–M' structure, geared towards the destruction of life. If people see and feel how they are cogs in a system that harms themselves, their families, the wider community, and the planet, a deep desire for breaking with it can emerge.

FROM CAPITAL TO FOSSIL CAPITAL

So, why is it that capitalism relies so much on the use of fossil fuels as the main source of power? Could it be otherwise? Could we not envisage a 'greener' capitalism based on the forces of the wind, the water and the sun? Some authors argue that fossil fuels are intrinsic to capitalism (e.g. Angus 2016) and Andreas Malm provides a particularly insightful account (Malm 2016) (Figure 2.2). His detailed historical study reveals how and why coal overtook water as the major source of power at the beginning of the Industrial Revolution; and it seems useful to briefly consider some of his findings here, to better understand what a transformation away from fossil fuels entails.

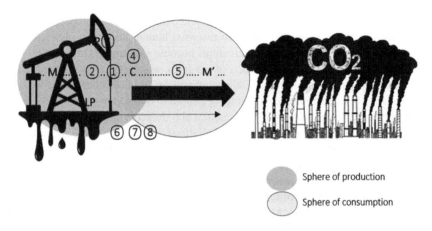

Figure 2.2   Spheres of production and consumption

The factory system that arose in Britain was originally based on waterpower. In 1800, there were 84 coal-fired engines compared with 1,000 water-powered cotton mills (Malm 2016: 67). The rise of the water mill led to massive improvements in productivity, high rates of profit, high output and reinvestments. And engineers had developed sophisticated plans to water-power the emerging industrial cities such as Manchester and Glasgow. The transition from water to steam in the British cotton industry did not occur because water was scarce, more expensive, or less technologically potent (which is what mainstream theories suggest). The contrary was the case: water was abundant, cheaper and technologically feasible. The transition occurred because coal had *social qualities* that water did not possess.

First, coal was a superior tool of *social control*. The spatial mobility of coal allowed producers to take advantage of the large labour supply that stood ready in cities. By 1851, already more than 50 per cent of the British population lived in cities – an unparalleled situation. Water sites, in contrast, were bound to locally specific places where flowing or falling water was available, which was typically in the sparsely populated countryside. Here, producers sourced people by offering them amenities (e.g. schools for their children) and by reverting to child labourers from orphanages. Both strategies were detrimental for producers, because forced labour does not perform as well as paid labour and paying for amenities was more expensive. Moreover, water-powered mills were reliant on the weather. In times of drought, mills stood still. Such shortfalls were typically compensated by flexible working hours and over-work at other times, but these options became more restricted after the passing of the Ten Hours Act in 1850 – a victory of the labour movement to limit working times. As a direct result, capitalists rushed to build steam mills. 'Workers might go on strike and water freeze' (Malm 2016: 213), but autonomous mechanical power could be controlled, managed, planned, governed and regulated with ease. Thus, 'the struggle against labour called for machinery, which called for steam power, which called for coal (Malm 2016: 222).

Moreover, coal allowed producers to *avoid collaboration* with other producers. As water is a common resource that cannot easily be divided or privatised, water-based schemes would have required closer coordination between mill-owners to share and distribute the resource. This was considered a restraint by capitalists and did not fit neatly with the trend towards more private property – the zeitgeist of the time. Coal, in contrast, did fit the logic of private property, being piecemeal, splintered, amenable to concentration and accumulation. It became a symbol of escape and independence from certain types of environmental and social constraint. In a nutshell, water-powered systems required 'emotional energy' (Malm 2016: 119) from which steam-powered systems were free, and so the unwillingness or inability of producers to submit to the planning, coordination and collective funding of water schemes led to their demise.

Malm provides historical evidence that capitalism centres on the exploitation and control of human labour, and is hence amenable to forms of power and infrastructures that enable it, such as cars, for example (Mattioli et al. 2020). Climate change and other crimes result as collateral damage. On this reasoning, climate change emerged *as a logical consequence* of the workings of capital, not in spite of it. If this is correct, any serious climate action starts with a sober confrontation of fossil capital as part of a programme to end capitalism (Mair 2019). We cannot afford to repeat past mistakes, yet today's debates of shifting towards renewables and a 'green economy' centre on the flawed ideas that Malm debunks as historically ungrounded: that a transition requires better technology, lower prices, and more funding. In the meantime, the fossil barons and their allies continue to drill Norwegian oil, Russian gas and Indonesian coal.

FROM FOSSIL CAPITAL TO FASCISM

It is quite clear what needs to happen to stop runaway climate change: leaving fossil fuels in the ground (that's about three quarters of the problem), stopping deforestation and transforming agriculture (that's most of the remaining one quarter) (Hayhoe 2020). This requires ending fossil fuel subsidies immediately and phasing out fracking, coal-fired power plants, and other fossil infrastructures (including fossil-using appliances such as cars) as first steps (Smith et al. 2019). It requires the reduction of demand and electrification of everything else – the heating and increasingly the cooling of homes, mobility and freight, the production of critical goods – powered by renewable energy (Grubler et al. 2018; Millward-Hopkins et al. 2020). It means a massive reduction of livestock for meat and dairy production (Carbon Brief 2020). It also requires the reparation of the damages that have been caused, as much as possible. All of this implies a redistribution of power in society, which does not echo well with existing elites and many currently dominant industries.

Instead of heavily investing in renewables and reinvention, fossil capital has decided to heavily invest in 'strategic communication' (Atkin 2020). The fossil fuel industry has told investors that the greatest threat they face is broad public anger over climate change, which is why they continue to spread misinformation about climate change, as they have done for 30 years (Supran and Oreskes 2017). They align with politics that distracts from the issue and divides people to slow down effective climate action. In pursuing such an objective, fossil fuel companies have regularly worked closely with the far-right. As fossil capital is threatened by the global climate justice movement and the associated politics that demands serious climate action – which means to shut them down – it supports the growing influence of leaders with neo-fascist characteristics, including Modi in India, Bolsonaro in Brazil, Orbán in Hungary, Erdoğan in Turkey, Putin in Russia, and Xi in China. In countries where they are not successful in carrying leadership, their influence pushes traditional right-wing parties to the far-right and their actions lead to division and violence, as has occurred in Greece, France, Sweden, Germany, Norway and many other places.

Links between fossil capital and the political far-right are very close. In the USA, the Trump administration was receptive to legislation drafted by the oil and gas industry to create criminal penalties of up to 20 years in prison for 'inhibiting the operation' of an oil or gas pipeline (Fang and Surgey 2019). On day one of Biden's presidency, Republican forces started fear-mongering on behalf of the fossil fuel industry by claiming that Biden's policies will plunge Americans into poverty (Atkin 2021). In India, Modi has direct ties with oligarchs, whose fossil and mining empires have benefited from subsidies and deregulation (Paranjoy Guha 2015). In Hungary, Victor Orbán has 'helped out' the German car industry to water down European legislation after the Volkswagen emissions scandal and, in return, companies such as Audi and Mercedes use their influence to dilute criticism against the Hungarian regime in the German political elite (Szabolcs 2018). Similar examples exist in, among others, Poland, Norway, Sweden, Spain and Brazil (Malm and Zetkin Collective 2021).

What do authoritarian (mis-)leaders do? They wrap a blanket of silence and deceit around the topic of climate emergency. They don't seriously address the issue of survival (Chomsky 2020) and at the same time discredit viable alternatives (Supran and Oreskes 2017) and demonise (and often jail, exile or kill) movements' leaders. Such strategies and the use of fake news are not new, but they are increasingly prevalent at a time when oligarchs and fossil capital benefit from a propaganda machinery of mass deception, denial and delay (Snyder 2017). Importantly, the rise of the far-right reminds us that the notion of a happy alliance between capitalism and democracy is a myth. Rather, capitalism uses democracy as a cover while making it impossible (Varoufakis 2020). The political system we call 'democracy', usually limited to representative democracy, was never fully developed. It could not be, because an egalitarian system of 'power of the people' would not allow for massive capitalist surplus which is predicated on the exploitation of people and planet (Smith 2018).

Solving problems of climate, biodiversity, and extreme inequalities of wealth, power and opportunity is not a utopian dream. Degrowth and Green New Deal initiatives show practical steps to a healthier world rooted in justice, care and ecological reparation (Aronoff et al. 2019; Kallis et al. 2020). Yet such ideas do not materialise just because they make sense: they must be fought for against extremely strong adversaries. This can only happen by strong social movement coalitions exercising continuous pressures on governments to make the required changes within the short period of time to stop runaway ecological damages. The Sunrise Movement in the USA and Ende Gelände in Germany are examples, working hard to bring planetary emergency to the core of public attention. But people who are critical, think and act are dangerous to power, as they have always been. This is why those who bring the message of hope, peace and support for people who need it are those who are bitterly attacked (Chomsky

2020). Extinction Rebellion (XR) is called an extremist and terrorist organisation by right-wing think-tanks such as Policy Exchange, who suggest that the state should step in to crack down on their peaceful protests (Mair and Steinberger 2019). This accusation is baseless, as XR's demands are reasonable and in line with the latest academic findings and practical action. But the sad truth is that freedom-fighters are all too often suppressed and criminalised. This is not news, but the planetary dimensions this struggle has now taken are.

The origins of capitalism – and hence of the M–C–M' structure – go back to long histories of exploiting women (Federici 2014), nature (Foster et al. 2010; Moore 2015) and colonies (Hochschild 2012). The evolution of capitalism remains deeply entangled with these violent roots. Today, the pattern of entangled discriminations that underpins M–C–M' in terms of race, class, age, sex, ability, nationality, and the brutality that is exercised to uphold it, becomes more visible:

> The same patriarchal power structure that oppresses and exploits girls, women, and nonbinary people … also wreaks destruction on the natural world. Dominance, supremacy, violence, extraction, egotism, greed, ruthless competition … these hallmarks of patriarchy fuel the climate crisis just as surely as they do inequality, colluding with racism along the way. (Johnson and Wilkinson 2020: xviii)

Capitalism is a system that destroys life: we need one that honours and protects it.

FREEDOM

The unfolding global struggle is about more than overcoming capitalism. In a longer-term view of human history, capitalism is just a relatively recent expression of the dominant way of excising violence and committing crimes against human and nonhuman beings. And yet, Marxian political economy remains essential because it offers a theory of current social relations. From this perspective, what's wrong is 'us'. The root problems (and solutions) are not with money, technology, the market, or a system that seems difficult to grasp and change but, much simpler and more profoundly, with everyday relationships – how we relate to ourselves, to other people and the natural world. New agreements at this level can change the world (Bishop 2021).

Capitalist social relations tend to accentuate competition and control. Competition implies that there is an 'I/we' *against* 'the other', rather than an 'I/we' *and* 'the other'. Competitiveness has long been justified as something intrinsically human and as necessary for developing technologies that enable wealthy, prosperous and free societies. In reality, competition goes *against* one of the most distinctive aspects of human beings: our propensity to cooperate (Kohn 1987; Bowles and Gintis 2013). The competitive spirit *legitimises*, rather than prevents, a pyramid system that benefits the very few,[4] at the expense of the majority of beings, because it rewards the winners of competitive struggles, and the resulting concentration of power undermines the conditions for all to thrive (Shaikh 2016).

In a deeper understanding of reality, we are all part of the web of life. All human and non-human beings are interconnected and dependent on each other, which implies that every one of us cannot be truly healthy and happy and free unless we organise in a way that makes sure that we are all just fine – which is actually what people enjoy doing! People thrive by caring for each other. If we align our actions with something greater than ourselves that is purposeful for others (i.e. by giving ourselves to create meaning), we become free (Bishop 2021).

There is no inherent contradiction between what is good for us and what serves the bigger whole. But it is essential to understand that in class-based societies people are prevented from seeing and doing exactly that.

The idea that capitalism paves the way to 'free societies' is one of the greatest myths of our times. It hides the fact that most people are inhibited from having their most fundamental needs met[5] – access to enough healthy food, decent housing, emancipatory education, and proper healthcare – things that should be provisioned unconditionally as human rights to enable dignified lives for all. But there is no unconditional care, even in supposedly 'rich' countries. For most people, if you don't sell your body and mind for a wage, and don't have a support network of friends and family, or savings, you are likely to end up on the street and/ or be treated like an outcast. This is not because society cannot be organised differently: we know that decent lives for all are possible (Millward-Hopkins 2020). It is because existing elites take advantage from most people sleepwalking and struggling, rather than fully living.

Radical theory lifts the veil of ignorance or confusion. It brings into people's consciousness the patterns of inequality, ignorance and brutality that underpin everyday interactions. This truth can be liberating,[6] because who wants to live in such a malfunctioning society? Who wants to live in a world that produces enough food for everyone, yet lets 820 million of us starve (United Nations 2021: 1)? These people represent a population greater than Europe, Australia and Oceania combined. Facing and feeling this viciousness creates a deep *willingness* for social change. At least this is what Marxian political economy has done to me. The clearer I see how deep structural violence is embedded in our institutions and how alienated it makes me feel, the more incapable I am of being at peace with it and unwilling to comply with it. All of us participate in systems of exploitation every day, for we live in the reality of existing arrangements. We cannot shake off these social relations on our own. Collectively however, we can nurture the capacities for breaking away from it.

What does freedom look like? How does she feel? A free world could be one in which we allow and support each other to discover and live our full potential; in which no one dominates and controls another; in which we act based on trust and generosity, rather than fear. It is a world that is light, joyous, playful, rich in meaning, good food, fun company. It would be a real home in which people are finally able, after centuries of oppression and suffering, to live together with all beings in respect, peace and love. The 'economy' – if you still prefer to call it that – would be grounded in care and creative potential. Human consciousness could be shifted to a new level, and we could have so much fun!

Such a vision is not a privileged, middle-class, spiritualist airy-fairy fantasy but something deeply human and, as such, within reach. Human beings are creative potential; dreaming big and aspiring to how we could live our lives as carers, lovers, healers – shining our light into the darker corners – seems essential to survive as a human collective. Flourishing is a necessity, not a luxury, especially in times of climate breakdown, because it unleashes the necessary energy, enthusiasm and creativity to turn the planetary disaster-tanker around (Pirgmaier 2020). Imagining the world for which we *deeply* long is not an alternative to political action, but the engine for it. Imagination awakens the possibilities that stretch far beyond the given frameworks of what exists (Bishop 2021).

The challenge is to invite and encourage enough people to tip the balance towards a society that is honest and healing. This requires a willingness and continuous practice of *living into* the desirable future by using our minds, hearts and bodies to work for the sake of the world. This includes decolonising, freeing ourselves from inherited beliefs and habits that no longer serve us, letting go of other- and self-exploitation, holding spaces for each other in which we can speak and live our truth and develop capacities for responsible choices, opposing existing power structures and creating solidarity with everyone who is victimised and marginalised by them. It involves learning from past struggles how rights were won through political organising, mass protest and civil disobedience – including that fighting out of fear and revenge is very different than fighting out of love and care.

CHOOSING TO STRENGTHEN THE FORCES OF LIFE

Climate change is often portrayed as this huge, complex, overwhelming issue, but actually, our response to it can be guided by reasonably straightforward questions such as: Do you want to support the forces of death, or do you want to strengthen the forces of life (Andrews 2020)? In a polarising world the choices of what to do – and what to stop doing – become easier. Not standing up, speaking up, and rising up for a rapid and radical transformation of society is a choice as well. It's an erroneous choice because all that evil needs to triumph is the silence of the good people (Ziegler 2020). As the old order falls apart, the choices presented to us are rather lucid: either we collectively organise and succeed in side-lining the powers that prevent people and other beings from living decent dignified lives, or the larger part of humanity and our fellow creatures will sink into deeper violence and disappear. We can learn to engage in this fight as if our life depended on it – because it does. What else are we here for? We are all part of this system; we participate in it every day. And we can learn, collectively and on our own, how to strengthen what needs to come to the fore, and how to let go of what needs to die, in every action we take. The times of blaming others and postponing action to tomorrow are over. The time is now, here, and it starts with you, with me, with us.

I end this chapter by giving the floor to Xiye Bastida (2020), who is an 18-year-old Mexican–Chilean climate activist, member of the indigenous Mexican Otomi-Toltec nation and co-organiser of Fridays for Future New York City. She presents ten ways how we can demonstrate our commitment for thriving life:

1. Don't start from scratch. There are hundreds of existing initiatives that you can join.
2. Maintain good communication with your peers and the adult organizations you partner with.
3. Take good care of yourself and others.
4. Make your activism intersectional; include all stakeholders in your decision making, and don't tokenize.
5. Don't do things the patriarchal way, the racist way, the exhausting way, or any way that excludes marginalized voices just to be "efficient" and do things fast.
6. At events you hold, invite Indigenous peoples to do land acknowledgments, and remember that Indigenous knowledge is the foundation for addressing the climate crisis.
7. Always convey that individual and structural change are both indisputably necessary.
8. Meet people where they're at. Not everyone knows the climate crisis back to front. Explain it and present solutions.
9. Use accessible language. Not everyone knows about ppm (parts per million) or the IPCC (Intergovernmental Panel on Climate Change).
10. Talk about greenwashing, environmental racism, green gentrification (or as I call it, *greentrification*), and what a just transition means.

That's enough for a start. Onwards.

NOTES

1. We have already left the Holocene, which was a very special time, starting 12,000 years ago, in which humanity invented agriculture, writing and cities. *Homo sapiens* is about 250,000 to 300,000 years old; *Homo genus* about two million years. At the current trajectory of 4–5 degrees of global warming by the end of the century, humanity is rolling back the climate clock by three million years by 2030, which is a climate that *Homo genus* has never experienced. If we aim for 2 degrees by immediately and massively reducing emissions, we will hit it by 2040. If we aim for 1.5 degrees, we will never get there at all (Burke et al. 2018).
2. Most planetary disaster reports still articulate drivers at a rather superficial level. Pressures of climate change and biodiversity loss are commonly attributed to land use change, the expansion of economic activity, trade and demand, rather than to the social relations that underpin them.
3. Many heterodox economists base their work on the M–C–M′ framework, which stands in contrast to the neoclassical conception of the economic system as C–M–C. The latter describes a simple commodity exchange economy (apples vs. oranges) in which money merely serves to facilitate barter.
4. Unleashing competitive capitalist dynamics under neoliberalism by waves of privatisation and deregulation has led to the spectacular inequalities we observe today. According to Oxfam (2020: 10): 'If you saved $10,000 a day since the building of the pyramids in Egypt you would have only one-fifth the average fortune of the 5 richest billionaires'.
5. Marxian scholars have long emphasised that what matters most for understanding the basic functioning and thriving of societies are the social-material foundations – the mental and physical infrastructures – that shape how societies provision what we need to live.
6. Radical theory is not automatically liberating, because revealing the flow of harm is not enough. It is not enough to sit on academic windowsills and preach how capitalism dehumanises people. If radical theorists remain content with criticism, or even worse, signal how difficult and impossible systemic change is, it easily leads to frustration, paralysis and cynicism – which is quite the opposite of kindling liberation. People need to feel empowered to fight for basic humanity. It is vital to highlight the real possibilities of a much better future within reach, and steps towards it, to stop the flow of harm and people who are complicit in it.

REFERENCES

Andrews, E. (2020) 'How Can I Celebrate the Jewish New Year When the Planet Is Burning?' *Grist Climate Column*, 26 Sept., accessed 6.6.2021 https://grist.org/article/how-can-i-celebrate-the-jewish-new-year-when-the-planet-is-burning/.

Angus, I. (2016) *Facing the Anthropocene: Fossil Capitalism and the Crisis of the Earth System*, New York: Monthly Review Press.

Aronoff, K., Battistoni, A., Cohen, D.A. and Riofrancos, T. (2019) *A Planet to Win: Why We Need a Green New Deal*, London: Verso.

Atkin, E. (2020) 'How Big Oil Defends Itself to Spooked Investors', *Heated*, 24 Feb., accessed 6.6.2021 at https://heated.world/p/how-big-oil-defends-itself-to-spooked.

Atkin, E. (2021) 'The Conservative Climate Fear-Mongering Begins', *Heated*, 21 Jan., accessed 6.6.2021 at https://heated.world/p/the-conservative-climate-fear-mongering.

Bastida, X. (2020) 'Calling In', in Johnson, A.E. and Wilkinson, K.K. (eds), *All We Can Save: Truth, Courage, and Solutions to the Climate Crisis*, New York: One World.

Benjaminsen, T.A. and Bryceson, I. (2012) 'Conservation, Green/Blue Grabbing and Accumulation by Dispossession in Tanzania', *Journal of Peasant Studies*, **39**, pp. 335–55.

Bishop, O. (2021) 'Conversations with Orland Bishop', accessed 6.6.2021 at https://charleseisenstein.org/program/conversations/orland-bishop-course-two/.

Bowles, S. and Gintis, H. (2013) *A Cooperative Species: Human Reciprocity and Its Evolution*, Princeton, NJ: Princeton University Press.

Brand, U. and Wissen, M. (2017) 'The Imperial Mode of Living', in Spash, C.L. (ed.), *Routledge Handbook of Ecological Economics: Nature and Society*, London and New York: Routledge, pp. 152–61.

Brown, A. (2007) 'Reorienting Critical Realism: A System-Wide Perspective on the Capitalist Economy', *Journal of Economic Methodology*, **14** (4), pp. 499–519.

Burke, K.D., Williams, J.W., Chandler, M.A, Haywood, A.M., Lunt, D.J. and Otto-Bliesner, B.L. (2018) 'Pliocene and Eocene Provide Best Analogs for Near-Future Climates', *Proceedings of the National Academy of Sciences of the United States of America*, **115** (52), pp. 13288–93.

Caesar, L., McCarthy, G.D., Thornalley, J.R., Cahill, N. and Rahmstorf, S. (2021) 'Current Atlantic Meridional Overturning Circulation Weakest in Last Millennium', *Nature Geoscience*, **14** (3), pp. 118–20.

Capra, F. (1975) *The Tao of Physics: An Exploration of the Parallels Between Modern Physics and Eastern Mysticism*, Boulder, CO: Shambhala Publications.

Capra, F. (1997) *The Web of Life: A New Synthesis of Mind and Matter*, London: Flamingo.

Carbon Brief (2020) 'What Is the Climate Impact of Eating Meat and Dairy?', accessed 6.6.2021 at https://interactive.carbonbrief.org/what-is-the-climate-impact-of-eating-meat-and-dairy/.

Chomsky, N. (2020) A Conversation with Noam Chomsky on Trump, Capitalism, and the U.S. Role in the New Cold War', accessed 6.6.2021 at https://www.youtube.com/watch?v=uiCeqySVhCE.

Cornforth, M. (1987) *Dialectical Materialism: An Introduction, Volume I: Materialism and the Dialectical Method*, 5th edn, London: Lawrence & Wishart.

Fairhead, J., Leach, M. and Scoones, I. (2012) 'Green Grabbing: a New Appropriation of Nature?', *Journal of Peasant Studies*, **39**, pp. 237–61.

Fang, L. and Surgey, N. (2019) 'Oil Lobbyists Attempt to Influence Pipeline Safety Legislation to Further Criminalize Pipeline Protests', *The Intercept*, accessed 6.6.2021 at https://theintercept.com/2019/09/27/pipeline-safety-legislation/.

Federici, S. (2014) *Caliban and the Witch: Women, the Body and Primitive Accumulation*, 2nd edn, New York: Autonomedia.

Foster, J.B., Clark, B. and York, R. (2010) *The Ecological Rift: Capitalism's War on the Earth*, New York: Monthly Review Press.

Freire, P. (1970) *Pedagogy of the Oppressed*, New York, London, New Delhi and Sydney: Bloomsbury.

Grubler, A., Wilson, C., Bento, N., Boza-Kiss, B., Krey, V., McCollum, D.L, Rao, N.D. et al. (2018) 'A Low Energy Demand Scenario for Meeting the 1.5°C Target and Sustainable Development Goals without Negative Emission Technologies', *Nature Energy*, **3** (6), pp. 515–27.

Hayhoe, K. (2020) 'How to Talk About Climate Change', in Johnson, A.E. and Wilkinson, K.K. (eds), *All We Can Save: Truth, Courage, and Solutions to the Climate Crisis*, New York: One World, pp. 108–13.

Hochschild, A. (2012) *King Leopold's Ghost: A Story of Greed, Terror and Heroism in Colonial Africa*, London: Pan Macmillan.

IPBES (2019) 'Summary for Policymakers of the Global Assessment Report on Biodiversity and Ecosystem Services of the Intergovernmental Science-Policy Platform on Biodiversity and Ecosystem Services', Bonn: IPBES.

IPCC (2018) 'IPPC Special Report 15: Global Warming of 1.5°C', accessed 6.6.2021 at https://www.ipcc.ch/sr15/.

Johnson, A.E. and Wilkinson, K.K. (2020) 'Begin', in *All We Can Save: Truth, Courage, and Solutions to the Climate Crisis*, New York: One World.

Kallis, G., Paulsen, S., D'Alisa, G. and Demaria, F. (2020) *The Case for Degrowth*, Cambridge: Polity Press.

Kohn, A. (1987) 'The Case Against Competition', accessed 6.6.2021 at https://www.alfiekohn.org/article/case-competition/.

Lewontin, R. and Levins, R. (2007) *Biology under the Influence. Dialectical Essays on Ecology, Agriculture, and Health*, New York: Monthly Review Press.

Luhmann, N. (1987) *Soziale Systeme: Grundriß Einer Allgemeinen Theorie*, Frankfurt: Suhrkamp.

Mair, S. (2019) 'Climate Change and Capitalism: A Political Marxist View', *New Socialist*, accessed 6.6.2021 at https://newsocialist.org.uk/climate-capitalism-political-marxism/.

Mair, S. and Steinberger, J.K. (2019) 'In the Age of Extinction, Who Is Extreme? A Response to Policy Exchange', *Open Democracy*, accessed 6.6.2021 at https://www.opendemocracy.net/en/oureconomy/age-extinction-who-extreme-response-policy-exchange/.

Malm, A. (2016) *Fossil Capital: The Rise of Steam Power and the Roots of Global Warming*, London and New York: Verso.

Malm, A. and Zetkin Collective (2021) *White Skin, Black Fuel: On the Danger of Fossil Fascism*, London: Verso.

Mattioli, G., Roberts, C., Brown, A. and Steinberger, J. (2020) 'Elements of a Political Economy of Car Dependence', *Energy Research & Social Science*, **66** (101486), pp. 1–18.

Meadows, D.H. (2009) *Thinking in Systems: A Primer*, London: Earthscan.

Millward-Hopkins, J. (2020) 'How 10 Billion People Could Live Well by 2050 – Using as Much Energy as We Did 60 Years Ago', *The Conversation*, October, accessed 6.6.2021 at https://theconversation.com/how-10-billion-people-could-live-well-by-2050-using-as-much-energy-as-we-did-60-years-ago-146896.

Millward-Hopkins, J., Steinberger, J.K. and Oswald, Y. (2020) 'Providing Decent Living with Minimum Energy: A Global Scenario', *Global Environmental Change*, **65** (102168).

Moore, J.W. (2015) *Capitalism in the Web of Life*, London and New York: Verso.

Murray, P. and Schuler, J. (2017) 'The Commodity Spectrum', *Continental Thought and Theory*, **1**, pp. 112–52.

Ollman, B. (1971) *Alienation: Marx's Conception of Man in Capitalist Society*, Cambridge: Cambridge University Press.

Ollman, B. (1993) *Dialectical Investigations*, New York and London: Routledge.

Oxfam (2020) 'Time to Care', Oxfam, accessed 6.6.2021 at https://www.oxfam.org/en/research/time-care.

Paranjoy Guha, T. (2015) 'The Incredible Rise and Rise of Gautam Adani: Part One', *The Citizen*, accessed 6.6.2021 at https://www.thecitizen.in/index.php/en/NewsDetail/index/1/3375/The-Incredible-Rise-and-Rise-of-Gautam-Adani-Part-One.

Pirgmaier, E. (2018) 'Value, Capital and Nature: Rethinking the Foundations of Ecological Economics', PhD thesis, University of Leeds.

Pirgmaier, E. (2020) 'Consumption Corridors, Capitalism and Social Change', *Sustainability, Science, Practice and Policy*, **16** (1), pp. 274–85.

Qin, Y., Xiao, X., Wigneron, J.P., Ciais, P., Brandt, M., Fan, L., Li, X. et al. (2021) 'Carbon Loss from Forest Degradation Exceeds that from Deforestation in the Brazilian Amazon', *Nature Climate Change*, **11** (5), pp. 442–8.

Shaikh, A. (2016) *Capitalism: Competition, Conflict, Crises*, New York: Oxford University Press.

Smith, C.J., Forster, P.M., Allen, M., Fuglestvedt, J., Millar, R.J., Rogelj, J. and Zickfeld, K. (2019) 'Current Fossil Fuel Infrastructure Does Not yet Commit Us to 1.5°C Warming', *Nature Communications*, **10** (1), pp. 1–10.

Smith, T. (1990) *The Logic of Marx's Capital*, New York: New York Press.

Smith, T. (2018) *Beyond Liberal Egalitarianism: Marx and Normative Social Theory in the Twenty-First Century*, Chicago, IL: Haymarket Books.

Snyder, T. (2017) *On Tyranny: Twenty Lessons from the Twentieth Century*, London: Vintage Publishing.

Steffen, W., Richardson, K., Rockström, J., Cornell, S.E., Fetzer, I., Bennett, E.M, Biggs, R., et al. (2015) 'Planetary Boundaries: Guiding Human Development on a Changing Planet', *Science*, **347** (6223), pp. 736–47.

Supran, G. and Oreskes, N. (2017) 'Assessing ExxonMobil's Climate Change Communications (1977–2014)', *Environmental Research Letters*, **12** (084019).

Szabolcs, P. (2018) 'How Orbán Played Germany, Europe's Great Power', *Direkt36*, accessed 6.6.2021 at https://www.direkt36.hu/en/a-magyar-nemet-kapcsolatok-rejtett-tortenete/.

Temper, L., Bene, D. del, and Alier, J.M. (2015) 'Mapping the Frontiers and Frontlines of Global Environmental Justice: the EJAtlas', *Journal of Political Ecology*, **22**, pp. 255–78.

Thiong'o, Ngũgĩ wa (1981) *Decolonising the Mind: The Politics of Language in African Literature*, Harare: Zimbabwe Publishing House.

United Nations (2021) '2020 – Hunger Map', United Nations World Food Programme, accessed 6.6.2021 at https://www.wfp.org/publications/hunger-map-2020.

Varoufakis, Y. (2020) 'What Comes after Capitalism?' accessed 6.6.2021 at https://www.yanisvaroufakis .eu/2020/09/19/why-we-need-a-progressive-international-that-must-plan-for-today-and-for-beyond -capitalism-keynote-at-the-pi-2020-summit-18-sep-2020/.

WWF (2020) 'Living Planet Report: Bending the Curve of Biodiversity Loss', Gland, Switzerland: World Wildlife Fund.

Ziegler, J. (2020) 'Die Schande Europas', Schrems: GEA Akademie, accessed 6.6.2021 at https://gea -waldviertler.at/alle-termine-veranstaltungen/jean-ziegler/.

PART II

IDENTIFYING FOUNDATIONAL APPROACHES TO POLITICAL ECONOMY

3. Classical political economy and its ongoing relevance

Jamie Morgan

Inquiring '*what* is Classical Political Economy?' (CPE) requires addressing the corollary questions of '*who* are the classical political economists?' and '*when* were their key works written?' The 'what' can, of course, be partly distinguished from the 'who' since, by definition, CPE is a synthesis. Its main architects could not conceive themselves in retrospect, nor could they position themselves in a history that had not yet happened (rendering them 'classical'). The classical political economists were inventing a subject before there was a discrete 'economics' discipline, and then the theoretical apparatus of CPE itself had to be invented. So, as synthesis, the 'what' and 'who' emphasise some aspects of work over others, and involves matters of interpretation, selection and omission. There is, therefore, a necessary historicity to CPE, but also retrospective contrasts and claims. The most readily familiar point of departure is Karl Marx, who coined the phrase 'CPE', mainly in contrast to 'vulgar political economy' – as discussed further below. Regardless, we now typically look to Marxists, Sraffians and scholars in the history of economic thought (HET) for answers to these questions of 'what' and 'who'. Simultaneously, it is important to contextualise this, since the contemporary relevance of CPE reflects a broader story of the evolution of mainstream economics. CPE, as with any body of knowledge, is only as relevant as it is allowed to be, and this can be based on more or less ignorance and more or less authoritative and justified claims.

Most broadly, CPE is associated with works written from the seventeenth century to the 1830s in the UK and France. Its undisputed core thinkers are Adam Smith and David Ricardo. Its canonical works are Smith's *An Inquiry Into the Nature and Causes of the Wealth of Nations* ([1776] 1976) and *The Theory of Moral Sentiments* ([1759] 2000), and Ricardo's *On the Principles of Political Economy and Taxation* ([1817] 1821) and his collected works (Ricardo 1951–73). Tony Aspromourgos (1996), however, notes the problem of merely referring to these 'usual suspects'. Instead, he distinguishes an early and mature CPE, whilst arguing – partly following Marx – that a broader grouping deserves recognition as contributing to CPE. Its less familiar names comprise a plethora of contributors whose work demonstrated something of a 'family resemblance'. Amongst others, these include William Petty ([1899] 1986) and James Steuart ([1767] 1966), as well as figures known in different contexts such as Benjamin Franklin and, to some degree, the Physiocrats. For present purposes, original CPE can be understood as a collective term for early and mature CPE, assuming sufficient family resemblance.

This chapter emphasises, however, that CPE has been interpreted and claimed in different ways, albeit without equal justification (see also Roncaglia 2006). This deliberation extends to disputes over who is legitimately 'classical' and, historically, who constitutes a transitional figure leading from CPE to modern economics. Myriad figures in the 1800s – such as Thomas Malthus ([1820] 1989, [1827] 1971), James McCulloch, Jeremy Bentham, James Mill ([1821] 2015), John Stuart Mill ([1848] 2017), and Jean Baptiste-Say – are contested as problematic for, or transitional from, CPE. Specifically, their work sits between early political economy and the rise of marginalism in the later 1800s, as well as later forms of neoclassical economics. Furthermore, the chapter positions CPE in terms of contemporary understandings of political economy and, with later chapters in this collection in mind, specifies how CPE remains relevant. This is a complex tale of uneven dynamics within the evolution of economics, based on different readings of, and claims made for, CPE.

The chapter first sets out some of the core commitments of an original CPE. It then considers matters of claims and complexity, focusing on continuity and discontinuity between CPE and the mainstream, before exploring some of the key themes of CPE. While contending that the limited mainstream perspective on CPE is mainly a product of ignorance, the chapter concludes by highlighting the relevance of CPE for contemporary political economy.

WHAT ORIGINAL CPE 'IS'

Providing a summary of CPE before discussing the complexity from which it emerges risks putting claims to legitimacy before the argument that justifies the case. That said, as a first-cut, CPE may be summarised as a collective and selective framework synthesised primarily from works written in the mid-to-late eighteenth century and early nineteenth century (with some contributions from the seventeenth century). These works took a new approach (less about the finances of government, more about wealth in general) when industrial capitalism was being born. Genealogically, the focus is primarily on the work of Adam Smith and David Ricardo, while also drawing on other lesser-known figures such as William Petty, Richard Cantillon, François Quesnay and James Steuart.

These works exhibit several common distinguishing features. First, a focus on how 'wealth' is *systematically* created and distributed. Second, an underlying methodological assumption that an economy has objectively determined features that affect creation and division of value. In turn, one can draw generalisations and aggregations on the ordinary functioning of an overall system – that is, reflect on features of an order (expressed as its typical or normal way of working). Third, a concomitant description of the emerging economic order as a system of capital accumulation, and an attempt to comprehend its variations around apparently underlying objectively determinable features. Fourth, a basic understanding that wages tend toward a given societal level. That is, there is a determined real wage dictated at minimum by subsistence, but which extends to conventional agreement on necessaries within a society. Fifth, a distinction between the proportion of wealth accruing to wages and other social groups. Sixth, a core idea that created wealth – the social product or total output – can then be split into that part necessary to reproduce the economy and a residual surplus. Seventh, some attempt to demonstrate or calculate the division of the social product between that necessary for reproduction – based on real wages, level of employment, a typical or given level of technical conditions of production, inputs and relative prices – and a surplus. Eighth, a basic insight that the *subsequent* surplus can be divided differently. This, in turn, can follow patterns and have consequences for profits, interest and rents, as well as the wage level and life conditions of labour. Ninth, a discussion of the role that power, motives and opportunity, and thus different social classes, play in determining the distribution of the surplus. Tenth, an argument about the proper or most effective functioning of an economy with more or less constraint on land use, market activity and international trade for the purposes of advancing wealth creation.

This list evokes a Sraffian–Marxian interpretation of original CPE. It implicitly contrasts CPE with marginalism's demand and supply approach to economy. In the latter, all aspects of an economy are simultaneously determined in a system of subjective preferences and factor prices, there is no distinctive role for labour, and little interest in social differences and power. In CPE, whilst prices, costs and wages may oscillate based on many (market) influences, labour has a central underlying role in determining value; and the economic system can be decomposed into distinct parts of a process (reproduction and subsequently distributable surplus) to analyse how its outcomes are determined. This Sraffian–Marxist take, and the myriad themes and nuances encompassing CPE are discussed further below. First, however, we consider how the term 'classical' has been constructed and disputed in economics.

CPE AND MATTERS OF CONTINUITY AND DISCONTINUITY IN POLITICAL ECONOMY

There is a longstanding claim that neoclassical economics is continuous with original CPE via marginalism (Cannan [1893] 1903; Bonar 1894; O'Brien 1975, 2004; Blaug 1978, 1987). This contrasts with the claim that neoclassical economics, and mainstream economics more generally, are discontinuous from CPE (Aspromourgos 1986, 2019). Moreover, from this second perspective, neoclassical and mainstream economics are not just significantly different, they are deficient. In contrast, other schools of thought (such as the Sraffians or neo-Ricardians, some post-Keynesians and neo-Marxists) have more legitimate claim to be both more adequate as political economy and as continuous from original CPE.

Our starting point is, thus, a necessarily obvious statement: continuity and discontinuity are disputed, and this is intimately bound up with how the 'relevance' of CPE is framed. This is as true today as in the period immediately following the 'birth' of CPE. For example, following John Stuart Mill's claim in *Principles of Political Economy* (1848) that 'there is nothing in the laws of value which remains for the present or any future writer to clear up', the early marginalist William Stanley Jevons explicitly rejects the Ricardian influence on political economy in the first Preface (1871) and a 'Ricardo–Mill school' in the second Preface (1879) to his *The Theory of Political Economy*, stating:

> When at length a true system of economics comes to be established, it will be seen that that able but wrong-headed man, David Ricardo, shunted the car of economic science on to a wrong line – a line, however, on which it was further urged towards confusion by his equally able and wrong-headed admirer, John Stuart Mill. (Jevons [1870, 1879] 1970: 72)

This sits awkwardly with the continuity thesis between CPE and marginalism. However, Jevons is more generous regarding Smith and Malthus. Further, one can contrast Jevons with Alfred Marshall's position in *Principles of Economics* ([1890] 1959), in which he claims to have preserved what was relevant in Smith and Ricardo. Marshall, for example, claims Ricardo as inspiration for his views on production and costs that form the basis of his approach to supply (within a demand and supply view of markets). Clearly, then, different marginalists relate to CPE according to different emphases. Concomitantly, subsequent interpretations – such as the link between Marshall and Thorstein Veblen and the transition to John Maynard Keynes – also illustrate this selective and purposive aspect of how later economists have related to original CPE.

Methodologically, Marshall saw his own work as combining induction and deduction. His *Principles of Economics* is replete with discussion of how socio-cultural complexity influences economic activity. Yet, his intent is to provide a theory of repetitive, regular behaviour which he expresses as law-like activity, and he relates this to a 'normal' over time – expressed in periods, such as the long run. The notion of 'normal' is a core concept of CPE, but it is contestable whether Marshall's use of the term is equivalent to that in CPE (discussed below). Regardless, this concept of 'normal' prompted Veblen to coin the term '*neo*classical' which, Tony Lawson (2015) has argued, was intended to capture a group of economists (Marshall, John Neville Keynes and others in the late nineteenth century) who recognised the organic nature of socio-economic change but were unable to adequately express this in their theory. Instead, the 'normal' amounts to a 'taxonomic science': a fixed categorisation of mechanistically repeating behaviours and outcomes that, whatever caveats are provided, is non-organic and unrealistic. Specifically, Marshall helped lay the grounds for theorising perfect competition as the template of an ideal market economy situation of convergent marginal 'efficiencies' – expressed by Arthur Pigou, formalised further by Frank Knight and, later, George Stigler and other Chicago school theorists (see Shackle [1967] 1983). Whilst there continues to be some dispute regarding what Veblen *did* mean by 'neoclassical', there is consensus that he did not use the phrase to suggest that neoclassical economists were true innovators along 'legitimately' classical lines (Morgan 2015, 2016a).

Writing in the decades after Veblen's articulation, John Maynard Keynes reaffirmed the classical link to the work of Marshall and others, based on a different emphasis and set of concerns. Keynes claimed that Say's law was core to classical economics and that the later economics of Marshall's generation, its marginalism notwithstanding, followed this line of reasoning. For Keynes, Marshall was also 'classical', as were others such as Pigou and Francis Edgeworth. Here, Keynes contrasted 'special cases' where Say's law applies with his own 'general theory', stating that the latter applies to the world *as it is* rather than as we might imagine it. Briefly, Say's law suggests that output induces demand through production and so further supply ultimately induces more demand, market to market, meaning a systematic shortage of demand cannot persist. For Keynes 'gluts', to use the classical term, were possible since effective demand could be systematically insufficient and so structural unemployment could arise – and had done so, at the time of the *General Theory*. Keynes acknowledges that his use of the term 'classical' is non-typical ('perpetrating a solecism'); nonetheless, his position indicates a degree of continuity between original CPE and the early progenitors of mainstream economics.

Beyond Keynes, Cambridge has also housed other scholars taking neoclassical economics as a failure and, in turn, seeking to develop CPE themes along more or less critical lines – such as Sraffa, Maurice Dobb, Joan Robinson, Richard Kahn, Luigi Pasinetti and Geoff Harcourt (along with Sraffa's executor at the University of Rome, Pierangelo Garegnani).[1] These scholars do not self-identify as 'classical', nor do they constitute a collective; yet, their work has greatly influenced interpretations of CPE over the previous century. This brings us to a more recognisably contemporary aspect of continuity and discontinuity between original CPE and subsequent developments, and closer to how the relevance of CPE remains *formally* disputed.

To reach this point, we first need to distinguish the different threads linking CPE to the current mainstream. Two threads may be readily distinguished. From a sociology of knowledge perspective, a general disciplinary attitude and understanding has developed in tandem with both how the field has developed and how economists have been socialised. Basic to this has been an ahistorical, asocial Whig history *presumption* that economics has evolved as a science and that classical economics is a historically specific set of canonical works from the origin of the discipline. Here, CPE works are prehistoric: both prior to economics as science and antiquated in language, context, discourse and theory. This perspective valorises Smith as a founding father, takes the 'invisible hand' as a dominant theme and then turns quickly to contemporary formulations of economics. Sociologically, this consequence stems from how the field has evolved pedagogically and how this is expressed for the majority: a textbook tradition that treats economics as though its concepts and theory amount to some equivalent of an engineering manual. Contemporary 'economics' is, thus, presented as a cumulative body of concepts, theory and applications. The state of the field is the state of the art, implicitly assuming 'economics' is constituted along a definite line of progress (more adequate knowledge, refined theory, better use of methods, improved empirical application and so forth). This narrative is self-perpetuating, based on the textbook tradition and corollary implication that there is no need for contemporary economists to be familiar with original CPE – only economic historians and philosophers and historians of economic thought have any need to explore it. The implication, inscribed in curricula, is that philosophy of economics and HET are sub-disciplinary specialisms, rather than integral to economics. As such, scholastic familiarity with original CPE becomes sub-disciplinary – tied to limited career prospects for its specialists. Further, teaching of CPE – if not eliminated entirely – is relegated to electives, with little apparent relevance to an engineering textbook perspective with its set of expectations of the future 'economist'. Thus, one thread of 'continuity' – the sociology of knowledge of the mainstream, with its presumption of linear progress in knowledge – trades on and reproduces ignorance of original CPE.

This first strand of 'continuity as ignorance' is coterminous with the widespread criticism that mainstream economics in general has followed a path dependence that has narrowed the field. Here, consensus is not absence of diversity nor development in sub-fields, but an underlying agreement of what economics is all about and how it best contributes as a social science. That is, the mainstream is constituted as a top-down disciplinary hierarchy maintained through control of PhD supervision and recruitment in prestige institutions and editorships of influential journals in a measured system of research activity, where place of publication matters for career prospects. This engenders a peculiar unity of methods, concepts and attitudes to what economics 'is'. This, in turn, is projected outwards as a universal toolkit to be applied to other social sciences – Gary Becker's version of George Stigler's positively posed 'imperial' project (Stigler 1984). This has been valorised over the years by proponents and beneficiaries according to a 'progress in knowledge' perspective, as simply mirroring a successful science.

To clarify, CPE is only as relevant as it is *allowed* to be, and the state of the field has provided the most significant, if silent, framework in which CPE has become essentially irrelevant for most economists. This is *not* because CPE is necessarily relevant (though the remainder of this chapter argues that it is), but because it is not possible to make an adequate determination from the perspective of ignorance (where Smith, for example, is reduced to passing comment on the invisible hand metaphor). The point, however, is not *really* about continuity of CPE with what follows, but the reproductive dynamics of the mainstream that affect the capacity to think about CPE, through the attitude towards it created by the evolution of the field.

Continuity *from* original CPE is merely a claim on the developmental trajectory of economics. This bring us to the second strand, and is more familiar when we ask ourselves questions such as, 'in what sense is CPE still relevant?' A useful bridging figure here is Paul Samuelson, since he looms large in both the intellectual history of economics and critical narratives of the state of the field by heterodox economists. Samuelson is a main source of formalism, one of the originators of the 'neoclassical new Keynesian synthesis', produced one of first mainstream-style textbooks, and often espoused Whig history opinion – despite that he was also a polymath and far more engaged with HET and its various professional bodies than later became the norm. He, thus, did a great deal to contribute to the 'learned ignorance' of the later mainstream regarding CPE. Equally, Samuelson's own work sits comfortably within what critics (originally Dobb 1972) refer to as 'counter-classical' work – a phrasing which rejects the appropriateness of the term 'neoclassical' because the work is not legitimately continuous from CPE. So, the second theme is the more nuanced discursive disputation in philosophy and HET and between schools laying claim to the legacy of original CPE.

The issue here is formal dispute over representation of CPE and, thus, claimed continuity (or lack of) *with* CPE. Clearly, the issue is not merely about the mainstream, but rather about how economists relate to the mainstream through CPE and vice versa. Its form is more sophisticated than the simple 'ignorance and progress' strand. Its most familiar construct to the interested non-specialist derives from such works as Robert Heilbroner's *The Worldly Philosophers* and *Teachings from the Worldly Philosophers*, and Joseph Schumpeter's *Ten Great Economists*. Schumpeter, of course, was also the author of the mammoth *History of Economic Analysis* – the typical point of departure for serious students embarking on postgraduate work and, thus, serves as a transition to more specialised works that add depth and insight to how we think about CPE.[2] In this regard, Tony Aspromourgos (1996, 2009) can reasonably claim to be among the most prominent historians of economic thought. His *On the Origins of Classical Political Economy* (1996), as indicated previously, argues that, prior to Smith's *Wealth of Nations*, original CPE owes much to Petty, Cantillon, Quesnay and Steuart. In *The Science of Wealth* (2009) he continues this theme: positing that whilst Smith may not have originated the term 'political economy', he provided the first coherent articulation of its main concepts and issues (a framework), such that political economy would develop on 'his terms'.

How Smith's work relates to the subsequent economics is, of course, a core issue for continuity, discontinuity and the continued relevance of CPE. Aspromourgos is relatively sympathetic to the Sraffian position and quite clear that the modern mainstream is discontinuous. As regards relevance, one cannot ignore Mark Blaug's *Economic Theory in Retrospect* (1978) and his entries in various dictionaries of economics (e.g. Blaug 1987). Blaug was a largely cautious advocate of mainstream economics and the claim that economics had made progress – that it had drawn selectively on and developed the work of the classics, albeit with improved technical expression. Conversely, he was also somewhat concerned by the apparent difficulty economics exhibits in applying Popperian falsification and demonstrating Kuhnian paradigm or Lakatosian research programme transition, and was, later, also a critic of formalism. Notably, Blaug frames his own approach to progress in contrast with both an 'ultra-Marxist' reading of history (theory merely reflects its time and place) and a free-floating economic theory 'for its own sake'. He is, however, ultimately unsympathetic to Sraffa by way of Ricardo. For Blaug, Ricardo was technically superior to Smith as an economist but had less breadth of vision. Generalisation of Ricardo's work on rent and income distribution via the problem of value led to Sraffa's contributions, which may have 'finally solved the mystery of an "invariable measure of value" […] However, what is in doubt is what we have gained by solving Ricardo's problem. Are we any the wiser about the functioning of an actual economic system as a result of it?' (Blaug 1978: 148). Sraffians, understandably, have responded to Blaug by questioning his interpretation of CPE and Sraffa (e.g. Garegnani 2002).

Evidently, there have been many different ways of relating to CPE, which have influenced the framing of its relevance. This is an important point, but it is also insufficient and easily misunderstood. It is one thing to suggest that different claims have been made on CPE and quite another to suggest that any claim on CPE is consistent with it and the purposes for which it is appropriated. Whilst common phrasing is not necessarily the same as common meaning, something is meant when claims are made. Different scholars may mean different things by CPE and use the term in different contexts for different purposes, but claims must be *justified* as adequate representations of the texts they draw from. Moreover, to be worthy of any serious claim to relevance, they must also be justified as providing plausible insight or argument with regard to their purported *purpose*: understanding economies in their various facets. That said, it is still possible that CPE has *multiple* useful things to tell us about contemporary economies, based on different developments, since plurality is not necessarily the same as incoherence. This can be illustrated by considering some aspects of the Sraffian claim on CPE, since this provides a segue into related ways CPE provides contemporary insight.

FROM SRAFFA BACK TO CPE VIA MARX

In addition to some of those already mentioned, there are many other prominent Sraffians and neo-Ricardians – John Eatwell, Christian Gehrke, Neri Salvadori, Ian Steedman and Heinz Kurz, to name just a few (see Kurz and Salvadori 2007, 2015; Vint et al. 2010; Gehrke et al. 2011; Faccarello and Kurz 2016). Kurz provides a useful summary of how Sraffians think about CPE:

> The litmus test of what is classical political economy is how its representatives approach the problem of value and distribution, that is, explain the sharing out of the product amongst the various claimants (workers, capitalists and landowners) and which system of relative prices supports this distribution […] the unifying element is that all [CPE authors] deal with the problem in essentially the same way: they explain the *general rate of profits* in the economy, the *rents* paid to the proprietors of the different types of land and the *ordinary or 'natural' prices* ruling in markets *at a given time and place* in terms of the following givens or *independent variables* (see Sraffa 1951, 1960):
> 1. The total quantities of the various commodities produced during a year.
> 2. The set of methods of production actually employed in producing these quantities, where this set reflects the technological knowledge available to producers.
> 3. The real wage rate (or, in the case of heterogenous labour, the set of real wage rates) in terms of a given bundle of commodities workers can afford with their money wage paid per unit of time (hour or work-day or […]).
> 4. The various qualities of land available in the economy to be used in production. (Kurz 2019: 29–30, original emphasis)

Clearly, this core aligns closely with the summary of what CPE 'is' above, while contrasting sharply with the *subjective* theory of value at the heart of marginalism and the subsequent development of much of mainstream economics (decontextualised and universalised demand and supply analysis based on individual preferences, marginal utility and marginal productivity of labour, and so forth). According to Sraffians, the focus of CPE is three groups or social classes with interests and the characteristics that arise from this. The subsequent economic analysis or framework explores an *objectively* conditioned set of circumstances (a system systematically theorised, as discussed in the next section of this chapter). At its core are conditional or contingent starting points (not to be confused with arbitrary starting points – they have reasons, but are not fixed) which, for Sraffians, are the institutionally given wage rate or profit rate. It is the system of wealth and the distribution of the 'social surplus' – what is available beyond the product of economic activity that is 'necessary' for the 'reproduction' of the system – that is the focus. Different starting points cause the system to adopt different manifest characteristics: for instance, different levels of power and influence for given groups, varying inequality and dynamism, and more or less of the surplus devoted to superfluous consumption rather than productive investment. This, in turn, leads to arguments for different institutional arrangements and policies.

Nuno Martins' contribution to this book (Chapter 8) reflects more deeply on the differing interpretations of Sraffa's system, developed after his editing, with Maurice Dobb, of Ricardo's papers (Ricardo 1951–73) and rejecting his original critique of Marshallian economics in the 1920s.[3] The main point here is that the Sraffian position is a claim on CPE, which takes the above as the core of CPE. Sraffians are typically to the left in their politics, which ostensibly sits awkwardly with the received impression that CPE is concerned with the superiority of a well-functioning liberal market economy (hence Blaug's comments that some aspects of Sraffian and neo-Marxist claims on Ricardo might seem odd as well as questionably 'realistic'). However, this simply serves to remind us that CPE 'is' an interpretive synthesis, even if it is not infinitely interpretable. Aspromourgos makes a similar point in reviewing Kurz and Salvadori (1998) which is worth quoting at length:

> At the risk of stating the obvious, 'classical economics' is a concept which had to be invented – it is not a mere 'natural' fact lying 'out there', only waiting to be (properly) discovered. As is well known, the notion of a classical economics was invented by Karl Marx, who deployed it to designate a group of economic writers from Petty and Boisguilbert in the seventeenth century to Ricardo and Sismondi in the early nineteenth century. Was this merely a chronological device? No [… it has] core substantive content built around the organising principle of production and distribution of surplus [… as] social net product […] net of necessary labour consumption as well as necessary inputs […] Subsequent to Marx the meaning of classicism shifted; and here Marshall's influence seems to have been the key factor [resulting in an interpretation of CPE as] a collection of more or less anticipatory elements of the marginalist approach, which led to a very different picture of the history of the science […] the great irony in all of this is that those historians of economics who now object to the Sraffian reconstruction of classical economics, as a kind of 'takeover' of the history of the discipline, are evidently oblivious to the possibility, or fact, that they themselves are latter-day foot-soldiers in an earlier usurpation of intellectual history by Marshall. The above characterisation supposes that Sraffa's conception of classicism more usefully captures our intellectual history than that of Marshall. (Aspromourgos 1999: 159)

This quotation brings together all the main issues: Marx's role in coining the term CPE, recognition of dispute regarding what it 'is', and the claim that there is a core to CPE and more or less adequate claims to be legitimately continuous with that core. So, we need to carefully consider what Marx meant and who he meant it about. Marx, of course, did not consider himself to be CPE – he wanted to identify a group who had oriented on questions deemed central and methods of interest. Moreover, he wanted to contrast this with what he considered a subsequent wrong turn, and contrast both with his own approach – substantively, *his* Labour Theory of Value and a class-based account of *why* it was unsurprising that a wrong turn might occur.

In *A Contribution to the Critique of Political Economy*, Marx ([1859] 1971: 52–63) first identifies CPE as work in Britain and France undertaken on labour and the commodity, beginning with Petty and Boisguilbert, taking in discussion of Benjamin Franklin, the Physiocrats, Steuart and Smith, and 'ending' with Ricardo and Sismondi. In the later *Theories of Surplus Value* (Marx 1951), he develops his constructive critique of the classical political economists (including the Physiocrats) in more detail. Here, Marx clearly defines CPE as an *attempt* to 'grasp the inner connection of the phenomena' under investigation. Finally in *Capital Volume I*, and most famously in the Second Preface (Marx [1867] 1954: 12–20), Marx contrasts between CPE as an early attempt at 'scientific examination' of what we today would call capitalism (Marx did not use this term) and 'apologetics' of 'vulgar' economics. Marx's underlying point is that CPE has some vulgar (apologetic) features and these increasingly come to the fore both in society and political economy scholarship. In the Second Preface, Marx holds that CPE exposes the 'antagonisms of class interests, of wages and profits, of profits and rent', and since 'class struggle' is a real facet of society, the subsequent response is both changes in law and a counter-movement in ideas. According to Marx, despite good intentions, John Stuart Mill begins a process of 'harmonising political economy' with the needs of the 'bourgeoisie' and starts to 'reconcile irreconcilables'. So, for Marx, Mill is not quite true to the original intent of CPE, such that original CPE begins to mutate or distort much earlier than with marginalism in the 1870s.

Whatever one's opinion of Marx's own work, the original designation of CPE refers to both a group and set of common concerns and commitments, and also served as a point of *contrast*. What this suggests, unsurprisingly, is that Sraffians can claim that their use of the term CPE is relatively consistent with Marx's, since both bring to the fore that CPE focuses on features of the economic system understood *objectively*.[4] As for the Sraffian claim that there is textual evidence for core common content of CPE and there is a 'litmus test', this too seems reasonably plausible. CPE may be, as Aspromourgos states, necessarily synthetic; but it is not reasonable to suggest its meaning can be endlessly 'plasticised' without doing violence to the intent of its original articulators. Earlier we suggested that both *claims about* CPE and its *relevance* must be justified. With this in mind, it is worth summarising some key features of original CPE and its contrasts with the mainstream, since these open up different pathways to explore how we might conceptualise CPE's continuing relevance.

CPE CONTRASTED WITH THE ECONOMIC MAINSTREAM

When balanced between reconstruction (exegesis) and synthesis, CPE becomes a system of thought: a set of concepts, problem domains and theories, all contained within a methodology and influenced by a 'spirit' of inquiry. This ordering is clearly open to different points of departure. The best way to start is to position the role of 'supply' and 'demand' in relation to CPE. This is not because this is what is most important in CPE. Rather, it is because the prevailing ideological projection of capitalism is dominated by the mainstream idea that subjective preference (marginal utility) constitutes *demand*, that marginal productivity underpins *supply*, and that these conjointly determine pricing and output in time in any one market and in all markets simultaneously. This is fundamental to a vision of the market economy as an equilibrating engine of dynamic efficiencies, whose harmonious progress is only interrupted by 'shocks', and which then variously tags on the state, crowding, distortions, inefficiencies, irrationalities and failures. Beginning with demand and supply allows a summary set of contrasting claims to be made that bring to the fore the difference between original CPE and the modern mainstream – some of which have already been foregrounded above.

It is trivially true that demand and supply exist and that market exchange 'occurs'. In production and trade processes, some organisations and persons provide demand for goods and services, which are supplied by other organisations, while *one* way in which this happens is through market exchange. Original CPE, however, highlighted the *significance* of production and trade for the national wealth, shifting attention from the sovereign to a *system* of wealth creation. Original CPE also shifted emphasis from the Physiocrats regarding the role of agriculture and land in wealth creation. The key point, though, is that it sought to explain how wealth was, and could best be, created. For CPE, demand and supply do not explain anything, not even the prices that arise in markets. There is an observable process of what Smith referred to as 'gravitation' where 'market prices' oscillate around some rough-and-ready level because of myriad disturbing influences on participant behaviour, but these 'market prices' are underpinned by 'normal' prices as determined by systemic forces (becoming relative prices). CPE focuses on these systemic forces and, thus, seeks a *systematic* explanation. Hence, CPE is objective-oriented, *not* subjective-focused in its explanations. Its normal is *not* that of Marshall.

To explain *how* a system of market exchange might operate, a concept of motivated participants is required, as some explanation is required of why polities might facilitate, and people might make, markets and engage in market activity. In CPE, Smith supplies this. In *The Wealth of Nations*, a 'double coincidence of wants' arises – one set of needs and wants is satisfied by another's set of needs and wants. There are many reasons wants and needs are met, though there is also a typical underlying convergent serving of self-interest on both sides: goods and services and reciprocating payment in market situations. Whilst this has historic social and cultural aspects, CPE roots it in a basic disposition to 'truck'. A 'division of labour' becomes possible from this disposition, and specialisation evolves through mutual self-interest, thereby serving economic ends. However, though self-interest is a fundamental aspect of economic activity, CPE holds that no person can be reduced to an economic isolate. Humans are social, and self-interest, in general, is other-regarding and involves constraint. The broader context is provided by Smith's *Theory of Moral Sentiments* (subject to reconciling the 'Adam Smith problem' of demonstrating compatibility between his works – see Göçmen 2007). Moral conventions emerge and evolve in societies based on 'mutual sympathy' and subject to continual monitoring processes (we ask ourselves: 'Is this right?' 'How do I feel about it?' 'How would others judge this?'). So, Smith's concept of self-interest has context and his economic individual is not a hedonistic calculative machine. Nor are greed and exploitation inadvertently condoned or valorised. Concomitantly, self-interest is *not* uncritically endorsed as necessarily leading to best possible outcomes. This is socio-historically conditioned. Self-interest is a good only as far as it is conducive to mutually beneficial outcomes and this, too, is conditional on its broader role in wealth creation.

Myriad theoretical, practical-policy and ethical themes evidently arise in CPE. One need not agree with claims made in CPE or based on it, yet, original CPE recognises that claims *must be* made, rather than merely assumed away in an ideal world, where the focus of the economist is reduced to an asocial depoliticised 'economic' domain. This latter viewpoint is circular and simply pushes intrinsic issues to the margins or makes them the concern of *different* social sciences.

Original CPE is antithetical to a naïve presumption that economic activity is necessarily mutually beneficial. In CPE, the social division of labour in its historic form is also a social stratification of classes, which returns us to CPE's focus on systemic forces underpinning economic explanations. This is the theoretical focus of an 'invariable measure of value' that, along with distribution, is for both Marx and Sraffians a 'litmus test' of whether something is CPE. As noted, this is core to Sraffian analysis of the relation between groups and relative prices in terms of the social surplus. This is also where Blaug applies pressure by positing no clear relevance in the Sraffian approach to real economies, whilst also suggesting left-leaning and Marxist claims on CPE are peculiar. Blaug's first point, however, is mainly a technical critique of the Sraffian model and many responses already exist (see the Sraffian collections previously referenced). Moreover, as philosophical counterargument (the parsing of argumentation), there is a distinction between acknowledging that Sraffa's work and Sraffian solutions to an 'invariable measure' are contestable (not least by Marxists), and acknowledging that Sraffian research attempts to provide solutions to problems and forms *set out* in original CPE. Again, this contrasts with the contemporary mainstream.

CPE clearly explores the objective measure of systemic interrelations by addressing wealth production and distribution. In CPE, the real wage can be known as far as convention dictates this – not necessarily equating subsistence to 'just at starvation level', but rather to what is deemed necessary to match social convention. The social product or total output can then be split between that necessary for economic reproduction (based on given technical conditions of production, inputs, level of employment, real wages and relative prices) and what remains to be divided between profit, interest and rent. In contrast to a supply and demand approach, the whole is not simultaneously determined, but there are clear links and interactions. The Sraffian approach to CPE is selective, but for the purposes of development of this core focus on the distribution of the surplus. Moreover, its proponents recognise the subtlety and differences in their CPE antecedents (ignorance is not the position) – such as Ricardo's critique of Smith on rent and use of a labour theory of value without conceiving labour as the sole determination of value in a system where anticipating the future affects present decisions (later addressed by Sraffians and Marxists).

Thus, as suggested in previous sections, the Sraffian system does not just stand alone; it has a reasonable claim to *authority*. Sraffians are mainly consistent with the *methodological* framing of original CPE, whilst the current mainstream is not. Yet, there remains scope for further philosophical debate over methodology, such as the ontological status of the Sraffian model of equations. This, however, involves a realist critique of the model form that determination takes in an *objectively* stated system. The critique is of the compatibility of intent, theory and its symbolic expression (the Lawson critique of heterodox consistency) rather than a critique of *all* aspects. One could take this in very different directions in relation to Blaug's general point regarding original CPE and Sraffians (and Marxists) on the problem of invariant value and insight on real economies. Yet, the point cannot be used to suggest that the subjective theory of the contemporary mainstream is consistent with original CPE.

Blaug's second point, regarding the politics of political economy, is more concerned with futures than history. As recognised by all detailed and biographical works on individual CPE theorists and CPE collectively, its articulators (and its more disputed figures) lived in a time of significant change: from the Enlightenment into early capitalism via a phase of technological change, land consolidation at home and appropriation abroad, slavery, whaling, establishment of early monopolising 'companies' (beginning with state charters), development of banking (and early central banking), war in Europe, financing of these wars and mercantile ventures, and expanded regional and global trade. This was neither 'liberal' nor 'free'. Nor was it harmonious, as demonstrated by Karl Polanyi (1945) and Eric Hobsbawn (1962, 1975). 'Market economy' had to be invented and the state played a major role in this in the UK and elsewhere.

The point, however, is that original CPE was deeply concerned by the real problems of its times. It was socially and politically observant and engaged, debating and exploring specific issues, such as currency exchange systems, gold standards, and state responses to downturns. Moreover, it was intimately concerned with not just theorising and explaining systems as a whole, but also debating their merits. For the casual reader, original CPE is associated with *advocacy* of free trade over mercantilism and freely exchanging domestic markets rather than more interventionist and state approaches. However, the question, 'is it odd, anachronistic or perverse for left-leaning economists to place a claim on original CPE?', is really a matter of the *degree* to which original CPE advocated a fully functioning liberal market, *why* they held those views, whether they *would* continue to hold them in changed circumstances, and whether CPE *can* engender reasonable arguments for different institutional, political and systemic situations.

The modern mainstream is not divorced from the contemporary world – it is a powerful influence on public policy – yet original CPE contains no similar implicit assumption of intrinsic *social cohesion*. There is no assumption that a market economy is a wealth-creating machine that, if left to its own devices, will operate ideally and 'grow' to the benefit of all. Scholars such as James Galbraith or Thomas Piketty periodically remind mainstream economics of its failure to adequately deal with inequality and distribution or the difference between wealth creation and wealth capture; yet, it has consistently failed to respond adequately (Fullbrook and Morgan 2014, 2021). Whatever the merits and limits of its arguments on theory and particular policy issues – with Ricardo on comparative advantage or Malthus on population being archetypal foci for this – CPE remains *different* to the modern mainstream in its fundamental framework of liberal market economy. Wealth creation is *conditional* on how surplus is created and evolves, which is deeply socio-political.

While original CPE does not assume society is harmonious or necessarily progressive, much of the theory is based on long runs and the 'normal'. There is something static about this, along with an implicit tendency to assume some systemic features as fixed in order to explore the determination of others. Both tendencies become features of more technical mainstream approaches after Marshall. However, to reiterate, the CPE system of normal is not that of Marshall, and perhaps deals more effectively with its overriding *purpose* as exploration of a dynamic situation (though this is arguable). CPE is, of course, dogged by controversy over Say's law (via James Mill in 1807 and John Stuart Mill later), but the primary problems discussed by Smith and Ricardo are the rate of capital accumulation, population change, the influence of distribution on technological and technical change, and the role of government in a domestic and international context. One does not have to agree with the arguments of original CPE, nor consider them exhaustive; yet, in this pre-disciplinary world, original CPE was socially engaged in a manner transcending the later 'science' of the mainstream (which has been criticised for its explanatory failure, ideological function and scientism).

It is also important to recognise what original CPE does acknowledge, because this nuance addresses the issue of 'degree' in the argument for a liberal market economy. Smith is clear that different social classes not only have different interests based on what can be distributed (as rent, profit and wages), but that each has different capacities to organise for influence and to understand their interests and how to pursue them. In turn, since landlords can earn rent indolently, they have less immediate reason to be well-informed; whilst merchants and masters are likely to be best informed by education and observation and workers least, except through experience of suffering. Moreover, merchants and masters have retained capital and so are most able to endure conflict. For Smith, the system is practically tilted towards masters and merchants, and there is a constant need to guard against their self-interest transitioning to become detrimental to the interests of wealth creation through influence on the law and state, and through monopolisation.

Capture of the state is a fundamental problem for Smith, no less than the need to ensure that trade works to the benefit of all in a system where it tends not to do so. In original CPE, it is the potential for wealth creation that underpins the *contingent* support for liberal market economy. In Smith, we have social stratification of classes, the social division of labour (specialisation of work categories) and technical division of labour affecting work categories. The last of these adds a new dimension to productive powers, which can be augmented through capital accumulation by enabling further improvements in productivity via the division of labour and socio-economic evolution, allowing for higher profits and incomes (as markets expand and deepen). This is *why* proponents of original CPE contingently advocated liberal market economy. There is no presumption of a magical 'invisible hand' in its modern form (Smith only uses the term three times across his works, and never in a significant or positive argument). Original CPE is, of course, *shaped* by its own time horizon (so both Blaug and Marx are focused on a relevant matter of socialisation) of what seems possible, but the advocacy is not uncritical. Continuing this theme, Ricardo argues that, if technical change is in service of luxuries consumed mainly by the few masters, merchants and rentiers, there will be no upward effect on general real wage rates. Meanwhile, substitution of capital for labour may reduce real wage rates for the deskilled and engender unemployment – there is, thus, textual scope in original CPE to contextualise Say's law along different lines. Moreover, there is a primary case in Ricardo's work to ensure that distributions enable growing consumption *across* the economy. There is, as such, no given dynamic of an economy, but different possible dynamics.

Regardless, in the Ricardian approach to rent there is a continual problem of transferring profit *to* rent (through relative rises in production costs of agricultural land and, thus, prices), offset by technological progress and based on conflict between extensive and intensive sources of rent and possibilities opened up by international trade.[5] Whilst Ricardo exploited his understanding of rent – becoming one of England's wealthiest landowners following the Napoleonic War and after making a fortune speculating on the stock exchange – he was, no less than Smith, systemically critical of the *role* of rent. Indeed, the very concept of rent and its negative connotations (as generalised unearned income) essentially disappear in later mainstream economics. Similarly, the concepts of 'capital', capital ownership and capital gains lose any sense of adequate distinctions and consequences in terms of metatheory: 'dynamic wealth creation' becomes a given of capital flows for essentially any form of asset, while investment, exploitation, appropriation and speculation are conflated.

So, one might argue that original CPE is a form of *critical* theory in relation to the issues of 'degree' and 'why', as set out above. Moreover, the scope of the state discussed by Smith and others is greater than a lay reader might imagine. Smith argues for banking regulation, state-financed primary education, infrastructure investment (albeit often through local tolls for financing), monitoring of monopoly tendencies (while assuming monopoly cannot be maintained forever because of the profit attraction and price problem), and services such as policing and modernised courts able to deliver *common* justice and security (including security of property to enable confidence in investment and ongoing capital accumulation). These were not givens in his time. Smith, of course, had a greater commitment to the emergence of order than Marx or later commentators on the instability of capitalism. Yet, he did not theorise this order as purely spontaneous, nor conflate it with the exceptional role of the few (rather than actions of the many) or with stability. Equally, Smith did not equate order with an argument for the state as some kind of stripped down 'nightwatchman'. Further, when acting as commissioner of customs, Smith assiduously enforced tariffs and trade restrictions that protected Scottish handicrafts. Following this theme, Ricardo's position on tax holds that taxes on rents affect only rentiers, whilst other forms of tax can be more readily shifted with adverse effects on other social classes and the scope for wealth creation. Ricardo advocated poor relief and was a social reformer in parliament: this reform commitment is a common theme of early CPE, shared by those Marx regarded with greater scepticism (Jeremy Bentham and both Mills).

Original CPE is, evidently, not some simple set of assertions regarding domestic and international free trade, nor a primitive precursor to the mainstream conception of a distinct economic domain matched by an economic theory excluding society, the state and politics based on a theory of necessary harmonies, equilibriums and benefits. Much more could be said regarding individual disputes: for example, CPE on the origins of money, commodity money and the role of money in banking, finance and growth. Equally, the contributions of individuals now deleted from popular history require further discussion – besides Petty, one should not neglect the work of Robert Torrens (a contemporary constructive critic of Ricardo) on comparative advantage, and his advocacy of conditional reciprocity in trade and major interventions on the Corn Laws, combinations and banking (see Robbins 1958; Torrens 2000). There is also a danger in shaping an argument contrasting the mainstream with constructive aspects and possible interpretations of CPE to convey the impression that CPE represents some theoretical zenith to the mainstream's nadir, which pre-empts every significant question and provides comprehensive answers. This would be overstatement. It is more reasonable to suggest, following Aspromourgos, that original CPE created a productive problem field, while the later mainstream has represented a wrong turn (see also Milonakis and Fine 2009). What a 'right turn' looks like remains an open question. What is not in question, however, is that the themes and spirit of original CPE, the current state of the mainstream notwithstanding, remains relevant, and we close with this.

CONCLUSION: THE CONTINUING RELEVANCE OF CPE

The very existence of the subsequent chapters in this collection indicates something of the legacy of CPE. Genealogically, this is hardly surprising given CPE came first. However, as is clear from the structure of this chapter, the Marxist and the neo-Ricardian schools are perhaps the most direct legacy, extending perhaps to post-Keynesians (see Kalecki 1971; Kaldor 1985). Yet, original CPE themes are to be found across non-mainstream economics. The development of institutional economics takes in the *methodenstreit* and Veblen on Marshall, so is quintessentially in a critical theory line of development from CPE. Likewise, social economics has roots in both Smith and the 'Adam Smith problem' and original institutionalism. In a more biographical vein, Gramsci and Sraffa influenced each other, and so there are personal links which stand behind the intellectual resonance of Gramscian and neo-Marxist approaches to political economy. Moreover, capital accumulation and social reproduction are fundamental to many political economy schools. Some are, of course, more critical and contrastive than others: feminist economics rejects self-interest as a cornerstone of society, since it omits care and, thus, renders invisible great swathes of motive, socio-economic activity and social relations. Equally, though CPE introduces the issue of 'steady-state' economies (found in Ricardo and John Stuart Mill as thought experiments), CPE and Marxism, no less than the mainstream, are dogged by criticism that they treat the world as an exploitable empty space rather than complex, balanced ecosystem. Though there is push back on these issues, they are a stark reminder that, though important questions may have been previously recognised in some form, their current interpretation can be quite different (see Dale 2021).

However, this chapter also suggested that it is still possible that CPE offers *multiple* useful insights about contemporary economies, based on different developments, since plurality is not necessarily the same as incoherence (see also Stilwell 2011; O'Hara 2012; Sinha and Thomas 2019). As such, it is worth mentioning a selection of recent works that share a CPE thread. Aspromourgos (1996: ch. 10) explores subsequent Sraffian and Keynesian themes. Similarly, Ajit Sinha has developed his own take on value theory from CPE, Marx and Sraffa (Sinha 2019), whilst Nuno Martins has advocated a hybrid of Sraffa, Keynes and Amartya Sen (Martins 2014; Morgan 2016b). This work takes the problem of the surplus as its point of departure; while this, along with interpreting the economy as a form of social provisioning, has remained central to heterodox economics (see Lee and Jo 2011; Lee and Cronin 2016; Jo et al. 2018).

Anwar Shaikh (2016), meanwhile, stakes a claim to the classical legacy, whilst also distancing himself from post-Keynesian and neoclassical approaches (claiming the latter is perfectionist and the former merely the imperfect version of this perfection via the visible hand of the state). He adopts an array of classical precepts (as well as its language – notably the demonstration of order–disorder and gravitation in long-term patterns of recurrence in 'real competition'). Amongst other things, Shaikh explores the classical treatment of the commodity and commodity money and Sraffian treatments of relative prices of production, arguing that, in a fiat money economy, national price levels are determined according to classical themes.[6]

What one can reasonably infer is that prominent figures are still drawing *new* inspiration from classical work and themes. One might describe much of this as diversely 'true to' original CPE without being slavishly tied to it. This hinges on Asproumorgos's point regarding 'plasticity', but it seems reasonable to suggest that CPE remains a relevant living body of knowledge. If we consider it as a spirit of inquiry, its relevance is broader still. For example, Michael Hudson, one of the most influential commentators on financialised economies (as well as the history of money), often contrasts the classical systemic critique of rent (siding against the rentier) with the ideological invisibility of rent in most modern mainstream work (Hudson 2017). As a final point, emphasis on the *classical* in CPE tends to evoke a historical period of transition; yet CPE is both a literature and cumulative legacy. It provides a permanent resource for critique of the current state of contemporary mainstream economics and alternatives to it. No modern economist should be comfortable with a position of ignorance in its regard.

48 *Handbook of alternative theories of political economy*

NOTES

1. For some indication of the general thread of debate, see Robinson (1962, 1971) and Harcourt (1983, 1984).
2. This is not to suggest that Schumpeter is the best source on CPE (various CPE scholars have disputed his reading). However, Schumpeter's *History* is also a reminder that focusing on CPE is just one strand in the complex history of economics. One can look back at CPE from myriad perspectives, which vary depending on context: 'Smithianismus' and the Methodenstreit, for example, take on different significance if one is interested in original institutionalism via Schmoller or if one were interested in later themes taken up by Max Weber.
3. For further context, see Meek (1950, 1961); Dobb (1972); Garegnani (1984); Hicks (1985); and Pasinetti (2007).
4. Further, Gehrke and Kurz (2018), for example, set out key differences based on how Sraffa approaches Marx's work; whilst Fine (2019) and Fine and Saad-Filho (2018) illustrate how this looks from the reverse.
5. For a comprehensive discussion of Ricardo on rent from a Marxist perspective, see Fine (2019).
6. Shaikh (2016) has attracted much attention (e.g. Patomäki 2017), not all of it complimentary (e.g. Toporowski 2020, on Shaikh's use of the classical treatment of interest and its links to money, credit and finance).

REFERENCES

Aspromourgos, T. (1986) 'On the origins of the term "neoclassical"', *Cambridge Journal of Economics* **10** (3), pp. 265–70.
Aspromourgos, T. (1996) *On the Origins of Classical Economics: Distribution and Value from William Petty to Adam Smith*, London: Routledge.
Aspromourgos, T. (1999) 'What is classical economics?', *History of Economics Review*, **30** (1), pp. 159–68.
Aspromourgos, T. (2009) *The Science of Wealth: Adam Smith and the Framing of Political Economy*, London: Routledge.
Aspromourgos, T. (2019) 'What is supply and demand? The Marshallian Cross versus Classical Economics', *Review of Political Economy*, **31** (1), pp. 26–41.
Blaug, M. (1978) *Economic Theory in Retrospect*, 3rd edn, Cambridge: Cambridge University Press.
Blaug, M. (1987) 'British classical economics', in Eatwell, J. et al. (eds), *The New Palgrave Dictionary of Economics*, Volume 1, Basingstoke: Macmillan.
Bonar, J. (1894) 'Classical economics', in Palgrave, R. (ed.), *Dictionary of Political Economy*, Volume 1, London: Macmillan.
Cannan, E. ([1893] 1903) *A History of the Theories of Production and Distribution in English Political Economy from 1776 to 1848*, 2nd edn, London: King.
Dale, G. (2021) 'Rule of nature or rule of capital? Physiocracy, ecological economics and ideology', *Globalizations*, **18** (7), pp. 1230–47.
Dobb, M. (1972) *Theories of Value and Distribution since Adam Smith: Ideology and Economic Theory*, Cambridge: Cambridge University Press.
Faccarello, G. and Kurz, H. (eds) (2016) *Handbook on the History of Economic Analysis: Volume II; Schools of Thought in Economics*, Cheltenham, UK and Northampton, MA, USA: Edward Elgar Publishing.
Fine, B. (2019) 'Marx's rent theory revisited? Landed property, nature and value', *Economy and Society*, **48** (3), pp. 450–61.
Fine, B. and Saad-Filho, A. (2018) 'Marx 200: the abiding relevance of the labour theory of value', *Review of Political Economy*, **30** (3), pp. 339–54.
Fullbrook, E. and Morgan, J. (eds) (2014) *Piketty's Capital in the Twenty-First Century*, London: College Books.

Fullbrook, E. and Morgan, J. (eds) (2021) *The Inequality Crisis*, Bristol: World Economics Association Books.

Garegnani, P. (1984) 'Value and distribution in the classical economists and Marx', *Oxford Economic Papers*, **36** (2), pp. 291–325.

Garegnani, P. (2002) 'Misunderstanding classical economics? A reply to Blaug', *History of Political Economy*, **34** (1), pp. 241–54.

Gehrke, C. and Kurz, H. (2018) 'Sraffa's constructive and interpretive work, and Marx', *Review of Political Economy*, **30** (3), pp. 428–42.

Gehrke, C., Salvadori, N., Steedman, I. and Sturn, R. (eds) (2011) *Classical Political Economy and Modern Theory: Essays in Honour of Heinz Kurz*, London: Routledge.

Göçmen, D. (2007) *The Adam Smith Problem*, London: Taurus.

Harcourt, G. (1983) 'On Piero Sraffa's contribution to economics', in Groenewegen, P. and Halevi, J. (eds), *Altro Polo: Italian Economics Past and Present*, Sydney: Frederick May Foundation, Chapter 4.

Harcourt, G. (1984) 'The end of an era: Joan Robinson (1903–83) and Piero Sraffa (1898–1983)', *Journal of Post Keynesian Economics*, **6** (3), pp. 466–9.

Hicks, J. (1985) 'Sraffa and Ricardo: a critical view', in Caravale, G. (ed), *The Legacy of Ricardo*, Oxford: Basil Blackwell, pp. 305–19.

Hobsbawm, E. (1962) *The Age of Revolution 1789–1848*, London: Weidenfeld and Nicholson.

Hobsbawm, E. (1975) *The Age of Capital 1848–1875*, London: Weidenfeld & Nicholson.

Hudson, M. (2017) *J is for Junk Economics*, Dresden: ISLET-Verlag.

Jevons, W. ([1871] 1970) *Theory of Political Economy*, London: Pelican.

Jo, T.-H., Chester, L. and D'ippolita, C. (eds) (2018) *The Routledge Handbook of Heterodox Economics: Theorizing, Analyzing and Transforming Capitalism*, London: Routledge.

Kaldor, N. (1985) *Economics Without Equilibrium*, London: Macmillan.

Kalecki, M. (1971) *Selected Essays on the Dynamics of the Capitalist Economy*, Cambridge: Cambridge University Press.

Kurz, H. (2019) 'Classical political economy', *Munich Social Science Review*, **2**, pp. 17–51.

Kurz, H. and Salvadori, N. (eds) (1998) *The Elgar Companion to Classical Economics*, Cheltenham, UK and Northampton, MA, USA: Edward Elgar Publishing.

Kurz, H. and Salvadori, N. (eds) (2007) *Interpreting Classical Economics: Studies in Long Period Analysis*, London: Routledge.

Kurz, H. and Salvadori, N. (eds) (2015) *The Elgar Companion to David Ricardo*, Cheltenham, UK and Northampton, MA, USA: Edward Elgar Publishing.

Lawson, T. (2015) *Essays on the Nature and State of Economics*, London: Routledge.

Lee, F. and Cronin, B. (eds) (2016) *Handbook of Research Methods and Applications in Heterodox Economics*, Cheltenham, UK and Northampton, MA, USA: Edward Elgar Publishing.

Lee, F. and Jo, T.-H. (2011) 'Social surplus approach and Heterodox Economics', *Journal of Economic Issues*, **45** (8), pp. 857–75.

Malthus, T. ([1820] 1989) *Principles of Political Economy*, 2 vols, Cambridge: Cambridge University Press.

Malthus, T. ([1827] 1971) *Definitions in Political Economy*, London: J. Murray.

Marshall, A. ([1890] 1959) *Principles of Economics*, 8th edn, London: MacMillan.

Martins, N. (2014) *The Cambridge Revival of Political Economy*, London: Routledge.

Marx, K. ([1859] 1971) *A Contribution to the Critique of Political Economy*, London: Lawrence and Wishart.

Marx, K. ([1867] 1954) *Capital: A Critique of Political Economy*, Volume 1, London: Lawrence and Wishart.

Marx, K. (1951) *Theories of Surplus Value: Selections*, London: Lawrence & Wishart.

Meek, R. (1950) 'The decline of Ricardian economics in England', *Economica*, **17** (65), pp. 43–62.

Meek, R. (1961) 'Mr Sraffa's rehabilitation of classical economics', *Scottish Journal of Political Economy*, **8**, pp. 119–36.

Mill, J. ([1821] 2015) *Elements of Political Economy*, London: Dalton.

Mill, J. S. ([1848] 2017) *Principles of Political Economy*, London: Pantios Classics.

Milonakis, D. and Fine, B. (2009) *From Political Economy to Economics*, London: Routledge.

Morgan, J. (2015) 'What's in a name? Tony Lawson on neoclassical economics and heterodox economics', *Cambridge Journal of Economics*, **39** (3), pp. 843–65.

Morgan, J. (ed.) (2016a) *What is Neoclassical Economics?* London: Routledge.

Morgan, J. (2016b) 'The contemporary relevance of a Cambridge tradition: economics as political economy, political economy as social theory and ethical theory', *Cambridge Journal of Economics*, **40** (2), pp. 663–700.

O'Brien, D. (1975) *The Classical Economists*, London: Oxford University Press.

O'Brien, D. (2004) *The Classical Economists Revisited*, Princeton, NJ: Princeton University Press.

O'Hara, P. (2012) 'Core general principles of political economy', *The Journal of Economic Analysis*, **3** (1), pp. 1–24.

Pasinetti, L. (2007) *Keynes and the Cambridge Keynesians: A Revolution in Economics to Be Accomplished*, Cambridge: Cambridge University Press.

Patomäki, H. (2017) 'Review: *Capitalism: Competition, Conflict, Crisis*', *Journal of Critical Realism*, **16** (5), pp. 537–43.

Petty, W. ([1899] 1986) *The Economic Writings of Sir William Petty*, ed. C. Hull, Volume 1, New York: A.M. Kelley.

Polanyi, K. (1945) *Origins of Our Time: The Great Transformation*, London: Victor Gollancz.

Ricardo, D. ([1817] 1821) *On the Principles of Political Economy and Taxation*, London: John Murray.

Ricardo, D. (1951–73) *The Works and Correspondence of David Ricardo*, 11 vols, collated and edited by P. Sraffa and M. Dobb, Cambridge: Cambridge University Press.

Robbins, L. (1958) *Robert Torrens and the Evolution of Classical Economics*, London: Macmillan.

Robinson, J. (1962) *Economic Philosophy*, London: Penguin.

Robinson, J. (1971) *Economic Heresies*, Basingstoke: Macmillan.

Roncaglia, A. (2006) *The Wealth of Ideas*, Cambridge: Cambridge University Press.

Shackle, G. ([1967] 1983) *The Years of High Theory: Invention and Tradition in Economic Thought 1926–1939*, Cambridge: Cambridge University Press.

Shaikh, A. (2016) *Capitalism: Competition, Conflict, Crises*, Oxford: Oxford University Press.

Sinha, A. (2019) *Essays on Theories of Value in the Classical Tradition*, Basingstoke: Palgrave Macmillan.

Sinha, A. and Thomas, A. (eds) (2019) *Pluralistic Economics and its History*, London: Routledge.

Smith, A. ([1759] 2000) *The Theory of Moral Sentiments*, New York: Prometheus Books.

Smith, A. ([1776] 1976) *An Inquiry into the Nature and Causes of the Wealth of Nations*, 2 vols, Oxford: Clarendon Press.

Sraffa, P. (1960) *Production of Commodities by Means of Commodities*, Cambridge: Cambridge University Press.

Steuart, J. ([1767] 1966) *An Inquiry into the Principles of Political Oeconomy*, 2 vols, Edinburgh: Oliver and Boyd.

Stigler, G. (1984) 'Economics: the imperial science?' *The Scandinavian Journal of Economics*, **86** (3), pp. 301–13.

Stilwell, F. (2011) *Political Economy: The Contest of Economic Ideas*, 3rd edn, Oxford: Oxford University Press.

Toporowski, J. (2020) 'Anwar Shaikh and the classical theory of interest: a critical note', *Cambridge Journal of Economics*, **44** (2), pp. 465–74.

Torrens, R. (2000) *Collected Works of Robert Torrens*, ed. G. de Vivo, 8 vols, London: Thoemmes Press.

Vint, J., Metcalfe, S., Kurz, H., Salvadori, N. and Samuelson, P. (eds) (2010) *Economic Theory and Economic Thought: Essays in Honour of Ian Steedman*, London: Routledge.

4. The Marxist tradition in political economy

Bill Dunn

The spectre of Marx haunts all critical political economy. Marx's visions of capitalism continue to resonate across the world, revealing it as a uniquely dynamic but disruptive system, a system of exploitation and economic crises, of imperialism and environmental destruction. Marxism epitomises the principle that theory should be dedicated not only to understanding the world but also to changing it; and it continues to inspire and inform new generations of activists. Even for Marxism's many opponents – and even through their often grotesque misrepresentations – Marxism remains an essential point of reference.

Because I cannot pretend to summarise more than 150 years of scholarship and activism here, this chapter simply identifies some basic principles and some particularly important work. The first section addresses the question of method: what makes Marxism? It argues that Marxism is anti-determinist but adopts conceptual priorities, focusing particularly on work and production as the keys to understanding capitalism and how it might be changed. The second section illustrates these principles, considering the core Marxist concepts of value, surplus value and capital accumulation, and showing how these continue to inform thinking about modern capitalism. The third section identifies issues which go beyond the letter of *Capital*, introducing Marxist arguments around uneven and combined development, imperialism, unequal exchange, dependency and the world-system, monopoly capitalism, and contemporary global restructuring. These themes only scratch the surface of Marxist scholarship, reflecting my own knowledge and its limits as well as my own prejudices. Other Marxists would undoubtedly emphasise different themes and interpret Marxism differently.

A NOTE ON MARX'S METHOD

There is a huge literature on Marx's method. He did different things and insisted there was no royal road to science (Marx 1976: 104). But it is possible to identify some basic principles. Marx's political economy is inescapably connected with his philosophy and politics. In politics, Marx was a radical democrat, seeking an egalitarian society in which a majority genuinely ruled. This is not a separate normative question, because writing about the world cannot be cleaved from questions of by whom and for what purpose it is written (MECW 5; Cox 1981). Marx's egalitarianism sits at the core of his understanding of the economy, with the concept of value hanging on the idea that human equality had 'acquired the permanence of a fixed popular opinion' (Marx 1976: 152).

In philosophy, Marx was profoundly influenced by Hegel, even if he tried to 'invert' or 'extract the rational kernel' from Hegel's idealist thought. Marx promised, but never produced, a summary of this philosophy, but at its core are ideas of totality and interrelation and of dynamic change. In common with other strands of non-mainstream economics, Marxists accordingly conceive the economy as inextricably connected to the rest of society, to politics and to history. At the same time, interconnectedness requires what can be difficult evaluations of relative importance: of wholes and parts, of structures and agents, of continuity and change.

Importantly, this interconnection of wholes and parts means that Marxism cannot be the crude materialism of its opponents' caricature. There are metaphors in Marx which, taken literally, can be read that way – of base and superstructure (Marx 1970: 20–21), of hand mills producing feudalism, steam mills producing capitalism, of people's social relations established in conformity with material productivity, producing 'also principles, ideas and categories, in conformity with their social relations' (Marx 1978b: 103). But it is ignorant or mischievous to claim this as the essence of Marx's thinking, as if ideas, institutions and politics do not matter. Lenin insisted that 'intelligent idealism is closer to intelligent materialism than stupid materialism' (Lenin 1961: 276). Marx saw a distinctiveness in human 'purposeful will' (Marx 1976: 284), but contrasted his materialist understanding with forms of idealism that, in his day as in ours, can deny anything beyond human consciousness. Brute realities of climate catastrophe and Covid-19 make some of the sillier contemporary idealism harder to sustain and Marx's approach can, by contrast, look more like a 'kind of common sense' (Anderson 1988: 337).

The interconnection of whole and parts also points to a recurring theme in the examples below that show how the economy should be understood as a global whole, not as a collection of individuals nor discrete national economies (Pradella 2014). Marxism is radically anti-nationalist. Marx's understanding of 'the social' – for example in 'socially necessary labour time' – only makes sense at the global level, albeit this is a multiply divided level in which states' actions often matter profoundly.

Marx also criticised 'the dialectic balancing of concepts, and not grasping the real relations' (1973: 90). Understanding the economy 'in the round', as a social process, produces problems of where to start and how to proceed (Arthur 1997). We cannot immediately understand everything, so we must prioritise conceptually. Everybody does this, knowingly or unknowingly, but Marxists are honest about it.

Marxists usually start with questions of labour: of work, the division of labour, production, exploitation and class struggle. People are a part of nature, not something radically apart, as the anti-humanism of wackier ecological thinking would have it. But, for Marx, people 'can be distinguished from animals by consciousness, by religion or anything else you like. They begin to distinguish themselves from animals as soon as they begin to produce their means of subsistence' (MECW 5: 31). Understanding what is produced, how it is produced, and by and for whom it is produced, provides crucial insights, obscured by the apparent separation of politics and economics and the apparent equality involved in market exchanges of money and commodities. Again, this priority of work and production does not reduce other aspects of social life to mere reflections of forces or relations of production. In Marx and Engels' formulation, people really do make history, just not in conditions of their own choosing.

Marx's (1970, 1973) method then involves moving between different levels of abstraction, with more abstract propositions informing analyses at more concrete levels but themselves being subject to testing and modification. Understood in this way, Marxism can be seen as something analogous to what Lakatos (1970) describes as a 'progressive research program'. Marxism's 'hard core' involves the historical materialist view which posits the centrality of labour, class formation and contest, economic development and social change. Then, as Burawoy writes, 'a progressive defence of the hard core takes the form of an expanding belt of theories that increase the corroborated empirical content and solve successive puzzles' (1989:

761: see also Lipietz 1985; Burawoy 1998; Blackledge 2006). But the more concrete empirical realities matter and have distinct moments of their own.

Accordingly, *Capital* moves from the most general to more specific determinations – 'from capital in general to many capitals' (Arthur 1997: 19). Similarly, Marx anticipated that he would write further volumes discussing the state, international relations and, finally, the world market (Marx 1973; Rosdolsky 1980). This movement from abstract to concrete should be treated somewhat cautiously. Abstract ideas do not descend from heaven: rather, there is a two-way process, such that the abstractions are subject to qualification and modification. Subsequent levels can therefore be informed by *Capital*'s analysis but never reduced to it, and what we knew, or thought we knew, from *Capital* must be subject to emendation.

USING MARX'S *CAPITAL*

The sheer size of *Capital* makes it foreboding and, while Marx often writes beautifully, sometimes the books can be heavy going. There are excellent introductions (e.g. Fine and Saad Fihlo 2004) which I will not try to recapitulate. Unfortunately, one important thing to understand about *Capital* is that it needs to be understood as a whole: it is easy to be misled by reading particular passages out of context. However, I will restrict myself here to brief comments on value, on surplus value and on capital's disorderly dynamics, showing how they continue to inform Marxist political economy.

Marx put labour at the core of his understanding of society and this provided the basis for his famous labour theory of value. This posits value as being determined by socially necessary human labour in the abstract, that is labour irrespective of its form (1976: 128). Marx dismissed demands for proof of this theory:

> The chatter about the need to prove the concept of value arises only from complete ignorance both of the subject under discussion and of the method of science. Every child knows that any nation that stopped working, not for a year, but let us say, just for a few weeks, would perish. (MECW 47: 67)

Mainstream economists continue to denounce Marxism for its failure to provide a fully adequate theory of prices, but this is their criterion, not Marx's. For Marx, political economy is something more ambitious. Value underpins price, sets the baseline or sea-level around which there can be huge variation with any determination of prices according to value inherently approximate and 'an average of perpetual fluctuations' (Marx 1981: 261). Indeed, 'the average price of commodities is *always different* from their value' (Marx 1969: 95). Value is instead better understood as a 'hard core' concept, not itself testable, but enabling the generation of other hypotheses about profit and growth and capital's dislocations.

This leaves open important questions of what constitutes socially necessary labour. Many Marxists insist on a narrow understanding, so that only specifically capitalist, commodity-producing labour 'counts'. There is an important tradition of quantitative Marxism which attempts to map Marxist concepts onto the available mainstream data to better calculate what is producing value and to discount all sorts of rubbish which nonetheless makes profits and satisfies conventional accounting techniques (Shaikh and Tonak 1994). Other Marxists adopt a broader understanding. For Campbell, value allows Marx to compare the masked exploitation of capitalism with the more naked forms of exploitation under slavery and feudalism: 'the difference between it and the others being that capitalism is indirectly rather than directly collective' (Campbell 1993: 151). Applying the 'fixed popular opinion' of human equality, value concepts might potentially inform a creative research agenda into interactions between different forms of labour, including those that are unpaid and those that produce commodities only indirectly (Dunn 2014).

Just as any society needs to work to survive, it can only expand if it produces surpluses that are invested rather than directly consumed. For there to be such surpluses, the immediate producers must be exploited. Marx saw the value of labour-power as also being determined 'by the labour-time necessary for the production and consequently also the reproduction, of this specific article' (Marx 1976: 274). The trick is that, even if workers sell their labour-power at its value, they can be worked longer and harder in production to produce more than is needed to reproduce themselves. There can be surplus value and profit. Exploitation is therefore what makes the capitalist world go round. It is essentially a technical term, identifying the ratio of surplus labour to necessary labour, and is distinct from the pejorative vernacular use. It is entirely possible for workers enjoying relatively good pay and conditions to be more exploited than those in sweatshops.

Workers have no choice but to accept exploitation because, under capitalism, they have no other way to make a living. In north-west Europe 'so called primitive accumulation' (Marx 1976) or what Harvey (2003) re-labels 'accumulation by dispossession' began centuries ago. In much of the world, it is an ongoing process as traditional ways of life and self-sufficient agriculture are destroyed, swelling the ranks of the urban dispossessed, who are then scolded for any failure to welcome the low-paid, menial jobs that are usually all that is available. Exploitation provides the basis for profit – which for almost all mainstream economists remains completely enigmatic, simply appearing as if by magic. By contrast, for Marxists, it is impossible to even begin to understand contemporary inequality without looking at questions of class and exploitation. The fact that it is predicated on exploitation also immediately queries the standard identification of success with economic growth (Selwyn 2020).

Without surplus value there can be no profit. However, as with translations from value to price, relations between surplus value and profit as it is recorded in company accounts are heavily mediated. There is a competitive sharing-out of profit amongst capitalists, including those which do not themselves produce value but live off surpluses made elsewhere. This leaves considerable empirical problems. Exactly which activities are productive and unproductive of value in Marx's sense continues to provoke controversy. It cannot be a crude material/immaterial distinction, and Marx made clear that writers, singers, schoolteachers and clowns can all be perfectly productive (Marx 1976: 1044, 644). Based on such considerations about where value is produced and how it is dispersed, Marxist research is informed by studying the production and (often unequal) exchange of value, not least about relations between finance and the productive economy (Fine 2010; Lapavitsas 2013) as well as between countries, as discussed below.

The need to make profit, always more profit, is also key to capitalism's disruptive dynamism. Competition produces an ever-present need to expand or go under. Even opponents admit the prescience of the *Communist Manifesto*'s depictions of capitalism's relentless expansion. The imperative to accumulate makes capitalism uniquely dynamic but also a system riddled with contradictions.

The most fundamental contradiction is between the exploiters and exploited, between capital and labour. As firms expand more and more workers are drawn in. For Marx, this ultimately produced the class of capitalism's gravediggers, a dispossessed proletariat. This was a class with radical chains, whose struggles had the potential to transform itself and thence the world. For each announcement of the working class's demise, and therefore of Marxism's obsolescence, spectacular growth, in sheer numerical terms, continues. When Marx and Engels announced the working class as the majority (MECW 5: 52), this was a distant prospect beyond a small corner of north-west Europe. It is now a global reality.

The conflicts between capital and labour also have potentially serious, shorter-term, economic consequences. Much as Ricardo argued, some Marxist accounts see wage rises undermining profits, sending the economy towards recession, inducing lay-offs and higher unemployment, which then undermines wages and restores profits (Glyn and Sutcliffe 1972; Goodwin 2014). This apparently neatly accounts for economic cycles and seems plausible as an explanation of at least some crises, including those in the 1970s. However, it hardly accounts for capitalism's subsequent stagnation and crises.

Conversely, as each individual capitalist tries to keep the wages paid to their workers to a minimum, workers' poverty (or relative poverty) limits consumption and checks expansion. As Marx argued, this is a '[c]ontradiction in the capitalist mode of production. The workers are important for the market as buyers of commodities. But as sellers of their commodity – labour-power – capitalist society has a tendency to restrict them to their minimum price' (Marx 1978a: 391). This provides the basis for an alternative view of crisis (Baran and Sweezy 1968; Foster and McChesney 2012). Now downturn exacerbates, rather than alleviates, problems of consumption, suggesting protracted stagnation. Such problems of demand have considerable plausibility in the current conjuncture of rich-country economies in the early twenty-first century, but again hardly seem adequate as an explanation of capitalism's many different crises. Theories that concentrate on immediate capital–labour relations and profit levels can also understate the importance and disruptiveness of inter-capitalist competition.

Capitalism's expansion is fundamentally anarchic: firms produce commodities in order to make money. This is the process of [M-C-M']. They need to produce something people want but the ultimate object is always more money. So, rather than intrinsically socially useful goods, more, always more, 'crappy shit' (Marx 1973: 273) needs to be pumped out in the hope of finding buyers. Therein lies the ever-present possibility of crisis. Therein too lies the root of environmental destruction – a problem about which Marxist ecologists have made enormous contributions (Foster 2000; Kovel 2002; Moore 2015), showing why 'green capitalism' is ultimately a mirage.

This process of expansion works unevenly, with a different pulse across economic sectors and across space. *Capital* Volume II introduces Marx's reproduction schema, with different departments of capital, different sectors, producing means of production and means of consumption. Marx develops a series of 'models' of what would be needed to sustain a 'balance' between sectors when moving from a situation of simple reproduction to a real world where capitalists make and reinvest profit and expand. These models were creatively reapplied by early generation Marxists including Luxemburg and Preobrazhensky. Of course, Marx is not suggesting that any balance will in fact occur; rather, his *Capital* Volume II has been interpreted as providing a theory of crises arising because of sectoral disproportionalities (Clarke 1994). Rather than smooth adjustments to market imperatives, economic imbalances can build up over time, to be released in mild tremors or terrifying quakes of unpredictable strength and consequence. Minimally, Marx anticipated by more than half a century Keynesian work on the 'traverse' and difficulties of sustaining balanced growth under capitalism (Howard and King 1992).

But everywhere competition forces capital to expand and to attempt to increase productivity. This creates a tendency to use more machinery, not least to replace workers who might resist capital's dictates. Marx called this a tendency for the 'technical composition of capital' to rise. Here again there is much controversy about how this translates in value terms, with devout followers of chapter 13 of Volume III insisting that more physical capital means relatively less exploitable labour and therefore a tendency for the rate of profit to fall. Of course, productivity increases simultaneously reduce the socially necessary labour time required to produce commodities and labour-power, so things become more complicated. The accounts developed by Fine (Fine and Harris 1979; Fine and Saad-Filho 2004) of uneven technological development and value creation across sectors provide a more subtle understanding of the basis for capitalism's contradictions. Different periods of capitalism may head in different directions and into different dislocations (Dumenil and Levy 2011; Dunn 2014).

Capital remained unfinished. Volume III was compiled by Engels from Marx's notes, with Engels admitting he sometimes struggled – and many critics insisting that he made a bad job of it. Volume III also begins to depict how capital is articulated with finance and with rent. As above, Marx also proposed further volumes on the state, international relations and the world market and crisis, all of which remained unwritten. We cannot know what he might have said and its relation to the earlier volumes. But Marx's method implies that what comes later cannot simply be deduced or derived from what goes before. While subsequent levels can be informed by the preceding analysis, each possesses its own specific moment.

AFTER *CAPITAL*

Many important creative innovations within Marxian political economy have occurred since Marx. This section of the chapter cannot provide much more than a list of examples and, in each case, rich literatures are introduced in indecent brevity. The general point I want to make is that, while insights are sometimes claimed as absolutes – as discoveries of new key determinants and overturning the Marxist 'hard core' – they might better by seen as more provisional hypotheses, potentially adding to or qualifying earlier Marxist work but needing careful empirical evaluation. They should be seen as inspiring Marxist research rather than as ready-made explanatory tools.

Uneven and Combined Development

Trotsky's (1969, 1977), ideas of uneven and combined development and permanent revolution provide a prime example of Marxism as a progressive research programme (Burawoy 1989). Rather than a 'naïve falsificationism', a babies and bathwater approach, where one disproved prediction – in this case that workers in the richest countries would lead the way to revolution – means abandoning the whole project, it leads to a creative and more sophisticated rethinking.

Marxists believe that capitalism creates its own gravediggers, workers. These were numerically and organisationally strongest where capitalism was most developed. Russia was backward in absolute terms, in its economic level or the proportion of urban workers to rural peasants. The 'objective' conditions for socialism had not been achieved. But what Trotsky argued was that Russia already contained elements of the most advanced capitalism, including some of the world's largest factories. State-led and foreign-financed capital meant that Russia was following a different path to that laid out in Britain centuries before. Accordingly, workers need not wait until after a successful bourgeois revolution and years of capitalist growth. They were already the most radical section of society and could be expected to lead any revolution. Having done so, rather than taking a self-denying ordinance to hand power back to the bourgeoisie, they could lead an ongoing or permanent revolutionary process involving peasant allies within Russia and workers in other countries where the 'objective' conditions for socialism had been achieved. After 1917, Trotsky appeared to have been brilliantly vindicated although, of course, by the late 1920s, Trotsky and his ideas were marginalised politically.

Trotsky's ideas have also been invoked mechanically to say that workers always and everywhere can lead a revolution, something quite distinct from his original analysis, full of rich empirical detail precisely about why this apparently unlikely outcome was possible in Russia. How, and to what extent, do Trotsky's ideas remain applicable now? Issues of how temporal and spatial combinations and unevennesses in economic development might be usefully understood and applied to contemporary capitalism and revolutionary strategy continue to provoke debate (Löwy 1981; Barker 2006; Davidson 2006; Rosenberg 2009, 2010). Most boldly, Rosenberg sees uneven and combined development providing the basis for a general theory of state formation. At the very least, thinking in terms of uneven and combined development can overcome the unhelpful binaries that posit globalisation against a world of discrete national economies. Instead, it can provide a framework for understanding global capitalism, the situation within it of national political economies, and the prospects for resistance and revolution. Some of the most useful thinking about contemporary global restructuring comes from radical geographers, not all of whom use the language of uneven and combined development but who seem to be working in similar ways, attempting to map shifting relations of economic and political power and thinking about possibilities for resistance (Cox 1997; Castree 2000; Herod 2000, 2018).

Imperialism

In the years after Marx's death, Marxists also turned to pressing questions of imperialism and war. A new wave of European colonisation built on older waves, for example the devastation wrought by the slave trade, weakened the ability to resist the European 'scramble for Africa'. But the late nineteenth-century imperialism had involved a major re-orientation and Marxists pioneered its study. They were not alone and could draw on other traditions, notably Lenin (1965) and the work of the English liberal Hobson. But Marxist priorities provided grounds for important original explanations based on the expansionary dynamic and changing character of capitalism in the European heartlands. The accounts varied, for example in terms of the emphasis put on the drive for cheap raw materials or final markets. Many also described how corporate growth and the merging of industrial and financial capital meant less competition 'at home' but how corporate influence pushed respective nation states into competition abroad. For Lenin, there was also the possibility that gains from imperialism could buy off at least sections of the metropolitan working class.

With the benefit of over a hundred years of hindsight, there are problems and enduring questions with some of these analyses. Depictions of corporate cartels and finance capital drew mainly on evidence from Germany and look less convincing in relation to Britain and France, the leading imperial powers. Meanwhile, where imperialism had been depicted as necessary to European capitalism's enduring success, countries with less empire or imperial ambition grew faster than Britain and France. Some contemporary Marxists reject the early twentieth-century theorising, not only as useless today but also on its own terms, arguing that it attempted to generalise what were very specific historical events (Radice 2014). Yet others still defend the core insights – the imperial project as underpinned by capitalism's expansionary dynamic, of shifting relations between monopoly and competition and between the need for national support and the need to overcome national boundaries. Minimally, as Hodgkin wrote nearly 50 years ago, it 'remains true that imperial expansion could not have occurred unless it had been willed by the dominant interest within the ruling classes of the imperial powers' (Hodgkin 1972: 107). Capitalist interests still drive inter-state competition and recent military adventures (Callinicos 2009). This is not to deny all sorts of historical contingency, with perhaps too little attention having been paid to how colonial experiences were conditioned by forms of resistance and collaboration within the colonies (Robinson 1972). But, at the very least, there are enduring lessons in how the second-generation Marxists attempted to apply Marxism creatively to new conditions; and their pioneering studies of imperialism remain vital reference points for serious contemporary work.

Unequal Exchange, Dependency and the World-system

The post-Second World War landscape saw a retreat from empire, at least formally. There could be some linguistic dexterity, with imperialism, originally applied to the military carve-up, now said to characterise economic relations even as formal colonies were abandoned. The term could become a catch-all indictment of bad things done by rich countries to poor ones. However, there was important and original re-thinking of an apparently post-imperial world in which international inequalities continued to widen rather than narrow. By the 1970s, three related ideas – of unequal exchange, dependency and the world-system – became particularly influential.

It has long been recognised that trade can be unequal and exploitative: Marx (1977: 269) mocked those who thought otherwise. More recent discussions of unequal exchange usually derive from Emmanuel (1972). Emmanuel argued that capital crossed national borders but that usually workers did not, creating a tendency to equalise profit rates but not to equalise wages. So high wages in the core were passed on as high prices, while low wages in the periphery meant low prices. International trade meant that, instead of exchanging goods at their value, the core sold dear and bought cheap, while the periphery sold cheap and bought dear. Thus, there was unequal exchange. Emmanuel conceded that productivity differences might, in principle, offset the inequalities but reasonably argued that, in many cases, the periphery held the advantages. Bananas grow better in tropical climates than temperate ones, whereas you can make a car or a shirt anywhere. Emmanuel's conclusions were uncomfortable for many Marxists. Workers in rich countries were the prime movers and prime beneficiaries of unequal exchange. Exploitation now occurred on a national, not a class, basis.

Ideas of unequal exchange were incorporated into much of the subsequent radical thinking about economic development. Not everyone working in what came to be called the 'dependency' tradition was a Marxist. However, the arguments of Frank (1970, 1978), Wallerstein (1974), Amin (1974) and others recaptured the important Marxist insight that the economy could not, or should not, be understood primarily in terms of discrete national economies but makes sense only when it is conceived as a global whole. In Wallerstein's phrase, it had to be understood as a 'World-System'. A self-contained economic system in one or more countries might, in principle, constitute a world-system but, with Europe's 'discovery' and colonisation of the new world, something close to a genuinely global economy emerged. One important implication, which Frank stressed, was that apparently 'backward' countries could not be understood in isolation. There were not 'stages of development', with poor countries merely at a lower rung on a developmental ladder. Nor could social relations within poor countries be understood just in local terms. The Latin American *latifundia* economy of giant estates and coerced labour might look more like feudalism than metropolitan capitalism. But there had never been feudalism in Latin America. The *latifundia* were a European imposition and their products were sold on the world market. Underdevelopment was itself a product of imperialism.

Some of this literature could 'up the ante' in terms of trade-based exploitation, seeing international politics, not class relations, as the essence of centuries of capitalism. One of the most powerful accounts in this tradition was Rodney's (1974) *How Europe Underdeveloped Africa*. However, whereas Frank's emphasis was on how metropolitan imperialism impoverished the periphery, in Rodney there was also a claim that it was this peripheral impoverishment that enriched the core. This would become a recurring theme. For Wallerstein (1974), European political power established a global division of labour, a core and a periphery, based on a systematic exploitation. The periphery was consigned to agriculture and mineral production, with perhaps a little basic manufacturing. Sophisticated manufacturing remained the preserve of the core. A semi-periphery might conduct some intermediate tasks and also play a vital political role – supervising the poorer countries as proxies for the imperialist powers and allowing the system some flexibility and the illusion that reform was possible, systemic revolution unnecessary. But the world-system meant trade was the basis of the continual enrichment of the core at the expense of the periphery.

Other Marxists were quick to criticise what they saw as third-world nationalism masquerading as Marxism. Of course, colonialism could underdevelop the periphery. Of course, trade could be unequal. But those insights become problematic when inflated into depictions of trade exploitation trumping class exploitation. Since wage differentials were, in most versions, the source of unequal exchange, peripheral-country rulers might simply have overcome this by allowing wage rises. Unsurprisingly, class priorities in practice won out (Raffer 1987). In emphasising exchange rather than production relations, the approach mirrored the mainstream, it was at best neo-Smithian Marxism (Kidron 1974; Brenner 1977; Skocpol 1977). Ultimately, only exploitation in production produced growth. Recent decades witnessed many poorer countries growing rapidly even as they became increasingly integrated into the global trade regime. Unequal exchange needs to be put in its proper place, critically investigated rather than taken as a general truth (Dunn 2017).

Monopoly Capital

Something similar can be said of trade-based exploitation within countries, and one of the most innovative and influential accounts of capitalism's twentieth-century transformation, written by Baran and Sweezy (1968). It argued that, since Marx's day, capitalism had changed fundamentally, and US monopoly forms should replace nineteenth-century competitive British forms as the model. The economy departs even further from liberal ideas of free-market capitalism, as giant corporations use their power and practices of mark-up pricing to increase profits at the expense of small firms and consumers. A nineteenth-century tendency for rates of profit to fall is superseded by a twentieth-century tendency for surpluses to rise, but with the corollary that there are perpetual problems of how these surpluses can be disposed, problems of underconsumption, and concomitant problems of underinvestment. Thence 'the *normal* state of monopoly capitalist society is stagnation' (Baran and Sweezy 1968: 113, original emphasis).

Corporate power is an essential reality of the modern economy and the monopoly capital tradition has considerable resonance explaining this. Amongst other things, the importance of low levels of investment alongside huge corporate profits and rising household debt were essential elements of the 2008 global financial crisis (Foster and McChesney 2012). However, for Marx, competition and monopoly were related processes, not alternatives. Relations between agglomeration and countertendencies to an increased roundaboutness in production are dynamic and changing (Marx 1976: 462, 776), with inter-capitalist competition remaining an often-brutal fact of economic life (Shaikh 2016). Later versions shifted from Baran and Sweezy's focus on the USA to the global economy, but this involves an interesting, if under-investigated, dynamic of increased competition within national markets even as global corporations expand. Ideas of mark-up pricing, inherited from the tradition of Keynes and Kalecki, better approximate the reality of corporate practice than price competition and warrant careful empirical investigation, although they can similarly occlude exploitation in production, the underlying determinant of any mark-up.

Challenges of Global Restructuring

Globalisation and New Economy became buzzwords in the 1990s and Marxists contributed to the buzz. The economy hurtled in new directions. Globalisation could be interpreted as confirming both Marx's predictions of capitalism's inexorable expansion and the need for genuine labour internationalism (Radice 2000). The new economy was predicated on capitalism's dynamism and technological innovation (Dumenil and Levy 2004; Howard and King 2008). Harvey's (1990) influential characterisation depicts dynamic temporal and spatial transformation as 'space-time compression'.

The discourses of transformation also often became vehicles for an anti-labour politics. They could claim that corporations could flit across the globe, setting workers in different places against each other and hollowing-out nation states as arenas of effective politics. The new or knowledge economy undermined traditional bases of labour organisation among the semi-skilled and, more remarkably, determined that politics became indeterminate, a question of rival ideas now cleaved from material interests (Castells 2000). Such political conclusions do not invalidate the claims and some people abandoned Marxism believing it had lost its agent, believing that globalisation or the new economy fundamentally transformed or eliminated the possibilities of class politics. But the political conclusions suggest the claims should be treated cautiously.

First, when conceiving the economy as global, it becomes misleading to conceive a process of national economies now slopping over boundaries. Rather, it is better to think in terms of an intrinsically global but uneven geography. Smith's (1984) 'see-saw' depicts waves of accumulation, with high wages at one point providing incentives to agglomeration through economies of scale, but then producing a counteracting impulse for capital to relocate to cheaper wage locations. Meanwhile, as Fine observes of space-time compression, 'to the extent that space and time are both compressed, absolutely nothing changes' (2004: 221). Shifting dynamics and new dislocations lie particularly in their uneven development which also potentially opens opportunities for labour at different scales (Herod 2000, 2018), without requiring the abandonment of organised labour's established strengths or of the state as an important arena of politics.

Second, reorganising production could be about 'management by stress' and intensifying exploitation rather than dynamic innovation (Parker and Slaughter 1988; Smith 2000). Labour organisation was always an achievement, never a straightforward product of material conditions. As 'rust-belt' industries disappear or are relocated, the 'new economy' also concentrates huge numbers of workers in new collectivities – in offices, call centres and distribution hubs, for example. Of course, class struggle continues, 'now hidden, now open' (MECW 6: 482) but, recalling industrial workers' bitter struggles in the first half of the twentieth century, there seem few reasons to assume that new work or workers are intrinsically harder, or easier, to organise.

Third, the narratives of economic novelty tend to ignore the politics of transformation, both high politics and the role of pro-capitalist governments in achieving change. They also ignore the importance of labour's defeats in the 1970s in shaping the new economic environment (Walker 1999). Amongst other things, putting labour's retreat at the core of the analysis solves the apparent puzzle of why the brutalities and rising inequalities of 'neoliberalism' have not met more resistance (at least in the old economic heartlands). Instead, the lack of resistance is the cause of the brutality and rising inequality. Only labour's strength made capital relatively benign. The political pessimism could also have a discordant rich-country accent. As I began writing this chapter in late 2019, there were near revolutionary situations in Chile, Hong Kong, Iraq, Lebanon and Sudan.

Fourth, rather than a new era of prosperity, capitalism lurched into new crises. The technical achievements in information and communications technologies and their possibilities are enormous; but more sanguine reflections, particularly after the 2008 crisis, suggested that social relations (not least the capacity of the super-rich to corner the gains) still fettered those technical achievements. Growth rates were unremarkable, even before coming to a juddering halt in 2009.

REDISCOVERING AND RE-THINKING MARX IN THE TWENTY-FIRST CENTURY

The left's political defeats over the last century marginalised Marxism and sometimes forced adherents into a defence of basic principles, even into a parroting of passages in *Capital*, rather than their creative application. But the enduring inequalities and injustices in the world – and the resistances they foster – generate new audiences for Marxist ideas and exciting new generations of Marxist scholarship.

This chapter has sketched some principles and problems. I regret that the limits of space and of my competence have meant that I could not detail how Marxists have contributed to, and learned from, several vital contemporary debates. To conclude, I will mention three examples – the rise of finance, the environmental crisis, and struggles for race and gender equality.

The rise of finance and recent financial crises pose new questions. Marx's own analysis of money and finance remained incomplete; and modern finance has also developed in ways hard to imagine in the nineteenth-century world of commodity money and the gold-standard.

Modern money presents important challenges, for example around the meaning and measure of value. Marxists are now conducting important work and engaging with other critical traditions, for which finance has been a more central preoccupation. But, if finance has a vital, disruptive moment of its own, which has been under-investigated, Marxist understandings of profits derived from exploitation in production and of (mis)management by specifically capitalist states can provide research on money and finance with an essential anchor.

The environmental crisis and struggles to redress it raise crucial questions around the relation between ecology and economy. Marxists have been central to both the conceptual debates about the relation between people and the rest of nature and in grappling with the difficult empirical questions. Important early formulations by O'Connor (1988) depicted environmental destruction also destroying the conditions of capitalism's own reproduction and therefore constituting a 'second contradiction of capitalism'. However, because the ecological crisis also can potentially lead to new opportunities for exploitation, Marxist political economists should beware too easy an assumption that all the angels can coalesce in a reconstituted green Keynesianism, saving capitalism and the planet.

Struggles for racial, gender and sexual equality and liberation present further conceptual challenges in understanding the inter-relation of different dimensions of oppression and resistance. Rather than this undermining Marxism and an alleged class reductionism, there are good reasons, as Matthaei (1996) argues, 'why feminist, Marxist and anti-racist economists should be feminist-Marxist-anti-racist economists'. The complexity and multiplicity of struggles has too often been used in academic social science to drive class off the agenda. Instead, it is better to recognise that those struggles and their potential are instead inextricably connected to class and that they can simultaneously be understood through, even as they enrich, a Marxist framework of analysis.

The point is a broader one. I am fond of Terry Eagleton's (2003: 33) example that Marxism cannot explain 'the quickest way to delouse cocker spaniels'. Marxism cannot do everything. But that leaves a vast terrain of political economy to which Marxism can be applied and thereby enriched and developed. There is much, much more research that has been done than this chapter could cover, and much, much more that needs to be done. The future of Marxism, of course, hangs most fundamentally on the revival of oppositional social movements, but Marxism continues to inform both how the world works and those struggles to change it.

REFERENCES

Amin, S. (1974) *Accumulation on a World Scale: A Critique of the Theory of Underdevelopment*, New York: Monthly Review Press.

Anderson, P. (1988) 'Modernity and revolution', in Grossberg, L. and Nelson, C. (eds), *Marxism and the Interpretation of Culture*, Urbana: University of Illinois Press, pp. 325–8.

Arthur, C. (1997) 'Against the logical-historical method', in Moseley, F. and Campbell, M. (eds), *New Investigations of Marx's Method*, Atlantic Highlands, NJ: Humanities Press, pp. 9–37.

Baran, P.A. and Sweezy, P.M. (1968) *Monopoly Capital*, Harmondsworth: Penguin.

Barker, C. (2006) 'Beyond Trotsky: extending combined and uneven development', in Dunn, B. and Radice, H. (eds), *100 Years of Permanent Revolution: Results and Prospects*, London: Pluto, pp. 78–87.

Blackledge, P. (2006) *Reflections on the Marxist Theory of History*, Manchester: Manchester University Press.

Brenner, R. (1977) 'The origins of capitalist development: a critique of neo-Smithian Marxism', *New Left Review*, 104, pp. 25–92.

Burawoy, M. (1989) 'Two methods in search of science: Skocpol versus Trotsky', *Theory and Society*, **18**, pp. 759–805.

Burawoy, M. (1998) 'The extended case method', *Sociological Theory*, **16** (1), pp. 4–33.

Callinicos, A. (2009) *Imperialism and the Global Political Economy*, Cambridge: Polity.

Campbell, M. (1993) 'Marx's concept of economic relations and the method of capital', in Moseley, F. (ed.), *Marx's Method in* Capital: *A Re-examination*, Atlantic Highlands, NJ: Humanities Press, pp. 135–55.

Castells, M. (2000) *The Information Age: Economy, Society and Culture, Volume 1*, Oxford: Blackwell.

Castree, N. (2000) 'Geographic scale and grass-roots internationalism', *Economic Geography*, **76** (3), pp. 272–92.

Clarke, S. (1994) *Marx's Theory of Crisis*, Basingstoke: Macmillan.

Cox, K.R. (1997) 'Globalization and geographies of workers' struggle in the late twentieth century', in Lee, R. and Wills, J. (eds), *Geographies of Economics*, London: Arnold, pp. 177–85.

Cox, R.W. (1981) 'Social forces, states and world orders', *Millennium: Journal of International Studies*, **10** (2), pp. 126–55.

Davidson, N. (2006) 'From uneven to combined development', in Dunn, B. and Radice, H. (eds), *100 Years of Permanent Revolution: Results and Prospects*, London: Pluto, pp. 10–26.

Dumenil, G. and Levy, D. (2004) *Capital Resurgent*, Cambridge, MA: Harvard University Press.

Dumenil, G. and Levy, D. (2011) *The Crisis of Neoliberalism*, Cambridge, MA: Harvard University Press.

Dunn, B. (2014) *The Political Economy of Global Capitalism and Crisis*, London: Routledge.

Dunn, B. (2017) 'Class, capital and the global unfree market: resituating theories of monopoly capitalism and unequal exchange', *Science & Society*, **81** (3), pp. 348–74.

Eagleton, T. (2003) *After Theory*, New York: Basic Books.

Emmanuel, A. (1972) *Unequal Exchange: A Study of the Imperialism of Trade*, London: New Left Books.

Fine, B. (2004) 'Examining the ideas of globalisation and development critically', *New Political Economy*, **9** (2), pp. 213–31.

Fine, B. (2010) 'Locating financialisation', *Historical Materialism*, **18** (2), pp. 97–116.

Fine, B. and Harris, L. (1979) *Rereading Capital*, London: Macmillan.

Fine, B. and and Saad-Filho, A. (2004) *Marx's Capital*, 4th edn, London: Pluto.

Foster, J.B. (2000) *Marx's Ecology*, New York: Monthly Review Press.

Foster, J.B. and McChesney, R. (2012) *The Endless Crisis*, New York: Monthly Review Press.

Frank, A.G. (1970) 'The development of underdevelopment', in Rhodes, R.I. (ed.), *Imperialism and Underdevelopment*, New York: Monthly Review Press, pp. 17–30.

Frank, A.G. (1978) *Dependent Accumulation and Underdevelopment*, London, Macmillan.

Glyn A. and Sutcliffe, B. (1972) *British Capitalism, Workers and the Profit Squeeze*, Harmondsworth: Penguin.

Goodwin, R.M. (2014) 'A growth cycle', paper presented at the First World Congress of the Econometric Society, Rome.

Harvey, D. (1990) *The Condition of Postmodernity: An Enquiry into the Origins of Cultural Change*, Oxford: Blackwell.

Harvey, D. (2003) *The New Imperialism*, Oxford: Oxford University Press.

Herod, A. (2000) 'Implications of just-in-time production for union strategy', *Annals of the Association of American Geographers*, **90** (3), pp. 521–47.

Herod, A. (2018) *Labor*, Cambridge: Polity.

Hodgkin, T. (1972) 'Some African and third world theories of imperialism', in Owen, R. and Sutcliffe, B. (eds), *Studies in the Theory of Imperialism*, London: Longman.

Howard, M.C. and King, J.E. (1992) *A History of Marxian Economics Volume II, 1929–1990*, Basingstoke: Macmillan.

Howard, M.C. and King, J.E. (2008) *The Rise of Neoliberalism in Advanced Capitalist Economies: A Materialist Analysis*, Basingstoke: Palgrave Macmillan.

Kidron, M. (1974) *Capitalism and Theory*, London: Pluto.

Kovel, J. (2002) *The Enemy of Nature*, Black Point, Nova Scotia: Fernwood.

Lakatos, I. (1970) 'Falsification and the methodology of scientific research programmes', in Lakatos, I. and Musgrove, A. (eds), *Criticism and the Growth of Knowledge*, Cambridge: Cambridge University Press, pp. 91–196.

Lapavitsas, C. (2013) *Profiting without Producing: How Finance Exploits Us All*, London: Verso.

Lenin, V.I. (1961) *Collected Works, Volume 38: Philosophical Notebooks*, London: Lawrence & Wishart.

Lenin, V.I. (1965) *Imperialism, the Highest Stage of Capitalism*, Peking: Foreign Languages Press.

Lipietz, A. (1985) *The Enchanted World*, London: Verso.

Löwy, M. (1981) *The Politics of Combined and Uneven Development: The Theory of Permanent Revolution*, London: Verso.

Marx, K. (1969) *Theories of Surplus Value Part 1*, Moscow: Progress.

Marx, K. (1970) *A Contribution to the Critique of Political Economy*, Moscow: Progress.

Marx, K. (1973) *Grundrisse*, New York: Random House.

Marx, K. (1976) *Capital, Volume I*, Harmondsworth: Penguin.

Marx, K. (1977) *Selected Writings*, ed. McLellan, D., Oxford: Oxford University Press.

Marx, K. (1978a) *Capital, Volume II*, Harmondsworth: Penguin.

Marx, K. (1978b) *The Poverty of Philosophy*, Peking: Foreign Languages Press.

Marx, K. (1981) *Capital, Volume III*, Harmondsworth: Penguin.

Matthaei, J. (1996) 'Why feminist, Marxist and anti-racist economists should be Feminist-Marxist-Anti-Racist economists', *Journal of Feminist Economics*, **2** (1), pp. 22–42.

MECW (various numbers) Marx, K. and Engels, F., *Collected Works*, London: Lawrence & Wishart, Electric Book.

Moore, J. (2015) *Capitalism in the Web of Life*, London: Verso.

O'Connor, J. (1988) 'Capitalism, nature, socialism: a theoretical introduction', *Capitalism, Nature, Socialism*, **1** (1), pp. 11–38.

Parker, M. and Slaughter, J. (1988) *Choosing Sides: Unions and the Team Concept*, Boston, MA: South End Press.

Pradella, L. (2014) *Globalization and the Critique of Political Economy: New Insights from Marx's Writings*, London: Routledge.

Radice, H. (2000) 'Responses to globalisation: a critique of progressive nationalism', *New Political Economy*, **5** (1), pp. 5–19.

Radice, H. (2014) *Global Capitalism: Selected Essays*, Abingdon: Routledge.

Raffer, K. (1987) *Unequal Exchange and the Evolution of the World System: Reconsidering the Impact of Trade on North-South Relations*, New York: St. Martin's Press.

Robinson, R. (1972) 'Non-European foundation of European imperialism', in Owen, R. and Sutcliffe, B. (eds), *Studies in the Theory of Imperialism*, London: Longman, pp. 117–42.

Rodney, W. (1974) *How Europe Underdeveloped Africa*, Washington, DC: Howard University Press.

Rosdolsky, R. (1980) *The Making of Marx's Capital*, London: Pluto.

Rosenberg, J. (2009) 'Basic problems in the theory of uneven and combined development: a reply to the CRIA forum', *Cambridge Review of International Affairs*, **22** (1), pp. 107–10.

Rosenberg, J. (2010) 'Basic problems in the theory of uneven and combined development. Part II: unevenness and political multiplicity', *Cambridge Review of International Affairs*, **23** (1), pp. 165–89.

Selwyn, B. (2020) 'Economic growth and the ideology of development', in Dunn, B. (ed.), *A Research Agenda for Critical Political Economy*, Cheltenham, UK and Northampton, MA, USA: Edward Elgar Publishing, pp. 35–46.

Shaikh, A. (2016) *Capitalism: Competition, Conflict, Crises*, Oxford: Oxford University Press.

Shaikh, A.M. and Tonak, E.A. (1994) *Measuring the Wealth of Nations: The Political Economy of National Accounts*, Cambridge: Cambridge University Press.

Skocpol, T. (1977) 'Wallerstein's World Capitalist System: a theoretical and historical critique', *American Journal of Sociology*, **82** (5), pp. 1075–90.

Smith, N. (1984) *Uneven Development*, Oxford: Basil Blackwell.

Smith, T. (2000) *Technology and Capital in the Age of Lean Production: A Marxian Critique of the 'New Economy'*, Albany: State University of New York Press.
Trotsky, L. (1969) *The Permanent Revolution and Results and Prospects*, New York: Pathfinder.
Trotsky, L. (1977) *The History of the Russian Revolution*, London: Pluto.
Walker, R.A. (1999) 'Putting capital in its place: globalization and the prospects for labor', *Geoforum*, **30**, pp. 263–84.
Wallerstein, I. (1974) *The Modern World-System*, New York: Academic Press.

5.   Institutional political economy

Arturo Hermann

This chapter analyses the significant contributions of institutional economics (in particular in its 'original' tradition, indicated as OIE or institutionalism) to political economy. It selects key authors and shows the concepts they use for understanding economic processes. These concepts include habits, instincts, evolution, technology, transactions, the legal and institutional foundations of the market, the imperfections of markets at micro and macro levels, social and instrumental value, the role of economic (in particular, democratic) planning, and the interdisciplinary perspective. Blending these features of the various currents within OIE creates important (and often overlooked) complementarities that address – both in theory and in policy action – the imbalances of contemporary capitalism.

The chapter begins with a brief introduction to the general character of this strand of political economy. It then considers the theoretical framework of Thorstein Veblen, with particular attention to its evolutionary perspective and the role of habits, instincts and technology. This is followed by a section on the contribution of John Commons and his theory of institutions and transactions. Attention then turns to analyses of market imperfections at micro and macro levels, and of the contributions by J.K. Galbraith and Gunnar Myrdal. Some consideration of the theory of democratic planning follows, emphasising institutionalist notions of social value and instrumental value. The final section argues for bringing out the synergy between these contributions through better collaboration between (and within) OIE and other heterodox fields of economics and social science.

THE INSTITUTIONAL ECONOMICS PERSPECTIVE

Institutional economics originated in the United States in the first few decades of the twentieth century, during which time it had considerable prominence, even a claim to be the dominant school of economic thought. Its cultural roots can be identified in the philosophy and psychology of Pragmatism – in particular, in the theories of Charles Sanders Peirce, John Dewey and William James – and in the German historical school, given impetus in the USA by Richard T. Ely, a scholar who had considerable influence on the formation of the first generation of institutionalists. The principal founders of institutional economics were Thorstein Veblen, John Commons, Walton Hamilton, Wesley Mitchell and Clarence Ayres. Further contributions came from, among others, L. Ardzooni, Adolph Berle, J.C. Bonbright, J.M. Clark, M.A. Copeland, Sumner Slichter, J. Fagg Foster, Robert Lee Hale, I. Lubin, Gardiner C. Means, Walter Stewart, and Rexford G. Tugwell. Later in the twentieth century, significant political economic work with important links to institutional economics was undertaken by John Kenneth Galbraith, Fred Hirsch, Albert Hirschman, Gunnar Myrdal, Karl Polanyi and Michael Polanyi.

Within institutional economics today, two main fields can be identified. One is the *old (or original) institutional economics* (OIE), a tradition shaped by the pioneering scholars just mentioned. The other is *new institutional economics* (NIE), created in the last few decades of the twentieth century by economists adopting principles derived from the neoclassical and Austrian schools of economic thought. Because this chapter is in a book focusing on political economic theories that challenge economic orthodoxy, the focus of what follows is exclusively on the *original institutional economics* (OIE, or institutionalism).

As noted by numerous authors, OIE does not present a completely unitary framework. Three main strands may be identified:

- An approach first expounded by Thorstein Veblen, stressing the evolutionary nature of economic systems; the dichotomy between ceremonial and instrumental institutions to which corresponds the distinction between pecuniary and industrial employments; the influence of habits of thought and action; the role of technology in moving the system from ceremonial and invidious distinctions of wealth and power to a serviceable economy based on the expression of the workmanship and parental bent instincts; and the role of the business enterprise in these complex dynamics.
- An approach initiated by John Commons, focusing attention on the evolutionary relations between economy, law and institutions; the nature of transactions, institutions and collective action; the role of conflicts of interest and of the social valuing associated with them; the evolution of ownership from a material notion of possession to one of relations, duties and opportunities; and the role of negotiational psychology for understanding economic and social phenomena.
- An approach developed by institutionalists such as Walton Hamilton and Wesley Mitchell, dealing with 'market imperfections' at micro and macro levels and their effects on economic systems. Here the focus is on market power, the duplication of firms and the inefficiency of many industrial sectors, the insufficient capacity to consume of middle- and low-income classes, and the dynamics of business cycles.

Despite differences between these approaches, the elements of convergence are remarkable. Whereas the differences tend to concern the issues that are addressed, the themes on which there is general agreement are: (i) recognition of the complex and interactive character of 'human nature' and the consequent importance of the social and institutional framework for its amelioration; (ii) strong emphasis on an inductive methodology based on case studies and statistical analysis, rejecting abstract and deductive forms of theorising that are detached from the observation of reality; (iii) an emphasis on the notion of 'social control', by which is meant a proactive role for institutions and policies in addressing economic and social problems; (iv) an interdisciplinary orientation, linking economics with the philosophy and psychology of pragmatism and other related contributions of social psychology in seeking a more realistic account of human nature in its individual and social unfolding.

In the last of these respects, there were, in OIE's heyday, several contributions that employed (and even created) a psychological approach to explaining economic behaviour. This new wave had its seats in some important American universities[1] – in particular, Amherst, Chicago, Columbia, Wisconsin – whose institutional economists fostered important collaborations with numerous research institutions and governmental bodies. The general sentiment pervading these initiatives was one of optimism about the possibilities of social progress. It was by no means confined only to institutional economists as it involved the philosophy and psychology of pragmatism, together with various strands of psychology, sociology and political science.

VEBLEN'S EVOLUTIONARY PERSPECTIVE

Thorstein Veblen's famous 1898 article 'Why is economics not an evolutionary science?' can be considered the initiation of the evolutionary and institutional approach in economics. It stressed that mainstream economics, based on simplistic hypotheses and a static approach, cannot succeed in analysing the complexity of economic phenomena. Instead, a deeper and more interdisciplinary analysis must analyse habits, instinct, evolution, and the role of technology in promoting social progress.

Habits, Instincts and Evolution

The existence of habits of thought and life that arise and change slowly and cumulatively implies, in Veblen's analysis, that people do not behave out of a supposed 'rational' decision-making process aimed at maximising their 'hedonism'. Thus, they do not react instantly to different economic circumstances as assumed within the neoclassical framework. Rather, following norms may itself be a goal, since norms reflect the values and criteria through which society classifies and appraises human conduct. Hence, norms can indicate to a person what is the appropriate behaviour.

Veblen's focus on habits also draws attention to important aspects of the nature of human development and the role played by *instincts* (sometimes called 'propensities'). His theory of instincts constitutes a neat departure from the neoclassical theory of utility maximisation because it brings under a unitary interpretative framework the complexity of the aspects making up human personality – biological, intellectual, affective – by considering them within their evolutionary pattern. This gives a different conception of human nature. In Veblen's words:

> According to this conception, it is the characteristic of man to do something, not simply to suffer pleasures and pains through the impact of suitable forces. He is not simply a bundle of desires that are to be saturated by being placed in the path of the forces of the environment, but rather a coherent structure of propensities and habits which seek realisation and expression in an unfolding activity. (Veblen [1914] 1990: 74)

In Veblen's further elaboration – particularly in his book *The Instinct of the Workmanship and the State of the Industrial Arts* – workmanship and parental bent are held to be the most important human instincts. Both are intended in a broad sense: 'workmanship' means not only technical abilities but the whole set of manual and intellectual activities, whereas 'parental bent' means an inclination to look after the common good that extends beyond the sphere of the family alone. These instincts are appraised by Veblen as complex entities. As he said: 'Instinct, as contra-distinguished from tropismatic action, involves consciousness and adaptation to an end aimed at [...] Hence all instinctive action is teleological. It involves holding to a purpose' (Veblen [1914] 1990: 4, 31).

In Veblen's view, these propensities tend, under ideal circumstances, to strengthen one another. This important insight is confirmed by studies in psychology and psychoanalysis that stress people's need to enhance their intellectual, social and emotional potential through the construction of adequate interpersonal relations. These propensities are likely to prevail in a situation where other instincts that can act at cross-purposes with them – for instance, predatory instincts which may be expressed through a framework of ceremonial and 'acquisitive' institutions based on invidious distinctions – have little social grounds to express themselves. Veblen supposes that the first stage of human life was of this kind but, since then, disturbing factors have caused progressive deviation. He posits that: 'the growth of institutions – usage, customs, canons of conduct, principles of right and propriety, the course of cumulative habituation as it goes forward under the driving force of the several instincts native to man – will commonly run at cross purposes with serviceability and the sense of workmanship' (Veblen [1914] 1990: 49–50).

The main disturbing factor is located by Veblen in the emergence of the business enterprises of the capitalistic system. To secure foreign markets and maximise profits, this system led to imperialist policies of national aggrandisement. Internally, the system is characterised by ceremonial institutions and invidious distinctions of wealth and status expressed through the phenomenon of 'conspicuous consumption'. Therein lies a tenuous relation, if any, between the serviceability of the product and the pecuniary gain.

The Role of Technology in Promoting Social Progress

In Veblen's theory (particularly Veblen 1914), a central factor steering social progress is the rationalising role of technological improvements. The expectation is that promoting more useful and rational habits of life would also promote more rational habits of thought. This process, in turn, would help eliminate ceremonial habits based on predatory and acquisitive tendencies and create a better environment for the expression of the instincts of workmanship and parental bent. For Veblen, the progress of the 'machine technology' of capitalism would have the power to disintegrate such system. As he puts it: 'In their struggle against the cultural effects of machine process, therefore, business principles cannot win in the long run ... with a free growth of the machine system business principles would presently fall into abeyance' (Veblen 1904).

These insights, though interesting, demand a better focus on whether, in fact, technological progress is sufficient, per se, to drive such a progressive course. What one can regularly witness in the course of human history (and more than a century after Veblen's analysis the situation is not much better) is that technological progress has been largely monopolised by the power and pecuniary interests of the stronger groups rather than oriented to instrumental objectives of public purpose. So, even if our societies seem more rational than older ones – in the sense that science and technology find a more widespread application to the solutions of human problems – this does not necessarily imply that the ceremonial, predatory and neurotic aspects play only a minor role in economic and social relations. Rather, the imbalances of mature capitalistic societies are still in the foreground.

To render Veblen's analysis more applicable to current policy issues, extensions are needed. First, there needs to be a broader conception of technological progress, corresponding to a wide notion of Veblen's instinct of workmanship (and of 'idle curiosity') – a conception including all advances taking place in natural, social and psychological sciences. This implies a broader and humanistic conception of scientific enquiry in which qualitative phenomena are also amenable to scientific analysis (for instance, in assessing the proficiency of a musician). Moreover, the assessment of even the most quantitative phenomenon should not be regarded as an automatic process: because it involves choice between different interpretations, it also involves qualitative assessment.

Veblen's theory also needs reconsideration of its treatment of institutions as a locus of power and ceremonialism standing in the way of the affirmation of the instrumental values driven by technological progress. As shown by a vast literature, technological progress is itself an inherently social process. It is we who choose to follow different scientific/technological options (or none at all) and their related application to the society. Hence, to orient technology towards the objective of social serviceability, we need to foster policy action explicitly informed by the 'instrumental value criterion' – a cornerstone of Veblen–Ayres's approach to institutional economics. This implies the use of technological progress for attaining moral values (Ayres 1961), a line of inquiry further developed by later institutionalists. An effective definition of the instrumental value criterion is the 'continuity of human life and the non-invidious re-creation of community through the instrumental use of knowledge' (Tool 1986).

COMMONS AND THE THEORY OF COLLECTIVE ACTION

Further important foundations for the OIE tradition were laid by John Commons. His theory of collective action sets out the foundations of the institutional analysis of the market. Core propositions are that collective action is a necessary element for the performance of individual action (Commons [1924] 1995, [1934] 1990); and that, for this reason, an increasingly significant part of individual action is carried out not in a *vacuum* but in institutions and organisations where dialectical and dynamic relations intervene between individual and collective action. As he wrote: 'the ultimate unit of activity, which correlates law, economics and ethics, must contain in itself the three principles of *conflict, dependence*, and *order*. This unit is a Transaction. A transaction, with its participants, is the smallest unit of institutional economics' (Commons [1934] 1990: 58).

Transactions are classified into three categories – bargaining, managerial and rationing – according to the relationship established between the parties involved. The first concerns the relations between individuals with equal rights – which do not necessarily correspond to equal economic power – for instance, between buyer and seller. The second refers to the relations between people organised within an institution, for instance between managers and collaborators. The third refers to the relations between the person and a kind of collective action where there is no direct involvement, particularly with the policy action of government. These three types of transactions are quite diverse according to the degree of direct intervention by collective action but they are closely intertwined. In their various combinations, they make up the tangled weft of collective action. Writing about this complex, conflicting and evolutionary role that institutions perform, Commons said: 'Since liberation and expansion for some persons consist in restraint, for their benefit, of other persons, and while the short definition of an institution is collective action in control of individual action, the derived definition is: collective action in restraint, liberation, and expansion of individual action' (Commons [1934] 1990: 73).

The importance attributed by Commons to 'human-wills-in-action' and his interpretation of collective action as a system of transactions does not imply, however, the adoption of a merely 'contractual' view of institutions that overlooks the role of coercion and unexpected consequences of human action. On that account, his definition of transactions and institutions makes it easier to scrutinise the various forms of collective action in the economic, social, cultural and psychological domains. In this connection, Commons ([1934] 1990) elaborated the concept of 'negotiational psychology', which can be employed for a better understanding of the complex relations underlying the various transactions in their individual and collective dimensions. Negotiational psychology embodies the idea of conflict between different feelings and values that find their manifold expressions at the various levels of collective action.

Reasonable Value and Policy Action

The analysis of transactions by Commons includes, in their mutual interaction, all kinds of social and economic relations – from the more individualistic to the more collective ones. A crucial element concerns the role played by all these transactions in making up policy action. These aspects, in turn, relate to the importance of the process of social value in the dynamics of collective action. Within this ambit, Commons elaborates the concept of reasonable value to draw attention to the conflicting and evolutionary nature of the process of social valuing. These concepts are expressed as follows:

> Each economic transaction is a process of joint valuation by participants, wherein each is moved by diversity of interests, by dependence upon the others, and by the working rules which, for the time being, require conformity of transactions to collective action ... Reasonable Value is the evolutionary collective determination of what is reasonable in view of all changing political, moral, and economic circumstances and the personalities that arise therefrom. (Commons [1934] 1990: 681, 683–4)

Thus, reasonable value can be regarded as an imperfect process whose characteristics can be interpreted as the synthesis of the conflicting and evolutionary components of collective action. The imperfection of reasonable value is also caused by its partly unconscious and conflicting character, often embodied in habits of thought and life.

The Articulation of Transactions and the 'Double' Definition of the Market

Commons regards the individual and collective elements as necessarily joint aspects of economic action. Even when the action seems utterly individualistic – for instance in the case of a bargaining transaction where the buyer and the seller seem to act exclusively out of their personal interests – there is present, often implicitly, a significant collective element. Seen from this perspective, it is possible to identify, for every transaction, the set of rights, duties, liberties and exposures that are exercised through a combination of performance, forbearance and avoidance behaviours.

For transactions that involve bargaining, the concept of market adopted by Commons acquires an interesting 'double' meaning – not only the sphere of exchange but also that of production. In this respect, Commons provides a historical reconstruction of the emergence of the market, underscoring the importance of deliberate public intervention in its creation. The origin of the market is located in the processes by which the justice courts decided disputes and thereby established the reasonable value. As he wrote:

> A market usually originated with a special monopolistic franchise, named a 'liberty', and granted to a powerful individual or ecclesiastical magnate, authorising him to hold concourse of buyers and sellers, with the privilege of taking tolls in consideration of the protection afforded [...] [in the course of time] [...] The courts, in their decisions, developed the principle of the 'market overt,' or the public, free and equal market [...] These principles were not something innate and natural but were actually constructed out of the good and bad practices of the time. The early physiocrat and classical

economists thought of them as handed down by divine Providence or the natural order. (Commons [1934] 1990: 775)

From this perspective, the market cannot realistically be considered as an abstract mechanism leading automatically – if it is sufficiently 'perfect' – to individual and social utility maximisation. Indeed, as a matter of fact, even the (seemingly) most atomistic and impersonal transaction occurring between individuals who are unknown to each other does not take place in an imaginary 'free market' world but within a complex institutional and legal framework that defines the 'working rules' of transactions, with the related set of 'rights', 'duties', 'liberties' and 'exposures'. This process, according to Commons,

> tells what the individual *must* or *must not* do (compulsion or duty), what they *may* do without interference from other individuals (permission or liberty), what they *can* do with the aid of collective power (capacity or right), and what they *cannot* expect the collective power to do in their behalf (incapacity or exposure). (Commons [1924] 1995: 6)

The institutional nature of the market implies that it is heavily embedded in the social and cultural domain and that it involves a process of social valuing. This kind of analysis explicitly considers transactions as a dynamic process. As Commons said: 'A transaction occurs at a point of time. But transactions flow one into another over a period of time, and this flow is a process' (Commons [1924] 1995: 7–8). By stressing the necessity to consider the temporal sequence of transactions, this analysis shows a further inadequacy of the static approach of neoclassical economics.

MARKET IMPERFECTIONS AT MICRO AND MACRO LEVELS

The foundational contributions to OIE, especially those by Commons, cast light on how markets are framed by a complex network of transactions and institutions and on how, through the process of social valuing, there arises a distinct policy dimension involving judicial decisions, the action of the various interest groups and government. This was a foundation on which subsequent institutionalists could deepen the analysis of market imperfections and how to deal with them. This was done – albeit without much synergy between them or with other strands of institutionalism – by scholars such as Albert Copeland, Wesley Mitchell and Walton Hamilton.

Copeland stressed the imperfections of the pecuniary standard in measuring – and hence apportioning between the parts – the integral (public and private) benefits and costs of a transaction. He pointed out that 'Any imperfections in that standard would necessarily have very serious consequences for economic welfare and justice' (Copeland 1924: 105). Because market prices do not necessarily accord with the costs in terms of human effort that go into making the goods, nor their significance for consumers' welfare, interesting questions arise about how those 'discrepancies' might be eliminated through social action. One line of enquiry – which can be traced back to Veblen's distinction between pecuniary and industrial employments – relates to how much the pecuniary valuation (the price) of a product is due to an increase of products or to an increase of profits. The two things should be carefully distinguished. If the objectives of profits and of making goods do not coincide – and all too often stand in opposition to each other – this implies that a similar distinction needs to be made in assessing the advantages of a transaction. Many examples can illustrate the discrepancy between differential and integral advantages originating from individual economic action. Among the most obvious are environmental degradation, waste of natural resources, cut-throat competition, instability of economic cycles, and chronic under-utilisation of human potential and productive capacity. Such imbalances are due to the largely unintended consequences of individual action. For instance, in a period of boom, firms have an interest in pushing up prices and producing more but, by making the economic wave higher, this makes more ruinous the subsequent fall. Similarly, the effects of depressions are reinforced by the often more than necessary cuts in production and employment.

Such discrepancies also arise in other instances that are (or appear) less controversial. For instance, a technological innovation leading, through to an increase of productivity, to lower costs, lower prices and more sales seems to present a clear social gain. However, for calculating the integral advantage, we need also to consider the impact on other firms employing the older technology that become suddenly obsolete. Or the case where a better standardisation of the components by complementary enterprises could increase integral advantage but does not occur because it pays more for differential advantage to maintain a needless duplication of these components. In such instances, prices presumably could be adjusted to reflect more precisely the integral advantage of the transactions. Copeland did not address the details of such policy interventions, only positing that policy action should preserve individual action, and should change the related economic incentives to mirror more accurately the real costs and benefits of transactions.

Somewhat similar concerns were addressed by Sumner Slichter in 'The organization and control of economic activities' (1924), which ponders how realistic is the claim that the system of 'free enterprise' is automatically conducive to social welfare. To realise or approximate this goal, the competition process associated with 'free enterprise' would have to lead to minimisation of costs and maximisation of consumers' utilities, as illustrated in neoclassical models. However, Slichter argued that not only do real capitalistic economies fail to realise such objectives but that they all too often move in the opposite direction. A central reason is that consumers have insufficient incentives to discourage actions not conducive to social welfare. So, for instance, cheaper prices are a powerful inducement to them to buy, even if they arise from harming the environment and/or evading labour and safety legislation. In most cases, consumers know little about these latter aspects and are often not interested to know more.

Another area where the system of free enterprise engenders a discrepancy between private profits and social welfare is that of want creation – an issue that J.K. Galbraith later developed as a cornerstone of his contribution to OIE. First, the firms in the consumer sector try to increase their sales by promoting goods that are 'visible carriers' of pecuniary success and of the invidious distinctions associated with it. In this respect, 'The precise things which philosophers and moralists of all ages have urged men to regard as of little consequence business presses on them as of great importance' (Slichter 1924: 312). Marketing experts do not merely create wants which only the buying of the goods may satisfy; they also create, as a part of the same process, apparent pains that can be avoided only by the purchasing of those goods. So, these marketing experts introduce new styles as soon as they can and then consumers tend to buy such items not so much for 'maximising' their utility but, rather, for avoiding the feeling of being out of fashion.[2] An important consequence is that, when one firm increases marketing expenses, all the others need to do likewise. Whether these expenses are beneficial to social welfare is, of course, much more doubtful.

If we move from the issue of 'utility maximisation' to 'cost minimisation', the situation is no better. As a matter of fact, the 'free enterprise system' tends actively to create various technical inefficiencies at the firm level. One reason for this relates to the excess of productive capacity, for which an important explanation lies in the dynamics of business cycles. Especially for big corporations, production capacity is increased during boom periods. Then, in normal or slack times, such capacity remains largely unchanged and therefore partly idle because of the costs and difficulty of reducing it. Waste can also persist where inefficiencies known to the workers directly engaged in the processes of production remain unresolved because those workers have no incentive to share this knowledge with the firm's management. What the workers fear (often with good reason) is that the benefits arising from their suggestions would go to the firm's profit and that tougher productive targets will be put on them. The workers' reluctance to cooperate with the firm in technical improvements may also be linked to how promotion prospects operate. Firms often fail to promote workers according to their merit: while their cleverness and reliability are relevant factors, other considerations, such as the network of influential social relations, play a more decisive role.

Another central reason for the market's weak capacity to economise costs is that is does not provide a mechanism[3] for limiting an uneconomical increase in the number of firms. Rather, as Slichter notes, when prices become higher than costs (i.e. the mark-up increases), the tendency is not for prices to be lowered, as claimed by neoclassical economics, but for costs to increase because of the multiplication of enterprises attracted by high profits. Ultimately, the root of these problems is traceable to the conflict between capital and labour. The firms' managers are appointed by the owners of the capital, while workers have but a scant voice in the process. And if the latter join a union, this tends to be considered as a disturbing factor. Only a more active role for the workers (and of consumers) in orienting the business policies could overcome the problems.

The Social Costs of Private Enterprise

The concerns about the structural imbalances arising in markets and capitalist enterprises have become key themes within OIE. Further foundations were laid by Karl Kapp, in his book, *Social Costs of Private Enterprise* (1950), and in subsequent articles. Kapp notes that firms working in capitalistic systems, but also in the countries of 'real socialism', have a structural tendency to shift to the collectivity the negative effects on environments of their activities. It is, in this sense, a much more pervasive phenomenon than is conveyed by the neoclassical notion of 'externality'. It is a phenomenon characterised by circular causation involving technological, social, and institutional aspects. Indeed, 'environmental disruption' happens only when the institutional system makes it possible. In Kapp's words:

> Speaking as an economist, I have long held the view and continue to believe that the institutionalised system of decision-making in a market economy has a built-in tendency of disregarding those negative effects (e.g. air and water pollution) which are 'external' to the decision-making unit [...] Thus, a system of decision-making, operating in accordance with the principle of investment for profit, cannot be expected to proceed in any other way but to try to reduce its costs whenever possible by shifting them to the shoulders of others or to society at large. (Kapp and Ullmann 1983: 42)

This situation, left to itself, tends to engender a vicious circle and is the result of a system that, under an appearance of private rationality, is overwhelmed by a collective destructive irrationality that finds expression in systematic damage of the environment. To address these problems, the objectives of environmental policies – in terms of social costs and benefits – should be appraised outside the market sphere, as socio-political entities. What Kapp suggests is an ex ante definition of the environmental objectives that should then be incorporated in investment decisions. A key factor for realising these objectives today rests in the systematic creation and widespread application of green technologies.

Contradictions of the 'Affluent Society'

Building on the earlier contributions to OIE, John Kenneth Galbraith became undoubtedly the most widely read of the institutional economists. Among his many books, the most famous was *The Affluent Society*, published for the first time in 1958 and then again in 1998 with an author's update. It addresses issues central to a critical understanding of the 'societies of abundance' during the decades following the Second World War. As an innovative and controversial interpretation, it points to (i) the imperative of production and consumption, with the excessive use of credit and pervasive advertising; (ii) the presence of a powerful 'techno-structure'; (iii) the systematic downplaying of public expenditure and public goods; (iv) the growing economic and social insecurity; (v) the environmental decay; and (vi) the limited possibility of conventional policies to influence these phenomena.

Galbraith presents a picture of an economic system in which 'real production' is usually identified almost exclusively with the private sector, while the public sector is considered, at best, a necessary evil, and, at worst, an obstacle to the free operation of market forces. In this view, he says, 'public services rarely lose their connotation of burden. Although they may be defended, their volume is almost certainly never a source of pride' (Galbraith [1958] 1998: 99–100). The result is a chronic shortage of the public goods needed for a balanced development of economic activities. It is also a situation of persistent inequality and 'poverty amidst affluence' because of the inadequate services (e.g. education) for poor people that would help to overcome their condition.

Meanwhile, the complex of large enterprises and their managers, which Galbraith names the 'technostructure', acquires the leading role in the creation and satisfaction of consumer needs. One of the indicators of this phenomenon consists in the costs of promoting the product, often equal to or even greater than the costs of production. In this sense, 'wants are increasingly created by the process in which they are satisfied' (Galbraith [1958] 1998: 129).

How can these problems be dealt with? Developing effective solutions to the problems of an affluent society, Galbraith argues, requires a growing public awareness of the imbalances – and this is the main objective of his contribution. However, he is not optimistic about the possibility of quickly realising this potential, ending his book by saying:

> To furnish a barren room is one thing. To continue to crowd in furniture until the foundation buckles is quite another. To have failed to solve the problem of producing goods would have been to continue man in his oldest and most grievous misfortune. But to fail to see that we have solved it, and to fail to proceed thence to the next tasks, would be fully as tragic. (Galbraith [1958] 1998: 260)

Yet a note of optimism may be added if his insights into the problems of the affluent society, interacting with other contributions from institutional economics and cognate social sciences, helps to identify a more comprehensive course of policy action.

The Relevance of Supranational Cooperation

Putting more emphasis on international issues, the Swedish economist Gunnar Myrdal has been another influential political economist within the institutionalist tradition. Among many other contributions, Myrdal elaborated the theory of circular and cumulative causation as a means of interpreting many phenomena addressed by institutional economists – for instance, the persistence over time of inefficient institutions (public and private) and of economic disparities such as those between developing and developed countries. This theory is further considered in Chapter 9 of this book.

Myrdal's work also offers an analysis of the insufficient level of supranational relations. In his 1957 lecture 'Why are international economic organizations so inefficient?' (reported on in Appelqvist and Andersson 2005) he argues, with prophetic insight, that, in a world where supranational cooperation becomes ever more necessary for addressing economic and social imbalances, the capacity to realise this goal remains dramatically deficient. There are inherent difficulties in treating complex matters in an enlarged dimension, of course, but the major political economic obstacle for such collaboration lies in the unwillingness of governments – supported by much public opinion – to renounce part of their sovereignty for attaining supranational objectives. One relevant reason for this attitude can be found in the psychological difficulty of expressing solidarity and empathy for anything we perceive as 'foreign' and outside our sphere of action (nations, regions, towns and villages, with the related social groups). Such localistic attitudes, however, are not conducive to reaping the advantages that would result from supranational cooperation.

What Myrdal proposes for overcoming nationalism and localism is an enlightened citizenship that could be fostered by a better knowledge of the gains of cooperation. There are, however, no precise suggestions as to how to speed up this process. In this regard, more might be done to draw from institutional economics and other social sciences to explain why progressive social change (including more supranational cooperation) is so difficult and slow. Relevant elements are the habits of thought and life that maintain the stability of social fabric, and how such habits can be influenced by the various propensities (positive and negative) of people in their interactions with the social system. So, if a society promotes predatory and aggressive propensities based on invidious distinctions of wealth and power, their embodiment in habits of thought and life can help to explain the difficulty of social change. Another work by the current author (Hermann 2020) shows how institutional theories, by interacting with pragmatist psychology and psychoanalysis, can provide a better understanding of the conflicts of individual and collective life and help to build a more equitable and sustainable society.

IMPLICATIONS FOR ECONOMIC PLANNING

Analysis of the process of planning is an important aspect of OIE's contributions to political economy. Should economic planning exist at all, and, if so, what kind is preferable? Exploring these questions fills a vacuum in mainstream economic thought. As this chapter has shown, the idea of a perfect and optimising market, conceived of as an exogenous and self-equilibrating mechanism, is a kind of wishful thinking. In real economies, markets are created and maintained by an evolving set of laws, institutions and policies that are typically oriented to serving the interests of the stronger groups. Furthermore, because markets cannot deliver various kind of public goods, direct public action is required. Some economic planning is therefore always necessary for attaining the objectives of policy action. The key question is what *kind* of economic planning is preferable. On that matter, OIE provides significant contributions (such as those of Clark [1939] 1969; Tool 1986; and Dugger 1988), enabling identification of three broad categories of economic planning: corporate, totalitarian and democratic.

Corporate planning is the reality of the 'concerted' capitalism of our time that sees a systematic interaction between the more powerful private groups and public action. In this system, the operation of 'free market forces' is heavily conditioned by the interests of big corporations that possess a wide array of instruments to influence policies in a direction conducive to their goals. In Dugger's words: 'The corporation is privately efficient [in the pursuit of its goals], but it is not socially efficient because its low-cost, high-productivity performance benefit those who control it, generally at the expense of those who depend upon it but frequently also at the expense of the society at large' (Dugger 1988: 239). Corporate planning is inherently hierarchical, the key decisions being made by top managers with little involvement of workers and citizens at large.

The second type is totalitarian planning, whereby a posited public purpose is pursued through a yet more strongly hierarchical institutional structure. Such organisations – although sometimes producing impressive results in infrastructure construction and poverty alleviation – are flawed by their fundamental lack of accountability and democratic representation. The central planners are appointed by the ruling (and single) political party. In such instances, there is no guarantee that the party is organised democratically and expresses the needs and experiences of all the groups and classes of society; nor are government members and public officials fully socially accountable for their behaviour. These institutional arrangements, by acquiring a marked self-referential character, make impossible any objective and pluralistic assessment of the policies adopted and the results achieved.

The third form is democratic planning. Although variable in practice and seldom 'working miracles', this is preferable for many reasons. Most obviously, by allowing a more complete expression of the experiences, motivations, and conflicts of the involved subjects, such a system improves the process of social valuation and the capacity of policy action to respond to the needs of society. Democratic planning, in contrast to corporate and totalitarian arrangements, has the capacity to self-correct – by a process of trial and error – its own shortcomings. In this regard, one key objective of democratic planning (see Tool 1986; Dugger 1988) is overcoming the dichotomy, first identified by Veblen, between the objectives of profit and serviceability related to the production of goods. This can be attained by reducing the artificial scarcity and the 'invidious distinctions' stemming from market power and ceremonial status, and by making better and more participatory use of the community's existing knowledge. All this is related to the fulfilment of John Dewey's democratic principle – that people affected by decisions must have a say in the decision-making and in assessing the results. It is this aspect that makes 'participatory processes dynamic and authoritarian processes so stultifying' (Dugger 1988: 245).

Democratic planning also offers flexibility, which is essential if it is to be applied to a wide array of contemporary issues, often reaching out to a supranational dimension. Of course, the objectives of the planning process and institutions will be interpreted differently according to each context. The key test lies in the process that democratic planning engenders for improving social valuation in decision-making. The 'instrumental value criterion' elaborated by Marc

Tool can usefully be integrated with the concept of 'reasonable value' elaborated by John Commons for analysis of its effectiveness in different contexts.

INSTRUMENTAL VALUE, SOCIAL VALUE AND INSTITUTIONAL PSYCHOLOGY

The preceding discussion, emphasising the relevance of realising a more equitable and democratic society, raises three important questions for the OIE tradition within political economy:

- Can economics endorse normative elements, in the sense of value judgements?
- If so, how can we decide about the intrinsic superiority or desirability of a more democratic, equitable and sustainable society?
- How can we decide which course of action is to be preferred?

For the first question, the answer is decidedly in the affirmative. Yet the dominant school of neoclassical economics fails to provide any coherent basis for such judgements. Its attempt to build a value-free theory of market transactions is illusory. Its two main neoclassical postulates – market perfection and (instrumental) rationality of economic agents – have the character of a wishful thinking which does not allow any verification of their realism. This comes about because any deviation from these postulates is explained as an unwelcomed exception deriving from 'exogenous factors'. But this is not the end of story because these unrealistic postulates betray the system of values of their supporters. This is a system of values considering modern capitalistic economies as largely unproblematic realities that enable any rational being to get the most from market exchange.

What alternative do institutionalists offer? They interpret and appraise economic behaviour as embedded in and intertwined with the evolution of social and cultural spheres, including all the related values, motivations, conflicts and contradictions at individual and collective level. Hence, only a careful study of the given situation can cast light on the real social and psychological forces underlying economic action. This approach shows the importance of being explicit about systems of values while keeping, as far as possible, such values distinct from the objective assessment of reality (which, of course, can never be fully 'neutral').

The second concern – identifying a basis for assessments of what constitutes social progress – is surely more tangled, but an institutional approach may offer a way forward. It recognises that comparison of the features of different social systems not only touches the issue of 'ultimate values' but also the notion of 'cultural relativism'. Although the latter notion is useful in counteracting the monism of conventional wisdom, it can lead to another kind of excess. In attempting to be 'neutral' and to avoid the dangers of 'simplification' and 'reductionism', cultural relativism may tend to treat the distinctive features of a given context – including aspects of violence and injustice contrary to our moral values – as expressions of cultural diversity and, as such, not appropriate for further ethical appraisal and scientific investigation. Both these limiting perspectives – cultural monism (which is a kind of reductionism) and the excesses of cultural relativism – must be overcome. The central question then becomes how to identify criteria for assessing the 'intrinsic validity', and hence the ethical foundations, of instrumental value criteria based on values of fairness and solidarity.

On this matter, the appraisal of adequacy of social systems can be found not so much in abstract universal principles of social good but, rather, in linking these principles to people's actual needs. In this respect, the notion of psychological soundness – namely, the extent to which persons are free from neurotic conflicts in their individual and collective action – can also help better clarify the central distinction between the instrumental value principle and ceremonialism resting on invidious distinctions of wealth and status. Moreover, if we assume, following insights from institutional economics, psychology and psychoanalysis, that the propensities of workmanship and parental bent lie at the heart of the needs of the person, the ethical principles of solidarity and participation become endowed with a more precise scientific content. They become based on a systematic analysis of the ontological foundations of human needs in their social and cultural expressions. On this reasoning, collaboration between these institutional theories and psychoanalysis can help to locate more precisely the multifarious and conflicting ways of expressing these instances within any context. On that basis, the formulation of policies can become more focussed on the profound needs and orientations of society.

This brings us to the third and final question – how can we decide what course of action is most appropriate for pursuing the social goals? For instance, should remunerations be equal for all workers, or should there be a premium related to merit, education, seniority or difficulty? And, if the latter applies, how large should any such premium be in connection to the various criteria? Similarly, how much profit (and relative market power) is fair and convenient to allow for realising policy objectives? Issues like these, and others of similar import, predictably stir intense debates. They go to the heart of the notion of social value, which is closely related to the notion of 'reasonable value' developed by Commons and addressed earlier in this chapter. As Marc Tool writes: 'The role of social value theory is to provide analyses of criteria in terms of which such choices are made' (Hodgson et al. 1994: 406–7). In this sense, social value is central to the very nature of political economy, conceived not an activity stemming from the application of abstract laws but as a collective and evolutionary decision-making process involving many institutions. Regarded in this way, political economy has a close relation with law and ethics. An interdisciplinary approach can also lead to a better understanding of the features and evolution of social valuing in any given context, finding expression in the complex frameworks of motivations, conflicts, and expectations, both at individual and collective levels.

CONCLUSION

There are many fields where institutional economics can contribute to a more effective analysis and forward-looking policy action. These include (but are not limited to) labour legislation, the role of unions, industrial and competition policies, the role of science and technology in economic and social progress, the social costs of private enterprise, addressing the contradictions of the 'affluent society', the nature of transactions, ownership and control of corporations, public utilities regulation, the analysis of business cycles, international relations, the links between law and economics, the role of economic planning, and the role of social psychology in casting more light on the motivations of economic action.

Some of these insights have been adapted in the 'new institutional economics'– a more recent perspective partly based on neoclassical economics. For example, as noted by Malcolm Rutherford:

> Recent work on the importance of property rights pursues a topic that was in the center of the institutionalist perspective. The concept of transactions costs was implicit in some of the older institutionalist literature, and its more recent explicit development has generated an explosive growth of literature on organisations, contracts, and the role of institutions in economic development. Much recent work in corporate finance and theories of agency and corporate control takes the pioneering work of institutionalists on the separation of ownership and control as its starting point. (Rutherford 2001: 187)

This 'new institutional economics' phenomenon has been investigated and assessed elsewhere (for instance, Yonay 1998; Rutherford 2001, 2011; Hodgson 2004; Hermann 2018a). Its impact during the post-Second World War period has contributed to a relative decline in the more far-reaching perspective of the original institutional economics.

To now revive and develop the broader potential of the original institutionalism requires overcoming the fragmentation (or limited collaboration) so often present in economic, social and psychological sciences. Institutionalism has itself been regrettably subject to these tendencies, from its inception until the late 1980s. The lack of systematic interactions and collaboration between institutionalist authors working within the different strands of institutionalism is evident in the paucity of reciprocal quotations.

Interactions with other fields of heterodox economics, especially Keynesian economics, have not always been constructive either. For instance, Gruchy (1972) describes Keynes' economics as an important but limited step, chiefly leading to 'manipulative fiscal and monetary policies'. That partial view fitted with the mechanistic interpretations of neo-Keynesian economics that was dominant in the USA in the early decades of the post-Second World War period and which showed little awareness of the structural imbalances of the system and of the usefulness of some form of democratic national planning.[4] But it overlooked the complexity and richness of Keynes' theory and of the subsequent strand of post-Keynesian economics. Significantly, Keynes considered, in the final part of *The General Theory* (1936), that a 'socialisation of investment' would be the only long-term solution to the capitalistic imbalances. Moreover, in the final part of *Essays in Persuasion* ([1931] 1963), he considered the economic system as potentially changing from being based on the profit motive to being oriented to creating more free time. Recognition of the structural imbalances of the system and the need of a new course of policy action continues to inform many post-Keynesian contributions to political economy. These features of the Keynesian tradition sit comfortably with institutional economics.

As observed by the sociologist Karl Mannheim (1952), a landscape can be seen only from a determined perspective, and without perspective there is no landscape. In this sense, observing a landscape (or phenomenon) from different angles (or disciplines) can help to acquire much clearer insights. An interdisciplinary perspective – by making endogenous many variables that orthodox economists treat as exogenous – can cast light on the real motivations of persons and how progress can be promoted, distorted or frustrated in economic and social life. Institutional economics, as a current within modern political economy that has a strong interdisciplinary inclination, is central to this undertaking.

Seen in this light, institutional economics offers promising research fields. These include studies of the motivations and conflicts underlying the various spheres of economic action – work, consumption, investment, saving – related to persons, groups, classes, public and private institutions, and how they impinge on the evolution of the system. For instance, are higher incomes sought only for 'material reasons'? Or does the drive for enrichment also result from the (partly unconscious) need to be accepted by following a socially approved behaviour?

The study of these aspects invites a closer analysis of the role of *superego* (and of the conflicts associated with it) in this process, and how these psychological aspects co-evolve with economic, social and cultures structures in any given context. Seen from this interdisciplinary perspective, institutional contributions can provide significant elements for the analysis of the imbalances and tensions of the economic system and the most effective policies for overcoming them.

NOTES

1. For more details on these developments, reference may be made to Hodgson (2004), Rutherford (2011), and Yonay (1998).
2. As noted in another work (Hermann 2015), in all these instances consumers are likely to be led also by neurotic influences and hence can hardly be maximising their 'utility'.
3. Since this analysis has striking parallels with the theories of underconsumption (see, for instance, Mummery and Hobson 1889), closer collaboration with these theories (and with post-Keynesian contributions) would be particularly useful for casting more light on these aspects.
4. This issue, with particular attention to sustainable policies, is also addressed in Hermann (2018b).

REFERENCES

Appelqvist, Ö. and Andersson, S. (eds) (2005) *The Essential Gunnar Myrdal*, New York: The New Press.
Ayres, C.E. (1961) *Toward a Reasonable Society*, Austin: University of Texas Press.
Clark, J.M. ([1939] 1969) *Social Control of Business*, 2nd edn, New York: A.M. Kelley.
Commons, J.R. ([1924] 1995) *Legal Foundations of Capitalism*, New Brunswick: Transaction Publishers.
Commons, J.R. ([1934] 1990) *Institutional Economics: Its Place in Political Economy*, New Brunswick: Transaction Publishers.
Copeland, A.M. (1924) 'Communities of economic interest and the price system', in Tugwell R.G. (ed.), *The Trend of Economics*, New York: Knopf, pp. 105–50.
Dugger, W.M. (1988) 'An institutionalist theory of economic planning', in Tool, M.R. (ed.), *Evolutionary Economics*, Volume II, New York: Sharpe.
Galbraith, J.K. ([1958] 1998) *The Affluent Society*, 2nd edn, New York: Mariner Books.
Gruchy, A.G. (1972) *Contemporary Economic Thought: The Contributions of Neo-Institutional Economics*, New Jersey: Augustus M. Kelley.
Hermann, A. (2015) *The Systemic Nature of the Economic Crisis: The Perspectives of Heterodox Economics and Psychoanalysis*, London and New York: Routledge.
Hermann, A. (2018a) 'The decline of the "Original Institutional Economics" in the post-World War II period and the perspectives of today', *Economic Thought*, 7 (1), pp. 63–86.
Hermann, A. (2018b) *United Nations Agenda 2030 for Sustainable Development between Progress and Problems: Insights from Environmental and Heterodox Economics*, Reading, UK: Green Economics Institute.
Hermann, A. (2020) 'The psychological contributions of pragmatism and of Original Institutional Economics and their implications for policy action', *Economic Thought*, 9 (1), pp. 48–71.
Hodgson, G. (2004) *The Evolution of Institutional Economics*, London and New York: Routledge.
Hodgson, G.M., Samuels, W.J. and Tool, M. (eds) (1994) *The Elgar Companion to Institutional and Evolutionary Economics*, Aldershot: Edward Elgar Publishing.
Kapp, K.W. (1950) *Social Costs of Private Enterprise*, Cambridge, MA: Harvard University Press.
Kapp, K.W. and Ullmann, J.E. (eds) (1983) *Social Costs, Economic Development and Environmental Disruption*, Lanham, MD: University Press of America.
Keynes, J.M. ([1931] 1963) *Essays in Persuasion*, New York: Norton.
Keynes, J.M. (1936) *The General Theory of Employment, Interest and Money*, London: Macmillan.

Mannheim, K. (1952) *Essays in Philosophy of Knowledge*, Oxford and New York: Oxford University Press.

Mummery, F.A. and Hobson, J.A. (1889) *The Physiology of Industry*, London, John Murray: reprinted 2015 by Leopold Classic Library.

Myrdal, G. (1957) 'Why are international organizations so inefficient?', lecture broadcast on Swedish radio, reported on in Appelqvist, Ö. and Andersson, S. (eds) (2005) *The Essential Gunnar Myrdal*, New York: The New Press.

Rutherford, M. (2001) 'Institutional economics: then and now', *Journal of Economic Perspectives*, **15** (3), pp. 173–94.

Rutherford, M. (2011) *The Institutional Movement in American Economics, 1918–1947: Science and Social Control*, Cambridge: Cambridge University Press.

Slichter, Sumner H. (1924) 'The organization and control of economic activities', in Tugwell, R.G. (ed.), *The Trend of Economics*, New York: Knopf, pp. 303–55.

Tool, M.R. (1986) *Essays in Social Value Theory: A Neoinstitutionalist Contribution*, New York: Sharpe.

Veblen, T. (1898) 'Why is economics not an evolutionary science?', *The Quarterly Journal of Economics*, **12** (4), pp. 373–97.

Veblen, T. (1904) *The Theory of Business Enterprise*, New York: Charles Scribner's Sons.

Veblen, T. ([1914] 1990) *The Instinct of Workmanship and the State of the Industrial Arts*, New Brunswick: Transaction Publishers.

Yonay, Y. (1998) *The Struggle over the Soul of Economics: Institutionalist and Neoclassical Economists in America between the Wars*, Princeton, NJ: Princeton University Press.

6. Post Keynesian economics

John E. King

Post Keynesian[1] economics is a dissident school in macroeconomics based on a particular interpretation of Keynes's *General Theory* (and, for some Post Keynesians, the work of Keynes's near-contemporary, the Polish economist Michał Kalecki). There is also a substantial body of work in Post Keynesian microeconomics, and some distinctive and controversial policy propositions.

There are six core propositions (Thirlwall 1993). First, employment and unemployment are determined in the product market, not the labour market. Unemployment is a *macroeconomic* problem that cannot be reduced to microeconomics, even though it does have a microeconomic dimension. Thus, an income–expenditure model underpins the Post Keynesian theory of employment and unemployment, which relies on a representation of the 'circular flow' of income. Without some version of this 'hydraulic model', the Keynesian multiplier makes no sense, and the effects on income and employment of changes in investment, government spending and net exports cannot be understood.

Second, involuntary unemployment is at least potentially, and often actually, a serious economic problem, which is caused by deficient effective demand. It is unlikely to be the result of labour market imperfections, and it would not be eliminated if such imperfections were removed. This follows directly from the first proposition, which rests on the distinction between demand-deficient and non-demand-deficient unemployment; only the latter can be reduced by making the labour market operate more efficiently.

Third, in the relationship between aggregate investment and aggregate saving that is fundamental to macroeconomic theory, causation runs from investment to saving, and not vice versa. In a capitalist economy the really important decisions are made by corporations, not by households or individual consumers. It is business investment spending that drives the simple income–expenditure model, if we abstract (as a first simplification) from government spending and net exports. Thus the level of investment spending is the independent variable determining aggregate employment, output and income, with consumption spending (and hence saving, as the difference between income and expenditure) as the dependent variable, which rises and falls as a result of increases and decreases in income. And business investment is a function of expected profitability.

Fourth, a monetary economy is very different from a barter economy. Since profit is defined as the difference between two sums of money (revenues and costs), this is rather obvious, but it is not apparent in the general equilibrium models that are used in mainstream macroeconomics. In this respect, Post Keynesians argue, a capitalist economy is very different from a barter economy, where there is no money and products are exchanged directly for other products. It follows that money is not 'neutral', and macroeconomic theory cannot be partitioned into 'real' and 'monetary' segments. Finance is very important, since investment projects require expenditures in advance of the expected profit flows. And debt matters, since there is a crucial asymmetry between debtors, who can be forced to reduce their expenditure, and creditors, who cannot be forced to increase theirs. It follows that a monetary economy cannot be analysed 'as if' it were a barter economy.

Fifth, the Quantity Theory of Money is seriously misleading, since it rests on the assumption that money is indeed neutral with respect to the determination of real output (and employment), and affects only the price level. In the mainstream Equation of Exchange, $MV = PT$, M represents the stock of money, V is the velocity of circulation, P is the price level, and T is the volume of turnover (a proxy for real output). Assume that T is determined by 'real' (that is, non-monetary) factors, above all by individual preferences for present and future consumption. Then, if V is constant, the Quantity Theory tells us that changes in M lead directly to changes in P, and *only* to changes in P. Thus, changes in the stock of money lead to changes in the price level but do not affect output or employment; and we must make a strict distinction between the real and the monetary sectors of the economy. Keynes rejected this 'classical dichotomy', and so denied both the neutrality of money and the Quantity Theory. He might have gone even further, recognising that money is endogenous to the system rather than exogenous, so that in the Equation of Exchange causation runs from right to left (from PT to MV), not from left to right (from MV to PT). Thus, in the Post Keynesian theory of inflation, increases in M are treated as the effect of inflation, not the cause.

Sixth, capitalist economies are driven by what Keynes described as the 'animal spirits' of investors, which determine investment decisions, rather than any precise calculations of future costs and revenues. Like many human activities, decisions to invest depend on 'spontaneous optimism rather than a mathematical expectation' of profit, in conditions of fundamental uncertainty about the future prospects for their profitability (Keynes 1936: 161). However, this does not mean that everything depends on waves of irrational psychology. For most of the time, most investors are content to apply rather conservative conventions and rules of thumb. Manias and panics do occur, but not often, and exactly what triggers them is itself a complicated and contentious question.

The implications of these six propositions are very clear and important. The crucial point is the *principle of effective demand*. Aggregate output and employment are normally demand-constrained, not supply-constrained. Say's law is false: increases in supply do not generally create increased demand. To achieve and maintain full employment often (perhaps normally) requires state intervention. Thus, Post Keynesians differ quite fundamentally from both 'Old Keynesian' and 'New Keynesian' macroeconomics, and also from the 'New Neoclassical Synthesis' (King 2015: ch. 3). They also disagree with the mainstream on critical questions of economic methodology, not least on the contested need to provide 'microfoundations' for macroeconomic theory (King 2012; 2015: ch. 4). As we shall see, there are also major implications for macroeconomic policy.

THE THREE SUB-SCHOOLS

The detailed exposition and elaboration of these six propositions differs significantly between three distinct sub-schools. The 'fundamentalist Keynesians' believe that they were all set out in the *General Theory*, although Keynes had not explained them as clearly as he might have done. The leading representative of this school is Paul Davidson (b.1930), who set out his position in the early 1970s and has not changed his thinking appreciably since then (Davidson 1972, 2011). According to Davidson, Keynes identified the three crucial axioms of 'classical' theory: ergodicity (the future can be reliably inferred from the past), gross substitution (price flexibility ensures that all markets clear), and the neutrality of money (the classical dichotomy: money affects prices, not output and employment, which depend only on the 'real' factors). All three axioms are wrong. The existence of fundamental uncertainty means that we live in a non-ergodic world, in which the future cannot be reliably inferred from the past. The axiom of gross substitution is false, so that price and wage flexibility does not guarantee full employment. And money is not neutral; it affects output and employment.

From this, Keynes derived the principle of effective demand that is summarised in Davidson's aggregate supply–aggregate demand diagram, which is very different from the mainstream textbook version. The latter is drawn in price level–real GDP or inflation–real GDP space. In contrast, in Davidson's version, the vertical axis measures expected sales proceeds and planned spending, while the level of employment is measured on the horizontal axis. The intersection of the aggregate demand and aggregate supply curves gives the point of effective demand, which determines the level of employment; this is less than the full employment level (Davidson 2011: fig. 2.5, p. 30). Davidson is a strong critic of what he describes as 'imperfectionism': the principle of effective demand, he insists, has nothing to do with imperfections in the labour market or the product market; and eliminating such imperfections, even if it were possible, would not reduce demand-deficient unemployment. A reduction in the real wage would not increase employment, which is determined in the product market, not in the labour market.

The second sub-school is associated with the Polish economist Michał Kalecki (1899–1970), who discovered the principle of effective demand more or less simultaneously with Keynes, but gave it a Marxist twist that emphasised the class nature of capitalist society (Kalecki 1954). The distinction between workers and capitalists is implicit in the *General Theory*, but Keynes does not pay it the attention that it deserves. For Kalecki and his followers, it is absolutely essential, since capitalist expenditure (above all on investment) is the key to the business cycle, and there is a very clear distinction between the savings propensities of capitalists and workers. Kalecki concludes from his simple macroeconomic model that workers spend what they get, while capitalists get what they spend.

His algebra is derived from the simplest income–expenditure model, which reveals that in a closed economy with no government, total profits are indeed equal to capitalists' expenditure. Write Y for total income, C for consumption (the suffixes w and p refer, respectively, to consumption spending by workers and capitalists, out of their wage and profit incomes), I for investment, W for total wages; and P for total profits. Then:

Total Expenditure $= C + I = C_w + C_p + I$

Total Income $= W + P$

Assuming that there is no saving by workers, so that $C_w = W$, equality of income and expenditure entails that:

$P = C_p + I$

Here causation runs from expenditure to income, that is, from right to left. Thus, in aggregate, profits are determined by capitalists' expenditure on consumption and (especially, since it depends on expected profits and is therefore much more volatile) on investment. The government and overseas sectors can also be taken into account, without substantially altering the conclusions.

Since the distribution of income between capital and labour plays a more important role in the Kaleckian macroeconomic model than it does for the fundamentalist Keynesians, the determination of relative shares is a central problem. For Kalecki, the profit share depends on the degree of monopoly in oligopolistic product markets (and on the outcome of class conflict in the labour market). There is also a strong tendency for chronic deficiency in effective demand, because the profit share is normally too high – and the wage share too low – to generate enough consumption expenditure to sustain full employment of labour or capital. Moreover, in a capitalist society, the ruling class will, for several reasons (Kalecki 1943), normally resist government deficit spending, even though it would increase total profits. In particular, capitalists view full employment as a threat to 'discipline in the factories'. Kalecki did eventually accept that post-1945 capitalism had undergone a 'crucial reform', in which rising real wages and higher state welfare spending had supplemented military expenditure and allowed the maintenance of full employment. But he argued – correctly, as subsequent events have shown – that this was a fragile, and probably also temporary, achievement (Kalecki and Kowalik 1971).

The third sub-school is based on the 'financial instability hypothesis' set out by Hyman Minsky (1919–1996). This is very different from Kalecki's model, but not fundamentally inconsistent with it. The central relationship in Minsky's 'Wall Street vision' of capitalism is not between the capitalist employer and the worker but rather between the investment banker and his capitalist client. Minsky's 'representative agent' is not a classless consumer (as in mainstream economic theory) or an industrial capitalist (as for Kalecki), but a financial capitalist. Borrowing and lending are the crucial transactions, not buying consumer goods or labour power.

Capitalism is inescapably cyclical and fluctuations in investment are crucial in explaining why. In a monetary economy, the availability of finance is central to investment. Minsky distinguished three phases: 'hedge finance' in the early stages of a cyclical upswing, when lenders only accommodate those borrowers whose projects are expected to be sufficiently profitable to allow them to make both the necessary interest payments and repay the principal; 'speculative finance', where lenders are less cautious, and no longer require that the repayment of the principal is guaranteed; and 'Ponzi finance', where lending standards become so lax that some borrowers can easily procure further loans in order to meet their interest obligations on already existing loans. The eventual, inevitable financial crisis results from a collapse in lenders' confidence. It leads to credit rationing, the forced liquidation of assets at 'fire sale' prices in order to repay loans, a sharp fall in investment, and a consequent decline in output and employment (Minsky [1986] 2008).

Late in his life, Minsky identified a new stage in the development of the financial sector – which he termed 'money manager capitalism' – in which consumer borrowing, and hence also consumer debt, had become more important (Minsky [1986] 2008). New financial instruments traded by new institutions in new markets, he argued, were continually eroding the bank share of assets and liabilities, forcing them into more and more risky forms of behaviour. Minsky would not have been at all surprised by the global financial crisis of 2007–09.

These three Post Keynesian sub-schools occupy a considerable area of common ground. They all agree that it is impossible to base macroeconomic theory on RARE (representative agents with rational expectations) microfoundations. Rational expectations are ruled out for

Davidson by non-ergodicity and fundamental Keynesian uncertainty, and for Minsky by the cyclical myopia and historical amnesia of his investment bankers. Kalecki, too, stresses the importance of irreducible 'borrowers' risk' and 'lenders' risk'. Neither is there any role for representative agents, since this would eliminate the 'bulls and bears' who are central to the economic analysis of Keynes and Davidson, the workers and capitalists who are emphasised by Kalecki, and the different types of debtors and creditors who are distinguished by Minsky.

It can be argued that Kalecki and Minsky need each other. In Kalecki's models, there is no substantial role for money or finance. It is not that he believed that capitalism could be analysed as if it were a barter economy, but simply that he chose to concentrate on other questions. Minsky's emphasis on cyclical variability in credit rationing and on asset price fluctuations might well have been useful to Kalecki in resolving the continuing problems that he had in specifying an acceptable macroeconomic investment function. And Minsky needed a theory of financial *resources* to complement his theory of financial commitments. Kalecki's theory of profits provides a clear and coherent theory of capitalists' aggregate financial resources, which can be used to explain when it is possible, and when it is not possible, for capitalists in aggregate (though not, of course, individually) to spend their way out of trouble.

MICROECONOMICS

Although their emphasis is on macroeconomics, Post Keynesians also have a distinctive position on many aspects of microeconomics, criticising the mainstream economists for making a host of unreal assumptions in their treatment of firms and markets. The Post Keynesian approach to price theory reveals little or no interest in models of pure or perfect competition. Instead, the focus is on the consequences of market power, in particular on price-setting in oligopoly (Coutts and Norman 2013). Since variable costs seem to be fairly constant with respect to output, and economies of scale are important, Post Keynesians maintain that the output of the firm is normally constrained by demand, not by rising marginal costs. From Kalecki (1954) to Fred Lee (1998), they have developed models of 'mark-up pricing', in which prices tend not to vary as a result of short-term shifts in product demand but are much more regularly affected by changes in production costs. This ties in with their approach to analysing firms' investment decisions, which stresses the role of internal finance ('retained earnings'). It is all very different from the price and investment theory of the neoclassical mainstream.

Strong criticism of mainstream microeconomics is also found in Post Keynesian labour economics. This begins by asserting the importance of macroeconomics, since a labour market characterised by full employment will behave very differently from one with significant involuntary unemployment. Post Keynesians also emphasise that the workplace is a social institution, which requires that attention be paid to questions of emulation, fairness and solidarity, in addition to the more narrowly defined variables of wages and hours of work. They argue that neoclassical theorists have neglected the role of power, and politics, in the operation of the labour market. The decline of trade union influence in recent decades has had important economic consequences, both macro (leading to a sustained decline in the share of wages and salaries in GDP) and micro – with growing insecurity of employment, the growth of a 'gig economy', and the increasingly important phenomenon of workers being denied their legal entitlements by employers – an epidemic of 'wage theft' that has emerged as a major macroeconomic problem (King 2019).

In consumer theory, Post Keynesians again stress the importance of fundamental uncertainty, which forces individuals to choose satisfactory rather than optimal outcomes; their rationality is 'bounded', as the institutionalist economist Herbert Simon used to say. Marc Lavoie (2014: ch. 2) identifies seven principles of Post Keynesian consumer theory that distinguish it from the mainstream. The first is 'procedural rationality', which involves the search for satisfactory rather than optimal outcomes. Consumer needs are both 'satiable' and 'separable', casting doubt on the importance of the substitution effect in the theory of consumption. For most individuals there is a 'hierarchy of needs', which rules out any single uniform measure of utility. The 'growth of needs' again suggests that income effects are more important than substitution effects. The 'non-independence of needs' reflects the fact that tastes are socially determined, so that an individual's preferences depend on the consumption decisions of others. Finally, the 'principle of heredity' indicates that choices are not independent of the order in which they are made.

In the 'Concluding Notes' to the *General Theory*, Keynes suggested that, if it were indeed possible to establish full employment via the *microeconomic* means he proposes, 'the classical theory comes into its own again from this point onwards' (Keynes 1936: 378). Here he was endorsing the *neoclassical* microeconomics of Alfred Marshall, who had taught him as a Cambridge undergraduate in the early years of the twentieth century. Post Keynesians would disagree with him quite strongly on this question, for all the reasons already noted.

There is still a lot to be done in Post Keynesian microeconomics, especially on matters of economic welfare and macroeconomic policy. Indeed, the marginal return to further work in microeconomics may be currently higher than in macroeconomics, and so Post Keynesian resources should be allocated accordingly (King 2015: 60).

GROWTH AND DEVELOPMENT

The Post Keynesian approach to questions of economic growth and development differs from that of the mainstream on two essential points. First, growth is predominantly demand-driven, not supply-driven. Second, no sharp distinction can be drawn between the short run, when there may be problems that require government intervention, and the long run, when everything is assumed to run smoothly. In the Harrod–Domar growth model that Post Keynesians broadly endorse, growth depends on business investment decisions, not on household decisions to save. Business investment itself is determined by expectations of future profitability, which are related to the desired capital–output ratio but are also subject to fundamental Keynesian uncertainty. On both counts, fluctuations in investment expenditure constitute a potentially serious source of macroeconomic instability.

Harrod identified a serious problem with the relationship between the actual growth rate and what he termed the 'warranted' (that is, the equilibrium) rate of growth, with entrepreneurs' attempts to bring the two together actually widening the gap between them. Post Keynesians reject the neoclassical solution to this problem, deeply embedded in the Solow–Swan growth model, in which full employment and macroeconomic stability are always maintained through capital–labour substitution in response to changes in the relative prices of capital and labour. The 'Cambridge controversies' in the theory of capital demonstrated that this substitution process cannot be relied upon (Harcourt 1972). This is an important point of agreement between the Post Keynesian and the Sraffian schools of thought, with the 'Sraffian super-multiplier' providing strong grounds for criticising the 'expansive austerity' claims of many mainstream theorists (Deleidi and Mazzacuto 2019).

There is an additional problem with the maintenance of full employment. What Harrod termed the 'natural' (that is, the maximum possible) rate of growth may exceed both the actual and the warranted rates, requiring government intervention to stimulate effective demand if full employment is to be achieved. The three growth rates will be equal only in what Joan Robinson termed a 'golden age', which may sometimes eventuate (as it did in advanced capitalist economies between 1945 and 1973), but cannot be relied upon.

Three further substantial complications must be taken into account (Thirlwall 2013). The first concerns the treatment of technical progress, which Post Keynesians regard as being endogenous to the economic system rather than exogenously determined. The second is the need to move away from the one-commodity Harrod–Domar model in order to distinguish consumption goods from investment goods, and to separate the primary, secondary and tertiary sectors of the economy. The third requires the analysis to be extended to an open economy, allowing export demand to play a critical role.

Nicholas Kaldor's early growth models relied heavily on endogenous technical progress (King 2009: ch. 4). He specified a 'technical progress function' in which the rate of growth of output per worker is strongly related to the rate of growth of capital per worker. That makes the natural rate of growth depend on the actual and/or warranted rates of growth, significantly reducing the degree of instability inherent in the Harrod–Domar model and introducing an element of path dependence. The Dutch theorist P.J. Verdoorn took this further, arguing that the strong positive relationship between the rate of growth of labour productivity and the rate of growth of output demonstrated the existence of dynamic increasing returns to scale.

In its original formulation, Verdoorn's Law applied only to manufacturing, and not at all to the service sector. It persuaded Kaldor to advocate a tax on tertiary employment (the notorious Selective Employment Tax introduced in 1966 by the then Labour government in the UK) to encourage faster growth of jobs in the secondary sector. In 2020, Kaldor might well have agreed with today's Post Keynesian growth theorists that more subtle distinctions are necessary – between high-tech and low-tech manufacturing, for example, and between the IT element of the service sector and its more traditional retailing, hospitality and care provision components.

Kaldor later came to stress the importance of the open economy. Exports, he now argued, are the only truly exogenous source of aggregate demand in any individual national economy. Drawing again on the experience of the British economy in the second half of the twentieth century, his biographer, A.P. Thirlwall, formalised this Kaldorian insight into a model of balance of payments-constrained growth. According to Thirlwall's law, the rate of growth in any individual country depends on three factors: the rate of growth of world income, the world's income-elasticity of demand for the country's exports, and the country's own income-elasticity of demand for imports (Thirlwall 2013: ch. 5).

These theoretical approaches and insights are relevant principally to the richer and more advanced parts of the world. Given the importance of history, institutions and socio-political factors in the Post Keynesian approach to the theory of growth, a rather different approach must be taken to the economics of development in poor and under-developed regions. Crucially, what Kalecki described as the 'tragedy of investment' – it raises effective demand but also increases the capital stock and so discourages further investment – does not apply to very poor countries, where (within limits) supply actually does create its own demand. There are clear parallels here with the structuralist school of development economics represented by Latin American theorists such as Raul Prebisch and the more recent centre–periphery or North–South models advocated by Post Keynesians such as Amitava Dutt (2002).

There are also important policy implications. The case for the liberalisation of trade and capital movements, and for reliance on currency depreciation to overcome balance of payments constraints, is much weaker than its neoclassical supporters in the International Monetary Fund and the World Trade Organization would admit. Such measures may well make things worse by giving rise to sharp and destabilising movements in exchange rates and producing instability and crises. Thus, government controls over capital movements and exchange rate fluctuations are preferable to financial liberalisation.

All this has helped to generate a distinctively Post Keynesian approach to the theory of international trade. Neoclassical trade theory assumes the full employment of capital and labour, with automatic and painless elimination of payments imbalances through changes in exchange rates. It takes an essentially static approach to the 'gains from trade', placing much too little emphasis on economic dynamics and thereby underestimating the impact of the dynamic external economies of scale that were stressed by Kaldor. This also has major implications for trade policy, with Post Keynesians presenting a strong case for the protection of infant industries, for controls over international capital flows, and for managed rather than freely floating exchange rates.

Two important methodological lessons can be drawn. First, path dependence, hysteresis and circular and cumulative causation are central in Post Keynesian theories of growth and development (Setterfield 2013). Second, the central role of investment spending confirms the point made at the beginning of this section – that growth is an inherently unstable process, so that no sharp distinction can be drawn between the ups and downs of cyclical disequilibrium in the short run and smooth equilibrium growth in the long run. As Kalecki once put it, the long run is nothing more than 'a slowly changing component of a chain of short-period situations'; it has no independent existence (Kalecki 1971: 165).

ECONOMIC POLICY

Post Keynesians have developed a distinctive approach to both the targets and the instruments of macroeconomic policy. Thus, their views on a very wide range of economic policy questions differentiate them clearly from the mainstream, and they have not forgotten the classic advice of the Dutch economist Jan Tinbergen: make use of at least as many policy instruments as you have policy targets, but do not rigidly attach specific instruments to particular targets. Post Keynesians generally advocate four macroeconomic targets, or policy objectives: full employment; a low but positive inflation rate; a fair distribution of income and wealth; and financial stability. This breadth of goals usually leads to the advocacy of a significantly wider range of policy instruments than are usually considered by mainstream economists, including (but not limited to) monetary policy, fiscal policy, prices and incomes policy, international economic policy issues, and environmental policy.

Before considering these economic policies and how they may contribute to the range of societal goals, something needs to be said about the underlying politics. Do Post Keynesians really share a common political position? I think it would be generally agreed that, as a general rule, they are left of centre, more so today than previous generations were. The first generation of Cambridge Post Keynesians were all social democrats of one sort or another, although Joan Robinson also developed Maoist sympathies that were based on what was known to her about Maoism at the time (Harcourt and Kerr 2009). In the United States, Hyman Minsky was a liberal Democrat, and Paul Davidson remains one. This was almost a centrist position in the 1960s but has more radical connotations half a century later.

There are good reasons for this affinity with the left. Post Keynesians have always insisted on the need for systematic regulation of markets – above all, vigilant regulation of financial markets – on the grounds that market failure is generally more dangerous than state failure. Their concern with income distribution also needs to be emphasised. For Post Keynesians, the first principle of an acceptable distribution of income is that it maintains macroeconomic stability, so that it is consistent with full employment without demand inflation. Given that poor people tend to spend a larger proportion of their incomes than rich people, there is a presumption in favour of greater equality in the personal distribution of income, together with a strong case for a stable or increasing wage share in GDP.

The underlying theoretical propositions that guide Post Keynesian thinking on *monetary policy* were summarised in a previous section: criticism of the classical dichotomy; insistence on the endogeneity of money; rejection of the loanable funds theory of interest and the notion of a 'natural' rate of interest; and recognition of the fragility of the financial system and the need to be constantly alert to the consequences of financial innovation. On these grounds, the first generation of Post Keynesians were strongly critical of monetarism, both as a theory and as a set of policy proposals. Inflation originates in the 'real' economy, in the product market and especially in the markets for labour and raw materials. Attempts to combat inflation by implementing a rigid rule for the growth of the money supply would not succeed and would more likely inflict serious damage on output and employment. Post Keynesians remain severely critical of mainstream monetary policy, not least for its dogmatic assertion that output price inflation is the only legitimate target. This has led to a dangerous neglect of other important targets, most notably asset price inflation and the stability of the financial system as a whole.

There is general acceptance by Post Keynesians that reliance on interest rates is inadequate; and that additional monetary policy instruments must be reinstated, including direct controls over lending and indirect controls that provide strong incentives for financial institutions to behave responsibly. One such proposal is for the imposition of asset-based reserve requirements that would, in effect, impose a higher tax on particular forms of lending to prevent the emergence of bubbles or to deflate them gradually (Palley 2004).

Because Post Keynesians are also inclined to question how much monetary policy actually can actually achieve in a world of endogenous credit money, they usually place much more emphasis on *fiscal policy*. Their starting-point is the rejection of the principle of 'sound finance', as expressed in Angela Merkel's famous statement of 'Swabian housewife logic' – 'every housewife knows that we cannot live beyond our means'. Instead, they assert the principle of 'functional finance' that was first stated by the economist Abba Lerner; the only thing that matters is the achievement of full employment and the avoidance of demand inflation. The government should run a deficit if private sector expenditure is expected to be inadequate to maintain full employment; and it should run a surplus if private sector spending is expected to be excessive and thus to generate demand inflation. A balanced budget is called for only in the exceptional case in which private sector spending is expected to be just right (Lerner 1943).

Contractionary fiscal policy ('austerity') is an appropriate weapon against demand inflation, but it is likely to be both ineffective and damaging when applied to cost inflation. In this case direct intervention in product and factor markets is required. Thus, Post Keynesians have always supported a *prices and incomes policy*, either through legally binding compulsory arbitration (as in Australia before 1990) or by agreement between the 'social partners' (as in many European countries).

Some Post Keynesians advocate an alternative way of restraining wage inflation. If the state were to act as an employer of last resort, Hyman Minsky suggested, offering a job at a low but socially acceptable wage to all those unable to find better-paid employment in the private sector, this would not only eliminate demand-deficient unemployment but would also help to control wage inflation. Recently this proposal has been strongly endorsed by the advocates of 'modern monetary theory' (Fullbrook and Morgan 2020).

Incomes policies of all types broke down during the stagflation crisis of the 1970s, since when trade unions have been very substantially weakened in almost all parts of the advanced capitalist world. Today, a rather different case can be made for an incomes policy, this time to avoid the dangers of *deflation* and a continually declining share of wages: instead of restraining real wages, an incomes policy now needs to make sure that wages rise at least as fast as labour productivity. A decline in the share of wages in national output will reduce consumption expenditure; but it will also tend to increase investment spending (by raising profits) and net exports (through the reduction in domestic costs and hence in the relative prices of exports and imports). If the negative effect on consumption is greater than the positive effect on investment and net exports, then there is scope for 'wage-led growth'; while, if it is smaller, there is scope for 'profit-led growth' (Stockhammer and Lavoie 2013). The evidence suggests that, for most rich countries, domestic demand is wage-led, so that the growing downward pressure on real wages has deleterious macroeconomic effects (King 2019).

There is some disagreement among Post Keynesians on the details of *international economic policy*, but broad agreement on the underlying principles, which include a substantial degree of re-regulation of global financial markets, prevention of neo-mercantilist strategies such as the deflationary wage policies that were criticised in the previous section, and acceptance that responsibility for correcting global trade imbalances should be shared by surplus and deficit countries, by creditors and debtors, as Keynes had unsuccessfully urged in 1944 at Bretton Woods. There is more general support for the reform of the International Monetary Fund to make it the world central bank that Keynes had envisaged: well-resourced and with a commitment to promoting full employment on a global scale. Similarly, there is a strong case for removing the residual traces of the 'Washington Consensus' from the current policies of the World Bank and for converting it into an agency that will promote the development of the poorest countries.

On *environmental policy*, Post Keynesians advocate several types of direct controls, including setting minimum environmental standards and renewable energy targets, measures to change consumer tastes and habits, and a public investment policy to promote innovation and overcome the constraints on green investment that may be imposed by credit rationing by lenders and fundamental uncertainty on the part of potential borrowers. Hence, there is strong Post Keynesian support for a Green New Deal (Dafermos and Nikolaidi 2019). In contrast to mainstream economists, they also recognise that there is an additional large and irreducibly macroeconomic dimension to the problem. If, to prevent dangerous and irreversible environmental damage from global warming, it is necessary to cut aggregate consumption, or at the very least substantially to reduce the rate of growth of consumption, how can this be achieved without initiating a serious recession? The move to an ecologically sustainable global economy requires growth that is 'slower by design, not disaster', to quote the sub-title of an influential book by Peter Victor (2019). Here, Post Keynesian thinking on fiscal policy and environmental policy come together.

Obviously, there is a lot more to be said on all these policy questions and on other aspects of Post Keynesian thinking. Key texts on the formal theoretical framework include: Hein (2012), Lavoie (2014) and Blecker and Setterfield (2019). For much more detailed discussion of the history of Post Keynesian economics, its critique of other 'Keynesian' models, the details of its distinctive approach to methodology, and its relations with other heterodox schools of thought, see King (2002; 2015: chs 3, 4 and 9).

POST KEYNESIAN ECONOMICS AND MARXIST POLITICAL ECONOMY

Post Keynesian economics, as described in this chapter, has a central place in modern political economy, alongside Marxian economics. It is pertinent to conclude this chapter with some observations on their relationship. They have a lot in common, especially (but not only) the Kaleckian stream of Post Keynesianism. Both schools deal explicitly with capitalist production for profit, not with exchanges between simple commodity producers. Hence the interests of different social classes are important, since they are a major influence on the outcome of individual decision-making, affecting the entire economy. Both schools of thought insist that economic theory must be historically and socially specific, changing with the different stages of capitalist development: so that the distinction between competitive and monopolistic capitalism is significant, along with any substantial increase in the degree of financialisation.

Marx himself anticipated some important elements of Post Keynesian theory in his models of what Keynes would later describe as a 'monetary production economy'. In volumes II and III of *Capital* he was quite close to the later Keynesian income–expenditure model of the determinants of total output and employment, and his account of the problem of 'realising' surplus value anticipates the question of ensuring that there is adequate effective aggregate demand in the economy. Marx, like the Post Keynesians, emphasises the economic activity of capitalist enterprises as opposed to individual consumers and households, focusing on the role of business investment in driving the business cycle and determining the rate of economic growth. Finally, and perhaps most important, both Marx and the Post Keynesians stress the need to explain the instability of the capitalist system. And Marx was, of course, a strong critic of Say's law.

However, some major qualifications are in order. First, and most obviously, Marx was writing more than a century and a half ago, and capitalism has moved on since then. It has also moved on since Keynes, of course, so how the most recent developments are interpreted depends on the standpoint from which they are viewed. The huge literature on Marxian political economy is also highly varied and extremely complicated, giving rise to serious problems in reconciling Marxism and Post Keynesian thought. Much of the Marxian literature would not be acceptable to twenty-first-century Post Keynesians, who reject the labour theory of value, the distinction between productive and unproductive labour, the theory of the falling rate of profit and (most fundamentally) the Marxian treatment of the relationship between production and exchange. A brief discussion of some of these issues can be found in Howard and King (1985: ch. 13).

There are also substantial differences concerning the economic role of the capitalist state. Should the state be seen as a powerful institution for the reform of capitalism in the interests, inter alia, of the working class, as most Post Keynesians would argue, or is it essentially an instrument of class repression, as the Marxists maintain? Many (if not all) Post Keynesians regard Marxism as an outdated form of obscurantism in political economy, while many (if not all) Marxists see Post Keynesian economics as a sophisticated apologetic for the exploitative class relations of capitalist society. Is some accommodation between the two strong positions possible and desirable, as Dow (2015), for example, advocates? The debate continues.

NOTE

1. There are four different ways of writing 'Post Keynesian', depending on whether or not a hyphen is used and the prefix is capitalised. I have always followed the practice of the founders of the *Journal of Post Keynesian Economics*, capitalising but omitting the hyphen, but nothing of any consequence is involved in these choices.

REFERENCES

Blecker, R.A. and Setterfield, M. (2019) *Heterodox Macroeconomics: Models of Demand, Distribution and Growth*, Cheltenham, UK and Northampton, MA, USA: Edward Elgar Publishing.

Coutts, K. and Norman, N. (2013) 'Post-Keynesian approaches to industrial pricing: a survey and critique', in Harcourt G.C. and Kriesler, P. (eds), *The Oxford Handbook of Post-Keynesian Economics, Volume 1: Theory and Origins*, Oxford: Oxford University Press, pp. 443–66.

Dafermos, Y. and Nikolaidi, M. (2019) 'Fiscal policy and ecological sustainability: a post-Keynesian perspective', in Arestis, P. and Sawyer, M. (cds), *Frontiers of Heterodox Macroeconomics*, Basingstoke: Palgrave Macmillan, pp. 277–332.

Davidson, P. (1972) *Money and the Real World*, London: Macmillan.

Davidson, P. (2011) *Post Keynesian Macroeconomic Theory: A Foundation for Successful Economic Policies for the Twenty-First Century*, 2nd edn, Cheltenham, UK and Northampton, MA, USA: Edward Elgar Publishing.

Deleidi, M. and Mazzucato, M. (2019) 'Putting austerity to bed: technical progress, aggregate demand and the supermultiplier', *Review of Political Economy*, **31** (3), pp. 315–35.

Dow, G. (2015) 'Marx, Keynes and heterodoxy', *Journal of Australian Political Economy*, **75**, pp. 60–98.

Dutt, A.K. (2002) 'Thirlwall's law and uneven development', *Journal of Post Keynesian Economics*, **24** (3), pp. 367–90.

Fullbrook, E. and Morgan, J. (2020) *Modern Monetary Theory and its Critics*, Bristol: World Economics Association Books.

Harcourt, G.C. (1972) *Some Cambridge Controversies in the Theory of Capital*, Cambridge: Cambridge University Press.

Harcourt, G.C. and Kerr, P. (2009) *Joan Robinson*, Basingstoke: Palgrave Macmillan.

Hein, E. (2012) *The Macroeconomics of Finance-dominated Capitalism – and its Crisis*, Cheltenham, UK and Northampton, MA, USA: Edward Elgar Publishing.

Howard, M.C. and King, J.E. (1985) *The Political Economy of Marx*, 2nd edn, London and New York: Longman.

Kalecki, M. (1943) 'Political aspects of full employment', *Political Quarterly*, **14** (4), October–December, pp. 322–31: reprinted in Osiatýnski, J. (ed.) (1990) *Collected Works of Michał Kalecki, Volume 1: Capitalism, Business Cycles and Full Employment*, Oxford: Clarendon Press, pp. 347–57.

Kalecki, M. (1954) *Theory of Economic Dynamics: An Essay on Cyclical and Long-Run Changes in Capitalist Economy*, London: Allen and Unwin: reprinted in Osiatýnski, J. (ed.), *Collected Works of Michał Kalecki, Volume 2: Capitalism, Economic Dynamics*, Oxford: Clarendon Press, 1991, pp. 205–348.

Kalecki, M. (1971) *Selected Essays on the Dynamics of the Capitalist Economy*, Cambridge: Cambridge University Press.

Kalecki, M. and Kowalik, T. (1971) 'Observations on the "crucial reform"', *Politica ed Economica* 2–3, pp. 190–6: reprinted in Osiatýnski, J. (ed.) (1990) *Collected Works of Michał Kalecki, Volume 1: Capitalism, Business Cycles and Full Employment*, Oxford: Clarendon Press, pp. 466–76.

Keynes, J.M. (1936) *The General Theory of Employment, Interest and Money*, London: Macmillan.

King, J.E. (2002) *A History of Post Keynesian Economics Since 1936*, Cheltenham, UK and Northampton, MA, USA: Edward Elgar Publishing.

King, J.E. (2009) *Nicholas Kaldor*, Basingstoke: Palgrave Macmillan.

King, J.E. (2012) *The Microfoundations Delusion: Metaphor and Dogma in the History of Macroeconomics*, Cheltenham, UK and Northampton, MA, USA: Edward Elgar Publishing.

King, J.E. (2015) *Advanced Introduction to Post Keynesian Economics*, Cheltenham, UK and Northampton, MA, USA: Edward Elgar Publishing.

King, J.E. (2019) 'Some obstacles to wage-led growth', *Review of Keynesian Economics*, **7** (3), pp. 308–20.

Lavoie, M. (2014) *Post-Keynesian Economics: New Foundations*, Cheltenham, UK and Northampton, MA, USA: Edward Elgar Publishing.

Lee, F.S. (1998) *Post Keynesian Price Theory*, Cambridge: Cambridge University Press.

Lerner, A.P. (1943) 'Functional finance and the federal debt', *Social Research*, **10** (1), pp. 38–51.

Minsky, H.P. ([1986] 2008) *Stabilizing an Unstable Economy*, New Haven, CT: Yale University Press, 2nd edn, New York: McGraw-Hill.

Palley, T. (2004) 'Asset based reserve requirements: reasserting domestic monetary control in an era of financial innovation and instability', *Review of Political Economy*, **16** (1), pp. 43–53.

Setterfield, M. (2013) 'Endogenous growth: a Kaldorian approach', in Harcourt, G.C. and Kriesler, P. (eds), *The Oxford Handbook of Post-Keynesian Economics, Volume 1: Theory and Origins*. Oxford: Oxford University Press, pp. 231–56.

Stockhammer, E. and Lavoie, M. (eds) (2013) *Wage-Led Growth: An Equitable Strategy for Economic Recovery*, London: Palgrave Macmillan.

Thirlwall, A. P. (1993) 'The renaissance of Keynesian economics', *Banca Nazionale del Lavoro Quarterly Review*, **186**, pp. 327–37.

Thirlwall, A.P. (2013) *Economic Growth in an Open Developing Economy: The Role of Structure and Demand*, Cheltenham, UK and Northampton, MA, USA: Edward Elgar Publishing.

Victor, P.A. (2019) *Managing Without Growth: Slower by Design not Disaster*, 2nd edn, Cheltenham, UK and Northampton, MA, USA: Edward Elgar Publishing.

7. Feminist political economy
Jennifer Cohen and Heidi Hartmann

There is a popular misconception in economics that feminist research is about *women's economic issues*. There are no such issues. Economic phenomena associated with women influence economic outcomes for people of all genders.[1] The gender wage gap offers a concrete example: women who are full professors of economics earn less than 75 per cent of similarly situated men in the discipline, a gap that has widened since 1995 (Ceci et al. 2014: 117). This inequity impacts women – and their children, families, and communities – including sons, brothers, partners and husbands, among others. The gender pay gap is not a women's economic issue, it is an economic issue. The same is true of all the economic issues that feminists research.

Even without the interdependence highlighted above, women's economic issues are economic issues, no qualifier needed, because women are economic agents in their own right. The 'women's issues' phrasing suggests that women and the work they do are marginal to the analysis of 'real economic issues'. Nothing could be further from the truth. Feminist political economy reveals how profoundly this simple point can contribute to economic analysis and to understanding the way actually existing economies operate.

Feminist political economic thought offers a broad view of what constitutes the economy, what counts as economic activity, and who acts as an economic agent. Feminist political economy (FPE) takes as its entry point the study of creating and sustaining life. It asks how societies provide the necessities of life to individuals and communities, and what role gender plays in provisioning (Power 2004).

This approach departs significantly from mainstream economics, which takes as its starting point how societies allocate scarce resources, focusing almost solely on market economies. Mainstream economists tend to ignore how people use what they acquire in markets in order to sustain themselves and others. Most of this work, called housework, carework or reproductive labour (Quick 2008), is done inside the household as non-market activity. It is essential to the functioning of any economy. In a market economy this work produces the labour power required for market-based production. The overall process is called *social reproduction.* Social reproduction includes activities traditionally assigned to women, so it is not surprising that feminist political economists, many of whom identify as women, would shine light on these activities and their foundational role in powering any economy. Economists, like other knowledge workers, are no doubt influenced by their own life experiences.

Feminist political economic thought is heterodox and relies on insights from institutional economics, Marxist economics, and classical and neoclassical economics, as well as from poststructural and postcolonial thought, feminist thought and political movements for women's liberation. Its historical roots date back to Harriet Taylor and John Stuart Mill in *The Subjection of Women*, published in 1844, but feminist thought in economics became firmly established in the late 1960s and early 1970s. In 1971, a critical mass of women economists in the Union for Radical Political Economy created a Women's Caucus in the organisation and spurred the creation of the Committee on the Status of Women in the Economics Profession

(CSWEP) within the American Economic Association (AEA) (Cohen 2019), which was also welcomed by women economists in the mainstream of the profession. One of CSWEP's primary activities since the mid-1970s has been tracking the representation of women in the discipline. Women's representation is not merely a question of demographics; it is an issue of gender-biased knowledge creation, policy recommendations, and disciplinary foci, all of which affect everyone.

FEMINIST POLITICAL ECONOMY

At the core of feminist political economy are three axioms.

First, there exist hierarchical relationships – inequities – between women and men which reflect power relations and can be changed. This commonly acknowledged male domination, often referred to as patriarchy, can be understood as having a material basis in men's control over women's labour in both the household and the market. It has ramifications for men and women, such as more leisure time, higher levels of personal consumption, and greater financial security for men than women, on average (Hartmann 1981; Rose and Hartmann 2018; Jacobsen 2020).

Second, feminist political economy makes an explicit normative commitment to improving the conditions under which people reproduce themselves intergenerationally and on a day-to-day basis (Cohen 2020a; Berik and Kongar 2021). This commitment is shared by most heterodox economists, even if their work is not focused on 'reproduction' and they do not articulate their commitment as such. In addition, however, feminist political economists seek to use their analyses to increase equity between women and men, a goal that not all heterodox economists share, much less place front and centre in their work, even when it is a likely result of a preferred policy.

Third, 'The Economy' as conceptualised in mainstream and much of heterodox economics is narrowly defined; economists tend to be fixated on a small portion of economic activity and economic behaviour, to the detriment of economic analysis (Hartmann and Markusen 1980; Albelda 1997). We take the first axiom as self-evident and return to the normative commitment later in the chapter. Here we focus on defining the economy.

The Economy

In FPE, the economy is understood as consisting of many interdependent systems and actors, shaped by history, culture and institutions that structure how people provision themselves and their communities. People are seen as necessarily driven not only to survive, but also to thrive, to achieve goals, and to experience a full range of emotions and connections with other living beings and with supportive social groups. A central focus of FPE is exploring the ways in which material life, the goods and services people need to thrive, can best be organised to provide a fulfilling quality of life for all.

In contrast to these human-focused analyses, mainstream, Marxist, and most heterodox economic theorists typically limit their attention only to the production of goods and services sold in the marketplace and the paid work this requires. The focus constitutes a pervasive productivist bias that constructs paid work as valuable and other activities as non-work. Productivism biases what most economists study, what they think is valuable, and ultimately what they understand to be 'The Economy', which in reality is a relatively limited sub-set of economic activities (Cohen 2018).

FPE's broader understanding of the economy is historical and applicable to all levels of the economy. For example, it takes into account how household production changes in response to macroeconomic phenomena or policies, with gendered effects. Researchers have found that encouraging girls to get more education through financial incentives for families, or by helping mothers modestly increase production for market exchange and thereby increasing their earned income, led to multigenerational improvements in children's health and well-being. Yet feminist scholars are also critical of how this information has been integrated into economic development theory and practice, which can seek to 'use' girls as instruments for development, instead of educating girls on the grounds of their intrinsic value (Chant and Sweetman 2012; Bergeron 2004). They point out that instrumentalism makes economic development the responsibility of women and girls in a context typically disadvantageous to them, often without addressing gendered structural and institutional issues.

Similarly, attempts to repay international debt can lead poorer countries to cut back on publicly provided services – a policy that lender countries and international financial institutions (IFIs) often require. Such cutbacks in public transportation or public health often force women to devote more time and labour to family care. In addition to increasing women's family care burden, this can reduce women's access to employment, girls' education and, more generally, lower economy-wide productivity with a negative effect on economic growth (Seguino 2021).

State failure to provide public services is not limited to countries in debt to IFIs like the World Bank and International Monetary Fund. During the 2020–21 Covid-19 pandemic in the United States, the failure of the Trump administration to provide supplies for personal safety – for example, masks and sanitiser (Cohen and Rodgers 2020) – led both consumers and workers to withdraw (Yan et al. 2021), making it impossible for the economy to rebound because an economy is composed of people and their activities. A focus on basic needs could have reduced the severity of the pandemic and resulted in less loss of life. It was an opportunity to place human well-being above concerns about economic output (although that would likely have benefited as well). Instead, when the spread of the new coronavirus first became public knowledge, and during the early months of the restrictions on economic activity, personal protective equipment and sanitisers were in extremely short supply, such that even health professionals in hospitals and nursing homes were unable to protect themselves and their patients (Cohen 2020b). Here, again, women were more negatively impacted by these failures than men (Cohen and Rodgers 2021).

Even generous and sophisticated welfare states, such as those in the Nordic countries, with family-friendly policies, such as long parental leaves and subsidised childcare, have not succeeded in raising their birth rates to the commonly cited population replacement rate of 2.1: several are at the lowest end of what demographers think can result in sustainable populations in an ageing society, 1.5–1.6 (Striessnig and Lutz 2014). This is a serious problem: spiraling population decline is not compatible with human thriving. The problem features in dystopian narratives such as the *Handmaid's Tale* (Atwood [1985] 2016), in which forced childbearing is used to keep human society from disappearing. Conservative and liberal views of the issue find explanations in eroded 'family values' and inadequate state support for parents (especially in the United States). However, as the Nordic case suggests, there are other forces at play. FPE points directly to a fundamental conflict between the aim of capital accumulation and the goal of human thriving and illuminates the conflict by focusing attention on human nurturing.

Productivism imposes a false division between economic activity associated with the production of goods and services for pay and the production of human beings; and this is intentional, not accidental. Historically, *household production* played a significant role in economies, including growing, raising and producing goods for exchange or sale. Indeed, the root of the word economics is the Greek word for household, *oikos*, and for means or managing, *nomos*. The study of economics as a separate field of knowledge is, however, typically dated to the publication of Adam Smith's *The Wealth of Nations* in 1776, by which time the wealth of some nations in the global North had expanded enormously through interdependent processes of colonisation, slavery and industrialisation; and much production and exchange was carried out by large-scale enterprises in relatively organised national and international markets. Nonmarket work still carried out in the household was decidedly left behind by the new 'science': '… economic activity taking place in the household, and carried out in great part by women, was relegated to a trivial status, if not made altogether non-existent in the minds of the theoreticians of capitalism' (Pujol 1992: 16).

Except for one page of the two volumes of *Wealth of Nations*, 'women are conspicuously absent from [Smith's] seminal discussion of the nature, organisation and operations of capitalist production' (Pujol 1992: 17). Instead, Smith assumes that the individual worker is male and that he supports a family financially, presumably in a household in which women reproduce the family through their unpaid reproductive labour. Smith argues that men are motivated by self-interest and engage in competitive struggle. Writing a century before Smith and positing a 'man-eat-man' world in which men had no obligations to any others, Thomas Hobbes was forced to use 'mushroom men' to obtain even the hypothetical conditions of men's imaginary independence. In his words, 'men sprung out of the earth and suddenly, like mushrooms, come to full maturity, without all kind of engagement to each other' – completely eliding their years of upbringing and nurturing (Folbre and Hartmann 1988: 187, citing DiStefano 1984).

Like Smith, Marx and Engels, writing approximately a century later, acknowledged that production has two sides, that of people and that of things, but largely ignored the former. In *Capital Volume 1*, Marx focused on the process of capital accumulation through production for exchange in which the drive for profits is met by paying workers less than the value of what they produce. From the capitalist's point of view, wrote Marx, the reproduction of the working class could 'safely be left to itself', arguing that (as paraphrased from *Capital Volume 1* in Hartmann 1979: 27, fn.14): 'The maintenance and reproduction of the working class is, and must ever be, a necessary condition to the reproduction of capital. But the capitalist may safely leave its fulfillment to the labourer's instincts for self-preservation and propagation'. Ignoring the scale and importance of household labour was a serious omission, a topic taken up by many Marxists and Marxist-feminists in the 1970s (Himmelweit and Mohun 1977). In much Marxist theory surplus value is extracted only in the 'hidden abode' of production. Some feminists have been critical of this formulation and argue that women are super-exploited through unpaid household work, which itself contributes to surplus value by creating and maintaining the paid workforce (Dalla Costa 1973; Mies 2001). The concept of super-exploitation highlights the dependence of surplus value in market-based production on the performance of unpaid labour in the household and beyond.

The further development of capitalism in the twentieth century and the increasing commodification of goods and services produced in households reconstructed the household as a space for consumption; and emphasised its role in constituting the demand for marketed production. Overlooked again, however, was the labour required to transform market goods, such as raw meat and vegetables, into consumable items, and the continued need for direct care to raise children and prepare adults for another day of activity. While many households no longer produce commodities, they continue to produce the human beings that become the labour supply on a daily and intergenerational basis. Moreover, those human beings are socialised into culturally acceptable identities (such as male or female, black or white, worker or owner), behaviours, and belief systems as part of the process of social reproduction.

Social Reproduction

In FPE, social reproduction is the day-to-day work required to 'maintain existing life and to reproduce the next generation' through a gendered division of labour in which women are disproportionately tasked with this typically unpaid or poorly paid work (Laslett and Brenner 1989: 383). Reproductive labour includes 'going into labour', the process of giving birth, the care and feeding of children, adults and the elderly, and the daily work of producing and maintaining well-socialised human beings, who collectively are often referred to as 'the labour supply'. People are not born alone, do not have lives completely separable from others, and typically do not die alone.

Increasingly, the work of producing well-socialised humans requires, in addition to unpaid work in the family, paid reproductive labour outside the household. This includes work by teachers and social workers, usually employed in the public sector, as well as food preparers in factories and restaurants who provide a substantial share of the typical family's meals in many wealthy societies. The work of community building, of creating networks that can sustain families in ways that public agencies cannot or will not is also often women's work (Cohen and Venter 2020). Community building has been especially important to people of colour, whose access to public safety nets is curtailed and who often face hostile practices by public agents (Banks 2020).

This definition of social reproduction is somewhat different from the way that Marx used the term. For Marx, social reproduction referred to the process of reproducing the social relations of production: 'the entire complex of social, cultural, and political processes required to reproduce capital-labor relations' (Rao and Akram-Lodhi 2021: 36). Nevertheless, in this very broad scope of social reproduction, Marx omitted the essential unpaid work done by women of providing the workforce, a gap that FPE attempts to fill, as Rao and Akram-Lodhi argue.

The phrase was adopted by social reproduction theory (SRT) as a 'declar[ation] of its heritage ... within the Marxist tradition' (Bhattacharya 2017). SRT picks up several threads from Marxist-feminist scholarship and from radical political economy. Two central points of SRT are, first, that capitalism is an integrated system (Luxton and Bezanson 2006; Vogel 2013) and second, that capital accumulation is in contradiction to (Weeks 2011) and takes precedence over (Gimenez 2005) 'life-making' (Arruzza et al. 2019). In comparison with some earlier formulations in feminist thought, SRT highlights how multiple forms of oppression are related to capitalist exploitation with an eye towards race and global labour processes.

Ultimately, research in FPE provides a dose of realism: production fundamentally depends on households and women's work within them. The limited portion of economic activity that is typically defined as production would not and could not exist without the reproductive labour that is disproportionately done by women. In capitalism, the ends of production – capital accumulation – dominate the ends of reproduction: human subsistence. Capital accumulation takes priority over meeting people's needs or ensuring that people have 'access to the necessary conditions for reproduction' (Gimenez 2005: 21). That subordination contributes to the over-valorisation of production in capitalism – and in economics – and obscures those two most fundamental insights of feminist research: that people are produced, and that capitalism relies on women's unpaid work (Cohen 2018).

ARE THERE *ANY* 'WOMEN'S ECONOMIC ISSUES'?

The previous sections have clarified how 'women's work' is central to all economic activity, which should make this work – regardless of who does it in practice – a major focus in the discipline. At the beginning of the chapter, we also pointed out that women's economic issues are economic issues, full stop, in part because interdependency means economic disadvantages for women impact men and boys. The concept of relationality helps capture a different facet of hierarchical relationships – the inequities benefiting men and boys – that reflect gendered power relations.

Hartmann (1979) points out that analyses focusing on capitalism alone do not adequately address the question of men's power over women. Capital benefits from women's domestic labour that produces and maintains the workforce, but men are also beneficiaries: gender roles that assign women unpaid work mean that men do not need to do all necessary unpaid work themselves. This insight also informs feminist economics, which often focuses on how members of the household do not necessarily have the same self-interests, and households cannot therefore be analysed as a single entity. Folbre (2020) notes that women tend to behave more altruistically than men, and they spend more time and energy caring for children and other dependent people. Folbre notes that '[c]oercive institutions have enforced women's specialisation in the work of caring for others' (2021: 56). Women are punished financially for this unpaid reproductive labour, which goes unrewarded.

The claim is not that men do not do *any* unpaid work; empirical evidence shows that men spend time on some household tasks, but that women spend much more time on this work than men. A 2021 report summarises the situation:

> Globally, women do three to ten times more unpaid care and domestic work than men. They also make up 70 percent of the global paid care workforce but represent only 25 percent of senior roles …
> At the current rate of change, the world is at least 92 years away from achieving equality in unpaid care work between men and women. (Barka et al. 2021: 16)

Hence, while individual men might contribute to the work of social reproduction, men as a group benefit from the *expectation* (women's and men's) that women are disproportionately responsible for this work, especially when young children are present. The temporary presence of young children does not, however, make women's responsibility temporary; women typically remain disproportionately responsible for unpaid work over the course of their lives. Moreover, the expectation systematically disadvantages women in the labour market in perpetuity, individually and as a group, because of discrimination by employers. Therefore, men have a two-fold incentive to maintain gender roles that *do not* assign them unpaid work: they benefit in both the household and the labour market.[2]

In the labour market, men, typically white, are able to reinforce these advantages by collectively seizing and monopolising the better-paying, higher-status positions (Hartmann 1976). This helps keep women dependent upon them and simultaneously sustains gendered responsibility for unpaid reproductive labour inside the household.[3] Relationality clarifies how this practice crowds women into a sub-set of less valued occupations, further reducing their wages, while it segregates occupations, restricting labour market competition and therefore raising men's wages (Bergmann 1974). The practice is present between occupational groups and within occupations, where men dominate the best paying positions even in professions equally, or nearly equally, populated by women and men, such as doctors and lawyers (Carter and Carter 1981; Sokoloff 1992). There is a long history of men seeking to exclude women from entering occupations over which they hold a monopoly (Abbott 1988; Sokoloff 1992; Bourdieu 2010) because they wish to resist the feminisation of the occupation. Feminisation is a demographic process as well as a process of *devalorisation*, or reduced status, so that men in feminised occupations are also likely to have lower earnings and status.

Academia broadly, and economics in particular, are not exceptions (McWilliams Tullberg 1998; Puojol 1992; Sokoloff 1992; Cohen 2019). To return to the example at the beginning of the chapter, in 2017 women represented 13.3 per cent of full professors of economics in the USA, and on average they earned about 73 per cent of men's earnings at the same rank (Ceci et al. 2014, p.117). Men's resistance to women 'entering' economics in larger numbers is captured symbolically in the minutes of the AEA's 1971 meeting. The minutes, and multiple accounts, describe a debate over adopting a resolution that read, 'Economics is not a man's field', but which was changed by amendment to read, 'Economics is not *exclusively* a man's field' (Cohen 2019). In other words, according to many of those present, economics *was* a man's field.

Men's resistance is captured in more concrete ways by women economists' accounts of discrimination, which include the refusal to hire women into tenure track positions; denial of tenure, promotions and leaves of absences for women faculty; and denial of funding for women graduate students. Olson and Emami (2002) illustrate this discrimination through interviews with prominent economists: Marianne Ferber (p. 35), Alice Rivlin (pp. 76–7), Suzanne Wiggins Helburn (p. 103), Myra Strober (p. 141), who entered the field in the 1950s and 1960s, all note that economics is (or was) a 'man's field'.

Men's resistance persists. In 2018 the AEA's Professional Climate Survey asked whether the AEA should expend more effort to make economics more diverse. One of the responses read:

> Devoting any time or attention to 'diversity' and 'inclusion' and 'climate' is a ridiculous 'politically correct' waste of time in the field of economics, as in most if not all fields of academia and work-places generally. While there are certainly cases of sexual harassment, these should not be lumped together with non-existent problems and non-existent issues. (AEA Committee on Equity, Diversity and Professional Conduct 2019: 70)

Diversity entails more than gender but, given the reference to sexual harassment, it is likely that the respondent had women in mind when they wrote that it is a 'ridiculous, politically correct waste of time'. It is also likely that the respondent is male, though that is unconfirmed.

Does men's resistance constitute a *women's* economic issue – or simply an economic issue? In other words, when class combines with oppression, does the combination designate inequities as 'problems' salient only for one group? Clearly women are more negatively and directly impacted by sexism than men, but interdependency and relationality mean that men are affected in multiple ways. From a relational perspective, when one population is relatively disadvantaged, the other is relatively advantaged. Relationality does not, however, imply that advantage and disadvantage are proportional or evenly distributed. Aside from interdependency and relationality, women are actualised actors, not a footnote to [men's] other or more important economic issues. Economic issues confronted by non-white and/or non-men people – *the majority of the population globally and in all countries* – are economic issues.

Further, class is not 'merely economic'. It is made up of concrete people, their communities, habitats and living conditions, their experiences, social ties and history, all produced and reproduced by activities and institutions that transcend the narrowly economic. Class constitutes not just relations of production but relations of reproduction. The holism of FPE – namely seeing the entirety of economic activity – renders it impossible to ignore oppression. In linking exploitation to oppressive social structures, gender and race join class as crucial components in a more holistic analysis.

INTERSECTIONALITY AND ECONOMICS

The economics discipline defines the aim of economic activity and therefore constructs which activities (and who) are popularly understood as valuable. Knowledge produced in an unrepresentative discipline is biased; it contributes to the devalorisation of activities associated with those not represented and elides (or misunderstands) the challenges confronted by the people who undertake those activities.

Understanding the experiences of people who are not men and/or who are not white requires an analytical approach that gets at the unique conditions that shape individual and group experiences. One such approach is intersectionality. A major point from intersectional theorists (and those who critique them), is that systems of oppression are not additive; they are connected (Crenshaw 1989, 1991; Hill Collins 1990; hooks [1984] 2000). How they are connected – whether they are axes, interlocking to form a matrix of domination, or are co-constituted systems – is the subject of some debate, with implications for theorising capitalism (Bhattacharya 2017; McNally 2017; Folbre 2020).

Some existing work in economics, especially that by black women, is explicitly or implicitly intersectional.[4] Feminist political economy has been criticised for a historical lack of race-consciousness, but an intersectional approach is increasingly recognised as a requisite for understanding collective conflict (Folbre 2020). Folbre's (2020, 2021) 'intersectional political economy' posits that group identities of many kinds, not only class and gender, can lead to collective action over the distribution of economic resources and that the power of these groups and sub-groups is structured by institutions.

Demographic data from the economics discipline are informative. The discipline has become more diverse in some ways, but several groups remain underrepresented. In the USA, in terms of race, the majority of faculty is white (56.2 per cent) or Asian (31.9 per cent). White men (44.6 per cent of 2017 economics faculty vs. 33 per cent of the 2017 US population), Asian men (23.0 per cent vs. 1.8 per cent), and Asian women (9.0 per cent vs. 2.1 per cent) are overrepresented compared with their respective populations at large; while black women (0.6 per cent vs. 4.9 per cent), black men (3.2 per cent vs. 4.0 per cent), Hispanic women (1.4 per cent vs. 4.9 per cent), and white women (11.6 per cent vs. 35.2 per cent) are underrepresented compared with the population, while Hispanic men (5.6 per cent vs. 5.0 per cent) are proportionally represented (Sharpe 2021).

Intersectionality facilitates an understanding of how systems of oppression and exploitation together shape experiences. Substantively, the importance of diverse demographic groups in economics lies partly in the ways their lived experiences inform their contributions to economic thought. While relationality indicates that economic disadvantage is simultaneously economic advantage to other populations, even those ostensibly committed to equity tend not to be critical of the status quo of which they are beneficiaries. Hence, a discipline dominated by white and Asian men (67.6 per cent of faculty but 34.8 per cent of the US population), in which black women are egregiously underrepresented (0.6 per cent of faculty compared with 4.9 per cent of the population), is not likely to pay much attention to historic and current economic disadvantages confronting black women.

In this foray into thinking about those who populate the economics discipline, we have not strayed as far from thinking about social reproduction as one might imagine. People, including economists, are produced through a gendered and racialised division of labour inside and outside the household. Slavery, apartheid, colonialism and imperialism are part and parcel of this production process and have profound and persistent impacts on who is represented in which occupations and with what status. In the economics discipline, they help determine who has the opportunity to contribute to the construction of economic knowledge. Many of the improvements to economic thought have come from the critical perspectives of non-white, non-male economists who find that existing theorisations are poor descriptions of their experiences. For example, women and people of colour have made significant advances in theorising discrimination (Bergmann 1974; Darity et al. 2017). Black women economists have brought entire sectors of the economy to light (Banks 2020; Hossein 2020), and economists from the global South have been critical of development policies that have failed to deliver the improvements they promise, and in many cases have been detrimental to the lives of women and marginalised groups (Zein-Elabdin and Charusheela 2003; Naidu and Ossome 2017).

A diverse and inclusive discipline would be more likely to entertain diverse ideas about what 'counts' as work, what an economy is for, and how it might function. Answers to these questions are critically important for theory and policy. For example, in regions where formal market relations are less pervasive, as in many places in the global South, nonmarket work is an even larger part of the economy that requires study and analysis to understand how life is sustained. Further, feminists have much to contribute to thinking about an economy in which the ends of social reproduction – human subsistence – would no longer be subordinate to the ends of production in capitalism – capital accumulation.

Knowledge production is important for many reasons, but one merits additional attention. Beyond being descriptive, knowledge creates and constrains possibilities. It is '… not just about things. Rather, knowledge adds to reality' (Barker and Kuiper 2003: 9). In other words, knowledge is world-making. Accordingly, feminist political economists seek to expand the world of what economics *is*, and to move from independent, isolated decision makers operating mostly in market-based production to a world of interdependency, power relations, solidarity, institutions, and norms that shape work, production and social aims.

Nancy Hartsock (1983: 41–2) imagines a society structured around the principle of nurture: 'One could begin to see the outline of a very different kind of community if one took the mother/infant relation rather than market exchange as the prototypic human interaction.' Indeed, Rao and Akram-Lodhi (2021) point out that in the current capitalist regime, human survival has been put at severe risk. The drive for profits is causing irreversible climate change and underinvestment in public health, making repeated pandemics increasingly likely; it also causes recurring crises and setbacks in growth and accumulation (as in the 2008 financial crisis). In fact, they argue, 'capitalism has no mechanism for automatically ensuring the reproduction of workers' (2021: 38). Rich capitalist countries pursue two strategies to make up for this gap in their economic system's functioning. First, they exploit the gendered and racialised division of labour in which unpaid and poorly paid labourers, many from the global South, do the care work that sustains human life in the global North; and second, they expand, although sometimes only temporarily, their publicly supported social safety nets to stave off evictions, ill-health and starvation, as the United States did in 2020 and 2021 in the face of the new Coronavirus pandemic.

Given these recurrent crises, it can be argued that human survival requires a major intervention in economic theory and policy that can be provided by FPE and its further development.

IMPACTS AND PROSPECTS FOR CHANGE

At present, feminist theory has had limited impact on mainstream and heterodox economics. The perceived presence of feminism may be heightened, but most journals and economists remain resistant to feminist analyses, even in radical political economy where one might expect it to be more welcome than in the discipline at large.

Although the first women's organisation in the discipline was formed in the Union for Radical Political Economics (URPE), fewer than 3 per cent of the articles published in their journal before 2019 (outside of special issues edited by members of the Women's Caucus) use a feminist lens, or are about women, girls or gender.[5] Feminist work is either missing or excluded. The production of people through a combination of reproductive labour and commodities, and the reliance of production on reproduction should be absolutely central for economists, as they are central to the reproduction of capitalism itself. Yet social reproduction goes unacknowledged by the vast majority of economists.

There are several reasons for this, but two stand out. First, economists misunderstand feminist research and the critique it presents. Second, and related, heterodox economists often do not see how feminism clarifies and strengthens their own arguments. Most economists simply assume that social reproduction is happening and will continue to happen. They ignore the work it requires, the people who do the work, and the fact that the work happens at all, and consequently dismiss its central relevance to the economy and therefore to economics. This oversight denies the value of women and 'women's work', relegating both to the sidelines of the discipline. It also denies the valuable contributions feminist political economy has made, and cheats economists of further feminist insight.

To return to the earlier point about shared normative commitments, ask yourself what your own economic analyses are ultimately *for*. Is the purpose related to improving the conditions under which people reproduce themselves intergenerationally and on a day-to-day basis? Improved conditions of social reproduction are *already* the normative commitment for most self-aware economists. Social reproduction makes a clear normative case for heterodox economists' analyses and policy recommendations. It is through social reproduction that many policies operate to improve people's lives. FPE aids in the identification of the gendered, racialised and classed people likely to benefit the most from those analyses and policies, strengthening the arguments for them.

In other words, heterodox economists' projects likely have more value and importance in the context of the normative commitment underlying them. Heterodox economists adopting a more reflexive view *of the work they are already doing*, locating it in relation to the *whole* of capitalism, and acknowledging that they are prompted to do so by feminist work would contribute a much richer understanding of capitalism and alternatives.

FPE clarifies how the crisis of social reproduction (identified in Bhattacharya 2017; Fraser 2017; Rao and Akram-Lodi 2021) is the result of a multitude of processes linked to capitalist production. Appropriate investment in environmental resources and public health will not be marshalled by private markets because they provide public goods. Therefore, the ecological crisis continues to deepen, responses to the Covid-19 pandemic remain inadequate in most nations, and the crisis of care is ongoing. Each of these crises reveals the life-crushing nature of an economic system in which capital accumulation – the reproduction of capital – dominates the reproduction of life itself.

Caring labour also cannot be accurately priced by the market, yet one cannot understand capitalism and its fundamental weaknesses without it. Economic analyses that do not consider the reproduction of humans are not merely incomplete, they are incorrect. Despite all its instability and voraciousness, for many, capitalism remains nearly unquestionable as *the* way to organise societies.

This is precisely why an FPE perspective is so necessary: it begins to flesh out an alternative principle around which to build an equitable way of provisioning, of sustaining life itself. Developing feminist political economy and spreading its approach throughout economic thought may well be critical to the survival of the human race, and of other life forms as well.

Economists working with feminist political economy in their tool case can explore what is required to construct economic institutions that have as their primary aim not the accumulation of capital but sustaining life and enhancing human opportunities.

NOTES

1.   Gender identity and expression are not fixed for individuals. Where we refer to 'women' and 'men' in this text, we indicate the socially constructed gendered roles, norms and constraints corresponding (however messily) to those expressions of gender among individuals in recent history. It is not our intention is to naturalise gender roles and/or reinforce stereotypes.
2.   Within a single generation this point may seem to apply only to cisgendered, heterosexual men but, from an intergenerational perspective, it is apparent that all men benefit from this expectation.
3.   This division of labour is rationalised by theorists such as Becker (1981), who argued – tautologically – that the partner earning lower pay should specialise in household work and that women earn lower pay due to their expectation to specialise in household work. Most women do not, in practice, specialise in household work; most combine paid and unpaid work.
4.   See, e.g. Glenn (1985, 1992); Williams (1993); Brewer et al. (2002); Bueno (2014); Banks (2020); Kim (2020); Holder et al. (2021).
5.   A brief audit of the top five mainstream and heterodox economics journals for the years 2000–2018 suggests that about 5 per cent of articles in top heterodox journals, and 4 per cent of articles in top mainstream journals, contain the words 'gender' or 'feminism' or 'woman' or 'women' or 'female' or 'females' or 'girl' or 'girls'. Of course, these words do not make research feminist: the percentage of articles from a feminist perspective is likely much lower. For details of this journal review process, see Cohen (2018). For a history of the formation of Women's Caucus within URPE, see Cohen (2019).

REFERENCES

Abbott, A.D. (1988) *The System of Professions: An Essay on the Division of Expert Labor*, Chicago, IL: University of Chicago Press.

AEA Committee on Equity, Diversity and Professional Conduct (2019) 'AEA Professional Climate Survey: Final Report', accessed 8/17/2021 at https://www.aeaweb.org/resources/member-docs/final -climate-survey-results-sept-2019.

Albelda, R.P. (1997) *Economics and Feminism: Disturbances in the Field*, New York: Twayne Publishers.

Arruzza, C., Bhattacharya, T. and Fraser, N. (2019) *Feminism for the 99%: A Manifesto*, London and New York: Verso.

Atwood, M. ([1985] 2016) *The Handmaid's Tale*, London: Random House.

Banks, N. (2020) 'Black Women in the United States and Unpaid Collective Work: Theorizing the Community as a Site of Production', *The Review of Black Political Economy*, **47** (4), pp. 343–62.

Barka, G., Garg, A., Heilman, B., van der Gaag, N. and Mehaffey, R. (2021) *State of the World's Fathers: Structural Solutions to Achieve Equality in Care Work*, Washington, DC: Promundo-US.

Barker, D.K. and Kuiper, E. (eds) (2003) *Toward a Feminist Philosophy of Economics: Economics as Social Theory*, London and New York: Routledge.

Becker, G. (1981) *A Treatise on the Family*, Cambridge, MA: Harvard University Press.

Bergeron, S. (2004) 'The Post-Washington Consensus and Economic Representations of Women in Development at the World Bank', *International Feminist Journal of Politics*, **5** (3), pp. 397–419.

Bergmann, B.R (1974) 'Occupational Segregation: Wages and Profits When Employers Discriminate by Race or Sex', *Eastern Economic Journal*, **1** (2), pp. 103–10.

Berik, G. and Kongar, E. (2021) 'The Social Provisioning Approach to Feminist Economics: The Unfolding Research', in Berik, G. and Kongar, E. (eds), *The Routledge Handbook of Feminist Economics*, London and New York: Routledge, pp. 3–21.

Bhattacharya, T. (2017) 'Introduction: Mapping Social Reproduction Theory', in Bhattacharya, T. (ed.), *Social Reproduction Theory: Remapping Class, Recentering Oppression*, London: Pluto Books, pp. 1–20.

Bourdieu, P. (2010) *Distinction: A Social Critique of the Judgement of Taste*, London and New York: Routledge.

Brewer, R.M., Conrad, C.A. and King, M.C. (2002) 'The Complexities and Potential of Theorizing Gender, Caste, Race, and Class', *Feminist Economics*, **8** (2), pp. 3–17.

Bueno, C. (2014) 'Stratification Economics and Grassroots Development: The Case of Low-Income Black Women Workers in Santo Domingo, Dominican Republic', *Review of Black Political Economy*, **42** (1–2), pp. 35–55.

Carter, M.J. and Carter, S.B. (1981) 'Women's Recent Progress in the Professions or, Women Get a Ticket to Ride after the Gravy Train Has Left the Station', *Feminist Studies*, **7** (3), pp. 476–504.

Ceci, S.J., Ginther, D.K., Kahn, S. and Williams, W.M. (2014) 'Women in Academic Science: A Changing Landscape', *Psychological Science in the Public Interest*, **15** (3), pp. 75–141.

Chant, S. and Sweetman, C. (2012) 'Fixing Women or Fixing the World? "Smart Economics", Efficiency Approaches, and Gender Equality in Development', *Gender & Development*, **20** (3), pp. 517–29.

Cohen, J. (2018) 'What's "Radical" about [Feminist] Radical Political Economy?', *Review of Radical Political Economics*, **50** (4), pp. 716–26.

Cohen, J. (2019) 'The Radical Roots of Feminism in Economics', *Research in the History of Economic Thought and Methodology*, **37** (May), pp. 85–100.

Cohen, J. (2020a) 'Feminist Political Economy and the Heterodoxy', *The American Review of Political Economy*, **14** (1). https://doi.org/10.38024/arpe.208.

Cohen, J. (2020b) 'Theorizing Entrepreneurial Price Gouging: Interdependency, Injustice, and Hand Sanitizer', *A Rethinking Marxism Dossier, The Pandemic*, 106263, accessed 8/6/2021 at http://rethinkingmarxism.org/Dossier2020/21_Cohen.pdf.

Cohen, J. and van der Meulen Rodgers, Y. (2020) 'Contributing Factors to Personal Protective Equipment Shortages during the COVID-19 Pandemic', *Preventive Medicine*, **141** (December), 106263, accessed 17.8.2021 at https://doi.org/10.1016/j..2020.106263.

Cohen, J. and van der Meulen Rodgers, Y. (2021) 'The Feminist Political Economy of Covid-19: Capitalism, Women, and Work', *Global Public Health*, **15** (8–9), pp. 1381–95.

Cohen, J. and Venter, W.D.F. (2020) 'The Integration of Occupational- and Household-Based Chronic Stress among South African Women Employed as Public Hospital Nurses', *PLOS ONE*, **15** (5): e0231693. https://doi.org/10.1371/journal.pone.0231693.

Crenshaw, K.W. (1989) 'Demarginalizing the Intersection of Race and Sex: A Black Feminist Critique of Antidiscrimination Doctrine, Feminist Theory and American Politics', *University of Chicago Legal Forum*, pp. 139–67. https://chicagounbound.uchicago.edu/cgi/viewcontent.cgi?article=1052&context=uclf.

Crenshaw, K.W. (1991) 'Mapping the Margins: Intersectionality, Identity Politics, and Violence against Women of Color', *Stanford Law Review*, **43** (6), pp. 1241–99.

Dalla Costa, M. (1973) 'Women and the Subversion of the Community', in Dalla Costa, M. and James, S. (eds), *The Power of Women and the Subversion of the Community*, 2nd edn, Bristol: Falling Wall Press, pp. 19–54.

Darity, W.A., Hamilton, D., Mason, P.L., Price, G.N., Dávila, A., Mora, M.T., Stockly, S.K., Flynn, A., Warren, D.T., Wong, F.J. and Holmberg, S.R. (2017) 'Stratification Economics: A General Theory of Intergroup Inequality', in Flynn, A., Warren, D., Wong, F. and Holmberg, S. (eds), *The Hidden Rules of Race: Barriers to an Inclusive Economy*, Cambridge: Cambridge University Press, pp. 35–51.

DiStefano, C. (1984) 'In Search of the Missing Mother: Maternal Subtexts in Political Theory', paper presented to the Eastern Division Fall Conference of the Society for Women in Philosophy, 3–4 November.

Folbre, N. (2020) *The Rise and Decline of Patriarchal Systems: An Intersectional Political Economy*, London and New York: Verso.

Folbre, N. (2021) 'Conceptualizing Patriarchal Systems', in Berik, G. and Kongar, E. (eds), *The Routledge Handbook of Feminist Economics*, Abingdon and New York: Routledge, pp. 53–61.

Folbre, N. and Hartmann, H. (1988) 'The Rhetoric of Self Interest: Gender Ideology in Economic Theory', in Klamer, A., McCloskey, D.N and Solow, R.M. (eds), *The Consequences of Economic Rhetoric*, Cambridge and New York: Cambridge University Press, pp. 184–203.

Fraser, N. (2017) 'Crisis of Care? On the Social-Reproductive Contradictions of Contemporary Capitalism', in Bhattacharya, T. (ed.), *Social Reproduction Theory: Remapping Class, Recentering Oppression*, London: Pluto Books, pp. 21–36.

Gimenez, M.E. (2005) 'Capitalism and the Oppression of Women: Marx Revisited', *Science and Society*, **69** (1), pp. 11–32.

Glenn, E.N. (1985) 'Racial Ethnic Women's Labor: The Intersection of Race, Gender and Class Oppression', *Review of Radical Political Economics*, **17** (3), pp. 86–108.

Glenn, E.N. (1992) 'From Servitude to Service Work: Historical Continuities in the Racial Division of Paid Reproductive Labor', *Signs: Journal of Women in Culture and Society*, **18** (1), pp. 1–43.

Hartmann, H. (1976) 'Capitalism, Patriarchy, and Job Segregation by Sex', *Signs: Journal of Women and Culture in Society*, **1** (3, Part 2), pp. 137–69.

Hartmann, H. (1979) 'The Unhappy Marriage of Marxism and Feminism: Towards a More Progressive Union', *Capital and Class*, **8** (Summer), pp. 1–33.

Hartmann, H. (1981) 'The Family as the Locus of Gender, Class, and Political Struggle: The Example of Housework', *Signs: Journal of Women and Culture in Society*, **6** (3), pp. 366–94.

Hartmann, H. and Markusen, A. (1980) 'Contemporary Marxist Theory and Practice: A Feminist Critique', *Review of Radical Political Economics*, **12** (2), pp. 87–94.

Hartsock, N. (1983) *Money, Sex, and Power: Toward a Feminist Historical Materialism*, New York: Longman.

Hill Collins, P. (1990) *Black Feminist Thought: Knowledge, Consciousness, and the Politics of Empowerment*, Boston, MA: Unwin Hyman.

Himmelweit, S. and Mohun, S. (1977) 'Domestic Labor and Capital', *Cambridge Journal of Economics*, **1** (1), pp. 15–31.

Holder, M., Jones, J. and Masterson, T. (2021) 'The Early Impact of Covid-19 on Job Losses among Black Women in the United States', *Feminist Economics*, **27** (1–2), pp. 103–16.

hooks, bell ([1984] 2000) *Feminist Theory: From Margin to Center*, revised edn, Cambridge, MA: South End Press.

Hossein, C.S. (2020) 'Racialized People, Women, and Social Enterprises: Politicized Economic Solidarity in Toronto', *Feminist Economics*, **27** (3), pp. 1–30.

Jacobsen, J.P. (2020) *Advanced Introduction to Feminist Economics*, Cheltenham, UK and Northampton, MA, USA: Edward Elgar Publishing.

Kim, M. (2020) 'Intersectionality and Gendered Racism in the United States: A New Theoretical Framework', *Review of Radical Political Economics*, **52** (4), pp. 616–25.

Laslett, B. and Brenner, J. (1989) 'Gender and Social Reproduction: Historical Perspectives', *Annual Review of Sociology*, **15**, pp. 381–404.

Luxton, M. and Bezanson, K. (eds) (2006) *Social Reproduction: Feminist Political Economy Challenges Neo-Liberalism*, Montreal: McGill-Queen's University Press.

McNally, D. (2017) 'Intersections and Dialectics: Critical Reconstructions in Social Reproduction Theory', in Bhattacharya, T. (ed.), *Social Reproduction Theory: Remapping Class, Recentering Oppression*, London: Pluto Books, pp. 94–111.

McWilliams Tullberg, R. (1998) *Women at Cambridge*, revised edn, Cambridge and New York: Cambridge University Press.

Mies, M. (2001) *Patriarchy and Accumulation on a World Scale: Women in the International Division of Labor*, London: Zed Books.

Naidu, S. and Ossome, L. (2017) 'Work, Gender, and Immiseration in South Africa and India', *Review of Radical Political Economics*, **50** (2), pp. 332–48.

Olson, P.I. and Emami, Z. (2002) *Engendering Economics: Conversations with Women Economists in the United States*, London and New York: Routledge.

Power, M. (2004) 'Social Provisioning as a Starting Point for Feminist Economics', *Feminist Economics*, **10** (3), pp. 3–19.

Pujol, M.A. (1992) *Feminism and Anti-Feminism in Early Economic Thought*, Aldershot and Brookfield: Edward Elgar Publishing.

Quick, P. (2008) 'Unpaid, Reproductive, Caring Labor? The Production of Labor Power? Theoretical and Practical Implications of Terms Used for Women's Work', *Review of Radical Political Economics*, **40** (3), pp. 308–14.

Rao, S. and Akram-Lodhi, A.H. (2021) 'Feminist Political Economy', in Berik, G. and Kongar, E. (eds), *The Routledge Handbook of Feminist Economics*, Abingdon and New York: Routledge, pp. 34–42.

Rose, S.J. and Hartmann, H.I. (2018) *Still a Man's Labor Market: The Slowly Narrowing Gender Wage Gap*, Washington, DC: Institute for Women's Policy Research.

Seguino, S. (2021) 'Gender and Economic Growth', in Berik, G. and Kongar, E. (eds), *The Routledge Handbook of Feminist Economics*, Abingdon and New York: Routledge, pp. 341–50.

Sharpe, R.V. (2021) 'The Quest for Inclusion in Economics in the US', in Berik, G. and Kongar, E. (eds), *The Routledge Handbook of Feminist Economics*, Abingdon and New York: Routledge, pp. 420–30.

Sokoloff, N.J. (1992) *Black Women and White Women in the Professions: Occupational Segregation by Race and Gender, 1960–1980*, Abingdon and New York: Routledge.

Striessnig, E. and Lutz, W. (2014) 'How Does Education Change the Relationship between Fertility and Age-dependency under Environmental Constraints? A Long-term Simulation Exercise', *Demographic Research*, **30**, pp. 465–92.

Vogel, L. (2013) *Marxism and the Oppression of Women: Toward a Unitary Theory*, Leiden: Brill.

Weeks, K. (2011) *The Problem with Work: Feminism, Marxism, Antiwork Politics, and Postwork Imaginaries*, Durham, NC: Duke University Press.

Williams, R.M. (1993) 'Race, Deconstruction, and the Emergent Agenda of Feminist Economic Theory', in Ferber, M.A. and Nelson, J.A. (eds), *Beyond Economic Man: Feminist Theory and Economics*, Chicago, IL: University of Chicago Press, pp. 144–53.

Yan, Y., Malik, A.A., Bayham, J., Fenichel, E.P., Couzens, C. and Omer, S.B. (2021) 'Measuring Voluntary and Policy-induced Social Distancing Behavior During the COVID-19 Pandemic', *Proceedings of the National Academy of Sciences of the United States of America*, **118** (16), 21 April 2020, updated 4 May 2021. https://doi.org/10.1073pnas.2008814118.

Zein-Elabdin, E. and Charusheela, S. (2003) *Postcolonialism Meets Economics*, London: Routledge.

8. Sraffian political economy

Nuno Ornelas Martins

Piero Sraffa's contribution is usually associated with his incisive critiques of various influential economic approaches, such as Alfred Marshall's partial (or particular) equilibrium analysis (Sraffa 1925, 1926), Friedrich Hayek's business cycle theory (Sraffa 1932), and the marginalist theory of value and distribution, a critique that provided the ground for the Cambridge controversies in the theory of capital (Sraffa 1960). The latter critique generated considerable debate in the academic world, paving the way for the emergence of what today is called Sraffian Political Economy. However, the fact that Sraffian Political Economy emerged at the same time as the Cambridge controversies in the theory of capital also shaped the way in which it was subsequently developed and interpreted.

Sraffa's contribution allowed the identification of important inconsistencies within the marginalist theory of value and distribution. However, when debating with mainstream economists, a tendency emerged for using their methods and language, which is radically at odds with Sraffa's careful reconstruction of the methods and language adopted by the classical political economists. This led to a widespread interpretation of Sraffa's own critique and overall contribution in terms of the methods and language of mainstream economics.

This latter tendency started to be reversed through research on Sraffa's unpublished papers at the Wren Library, Trinity College, Cambridge, leading to various disputes concerning the proper interpretation of Sraffa's contribution. My characterisation of Sraffian Political Economy in this chapter takes into account various interpretations that emerged through this process, and its relevance for contemporary political economy. I start by addressing Sraffa's own contribution, and then explain how the different interpretations of this contribution led to various strands in Sraffian Political Economy. To conclude, I will also point out some possible avenues for collaboration between Sraffian Political Economy and other alternative theories of political economy. This conclusion also shows the significance for the further development of political economic analysis of what, at first sight, may seem somewhat arcane debates about the interpretation of Sraffa's work. Joan Robinson (1985) argued that Sraffa's theory could be used as the basis for a reconstruction of economic theory. Her call for a reconstruction of economic theory, and the role of Sraffa's contribution in such a project, remains as relevant as ever, as I shall argue in the conclusion. Albeit Sraffa's theory is often seen essentially as a critique of marginalist theory, there is also a constructive dimension in Sraffa's overall project (Chiodi 2008; Porta 2018).

INDUSTRIAL ORGANISATION AND IMPERFECT COMPETITION

Piero Sraffa personally published relatively little, but his contributions had a significant impact. After writing a thesis on monetary inflation in Italy and achieving the post of Professor of Political Economy at Cagliari, Sraffa moved to Cambridge through the intermediation of John Maynard Keynes, who was impressed with Sraffa's critique of Alfred Marshall's ([1890]

1920) partial (or particular) equilibrium analysis, first published in Italian (Sraffa 1925) and subsequently in English (Sraffa 1926). Sraffa's critique of Marshall's theory led to a debate with leading Marshallians such as Dennis Robertson and Gerald Shove (Robertson et al. 1930) and contains many insights on what came to be known as imperfect competition (Robinson 1933).

A central aspect noted by Sraffa (1925, 1926) in his critique of Marshallian partial equilibrium analysis is the interconnection between various industries. Using Marshall's terminology, Sraffa argues that an industry as whole has external returns, in the sense that it depends upon factors of production which are produced by other industries. The rationale behind Sraffa's reasoning is that many firms specialise in the production of components for end products across various industries. This brings the possibility of moving to a different industry that has become more attractive due to price variations, leading to changes in the corresponding supply and demand curves, as noted by Sraffa (1925, 1926). Furthermore, since those components are used in various industries, changes in a given industry have repercussions in the prices of various factors of production across various industries, even if there is no entry or exit of firms. Supply and demand curves cannot then move independently, and a full analysis of the industrial process is required.

These effects occur not only in the context of diminishing returns, but also in the case of increasing returns. Citing Marshall's ([1919] 1923: 188) *Industry and Trade*, Sraffa (1926: 540) writes:

> As Marshall has said in the work in which he has intended to approach most closely the actual conditions of industry, 'the economies of production on a large scale can seldom be allocated exactly to any one industry: they are in great measure attached to groups, often large groups, of correlated industries.'

This analysis is still very relevant for understanding how groups of correlated industries lead to what is usually termed a supply chain or value chain. It also contains important insights concerning the impact of industrial organisation on competition.

The case of increasing returns is also a situation where the key limitation found by firms when increasing production is not a higher cost of production, since the latter will typically be lower with the production of an increasing quantity, but rather the difficulties of selling an increasing quantity at the same price. Thus, Sraffa (1926: 543) writes:

> The chief obstacle against which they have to contend when they want gradually to increase their production does not lie in the cost of production – which, indeed, generally favours them in that direction – but in the difficulty of selling the larger quantity of goods without reducing the price, or without having to face increased marketing expenses.

The price depends on various factors that may lead buyers to be willing to pay 'something extra in order to obtain the goods from a particular firm rather than from any other'. In this regard, Sraffa notes:

> The causes of the preference shown by any group of buyers for a particular firm are of the most diverse nature, and may range from long custom, personal acquaintance, confidence in the quality of the product, proximity, knowledge of particular requirements and the possibility of obtaining credit, to the reputation of a trade-mark, or sign, or a name with high traditions, or to such special features of modelling or design in the product as – without constituting it a distinct commodity intended for

the satisfaction of particular needs – have for their principal purpose that of distinguishing it from the products of other firms. (1926: 544)

The enumeration of various factors that may lead buyers to be willing to pay 'something extra' 'from a particular firm' constitutes an analysis within what is termed today imperfect competition, a topic subsequently elaborated by Joan Robinson (1933), the ingredients of which can already be found in Sraffa's (1925, 1926) critique of Marshallian partial equilibrium analysis.

Sraffa's contributions to industrial organisation and imperfect competition would have been enough to give Sraffa a place in the history of economic thought. But Sraffa's subsequent contribution became focused on developing a different framework of analysis, one that would not fall into the inconsistencies he found in the Marshallian framework. The pursuit of this different framework of analysis led Sraffa to a revival of classical political economy (Meek 1961), moving away from theories that determine prices and quantities in terms of supply and demand (Bharadwaj 1978), while also providing the ground for a subsequent critique of marginalist economic theory.

THE REVIVAL OF CLASSICAL POLITICAL ECONOMY AND MARX

After coming to Cambridge, Sraffa started to express his analysis of the problem of value in terms of equations. These equations, originally elaborated in 1927, led to the 1960 book *Production of Commodities by Means of Commodities*, after an unusually long period of maturation. Sraffa (1960) presents these equations in three different forms: (1) Production for subsistence without a surplus; (2) Production with a surplus without explicitly identifying the quantity of labour in the equations (instead, the equations contain the quantities of commodities used as means of subsistence by the workers); (3) Production with a surplus while explicitly identifying the quantity of labour in the equations (instead of the quantities of commodities used as means of subsistence by the workers). The third form is the one usually adopted, and can be represented in the following way:

$$(A_a p_a + B_a p_b + \ldots + K_a p_k)(1 + r) + L_a w = A p_a$$

$$(A_b p_a + B_b p_b + \ldots + K_b p_k)(1 + r) + L_b w = B p_b$$

$$\ldots\ldots\ldots$$

$$\ldots\ldots\ldots$$

$$(A_k p_a + B_k p_b + \ldots + K_k p_k)(1+r) + L_k w = K p_k$$

$$L_a + L_b + \ldots + L_k = 1$$

$$[A-(A_a + \ldots A_k)] p_a + \ldots + [K-(K_a + \ldots K_k)] p_k = 1$$

L_i is the proportion of labor used to produced commodity 'i', since Sraffa normalises the sum of labor terms to unity. He also considers that national income, that is, the difference between the value of outputs and the value of inputs in a given year, is equal to unity. A, B, ..., K are the quantities of commodities produced as outputs, A_i, B_i, ..., K_i the quantities of each of those commodities used as inputs for commodity 'i', p_i is the price of commodity 'i', 'r' is the rate of profit, and 'w' is the wages paid. The wage term 'w' can be re-written as $w = w_s(1+r)$, where 'w_s' denotes the subsistence wage, since Sraffa (1960) defines the wage 'w' as a share of the surplus, which includes not only the component of subsistence w_s (a lower bound below which the wage cannot fall), and also a share of profits (1+r).

Pierangelo Garegnani (1984: 310) presents the equations above in an alternative form using the subsistence wage, while considering the wage as 'the quantity of labour necessary to produce the given real wage'. These equations are also expanded by Sraffa (1960) in order to include joint production, so as to subsequently include fixed capital as a joint output of production, and also in order to include land, so as to conceptualise rent. Furthermore, Sraffa (1960) also introduces the notions of Standard commodity and Standard net product (which replaces the last equation that is normalised as unity), and re-writes the equations above in terms of a Standard system.

There is considerable debate on how Sraffa reached these equations. Those debates result from competing interpretations of Sraffa's unpublished papers, kept at the Wren Library. While those debates often seem to spring from an excessive emphasis on minute detail, they are important for understanding Sraffa's project of engaging in a revival of classical political economy. Furthermore, the various approaches to Sraffian political economy that have emerged are a result of those competing interpretations on how Sraffa reached his equations.

Giorgio Gilibert (2003) and Giancarlo de Vivo (2003) argue that Sraffa's perspective was inspired by Marx's ([1885] 1978) reproduction schemes. Ricardo Bellofiore (2008) and Scott Carter (2014) also highlight Marx's influence on Sraffa, and argue that Sraffa's equations are designed in order to represent Marx's view that the surplus corresponds to the quantity of labour. This would be inferred from the fact that, as noted above, the normalisation of the quantity of labour and of the difference between the value of outputs and the value of inputs (i.e. the surplus), by making both equal to unity, implies that the surplus is equal to the quantity of labour.

Heinz Kurz and Neri Salvadori (2005: 416), in contrast, argue that '[a]t the beginning of his academic career Sraffa appears to have adopted by and large the received Marshall's interpretation of the classical economists as early and rude types of demand and supply theorists with the demand side still in its infancy'. Kurz and Salvadori (2005: 416) note, however, that Sraffa 'gradually came to see that this interpretation implied a travesty of facts', and '[t]he radical change of his view of the classical authors received some support from his reading in 1927 and 1928 of the French translation of Marx 1924–25', rather than being originally inspired in Marx.

Kurz and Salvadori (2010: 190) argue that Sraffa was then led to what he called a value theory of labour (rather than Marx's labour theory of value), where Marx's results were expressed in terms of an objectivist approach that, according to Kurz and Salvadori (2010: 192), Sraffa traced back to William Petty's ([1690] 1899: 244) emphasis on expressing himself in terms of 'Number, Weight, or Measure' (see also Saverio Fratini (2018) on Sraffa's analysis of the evolution of the notion of cost from Petty's objective conception towards an increasingly subjective approach). Kurz and Salvadori (2005) then argue that it is Sraffa's objectivist approach that led to a gradual change in Sraffa's interpretation of classical political economy and Marx (see also Kurz and Salvadori (2015), especially chapters 1, 10 and 11).

Pierangelo Garegnani (2005: 488) refers to the above interpretation of Kurz and Salvadori (2005), arguing that '[t]he change in the interpretation of the classical authors does not appear to have been gradual, but to have rather been a matter of months, if not weeks, early in the Autumn of 1927, as Sraffa arrived at the "equations"'. Furthermore, Garegnani (2005: 488–9) argues that

> [i]f Sraffa's question had then been to achieve 'objectivism', rather than that of having stumbled on an alternative theory of relative prices and distribution, based on the notion of surplus, he would probably have thought to have conquered that 'objectivism' already in his 1925–26 synthesis, when he was determining prices independently of a demand, which, in any case, he held to be definable with no recourse to subjective utility.

Garegnani's interpretation can be reconciled with the idea that Sraffa was essentially inspired by Marx, and Garegnani (1984, 2018) indeed held this conviction throughout his career.

The influence of Marx is also relevant for understanding Sraffa's interpretation of David Ricardo ([1817] 1821), whose works Sraffa edited after a considerable period of gestation, and with the help of Maurice Dobb in its final stages. Ajit Sinha (2016: 171) argues that the evidence in Sraffa's notes of 1942–43 provides support to the long-standing thesis of Pier Luigi Porta (1986, 2012) that Sraffa's interpretation of Ricardo is much influenced by Marx's ([1894] 1981) transformation problem. But, like Kurz and Salvadori (2005), Sinha (2016: 72–5) also stresses the influence of natural scientists on Sraffa, especially those concerned with the development of quantum physics.

Drawing on Garegnani's analysis of Sraffa's papers, Nerio Naldi (2020: 19) noted more recently that Sraffa's equations were developed in order to represent 'a community that produces just what is sufficient to keep it going', so as to avoid the problems raised by the existence of substitutes when trying to determine value in terms of commodities used in the production of other commodities. Using this determination of value, it is then possible to define a physical net product as the surplus, so as to engage in the analysis of distribution. Naldi notes that Sraffa's reference to an 'extremely simple society which produces just enough to maintain itself' (Sraffa 1960: 3) in his book shows how 'material conditions of production lay at the bottom of the whole analysis of prices and how the existence of a physical net product is a necessary condition to the existence of any distributive variable' (Naldi 2020: 20).

This leads to a consistent analytical framework in which the distribution of the social surplus, a central topic for the classical political economists and Marx, can be analysed. Furthermore, the emphasis on physical real costs as the basis for defining the surplus also ties in well with what John Davis (2012, 2017) calls the physicalist orientation of Sraffa, connected to his studies of natural sciences. Davis argues that we can distinguish the outside causes that operate on Sraffa's system, such as various factors influencing the distribution of the surplus, but taking into account that those outside causes work within the system by modifying its way of functioning.

It seems clear that Sraffa received influence both from contributions to quantum physics and from the classical political economists and Marx. But in *Production of Commodities*, Sraffa (1960: 94) refers only to the latter as relevant literature for interpreting his equations. Porta (2018: 11–12) stresses that Sraffa was concerned with a research programme of how economics would have evolved from the contributions of the classical authors if this line of thought had not been broken down by marginalism (see also Maria Cristina Marcuzzo and Annalisa Rosselli (2011) on Sraffa's critique of marginalism). According to Porta (2018: 10), a 'proper understanding of Sraffa's ideas on Classical Economics requires us to take into account two historico-analytical elements', namely 'the large inspiration, on the constructive side, of Marx's *Theorien über den Mehrwert* and 'the pervasive need – on the negative and destructive side – to counter the Marshallian synthesis in economics'.

Porta notes that his interpretation of Sraffa is in line with Luigi Pasinetti's (2007) idea that 'Piero Sraffa had conceived an *impossibly grand research programme* at the very beginning of his research years' (Porta 2018: 7, original emphasis). However, Porta also notes that Sraffa felt the need of focus more and more on analytical aspects, by-passing the broader historico-analytical treatment that he intended to undertake in the original set-up of his research programme.

This emphasis on the analytical aspect, in detriment to the broader historico-analytical programme, led to many difficulties in identifying the relative importance of each classical author, and of Marx, in the formation of Sraffa's political economy. Here it is important to note that, while the connection of Sraffa's (1960) contribution to the classical standpoint of Adam Smith and Ricardo has been less controversial (hence the usual designation of Sraffian political economy as 'neo-Ricardian' political economy), the connection to Marx has raised more controversy, not least in light of contributions which see Sraffa's (1960) contribution as a way to do away with concepts often seen as central to Marx's theory, such as the labour theory of value (Steedman 1977). These divergences have contributed, amongst other factors, to the emergence of various Sraffian research programmes, which can largely be seen as a result of a tendency to focus more on one aspect or another of the classical authors and Marx.

THE SRAFFIAN RESEARCH PROGRAMMES

Alessandro Roncaglia (2000) distinguishes various research programmes that stem from Sraffa's revival of classical political economy, depending on whether the emphasis is on a 'Marxian' approach followed by Garegnani, a 'Ricardian' approach which Roncaglia associates with Luigi Pasinetti, and a 'Smithian' approach which Roncaglia identifies with Paolo Sylos Labini. Pasinetti (1981) also contributed much to a Smithian view, while stressing the need of seeing Sraffa's theory as a theory of production, rather than a theory of exchange like the marginalist theory (Pasinetti 2005, 2007). Indeed, Hilary Putnam and Vivian Walsh (2012) identify Pasinetti and Amartya Sen as two fundamental authors for the recovery of a Smithian view of the economy and society, in line with Sraffa's overall project of a revival of classical political economy.

The interpretation of Sraffa's equations raises questions not only regarding their origin (and the influence of Marx in particular) but also their meaning. Sraffa (1960) provides an economic system where we can determine the various prices of commodities if we know only: (i) the quantities and composition of inputs and outputs, and (ii) either the rate of profits or the wages. But Sraffa leaves the wages, the rate of profits, and the quantities and composition of inputs and outputs as exogenous variables, opening the way for combining his economic theory with other theories that provide a determination of any of these magnitudes.

Garegnani (1978, 1979a) and Pasinetti (1981, 1993, 2005, 2007) showed how to combine Sraffa's economic theory with the Keynesian principle of effective demand, thus determining the quantities of outputs through Keynesian theory. This leads to a Sraffian project 'augmented by effective demand' (Aspromourgos 2004: 182). As for the wage, Sraffa suggests (in the first pages of his book until page 33) determining wages through the subsistence level, as the classical authors did (Sraffa 1960: 33). Subsequently, however, Sraffa also considers another way of conceiving how his system can be connected to the outside world. More specifically, he argues that the rate of profit is determined by the money rate of interest (Sraffa 1960: 33). There is a choice to be made here regarding how to connect Sraffa's system to the real world. For once we define one of these magnitudes – either the wage level or the rate of profit – the other is already determined within Sraffa's system.

The fact that Sraffa's equations can be interpreted in various ways, and that their magnitudes can be determined in various ways too, depending on which one we choose to 'close' the system, further contributed to the existence of a variety of research programmes springing from his equations (Aspromourgos 2004). Thus, it is not only the historico-analytical dimension (Porta 2018) that led to the emergence of various Sraffian research programmes, depending on whether the emphasis was on a given classical author (typically Smith or Ricardo) or Marx (Roncaglia 2000). The analytical element on which Sraffa came increasingly to focus, at the expense of the historico-analytical element (Pasinetti 2007; Porta 2018), also opened the door to the emergence of various Sraffian research programmes at an analytical level too, depending on how the Sraffian equations are combined with other theories that can be used to determine the exogenous variables of Sraffa's system. Thus, Tony Aspromourgos argues that, '[r]ather than a comprehensive theory of human and social economy then, what the Sraffian project augmented by effective demand stands upon is a small set of fundamental propositions, from which a *variety* of research programmes can proceed' (2004: 182, original emphasis).

In order to further refine the determination of the wage from a Sraffian perspective, Vivian Walsh (2003) argues that the level of wages can be set by drawing on Amartya Sen's capability approach when defining a given standard of living, bringing a moral dimension to Sraffa's analysis. In fact, Walsh argues that this is broadly in line with the spirit of the classical authors' view of a subsistence wage. This leads to a research programme combining Sraffa's revival of classical economic theory with Sen's revival of the moral anthropology of the classical authors and Marx (Putnam and Walsh 2012; Martins 2013).

But if we reach the conclusion that, in a given economy such as a capitalist economy, the wage level is not determined by moral considerations on the standard of living, the proposal above constitutes a normative ideal rather than a description of the actual economy and society. Sraffa (1960: 33) himself seems to have thought that, in actually existing capitalism, the rate of profit is the magnitude determined from outside the system, by the rate of interest as noted above. In this regard, Aspromourgos (2004) notes that there are various ways of determining the rate of profits, such as seeing it determined by or identified with a rate of growth (on which, see also Dobb (1969: 176–82) or Walsh (2003: 363–9)) or seeing it as determined by the rate of interest (as Sraffa himself suggests).

Sraffa's system also shows that it is not possible to attend both to the standard of living, and to the rate of interest, when closing his system. Either the wage is set by attending to a given standard of living, and the rate of profit is thus determined too, or the rate of profit is determined by the money rate of interest, thus enforcing a given wage (Sraffa 1960: 33). In fact, Sraffa shows that wages and the rate of profit are inversely related, thus highlighting the tension between the attempt to set a given standard of living through a certain wage level, and the demands of the financial system when setting a rate of interest. This also opens the door to the possibility of a normative analysis of capitalism drawing on Sraffa's (1960) system (Putnam and Walsh 2012; Martins 2013). It is important to note that Sraffa did not engage in any such analysis himself, at least in his published writings, even if Sraffa's interactions with Antonio Gramsci (Naldi 2000; Roncaglia 2000; Davis 2002; Sen 2003; McGuiness 2008) reveal much of his views on these matters.

THE METHODOLOGY OF SRAFFIAN POLITICAL ECONOMY

The methodology underlying Sraffa's equations is also relevant to understand how to develop a Sraffian (or the various Sraffian) research programme(s). Alessandro Roncaglia (1978, 2000) interprets Sraffa's equations as an 'instantaneous photograph', a snapshot of the economy at a given moment in time. This interpretation is also consistent with the interpretation of Sraffa's system provided by Harcourt and Massaro (1964: 716), who note that the relationships analysed in Sraffa's system refer to one year only.

This is also the interpretation followed by Joan Robinson (1985), who criticises Garegnani's (1978, 1979a) reference to the long period and to a normal rate of profit that prevails in the long period. Regarding Garegnani's normal rate of profit, Robinson (1979: 180) asks whether Garegnani means 'what the rate of profit on capital will be in the future or what it has been in the past or does it float above historical time as a Platonic Idea?' Garegnani, in turn, argues that the normal rate of profit must be located in the present, since '[i]t corresponds to the rate which is being realised *on an average* (as between firms and over time) by the entrepreneurs who use the dominant technique' (1979b: 185, original emphasis).

The idea of an average rate of profit implies the existence of several rates of profit between firms and over time. The various rates of profit would then gravitate towards the normal rate of profit, in the long period, which Garegnani sees as the frame of reference of the classical analysis that Sraffa is recovering. In Garegnani's conception, the classical notion of gravitation is aimed at capturing a connection between empirical reality and the theory of prices.

In this connection, Garegnani (2012) also distinguishes Léon Walras's ([1874] 1926) contribution from the neo-Walrasian approach of Kenneth Arrow, Gérard Debreu and Lionel McKenzie. According to Garegnani, Walras's reference to a general rate of return presupposes a normal position toward which the economy tends through a *tâtonnement* process, that is, a process of trial and error through which market clearing prices are reached. John Hicks (1939) advanced subsequently a new conception of equilibrium, where the economy is always in equilibrium as it moves from a temporary equilibrium to the next one through an intertemporal equilibrium path (Petri 2004: ch.4; Lazzarini 2011: ch. 6; Dvoskin and Lazzarini 2013; Martins 2013: 61–3; Fratini 2019). Garegnani's emphasis on the long period is not in line with the notion of equilibrium adopted in neoclassical economics after Hicks (1939), even if it has some affinity with the methodology of Walras and Marshall, albeit not with their underlying theory of equilibrium, be it Walrasian general equilibrium or Marshallian partial (or particular) equilibrium.

Roncaglia (2010: 183–4), however, notes that Garegnani's emphasis on a long period, which is shared by the classical authors and by early neoclassical authors such as Walras and Marshall, may divert attention from the fact that prices and quantities are determined separately in the classical analysis, but simultaneously in the neoclassical analysis. The interpretation of Sraffa's equations as a snapshot of the economy, advocated by Roncaglia (and also implied in Joan Robinson's interpretation), would avoid this problem. It is, however, possible to reconcile the idea that Sraffa's system refers to a given moment in time with the idea that it expresses a centre of gravitation (Harcourt 1981; Martins 2013), as long as the idea of gravitation is seen as a mere empirical counterpart rather than the subject of theoretical analysis (Martins 2013, 2019). For Sraffa's perspective seems to be incompatible with attempts to engage in a theoretical analysis of gravitation (Martins 2013, 2019; Sinha, 2016), especially if we follow the tools of neoclassical economics in so doing (Martins 2013: 20–22).

There has been, however, a tendency to draw upon the tools of neoclassical economics when interpreting Sraffa's theory. Richard Arena (2015: 1088) distinguishes what he sees as two predominant interpretations of the analytical message delivered by Sraffa's (1960) *Production of Commodities by Means of Commodities* (*PCMC*), where '[t]he first considers Sraffa's *PCMC* as a specific version of the theory of general equilibrium, whereas the second interprets it as the final outcome of a process of gravitation of market prices around natural or production prices'. While the second interpretation is Garegnani's, the first one is associated with Claudio Napoleoni (1965) whose book on general equilibrium 'suggests the existence of a natural progressive formal evolution from Walras's to Sraffa's models' (Arena 2015: 1089). Christian Bidard (1991) also argued for the compatibility between neo-Walrasian theory and Sraffian price theory.

Vivian Walsh and Harvey Gram (1980), in contrast, argued that Sraffa's theory is a classical variant of general equilibrium, which is radically different from the neoclassical variant. Walsh and Gram carefully distinguish Sraffa's classical approach from the neoclassical approach to general equilibrium. But there has been also a tendency to interpret Sraffa's theory as a particular case of the neoclassical approach to general equilibrium. Thus, Frank Hahn (1975: 362) asserts that 'there is not a single formal proposition in Sraffa's book which is not also true in a General Equilibrium model constructed on his assumptions'.

The tendency for interpreting Sraffa's contribution in terms of neoclassical general equilibrium theory springs also from the specific context in which Sraffa's came to be known worldwide after the publication of *PCMC*. Sraffa subtitled this book as a 'prelude to a critique of economic theory'. The book captured the attention of mainstream economists such as Paul Samuelson, who recognised the validity of Sraffa's critique (Samuelson 1966), and tried to provide technical solutions to the problems raised by Sraffa, the last one through what Samuelson (2010: 169) calls a 'Clark–Solow "anti-Sraffa" production function'. This production function is meant to overcome the problems of the neoclassical production function identified by Joan Robinson (1953–54) and Sraffa within the Cambridge controversies in the theory of capital (on which, see Bliss (1975) and Harcourt (1972) for early approaches from different angles, Cohen and Harcourt (2003) for a retrospective, and Backhouse (2014) and Gram and Harcourt (2017) for more recent assessments, again from different angles).

The context provided by the Cambridge controversies in the theory of capital led to a tendency to interpret Sraffa's contribution in terms of neoclassical approaches, such as general equilibrium theory, or other approaches, such as the approach to linear programming that Samuelson and Solow were developing with Robert Dorfman (Dorfman et al. 1958). Solow (2014: 63) made an assessment of Sraffa's contribution following the latter perspective, arguing that Sraffa adopted 'primitive tools' such as 'Simple Leontief Models' while others (including Samuelson and Solow himself) had developed 'Generalised Leontief Models (that allow for choice of technique within each industry)'. Solow also presupposes, like Samuelson (2010), that Sraffa produced a more limited linear model with constant returns to scale.

However, in Sraffa's theory both the inputs and the outputs are exogenous variables, so there is no functional relationship from inputs to outputs, and so no assumption is made on returns to scale (Sraffa 1960; Eatwell 1977; Sen 2003). Sraffa's manipulations of his system aim at *constructing*, rather than *deducing*, certain results (Martins 2013). We can have any given technology, and then write down the inputs and outputs in Sraffa's system, since the relationship between them is not determined mathematically, as Sen (2003) also notes.

There is a tendency to engage in mathematical analysis drawing on Sraffa's equations, focusing on what Porta (2018) calls the analytical aspect of Sraffa's contribution, which became the central emphasis of Sraffa himself as he realised the difficulties in pursuing the more complete historico-analytical project with which he was initially engaged (Pasinetti 2007; Porta 2018). Some of those analytical contributions capture adequately Sraffa's standpoint, especially when taking into account the mathematical methodology that Sraffa employed (Velupillai 2008). Others end up interpreting Sraffa drawing on the neoclassical theory, for example imposing constant returns to scale on Sraffa's equations, a procedure that Sraffa acknowledged to be possibly pedagogical as a first step, not least given the widespread use of neoclassical tools and the difficulties in recovering the submerged classical standpoint he was attempting to recover. However, Sraffa made it clear that the latter interpretation does not correspond to how he viewed his equations.

Stephen Pratten (1999) provides an ontologically informed analysis of how many (if not most) Sraffian scholars end up reducing economic reality to mathematical models, at least as a first stage for subsequent analysis. Garegnani (1984) and Pasinetti (1993) argue that this first stage constitutes a 'core' (to use Garegnani's expression) or 'pure theory' (to use Pasinetti's expression) that must be subsequently combined with what Pasinetti (1993) calls 'institutional analysis'. The stage of 'institutional analysis' is where we are led back to Sraffa's more ambitious historico-analytical programme (Pasinetti 2007; Porta 2018), which also provides the ground for engaging in a dialogue between Sraffian political economy and other alternative theories of political economy. It seems that, in order to attain an adequate view of Sraffian political economy, it is necessary to recover this historico-analytical aspect, which is revealed especially in Sraffa's interactions with Antonio Gramsci and Ludwig Wittgenstein.

CONCLUDING REMARKS

The historico-analytical nature of Sraffa's original formulation of his research programme (Pasinetti 2007; Porta 2018) can help us grasp more fully Sraffa's methodological vision at a broader level. As Sen (2003) writes, Sraffa's interactions with Ludwig Wittgenstein (on which, see also Roncaglia (2000), Davis (2002, 2012), Arena (2015), Sinha (2016), or Cesaratto and Bucchianico (2021)) show that Sraffa's own approach to studying societies is what may be termed an ethnological or anthropological approach, which cannot be reduced to mathematical models. Sen writes, drawing on Ray Monk's (1990) biography of Wittgenstein, that Wittgenstein told Rush Rees how 'the most important thing that he got from Sraffa is an "anthropological way" of seeing philosophical problems'. Brian McGuinness also emphasises, when discussing Wittgenstein, 'the ethnological or anthropological way of looking at things that came to him from the economist Sraffa' (Sen 2003: 1242), and the letters between Sraffa and Wittgenstein edited by McGuiness (2008) highlight this issue again.

A central concept at stake here, which needs to be further explored when addressing the broader historico-analytical nature of Sraffa's programme (Pasinetti 2007; Porta 2018), is the notion of 'mode of life', or 'form of life'. In *The German Ideology*, Marx and Engels (1974: 42) refer to a 'definite *mode of life*', a mode for individuals for expressing their life, while also referring to this notion when defining human essence in terms of human conditions of existence (Marx and Engels 1974: 61). Antonio Gramsci (2007: 321) draws upon Marx's definition of human essence as an ensemble of social relations in his *Theses on Feuerbach* (Martins 2017: 92), and Gramsci (1992: 167) also uses the notion of 'form of life' (Martins 2017: 84). It is plausible to assume that the idea of immersion in a given 'form of life' used by Wittgenstein ([1953] 1963) can be traced back to Gramsci (and from Gramsci to Marx) through the intermediation of Sraffa (Martins 2017: 84). The emphasis on human practices as the basis for the interpretation of the mode or form of life is the basis of the anthropological approach that Wittgenstein took from Sraffa.

Further research into Sraffa's anthropological approach would also help addressing important critiques of Sraffian political economy for lacking a theory of agency. Frederic Lee, when advancing the institutionalist notion of 'going concern' within his heterodox surplus approach (Lee and Jo 2011), writes that: 'One way to depict a *going concern economy* is the Sraffian social surplus approach; but it has no room for the agency of acting persons' (2018: 39). Lee further notes that 'agents in the heterodox surplus approach (and heterodox economics in general) are distinctively different from the mainstream notion of agent that Sraffa rejected when adopting his objectivist methodology' (2018: 188). This is certainly an important aspect that Sraffian scholarship must address.

Sraffian Political Economy became well-known worldwide because it provided the basis for a critique of the neoclassical production function. But Sraffa's overall vision also possesses the basis for a critique of subjective utility (and consequently the neoclassical utility function) within an anthropological approach. This anthropological approach, expressed in Wittgenstein's ([1953] 1963) later writings, stresses the role of human conventions, which are also central in Keynes's (1936) approach (Favereau 1988), and constitutes an alternative to the study of human agency in terms of the subjective motivations that would presumably trigger human activity. This view of human practices is in fact part of the overall Cambridge tradition in the days of Keynes, Sraffa and Wittgenstein (Martins 2013).

The role of human conventions within an anthropological approach can also help addressing important issues concerning Sraffa's theory of production, his approach to prices and the rate of profits. Hicks (1985: 306), when addressing price-fixing, notes that the rate of profits used to establish a mark-up is a conventional one, and one can thus interpret the uniformity of the rate of profits in Sraffa's system in terms of a uniformity of convention (see also Sinha (2016: 214)). This approach can also be fruitfully combined with Lee's (1998) approach to price theory (Martins 2015: 216–20) and earlier approaches to price theory such as Michal Kalecki's (1971) work, contributing to the development of an alternative economic theory that fruitfully combines contributions from alternative theories of political economy while also addressing Richard Kahn's concern with the lack of a foundation for the mark-up in Kalecki's analysis.

Joan Robinson, who engaged in frequent dialogue with Kahn, suggests focusing on Sraffa's view of prices for the Marshallian long period, and Kalecki's view of mark-up prices for the Marshallian short period (Marcuzzo and Rosselli 2005). More importantly, she tried to find a synthesis between Sraffa's social surplus approach and the principle of effective demand developed by Kalecki and Keynes. Significantly, Joan Robinson (1985: 165) argues that

Sraffa's theoretical framework provides the basic framework for accommodating Keynesian ideas, and writes that: '[t]here does not seem to be much point in making further systematic generalisations', since in Sraffa's theory we have 'a broad frame within which detailed studies of actual history can be carried out', and '[t]his is where Sraffa leaves us and hands us over to Keynes'.

When commenting on the Cambridge school of Keynesian economics, Luigi Pasinetti (2005, 2007) also suggests using Sraffa's theory as a basis for accommodating Keynesian ideas, such as the principle of effective demand and monetary aspects, while noting Keynes's own use of the expression *monetary theory of production* in order to highlight the central role of money in production. The combination of a social surplus approach (very much in line with Sraffa's revival of classical political economy) with the Keynesian principle of effective demand and a monetary theory of production has also been recently advanced as core foundational principles for heterodox economic theory (Lee and Jo 2011). The development of a heterodox economic theory – built upon the social surplus approach, the Kaleckian–Keynesian principle of effective demand, and a monetary theory of production – can benefit greatly from greater interaction with Sraffian political economy (Cesaratto 2020). Combining ideas like these (social surplus approach, Keynesian effective demand and a monetary theory of production) has already been pursued within Sraffian political economy (Garegnani 1978, 1979a; Pasinetti 1993, 2007), focusing essentially on analytical aspects, providing important lessons when seeking to develop alternative theories of political economy. However, the analytical aspects typically addressed within Sraffian political economy should be scrutinised together within Sraffa's anthropological approach. In this way, a broader historico-analytical dimension for Sraffian political economy can be reached, while also contributing to the development of alternative theory through interaction with other schools of political economic thought.

REFERENCES

Arena, R. (2015) 'Order, process and morpohology: Sraffa and Wittgenstein', *Cambridge Journal of Economics*, **39** (4), pp. 1087–108.

Aspromourgos, T. (2004) 'Sraffian research programmes and unorthodox economics', *Review of Political Economy*, **16** (2), pp. 179–206.

Backhouse, R. (2014) 'MIT and the other Cambridge', *History of Political Economy*, **46** (suppl. 1), pp. 252–71.

Bharadwaj, K. (1978) *Classical Political Economy and Rise to Dominance of Supply and Demand Theories* (R.C. Dutt lectures on political economy), Calcutta: Orient Longman.

Bidard, C. (1991) *Prix, Reproduction, Rareté*, Paris: Economica.

Bellofiore, R. (2008) 'Sraffa and Marx: an open issue', in Chiodi, G. and Ditta, L. (eds), *Sraffa and an Alternative Economics*, Basingstoke: Palgrave Macmillan, pp. 68–92.

Bliss, C.J. (1975) *Capital Theory and the Distribution of Income*, Amsterdam: North-Holland.

Carter, S. (2014) 'From "pool of profits" to surplus and deficit industries: archival evidence on the evolution of Piero Sraffa's thought', *Research in Political Economy*, **29**, pp. 3–61.

Cesaratto, S. (2020) *Heterodox Challenges in Economics: Theoretical Issues and the Crisis of the Eurozone*, Cham: Springer.

Cesaratto, S. and Di Bucchianico, S. (2021) 'The surplus approach, institutions and economic formations', *Contributions to Political Economy*, **40** (1), pp. 26–52.

Chiodi, G. (2008) 'Beyond capitalism: Sraffa's economic theory', in Chiodi, G. and Ditta, L. (eds), *Sraffa or an Alternative Economics*, London: Palgrave Macmillan, pp. 187–98.

Cohen, A. and Harcourt, G.C. (2003) 'Whatever happened to the Cambridge Capital Theory controversies?', *Journal of Economic Perspectives*, **17** (1), pp. 199–214.

Davis, J. (2002) 'Gramsci, Sraffa, Wittgenstein: philosophical linkages', *European Journal of the History of Economic Thought*, **9** (3), pp. 384–401.

Davis, J.B. (2012) 'The change in Sraffa's philosophical thinking', *Cambridge Journal of Economics*, **36** (6), pp. 1341–56.

Davis, J.B. (2017) 'Sraffa on the open versus "closed systems" distinction and causality', *Research in the History of Economic Thought and Methodology*, **35** (B), pp. 153–70.

De Vivo, G. (2003) 'Sraffa's path to *Production of Commodities by Means of Commodities*: an interpretation', *Contributions to Political Economy*, **22** (1), pp. 1–25.

Dobb, M. (1969) *Welfare Economics and the Economics of Socialism*, Cambridge: Cambridge University Press.

Dorfman, R., Samuelson, P.A. and Solow, R.M. (1958) *Linear Programming and Economic Analysis*, New York: McGraw Hill.

Dvoskin, A. and Lazzarini, A. (2013) 'On Walras's concept of equilibrium', *Review of Political Economy*, **25** (1), pp. 117–38.

Eatwell, J. (1977) 'The irrelevance of returns to scale in Sraffa's analysis', *Journal of Economic Literature*, **15**, pp. 61–8.

Favereau, O. (1988) 'La Theorie Générale: de l'economie conventionnelle à l'economie des conventions', *Cahiers d'économie politique*, **14–15**, pp. 197–220.

Fratini, S.M. (2018) 'Sraffa on the degeneration of the notion of cost', *Cambridge Journal of Economics*, **42** (3) pp. 817–36.

Fratini, S.M. (2019) 'On the second stage of the Cambridge capital controversy', *Journal of Economic Surveys*, **33** (4), pp. 1073–93.

Garegnani, P. (1978) 'Notes on consumption, investment and effective demand: I', *Cambridge Journal of Economics*, **2** (4), pp. 335–53.

Garegnani, P. (1979a) 'Notes on consumption, investment and effective demand: II', *Cambridge Journal of Economics*, **3** (1), pp. 63–82.

Garegnani, P. (1979b) 'Notes on consumption, investment and effective demand: a reply to Joan Robinson', *Cambridge Journal of Economics*, **3** (2), pp. 181–7.

Garegnani, P. (1984) 'Value and distribution in the classical economists and Marx', *Oxford Economic Papers*, **36**, pp. 291–325.

Garegnani, P. (2005) 'On a turning point in Sraffa's theoretical and interpretative position in the late 1920s', *European Journal of the History of Economic Thought*, **12** (3), pp. 453–92.

Garegnani, P. (2012) 'On the present state of the capital controversy', *Cambridge Journal of Economics*, **36** (6), pp. 1417–32.

Garegnani, P. (2018) 'On the labour theory of value in Marx and in the Marxist tradition', *Review of Political Economy*, **30** (4), pp. 618–42.

Gilibert, G. (2003) 'The equations unveiled: Sraffa's price equations in the making', *Contributions to Political Economy*, **22** (1), pp. 27–40.

Gram, H. and Harcourt, G.C. (2017) 'Joan Robinson and the MIT', *History of Political Economy*, **49** (3), pp. 437–50.

Gramsci, A. (1992) *Prison Notebooks: Volume I*, edited with an introduction by J.A. Buttigieg, translated by Joseph Buttigieg and Antonio Callari, New York: Columbia University Press.

Gramsci, A. (2007) *Prison Notebooks: Volume III*, edited with an introduction by J.A. Buttigieg, translated by Joseph Buttigieg and Antonio Callari, New York: Columbia University Press.

Hahn, F. (1975) 'Revival of political economy: the wrong issues and the wrong argument', *Economic Record*, **51** (135), pp. 360–65.

Harcourt, G.C. (1972) *Some Cambridge Controversies in the Theory of Capital*, Cambridge: Cambridge University Press.

Harcourt, G.C. (1981) 'Marshall, Sraffa, and Keynes: incompatible bedfellows?', *Eastern Economic Journal*, **7**, pp. 39–50, reprinted in Kerr, P. (ed.) (1982) *The Social Science Imperialists: Selected Essays of G.C. Harcourt*, London: Routledge and Kegan Paul, pp. 250–64.

Harcourt, G.C. and Massaro, V.G. (1964) 'A note on Mr. Sraffa's sub-systems', *Economic Journal*, **74**, pp. 715–22.

Hicks, J.R. (1939) *Value and Capital*, London: Oxford University Press.

Hicks, J.R. (1985) 'Sraffa and Ricardo: a critical view', in Caravale, G.A. (ed.), *The Legacy of Ricardo*, Oxford and New York: Basil Blackwell, pp. 305–19.

Kalecki, M. (1971) *Selected Essays on the Dynamics of the Capitalist Economy*, Cambridge: Cambridge University Press.

Keynes, J.M. (1936) *The General Theory of Employment, Interest and Money*, London: Macmillan.

Kurz, H. and Salvadori, N. (2005) 'Representing the production and circulation of commodities in material terms: on Sraffa's objectivism', *Review of Political Economy*, **17** (3), pp. 69–97.

Kurz, H. and Salvadori, N. (2010) 'Sraffa and the labour theory of value', in Vint, J., Metcalfe, S.S., Kurz, H., Salvadori, N. and Samuelson, P. (eds), *Economic Theory and Economic Thought*, London: Routledge, pp. 189–215.

Kurz, H. and Salvadori, N. (2015) *Revisiting Classical Economics: Studies in Long-period Analysis*, London: Routledge.

Lazzarini, A. (2011) *Revisiting the Cambridge Capital Theory Controversies: A Historical and Analytical Study*, Pavia: Pavia University Press.

Lee, F.S. (1998) *Post Keynesian Price Theory*, Cambridge: Cambridge University Press.

Lee, F.S. (2018) *Microeconomic Theory: A Heterodox Approach*, ed. Tae-Hee Jo, London and New York: Routledge.

Lee, F.S. and Jo, T.-H. (2011) 'Social surplus approach and heterodox economics', *Journal of Economic Issues*, **45** (4), pp. 857–75.

Marcuzzo, C. and Rosselli, A. (eds) (2005) *Economists in Cambridge: A Study through their Correspondence, 1907–1946*, London: Routledge.

Marcuzzo, M.C. and Rosselli, A. (2011) 'Sraffa and his arguments against "marginism"', *Cambridge Journal of Economics*, **35** (1), pp. 219–31.

Marshall, A. ([1890] 1920) *Principles of Economics*, London: Macmillan.

Marshall, A. ([1919] 1923) *Industry and Trade*, London: Macmillan.

Martins, N.O. (2013) *The Cambridge Revival of Political Economy*, London and New York, Routledge.

Martins, N.O. (2015) 'Advancing heterodox economics in the tradition of the surplus approach', in Jo, T.-H. and Todorova, Z. (eds), *Advancing the Frontiers of Heterodox Economics: Essays in Honor of Frederic S. Lee*, London: Routledge, pp. 213–29.

Martins, N.O. (2017) 'Spatial dimensions of Antonio Gramsci's contribution', *Regional Science Policy and Practice*, **9** (2), pp. 83–99.

Martins, N.O. (2019) 'The Sraffian *methodenstreit* and the revolution in economic theory', *Cambridge Journal of Economics*, **43** (2), pp. 507–25.

Marx, K. ([1885] 1978) *Capital*, Vol. II, trans. D. Fernbach, London: Pelican Books.

Marx, K. ([1894] 1981) *Capital*, Vol. III, trans. D. Fernbach, London: Pelican Books.

Marx, K. and Engels, F. (1974) *The German Ideology*, 2nd edn, London: Lawrence and Wishart.

Meek, R. (1961) 'Mr. Sraffa's rehabilitation of classical economics', *Scottish Journal of Political Economy*, **8**, pp. 119–36.

McGuiness, B. (2008) *Wittgenstein in Cambridge: Letters and Documents 1911–1951*, Oxford: Blackwell.

Monk, R. (1990) *Ludwig Wittgenstein: The Duty of Genius*, London: Jonathan Cape.

Naldi, N. (2000) 'Piero Sraffa and Antonio Gramsci: their friendship between 1919 and 1927', *European Journal of the History of Economic Thought*, **7** (1), pp. 79–114.

Naldi, N. (2020) 'The origins of Piero Sraffa's equations', *Contributions to Political Economy*, **39** (1), pp. 1–22.

Napoleoni, C. (1965) *L'equilibrio Economico Generale: Studio Introduttivo*, Milan: Boringhieri.

Pasinetti, L.L. (1981) *Structural Change and Economic Growth: A Theoretical Essay on the Dynamics of the Wealth of Nations*, Cambridge: Cambridge University Press.

Pasinetti, L.L. (1993) *Structural Economic Dynamics*, Cambridge: Cambridge University Press.

Pasinetti, L.L. (2005) 'The Cambridge school of Keynesian economics', *Cambridge Journal of Economics*, **29**, pp. 837–48.

Pasinetti, L.L. (2007) *Keynes and the Cambridge Keynesians: A 'Revolution in Economics' to Be Accomplished*, Cambridge: Cambridge University Press.

Petty, W. ([1690] 1899) *The Economic Writings of Sir William Petty*, Vols I–II, ed. Hull, C.H., Cambridge: Cambridge University Press.

Petri, F. (2004) *General Equilibrium, Capital and Macroeconomics: A Key to Recent Controversies in Equilibrium Theory*, Cheltenham, UK and Northampton, MA, USA: Edward Elgar Publishing.

Porta, P.L. (1986) 'Understanding the significance of Piero Sraffa's standard commodity: a note on the Marxian notion of surplus', *History of Political Economy*, **18** (3), pp. 443–54.

Porta, P.L. (2012) 'Piero Sraffa's early views on classical political economy', *Cambridge Journal of Economics*, **36** (6), pp. 1357–83.

Porta, P.L. (2018) 'The formative stages of Piero Sraffa's research program', *History of Economic Review*, **70** (1), pp. 2–22.

Pratten, S. (1999) 'The "closure" assumption as a first step: neo-Ricardian economics and post-Keynesianism', in Fleetwood, S. (ed.), *Critical Realism in Economics: Development and Debate*, London: Routledge, pp. 21–41.

Putnam, H. and Walsh, V. (eds) (2012), *The End of Value-Free Economics*, London and New York: Routledge.

Ricardo, D. ([1817] 1821), *On the Principles of Political Economy and Taxation*, London: John Murray.

Robertson, D.H., Sraffa, P. and Shove, G.F. (1930). 'Increasing returns and the representative firm', *The Economic Journal*, **40**, pp. 79–116.

Robinson, J. (1933) *The Economics of Imperfect Competition*, London: Macmillan.

Robinson, J. (1953–54) 'The production function and the theory of capital', *Review of Economic Studies*, **21** (2), pp. 81–106.

Robinson, J. (1979) 'Garegnani on effective demand', *Cambridge Journal of Economics*, **3** (2), pp. 179–80.

Robinson, J.V. (1985) 'The theory of normal prices and the reconstruction of economic theory', in Feiwel, G. (ed.), *Issues in Contemporary Macroeconomics and Distribution*, London: Macmillan, pp. 157–65.

Roncaglia, A. (1978) *Sraffa and the Theory of Prices*, Chichester: John Wiley and Sons.

Roncaglia, A. (2000) *Piero Sraffa and His Life, Thought and Cultural Heritage*, London: Routledge.

Roncaglia, A. (2010) 'The notion of production prices: notes', in Vint, J., Metcalfe, J. S., Kurz, H., Salvadori, N. and Samuelson, A. (eds), *Economic Theory and Economic Thought: Essays in Honour of Ian Steedman*, London: Routledge, pp. 174–88.

Samuelson, P.A. (1966) 'A summing up', *Quarterly Journal of Economics*, **80** (4), pp. 568–83.

Samuelson, P.A. (2010) 'Testing whether the "capital reversal" syndrome mandates deadweight loss in competitive intertemporal equilibrium', in Vint, J., Metcalfe, J. S., Kurz, H., Salvadori, N. and Samuelson, A. (eds), *Economic Theory and Economic Thought: Essays in Honour of Ian Steedman*, London: Routledge, pp. 167–73.

Sen, A.K. (2003) 'Sraffa, Wittgenstein, and Gramsci', *Journal of Economic Literature*, **41** (4), pp. 1240–55.

Sinha, A. (2016) *A Revolution in Economic Theory: The Economics of Piero Sraffa*, Cham: Springer International.

Solow, R. (2014) 'Comments on Scott Carter', *Research in Political Economy*, **29**, pp. 63–7.

Sraffa, P. (1925) 'Sulle relazioni fra costo e quantita prodotta', *Annali di economia*, **2**, pp. 277–328.

Sraffa, P. (1926) 'The laws of returns under competitive conditions', *Economic Journal*, **36**, pp. 535–50.

Sraffa, P. (1932) 'Dr. Hayek on money and capital', *Economic Journal*, **42**, pp. 42–53.

Sraffa, P. (1960) *Production of Commodities by Means of Commodities: Prelude to a Critique of Economic Theory*, Cambridge: Cambridge University Press.

Steedman, I. (1977) *Marx after Sraffa*, London: Verso.

Velupillai, V. (2008) 'Sraffa's mathematical economics: a constructive interpretation', *Journal of Economic Methodology*, **15** (4), pp. 325–48.

Walsh, V. and Gram, H. (1980) *Classical and Neoclassical Theories of General Equilibrium*, Oxford: Oxford University Press.

Walras, L. ([1874] 1926) *Elements d'economie politique pure; ou, theorie de la richesse sociale*, Paris: Pichon et Durand-Auzias.

Walsh, V. (2003) 'Sen after Putnam', *Review of Political Economy*, **15** (3), pp. 315–94.

Wittgenstein, L. ([1953] 1963) *Philosophical Investigations*, trans. G.E.M. Anscombe, Oxford: Blackwell.

PART III

ANALYSING THE DYNAMICS OF ECONOMIC SYSTEMS

9.   Circular and cumulative causation

Phillip Toner and Gavan Butler

Circular and cumulative causation (CCC) is a principle in political economy rather than a specific theory. It is a way of seeing and understanding processes that, over time, tend to amplify economic expansion or decline, not convergence to any condition of equilibrium. CCC can be applied to interpret economic phenomena such as economic growth, but also to an array of broader social phenomena. It can also illuminate relationships *between* economic and social variables. In a process of CCC, 'history always matters': indeed, the process is *inherently* historical.

This chapter explains the nature and meaning of CCC and shows some of the various ways in which it has been fruitfully applied. The first section introduces the principle, pointing to the feedback processes that create what are sometimes described as the 'virtuous cycle' and 'vicious cycle' aspects of cumulative change. The second section notes the foundational contribution of Swedish political economist Gunnar Myrdal, and then considers the diverse settings in which the CCC principle has been applied, such as study of institutions, the developmental state, evolution, path-dependency, geographical agglomeration, and migration. The third section notes the important role of Nicholas Kaldor in developing a more formal model of CCC applied to the study of industry development, economic growth, and industry, trade and regional policies. The concluding section points to some current challenges for further development of CCC in political economy.

FUNDAMENTAL FEATURES OF CIRCULAR AND CUMULATIVE CAUSATION

Many economic and social processes of change have a *cumulative* character, whereby a change in a social or economic variable causes that variable to change further in the same direction. Thus, an initial small change can be magnified. For example, seeing their children begin to learn in a new school in an area that has previously had no school may stimulate the parents' respect for learning and lead them to enthuse their children to learn more and to remain at school – in other words the change in schooling is self-reinforcing. Moreover, a change in one variable may lead to change in a second variable, which in turn enables further change in the first variable. *Circularity* is at the heart of cumulativeness (Schmid 1999: 87). It arises wherever the outcome of a process feeds back into the process of change itself, stimulating or promoting it. So, circular and cumulative causation involves reinforcement and feedback. These processes of CCC may be depicted as 'virtuous' (a positive change brings about a further positive change, or progress) or as 'vicious' (a negative change brings about a further negative change, or regress). What is depicted as 'virtuous' and what is depicted as 'vicious' obviously depends on the value judgements – and/or on the material interests – of the beholder.

The positive aspects of CCC processes are commonly observed in manufacturing industries, where an increasingly detailed division of labour and creation of specialised lines of production leads to the establishment of other firms that produce capital goods (Argyrous 2011: 145). These manufacturers of capital goods supply the machines and other equipment tools needed for the manufacture of consumer goods: but they may also create other capital goods, including machine tools. The specialisation in these manufacturing industries also enables the development of new techniques, cheapens production overall and thereby becomes self-reinforcing. As the output and range of activities expand, production becomes more complex – more 'roundabout' – and capital deepening occurs. This type of industrial growth need not be limited by a 'shortage of capital', although that may be the case if there is a constraint on the CCC process. Such a constraint could arise from: (i) producers experiencing a shortage of liquidity with which to finance production; (ii) disproportionality between the installed capacities for producing capital goods and consumer goods or disproportionalities between the rates of production of various sorts of capital goods; and (iii) vital technical knowledge being held exclusively and deployed strategically by specific corporations. Overall, a limit on expansion is set only by the level of aggregate demand for consumer goods, which must be sufficient to absorb its entire productive capacity at any time.

While increasing specialisation and scale of production both cheapen resources, thereby enabling further expansion of the scale of production (either at the level of an enterprise or of an industry), CCC is about more than increasing returns. It is also a means of understanding complex processes that can occur simultaneously and interact with each other, either positively or negatively. As Gunnar Myrdal, the great proponent of CCC, wrote in relation to his conditions of a social system, the various processes influencing development do not necessarily exert their influence in the same direction (Myrdal 1968). For example, the processes comprising the 'green revolution' in the agricultural practices of some developing nations involved the introduction of high-yielding seed varieties, but also the application of inorganic fertilisers and pesticides with adverse long-term effects. That said, human learning is also a circular and cumulative process; and – in this case – humans were able, from observing destructive practices, to discover more about the vulnerability of the natural environment and the accumulation of toxins in animal/human tissues. The CCC process may also entail qualitative, as well as quantitative, changes in variables, such as the honing of skills in teamwork. Furthermore, the CCC process may also draw into itself, in complex and unpredictable ways, economic, social and technological variables other than the initially changing variable; and these additional variables may then also undergo qualitative change.

The principle of CCC can be seen to play a role in explaining a wide range of aspects of an economy and society. For example, Stilwell (2011: 224) argues, in terms of CCC, that 'economic inequalities, once established, tend to self-perpetuate and grow'. Central to a CCC process are 'feedback mechanisms', 'backwash effects' and 'spread effects' through which the process may be replicated or extended with the passage of time.

Other areas to which CCC can contribute to analysis include:

- studies of innovation, demonstrating the 'complementarities' in technical change and the 'path dependency' of such change (Cimoli et al. 2009);
- the evolution of rules or institutions governing production and the distribution of income, such as the cumulative interaction between skills formation systems, production systems and localised technology specialisation, as demonstrated in the 'Varieties of Capitalism' literature (Hall and Soskice 2001);
- the changing patterns of human migration (Fussell 2010).

Clearly, the range of applications of the CCC principle in political economic analysis and research is diverse. Two broad clusters can be identified: one using the CCC concept as a flexible tool for studying a wide range of political economic, social and geographical phenomena; and the other situating CCC in a post-Keynesian tradition where the focus is more specifically on specialisation in production and its implications for industries and economic growth. The next two major sections of this chapter explore each cluster in turn.

BROAD SETTINGS OF THE STUDY OF CIRCULAR AND CUMULATIVE CAUSATION

The Pioneering Work of Gunnar Myrdal

The work of Gunnar Myrdal is celebrated for having illuminated the broad significance of CCC. In his *The American Dilemma* (1944), Myrdal argued forcefully that the impoverishment of African Americans creates their ongoing impoverishment. Their poverty leads to attenuated education and poor schools, malnutrition and a poor standard of public health, a neglect of preventative healthcare, inaccessible and poor curative medicine for individual families, unemployment or underemployment, as well as many other blights, such as inadequate care of the aged, domestic violence and drug addiction financed by street crime. This is a regressive CCC process of the 'vicious cycle' type.

In contrast, Myrdal's *Asian Drama* (1968), though set in South Asia, anticipated the rise of the developmental state in East Asia, to which we return shortly. Myrdal was concerned with engendering a 'virtuous cycle' type of CCC process and sought in his monumental work on Asian development and underdevelopment to promote recognition of 'general interdependencies among factors involved in the process of social change'. To initiate and accelerate development, induced changes in social conditions and relationships are taken to be 'instrumental or even to play a strategic role in the cumulative causation of a development process' (Myrdal 1968: 43). When looking back at his work five years later, Myrdal emphasised that his approach had eschewed GDP fetishism in favour of the idea of the betterment ('upward movement') of the 'entire social system' in which there are many interdependencies such that 'a change in one "condition" tends to move other conditions in the same direction and [bring about] further changes of the same type in the whole system' (Myrdal 1975: 190). He concluded his summary statement on 'A System Analysis' by writing: 'I call this circular causation with cumulative effects'.

Path Dependency

The notions of 'interdependencies among factors involved in the process of social change' and of self-reinforcement imply that development within each social formation tends to proceed along an established path. As it is most generally expressed, the idea of path dependency is that past events condition current and future events – history matters. Thus, experience of a past event tends to determine the shape of future events in similar circumstances – for good or ill. In the words of Setterfield (1999), the mechanisms by which such feedback occurs 'imbue economic systems with memories …'. Alternatively, institutions plus habits of thought and habitual practices may lay down paths of behaviour into the future. Indeed, institutional development may itself be path-dependent.

On this reasoning, it is possible to present a quite straightforward conception of CCC and path dependencies relating to growth and development, as follows. The development of one industry is likely to stimulate the development of other industries that are associated with it, whether by supplying inputs, being major users of the first industry's product, or being linked into previously established supply chains. New investment in an economy is more likely to occur in the already established industrial structure and, within an industry, in lines of production that have long existed (within the automobile industry, in the production of cars driven by internal combustion engines rather than electric motors, for example). As Luigi Pasinetti (1981) argues, it is more likely to occur either within established 'vertically integrated industries' or in expanding them: the patterns of (new) investment reflect the established industry structure but also changes in linkages within that structure.

It is also important to recognise, however, that path dependencies may not persist in the face of exogenous factors: paths may be abandoned. Moreover, an individual entrepreneur may be induced to step off the path by the prospect of 'first mover advantage'.

Evolutionary Economics

Writers in the CCC tradition, such as Myrdal and Veblen, are acknowledged as key initiators of evolutionary economics (Berger and Elsner 2007). Gunnar Myrdal's vision of change in entire social systems is totally consonant with what that field has come to be. Thorstein Veblen had earlier written a dense, albeit now famous article which was published in the *Quarterly Journal of Economics* in 1898 on 'why economics is not an evolutionary science'. He argued that 'the process of cumulative change that is to be accounted for is the sequence of change in the methods of doing things – the methods of dealing with the material means of life' (Veblen 1898: 387). He went on to state that 'it appears that an evolutionary economics must be the theory of a process of cultural growth as determined by the economic interest, a theory of a cumulative sequence of economic institutions stated in terms of the process itself'. Geoffrey Hodgson, probably the pre-eminent contemporary writer in the field, has written that evolutionary economics sets out to describe and explain dynamic change in economies and society (Hodgson 1999: 294–8). Of Veblen's work in particular, he wrote that Veblen 'attempted to develop a theory of socioeconomic evolution that drew upon the three Darwinian principles of inheritance, variation and selection'. Instincts, habits and institutions were what were heritable; and the selection of institutions takes place in circumstances that are constantly changing, most importantly as technologies change.

Another chapter in this current book presents evolutionary economics more fully, so here we simply note some important themes in evolutionary economics which are relevant to CCC. Among these is, first, that evolutionary economics is centrally concerned with the role of institutions as enablers of or constraints on change and adaptation and more specifically on processes of CCC. At one remove, as Reinert (2007: 62) asserts, the mode of production of a society drives institutional development (the demand for and shaping of new institutions). At another remove, the rules that govern social interactions are, in turn, continuously being reconstituted in the light of the evident experience of underlying conflicts and contradictions arising as the productive system changes. Second, those institutions that are of greatest importance to CCC include the institutions of the state which play roles in initiating and maintaining

CCC growth processes, as well as other institutions governing the generation and transmission of new technologies across firms and the workforce. The institutions of the market are but a sub-set of all the important institutions. However, the formal model of CCC, or quantitative and econometric approaches in the post-Keynesian tradition (see the following section of this chapter), is silent on the interaction of *non-market institutions* and cumulative growth. This silence diminishes the completeness of the model – all the more so since Myrdal, who was acknowledged by Kaldor as a key contributor to CCC theory, gave equal weight to productive processes and institutions in the explanation of development and underdevelopment.

In a recent, detailed review of work in the field of evolutionary economics, Hodgson (2019) has written that the diversity of approaches in evolutionary economics is so great as to render evolutionary economics amorphous. However, he has also observed that there is an 'invisible college of evolutionary thought', the members of which share the following views: (i) that the world in which we live is a world of change; (ii) that a feature of this world is the generation of novelty (there is constant innovation); (iii) that an essential feature of economic systems is their complexity; (iv) that human agents have limited cognitive capacities ('bounded rationality') – and so we use 'rules of thumb'; and (v) that complex phenomena emerge through piecemeal iteration in social interactions, rather than from deliberate design. The shared overall view can be said to be that there is constant and actively pursued change in complex production systems that is prompted by changes in technology and thereupon guided by rules that may emerge from the collective experience of the agents of production. CCC sits comfortably in this company, all the more so because it directs attention to the institutions engaged in the evolutionary processes.

Institutions

Institutions have been described as the 'rules of the game', in the felicitous phrase used by Douglass North (1991: 97); they are the rules that govern social interactions between the members of a society/community. Among those which concerned Myrdal (1958) are the laws and customs governing the tenure of land, persistently feudal social structures, and the laws and customs that specify the places of different races, classes or castes in the economic system. This view implicitly rejects the (neoclassical) prioritisation of property rights. Institutions may come to be regarded as inadequate in some sense, as unacceptably biased in effect, as being offensive to contemporary notions of human rights, or as having otherwise failed to command the continuing respect of significant proportions of the people to whom they apply. On the other hand, they may strengthen if they demonstrably govern conflicts in social interactions. In principle, they are able to evolve (and initially to be established) through 'social iteration' – a broad process (to which Hodgson obliquely alluded in his 2019 review of evolutionary economics) by which people experiment together, observe, test out, evaluate, refine or reject possible rules. It is a process that is in some measure inclusive – involving the governed and their insights and knowledge. Lest it be thought, however, that the evolution of institutions is always organic, it must be recognised that the rules may instead be laid down by a particular segment of a society – a ruling class. The rules are both formal and informal, with formal and informal rules often being mutually supportive.

In the case of the development or evolution of formal rules established by the state in a democracy, a parliament is an important contributor to the broad process. Of course, democratic outcomes may be thwarted, repudiated or set aside by hostile political and social forces or by the power of private corporations. Where there are deep class divisions, a ruling class may repudiate 'social iteration' even to the point of sparking rebellion. In an authoritarian polity there can anyway be no 'social iteration': the rules may change but they do not do so in this way because the rules and changes to them are dictates.

Institutions govern social interactions and thus social production as a whole. In a *neoclassical* world this means that the market and exchange, backed by private property and the law of contract, are deemed capable of an optimal allocation of resources and distribution of income. In a *non-neoclassical* world with CCC characteristics, the various and multiple processes of production, distribution and 'dis-equilibrium growth' are governed by similarly various and multiple – and contradictory and changing – non-market institutions. Among these, the state – or the institutions of the state – is paramount.

The Developmental State

In neoclassical growth theory, increases in output and productivity reflect the drive of 'entrepreneurs' to maximise profit in the face of price fluctuations. In this theoretical framework, the rules to ensure that markets are cleared by changes in relative prices are the over-arching institutions. However, once one leaves the confines of neoclassical economics the question arises as to how the disparate parts of an economy are coordinated with each other.

In the dynamic world to which CCC relates, the environment of any enterprise is uncertain. Relative price movements cannot be depended upon to signal appropriate short-term and long-term enterprise decisions. Therefore, for any enterprise, there are substantial risks to profitability in decision-making. In these conditions, the coordination of investments to achieve development across an economy requires consultation, planning and centralised direction. Studies of the 'developmental state', or the post-Second World War East Asian 'economic miracle', argue that the state was integral to such coordination. The coordination and planning is achieved by the likes of a statutory planning commission, such as the Japanese Ministry of International Trade and Industry (or Ministry of Economy, Trade and Industry as it now is), or a centrally organised conglomerate (a Korean *chaebol*, perhaps), or a network of enterprises (a Japanese *keiretsu*, perhaps), or *both* public and 'private' sector organisations (Johnson 1982; Wade 2004).

The developmental state is a state that invests public resources in linked industries and that guides, cajoles or induces the private sector to collaborate. It can 'harvest' external benefits of private investment projects ('positive externalities'), at least those which manifest as higher taxable income, and regulate the creation of external costs ('negative externalities'). A wide spread of industrial enterprises can be encouraged to direct production systematically to export markets, thus generating economies of scale and revenue for financing further investment, sustaining productivity growth and social provisioning. One of the leading scholars of the developmental state in East Asia is Robert Wade. In a conversational exchange with a group of scholars, including the present authors, about a new introduction to his seminal *Governing the Market* which is focused on Taiwan, Wade represented CCC as explaining the efficacy of industry policy as a critical dimension of the developmental state, arguing that 'the purpose of industrial policy (*sic*) is to exploit increasing returns, externalities and complementarities so as to accelerate income growth and structural change' (Toner and Butler 2009: 58). The developmental states of East Asia have also understood the importance of the complementary promotion of exports as a major component of the demand that is the primary driver of growth. So, too, they recognise the importance of managing the balance of payments, since imports required for industrial growth (*and* export growth) must be financed by exports. Lest one be inclined to see the developmental states of East Asia as conceding in recent decades to neoliberalism, it has been argued – for the case of Korea at any rate – that the developmental state (thus 'state-led capitalism') has persisted rather than retreated. That this should be so has been explained either as reflecting *continuity because of change*, such as the change from the later decade of the twentieth century when the developmental state worked with the *chaebols* to the current situation where it works with decentralised research consortia (Kim 2021), or as reflecting the 'stickiness of institutions'.

Geographic Agglomeration and Migration

CCC also has considerable relevance for the study of spatial political economy. Early human settlement and historical locations of agriculture, the timber industry and the beginnings of industrialisation were largely dictated by geographic features – such as rivers and the alluvial soils of river valleys, forests, and natural harbours. As Argyrous and Bamberry have argued, the consequent regional markets were important 'at the "embryonic" stage of firm development' (2009: 74). Production progressed from primary to secondary to tertiary activities, with concomitant development of the firm. Immigrant workers were attracted by the availability of jobs, and apprenticeships expanded the local availability of skills. Over time, income disparities have grown between centres and peripheries. Retailing and household services dependent on households' having discretionary incomes were concentrated in the centres. The progression accentuated the geographic concentration of economic activities. In one of Myrdal's less widely celebrated books, he developed these ideas into a comprehensive overview of regional inequalities, both between and within nations (Myrdal 1958).

Paul Krugman is commonly credited with explicitly introducing the idea of CCC into economic geography. Krugman's studies in the 1990s employed the notion of economies of scale, along with transportation costs, to model the concentration of manufacturing and the agglomeration of population in certain regions of a country, providing a basis for regional disparities in growth and development and the rise of core–periphery structures (see Krugman 1991). However, Krugman's modelling of industrial and population agglomeration was developed within the method and constraints of equilibrium economics: it was about shifts from one equilibrium to another and about the sustainability of an equilibrium (Martin 1990). As such, it was not really about CCC as understood in political economy, notwithstanding references by Krugman and his followers to 'circular causation' and 'circularity'.

CIRCULAR AND CUMULATIVE CAUSATION, INDUSTRIES AND GROWTH

Alongside the foregoing applications of CCC to the study of various socio-economic processes, much of what has been written on CCC relates more specifically to growth theory and its policy implications. The latter literature sits in a post-Keynesian tradition in which the Keynesian emphasis on aggregate demand is linked to concerns with specialisation in production in the tradition of Adam Smith's political economy.

The Formal Model

A formal CCC model of growth can be developed from the central proposition that growth is demand constrained. Increases in total output, 'factor inputs' and output per worker (productivity growth) are taken to be a function of the growth of demand for goods and services. In this demand-led model, key variables, including consumer preferences, technological change and factor supply, are endogenous. CCC is fundamentally a model of dis-equilibrium growth: each increment in demand induces changes in supply – especially technological changes, 'factor proportions' and consumer tastes that act to induce a further increase in demand. Cumulative expansion may thereby occur.

The key processes underlying the growth relate to the stimulus that growth in the size of the market provides for increasing returns, overcoming indivisibilities in investment and innovation in new production processes, products and services. Productivity growth induces growth of real income and output, which further expands the scope for the division of labour, or the specialisation of inputs and outputs within and across firms and industries. The more detailed division of labour leads to the introduction of more efficient, capital-intensive techniques of production and work organisation methods. Growth in total output is absorbed, as CCC theory assumes that goods subject to increasing returns – that is, manufactures – have both high 'price elasticity of demand' (so that a reduction in their unit prices leads to a more than proportionate increase in demand) and a high 'income elasticity of demand'. Causation is cumulative in that the self-reinforcing effect of increasing returns, endogenous technical change and the apparently insatiable demand for variety in products and services in a market industrial economy creates virtuous cycles of development. In Allyn Young's famous aphorism: 'the division of labour depends upon the extent of the market, but the extent of the market also depends upon the division of labour' (Young 1928: 539).

This was the vison of self-sustaining growth in an industrial economy that Young propounded in his foundational work on CCC (Young 1928). It can be regarded as a synthesis of ideas from J.B. Say and Adam Smith in which the classical spectre of internal economic contradictions – the dismal prospect of finite resources and diminishing returns – had been abolished. Conversely, later writers in the CCC tradition identified binding market barriers to per capita income growth, especially in the transition from a low-income to high-income economy. Crucially, however, they also proposed the means of *un*binding them. In Myrdal's view: '[t]he hypothesis of circular and cumulative causation, which tends to be the doctrine of despair for the poorer countries as long as they leave things to take their natural course, holds out glittering prizes for a policy of purposive interferences' (Myrdal 1958: 85). For these writers, the processes of CCC foreshadow, in the absence of countervailing measures, an ever-widening divergence in growth prospects both within nations and across nations.

The barriers to growth and the means of their redress were the central concerns of mid-twentieth-century development economists inspired by CCC. Foremost were the 'Balanced Growth' model of Rosenstein-Rodan (1943) and the 'Unbalanced Growth' model of Hirschman (1958). The latter pioneered the use of input–output techniques to quantify Young's model where incremental increases in demand and supply were conceived in terms of intensified intra- and inter-industry input–output transactions. Further, the input–output transaction table could be used to identify gaps in a developing nation's industrial structure that would otherwise be filled by imports. This model demonstrated how input–output multipliers create a virtuous cycle of increases in domestic demand and supply. In essence, for

Hirschman (and also for the 'father' of input–output analysis, Wassily Leontief), development consists essentially in 'filling-in' previous gaps in the national input–output matrix. Later empirical work by Hollis Chenery (1961, 1979) identified the systematic transformations in the input–output structure of economies moving through different levels of per capita income or successive stages of development. These empirical regularities support the CCC claim of a causal connection between per capita income growth and increases in both the diversity of industries and the density of intra- and inter-industry transactions. The view that growth in total output and per capita income is causally associated with an increase in the density of national input–output tables is also supported by the stylised fact that intra-industry trade is the dominant form of non-commodity international trade among high-income nations.

Writers such as Rosenstein-Rodan and Hirschman identified self-reinforcing barriers, or vicious cycles, that impede development in poor nations. These barriers include the small size of the market in developing nations that make it difficult to justify private investment in modern, efficient, large-scale manufacturing and infrastructure. Indivisibilities in investment projects, combined with the expense and imperfect nature of information available to private investors, result in uncertainty, risk and coordination failures in the sequencing and sizing of potentially self-sustaining investments. Shortages of both skilled labour and 'learning by doing' in production, both of which are by-products of inadequate past industrial output, constrain future growth in output. Developing country dependence on the export of unprocessed agricultural and mineral commodities also inhibits development due to limited input–output linkages to any nascent, local industrial sector and causes a leakage of scarce effective demand into imported goods.

In sum, international free trade – without state interventions to redress barriers to industrial development – may constrain the economic opportunities of low-income nations. These CCC-inspired development economists proposed interventions such as the coordination of investments that have strong input–output linkages and the imposition of temporary restraints on competing imports.

Nicholas Kaldor

The most sophisticated and fully articulated CCC model was provided by the leading post-Keynesian, Nicholas Kaldor (1966, 1972). He accepted Allyn Young's vision of growth in advanced industrial economies, based on a virtuous cycle of growth in demand and supply. The growth process occurs under conditions where the production of commodities is subject to increasing returns, leading to consequent real price reductions; where the commodities have high price and income elasticities of demand; and where the supply of factors of production is elastic.

Empirical support for increasing returns, Kaldor (1966) held, is given by the 'Verdoorn Law'. This is the proposition, based on apparent empirical regularity, that there exists a statistically reliable connection between growth of industrial output and growth of productivity. Regressing growth in labour productivity in manufacturing against growth in manufacturing output reveals that a 1 per cent increase in manufacturing output is associated with a 0.5 per cent increase in manufacturing productivity. Kaldor took this positive coefficient as evidence for generalised increasing returns to industrial activities and endogenous technical change, such as learning by doing. Importantly, the equivalent coefficient for other industries is weak, which confirms – Kaldor argued – that manufacturing industry alone possesses the necessary properties for a strong CCC process to occur.[1]

Kaldor combined this classically inspired model, where commodities exchange against commodities, with a money economy and, specifically, Keynesian 'effective demand'. The key concepts employed by Kaldor in his analysis of effective demand were the income multiplier, investment accelerator and a central role for the state in redressing the constraints to a virtuous cycle of growth in demand and supply. Specifically, Kaldor focused on the state creating an accommodative money supply, maintaining demand through regulating business cycles and encouraging positive cumulative growth processes for manufacturing, while also redressing negative feedback loops via industry and regional policies. Finally, Kaldor, following Harrod (1957), identified the key role of exports as an 'autonomous' source of demand. Exports are regarded as particularly important in this context. First, more directly, they are a discrete source of demand. Second, less directly, they fund a higher level of imported intermediate and capital goods, permitting a higher level of output to be attained. Competitive imported capital and intermediate inputs may also embody more productive new technologies than their domestic equivalents.

In this model, it is the growth of exports relative to imports that is the key determinant of total national output. Specifically, 'the growth rate of exports, together with the *income* elasticity of imports, govern the growth rate of the economy' (Kaldor 1985: 67). This relates to what has come to be known as 'the balance of payments constraint to growth' (BPCG) (McCombie and Thirlwall 1994). Put simply, over the long run, a nation must adjust its level of output and income to its volume of net imports to achieve current account balance. '[T]rade is kept in balance by variations of production and incomes rather than by price variations: a proposition which implies that the income elasticity of demand of a country's inhabitants for imports and those of foreigners for its exports are far more important explanatory variables than price elasticities' (Kaldor 1985). The fundamental determinant of the income elasticities of a nation's demand for imports, and of other countries' demands for its exports, is its industrial structure or, more specifically, its capacity to produce goods and related services which compete on both price and non-price features – the latter including high quality, performance, design, customisation, embodied leading technologies and marketing (Kaldor 1985: 69; UNIDO 2018). Kaldor did not deny that price elasticities are important for some low-value goods or bulk commodities, but this raises the prospect of adverse terms of trade, with the adverse consequences described by Prebisch (1950).

The balance of payments constraint to growth derives from a profound scepticism among CCC writers about both exchange rates adjustment mechanisms and domestic relative prices as means of redressing external imbalances and reallocating resources to more productive industries. Kaldor, like all CCC writers, rejected 'comparative advantage' as a principle of national and international resource allocation, mainly because of its assumptions of constant returns in all industries, identical technology across nations, and the possibility that a nation could specialise in industries with adverse terms of trade and low scope for productivity growth (Kaldor 1985: 62–3). Countries subject to severe BPCG experience a vicious cycle, with low initial growth and specialisation in industries such as bulk commodities or low-value goods. These are industries with low scope for productivity and technological change and few input–output linkages with other local industries. In such a nation or region, there is also likely to be an absence of positive externalities, such as a skilled and occupationally diverse workforce, research facilities and infrastructure.

As Thirlwall (2002: 54) argued, the BPCG 'leads into centre-periphery models of growth and development which ... predict divergence between regions and countries in the world economy'. A distinguishing feature of 'the industrially developed countries [is that] high income elasticities for exports and low income elasticities for imports frequently go together' (Kaldor 1985: 69). Kaldor (1970) employed similar 'vicious or virtuous cycle' arguments to explain *regional growth disparities within nations*, not through a strict BPCG (since regions share a common currency and border each other), but through differences in the income elasticity of demand for their 'exports' and 'imports'.

Whilst Keynes argued for the central role of the state in managing business cycles, the control of which may require far-reaching extension of public ownership and limitations on the disposition of private capital, the level of analysis remained the macro economy. Keynes was largely silent on the impact of industrial structure and of industrial development policies on macroeconomic performance. For Kaldor and other CCC writers after Young, however, cumulative growth processes – such as the realisation of external economies and increasing returns – may be inherent in the growth of markets, although there are also substantial barriers to the growth of demand and productive capacity in *both* developing and developed economies. Indeed, for Kaldor the *initiation* and *maintenance* of these growth processes requires significant state action in both developing and developed economies.

Kaldor's identification of the key role of the state in overcoming the small size of the market drew on the study of the early industrialisation of Germany and the USA. He wrote that '[w]hat distinguishes the successful industrialisers from the others was the use of relatively moderate tariffs – no greater than was necessary to make domestic industries profitable – and a protective tariff that was carefully designed in favour of those industries that had the capability of developing an export potential, and not just a substitute for imports' (Kaldor 1985: 66). Kaldor also identified multiple barriers to growth within *developed* economies, notably the UK, due to factors such as the inability of the market to generate a sufficient supply of skilled labour and the operation of vicious growth cycles that had created large regional income disparities that lowered the growth of aggregate demand. He further pointed out how balance of payments constraints limit the development of advanced manufactures which, in turn, reinforces this constraint. Redressing each of these barriers in developed economies requires specific industrial, regional, technological and tax policies.

Kaldor's contribution to CCC effectively laid out an alternative epistemology to neoclassicism. Social reality is treated as fundamentally different – founded on consciousness and intentionality; and with complex feedback loops that make it difficult or impossible to separate cause and effect. Change is the only constant in social life. Controlled experimentation, analogous to that in the physical sciences, is impossible in economic analysis that relates to the real world. Accordingly, research should proceed inductively, identifying 'empirical regularities' or 'stylised facts' which are, however, historically contingent, changing over time with transformations in the economic system. Thus, 'it is impossible to distinguish facts that are precise and at the same time suggestive and intriguing in their implications, and that admit of no exception' (Kaldor 1985: 8–9). On this reasoning, the objective of CCC is not to construct a grand unified theory accounting for all empirical regularities: rather, separate theories may be required for each 'stylised fact' (Kaldor 1985: 8).

CONCLUDING REMARKS

The influence of CCC, both as a formal model and a general principle, in understanding economic and social change has been substantial, as described in this chapter. Yet big challenges exist for extending the usefulness of this current within political economic analysis. We conclude by noting three, relating to research method, service industries and the effects of financialisation.

CCC is deeply critical of mainstream economics for the priority it gives to the construction of mathematically determinate equilibrium models and for how this determines both its assumptions and objects of study. Ironically, a related criticism can also be made of trying to model CCC growth processes and outcomes in ways that can be empirically tested by using official economic statistics. Whilst it is critical to be able to test any theory's core propositions, many of the core propositions of CCC are not readily capable of refutation by using econometric methods. This is true of key propositions relating to institutions, technical innovation and knowledge spillovers, workforce skills, inter-firm coordination, and efficacy of state industry and economic policy. These variables are not measured in standard national economic accounting frameworks; and their workings and effects are difficult to test by way of null hypotheses. Other research methods and means of weighing evidence, such as case studies of public policies and their effectiveness (see Wade 2004), must be deployed to study these variables.

The specific issue of increasing returns also needs further consideration. This is a key aspect of the CCC approach and, from Young and Kaldor to the present, increasing returns have been regarded as pertaining primarily to manufacturing industry. What then of service industries? Leading CCC scholars, such as Thirlwall (2002), have noted that evidence for 'the increasing-returns character of service industries is steadily strengthening': but these have not yet been subjected to comparably extensive analysis nor greatly modified the standard CCC model. As leading innovation scholar W. Brian Arthur (1996) has observed: 'increasing returns reign in ... knowledge-based industries'. This applies especially to 'service' industries where production processes and/or outputs are digitised, including software, ICT, telecoms, banking, insurance, publishing and logistics (e.g. Amazon). Key questions include: what are the sources of increasing returns in these service industries, how do they differ from those in manufacturing, and what are their implications for the CCC macro growth model?

Finally, CCC also needs to engage with analyses of financialisation. CCC evolved to explain the revolutionary character of a nascent Industrial Revolution and remains well adapted to explaining the growth dynamics of a modern industrial economy. However, CCC theorists have been largely silent on the factors driving the rapid growth of the current 'financialised' economy and its apparently constraining effects on both demand – through intensifying income and wealth inequality within nations – and incentives to invest in manufacturing and innovation (Storm 2018). Here too there is scope for further development and progress in the contribution of CCC in political economic research.

NOTE

1. McCombie et al. (2002) provide a comprehensive discussion of methods, interpretation and implications of Verdoorn's Law. Somewhat confusingly, the Verdoorn Law and several other related propositions are also referred to as Kaldor's Laws: see Thirlwall (2002).

REFERENCES

Argyrous, G. (2011) 'Economic Evolution and Cumulative Causation', in Argyrous, G. and Stilwell, F. (eds), *Readings in Political Economy: Economics as a Social Science*, 3rd edn, Sydney: Pluto Press, pp. 144–51.

Argyrous, G. and Bamberry, G. (2009) 'Cumulative Causation and Industrial Development: The Regional Stage', in Berger, S. (ed.), *The Foundations of Non-Equilibrium Economics: The Principles of Circular and Cumulative Causation*, London and New York: Routledge, pp. 65–76.

Arthur, W.B. (1996) 'Increasing Returns and the New World of Business', *Harvard Business Review*, **74** (4), pp. 100–109.

Berger, S. and Elsner, W. (2007) 'European Contributions to Evolutionary Institutional Economics: The Cases of "Cumulative Circular Causation" (CCC) and "Open Systems Approach" (OSA): Some Methodological and Policy Implications', *Journal of Economic Issues*, **41** (2), pp. 529–37.

Chenery, H. (1961) 'Comparative Advantage and Development Policy', *American Economic Review*, **51** (1), and in Chenery, H. (1979) *Structural Change and Development Policy*, Washington, DC: Oxford University Press for the World Bank, pp. 272–308.

Chenery, H. (1979) *Structural Change and Development Policy*, Washington, DC: Oxford University Press for the World Bank.

Cimoli M., Dosi, G. and Stiglitz J.E. (2009) *Industrial Policy and Development: The Political Economy of Capabilities Accumulation*, New York: Oxford University Press.

Fussell, E. (2010) 'The Cumulative Causation of International Migration in Latin America', *The Annals of the American Academy of Political and Social Science*, **630** (1), pp. 162–77.

Hall, P.A. and Soskice, D. (eds) (2001) *Varieties of Capitalism*, Oxford: Oxford University Press.

Harrod, R.F. (1957) *International Economics*, 4th edn, Cambridge: Cambridge University Press.

Hirschman A. (1958) *The Strategy of Economic Development*, New Haven, CT and London: Yale University Press.

Hodgson, G.M. (1999) *Evolutionary Economics: Its Nature and Future*, Cambridge: Cambridge University Press.

Hodgson, G.M. (2019) *Evolutionary Economics: Its Nature and Future*, Cambridge: Cambridge University Press.

Johnson, C. (1982) *MITI and the Japanese Miracle: The Growth of Industrial Policy, 1925–1975*, Stanford, CA: Stanford University Press.

Kaldor, N. (1966) *Causes of the Slow Rate of Economic Growth of the United Kingdom*, Cambridge: Cambridge University Press.

Kaldor, N. (1970) 'The Case for Regional Policies', *Scottish Journal of Political Economy*, **17** (November), pp. 337–48.

Kaldor, N. (1972) 'The Irrelevance of Equilibrium Economics', *The Economic Journal*, **82** (328), pp. 1237–55.

Kaldor, N. (1985) *Economics Without Equilibrium*, New York: M.E. Sharpe.

Kim, K.M. (2021) 'Persistence or Change: Evolution of the Korean Developmental State', *Journal of Australian Political Economy*, **87**, pp. 121–44.

Krugman, P. (1991) *Geography and Trade*, Cambridge, MA: MIT Press.

Martin, R. (1999) 'The New "Geographical Turn" in Economics: Some Critical Reflections', *Cambridge Journal of Economics*, **23** (1), pp. 63–91.

McCombie, J. and Thirlwall, A.P. (1994) *The Balance of Payments Constraint to Growth*, New York: St. Martin's Press.

McCombie, J., Pugno, M. and Soro, B. (eds) (2002) *Productivity Growth and Economic Performance: Essays on Verdoorn's Law*, London: Palgrave Macmillan.

Myrdal, G. (1944) *An American Dilemma: The Negro Problem and Modern Democracy*, 2 vols, New York: Harper and Row.

Myrdal, G. (1958) *Economic Theory and Underdeveloped Regions*, London: Methuen.

Myrdal, G. (1968) *Asian Drama: An Inquiry into the Poverty of Nations*, New York: Twentieth Century Fund.

Myrdal, G. (1975) *Against the Stream: Critical Essays in Economics*, New York: Vintage Books.

North, D.C. (1991) 'Institutions', *Journal of Economic Perspectives*, **5** (1), pp. 97–112.

Pasinetti, L. (1981) *Structural Change and Economic Growth: A Theoretical Essay on the Dynamics of the Wealth of Nations*, Cambridge: Cambridge University Press.

Prebisch, R. (1950) *The Economic Development of Latin America and Its Principal Problems*, New York: United Nations, Economic Commission for Latin America.

Reinert, E.S. (2007) 'Institutionalism Ancient, Old and New: A Historical Perspective on Institutions and Uneven Development', in Chang, H.-J. (ed.), *Institutional Change and Economic Development*, Tokyo and New York: United Nations University Press and Anthem, pp. 53–74.

Rosenstein-Rodan, P.N. (1943) 'Problems of Industrialisation in Eastern and South-Eastern Europe', *Economic Journal*, **58**, reprinted in Agarwala, N. and Singh, S.P. (eds) (1975), *The Economics of Underdevelopment: A Series of Articles and Papers*, Delhi: Oxford University Press, pp. 245–55.

Schmid, A.A. (1999) 'Circular and Cumulative Causation', in O'Hara, P.A. (ed.), *Encyclopedia of Political Economy, Volume 1*, London and New York: Routledge.

Setterfield, M. (1999) 'Path dependency', in O'Hara, P.A. (ed.), *Encyclopedia of Political Economy, Volume 2*, London and New York: Routledge, pp. 841–3.

Stilwell, F. (2011) *Political Economy: The Contest of Economic Ideas*, 3rd edn, Melbourne: Oxford University Press.

Storm, S. (2018) 'Financialization and Economic Development: A Debate on the Social Efficiency of Modern Finance', *Development and Change*, **49** (2), pp. 302–29.

Thirlwall, A.P. (2002) *The Nature of Economic Growth*, Cheltenham, UK and Northampton, MA, USA: Edward Elgar Publishing.

Toner, P. and Butler, G. (2004) 'Some Reflections on "Governing the Market"', *Issues and Studies: A Quarterly Journal on China, Taiwan and East Asia*, **40** (1), pp. 81–102.

Toner, P. and Butler, G. (2009) 'Cumulative Causation and Northeast Asian Post-war Industry Policy', in Berger, S. (ed.), *The Foundations of Non-Equilibrium Economics: The Principles of Circular and Cumulative Causation*, London and New York: Routledge, pp. 43–64.

UNIDO [United Nations Industrial Development Organization] (2017) *Industrial Development Report 2018. Demand for Manufacturing: Driving Inclusive and Sustainable Industrial Development*, Vienna: UNIDO ID/448.

Veblen, T. (1898) 'Why Economics is not an Evolutionary Science', *Quarterly Journal of Economics*, **12** (July), pp. 373–97.

Wade, R. (2004) *Governing the Market: Economic Theory and the Role of Government in East Asian Industrialization*, 2nd edn, Princeton, NJ: Princeton University Press.

Wade, R. (2004) 'The Reprinting of Governing the Market: A Dinner Table Conversation', *Issues and Studies*, **40** (1), pp. 103–34.

Young, A. (1928) 'Increasing Returns and Economic Progress', *Economic Journal*, **38** (December), pp. 527–42.

10. Evolutionary political economy

Tae-Hee Jo

Evolutionary economics is a wide-ranging branch of economics whose borders are difficult to demarcate. For most mainstream evolutionary economists, evolution is treated mainly as a quantitative change in economic variables. For evolutionary political economists (or heterodox evolutionary economists),[1] evolution is historical, social and cultural change that cannot be properly comprehended by deploying purely mechanistic, biological, static and equilibrium methods. That is, evolution is a cumulative, path-dependent and open-ended process (or, in Veblen's language, a 'blind drift' process) that inevitably involves changes in institutional arrangements and social relationships. Nothing in society remains permanently fixed: the entire cultural and social system and its constituents are subject to change.

The aim of this chapter is to characterise evolutionary political economy as a study of social evolution, which is an alternative to mainstream economics. A case study approach is deployed to support this general argument.[2] Specifically, the Marshallian and mainstream evolutionary economics represented by Nelson and Winter (1982) is examined and critiqued. The key argument is that, while Nelson and Winter's evolutionary theory provides a more realistic account of firms' behaviour than Marshallian neoclassical theory does, it is a mainstream evolutionary theory in much the same sense as Marshall's economics is quasi-evolutionary neoclassical economics. In other words, the type of critique that Veblen ([1900] 1961b) long ago made of Marshall's evolutionary economics can be updated and extended to reveal the underlying problems in Nelson and Winter's evolutionary theory. Given this, the latter theory is best understood as a protective modification of neoclassical economics and is antithetical to proper evolutionary political economy.

This chapter is organised in the following manner. The first section discusses the basic characteristics of evolutionary approaches whose lineage extends back to classical political economy and Thorstein Veblen's economics. The second section contrasts Veblen's evolutionary economics to Alfred Marshall's economics. Having established these foundations, the third section examines the theoretical and methodological commitments of Nelson and Winter's evolutionary theory which has significantly influenced evolutionary approaches since the early 1980s. By examining its concepts of rationality, optimisation, equilibrium and evolution, Nelson and Winter's evolutionary analysis of institutions (markets and firms) is shown to be fundamentally different from evolutionary political economy in the tradition of Thorstein Veblen. The final section concludes the chapter by arguing that evolutionary political economy can be a radical intellectual enterprise in modern heterodox economic analysis.

EVOLUTIONARY APPROACHES IN ECONOMICS

In the vast body of economics literature, the term 'evolution' is used in quite general and diverse ways. It denotes, for example, change, dynamics, growth, development, progress or transformation. These interpretations are manifest in various evolutionary approaches in economics that have dealt with different aspects of socio-economic changes.

Classical political economy in the eighteenth and nineteenth centuries, even before the emergence of evolutionary theories in biology, held an evolutionary view in regard to, inter alia, the process of (re)production, the accumulation of wealth and capital, and the changes in social institutions and relationships in historical time.[3] Adam Smith, for example, one of the Enlightenment thinkers, viewed the social order (and institutional arrangements therein) of his time as the outcome of the past evolutionary process which set the course of future social developments. Smith's view, however, does not imply that social evolution is always progressive, or the capitalist market system would invariably lead to human flourishing (Alvey 2003; Roncaglia 2005: 83). Another example is Karl Marx, often considered as the precursor of evolutionary-institutional analysis (Gruchy [1947] 1967: 275). Marx's theoretical system entails both gradual and radical changes in the social structures, which are endogenously driven by class conflict and technical development. To quote Marx: 'There is a continual movement of growth in productive forces, of destruction in social relations, of formation of ideas; the only immutable thing is the abstraction of movement' (Marx [1847] 1963: 110). Evolution in Marx's system is not predetermined but unfolding in the complex socio-historical context (Sowell 1985: 24; Henry 1990: 48–50; Dugger and Sherman 2000: 4–9).

The most important figure in the development of evolutionary political economy is Thorstein Veblen, who was influenced by Darwin's evolutionism and the German historical school. Veblen explicitly addressed the importance of evolutionary thinking in economics and articulated it, although not fully developed, as a critique of, and an alternative to, the utilitarian version of classical economics. Veblen's evolutionary economics is historical, social, cultural, institutional, endogenous, cumulative and non-teleological. For Veblen, evolution is a 'cumulative unfolding process or an institutional adaptation to cumulatively unfolding exigencies' (Veblen [1900] 1961b: 73) and, accordingly, 'evolutionary economics is the theory of a process of cultural growth as determined by the economic interest, a theory of cumulative sequence of economic interactions stated in terms of the process itself' (Veblen [1898] 1961c: 77). As such, central to Veblen's evolutionary economics is the vision that nothing is natural and normal in social evolution, since any change is driven by purposeful actions in the social context without a predetermined end.

Essentially, from the perspectives of classical political economists and Veblen, the velocity, direction and outcome of social evolution is open-ended. In other words, it is non-teleological. Nor does social evolution mirror natural evolution. Although classical political economy bears an evolutionary vision of economy and society, its theoretical system is not truly evolutionary to the extent that the principal problem, as understood by key figures such as Ricardo and Mill, was to 'determine the laws which regulate this distribution [of rent, profit and wages]' (Ricardo [1817] 1951: 5) and to find the 'laws of human nature' that account for the 'production and distribution of wealth' (Mill [1836] 1967: 318). This principal problem was usually pursued in quite mechanistic terms, seeking to find equilibrium outcomes or tendencies. As Hamilton writes:

> The classicist has always viewed change as discontinuous and has held that it is a re-establishment of an equilibrium or state of quiescence. The cause of change is independent of the economy; change is caused by disturbing elements from without the system. A new adjustment must be made in response to the disturbance caused by these elements. (Hamilton 1970: 17)

On the contrary, the evolutionary institutionalist

> considers change to be a part of the economic process. Instead of viewing the economy as a fixed system periodically prodded into movement to a new point of non-motions, he holds that economy is at all times undergoing a process of cumulative change, and that the study of economics is the study of [evolutionary] process. (Hamilton 1970: 17)

The evolutionary view of the economy thus demands a theoretical system radically different from static and equilibrium-centred economics. Various schools within heterodox economics, particularly evolutionary institutionalists in the United States and economists associated with the European Association for Evolutionary Political Economy (which also includes other streams in evolutionary economics and heterodox economics), have taken Veblen's evolutionary ideas very seriously (Lee 2009).[4] However, Veblen's ([1898] 1961c) call for an evolutionary science has been not understood or not heeded by mainstream economists. Those who are sympathetic to an evolutionary theorising rely mainly on Spencerian–Marshallian ideas.

ORIGINS OF MAINSTREAM EVOLUTIONARY THEORY: MARSHALL AND SPENCER

Alfred Marshall's economics is multi-faceted. In it we see the difficulties, and likely the impossibility, of trying to reconcile two fundamentally different ways of doing economics. Marshall's pre-analytical vision is evolutionary, holding that: 'economics, like biology, deals with a matter, of which the inner nature and constitution, as well as the outer form, are constantly changing' (Marshall [1890] 1920: 772). If something is constantly in motion, nothing is preordained. This is the gist of evolutionary thinking that implies the open system in which interactions between agents and surrounding environment lead to change. Such an evolutionary open-system view is implied by Marshall when he writes:

> 'Progress' or 'evolution,' industrial and social, is not mere increase or decrease. It is organic growth chastened and confined and occasionally reversed by the decay of innumerable factors, each of which influences and is influenced by those around it; and every such mutual influence varies with the stages which the respective factors have already reached in their growth. (Marshall [1898] 1966: 317)

Despite this clearly specified evolutionary vision, Marshall regularly deploys static and partial methods. Furthermore, the theory for which he is best known is utilitarian and marginalist (Veblen [1900] 1961b; Henry 1990: 211–18; Thomas 1991; Pratten 1998; Laurent 2000; Lawson 2016). Marshall's static and partial analysis presupposes a closed system in which a law-like tendency towards an equilibrium state is the norm. Such a mechanical process within the mentally constructed closed system is predicated on the utilitarian-marginalist axioms, such as relative scarcity, optimising behaviour and competition under the 'normal' conditions of life (Henry 1990: 156; Thomas 1991). Thus, Marshall's economics bears an obvious contradiction between his vision and his theory-method. To put it another way, his theoretical system and method are inadequate to account for ever-changing reality (Pratten 1998: 122; Mayhew 2016: 132). This is Marshall's 'dilemma' (see Hart, 2003, 2012). And this is precisely the reason Veblen called Marshall's economics 'neoclassical' in the sense that Marshall's economics both continues (in terms of taxonomic methods) and discontinues (in terms of the evolutionary vision) the utilitarian version of classical economics (Veblen [1900] 1961b: 171–3; Lawson 2016).

How is it possible that these two seemingly contradictory elements – an evolutionary vision and a static theory-method – constitute Marshall's economics? Trying to escape the contradiction, Marshall separates 'pure theory' from 'applied theory'. It is the pure theory from which Marshall's 'general theory' is derived: 'the general theory of the equilibrium of demand and supply is a Fundamental Idea running through the frames of all the various parts of the central problem of Distribution and Exchange' (Marshall [1890] 1920: viii). Marshall's timeless supply–demand engine results in a mechanical equilibrium, which is at odds with the evolutionary process (Thomas 1991). Insofar as Marshall's *Principles of Economics* ([1890] 1920) is concerned, his applied evolutionary view of the economy is an add-on to the pure general theory to the extent that change occurs within the fixed and closed system. Thus, evolution is putative, quantitative and adaptive, rather than being historical, qualitative and transformative. Such a conception of evolution is neither Darwinian nor Veblenian (see, for example, Veblen [1898] 1961c; Hamilton 1970; Hodgson 1993; Mayhew 1998).

What exactly, then, is the evolutionary vision in Marshall's economics? Consider the following passage:

> The doctrine that those organisms which are the most highly developed [...] are those which are most likely to survive in the struggle for existence, is itself in process of development [...] The law of 'survival of the fittest' states that those organisms tend to survive which are best fitted to utilize the environment for their own purposes. (Marshall [1890] 1920: 241–2)

As in Marshall's famous biological analogy of the 'trees in the forest', individuals struggle (or compete) for existence and only the best fitted to their environment survive and grow (Marshall [1890] 1920: 315–16). This is the law of the survival of the fittest or the natural selection doctrine of Herbert Spencer, applied to social organisations as well as every living organism. As noted previously, Marshall's view of evolution presumes the 'fixed' environment – that is, the competitive market system that is assumed to be natural, normal, universal and, thereby, unalterable and unquestionable. How the environment emerged and has evolved into the present state is never taken into account. From Veblen's perspective, such an evolutionary approach is pre-Darwinian (Spencerian) and taxonomic in the sense that it is predominantly of the 'normal' conditions (Veblen [1898] 1961c: 67; Henry 1990: 211–18; Jennings and Waller 1998: 209–11; Lawson 2016: 42). When evolution is looked at through the lens of Spencerian evolutionism, society is an organic whole; its evolution amounts to progress; progress is gradual and unhurried; and evolution brings about the harmonious equilibrium state (Spencer [1862] 1890: 524–5; Hofstadter [1944] 1955; Bannister 1979; Laurent 2000; Beck 2013).

If evolution is such a unidirectional progressive process, the present is the best outcome of the past processes, and a better future is predetermined by the natural selection process at work. The causality goes from nature (environment) to organisms (agents). In short, the Spencerian doctrine promotes a view that people have no power to change their social environment since it is the result of the 'material process of inexorable evolution' (Noble 1958: 61).

Similarly, Marshall's evolution presumes a change towards the equilibrium position at which inefficient and incompetent individuals are squeezed out. Provided that the socio-economic environment, along with fixed preferences and behavioural patterns, is a given datum, the selection of the fit is predetermined rather than open-ended. For both Spencer and Marshall, the leisure class, the rich, ruling elites, thriving business enterprises and their owners and managers are the naturally selected social classes, because they are allegedly most efficient and competent. The fit as well as the given are, therefore, legitimated – that is to say, 'the existing is normal and the normal is right' (Hofstadter [1944] 1955: 155; see also Henry 1995: 81).

On the contrary, from Veblen's social evolutionary perspective, 'the fit' in the Spencer and Marshall's evolutionism are, in effect, the socially unfit in that they are the predatory who expropriate the social surplus created by the working class and the community at large (Edgell 1975; Adams 1991; Dugger 2006; Martins 2018). They are the wasteful who use the expropriated surplus or the accumulated wealth in a socially disserviceable manner (e.g. conspicuous consumption and military spending). They are detrimental to social welfare in that they control the production of goods and services in their own interest of pecuniary gain (e.g. business control of industry such as 'sabotage of production'). Moreover, they are the socially inefficient whose wasteful expenditure and irresponsible behaviour generate social costs (Veblen [1901] 1961a: 299; [1914] 1964b: 123, 144; Edgell and Tilman 1989: 1009; Frigato and Santos-Arteaga 2012: 83). Underlying the reversal between the fit and the unfit is the Veblenian view that the system of institutions under capitalism is organised in such a way as to distribute the social surplus in favour of the unfit who are least desirable and serviceable to the progress of the entire society. Thus, evolution cannot be equated to progress. As for the Spencerian–Marshallian doctrine of the survival of the fittest, Veblen ([1896] 1973: 451–2) puts it that:

> It is [...] only by injecting a wholly illegitimate teleological meaning to the term 'fittest' as used by Darwin and the Darwinists that the expression 'survival of the fittest' is made to mean a survival of the socially desirable individuals [...] the present competitive system does not by any means uniformly results in a working out of favorable result by a process of natural selection.

In order to legitimate the existing economic system, it is therefore necessary to hide the social foundations of the system (e.g. class differentiation and exploitation) as if the society were an organic whole which has naturally evolved into the most desirable state and in which there exists a common interest of all the members of the society (Henry 2018). Marshall's economics, inspired by Spencer's evolutionism, is the case in point. Hiding the social foundations is done by equating human society to nature in which the natural selection mechanism is alleged to be the driver and cause of the evolutionary process, by normalising and naturalising the given system, and by replacing deliberate human agency with the hypothetical, asocial 'representative agent' or the 'lighting calculator of pleasures and pains' (Veblen [1898] 1961c: 73). By contrast, in Veblen's evolutionary economics, society is not an organic, harmonious whole. It is a class-based capitalist system with no common interest. Its cumulative unfolding process is driven by purposeful human agency. Therefore, social evolution does not entail unidirectional progress or the equilibrium state (Henry 2018).

Marshall's economics, coupled with Spencerian evolutionism, forcefully lends support to the view that any institution which serves vested interests should remain fixed. This is a theoretical and ideological defence of the existing social order and vested interests therein. For this and other reasons, Veblen was critical of Marshall's evolutionary economics:

> Any sympathetic reader of Professor Marshall's great work – and that must mean every reader – comes away with a sense of swift and smooth movement and interaction of parts; but it is the movement of a consummately conceived and self-balanced mechanism, not that of a cumulatively

unfolding process or an institutional adaptation to cumulatively unfolding exigencies. The taxonomic bearing is, after all, the dominant feature. (Veblen [1900] 1961b: 173)

According to Veblen, Marshall's theory bears 'an air of evolutionism', which is nothing but a 'quasi-evolutionary tone of neo-classical political economy', since Marshall's law-like theories under the postulate of normality are not capable of explicating deliberate or transformative human agency and its reciprocal and cumulative relationship with institutional changes (Veblen [1900] 1961b: 175, 178). Essentially, such a quasi-evolutionary theory, anchored in the conception of normality and the doctrine of the survival of the fittest, is incompatible with Veblen's evolutionism (and with classical political economy's vision of social evolution). As discussed in the following section, it is Marshall's quasi-evolutionary thinking that is kept and revived by Nelson and Winter (1982), the most influential contribution to mainstream evolutionary economics.

NELSON AND WINTER'S EVOLUTIONARY THEORY

Since the publication of Nelson and Winter's *An Evolutionary Theory of Economic Change* (1982), evolutionary economics has been given new attention from economists.[5] Among heterodox economists, however, the reception of Nelson and Winter's (hereafter NW) evolutionary theory is divided. Proponents think that NW's theory is a revival of the long-neglected evolutionary tradition in economics. Hodgson (2019: 111), for example, considers NW's theory 'heterodox' in the sense that it resembles Veblen's post-Darwinian evolutionary economics and that it emphasises the 'complexity, uncertainty, and ongoing change in the real world'. Hodgson (2007: 311) also holds that NW has 'inspired an entire new generation of evolutionary economists and played a major role in the development of an evolutionary alternative to neoclassical theory'. In a similar vein, Becker and Knudsen (2012: 243, 252) extol that 'Nelson and Winter provided the foundation for evolutionary economics and the evolutionary theory of the firm [...] [which] has been decisive in advancing our knowledge about the origins and evolution of firm structure and boundaries'. Other 'heterodox' proponents also argue that the NW's theory is either compatible with or complementary to 'original' evolutionary-institutional economics (see, for example, Foss 1998; Nightingale and Potts 2003; Hodgson and Knudsen 2004; Hodgson 2013). Such a favourable reception of NW's theory within heterodox economics is exemplified by the fact that the Association for Evolutionary Economics granted Richard Nelson the prestigious Veblen–Commons Award in 2007.

Yet, other heterodox economists are critical of NW's theory. They argue that it does not offer a novel theoretical framework grounded in the actual socio-historical context and, hence, that it does not transcend the standard neoclassical framework (Mirowski [1983] 1998; Boulding 1984; Ramstad 1994; Vromen 1995, 2001; Mayhew 2000; Frigato and Santos-Arteaga 2012). Expanding this line of critique, I argue that NW's theory is an anti-Veblenian project that is akin to neoclassical economics: it offers a neoclassical alternative to Veblenian evolutionary theory. This argument is predicated on the examination of evolution, rationality, equilibrium, institutions and uncertainty in NW's theory. The purpose of this examination is to delineate distinctive features of an evolutionary political economy that has a more productive role in heterodox economics.

Rationality, Optimisation, Equilibrium and Evolution

The origins of NW's evolutionary theory can be found in Spencer's evolutionism and Marshall's neoclassical economics, rather than Darwin's evolutionism and Veblen's evolutionary economics.[6] This has profound implications for understanding NW's theory in particular and mainstream evolutionary economics in general – its methodological and theoretical foundations and its place in economics.

It is widely thought that NW's evolutionary theory is, as NW (1982: 94) themselves claim, an alternative to the Marshallian–neoclassical theory of the firm. This is due largely to the fact that NW modified the Marshall's assumption of profit maximisation. However, this does not amount to NW taking an anti-Marshallian or anti-neoclassical position. Both Marshall's Spencerian evolutionary vision delineated above and most of the principal neoclassical preconceptions and methods are kept intact in NW's theory. This argument can be developed more fully by considering the theoretical background from which NW's theory emerged.

One of the building blocks of neoclassical economics is the rationality assumption. In its original form, rationality is translated into optimising behaviour, given scarce resources and complete information as to the economic environment. Firms maximise profits by equating marginal cost to marginal revenue. This marginalist principle was challenged by, amongst others, the Oxford Economists' Research Group in the UK and Richard Lester in the USA between the 1930s and 1950s. The challengers argued that real-world business enterprises do not calculate marginal cost and marginal revenue and, hence, that profit maximisation is meaningless in the real world; nor do enterprises consider wage rates (or the marginal labour costs) as a significant factor in employment decisions. This means that the Marshallian demand–supply framework – and any theory based upon the marginalist doctrine – is flawed in view of real-world business activities (Lee 1981, 1984, 1990–91; Vromen 1995: ch. 2).

Reacting against these challenges, neoclassical economists, such as Armen Alchian and Milton Friedman, defended their conceptions of firms' rationality. Alchian's (1950) defence is that, in an uncertain market environment, whether an individual firm actually maximises profits is not important. Rather, firms are rational in the sense that they seek profit, be it maximum or otherwise, in order to survive and to grow: what is important to them is adjusting to the given market environment – that is, its searching for more profitable actions. Different in character, the argument put by Friedman (1953: 22) is that a surviving or growing firm should be assumed to be maximising profits because the natural (market) selection process drives non-optimising firms out of the market. Thus, Alchian's and Friedman's respective arguments sought to rescue the rationality assumption by extending the meaning of rationality – one by introducing uncertainty and search behaviour and the other by adding the market selection mechanism to profit-maximising behaviour. Both modifications are consonant with the Marshallian–Spencerian principle of the survival of the fittest and natural selection. Furthermore, the 'extended' marginalist doctrine is made compatible with a range of flexible firm behaviours, such as rule-of-thumb behaviour under uncertainty or with bounded rationality, opportunistic behaviour and transaction cost minimisation (Lee 1984; Ramstad 1994: 73–8; Vromen 1995: ch. 2). Either in its original or extended form, the rationality assumption not only prioritises the natural selection principle but also, thereby, divests human beings and organisations of power to change the institutional environment.

NW's evolutionary theory emerged out of this theoretical context. It rejects the standard profit maximisation assumption, due to its lack of a market selection mechanism which takes place over time. Instead, inspired by Alchian, NW argue that a firm should be understood as a profit-seeking organism that, facing competitive pressure and unpredictable external changes in the market environment, has to alter its decisions and behaviour to stay alive by making positive profits, if not maximum profits. In this 'evolutionary' context, optimising firm behaviour in the standard textbook does not adequately explain a firm's struggle for survival, such as learning by doing, trial and error, feedback and imitation (Nelson and Winter 1982: 31–3). NW's position is 'more realistic' than that of orthodox neoclassical economists who stick to the standard rationality assumption.

However, being more realistic does not mean that NW reject the entire neoclassical paradigm. Nor do NW envisage a completely alternative approach that would overcome the static and equilibrium-oriented analysis of neoclassical economics. Instead of taking a 'radical' route which Veblen ([1898] 1961c) envisioned, NW sought to extend neoclassical economics by incorporating evolutionary reasoning and methods. This is because neoclassical economics is, from NW's viewpoint, 'flexible and ever-changing' and 'more subtle and flexible than the image of it presented in the intermediate texts' (Nelson and Winter 1982: 6–7, 362). NW demonstrate that neoclassical economics can accommodate evolutionary reasoning if the latter is formulated in neoclassical terms. Seen in this way, NW's theory is 'better viewed as an explication and extension of the basic belief of "orthodox" theorists such as Alchian and Friedman' (Vromen 1995: 66).

To be clear, the neoclassical concepts of rationality and optimisation are not discarded completely in NW's theory; rather, rational-optimising behaviour is treated as a special case, while profit-seeking behaviour under uncertainty and complexity is the general case. External complexity is translated into agents' cognitive limitations which bind rational-optimising behaviour. In this respect, firms may and could maximise profits '[i]n a sufficiently calm and repetitive decision context' (Nelson and Winter 1982: 31). This implies that NW's firm is both rational in the normal situation and boundedly rational in the evolutionary context.

As such, bounded rationality (à la Herbert Simon) is one of the core assumptions for firms' behaviour in NW's theory. It should be noted that the concept of bounded rationality is not necessarily contradictory to the neoclassical framework, as it has been used in behavioural economics as a way of extending and protecting the idea of *homo economicus* (see Primrose 2017). If firms are boundedly rational they cannot optimise profits in the standard neoclassical sense since optimisation requires complete information about the future outcomes, but firms can still behave rationally by seeking profits and following rules. Such 'satisficing' behaviour (e.g. routine- or rule-following behaviour) leads to a 'sub-optimal' equilibrium. Thus, rules or routines take the place of optimisation in NW's theory. In this setting, uncertainty is taken into account but it is not 'fundamental' uncertainty (à la Keynes). Rather, it is uncertainty that is reconstituted into calculable risk or a probability distribution, which is consistent with the notion of cognitive limitation or imperfect information (Dunn 2001; Lee and Keen 2004; Henry 2012). The gist is that bounded rationality is a variant of rationality, which allows NW not only to sidestep the straitjacket of the static maximisation and rationality assumptions but also to remain comfortably in the neoclassical framework.

There are other similar self-contradictions (if seen from the Veblenian perspective) in NW's theory. In their evolutionary process driven by the competition for survival – that is, a process of dynamic technological changes (perceived as 'disequilibrium' and 'stochastic' processes) such as innovative and imitative behaviours undertaken by firms in search of a more profitable routine or behavioural rule – there emerges a 'stable equilibrium' state at which competitive forces grow at a constant rate of change (Nelson and Winter 1982: 32, 203, 236, 282). Indeed, greater emphasis is placed on disequilibrium rather than on equilibrium, as the latter is an essential feature of the neoclassical orthodoxy with which NW contend. Like profit maximisation, however, NW's concern is not about the equilibrium concept per se but about the disequilibrium 'process' leading to an equilibrium state.

In short, in NW's evolutionary theory, the equilibrium concept is not rejected but extended by emphasising the disequilibrium process. If one rejects equilibrium (or optimality) entirely, disequilibrium (or sub-optimality) cannot be defined, since the latter refers to the former. The mix of evolution and equilibrium is certainly puzzling. In Veblen's evolutionary approach, it is not possible to conceive of equilibrium along with evolution since Veblen's evolution takes place in the social context over historical time in which both equilibrium and disequilibrium have no meaning (Veblen [1898] 1961c; 1909). Yet, 'evolutionary equilibrium' is conceivable and possible in NW's approach, as in Marshall's economics, since evolution is conceptualised as an ahistorical and asocial change.

Institutions: Markets and Firms

NW's analysis of the market and firm also deserves critical discussion as to how institutions are treated. NW (1982: 266–8) define the market as the 'selection environment' composed of a set of routines or rules of the game, which determines whether a firm is profitable or not. Since only innovative and profitable firms survive, the market is crowded with efficient firms and, hence, is an institution of efficient resource allocation. NW's markets are thus redolent of the new institutionalist notion of institutions – that is, formal and informal constraints (or 'rules') defining individual choice sets and costs (North 1991: 97).

In NW's theory, boundedly rational individuals adjust themselves to the market. In an orderly market assuming the standard demand and supply curves, the competitive market equilibrium is achieved through individual consumers' and seller's satisficing, rule-following behaviours. This means that market transactions are made at the equilibrium, and the market price mechanism – that is, Marshall's supply–demand engine – functions as the organising principle of economic activities. In the long-run context, however, the market order is disturbed by innovative firm behaviour. In reaction to market disorder, individual firms search for new routines to stay alive and to grow. Consequently, either a new market order is established or at least the market moves towards a new equilibrium. In either circumstance, the market price mechanism rules the roost (see Mirowski [1983] 1998: 165, for a critique of NW's assumption of the standard demand curve).

A change in the market – that is, a shift from one equilibrium to another through the disequilibrium adjustment process or the probabilistic 'Markov' process – occurs largely because of each individual agent's struggle for survival. In this evolutionary process actions taken by individual agents are passive and adaptive in the sense that it is the exogenous market order that selects the fit (profitable firms) over the unfit (unprofitable firms) (Nelson and Winter 1982: 18–20, 266–8). Central to the market order is the price mechanism, the functional relationship between price and quantity. This is nothing but an extension of the neoclassical price theory. In other words, the neoclassical price theory in the short-run stable market is combined with the evolutionary theory in the long-run dynamic market. As a result, the standard market price mechanism is legitimated. This is precisely what NW's evolutionary theory is designed to do: '[r]eformulating basic assumptions of price theory so as to make things like demand and supply more compatible intellectually with the perspective of evolutionary theory' (Nelson 2013: 36).

Then what exactly is the firm in NW's theory? The firm is portrayed as a set of 'capabilities and decision rules', or set of behavioural routines, whose only and explicit objective is making profits (Nelson and Winter 1982: 4, 30). Although NW's theory of the firm is conceptually broader and more realistic than the neoclassical theory, it is still too simple and abstract to explain the real-world business enterprise. Still unknown are firms' internal organisational and ownership structures, their strategic decision-making processes and their places in and relation to the society beyond the economy. Furthermore, firm behaviour is directed by routines in a semi-automatic manner – as if genes determine the behaviour of the living organism – and is subject to the market conditions (Nelson and Winter 1982: 134–46). Like the Marshallian–neoclassical firm, NW's firm is nothing but a 'tree in the forest', a 'bowl of capital-jello', a black box and a production function (Mirowski [1983] 1998: 166; Vromen 1995: 77; Mayhew 2000: 58).

In short, NW's theory accounts for the evolution of the firm and its adjustment to the given and relatively stable market order. Such a relationship between the firm and the market is reversed in Veblen's theory, since Veblen was concerned primarily with the evolution of the system of institutions driven by the business enterprise (Mayhew 2000: 55; Jo 2019). Veblen's institutions are not given or fixed; nor are they taken for granted; nor do they emerge and evolve naturally. In Veblen's theory, an enquiry into the business enterprise as a driving force of social evolution in a particular historical context requires the analysis of the prevailing institutions, which are established, maintained and modified by human agents (Henry 2018: 163). The point of departure is the investigation of social institutions – that is, the way in which the 'settled habits of thought' and action in the 'community's scheme of life' is organised (Veblen 1909: 626–7). The industrial society Veblen was analysing is 'credit economy', the social institutions of which were organised in such a way as to make monetary profits in the interest of the business enterprise and its absentee owners and managers, as opposed to making serviceable goods in the interest of the population. Credit economy thus runs counter to 'money economy' in which good-making activity ('industry') is given priority over money-making activity ('business'). Absent in both Marshall's and NW's theories is the Veblenian view that, in the capitalist system, industry depends upon business or, to put it another way, the social provisioning process depends upon the business enterprise's money-making activities (Veblen [1901] 1961a: 298–9; 1904: 50–51, 150–51; Mayhew 2000: 58–9; Frigato and Santos-Arteaga 2012: 73–4; Jo and Henry 2015: 24–8; Jo 2018: 201).

Then how does Veblen conceptualise and explain the business enterprise vis-à-vis social evolution? In contrast to NW's narrowly defined and ahistorical firm, Veblen's business enterprise is a 'going concern' whose objective is survival and growth in size and power. The business enterprise engages in strategic management and production activities under fundamental uncertainty. In this context, business enterprise activities do not guarantee that goals are achieved even in a probabilistic sense. Investments or innovative activities, for example, do not necessarily lead to an expected increase in productive capital stock. Strategic enterprise activities may lead to the demise of the business enterprise, not because decisions are made poorly but because consequences are not predetermined or known a priori. Therefore, much effort goes into reducing uncertainty by, for example, enterprises making enduring working rules and decision-making structures, establishing 'goodwill' relationships with other actors in the society, engaging in aggressive pecuniary activities (for example, planned obsolescence and 'industrial sabotage'), and controlling the market environment including competition and the rules of the game. This means that the business enterprise is, in effect, created to reduce uncertainty and complexity in the real world in order to remain ongoing: it is not, as in NW's theory, a carrier of complexity that reacts passively to the external conditions (Valentinov 2013; Jo and Henry 2015; Jo 2019). Veblen's theory of the business enterprise is therefore incompatible with the mainstream evolutionary view that the competitive market is the selector and controller of the firm, as the selection mechanism is a creation of the business enterprise (Watkins 2010).

A yet more fundamental difference between NW's firm and Veblen's business enterprise is found in their respective functions in society. NW's firm is assumed to be a socially desirable and socially efficient institution whose survival and growth is in large part determined by the market and, consequently, whose normal productive activity provides necessary goods and services for society. Veblen's business enterprise is a socially predatory and socially inefficient institution that survives and grows by making monetary profits at the expense of welfare of the common people – thus, its efficiency in money terms becomes disserviceable and wasteful from a community's point of view. Such irreconcilable views are, as discussed thus far, predicated on the different notions of, and relationship between, evolution and institution. Essentially, Veblen's business enterprise is the 'master institution' of the capitalist economy, having the capacity to make socio-economic conditions in favour of itself and of the corporate managers and absentee owners whose interests are vested in the business enterprise (Veblen [1923] 1964a: 86–9). Such socio-economic contradictions as manifest in the uncertain evolutionary process of institutions are what Veblen's theory of business enterprise explains. NW's theory of the firm, however, does not offer any significant insight into how a socio-economic system actually evolves. Instead, it explains how the firm evolves and is selected by the market; hence it conforms to the ceremonial adequacy of neoclassical economics (Dugger 2006; Frigato and Santos-Arteaga 2012).

CONCLUSION

Evolutionary political economy is the study of social evolution that is an open-ended unfolding process pertaining to the organisation and reproduction of the economic system and its constituents in historical context. Social evolution is neither natural nor universal, as it is driven by purposeful actions embedded in social relationships. Such an evolutionary vision is manifested, if not invariably, in classical political economy's analysis of the process of (re)production, the accumulation of wealth and capital, and the changes in social institutions and relationships. Classical political economists, however, did not fully flesh out this vision into an evolutionary analysis because their primary concern was finding law-like tendencies in the capitalist system. This conflict between the evolutionary vision and the teleologic and taxonomic method led Veblen to argue that economics should be an evolutionary science – as an alternative to classical and neoclassical economics. Being an evolutionary science, economics should provide a historical and social account of how the economic system works and evolves over time and what drives changes in society. Veblen was sceptical about economics actually becoming an evolutionary science, however, since it is hard to break the hold of prevailing social institutions on how the economics discipline favours already received ideas and methods (see Jo 2021).

To distinguish evolutionary political economy from its mainstream counterpart, a significant portion of this chapter has been devoted to discussing how mainstream evolutionary economics developed in Marshall's footsteps. Essentially, in mainstream economics, evolution is perceived as ahistorical quantitative changes, coupled with the Spencerian doctrine of the survival of the fittest, and formulated in marginalist language including concepts such as rationality, optimisation and equilibrium. There is little consideration of purposeful actions coping with unpredictable historical processes, nor of transformative agency changing existing institutional arrangements. Nelson and Winter's evolutionary theory is in this mainstream tradition which reinforces Spencerian and marginalist doctrines. It is a vulgarisation of evolutionary political economy to the extent that it shifts attention from the social relationships and institutions underlying the historical dynamics of the economic system to the superficial phenomena by 'systemizing in a pedantic way, and proclaiming for everlasting truths, the banal and complacent notions held by the bourgeois agents of production about their own world, which is to them the best of all possible worlds' (Marx [1867] 1990: 174–5). Mainstream evolutionary economics is limited in explaining the underlying structural causes and effects of anomalies in society, such as economic, social and ecological crises.

In the economics discipline, the vulgarisation and marginalisation of relevant ideas is not unusual (see Lee 2009). It is not the most relevant, theoretically and empirically sound approach that is widely received in academia and society. Challenging this situation, evolutionary political economy has a more transformative role to play. This evolutionary view – be it classical, Marxian or Veblenian – is one of the building blocks of many heterodox research programmes. Moreover, various strands in heterodox economics, such as original institutional economics, post-Keynesian economics, radical political economy, regulation theory and the social structures of accumulation approach, have been developing an evolutionary theory that is in line with evolutionary political economy in its broader sense. Evolutionary political economy is a radical intellectual enterprise, presenting an alternative to the mainstream view that the economy is self-adjusting and governed by preordained market rules.

ACKNOWLEDGEMENT

This chapter is a revised version of the article, 'A Veblenian critique of Nelson and Winter's evolutionary theory', published in the *Journal of Economic Issues*, **55** (4), pp. 1101–17, December 2021. I thank William Waller, the editor of the *Journal*, the Association for Evolutionary Economics and Taylor & Francis for giving me permission to reproduce a significant part of the article.

NOTES

1. I use the term 'heterodox economics' and 'political economy' interchangeably. Heterodox economics refers to a group of economic schools of thought that collectively provide a scientific analysis of how the real-world capitalist economy works and evolves in historical and social context – or, in short, the social provisioning process under capitalism: see Lee (2008) and Jo et al. (2018).
2. Due to constraints of space, I do not examine all the evolutionary approaches in economics, such as Austrian–Hayekian, neo-Schumpeterian, evolutionary game theory and evolutionary complexity theory.

3. See Chapter 3 in this volume by Jamie Morgan where he describes the evolutionary viewpoint as one of the distinctive features of classical political economy, even though Smith did not use the term 'evolution'. Also note that 'evolutionary-institutional' economics in my chapter refers to the theoretical tradition following Veblen, Commons and Ayres, whose main concern is the evolution of social institutions. See David Hamilton (1970) for a detailed history of the evolutionary approach written from an evolutionary-institutional perspective.
4. In this chapter, neoclassical economics refers to a system of enquiry informed by deductivist-individualist methodology and built on a set of utilitarian-marginalist assumptions. Mainstream economics refers to a currently dominant group of economics schools of thought that share core neoclassical assumptions and methodology. A specific mainstream theory, model or policy may at times relax or modify one or more core assumptions but still retain overall continuity with the neoclassical core.
5. I deal mainly with Nelson and Winter (1982) in this chapter because of this book's importance and popularity in the field of 'modern' evolutionary economics. Hodgson (2019: 125) rightly notes that modern evolutionary economics has not much developed since Nelson and Winter's work in terms of the 'theoretical hard core'.
6. Although it is commonly assumed that the origins of NW's evolutionary economics stem from the economics of Joseph Schumpeter and Armen Alchian, NW hold that: 'our evolutionary theory is closer to the original Marshallian doctrine than is contemporary orthodoxy' (Nelson and Winter 1982: 45).

REFERENCES

Adams, J. (1991) 'Surplus, surplus, who's got the surplus? The subtractivist fallacy in orthodox economics', *Journal of Economic Issues*, **25** (1), pp. 187–97.
Alchian, A. (1950) 'Uncertainty, evolution, and economic theory', *Journal of Political Economy*, **58** (3), pp. 211–21.
Alvey, J. (2003) *Adam Smith, Optimist or Pessimist?* Aldershot: Ashgate.
Bannister, R. (1979) *Social Darwinism: Science and Myth in Anglo-American Social Thought*, Philadelphia, PA: Temple University Press.
Beck, N. (2013) 'Social Darwinism', in Ruse, M. (ed.), *The Cambridge Encyclopedia of Darwin and Evolutionary Thought*, Cambridge: Cambridge University Press, pp. 195–201.
Becker, M. and Knudsen, T. (2012) 'Nelson and Winter revisited', in Dietrich, M. and Krafft, J. (eds), *Handbook on the Economics and Theory of the Firm*, Cheltenham, UK and Northampton, MA, USA: Edward Elgar Publishing, pp. 243–55.
Boulding, K. (1984) 'Review of *An Evolutionary Theory of Economic Change* by Nelson, R. and Winter, S.G.', *American Journal of Agricultural Economics*, **66** (4), pp. 535–6.
Dugger, W. (2006) 'Veblen's radical theory of social evolution', *Journal of Economic Issues*, **40** (3), pp. 651–72.
Dugger, W. and Sherman, H. (2000) *Reclaiming Evolution: A Dialogue between Marxism and Institutionalism on Social Change*, London: Routledge.
Dunn, S. (2001) 'Bounded rationality is not fundamental uncertainty: a Post Keynesian perspective', *Journal of Post Keynesian Economics*, **23** (4), pp. 567–88.
Edgell, S. (1975) 'Thorstein Veblen's theory of evolutionary change', *American Journal of Economics and Sociology*, **34** (3), pp. 267–80.
Edgell, S. and Tilman, R. (1989) 'The intellectual antecedents of Thorstein Veblen: a reappraisal', *Journal of Economic Issues*, **23** (4), pp. 1003–26.
Foss, N. (1998) 'The competence-based approach: Veblenian ideas in the modern theory of the firm', *Cambridge Journal of Economics*, **22** (4), pp. 479–95.
Friedman, M. (1953) *Essays in Positive Economics*, Chicago, IL: University of Chicago Press.
Frigato, P. and Santos-Arteaga, F. (2012) 'Planned obsolescence and the manufacture of doubt: on social costs and the evolutionary theory of the firm', in Ramazzotti, P., Frigato, P. and Elsner, W. (eds), *Social Costs Today: Institutional Analyses of the Present Crises*, London: Routledge, pp. 73–95.

Gruchy, A. ([1947] 1967) *Modern Economic Thought: The American Contribution*, New York: Augustus M. Kelley.

Hamilton, D. (1970) *Evolutionary Economics: A Study of Change in Economic Thought*, Albuquerque: University of New Mexico Press.

Hart, N. (2003) 'Marshall's dilemma: equilibrium versus evolution', *Journal of Economic Issues*, **37** (4), pp. 1139–60.

Hart, N. (2012) *Equilibrium and Evolution: Alfred Marshall and the Marshallians*, New York: Palgrave Macmillan.

Henry, J. (1990) *The Making of Neoclassical Economics*, Boston, MA: Unwin Hyman.

Henry, J. (1995) 'God and the marginal product: comparative perspective – religion and the development of J. B. Clark's theory of distribution', *Research in the History of Economic Thought and Methodology*, **13**, pp. 75–101.

Henry, J. (2012) 'Time in economic theory', in King, J. (ed.), *The Elgar Companion to Post Keynesian Economics*', 2nd edn, Cheltenham, UK and Northampton, MA, USA: Edward Elgar Publishing, pp. 528–33.

Henry, J. (2018) 'Society and its institutions', in Jo, T.-H., Chester, L. and D'Ippoliti, C. (eds), *The Routledge Handbook of Heterodox Economics*, London: Routledge, pp. 163–75.

Hodgson, G. (1993) *Economics and Evolution*, Ann Arbor: University of Michigan Press.

Hodgson, G. (2007) 'The 2007 Veblen–Commons Award recipient: Richard R. Nelson', *Journal of Economics Issues*, **41** (2), p. 311.

Hodgson, G. (2013) 'Understanding organizational evolution: toward a research agenda using generalized Darwinism', *Organization Studies*, **34** (7), pp. 973–92.

Hodgson, G. (2019) *Is There a Future for Heterodox Economics?* Cheltenham, UK and Northampton, MA, USA: Edward Elgar Publishing.

Hodgson, G. and Knudsen, T. (2004) 'The firm as an interactor: firms as vehicles for habits and routines', *Journal of Evolutionary Economics*, **14** (3), pp. 281–307.

Hofstadter, R. ([1944] 1955) *Social Darwinism in American Thought*, revised edn, Boston, MA: Beacon Press.

Jennings, A. and Waller, W. (1998) 'The place of biological science in Veblen's economics', *History of Political Economy*, **30** (2), pp. 189–216.

Jo, T.-H. (2018) 'A heterodox theory of the business enterprise', in Jo, T.-H., Chester, L. and D'Ippoliti, C. (eds), *The Routledge Handbook of Heterodox Economics*, London: Routledge, pp. 199–212.

Jo, T.-H. (2019) 'The institutionalist theory of the business enterprise: past, present, and future', *Journal of Economic Issues*, **53** (3), pp. 597–611.

Jo, T.-H. (2021) 'Veblen's evolutionary methodology and its implications for heterodox economics in the calculable future', *Review of Evolutionary Political Economy*, **2** (2), pp. 277–95.

Jo, T.-H., Chester, L. and D'Ippoliti, C. (2018) 'The state of the art and challenges for heterodox economics', in Jo, T.-H., Chester, L. and D'Ippoliti, C. (eds), *The Routledge Handbook of Heterodox Economics*, London: Routledge, pp. 3–26.

Jo, T.-H. and Henry, J. (2015) 'The business enterprise in the age of money manager capitalism', *Journal of Economic Issues*, **49** (1), pp. 23–46.

Laurent, J. (2000) 'Alfred Marshall's annotations on Herbert Spencer's principles of biology', *Marshall Studies Bulletin* 7, accessed 20.4.2021 at www.disei.unifi.it/upload/sub/pubblicazioni/msb/2000/laurent7.pdf.

Lawson, T. (2016) 'What is this "school" called neoclassical economics?', in Morgan, J. (ed.), *What is Neoclassical Economics?* London: Routledge, pp. 30–80.

Lee, F. (1981) 'The Oxford challenge to Marshallian supply and demand: the history of the Oxford Economists' Research Group', *Oxford Economic Papers*, **33** (3), pp. 339–51.

Lee, F. (1984) 'The marginalist controversy and the demise of full cost pricing', *Journal of Economic Issues*, **18** (4), pp. 1107–32.

Lee, F. (1990–91) 'Marginalist controversy and Post Keynesian price theory', *Journal of Post Keynesian Economics*, **13** (2), pp. 252–63.

Lee, F. (2008) 'Heterodox economics', in Durlauf, S. and Blume, L. (eds), *The New Palgrave Dictionary of Economics*, 2nd online edn, London: Palgrave Macmillan, accessed 20.4.2021 at https://doi.org/10.1057/978-1-349-95121-5.

Lee, F. (2009) *A History of Heterodox Economics: Challenging the Mainstream in the Twentieth Century*, London: Routledge.

Lee, F. and Keen, S. (2004) 'The incoherent emperor: a heterodox critique of neoclassical microeconomic theory', *Review of Social Economy*, **62** (2), pp. 169–99.

Marshall, A. ([1890] 1920) *Principles of Economics*, 8th edn, London: Macmillan.

Marshall, A. ([1898] 1966) 'Mechanical and biological analogies in economics', in Pigou, A.C. (ed.), *Memorials of Alfred Marshall*, New York: Augustus M. Kelley, pp. 312–18.

Martins, N. (2018) 'The social surplus approach: historical origins and present state', in Jo, T.-H., Chester, L. and D'Ippoliti, C. (eds), *The Routledge Handbook of Heterodox Economics*, London: Routledge, pp. 41–53.

Marx, K. ([1847] 1963) *The Poverty of Philosophy*, New York: International Publishers.

Marx, K. ([1867] 1990) *Capital, Volume I*, New York: Penguin Books.

Mayhew, A. (1998) 'On the difficulty of evolutionary analysis', *Cambridge Journal of Economics*, **22** (4), pp. 449–61.

Mayhew, A. (2000) 'Veblen and theories of the "firm"', in Louçã, F. and Perlman, M. (eds), *Is Economics an Evolutionary Science? The Legacy of Thorstein Veblen*, Cheltenham, UK and Northampton, MA, USA: Edward Elgar Publishing, pp. 54–63.

Mayhew, A. (2016) 'Lawson, Veblen and Marshall', in Morgan, J. (ed.), *What is Neoclassical Economics?* London: Routledge, pp. 119–34.

Mill, J. ([1836] 1967) 'On the definition of political economy', in Robson, J. (ed.), *Collected Works of John Stuart Mill: Essays on Economics and Society*, Vol. V, Toronto: University of Toronto Press, pp. 209–340.

Mirowski, P. ([1983] 1998) 'Nelson and Winter's *Evolutionary Theory of Economic Change*', in *Against Mechanism: Protecting Economics from Science*, Totowa, NJ: Rowman & Littlefield, pp. 161–70.

Nelson, R. (2013) 'Demand, supply, and their interactions on markets, as seen from the perspective of evolutionary economic theory', *Journal of Evolutionary Economics*, **23** (1), pp. 17–38.

Nelson, R. and Winter, S. (1982) *An Evolutionary Theory of Economic Change*, Cambridge, MA: Harvard University Press.

Nightingale, J. and Potts, J. (2003) 'An alternative framework for economics', in Fullbrook, E. (ed.), *The Crisis in Economics*, London: Routledge, pp. 180–82.

Noble, D. (1958) *The Paradox of Progressive Thought*, Minneapolis: University of Minnesota Press.

North, D. (1991) 'Institutions', *Journal of Economic Perspectives*, **5** (1), pp. 97–112.

Pratten, S. (1998) 'Marshall on tendencies, equilibrium, and the statical method', *History of Political Economy*, **30** (1), pp. 121–63.

Primrose, D. (2017) 'The subjectification of *homo economicus* in behavioural economics', *Australian Journal of Political Economy*, **80**, pp. 88–128.

Ramstad, Y. (1994) 'On the nature of economic evolution: John R. Commons and the metaphor of artificial selection', in Magnusson, L. (ed.), *Evolutionary and Neo-Schumpeterian Approaches to Economics*, Boston, MA: Kluwer, pp. 65–121.

Ricardo, D. ([1817] 1951) *Principles of Political Economy and Taxation*, in Sraffa, P. (ed.), *The Works and Correspondence of David Ricardo*, Vol. I, Cambridge: Cambridge University Press.

Roncaglia, A. (2005) *The Wealth of Ideas: A History of Economic Thought*, Cambridge: Cambridge University Press.

Sowell, T. (1985) *Marxism: Philosophy and Economics*, London: George Allen & Unwin.

Spencer, H. ([1862] 1890) *First Principles*, 5th edition, London: Williams and Norgate.

Thomas, B. (1991) 'Alfred Marshall on economic biology', *Review of Political Economy*, **3** (1), pp. 1–14.

Valentinov, V. (2013) 'Veblen and instrumental value: a systems theory perspective', *Journal of Economic Issues*, **47** (3), pp. 673–88.

Veblen, T. (1904) *The Theory of Business Enterprise*, New York: Charles Scribner.

Veblen, T. (1909) 'The limitations of marginal utility', *Journal of Political Economy*, **17** (9), pp. 620–36.

Veblen, T. ([1901] 1961a) 'Industrial and pecuniary employments', in *The Place of Science in Modern Civilisation and Other Essays*, New York: Russell & Russell, pp. 279–323.

Veblen, T. ([1900] 1961b) 'The preconceptions of economic science III', in *The Place of Science in Modern Civilisation and Other Essays*, New York: Russell & Russell, pp. 148–79.

Veblen, T. ([1898] 1961c) 'Why is economics not an evolutionary science?', in *The Place of Science in Modern Civilisation and Other Essays*, New York: Russell & Russell, pp. 56–81.

Veblen, T. ([1923] 1964a) *Absentee Ownership and Business Enterprise in Recent Times: The Case of America*, New York: Augustus M. Kelley.

Veblen, T. ([1914] 1964b) *The Instinct of Workmanship and the State of the Industrial Arts*, New York: Augustus M. Kelley.

Veblen, T. ([1896] 1973) 'Review of *Socialisme et science positive* by Enrico Ferri', in Dorfman, J. (ed), *Thorstein Veblen: Essays, Reviews and Reports*, Clifton, NJ: Augustus M. Kelley, pp. 449–55.

Vromen, J. (1995) *Economic Evolution: An Enquiry into the Foundations of New Institutional Economics*, London: Routledge.

Vromen, J. (2001) 'Ontological commitments of evolutionary economics', in Mäki, U. (ed.), *The Economic World View*, Cambridge: Cambridge University Press, pp. 189–224.

Watkins, J. (2010) 'Mainstream efforts to tell a better story – natural selection as a misplaced metaphor: the problem of corporate power', *Journal of Economic Issues*, **44** (4), pp. 991–1008.

11. Neo-Schumpeterian economics

Rinaldo Evangelista

In the context of contemporary capitalism, technological innovation and its socio-economic impacts have increasingly come to occupy a central place in scholarly and policy-based discourse. Seeking to comprehend these processes, this chapter makes the case for a 'political economy' approach to the complex and potentially contradictory nature of relations between technological progress, economic growth and social development under capitalism, while also pointing to the need to re-think technology policies from a heterodox perspective. Developing this perspective requires critically engaging with the recent neo-Schumpeterian Economics (NSE) literature that has sought to re-centre technological processes within economic theory. The chapter posits that, despite providing fundamental contributions to our understanding of innovation, this NSE tradition has buttressed an optimistic reading of technology–economy–society relations. Contrary to other influential heterodox economic schools and Schumpeter himself, NSE rarely associates technology with the cyclical occurrence of systemic economic crises, structural unemployment, and the growth of social and economic inequalities. Concomitantly, the chapter urges re-opening the debate on the role and scope of technology policies and, more broadly, on the long-term options for social and institutional mechanisms governing the pace and direction of technological change. Such a move requires re-framing the analysis of the technology–economy relationships within a macroeconomic, structural and institutional framework, whereby the dynamic interactions between technological change, structural transformations of the economy, demand and income distribution inform a new theoretical and empirical agenda.

This chapter is organised in six principal sections. The first locates the genesis of the renewed interest in Schumpeter's ideas in a historical setting. The second recalls the main heterodox features of Schumpeter's works that have inspired the NSE research agenda. Next, the main strands of the literature following the legacy of the Austrian scholar are synthetically sketched. This is followed by a section that highlights some key methodological and conceptual traits of NSE that hinder its capacity to conceptualise the socially embedded and contradictory nature of technological change under capitalism. The final section, preceding some general conclusions, examines the rationale for a new round of industrial and technology policies grounded in NSE insights, while also positing the need for a thorough, more heterodox, re-thinking of the role and scope of technology policies.

NEO-SCHUMPETERIAN ECONOMICS IN HISTORICAL CONTEXT

Over the last 150 years, the discipline of political economy has been largely dominated by the neoclassical school. This is characterised by a (supposed) high level of internal methodological and formal rigour. Beyond the internal logical inconsistencies of the marginalist theory of value, capital and distribution highlighted a century ago by Piero Sraffa (Roncaglia 2009), the neoclassical framework is limited by conceptually restrictive and unrealistic axioms concerning economic agents, markets and economic systems. These assumptions function to preserve the internal methodological coherence of neoclassical models, and also (perhaps more importantly) to proving the virtues of markets – particularly the capacity of the 'invisible hand' to guarantee an objectively 'efficient' (Pareto optimal) allocation of resources. Neoclassical modelling is, thus, designed to prove that market economies consist of harmonic, efficient and non-conflictual socio-economic systems. The functioning of market forces is, in turn, the ideal means to resolve the 'economic problem' faced by individuals and society: how to most efficiently utilise a scarce pool of resources to satisfy unlimited wants (Robbins 1932).

In the standard neoclassical framework, innovation and technological change are considered as exogenous variables: elements not essential to understanding the behaviours of economic agents, the functioning of markets, or the aggregate performances of economic systems. Moving away from the 'Classical tradition', the bulk of neoclassical theory has, in fact, focused on the static and equilibrium properties of markets, assuming as exogenous all the factors explaining 'from within' the dynamism and qualitative changes of market economies, as well as their social structure (Schumpeter [1912] 1938, [1942] 1950). Thus, technology has traditionally been treated as a 'black box' (Rosenberg 1983), merely reflected in a set of static quantitative input–output relationships within the straitjacket of production functions. Since the late 1980s, starting with the contributions of Lucas and Romer, there have been various attempts at endogenising innovation and technological change within formal neoclassical models of economic growth (e.g. Lucas 1988; Romer 1990, 1994; Aghion and Howitt 1992, 1998). However, the basic conceptual and methodological structure of these models has not significantly changed: remaining anchored to methodological individualism, trusting the functioning of Say's law and the equilibrium properties of markets, and assuming that systemic economic processes reflect the individual choices of fully rational maximising agents coordinated by efficient markets (Verspagen 2002, 2005).

To find an endogenous, socially and institutionally embedded treatment of technological change, one must look beyond orthodox economics. In fact, a more complex political economy of technology requires returning to the insightful, albeit still embryonic formulations of Classical authors such as Smith and Ricardo, the titanic works of Marx and Schumpeter, and important contributions from the post-Keynesian school (Kaldor 1961; Kalecki [1935] 1971, [1954] 1991) and institutional economics (Kapp 1950, 1963, 1970). With the partial exception of Smith and Ricardo, these heterogeneous schools and scholars share some common heterodox traits. These include:

- acknowledgement of the intrinsic instability of capitalism conceived as a historically specific socio-economic system,
- an analytical focus on the factors, forces and conditions engendering disequilibrium conditions,
- the idea that perfect competition is an abstract, irrelevant theoretical reference point, and
- the endogenous character of technological change, as a phenomenon central to processes of capital accumulation and institutional, social and structural change.

In the last case, the socially and institutionally embedded dimensions of technological change (affecting both the pace and direction of scientific advancements and their economic use) are inter-related with the specific class structure of capitalism and its modus operandi, characterised by conflictual relationships over the control and use of means of production and on income distribution (Courvisanos 2012).

Despite its serious heuristic caveats, the neoclassical approach has been largely dominant over the last 150 years. Explaining why is beyond the scope of this contribution, but it is pertinent to remark that the re-affirmation of the neoclassical apparatus during the last four decades may be understood in the context of social and political changes, especially the widespread introduction of neoliberal policies and reforms (Bellofiore 2013). It is in this 'neoclassical counter-reform climate' that Schumpeter has also been 're-discovered', becoming a heterodox reference point for a new field of research specifically dealing with the economics of technology and innovation. The holistic methodological approach of this Austrian economist, his out-of-equilibrium, evolutionary, historical view of economic processes, his focus on the role of innovation as the engine of competition, structural change and economic growth, have all been a strong source of attraction and inspiration for a new generation of economists and scholars.

Since the 1980s, the acceleration of scientific and technological change engendered by the emergence and diffusion of information and communication technology (ICT) has contributed to the rapid growth of a new tradition building on Schumpeterian insights – variously labelled 'economics of technological change', 'economics of innovation', 'Schumpeterian economics', or 'evolutionary economics'.[1] For the sake of simplicity (and with a certain degree of approximation), the chapter labels this rapidly growing research area, and related literature, as 'neo-Schumpeterian'.

SCHUMPETER AS A HETERODOX THINKER

Despite being often depicted as a conservative, there is little doubt that Schumpeter should, in many respects, be considered a heterodox economist – that is, a scholar pushing beyond the strict methodological and theoretical boundaries of neoclassical economics, and explicitly acknowledging his intellectual debt to Marx (Rosenberg 2011). Schumpeter's theoretical interests do not revolve around the analytical treatment of the static equilibrium conditions of rational economic agents and efficient markets, the clearing features of the price mechanism and the associated conditions of Pareto optimality. According to Schumpeter, these features relate only to a stationary state of the economy – one comprising the mere circular reproduction of the system – not reflecting the prevailing dynamic and out-of-equilibrium characteristics of market economies.

Instead, Schumpeter adopts a view on the nature of competition and entrepreneurial activities antithetical to the neoclassical conceptualisation, in which real (capitalist) economies are driven by the continuous search for, and use of, novelties, rather than pursuing static efficiency and price/cost reductions. Following the Classical tradition, and Marx in particular, Schumpeter is interested in studying the nature of capitalism, conceptualised as 'a form or method of economic change and not only never is but never can be stationary' (Schumpeter 1950: 82). To provide a synthetic representation of the restless and immanently transformative character of capitalism, he introduced the well-known concept of 'creative destruction' – that is, 'a process of industrial mutation [...] that incessantly revolutionises the economic structure from within, incessantly destroying the old one, incessantly creating a new one' (Schumpeter [1942] 1950: 83). From this perspective, the primary driver of economic activity and processes of structural change is innovation, conceptualised broadly as including new products unfamiliar to consumers, new methods of production or new ways of handling commodities, opening up new markets, new sources of supply of raw materials or half-manufactured goods, and new organisation of the competitive structure of an industry (Schumpeter [1912] 1938).

Schumpeter analysed the 'process of creative destruction' in his three main scholarly works – *The Theory of Economic Development* (1912), *Business Cycles* (1939) and *Capitalism Socialism and Democracy* (1942) – each book looking from different, albeit complementary, angles. Specifically, across his works, he examined it at different levels of analysis (micro, meso and macro), within different time-scale frameworks (short- versus long-term), while also placing emphasis on different types of actors (entrepreneurs, small firms, large corporations, industries, social behaviours and structures, institutions) and competitive contexts (competitive versus 'trustified' market structures). This broad perspective on the sources and drivers of structural change is consistent with his concept of innovation, conceived as a multifaceted phenomenon substantiating and affecting all possible levels of the economic space, the behaviors of entrepreneurs, the strategies of firms and the dynamics of industries and markets, as well as long-term macroeconomic processes.

A distinctive feature of Schumpeter is also his holistic approach to the analysis of innovation and economic change, and his attention to both quantitative and qualitative dimensions of such processes in their structural and behavioral dimensions. Additional elements of this eclecticism are evident in the importance attached to the financial sector in supporting the most innovative firms and industries, as well as the attention given to the specific historical and institutional settings in which innovation occurs. In the light of all this, it is somewhat surprising that the richness of Schumpeter's approach and the important contributions contained in his works have somewhat remained in the shadows both during and after his lifetime. Rather, Schumpeterian insights have been kept at the margin of the theoretical battle between the neoclassical and Keynesian schools (Phillimore 1998), both paying little attention to the endogenous sources of qualitative economic transformations and the role of innovation in such processes.

MAIN RESEARCH STREAMS IN NEO-SCHUMPETERIAN ECONOMICS

Conversely, scholars in the NSE tradition have sought to bring Schumpeterian insights into the limelight. Most prominently, NSE has the fundamental merit of returning (after Marx and Schumpeter) technology and innovation to the centre of economic theory and analysis. This research stream builds on Schumpeter's position that technology and innovation (along with diffusion) are the distinctive and most important drivers of competition, the real fuel of the process of economic change – that is, the processes engendering the birth and death of firms, the emergence and decline of markets and industries, as well as the dynamic performance of economies at large.[2] Drawing from Evangelista (2018), as well as from previous surveys of this research field (Castellacci 2007; Hanusch and Pyka 2007), four major strands of NSE can be identified, each one starting from (and further developing) the contributions and ideas contained in Schumpeter's works.

Innovation and Business Cycles

The NSE literature on long waves, inspired by Schumpeter's *Business Cycles*, presents a technological interpretation of the long-term cyclical patterns of capitalism. These studies have, in fact, further developed the Schumpeterian idea regarding the existence of a strong nexus between the cyclical trend of economic systems and the discontinuous nature of technological change. The underlying proposition is that, far from being a linear and smooth process, innovations tend to cluster in certain historical periods and sectors of the economy. Capitalism evolves through up-swing and down-swing stages, with the length and intensity of the up-swing stages of development depending on the level of radicalness and pervasiveness of technological change. Radical innovations and technological revolutions can sustain phases of long-term economic growth, which are followed by stagnation periods due to exhaustion of the previous set of dominant technologies. Research within this stream has focused on the degree of endogeneity/exogeneity of technological change with respect to the dynamics of the business cycle, as well as the role played by demand- or supply-side forces in explaining the dynamics of innovation (Mowery and Rosenberg 1979; Dosi 1982; Coombs et al. 1987).

Freeman and Perez (1986, 1988), Freeman and Louçã (2001), Perez (2002, 2010, 2013) and Louçã (2021) have sought to provide a more holistic, complex and less deterministic interpretation of the relationship between economic cycles and technological change. These theorists attribute the upswing stage of long waves not only to the emergence of a new set of pervasive technologies, but also to necessary changes in the economic, cultural, social and institutional context. From this perspective, the main long-term surges in development experienced by capitalist economies over the last two centuries are interpreted as resulting from the emergence and consolidation of different 'techno-economic paradigms' – that is, radical changes in the cost structures, nature and organisation of innovation activities, and broader criteria and principles according to which economic systems operate (Freeman and Louçã 2001; Perez 2010). This more comprehensive and long-term view on the discontinuous and transformative character of economic and technological systems allows theorists to explain the difficulties encountered by new technological paradigms in emerging and fully exerting their economic and social potentialities. Specifically, they should be accompanied and supported by fundamental changes in the structure and functioning of socio-economic systems. This may include development of new infrastructural networks, introducing new organisational models and structures into firms and industries, new patterns of location of investment, the formation of new skills, competences, educational and training schemes, and different patterns of consumption and styles of living (Freeman and Perez 1988). As Perez (2002: 1) states when conceptualising the prevailing techno-economic paradigm during the early twenty-first century:

> Reaping the higher productivity will require the unlearning of many of the old behaviours, the abandonment of what seemed obvious 'common sense' and the systematic learning of the new best practices. In the previous surge it was the adoption of mass production and scientific management; in the current one it has been the shift from pyramids to networks, from human resources to human capital, from inter-nationalization to globalization and so on.

As discussed later in this chapter, the limited coherence between the revolutionary character of the previous technological paradigm (ICT) and other broader (and inertial) organisational and institutionalised socio-economic factors is considered by these NSE scholars as a key factor explaining the lack of a stable new accumulation regime over the course of the last four decades (Freeman and Louçã 2001; Perez 2002; Louçã 2021).

The Technology-gap Approach

Studies following the so-called technology-gap approach have sought to explain the lack of economic and technological convergence between more wealthy and poorer countries, as well as those factors that facilitate processes of catching-up and following-behind (Dosi et al. 1990; Fagerberg 1994; Fagerberg et al. 2007). From this perspective, the lack of technological convergence is deemed to arise from the nature of technology and innovation itself. Far from having a public-good character, the latter are depicted as being partly appropriable, and difficult to adopt and transfer to economic, cultural and institutional contexts different from those in which they were first generated and exploited. Innovation processes are, therefore, viewed as being characterised by high levels of cumulativeness and irreversibility, giving the growth and development a path-dependent character.

The Systemic Nature of Innovation

Another important strand of NSE literature has highlighted the systemic nature of technological change, the importance of linkages and interactions between the different actors involved in processes of innovation and diffusion, and the important role played by several types of institutions in underpinning innovation. From this perspective, the innovation process is seen as more than the mere sum of individual firms' behaviours and strategies. Instead, it constitutes the outcome of the systemic interactions, technological interdependencies and knowledge flows taking place within and between firms and industries, and between the latter and other scientific and technological institutions (both public and private). Accordingly, this literature has highlighted the presence of various types of National Systems of Innovation (NSI), each one rooted in different, historically determined, industrial structures and cultural and institutional contexts.[3]

The Evolutionary Stream

A fourth, and nowadays dominant, NSE stream is that inspired by the seminal contribution of Nelson and Winter (Nelson and Winter 1982; Nelson et al. 2018), which interpreted the innovative behaviours of firms, the dynamics of industries and economic growth, as resulting from an evolutionary (continuous) process of generation of variety (innovation) and market selection. For the sake of simplicity, we label this fourth strand of literature as 'evolutionary'. As discussed at more length in the following section, while the first three streams of NSE privilege a macro and institutional perspective on the effects exerted by technology on the economy and society, the evolutionary stream is explicitly micro-founded and very much focused on looking inside the 'black box' of innovation and the innovative behaviours of firms.

Pertinently, the microeconomic foundations of this evolutionary economics are antithetical to those of neoclassical economics. The former rejects ideas of equilibrium, representative agents, full rationality of economic agents and the public nature of technology (i.e. assimilation of technology to pure information) (Dosi 1988). Instead, the evolutionary school emphasises the role of routines, seen as an operational way in which firms, based on their past experience and accumulated competencies, allocate resources, organise production inputs, and define their competitive and innovative strategies (Nelson and Winter 1982; Dosi 1988; Nelson 1994). In this approach, a clear understanding and specification of the behaviours of firms, operating in competitive contexts characterised by technological rivalry and uncertainty, is also considered vital to explain the aggregate properties of industries and economic systems (Dosi 2013). In fact, the explicit and most ambitious challenge of Nelson and Winter's model consists precisely in building an out-of-equilibrium narrative and micro-based modelling of economic growth and change. This, in turn, is said to 'provide an analysis that at least comes close to matching the power of neoclassical theory to predict and illuminate the macroeconomic patterns of growth' (Nelson and Winter 1982: 206).

EMERGING TRENDS AND LIMITATIONS IN NEO-SCHUMPETERIAN ECONOMICS

The heterogeneity of the NSE approaches is not surprising, especially considering the eclectic scientific profile of Schumpeter and the wide spectrum of his theoretical interests. Along with stressing the richness of the theoretical developments originating from Schumpeter's works, this chapter also seeks to critically examine the specific long-term trajectory of neo-Schumpeterian studies. In this regard, three broad trends can be identified. The first entails the analytical focus on technology–economy relations progressively shifting from a macro- to microeconomic level. The second trend involves the progressive reinforcement of a supply-side view of relations between the generation, diffusion and use of technology and primary economic phenomena, with the role of demand largely neglected. The third element is the emergence of an (implicitly) optimistic view of the economic and social role technology plays in capitalist economies (Soete 2013). These trends are discussed and elaborated at length in Evangelista (2018) and summarised in what follows.

NSE examines technology–economy relations in a manner diverging from Classical Political Economy, and even more so from post-Keynesianism. The main differences concern the level of analytical aggregation, the level of generalisation of the relationships examined, and the relative importance accorded to demand- and supply-side drivers of growth. In fact, since its origin, NSE has demonstrated little interest in the traditional macroeconomic variables and dynamic mechanisms considered in the post-Keynesian tradition, with the latter analysing the dynamic interplay between investment, capital accumulation, productivity growth, income distribution and effective demand. Rather, NSE has progressively privileged a fully supply-side view of the dynamics of macroeconomic forces, with technology perceived as the foundational driver of myriad economic performance variables, especially economic growth (explored in Nelson and Winter's 1982 model) and observed cross-country disparities in productivity growth and international competitiveness (in the technology gap approach).

More significantly, the role of demand, and its relationship with the rate and direction of technological change, has been largely neglected by NSE, particularly by the evolutionary stream. As explicitly stated by Dosi et al. (2010: 1749), 'evolutionary models, as pioneered by Nelson and Winter (1982), are driven by a Schumpeterian core with endogenous innovation, but largely neglect too any demand-related driver of macroeconomic activity'. Courvisanos (2012: 27) notes that: 'The lack of an aggregate demand element in neo-Schumpeterian economics has been long recognised, but only limited research has been conducted in this area.'[4]

In fact, in most theoretical and empirical NSE accounts, economic growth (associated with the process of creative destruction) is never constrained by aggregate demand, and the latter is automatically expanded by technology through the emergence of new markets, industries and products.[5]

In this supply-side (competitive-based) view of technology–economy relations, the micro-level mechanisms governing the fabric of innovation processes have become a key area of investigation and theoretical concern. This has primarily been found in the search for robust micro-economic theoretical foundations (and empirical support) for the evolutionary models of competition, economic growth and industrial dynamics (Dosi 1988; Dosi and Nelson 2010).[6] As explicitly stated by Nelson and Winter (1982: 229), 'The question of the nature of "search" processes would appear to be among the most important for those trying to understand economic growth, and the evolutionary theory has the advantage of posing the question explicitly.'

This literature has explored myriad areas and contributed much to our understanding of innovation, firms' behaviours and industrial dynamics (Dosi 2013; Winter 2014). However, the supply-side perspective and micro-economic focus adopted by the bulk of NSE studies have also contributed to the emergence of an optimistic vision of the role technology plays in the economy and society. Innovation is fetishised as playing a thaumaturgic role: being able to explain almost everything from the performance of firms, industries, regions and countries to the destiny of individuals and workers. This view, in turn, assumes that technological competition always comprises a socio-economic positive-sum game – that this was true in the past, holds in present times and will continue to be so in the future. This has contributed to a simplified picture of the political economic processes associated with the advancement of technologies and their use in capitalist economies.

The analytical simplification of the macroeconomic character of the determinants and effects of technological change can be seen as the result of the excessive transposition of microeconomic relationships and mechanisms to the macroeconomic level. Indeed, most of the NSE literature conveys a Schumpeterian version of Say's law, which could be re-phrased as follows: 'each technology creates its own demand' at both the micro and macro levels. More specifically, this approach neglects or underplays crucial macroeconomic issues addressed in heterodox strands of political economy (especially in Marx's writings and the post-Keynesian tradition) – especially those concerning the possible mismatch between interrelated phenomena such as dynamics of investment and technology, corresponding changes in supply forces (productivity), and changes in income distribution and demand conditions (Courvisanos 2012). These incongruities are at the basis of potential contradictions or crises stemming from over-capacity, under-consumption, misallocation and waste of resources (human, tangible and intangible), or static and dynamic efficiency losses.

The relevance of macroeconomic relationships governing the pace and direction of technological change, and the risk associated with the bulk of NSE studies neglecting such insights, is acknowledged by Christopher Freeman (quoted in Fagerberg et al. 2011: 907):

> I think the main area that needs to be strengthened is the main core of economic theory, macroeconomic theory, and I think you can't shift the main central core of neoclassical economic theory simply with microeconomic studies […] Most of the people working on innovation systems prefer to work at the micro-level. They are a bit frightened still of the strength of the neoclassical paradigm at the macroeconomic level. But I think that's where they have to work. You have to have an attack on the central core of macroeconomic theory. It is happening but not happening enough.

The methodological and theoretical traits of NSE highlighted above have, in turn, led to the marginalisation of broad macroeconomic and socially relevant themes concerning the role and socio-economic impact of technological change – topics deeply rooted in the Classical tradition as well as post-Keynesianism. Three such neglected themes may be highlighted.

Technology and Employment

This topic has long been theorised within political economy. Surprisingly, however, after the pioneering contributions of early NSE scholars such as Freeman, Clark and Soete (Freeman et al. 1982; Freeman and Soete 1994), this theme has been progressively marginalised within NSE.[7] This disinterest stems from an (implicit) belief that technology is potentially able to foster economic growth at a pace sufficient to engender full employment. Of course, labour-displacing effects are not ruled out, but are assumed to primarily affect low-skilled jobs, while the overall employment impact is deemed to be positive. However, there is no empirical evidence supporting this optimistic view, given the difficulty of modelling and estimating the net long-term aggregate effect of technological change on employment (Vivarelli 2013). The functioning and strength of so-called 'compensation' mechanisms (Vivarelli 1995; Vivarelli and Pianta 2000) depends on rather axiomatic conditions, such as the existence of perfectly competitive markets, perfect and continuous input substitutability, and the validity of Say's law, which guarantees that changes in 'supply conditions' (productivity growth and supply of new products) always generate corresponding (market clearing) changes in demand. The net aggregate employment impact of technological change becomes even more difficult to assess in the case of the diffusion of digital technologies. This is because of the pervasiveness of these technologies and their widespread impact on almost any domain of economic and social life (Evangelista et al. 2014; Balliester and Elsheikhi 2018). Consequently, the prevailing optimistic and supply-side view of the relationship between technological change and employment within NSE, as well as the minimal attention it accords to this crucial and socially relevant theme, is puzzling.

Technology and (Functional) Income Distribution

This is another theme central among Classical political economists and also considered by post-Keynesian scholars, yet somehow surprisingly expelled by the NSE research agenda. For the Classicals, along with Kalecki, the rate and direction of technological change are heavily influenced by 'class structure' – that is, the social and economic relationships shaping the structure and functioning of capitalism (Courvisanos 2009, 2012). From a Marxian perspective, technological change within capitalism has a capital deepening and labour-saving nature over the long term, which affects both income distribution between classes and, consequently, the composition and volume of aggregate demand. From this perspective, the cyclical occurrence of phases of over-production, unemployment, under-consumption, skewed income distribution and insufficient demand are strictly inter-connected phenomena associated with the very nature of capital accumulation, inter-capital competition and the non-coordinated nature of investment decisions. Concomitantly, technological change simply amplifies the contradictory nature of these processes, fuelling divergence between the development of production forces (labour productivity), distribution relationships and the capacity of the market (in particular, final demand) to absorb all production output. Both Marx and Kalecki emphasise this point by stressing the structural asymmetry between capital accumulation and demand, with the latter constrained by insufficient wage dynamics (Sebastiani 1989). This asymmetry is, thus, at the core of the contradictory and cyclical nature of capitalist development.[8]

Conversely, following Schumpeter, the most recent NSE literature underplays the role of technological change within capitalism as a system characterised by conflictual capital–labour relationships. Relatedly, NSE accords little concern to the influence that this institutional setting can exert on the 'distribution outcome' of technological change (Smith 2010). Technological change ceases to have a predominantly labour-saving character, nor is it conceptualised as developing within highly asymmetric and conflictual social relations. The process of creative destruction is, in fact, conceived as primarily associated with the rise and expansion of new products and industries. Relatedly, this literature implicitly assumes that productivity gains obtained via technological change are so large and widespread that 'income distribution' becomes a marginal issue or one with little relevance to the rate and direction of technological change. NSE, thereby, fails to investigate relations between long-term changes in the functional income distribution – namely, from labour to capital – observed in most industrialised countries and the new technological regime (in conjunction with the dominance of financial capital) centred on the use and diffusion of digital technologies and platforms in manufacturing and service industries, and society more broadly (Fuchs and Mosco 2016; Srnicek 2017).

Technology and Socio-economic Progress

The intertwined relationship between technological change and long-term transformation of economic and social conditions (socio-economic progress) is another broad theme in the research agenda of early NSE, but marginalised in recent evolutionary literature. In fact, despite being central to some pioneers of NSE, such as Christopher Freeman and Carlota Perez (Freeman et al. 1982; Freeman and Perez 1988), this topic has been gradually narrowed or even exorcised from the research agenda of innovation studies in recent decades. Specifically, the socio-economic effects of technology have been primarily investigated through shifting the focus from conceptualising the qualitative character of technology–development relations to a mere quantification of the effects of technology on productivity, economic growth, international competitiveness.

This account, thereby, encounters difficulty in interpreting the mismatch between the substantial opportunities engendered by technological advances and the pervasive social problems associated with contemporary capitalism, such as increased socio-economic inequalities, pervasive human needs remaining unsatisfied, and unsustainable pressures exerted on ecological processes (Courvisanos 2009; Pagano and Rossi 2011). This is the central macroeconomic paradox that has become more evident in the last three decades. Despite the emergence of the third and fourth industrial and technological revolutions associated with the widespread socio-economic diffusion of ICT and digitalisation processes, the global economy has only grown at a sluggish pace. As already mentioned, NSE scholars such as Freeman, Perez and Louçã (Freeman and Perez 1988; Freeman and Louçã 2001; Louçã 2021) have interpreted this paradox as highlighting the inertia and the limited capacity of the broader socio-institutional system to keep-up with the paradigm-shifting nature of the new technologies (the 'mismatch' hypothesis). The same type of argument is put forward by Paul David in connection with the 'general purpose' nature of ICT (David 1991; David and Wright 1999; Bresnahan 2010). This line of argument usefully highlights the presence and implications of the socio-economic and institutional inertia characterising transition phases between different techno-economic paradigms. However, the mismatch hypothesis risks progressively losing its explicative power and plausibility, considering the long time that has passed since ICT first appeared and the pervasive, entrenched role that digital technologies play in contemporary political economic and social processes.

TOWARDS A HETERODOX VIEW ON INDUSTRIAL AND TECHNOLOGY POLICIES

Neoclassical economics acknowledges that the functioning of the markets can lead to 'inefficiencies' and, thus, 'market failures'. Yet, because these are largely downplayed as constituting exceptional cases and having only a microeconomic character, limited scope is accorded for industrial policies.

Conversely, NSE considers industrial, science and technology policies as vitally important and supported by robust theoretical bases. Building on a theory of the firm and competitive models diverging from those found in neoclassical economics, evolutionary scholars have partly corrected the mainstream public-good view of technology and innovation. Instead, they emphasise the tacit component and the sticky nature of most technological knowledge developed and used by firms, and conceptualise such technological processes as occurring in contexts characterised by substantial uncertainty and bounded rationality (Metcalfe 1994). This latter perspective provides strong support to innovation policies devoted to accelerating learning processes and competence building by firms, and support for institutionalising framework conditions that engender technological variety by simultaneously enabling an effective selection mechanism, while avoiding processes of technological lock-in (Smith 1991; Cantner and Pyka 2001; Dodgson et al. 2011; Edler and Fagerberg 2017).

A Schumpeterian rationale for industrial policies can also been found in the search for medium- and long-term improvements in static and dynamic efficiency at more systemic and meso levels (Lundvall and Borràs 2005). In this more 'structural' and 'mission oriented' perspective, public policies should be explicitly devoted to favouring emerging technologies and firms located in strategic and dynamic sectors. These include industries and markets characterised by strong learning processes, high levels of technological opportunities, productivity increases, dynamic economies of scale, internationalisation, and rapid demand growth (Chang 1994; Chaminade and Edquist 2006; Pianta et al. 2020).

More recently, policy-oriented research has progressively recognised the need to move towards a more vigorous, structural and long-term regime of industrial and technology strategies.[9] This change of perspective is primarily informed by three political economic logics (Pianta 2014). The first is rooted in macroeconomic analysis and adopts a Keynesian rationale. Specifically, emerging from the current global economic stagnation (especially in the EU context) – produced by the effects of the 2007/08 global financial crisis and subsequent global Coronavirus crisis – requires a substantial increase in demand, which could be driven by large-scale public investment policies. The Next Generation EU clearly adopts such a perspective. Second, a new industrial and technology policy is required to buttress knowledge-intensive, high skill and wage activities consistent with the EU Lisbon strategy, the Next Generation EU programme and targets enunciated in many policy documents around the world.[10] Third, a new industrial policy is required to accelerate the ecological transition of capitalism toward a more sustainable socio-economic form.

These three lines of intervention represent the pillars of a novel policy agenda informed by both Keyensianism and Schumpeterian logics (Dosi et al. 2016, 2017). The Keynesian flavour of this framework derives from the use of tax incentives, fiscal stimuli and public procurement as a leverage to foster the transition to a digital and sustainable model of economic development. Along with expanding public budgets, this approach requires a qualitative extension of the role of the state in economic activity and science and technology (Mazzucato 2013). These state-led activities may include ambitious tasks, such as

- setting political economic priorities favouring a broad range of socio-ecological objectives,
- engaging in large-scale public investment that creates employment opportunities and supports the organisation of new markets,
- development of competences and entrepreneurship,
- ensuring public access to capital,
- securing production of public goods such as knowledge, environmental quality, social well-being and integration, and territorial cohesion.

Re-orienting industrial and technology policies along these lines would represent somewhat of a Copernican Revolution away from the prevailing neoliberal approach. This broader perspective echoes the literature examining the existence and viability of alternative models of capitalism (Hall and Soskice 2001; Crouch 2005), as well as contributions addressing the more fundamental issue of 'rethinking capitalism' (Jacobs and Mazzucato 2016).

However, most debate on new directions for industrial and technology policies continues to fall well short of envisaging any such possibilities for a more radical transformation of the political economic logic driving generation and use of knowledge. Driving scholarly research and policy processes further towards this more heterodox agenda would require further consideration be given to a range of other questions. For instance, what is the political scope to 'rethink and reform capitalism' in its current highly globalised and financialised form, seeking to secure socio-ecological benefits from its progressive technological forces while also controlling its destructive power? Or has the time come to consider other institutionalised forms of social democratic planning that would enable social control and coordination of the knowledge generation processes and their application? At which geo-political scale could such alternative models be trialled or practised, and what economic and social actors should be involved in such processes? Would a substantial expansion of the state from basic research to the direct ownership and management of strategic economic sectors represent a desirable transition to a different political economic system? Complex questions and issues like these should be central to future debates amongst heterodox schools of thought.

CONCLUSIONS

This chapter has highlighted the dominant optimistic view of the relations between technology, economy and society that permeates both mainstream economics and much of the most recent NSE literature. This optimistic view clashes with the practical disjuncture experienced in recent decades between accelerating scientific and technological change and the limited capability of contemporary capitalism to adapt these to address human needs and secure sustainable development. Explaining this paradox, understanding its deep economic, social and institutional bases, requires acknowledging the complex, non-linear and potentially contradictory nature of the relations between technological progress, economic growth and social development under capitalism – especially its current globalised, financialised and neoliberal form. This was the perspective adopted by heterodox thinkers such as Marx and Kalecki, albeit rejected by the neoclassical school and marginalised by most heterodox schools during the twentieth century. Conversely, much of the NSE literature has contributed to reinforcing an optimistic and supply-side reading of the relations between technology, economy and society, with technology being able to guarantee strong economic growth and (implicitly) social welfare. Contrary to the Classicals, and Schumpeter himself, NSE (especially in the evolutionary stream) only rarely associates technology with systemic crises, structural unemployment, and the growth of social and economic inequalities. Instead, NSE retains its faith in the economically and socially progressive nature of the Schumpeterian process of creative destruction driven by market forces, especially when properly supported by public policies.

This optimistic presumption within the NSE literature concomitantly marginalises socially relevant themes addressed by more established heterodox schools, such as the relationship between technology and development, and the complex interactions between technological change, employment, income distribution and demand. It has contributed to an impoverished theoretical debate by diminishing the capacity of NSE to explore the complex and non-linear links between technological progress, economic change and societal development. There is, therefore, evidently a need for reorientation of NSE, focusing on the new economic, societal and environmental challenges generated by contemporary capitalism. This requires re-framing the analysis of technology–economy interactions within a macroeconomic and institutional framework, highlighting the dynamic interaction between changes in technology, income distribution and demand. There is an urgent need to re-open the debate among heterodox scholars on the role and scope of technology policies and, more broadly, on the social and institutional mechanisms governing the pace and direction of technological change.

NOTES

1. See Dosi et al. (1988); Dodgson and Rothwell (1994); Stoneman (1995); Fagerberg et al. (2005); Fagerberg and Verspagen (2009); Hall and Rosenberg (2010).
2. See Dosi et al. (1988); Dodgson and Rothwell (1994); Stoneman (1995); Fagerberg et al. (2005); Hall and Rosenberg (2010); Fagerberg et al. (2012); Dosi (2013); Fagerberg (2013); Winter (2014).
3. See Nelson (1994); Godin (2009); Lundvall (2010); Acs et al. (2017).
4. The supply-side bias of modern evolutionary economics is also well reflected in the evocative and provocative title given to the 2001 special issue of the *Journal of Evolutionary Economics*: 'Economic growth – what happens on the demand side?' (Witt 2001).
5. Among the few exceptions, see Dosi et al. (2010, 2016).
6. There is no need to say that the 'microeconomic foundations' of evolutionary economics are antithetic to those of neoclassical economics. In particular, the evolutionary school rejects most of the original microeconomic neoclassical assumptions, such as the idea of representative agents, the presence of full rationality of economic behaviours, the public nature of technology, and the assimilation of technology to pure information (Dosi 1988).
7. The works of Vivarelli and Pianta represent, in this respect, relevant exceptions (Vivarelli 1995; Vivarelli and Pianta 2000; Pianta 2005).
8. According to Marx (1981: 353), 'the more productivity develops, the more it comes into conflict with the narrow basis on which the relations of consumption rests'. Kalecki ([1935] 1971: 32)

expresses a similar point in stating that the most remarkable paradox of the capitalist system concerns the fact that 'the expansion of the capital equipment, i.e. the increase in the national wealth, contains the seed of depression in the course of which the additional wealth proves to be only potential in character.'

9. See Stiglitz and Lin Yifu (2013); Rodrik (2014); Cimoli et al. (2015); European Commission (2012, 2014, 2017); Savona (2018); Pianta et al. (2020).
10. For a more in-depth discussion of the relevance and rationale for a new industrial policy at the European level, see Pianta (2014, 2015) and Pianta et al. (2020).

REFERENCES

Acs, Z.J., Audretsch, D.B., Lehmann, E.E. and Licht, G. (2017) 'National systems of innovation', *The Journal of Technology Transfer*, **42**, pp. 997–1008.

Aghion, P. and Howitt, P. (1992) 'A model of growth through creative destruction', *Econometrica*, 60, pp. 323–51.

Aghion, P. and Howitt, P. (1998) *Endogenous Growth Theory*, Cambridge, MA: MIT Press.

Balliester, T. and Elsheikhi, A. (2018) 'The future of work a literature review', *ILO Working Papers*, Geneva: International Labour Organization.

Bellofiore, E. (2013) 'Two or three things I know about her: Europe in the global crisis and heterodox economics', *Cambridge Journal of Economics*, 37, pp. 497–512.

Bresnahan, T. (2010) 'General purpose technologies', in Hall, B.H. and Rosenberg N. (eds), *Handbook of the Economics of Innovation*, Amsterdam: North Holland.

Cantner, U. and Pyka, A. (2001) 'Classifying technology policy from an evolutionary perspective', *Research Policy*, 30 (5), pp. 759–75.

Castellacci, F. (2007) 'Evolutionary and new growth theories: are they converging?' *Journal of Economic Surveys*, 21 (3), pp. 585–627.

Chaminade, C. and Edquist, C. (2006) 'From theory to practice: the use of the systems of innovation approach in innovation policy', in Hage, J. and De Meeus, M. (eds), *Innovation, Learning and Institutions*, Oxford: Oxford University Press, pp. 141–63.

Chang, H.J. (1994) *The Political Economy of Industrial Policy*, Basingstoke: Macmillan.

Cimoli, M., Dosi, G. and Stiglitz, J. (2015) 'The rationale for industrial and innovation policy', *Intereconomics*, **50** (3), pp. 125–55.

Coombs, R., Saviotti, P. and Walsh, V. (1987) *Economics and Technological Change*, Totowa, NJ: Rowman and Littlefield.

Courvisanos, J. (2009) 'In search of new Atlantis: what can HET on innovation reveal about the path out of the 2009 Great Recession?' Paper presented at 22nd Conference of the History of Economic Thought Society of Australia, 14–17 July, Freemantle: University of Notre Dame.

Courvisanos, J. (2012) *Cycles, Crises and Innovation*, Cheltenham, UK and Northampton, MA, USA: Edward Elgar Publishing.

Crouch, C. (2005) 'Models of capitalism', *New Political Economy*, **10** (4), pp. 439–56.

David, P.A. (1991) 'Computer and dynamo: the modern productivity paradox in a not-too-distant mirror', in *Technology and Productivity*, Paris: OECD, pp. 315–47.

David, P. and Wright, G. (1999) *General Purpose Technologies and Productivity Surges: Historical Reflections on the Future of the ICT Revolution*, Discussion Papers in Economic and Social History, no. 31, University of Oxford.

Dodgson, M. and Rothwell, R. (eds) (1994) *The Handbook of Industrial Innovation*, Aldershot: Edward Elgar Publishing.

Dodgson, M., Hughes, A., Foster, J. and Metcalfe, S. (2011) 'System thinking, market failure, and the development of innovation policy: the case of Australia', *Research Policy*, **40**, pp. 1145–56.

Dosi, G. (1982) 'Technological paradigms and technological trajectories', *Research Policy*, **76** (2), pp. 332–7.

Dosi, G. (1988) 'Sources, procedures and microeconomic effects of innovation', *Journal of Economic Literature*, **26**, pp. 1120–71.

Dosi, G. (2013) 'Innovation, evolution, and economics: where we are and where we should go', in Fagerberg, J., Martin, B. and Andersen, E.S. (eds), *Innovation Studies: Evolution and Future Challenges*, Oxford: Oxford University Press, pp. 111–33.

Dosi, G. and Nelson, R. (2010) 'Technological change and industrial dynamics as evolutionary processes', in Hall, B.H. and Rosenberg, N. (eds), *Handbook of the Economics of Innovation*, Amsterdam: North Holland, pp. 51–127.

Dosi, G., Pavitt, K. and Soete, L. (1990) *The Economics of Technical Change and International Trade*, London: Harvester Wheatsheaf.

Dosi, G., Fagiolo, G. and Roventini A. (2010) 'Schumpeter meeting Keynes: a policy-friendly model of endogenous growth and business cycles', *Journal of Economic Dynamics & Control*, **34**, pp. 1748–67.

Dosi, G., Napoletano, M., Roventini, A. and Treibich, T. (2016) 'The short- and long-run damages of fiscal austerity: Keynes beyond Schumpeter', in Stiglitz, J. and Guzman M. (eds), *Contemporary Issues in Macroeconomics*, New York: Palgrave Macmillan, pp. 79–100.

Dosi, G., Napoletano, M., Roventini, A. and Treibich, T. (2017) 'Micro and macro policies in the Keynes+Schumpeter evolutionary models', *Journal of Evolutionary Economics*, **27** (1), pp. 63–90.

Dosi, G., Freeman, C., Nelson, R., Silverberg, G. and Soete, L. (eds) (1988) *Technical Change and Economic Theory*, London: Pinter.

Edler, J. and Fagerberg, J. (2017) 'Innovation policy: what, why, and how', *Oxford Review of Economic Policy*, **33** (1), pp. 2–23.

European Commission (2012) *A Stronger European Industry for Growth and Economic Recovery*, COM (2012) 582 final.

European Commission (2014) *For a European Industrial Renaissance*, COM (2014) 14 final.

European Commission (2017) *Investing in a Smart, Innovative and Sustainable Industry: A Renewed EU Industrial Policy Strategy*, COM (2017) 479 final.

Evangelista, R. (2018) 'Technology and economic development: the Schumpeterian legacy', *Review of Radical Political Economy*, **50** (1), pp. 136–53.

Evangelista, R., Guerrieri, P. and Meliciani, V. (2014) 'The economic impact of digital technologies in Europe', *Economics of Innovation and New Technology*, **23** (8), pp. 802–24.

Fagerberg, J. (1994) 'Technology and international differences in growth rates', *Journal of Economic Literature*, **32** (3), pp. 1147–75.

Fagerberg, J. (ed.) (2013) *Innovation Studies: Evolution and Future Challenges*, Oxford: Oxford University Press.

Fagerberg, J. and Verspagen, B. (2009) 'Innovation studies: the emerging structure of a new scientific field', *Research Policy*, **38** (2), pp. 218–33.

Fagerberg, J., Fosaas, M. and Sapprasert, K. (2012) 'Innovation: exploring the knowledge base', *Research Policy*, **41** (7) pp. 1132–53.

Fagerberg, J., Mowery, D. and Nelson, R. (eds) (2005) *The Oxford Handbook of Innovation*, New York and Oxford: Oxford University Press.

Fagerberg, J., Srholec, M. and Knell, M. (2007) 'The competitiveness of nations: why some countries prosper while others fall behind', *World Development*, **35** (10), pp. 1595–620.

Fagerberg, J., Fosaas, M., Bell, M. and Martin B.R. (2011) 'Christopher Freeman: social science entrepreneur', *Research Policy*, **40** (2), pp. 897–916.

Freeman, C. and Louçã, F. (2001) *As Time Goes By. From the Industrial Revolutions to the Information Revolution*, Oxford: Oxford University Press.

Freeman, C. and Perez, C. (1986) 'The diffusion of technical innovations and changes in technoeconomic paradigms', Paper to the Venice Conference on Innovation Diffusion, manuscript.

Freeman, C. and Perez, C. (1988) 'Structural crises of adjustment, business cycles and investment behaviour', in Dosi, G., Freeman, C., Nelson, R., Silverberg, G. and Soete, L. (eds), *Technical Change and Economic Theory*, London: Pinter, pp. 38–66.

Freeman, C. and Soete, L. (1994) *Work for All or Mass Unemployment? Computerised Technical Change in the Twenty-First Century*, London: Pinter.

Freeman, C., Clark, C. and Soete, L. (1982) *Unemployment and Technical Innovation*, London: Frances Pinter.

Fuchs, C. and Mosco, V. (eds) (2016) *Marx in the Age of Digital Capitalism*, Leiden: Brill.

Godin, B. (2009) 'National innovation system: the system approach in historical perspective', *Science, Technology & Human Values*, **34** (4), pp. 476–501.

Hall, B.H. and Rosenberg, N. (eds) (2010) *Handbook of the Economics of Innovation*, Amsterdam: North Holland.

Hall, P.A. and Soskice, D. (2001) *Varieties of Capitalism: The Institutional Foundations of Comparative Advantage*, Oxford: Oxford University Press.

Hanusch, H. and Pyka, A. (2007) 'Principles of neo-Schumpeterian economics', *Cambridge Journal of Economics*, **31** (2), pp. 275–89.

Jacobs, M. and Mazzucato, M. (eds) (2016) *Rethinking Capitalism: Economics and Policy for Sustainable and Inclusive Growth*, London: Wiley-Blackwell.

Kaldor, N. (1961) 'Capital accumulation and economic growth', in Lutz, F.A. and Hague, D.C. (eds) *The Theory of Capital*, New York: St. Martin's Press, pp. 177–222.

Kalecki, M. ([1935] 1971) 'The mechanism of business upswing', in Kalecki M. (ed.), *Selected Essays on the Dynamics of the Capitalist Economy 1933–1970*, Cambridge: Cambridge University Press, pp. 26–34.

Kalecki, M. ([1954] 1991) 'Theory of economic dynamics', in Osiatynski, J. (ed.), *Collected Works of Michal Kalecki, Volume II: Capitalism—Economic Dynamics*, Oxford: Clarendon Press.

Kapp, K.W. (1950) *The Social Costs of Private Enterprise*, Cambridge, MA: Harvard University Press.

Kapp, K.W. (1963) 'Social costs and social benefits: a contribution to normative economics', in von Beckerath E. and Giersch H. (eds), *Probleme der normativen Ökonomik und derwirtschaftspolitischen Beratung*, Berlin: Duncker & Humbolot.

Kapp, K.W. (1970) 'Environmental disruption and social costs: a challenge to economics', *Kyklos*, **23** (4), pp. 833–46.

Louçã, F. (2021) 'As time went by – why is the long wave so long?' *Journal of Evolutionary Economics*, 6 March, https://doi.org/10.1007/s00191-021-00724-9.

Lucas, R.E. (1988) 'On the mechanisms of economic development', *Journal of Monetary Economics*, **22** (1), pp. 3–42.

Lundvall, B. (eds) (2010) *National Systems of Innovation: Toward a Theory of Innovation and Interactive Learning*, London: Anthem Press.

Lundvall, B. and Borràs, S. (2005) 'Science, technology and innovation policy' in Fagerberg, J., Mowery, D. and Nelson, R. (eds), *The Oxford Handbook of Innovation*, New York and Oxford, Oxford University Press, pp. 599–631.

Marx, K. (1981) *Capital, Volume 3*, New York: Penguin Books.

Mazzucato, M. (2013) *The Entrepreneurial State*, London: Anthem Press.

Metcalfe, J.S. (1994) 'Evolutionary economics and technology policy', *The Economic Journal*, **104** (425), pp. 931–44.

Mowery, D. and Rosenberg, N. (1979) 'The influence of market demand upon innovation: a critical review of some recent empirical studies', *Research Policy*, **8** (2), pp. 102–53.

Nelson, R.R. (1994) 'The co-evolution of technology, industrial structure and supporting institutions', *Industrial and Corporate Change*, **3** (1), pp. 47–64.

Nelson, R. and Winter, S. (1982) *An Evolutionary Theory of Economic Change*, Cambridge, MA: Harvard University Press.

Nelson, R., Dosi, G., Helfat, C., Pyka, A., Saviotti, P., Lee, K., Dopfer, K., Malerba, F. and Winter, S. (2018) *Modern Evolutionary Economics: An Overview*, Cambridge: Cambridge University Press.

Pagano, U. and Rossi, M.A. (2011) 'Property rights in the knowledge economy', in Brancaccio, E. and Fontana, R. (eds), *The Global Economic Crisis*, Abingdon: Routledge, pp. 284–97.

Perez, C. (2002) *Technological Revolutions and Financial Capital: The Dynamics of Bubbles and Golden Ages*, Cheltenham, UK and Northampton, MA, USA: Edward Elgar Publishing.

Perez, C. (2010) 'Technological revolutions and techno-economic paradigms', *Cambridge Journal of Economics*, **34** (1), pp. 185–202.

Perez, C. (2013) 'Unleashing a golden age after the financial collapse: drawing lessons from history', *Environmental Innovation and Societal Transitions*, **6**, pp. 9–23.

Phillimore, J. (1998) 'Neo-Schumpeterian economics: political possibilities and problems', *Journal of Australian Political Economy*, **42**, pp. 48–74.

Pianta, M. (2005) 'Innovation and employment', in Fagerberg, J., Mowery, D. and Nelson, R. (eds), *The Oxford Handbook of Innovation*, Oxford: Oxford University Press.

Pianta, M. (2014) 'An industrial policy for Europe', *Seoul Journal of Economics*, **27** (3), pp. 277–305.

Pianta, M. (2015) 'What is to be produced? The case for industrial policy', *Intereconomics*, **50** (3), pp. 130–37.

Pianta, M., Lucchese, M. and Nascia, L. (2020) 'The policy space for a novel industrial policy in Europe', *Industrial and Corporate Change*, **29** (3), pp. 779–95.

Robbins, L. (1932) *An Essay on the Nature and Significance of Economic Science*, London: Macmillan.

Rodrik, D. (2014) 'Green industrial policy', *Oxford Review of Economic Policy*, **30** (3), pp. 469–91.

Romer, P. (1990) 'Endogenous technological change', *Journal of Political Economy*, **98**, pp. 71–102.

Romer, P. (1994) 'The origins of endogenous growth', *The Journal of Economic Perspectives*, **8** (1), pp. 3–22.

Roncaglia, A. (2009) *Piero Sraffa*, Basingstoke: Palgrave Macmillan.

Rosenberg, N. (1983) *Inside the Black Box: Technology and Economics*, Cambridge: Cambridge University Press.

Rosenberg, N. (2011) 'Was Schumpeter a Marxist?' *Industrial and Corporate Change*, **20** (4), pp. 1215–22.

Savona, M. (2018) 'Industrial policy for a European industrial renaissance: a few reflections', Science Policy Research Unit Working Paper Series no. 7, Brighton.

Schumpeter, J.A. ([1912] 1938) *The Theory of Economic Development*, Cambridge, MA: Harvard University Press.

Schumpeter, J.A. (1939) *Business Cycles*, New York: McGraw-Hill.

Schumpeter, J.A. ([1942] 1950) *Capitalism, Socialism and Democracy*, New York: Harper and Brothers.

Sebastiani, M. (1989) 'Kalecki and Marx on effective demand', *Atlantic Economic Journal*, **17** (4), pp. 22–8.

Smith, K. (1991) 'Innovation policy in an evolutionary context', in Saviotti, P. and Metcalfe, J.S. (eds), *Evolutionary Theories of Economic and Technological Change*, London: Routledge, pp. 256–75.

Smith, T. (2010) 'Technological change in capitalism: some Marxian themes', *Cambridge Journal of Economics*, **34**, pp. 203–12.

Soete, L.G. (2013) 'Is innovation always good?' in Fagerberg, J., Martin, B. and Andersen, E.S. (eds), *Innovation Studies: Evolution and Future Challenges*, Oxford: Oxford University Press, pp. 134–46.

Srnicek, N. (2017) *Platform Capitalism*, Cambridge: Polity Press.

Stiglitz, J. and Lin Yifu, J. (eds) (2013) *The Industrial Policy Revolution I: The Role of Government Beyond Ideology*, Basingstoke: Palgrave Macmillan.

Stoneman, P. (eds) (1995) *Handbook of the Economics of Innovation and Technological Change*, Oxford: Blackwell.

Verspagen, B. (2002) 'Evolutionary macroeconomics: a synthesis between neo-Schumpeterian and post-Keynesian lines of thought', *The Electronic Journal of Evolutionary Modeling and Economic Dynamics*, 1007, https://citeseerx.ist.psu.edu/viewdoc/download?doi=10.1.1.514.9951&rep=rep1&type=pdf.

Verspagen, B. (2005) 'Innovation and economic growth', in Fagerberg, J., Mowery, D. and Nelson, R. (eds), *The Oxford Handbook of Innovation*, New York and Oxford: Oxford University Press.

Vivarelli, M. (1995) *The Economics of Technology and Employment*, Aldershot: Edward Elgar Publishing.

Vivarelli, M. (2013) 'Technology, employment and skills: an interpretative framework', *Eurasian Business Review*, **3** (1), pp. 66–89.

Vivarelli, M. and Pianta, M. (eds) (2000) *The Employment Impact of Innovation: Evidence and Policy*, London: Routledge.

Winter, S. (2014) 'The future of evolutionary economics: can we break out of the beachhead?' *Journal of Institutional Economics*, **10** (4), pp. 613–44.

Witt, U. (2001) Special issue: Economic growth – what happens on the demand side? 'Introduction'. *Journal of Evolutionary Economics*, **11**(1), pp. 1–5.

12. The regulation approach
Brett Heino

The orthodox Marxist thought that took shape in the late nineteenth and early twentieth centuries generally took as a given that capitalism was living on borrowed time. Marx and Engels' ([1848] 2002: 225) evocative casting of modern bourgeois society as a 'sorcerer ... who is no longer able to control the powers of the nether world whom he has called up by his spells' created a dominant conception of capitalism as prone to increasing instability and eventual ruin. This strongly teleological perspective informed the character and policies of the global communist movement, particularly insofar as it came under the stifling influence of Stalinism.

The post-Second World War long boom, however, forced a fundamental rethink. From 1945 through to the early 1970s, capitalism entered an epoch of unrivalled growth and stability in the West, with increased production, productivity improvements and high profit margins being complemented by full employment, rising real incomes and a redistributive welfare state (Elam 1994; Vidal 2013). Mainstream economics, dominated on its macroeconomic side by Keynesianism, spoke of the demise of the traditional business cycle and the crises of overproduction Marxism holds dear (Boyer 1990). Despite the immanent crisis tendencies so carefully dissected by Marx, it was thus clear that capitalism could be made comparatively stable and prosperous for a significant period of time. This situation highlighted the need for intermediate accounts of capitalist development that, whilst employing a Marxist methodology and cognisant of Marx's long-run observations, were able to account for stabilising forces in the short to medium term.

A number of theories geared towards providing just such accounts have been bundled together under the rubric of the 'regulation approach'. This chapter will briefly summarise these theoretical traditions before zeroing in on the Parisian school, which is the most well-known and influential. Its method of theory construction will be elucidated before considering some of its most important concepts. A survey of key criticisms of the approach will then be made, leading into some thoughts on what the future holds for the regulation approach. The continuing vitality and analytical utility of regulationist work entitles us to look to this future with optimism.

THE REGULATION APPROACH: AN OVERVIEW

When most political economists hear the term 'regulation approach',[1] they think almost automatically of the Parisian regulation approach or Parisian school. Indeed, the Parisian school is the most influential current and, unless one is tuned into the field, it is normally seen as being synonymous with the approach as a whole. Because it also 'enjoys the greatest international impact' (Jessop and Sum 2006: 23), it is the principal focus for this chapter. However, it is important to note that there are influential scholars who maintain that the Parisian school is just one amongst others in a more broadly defined regulation approach. Drawing on the typology created by Torfing (1998) and Jessop and Sum (2006), these other variants can be described as a means of introducing some general concerns and key concepts.

The Grenoble school, centred on the *Groupe de recherche sur la régulation de l'économie capitaliste* (GRREC), traces the articulation of two key Marxist laws of social development: the tendency of the rate of profit to fall and the tendency to equalisation of profits across different branches of production (Robles 1994). The articulation of these laws is seen as being guaranteed by social institutions, the coherence of which is described as a mode of regulation (Robles 1994; Jessop and Sum 2006). Scholars in this tradition have posited the existence of three main epochs of capitalism: competitive capitalism, monopoly capitalism, and state monopoly capitalism (Torfing 1998).

A second variant of the regulation approach comes from a group of economists associated with the French Communist Party, led by Paul Boccara. This work stemmed from the state monopoly capital tradition and is focused on how the fundamental survival of capitalism has depended upon the devalorisation of capital (Torfing 1998; Jessop and Sum 2006). This process is handled differently in different historical periods and involves the state and 'anthroponomic factors' which internalise societal norms and values (Hoogvelt 2001: 133). Whilst accepting a periodisation that distinguishes between competitive, monopoly and state capitalist epochs, Boccara, in a point of contrast to the Parisians, rejected 'the myth of Fordism' (quoted in Torfing 1998: 98).

The West German school offers another variation on the regulationist theme. It emerged from the state derivation debate of the 1970s (see, for example, Holloway and Picciotto 1978). Jessop and Sum (2006) note that this school has shared the French concern to explain how capitalism can be reproduced when the forms to which it gives rise (such as value and the state) cannot secure this reproduction in and of themselves. The answer proffered, a mode of societalisation or 'society effect' (*Vergesellschaftungsmodi*), denotes 'processes of structuration and regulation at a societal level' that combine 'a regulation approach to political economy with its own account of the capitalist state' (Jessop and Sum 2006: 46). Using the insights of Gramsci and Poulantzas, scholars in this vein (such as Hirsch and Esser) have explored how techniques for ensuring structural coherence and an integration of the masses could result in a more or less stable 'historical bloc' (Torfing 1998).

The Amsterdam school, sometimes referred to as the Amsterdam School of Transnational Historical Materialism (Staricco 2017), is yet another variant. Scholars in this tradition have stressed the importance of the transnational scale in the constitution of capitalism, particularly insofar as 'the formation of (capitalist) classes transnationally is […] seen as a key process through which politics itself is increasingly transnationalized' (van Apeldoorn 2004: 111). Projecting the notion of 'class fractions' into the study of international politics, the Amsterdam school seeks to explore how this space is structured through 'comprehensive concepts of control' which represent the interests of a specific class fraction as the general interest (Overbeek 2019). Van der Pijl has stated that

> [c]oncepts of control denote a temporary synthesis between the perspective generated by an ascendant trend in the economy articulated by particular 'moments' in the capitalist cycle (the financial, the productive, the commercial, the national or world market, etc.); and the capacity of a set of social forces operating in the context of one or several state(s) to translate this perspective into a general ('comprehensive') programme for society as a whole. (2004: 182)

Neoliberalism is, on this score, an example of a particular comprehensive concept of control (van Apeldoorn 2004).

Finally, affinity with the regulation approach is evident in the social structures of accumulation (SSA) approach to political economy, derived from the work of American political economists such as Gordon, Edwards and Reich (1982). Accepting that capitalism is inherently prone to crisis, scholars in this tradition argue that social structures of accumulation underwrite distinct periods of capitalism. The SSA approach 'aims to explain the stages of capitalism and describes and analyses the institutional arrangements which prevail on each of these stages' (Hein et al. 2014: 12). Although initial exponents of the SSA approach stressed the linkage between a social structure of accumulation and robust capital accumulation, subsequent lines of research have posited that this linkage is a historically contingent one (and one based moreover on the post-Second World War experience – see, for example, Rey Araujo 2018). In keeping with the need to periodise capitalism whilst responding to the challenge posed by the persistence of low growth/low investment neoliberalism, Kotz has suggested the concept of an 'institutional structure', comprising 'a coherent set of economic, political, and cultural/ideological institutions that provides a structure for capitalist economic activity'. Kotz distinguishes between a regulated and liberal institutional structure, differing 'along four dimensions: state-economy relations, capital-labor relations, capital-capital relations, and the character of the dominant ideology' (factors which bear some resemblance to the 'institutional forms' that the Parisians regard as constituting a mode of regulation, as explored further below) (Kotz 2003: 264).

Despite their differences, these currents of a broadly defined regulation approach share a commitment to understanding how, despite immanent crisis tendencies, capitalism can be reproduced through time by the mediation of economic, political and social institutions. Moreover, the study of the arrangement of these institutions and their articulation with capital accumulation gives a solid conceptual basis for attempts to periodise capitalism.

It is worth noting, however, that the contemporary status of these schools is quite variegated. Some strands, such as the scholarship associated with Boccara and the West German state theorists, have generated highly useful concepts but have not continued as coherent, distinct and vibrant research agendas. Their analytical concerns were tied quite tightly to the political economic issues of their time.

Other currents, however, remain active, cohesive and fertile research paradigms. SSA scholarship, for example, remains strong and has grown from its American roots to become a useful tool of analysis in other contexts (see, for example, the work of O'Hara 2008 on Australian capitalism). The Amsterdam school has evolved into a significant current within international political economy and is presently involved in important ontological and methodological debates with Jessop's 'cultural political economy', the latter owing much to the influence of the Parisian school (see, for example, Staricco 2017 and Jessop and Sum 2017). The Parisian regulation approach, for its part, remains the source for a large volume of work on the nature, periodisation and institutional structures of capitalist societies (see, for example, Workman 2009; Boyer 2015, 2018; Christophers 2016; Heino 2017; Neilson 2020; and Uemura 2019). The rest of this chapter focuses on this current: its methods of theory construction, concepts, criticisms and future prospects.

THE PARISIAN REGULATION APPROACH

The Parisian regulation approach (PRA) emerged in France in the late-1970s, stemming from Michel Aglietta's (1979) ground-breaking account of the development of US capitalism. Notable scholars who kick-started it, including Aglietta, Robert Boyer and Alain Lipietz, were heavily influenced by Althusserian structuralism, even if they rejected its problematic construction of reproduction as quasi-automatic and its piecemeal treatment of contradiction (Lipietz 1993). As Neilson (2012: 160) writes: 'Central to the appeal of Althusser's French Regulation School (FRS) "rebel sons" was the implicit promise of a mid-range theory of capitalist development that could complement Marx's long-range account.'

In common with the other regulationist schools discussed above, the Parisians stressed the fact that political, economic and social institutions can help structure the crisis-prone process of capital accumulation. This process could be guided and regularised through a contingent, historically varying combination of economic and extra-economic factors in a distinctive institutional matrix, handling, to varying degrees, the different crisis tendencies of capitalist social relations. Aglietta states eloquently:

> To speak of the regulation of a mode of production is to try to formulate in general laws the ways in which the determinant structure of society is reproduced [...] *[A] theory of social regulation is a complete alternative to the theory of general equilibrium* [...] The study of capitalist regulation, therefore, cannot be the investigation of abstract economic laws. It is the study of the transformation of social relations as it creates new forms that are both economic and noneconomic, that are organized in structures and themselves reproduce a determinant structure, the mode of production. (1979: 13, 16; emphasis added)

This definition pays clear homage to the structural Marxist roots of the approach, and is echoed by Lipietz (1988) who, recognising the dialectical link between regulation and crisis, notes that the former describes a situation where there is a temporary, relative primacy of unity over struggle in a deeply contradictory society. Neilson (2012: 161) adds that 'regulation politically modifies the economic process to temporarily stabilise, or contain, the contradictory core of capitalism'. Through understanding the twists and turns of capital accumulation and the success or failure of attempts to regulate it, powerful mid-range accounts can be produced to explain the trajectory of particular capitalist societies.

A critical precondition of the attempt to create these mid-range accounts is a theory armed with a range of concepts of varying compass, occupying different locations on the plane from abstract to concrete. This is evident in the spiralling method of analysis advocated by the regulationists, which employs a *dialectical* movement along the plane from abstract-simple to concrete-complex (Treuren 1997a).

Aglietta describes this spiral:

> It follows that concepts are not introduced once and for all at a single level of abstraction. They are transformed by the characteristic interplay which constitutes the passage from the abstract to the concrete and enables the concrete to be absorbed within theory. Theory, for its part, is never final and complete, it is always in the process of development. (1979: 15)

In generating these spiralling, intermediate-level accounts of the trajectory of capitalist development, it follows that regulationist scholars must be equipped with concepts at a lower level of abstraction that, while taking their methodological lead from Marx, are nevertheless more concrete and historically sensitive in their operation. Broadly speaking, four such concepts are apparent within the school. They are

- industrial paradigm
- accumulation regime
- mode of regulation
- model of development.

In the following sections we explore the content of these concepts, demonstrating how, in combination, they offer a powerful framework for understanding the physiology of various epochs of capitalism.

Industrial Paradigm

Absolutely central to the early work of Aglietta and Lipietz is a dominant 'industrial paradigm' or labour process model. The organisation of the labour process, particularly the manner in which it produces surplus value for the capitalist, has a powerful influence on the architecture of a capitalist society, a reality that Lukács (1971: 90) grasped when he stated that the organisation of the factory 'contained in concentrated form the whole structure of capitalist society'. In this light, it is somewhat surprising that an industrial paradigm does not generally have the status of a discrete concept in later regulationist work (Dunford 1990), although there are promising signs of a renewed emphasis on the labour process (see, for example, Vidal's 2011 and 2020 work on the post-Fordist labour process).

Generally, early regulationist labour process analysis was closely related to Braverman's (1974) influential account. Aglietta describes neatly how

> Capitalist production is the unity of a labour process and a process of valorization, in which the valorization is dominant [...] On the one hand, we have defined the wage relation, the appropriation of labour-power as a commodity, as *the* fundamental relation of production. On the other hand, we said that capitalist relations of production present a dual character of antagonism and cooperation. In showing how the labour process is transformed under the impulse of the struggle for surplus-value, we must acquit a task that is essential for the transition from the abstract to the concrete in any theory of accumulation: namely to demonstrate that the transformation of the labour process creates relationships within production that adapt the cooperation of labour-power to the domination of the wage relation. (1979: 111; original emphasis)

The particular nexus between valorisation and production, together with the state of technology, results in an industrial paradigm, which can be thought of as a dominant model of labour process organisation that governs the social and technical division of labour. Examples of such paradigms include mass production on semi-automatic production lines and flexible production based on advanced, multi-purpose technologies and 'just-in-time' methods (Aglietta 1979; Vidal 2011). This does not necessarily imply that all branches of the economy are organised according to these same principles: it is enough that the leading sectors revolve around them (Jessop 1991).

Accumulation Regime

Boyer (1990: 35) describes an accumulation regime as a 'set of regularities that ensure the general and relatively coherent progress of capital accumulation'. It is a structure of economic and social patterns governing the composition of social demand corresponding to productive capacity, the time horizons of capital valorisation and the distribution of value within and between classes (Boyer 1990). Such a regime is necessary in the attempt to contain capitalism's contradictions. Of particular importance is the awkward reality that, within capitalist social formations, the factors that favour profitability in the sphere of production are the same factors which impinge upon the realisation of surplus value in the sphere of circulation (Boyer 1990). In a very general sense, a viable accumulation regime must then articulate production and consumption at the macro-level in a stable, reproducible fashion (Jessop 2013). Building on this, and in concert with a redefinition of a mode of regulation, an accumulation regime can essentially be conceived as a concrete arrangement of the economic forms of capital – of the circuit of capital as an *economic process*, conceptually distinct, that is, from its juridic forms (Heino 2017).

In Volume II of *Capital*, Marx (1991) identified the difficulties facing the achievement of such stability, due in part to the restricted nature of working-class purchasing power and the disjunction between the two great departments of the economy (namely, Department I, producing means of production, and Department II, producing means of consumption). Unless surplus value were reduced to nought, workers could never have the purchasing power to procure all they had made, while the interlocking demand of capitalists in one department for the products of the other is beset by a host of temporal irregularities and discontinuities.

Aglietta (1979), using Marx's reproduction schemas, demonstrated how an accumulation regime could help combat this tendency towards instability by the development of particular linkages between the two departments. Specifically, he developed a notion of *extensive* versus *intensive* accumulation. While the former revolves around transformations of the labour process narrowly construed, the latter involves a simultaneous development of both the labour process and the proletariat's conditions of existence through a commodification of individual consumption. Put another way, extensive accumulation (which characterised capitalism in America and other capitalist countries up to the 1920s) was, in the face of continued petty-bourgeois production of working-class subsistence goods and the poverty of the proletariat, dependent primarily on increasing the scale of production in Department I, resulting in recurrent obstacles to the pace of accumulation. Intensive accumulation, through extending the field of capitalist production to the very necessities of life, permitted a more organic series of linkages between the two departments, allowing the creation of a social consumption norm and a more rapid and regular increase in the rate of accumulation (Aglietta 1979). Intensive accumulation thus denotes more than the link between rapid technological change and surplus value; it is a specific mechanism by which social reproduction is mediated.

This outwardly simple typology of regimes of accumulation has become increasingly nuanced and complicated, particularly as the school has expanded its ambit of study beyond advanced industrialised economies. Boyer (1990) notes the profusion of regimes of accumulation in the developing world, including those of pre-industrial, rentier and inward-looking industrialising states.

Mode of Regulation

An accumulation regime cannot in isolation secure the continued reproduction of capital. For this, it requires an attendant mode of regulation, which Jessop and Sum (2006: 42) have described as an 'emergent ensemble of norms, institutions, organisational forms, social networks and patterns of conduct that can temporarily stabilise an accumulation regime'. Typically, this includes coherent and compatible 'institutional forms', of which five are commonly posited: wage relations, state forms, enterprise forms and linkages, money and (arguably) international relations (Jessop 1997, 2013). Like the manner in which the author conceived of an accumulation regime as a concrete arrangement of capital's economic forms, a mode of regulation can be regarded as a concrete hierarchy of capital's juridic forms – the extra-economic struts that allow capital to move through its circuit. This conception best captures the reality that capital has a juridic, as well as economic, existence. Elam hits upon this truth when he states of the regulation approach:

> The result of this marriage between Marxist political economy and institutionalist tradition is a conceptualization of qualitative change within capitalism which posits the existence of not one, but *two*, fundamental dynamics forcing change. Two dynamics growing out of the same discordant soil of capitalist social relations. One giving rise to specific *regimes of accumulation*, the other to particular *modes of regulation*. (1994: 57; original emphasis)

A functioning mode of regulation, however it is defined, both channels the crisis tendencies of a particular capitalist society through institutional pathways and modifies the behaviour of actors (both individual and collective) to accord with the rhythms of the accumulation regime. In containing, ameliorating or deferring the contradictions of an accumulation regime, a mode of regulation can ensure a period of relative stability and growth in capital accumulation (Tickell and Peck 1995: 360). Alternatively, to the extent that modes of regulation contain certain capitalist contradictions at the expense of others and shape economic and social relations in a path-dependent manner, they routinely undermine the very source of their success and become barriers to new modalities of capitalist growth (1995: 360). Moreover, if we move beyond a reductionist conception of capitalism as a purely economic concern, and instead perceive capitalist social relations as assuming both economic *and* extra-economic forms, then it follows that a political handling of capitalism's contradictions does not dispel them – they merely assume a different form.

Model of Development

A model of development is the most all-embracing regulationist concept. Neilson (2012: 162) describes a model of development as a 'stable regime of accumulation or virtuous cycle of production, investment, and consumption engineered by the stabilising regulation of unstable tendencies of the capitalist mode of production'. Boyer and Saillard (2002: 41) proffer a somewhat more dynamic definition that recognises the dialectical unfolding of regulation and crisis, describing a 'mode' of development as the 'way in which an accumulation regime and a type of *régulation* stabilize themselves over the long term and how they enter into a period of crisis and then renew themselves'. Lipietz's (1992) conception is perhaps the most embracing, defining a model of development as *a coherent combination of an industrial paradigm, accumulation regime and mode of regulation*.

This definition of Lipietz's is the most holistic and most useful, particularly as it conceives of a structured totality of economic, political and social forms (thus allowing the PRA to escape a perceived economistic bias, as will be discussed below). Given this, it is odd that his concept has not really achieved broader traction. Heino (2017) has attempted to reinvigorate the concept, arguing that the model of development concept can be pitched at varying levels of abstraction, depending upon the generality or specificity accorded to the model.

With this basket of concepts and a spiralling method of theory construction, the Parisian regulation approach is ideally placed to deliver theoretically sophisticated yet empirically rigorous mid-range accounts of the development of capitalist societies, accounts that both recognise the presence of entrenched structures while affirming the role of human agency.

FORDISM AND POST-FORDISM

To demonstrate how the foregoing concepts work together, it useful to deploy the constructions for which the Parisian school is most well-known: Fordism and post-Fordism. At the outset, it is necessary to point out that, despite the fact that both concepts are central to the regulationist analysis of capitalism since the Second World War, there is considerable diversity in the way they are used and the structures to which they refer. For example, they have been employed variously to describe an industrial paradigm, an accumulation regime and a mode of regulation (Jessop and Sum 2006). However, there is basic agreement as to the main institutional features, mechanisms of coherence and trajectories of crisis of the epochs of capitalism to which they refer. My view is that the most persuasive of the accounts of Fordism and post-Fordism are those that pitch them as models of development – and it is at this level that the following descriptions take place.

Lipietz (1992, 2013) is the scholar who has most consistently and rigorously described Fordism as a model of development. According to him, Fordism combines:

- a Taylorist, mechanised labour process paradigm within large, multi-department firms;
- an autocentric mass production/mass consumption intensive accumulation regime synthesising full employment with rising productivity and real wages; and
- a mode of regulation involving a Keynesian Welfare National State that guaranteed effective demand through protective social legislation and the generalisation of mass consumption norms (Lipietz 1992: 3–7).

Each of these structures had its roots in the late nineteenth and early twentieth centuries. However, it was only after the Second World War – which simultaneously soaked up Depression-era unemployment, intensified industrial production, resulted in a massive devalorisation of capital and forged a new international hierarchy – that these elements could cohere into the Fordist model of development.

Using Lipietz's formulation, we can schematically show how these concepts work together to create an interpretation of how Fordism functioned and achieved coherence for the best part of three decades. The application of Taylorist, mass production principles in the labour process resulted in substantial productivity gains for capitalists. In exchange for accepting the enhanced managerial prerogative and labour intensification consequent upon this development, workers were given liberal rights to organise, assured employment security and growth in their real wages in line with productivity improvements (Neilson 2007). The resultant increased purchasing power in the proletariat's hands allowed it to consume a greater proportion of the goods and services it created, ensuring both high utilisation of capital capacity and further opportunities for capitalists to expand the scale of production. As this increased demand begat further productivity improvements, the cycle began afresh. To fortify and guarantee this process, the national state adopted policies designed to maintain full employment, smooth the business cycle and support the stability of demand by ensuring those temporarily out of work or not a part of the labour force could nevertheless consume. This in turn presupposed both the capacity and willingness of the state to directly involve itself in the circuit of capital.

The result was a self-reinforcing virtuous circle, serving to offset and/or defer the crisis tendencies of capitalism, albeit in a provisional and ultimately self-defeating way. Vidal notes that

> The profit rate in the Fordist period was high initially because it followed a massive decline in the value of physical capital and the nominal value of financial assets during the Great Depression and World War II. A rise in the technical composition of capital was offset by a continuous rise in productivity generated by intensive growth, underconsumptionism offset by rising real wages and overproduction moderated through nationally bound, oligopolistic competition, again with balanced growth via standardized mass production and institutional supports for mass consumption. (2013: 458)

Fordism at this level of abstraction is an ideal type, a means of identifying causal relationships and broad structures. In this sense, it does not describe the concrete experience of any particular society but serves as the basis for a sensitisation to those contexts that can.

Using a similar conceptualisation, and cognisant of the comments just made about the status of ideal-types as abstractions, we can define post-Fordism (or 'liberal-productivism', to use Lipietz's term) as the union of

- an intensification and deepening of Taylorism into the tertiary sector, together with the rise of 'lean' production;
- an intensive accumulation regime that disassociates wages and productivity (and is thus debt-fuelled); and
- a neoliberal mode of regulation in an increasingly complex global division of labour.

Each of these structures has its root in the disintegration of Fordism in the 1970s, and answers, in a provisional and contingent way, the crisis tendencies of that model of development. Despite being pregnant with their own contradictions (the manifestations of which can be seen in events such as the global financial crisis of the late 2000s and the economic dislocation consequent upon the Coronavirus pandemic), these post-Fordist structures remain more or less extant today. In terms of post-Fordism's mechanisms of coherence, the application of intensified Taylorism and lean production within both the manufacturing and service sectors has the effect not only of raising productivity but of further deepening managerial control of the labour process. Companies are thus able to appropriate a greater share of surplus value, resulting in extremely high profit shares of national income (and concomitantly low labour shares) even while profit rates are below those achieved during the period of Fordist coherence. In the midst of a continuing tendency towards global overproduction, finance often proves the more attractive investment for these profits; and it is finance capital which provides the engine of the accumulation regime. Cheap credit emanating from the financial system covers the gap between worker demand and worker purchasing power, expressed in hard money. This cheap credit, a function of the financialisation of capital investment and the hypermobile, international capital flows it begets, now provides the motive force of intensive accumulation. A neoliberal mode of regulation is both constitutive of and constituted by these developments. As part of this mode of regulation, the state is transformed, performing a variety of functions, including the recasting of labour as a commodity like any other, the subordination of social policy to the increasingly deregulated labour market, and reducing fetters on the free movement of commodities and capital across an increasingly connected yet variegated global space.

The analytical utility of the concepts of Fordism and post-Fordism should now be clear. They provide a means of understanding how the long-term crisis tendencies of capitalism were/are managed in a particular time and place through the mediating role of economic, political and social institutions. More specifically, both Fordism and post-Fordism highlight key aspects of the capitalist mode of production, such as the labour process, the circuit of capital and the state, providing coherent and wide-ranging accounts of capitalist epochs that are both more empirically sensitive than much orthodox Marxist theory and more theoretically rigorous than pure institutionalism. Unlike the latter, these concepts tie institutional function and development to the deep-seated tendencies in the capitalist mode of production. Thus, they provide a solid conceptual basis to attempts to periodise capitalism. Through identifying its mechanisms of coherence and trajectories of crisis, Fordism and post-Fordism, as models of development, indicate the specificity of their respective historical epochs.

Despite the strength of analysis made possible by such concepts, however, there have been numerous criticisms made of the approach. It is to these we now turn.

CRITICISMS

The 'golden age' of regulation theory in political economy was probably the 1980s and early 1990s. During that period, its insights and its concepts animated research around the world. Notions of Fordism and post-Fordism entered the scholarly and public discourses, informing political discussion and serving as the basis of often vigorous and long-lived debates. As time passed, however, it appeared that some of the shine was taken off the approach. James (2009: 182) noted that 'the Régulation approach has fallen from the academic limelight in recent years, without much explanation'. Vidal (2011: 273), talking about the concepts of Fordism and post-Fordism (with which, it is important to note, the regulation approach is not reducible or synonymous), opined that, 'while they continue to be used in the social science literature, they have been used as core concepts framing research much less frequently in the 2000s than in the 1980s and 1990s'.

Was this decline a matter of academic faddishness? Or was it was due to inherent weaknesses or shortcomings in the regulation approach, reflecting the various criticisms that have been levelled against its concepts, methodology and political implications? Some of the more significant charges include:

● Reification of capitalist social production relations, leading to a functionalist and undialectical separation of capitalist structures and class struggle (Holloway 1988; Kennedy 2001). The essence of criticism on this point is that regulationists allegedly subscribe to a conception of capitalism as dominated by a set of self-contained and self-sufficient objective laws, presenting a structuralist view that is devoid of the motive force of class struggle (Bonefeld 1987).

- Weakness of mid-range theorising. This charge implies a divorce from a broader theory of the capitalist mode of production and the creation of historically vacuous models of real epochs within capitalism (Brenner and Glick 1991; Mavroudeas 1999).
- Cavalier use of concepts such as Fordism and post-Fordism which, if applied across different societies in an abstract way, reify the experience of those states which most closely match 'the model' (Treuren 1997b).
- Inadequate treatment of the state. Some have alleged that the approach's theory of the state is either underdeveloped or borrowed from other disciplines (Boyer 1990), whilst others accuse it of a narrow, functionalist account of state action (Clarke 1992). Such a charge is related to the claim that the approach is characterised by an innate economism. A leading scholar of the Amsterdam school has pointed to a 'lack of elaboration of the political sphere as a terrain of struggle and a relative neglect of the transnational sphere in favour of a national focus' (van der Pijl 2004: 182).
- Implicit political reformism. Due to its focus on the means through which capitalism's crisis tendencies can be handled through institutions (albeit provisionally and temporarily), the argument has been made that the political implications of the approach favour trying to better regulate capitalism rather than fundamentally challenging its tenets.

Specific responses to most of these criticisms has been provided elsewhere (Heino 2017). In broad terms, it can be said that, whilst the criticisms sometimes point to historical shortcomings, none strike a mortal wound to the central regulationist methodology and/or concepts. By way of illustration, we can consider how the charges relating to the cavalier use of ideal-type models and the treatment of the state can be surmounted from within a regulationist paradigm.

The models of Fordism and post-Fordism have sometimes been applied rather mechanically and abstractly to the experiences of different societies, often by people working outside of the approach (Hampson 1991) and often with a fixation on the labour process in some of the cruder applications of regulation theory. In such uses, the model is confused for an exact account of the experience of the society under study, thereby losing its explanatory potential as more and more caveats and qualifications have to be added in the face of any infinitely complex reality.

However, sophisticated regulationist analysis avoids these pitfalls by sensitising the historical models with which it works to each society that those models are meant to illuminate. This is particularly the case regarding the 'model of development' concept. When pitched at its highest operational level of abstraction, Fordism is an ideal type which, in the manner of Marx (1973: 85–8), 'brings out and fixes the common element'. The ideal-typical model of development does not describe the concrete experience of any particular society in the absence of sensitisation to specific national contexts. Rather, as Treuren (1997a) notes, it forms a vital intermediate link in the movement from abstract to concrete. It has a dialectical relationship with concrete existence in which the model identifies causal relationships while empirical study comments on the adequacy of the theoretical construct.

The charge that the PRA inadequately treats the state is also a criticism that may hold true in certain circumstances, something Jessop and Sum (2006) attribute to an innate economism. However, it is important to distinguish between historical lacunae and shortcomings that are inherently inscribed in the concepts and methodology of the school itself. Sophisticated treatments of the state from a regulationist standpoint demonstrate that rich state analysis is possible from this perspective (see, for example, Théret 1994 and André 2002). Most recently, Neilson and Stubbs (2016) have continued to meet the criticism that regulationists do not have an adequate conception of the state by contributing towards the development of 'third generation' state analysis focused on the notion of the 'competition state', creating a line of enquiry that promises to further deepen the regulationist treatment of the state. This example shows how critical concerns can be remedied by a redoubling of the approach's methodology and further development of its concepts.

Some regulationist scholars, such as Neilson (2012) and Heino (2017) have criticised developments within the trajectory of the regulationist approach. As previously noted, the first generation of regulationist scholars were heavily influenced by Althusserian structuralism, focusing on how the economic, political and social spheres combine to produce and reproduce capitalism. Although the regulationists sought to analyse and problematise this process of reproduction more intimately, the continuities with structural Marxism are manifest in the former's desire to understand and articulate, in a non-reductionist manner, both the economic and extra-economic aspects of a capitalist society. This emphasis reflects a deep connection with Marxist political economy that focuses on the long-term tendencies of capitalism.

Given this heritage, it is important to note the gradual movement away from an explicitly Marxist political economy that has been evident in the approach during the last few decades. For example, the overall state of the labour theory of value is uncertain, with some scholars abandoning it, others holding to it, and yet others not specifying their conception of it (Jessop and Sum 2006). More broadly, there is an increasing eclecticism and desire to seek *rapprochement* with other heterodox currents, such as the Varieties of Capitalism school, which are not necessarily theoretically commensurable (Neilson 2012). Neilson (2012: 161) attributes the sources of this estrangement to a 'focus on national difference, linked with a de-emphasis of the Fordist model of development and the absence altogether of a model of development in the analysis of the contemporary era'. This stymies the approach in delivering on its initial promise of a powerful mid-range Marxist analysis of capitalist development and tends to render it just another institutional theory.

Neilson (2012) and Heino (2017) argue that the regulationist research programme must be put back on course to deliver on its promise of a mid-range Marxist account of the dynamics and trajectories of capitalist social formations. This involves both re-establishing the links between the PRA and the deep-seated tendencies of the capitalist mode of production and the reaffirmation of the utility of ideal type models such as Fordism as a means of identifying causal relationships and broad structures.

Looked at in this way, the regulation approach may be seen as an important bridge between Marxism and other currents of political economy, particularly institutionalism. More than that, it offers a framework for understanding the evolving character of capitalism, responding to recurrent contradictions and crises by developing new structures and means of producing and extracting economic surplus.

THE FUTURE

Vidal (2013: 452) notes that criticism of some simplistic accounts of post-Fordism saw, to a certain degree, the regulationist baby being thrown out with the bathwater. This was never total, particularly given the steady stream of work from leading regulationist scholars, most notably Boyer (e.g. Boyer 2015). Moreover, the regulation approach has been galvanised in recent years by a range of new studies, several of which can be mentioned to indicate its continued vitality and wide range of applicability. Vidal (2011, 2020) has sought to re-interrogate the labour process through the concepts of Fordism and post-Fordism, which represents a welcome re-focusing on what was a central object of analysis in Aglietta's seminal 1979 work. In another important development, Vidal (2013) has also proposed a fundamental shake-up of regulationist concepts, discarding the idea of a mode of regulation and redefining the confluence of its institutional forms as an accumulation regime (which he then regards as functional or dysfunctional according to the application of certain criteria). Such a move represents a welcome test of regulationist 'orthodoxy' and a challenge to those who argue for the retention of the mode of regulation concept. Neilson (2019) has also outlined the parameters and dynamics of a 'neoliberal model of development', a concept that enables us to much more rigorously appreciate the epoch of capitalist development in which we currently live. Christophers (2016) and Heino (2017) have sought to extend the insights of regulation theory to legal analysis, exploring how competition/intellectual property law and labour law respectively are imbricated in their epochs of capitalism. Lastly, regulationist concepts remain important in the burgeoning new field of 'cultural political economy' spearheaded by Jessop (see Chapter 25 in this book). As mentioned above, work also continues in other fields of the broader regulation approach, particularly the SSA and Amsterdam schools.

Overall, the regulation approach remains a potent tool for explaining the structure and dynamics of capitalist societies. Born of a history of rapid political and economic change in the 1970s and 1980s, the regulation approach is, by its nature, geared towards understanding the effects of crisis on economic, political and cultural institutions. In today's climate of profound economic stagnation and political upheaval, the need for such a perspective is clear.

NOTE

1. Confusingly, mainstream economists hearing the term think of regulation as government restrictions that limit what economic actors (households, businesses, banks) might otherwise do. This conventional 'market versus state' perspective is an entirely different paradigm.

REFERENCES

Aglietta, M. (1979) *A Theory of Capitalist Regulation: The US Experience*, London: New Left Books.
André, C. (2002), 'The Welfare State and Institutional Compromises: From Origins to Contemporary Crisis', in R. Boyer and Y. Saillard (eds), *Régulation Theory: The State of the Art*, London: Routledge, pp. 94–100.
Bonefeld, W. (1987) 'Reformulation of State Theory', *Capital and Class*, 11 (3), pp. 96–127.
Boyer, R. (1990) *The Regulation School: A Critical Introduction*, New York: Columbia University Press.
Boyer, R. (2015) *Économie politique des capitalismes: Théorie de la régulation et des crises*, Paris: La Découverte.
Boyer, R. (2018) 'Marx's Legacy, *Régulation* Theory and Contemporary Capitalism', *Review of Political Economy*, 30 (3), pp. 284–316.
Boyer, R. and Saillard, Y. (2002) 'A Summary of Régulation Theory', in Boyer, R. and Saillard, Y. (eds), *Régulation Theory: The State of the Art*, London: Routledge, pp. 36–44.
Braverman, H. (1974), *Labor and Monopoly Capital: The Degradation of Work in the Twentieth Century*, New York and London: Monthly Review Press.
Brenner, R. and Glick, M. (1991) 'The Regulation Approach: Theory and History', *New Left Review*, 188, pp. 45–119.

Christophers, B. (2016) *The Great Leveller: Capitalism and Competition in the Court of Law*, Cambridge, MA: Harvard University Press.

Clarke, S. (1992) 'The Global Accumulation of Capital and the Periodisation of the Capitalist State Form', in Bonefeld, W., Gunn, R. and Psychopedis, K. (eds), *Open Marxism Volume I: Dialectics and History*, London: Pluto Press, pp. 133–50.

Dunford, M. (1990) 'Theories of Regulation', *Environment and Planning D*, **8** (3), pp. 297–321.

Elam, M. (1994) 'Puzzling out the Post-Fordist Debate: Technology, Markets and Institutions', in Amin, A. (ed.), *Post-Fordism: A Reader*, Oxford: Blackwell, pp. 43–70.

Gordon, D.M., Edwards, R. and Reich, M. (1982) *Segmented Work, Divided Workers: The Historical Transformation of Labor in the United States*, Cambridge and New York: Cambridge University Press.

Hampson, I. (1991) 'Post-Fordism, the "French Regulation School", and the Work of John Mathews', *Journal of Australian Political Economy*, **28**, pp. 92–130.

Hein, E., Dodig, N. and Budyldina, N. (2014) 'Financial, Economic and Social Systems: French Regulation School, Social Structures of Accumulation and Post-Keynesian Approaches Compared', *Financialisation, Economy, Society and Sustainable Development*, Berlin School of Economics and Law, Institute for International Political Economy, Working Paper Series No. 22.

Heino, B. (2017) *Regulation Theory and Australian Capitalism: Rethinking Social Justice and Labour Law*, London: Rowman and Littlefield.

Holloway, J. (1988) 'The Great-Bear, Post-Fordism and Class Struggle: A Comment on Bonefeld and Jessop', *Capital and Class*, **12** (3), pp. 93–104.

Holloway, J. and Picciotto, S. (eds) (1978) *State and Capital: A Marxist Debate*, London: Edward Arnold.

Hoogvelt, A. (2001) *Globalization and the Postcolonial World*, Basingstoke: Palgrave.

James, T.S. (2009) 'Whatever Happened to Régulation Theory? The Régulation Approach and Local Government Revisited', *Policy Studies*, **30** (2), pp. 181–201.

Jessop, B. (1991) 'Thatcherism and Flexibility: The White Heat of a Post-Fordist Revolution', in Jessop, B., Kastendiek, H., Nielsen, K. and Pedersen, O.K. (eds), *The Politics of Flexibility: Restructuring State and Industry in Britain, Germany and Scandinavia*, Aldershot: Edward Elgar Publishing, pp. 135–61.

Jessop, B. (1997) 'Survey Article: The Regulation Approach', *Journal of Political Philosophy*, **5** (3), pp. 287–326.

Jessop, B. (2013) 'Revisiting the Regulation Approach: Critical Reflections on the Contradictions, Dilemmas, Fixes and Crisis Dynamics of Growth Regimes', *Capital and Class*, **37** (1), pp. 5–24.

Jessop, B. and Sum, N.-L. (2006) *Beyond the Regulation Approach: Putting Capitalist Economies in Their Place*, Cheltenham, UK and Northampton, MA, USA: Edward Elgar Publishing.

Jessop, B. and Sum, N.-L. (2017) 'Putting the 'Amsterdam School' in its Rightful Place: A Reply to Juan Ignacio Staricco's Critique of Cultural Political Economy', *New Political Economy*, **22** (3), pp. 342–54.

Kennedy, P. (2001) 'Beyond the Objective & the Subjective: Putting Value Back into the Social', *Critique: Journal of Socialist Theory*, **29** (1), pp. 227–44.

Kotz, D.M. (2003) 'Neoliberalism and the social structure of accumulation theory of long-run capital accumulation', *Review of Radical Political Economics*, **35** (3), pp. 263–70.

Lipietz, A. (1988) 'Reflections on a Tale: The Marxist Foundations of the Concepts of Regulation and Accumulation', *Studies in Political Economy*, **26**, pp. 7–36.

Lipietz, A. (1992) *Towards a New Economic Order: Postfordism, Ecology and Democracy*, Cambridge: Polity Press.

Lipietz, A. (1993) 'From Althusserianism to "Regulation Theory"', in Kaplan, E.A. and Sprinkler, M. (eds), *The Althusserian Legacy*, London and New York: Verso, pp. 99–138.

Lipietz, A. (2013) 'Fears and Hopes: The Crisis of the Liberal-Productivist Model and Its Green Alternative', *Capital and Class*, **37** (1), pp. 127–41.

Lukács, G. (1971) *History and Class Consciousness: Studies in Marxist Dialectics*, London: Merlin Press.

Marx, K. (1973) *Grundrisse*, London: Allen Lane.

Marx, K. (1991) *Capital: A Critique of Political Economy Volume III*, London: Penguin Classics.

Marx, K. and Engels, F. ([1848] 2002) *The Communist Manifesto*, London: Penguin Classics.

Mavroudeas, S. (1999) 'Regulation Theory: The Road from Creative Marxism to Postmodern Disintegration', *Science and Society*, **63** (3), pp. 310–37.

Neilson, D. (2007) 'Formal and Real Subordination and the Contemporary Proletariat: Re-Coupling Marxist Class Theory and Labour-Process Analysis', *Capital and Class*, **31** (1), pp. 89–123.

Neilson, D. (2012) 'Remaking the Connections: Marxism and the French Regulation School', *Review of Radical Political Economics*, **44** (2), pp. 160–77.

Neilson, D. (2020) 'Bringing in the "Neoliberal Model of Development"', *Capital and Class*, **44** (1), pp. 85–108.

Neilson, D. and Stubbs, T. (2016) 'Competition States in the Neoliberal Era: Towards Third-Generation Regulation Theory', *Competition and Change*, **20** (2), pp. 122–44.

O'Hara, P.A. (2008) 'A Social Structure of Accumulation for Long Wave Upswing in Australia?', *Journal of Australian Political Economy*, **61**, pp. 88–111.

Overbeek, H. (2019) 'Introduction – Political Economy, Capital Fractions, Transnational Class Formation: Revisiting the Amsterdam School', in Jessop, B. and Overbeek, H. (eds), *Transnational Capital and Class Fractions: The Amsterdam School Perspective Revisited*, Abingdon and New York: Routledge.

Rey Araujo, P.M. (2018) 'Institutional Change in Social Structures of Accumulation Theory: An Anti-essentialist Approach', *Review of Radical Political Economics*, **50** (2), pp. 252–69.

Robles, A.C. (1994) *French Theories of Regulation and Conceptions of the International Division of Labour*, Basingstoke: Macmillan Press.

Staricco J.I. (2017) 'Putting Culture in its Place? A Critical Engagement with Cultural Political Economy', *New Political Economy*, **22** (3), pp. 328–41.

Théret, B. (1994) 'To Have or to Be: On the Problem of the Interaction between State and Economy and Its "Solidarist" Mode of Regulation', *Economy and Society*, **23** (1), pp. 1–46.

Tickell, A. and Peck, J.A. (1995) 'Social Regulation *after* Fordism: Regulation Theory, Neoliberalism and the Global-Local Nexus', *Economy and Society*, **24** (3), pp. 357–86.

Torfing, J. (1998) *Politics, Regulation and the Modern Welfare State*, Basingstoke: Macmillan Press.

Treuren, G. (1997a) 'State Theory and the Origins of Federal Arbitration Legislation in Australia', *Policy, Organisation and Society*, **13**, pp. 56–81.

Treuren, G. (1997b) 'Regulation Theory and Australian Theorising of Institutional Change in Industrial Regulation', paper presented at the 11th Conference of the Association of Industrial Relations Academics of Australia and New Zealand, Brisbane, 20 January–1 February.

Uemura, H. (2019) 'Social Preference and Civil Society in the Institutional Analysis of Capitalisms: An Attempt to Integrate Samuel Bowles' *The Moral Economy* and Robert Boyer's *Régulation Theory*', *Evolutionary and Institutional Economics Review*, **16** (2), pp. 433–53.

van Apeldoorn, B. (2004) 'Transnational Historical Materialism: The Amsterdam International Political Economy Project', *Journal of International Relations and Development*, **7** (2), pp. 110–12.

van der Pijl, K. (2004) 'Two Faces of the Transnational Cadre Under Neo-liberalism', *Journal of International Relations and Development*, **7** (2), pp. 177–207.

Vidal, M. (2011) 'Reworking Postfordism: Labor Process versus Employment Relations', *Sociology Compass*, **5** (4), pp. 273–86.

Vidal, M. (2013) 'Postfordism as a Dysfunctional Accumulation Regime: A Comparative Analysis of the USA, the UK and Germany', *Work, Employment and Society*, **27** (3), pp. 451–71.

Vidal, M. (2020) 'Contradictions of the Labour Process, Worker-Empowerment and Capitalist Inefficiency', *Historical Materialism*, **28** (2), pp. 170–204.

Workman, T. (2009) *If You're in My Way, I'm Walking: The Assault on Working People Since 1970*, Black Point, Canada: Fernwood Publishing.

13. Social structures of accumulation

Terrence McDonough and David M. Kotz

In a capitalist system, class divisions and capitalist competition, combined with the central role of profit-making, lead to periodic economic and institutional instabilities which bring about an interruption of accumulation. For stable accumulation to resume, these sources of instability must be countered through the construction of a new set of enduring economic, political and ideological institutions. The construction of such a social structure underpins the profit rate and creates secure expectations that stimulate long-term investment. This is the basis of a new period of accumulation and the new stage of capitalism. The ensemble of these institutions is the social structure of accumulation (SSA).

As accumulation proceeds, the institutions of an SSA are eventually undermined by class conflict, capitalist competition, and the process of accumulation itself. These forces and the interdependence of the institutions eventually bring an end to the ability of the SSA to promote accumulation, initiating a period of crisis, which is manifested in some combination of sharply reduced accumulation, a falling rate of profit, and/or a high degree of macroeconomic instability. The crisis is only overcome with the construction of a new set of institutions. Thus, capitalist stages are constituted by distinct sets of interdependent economic, political and ideological institutions that underpin relatively successful long periods of accumulation, following one another and separated by periods of crisis.[1]

SSA theory is both a theory of stages of capitalism and a theory of economic crisis. Capitalist stage theory focuses on periods intermediate in length between a short-run business cycle and overall capitalist history. These periods consist of a long period of relatively stable capital accumulation followed by a relatively long and/or deep period of crisis and breakdown. Each of the periods of accumulation is underpinned by a set of institutions designated as an SSA. Examples from the United States include the competitive capitalist SSA that emerged in the mid-nineteenth century followed by a crisis in the last decades of that century, the monopoly capitalist SSA established at the beginning of the twentieth century and ending in the Great Depression, and the post-war SSA, which led to a crisis of rising inflation, unemployment and economic instability in the 1970s.[2] Looking from this perspective, the key challenge now is to identify the characteristics of the SSA in the era of neoliberalism, the different crisis tendencies to which it gives rise, and the prospects for the next SSA. This chapter addresses these issues in successive sections that consider the analytical framework, its applications, the current political economic context, and future prospects.

ANALYTICAL FRAMEWORK

The SSA framework arose in the United States in the wake of the collapse of what many have termed the 'Golden Age' of capitalism, which is generally understood to span the period from 1950 to 1973 and which applies to the USA and most other developed economies. In contrast to that 'Golden Age', the mid-1970s was a period of capitalist crisis characterised by simultaneously high levels of unemployment and high levels of inflation. This so-called 'stagflation' ran counter to the neoclassical version[3] of Keynesian economics, which posited that inflation and unemployment should not increase simultaneously. The contradiction of this particular type of Keynesian theory, along with the failure of its recommended fiscal and monetary policies, was not seen as an opportunity to embrace the more coherent post-Keynesian theory that was on offer, but instead provided an opportunity for long-time critics of Keynesian economics. Monetarism and a variety of new free-market economic theories (such as supply-side economics, rational expectations, and real business cycles) increasingly came to dominate establishment economics. These had in common a different role for government – lower taxes, deregulation, and shifting income away from labour – policies that have been termed neoliberal. By contrast, post-Keynesians emphasised uncertainty undermining investment, distributional conflict driving inflation, and the role of various institutional and contextual factors in explaining the crisis. Some Marxian thinkers saw this new crisis as another crisis of capitalism similar to the two 'Great Depressions' – the long depression at the end of the nineteenth century and the more familiar Great Depression of the 1930s (Bowles and Edwards 1985; Kotz 1987).[4] This observation would lead to the promulgation of general theories of capitalist stages and their subsequent crises.

Traditional Marxist theories of capitalist crisis had tended to locate the crisis of the 1970s in fundamental tendencies of the capitalist economy which were always potentially present. These tendencies included the tendency of the rate of profit to fall, disproportionalities among economic sectors, and either overproduction or underconsumption. Thus, the emergence of crisis would be the expression of these long-run tendencies. The new theories that arose in the 1970s and early 1980s in the wake of the 1970s crisis did not share the same emphasis on the historical ubiquity of these tendencies. Crises could arise from the squeezing of profits due to successful distributional class struggle, or from the breakdown of the institutional framework that had conditioned the previous period of capitalist expansion. Some of the previously identified classical Marxian secular crisis tendencies could play a role in the breakdown of a particular SSA as institutional configurations which held them in check ultimately failed, but they would not all necessarily be present in every crisis. SSA theory defined recurring crisis periods as more serious than downward fluctuations of the ordinary business cycle, but not necessarily as the expression of an ultimate crisis of capitalism.

In defining crisis in this way, these theories drew on another tradition within the Marxian literature. This was a stage-theoretic tradition that began with Hilferding's ([1910] 1980) seminal work on finance capital. Hilferding sought to explain the recovery of capitalism after the long depression at the end of the nineteenth century. While emphasising the emerging dominance of finance capital, he developed a multi-institutional analysis which identified important transformations in capitalism that served to resolve the long depression and inaugurate an era of renewed capitalist expansion. Nicolai Bukharin ([1915] 1973) recapitulated Hilferding's multi-factoral argument, while also emphasising the globalisation of economic activity. This highlights the holistic character of this kind of analysis. In *Imperialism, the Highest Stage of Capitalism*, Lenin ([1917] 1969) summarised Hilferding's argument but also moved beyond it by laying emphasis on the emergence of capitalism's monopoly stage. It was clearly possible in this type of analysis for the emergence of finance capital or imperialism to temporarily resolve a crisis and set the foundations of a new stage of capitalism. This research tradition was to be carried forward in the work of Ernest Mandel (1970, 1978, 1980) and Paul Sweezy and Paul Baran (Sweezy 1968; Baran and Sweezy 1966).

This stage-theoretic perspective emphasised not only recurring periods of crisis but also the periods of capitalist stability and expansion that preceded the crises. Crises arose after long periods (averaging 25 to 30 years) of relatively unproblematic capitalist reproduction and accumulation. This research supplied some of the foundations required to understand the serious character of the crisis of the 1970s and for the formulation of theories of long periods of stable capitalist growth as well as long periods of capitalist crisis. These were variously characterised as theories of long waves in capitalist history and theories of capitalist stages (McDonough 1994). The new theories thus proposed an intermediate level of capitalist crisis between business cycle downturns and capitalist breakdown: in other words, a new theory of long waves in capitalist history and a theory of capitalist stages.

Two strands of this approach arose in Europe. Ernest Mandel contributed his monumental work *Late Capitalism* (1978), but his work on long waves was not extensively developed by subsequent authors. The French Regulation school has been much more influential: Michel Aglietta's *A Theory of Capitalist Regulation* (1979) became its founding document. The proponents of the latter school contended that the dynamic tendencies of capitalism had to be institutionally 'regulated' if they were not to prompt instability and crisis. It identified different 'regimes of accumulation' that united varieties of production regimes with the social consumption norms needed to realise profits. It also theorised 'modes of regulation' which brought in other institutions such as money and the state. The regime of accumulation and an associated mode of regulation could create a period of capitalist stability like the post-Second World War 'Fordist' era. According to the Regulation school, however, the potential of these institutional arrangements to underpin growth would eventually become exhausted, leading to a period of crisis.

At roughly the same time as these European developments, the SSA framework emerged in the United States. Its major founding document was *Segmented Work: Divided Workers: The Historical Transformations of Labor in the United States,* written by David Gordon, Richard Edwards, and Michael Reich (Gordon et al. 1982). David Gordon (1978, 1980) had previously published two articles that developed an approach to long cycle theory and stages of capitalist development. His innovations were undertaken against the background of the American Monopoly Capital school, founded earlier by Paul Baran and Paul Sweezy. The Monopoly Capital school saw the Great Depression years as the expression of the long run stagnation tendency of monopoly capital (as first described by Lenin), which was only temporarily interrupted by the post-Second World War expansion. In Baran and Sweezy's view, this expansion was consequent on a unique set of historical circumstances that were unlikely to be repeated, so that the stagnation tendency of monopoly capitalism was bound to reassert itself.

The question that Gordon's long wave reformulation posed to the monopoly stage of capitalism tradition was whether the post-war expansion was not simply a confluence of circumstances but a powerful institutional reorganisation of American capitalism historically analogous to the earlier organisation of monopoly capitalism as described by Hilferding, Bukharin and Lenin. Gordon proposed a set of newly historically constituted institutions that accounted for the long period of American post-war prosperity. These included multinational corporations, dual labour markets, American international hegemony, a conservative version of Keynesianism, relatively peaceful collective bargaining, and bureaucratic systems of workplace control. The crisis of the 1970s was a result of the breakdown of the ability of these institutions to underpin further successful accumulation.

The addition of a new period of profound institutional transformation to the previously ana-lysed transition to monopoly capitalism raised the following question: Could these successive institutional transformations be generalised into a comprehensive theory of staged capitalism? Gordon et al. (1982) decisively answered this question in the affirmative by proposing that both the monopoly capital transition and the post-Second World War transition rested on the construction of a social structure of accumulation. The construction of an SSA formed the institutional basis for a new stage of capitalism. The shift of an SSA from promoting to obstructing accumulation marked the beginning of the crisis phase of an SSA.[5]

In *Segmented Work* the framework of SSA theory was refined and, perhaps more impor-tantly, applied to explain the history of capital–labour relations in the United States. The three authors had earlier brought segmented labour market theory together with the earlier theorisation of the transition to monopoly capital. Yoking the SSA approach to the history of capital–labour relations provided a clarifying framework for this history and, at the same time, provided a powerful illustration of the potential utility of the SSA theory. Gordon, Edwards and Reich had constructed a theory of long waves of growth and stagnation, a theory of capi-talist stages, an intermediate theory of capitalist crisis, and a framework for the understanding of major transitions in the history of capitalist institutions.

All the theories of capitalist stages have undergone changes and developments over the last few decades. Orthodox Marxists have generally rejected theories of capitalist stages, perhaps because Marxists in the value-theoretic tradition that emphasises the law of the tendency of the rate of profit to fall have been concerned to develop a secular theory of crisis. This approach has denied that the global neoliberal era that succeeded the post-war SSA represented a reso-lution, however temporary, of the 1970s crisis. By contrast, these analysts have seen the entire period since the mid-1970s as one of uninterrupted crisis. Accordingly, Mandel's hypothesis of the possibility of capitalist recovery despite his affirmation of the falling rate of profit has lost contemporary relevance for these theorists.

INFLUENCE AND DEVELOPMENTS

Many concepts used by the Regulation school have been widely diffused in the radical academy. The concept of 'post-Fordism' became pervasive as a description of the post-war regime of accumulation that combined mass production with a linking of wages and produc-tivity and then mass consumption. This conception was widely discussed in conjunction with the 'crisis of Fordism' and speculation on the nature of the 'post-Fordism' that was succeeding the earlier regime (see Jessop 2001; Boyer and Saillard 2002). Despite this recognition and success, the Francophone Regulation school shifted its theoretical moorings. Renouncing Marxian theory, the French Regulation school has searched for an alternative theoretical framework in institutionalism and a microeconomics of conventions. Coincident with this retreat, radical analysts came to see the post-1970s social structure as affirmatively neoliberal, rather than as the end of mass production linked with mass consumption norms.

Although the SSA framework has attracted more subsequent work than Mandel's theory of long waves, it has not been as widely utilised as the Regulation school's characterisation of Fordism and post-Fordism. At the same time, it has largely retained its theoretical coherence. Michael Reich (1997) identified the SSA perspective as rooted in 'Marxian insights concern-ing class conflict over production and distribution at the workplace and in the political arena, and by Marxian and Keynesian macroeconomic analyses'. This characterisation is still basically accurate, although the American institutionalist tradition should also be acknowledged.

Another early and influential work in the SSA framework was the macro-modelling of Samuel Bowles, David Gordon and Thomas Weisskopf in examining the 'rise and demise' of the post-war SSA. In *Beyond the Wasteland: A Democratic Alternative to Economic Decline*, Bowles et al. (1983) argued that the post-war SSA rests on three buttresses, Pax Americana, the limited capital–labour accord, and the capitalist–citizen accord.[6] These institutions originally raised the profit rate, and their disintegration brought lower profit rates and the onset of crisis. This argument was further developed in a series of academic articles (Weisskopf et al. 1983; Bowles et al. 1986, 1989). One (Weisskopf et al. 1983) found econometric support for the hypothesis that variations in profitability can be explained by variations in quantitative indicators of capitalist power in the post-war SSA. This modelling has been extended to Greece and South Korea (Mihail 1983; Jeong 1997), although it has not been a major focus of the SSA literature in recent years.

Following the initial focus of SSA studies on the USA, identification of long waves of accumulation has become more international (Goldstein 1997; Li et al. 2007). William Robinson (2003, 2004, 2008) has developed comprehensive accounts of the history of SSAs in Latin America, addressing both Central and South America. He has located these developments in the context of his broader work which argues that globalisation is a qualitatively new epoch in world capitalism, characterised by the emergence of a transnational capitalist class and the re-articulation of most countries into a global production and financial system. The SSA framework has also been controversially applied to understanding apartheid in South Africa (Nattrass 1992; Heintz 2002).

India has also proven to be an interesting arena for SSA studies. In *India Working*, Barbara Harriss-White (2003) applies an SSA approach that emphasises the social institutions which condition accumulation at a given point in time. The study also includes an incisive analysis of the informal economy outside the major urban areas. Gender, religion, space, classes, and the state are all central to the analysis. Shilpa Ranganathan and Harland Prechel (2007) develop a more historical analysis of SSAs in India. They identify a transition from colonial capitalism to national capitalism in the immediate post-colonial era. Significantly, another transition occurs to a more transnational form of capitalism following a debt crisis in 1991.

The SSA framework has also been used to analyse the history of specific institutions. Prominently, a 'spatialisation' school has sought to directly extend Gordon, Edwards and Reich's history of labour control strategies into the modern era. Gordon, Edwards and Reich identified successive labour control strategies in proletarianisation, homogenisation, and segmentation. Michael Wallace and David Brady (2010) identify a spatialisation strategy based on controlling labour through capital mobility and the threat of capital flight. Following the original argument in *Segmented Work*, they argue that this strategy forms the basis of the current SSA.

In addition to labour control, another strand of the literature has taken up the broader issue of social control in general. One study (Barlow et al. 1993) presents a careful long wave/SSA history of criminal justice policy in the USA from 1789 to the present day. The authors observe that

> the criminal justice system is a vital component of the social structure of accumulation in capitalist societies. As the capitalist state's most openly coercive form of social control, criminal justice plays

a critical role in maintaining social order, and thereby, establishing a favourable business climate. (Barlow et al. 1993: 146)

Raymond Michalowski and Susan Carlson (2000) examine the relationship between unemployment, crime and imprisonment. They accord great importance to distinct phases *within* SSAs. Phillip O'Hara (1995) adds the family to the set of institutions that are crucial to conditioning accumulation in the USA in the post-war period. He also emphasises the importance of household labour in general within capitalist economies. Racial questions are addressed by Francisco Valdes and Sumi Cho (2011), using the SSA perspective as one source for the development of a critical race materialism. This allows a reframing of the SSA analysis including racial dynamics.

Other studies have further broadened the fields of application. Martin Wolfson (2013) has used the SSA framework as a backdrop to understand the history of finance in the United States. On a more microeconomic level, Harland Prechel (2000) has developed an SSA analysis of transitions in corporate form and strategy. Kent Klitgaard and co-authors (Hall and Klitgaard 2012; Klitgaard and Krall 2012) have argued that ecological economics has made progress in understanding how the human economy is necessarily embedded in the larger biophysical ecosystem, drawing sustenance from that system and in turn affecting it. They contend, on the other hand, that ecological economics has an insufficiently sophisticated theory of the internal dynamics of the capitalist economy and its limits are expressed in recurrent crises. They have proposed that SSA theory is well positioned to fill this gap.

SSA theory has been brought up to date through a discussion of the emergence of a new SSA after the 1970s crisis. The focus is on institutional changes such as neoliberalism, globalisation, financialisation and the weakening of labour. In parallel with the first writing on capitalist stages at the turn of the twentieth century, the analysis is multi-factoral, but with different writers placing particular emphasis on different institutions. Kotz and McDonough (2010) characterise the current SSA as global neoliberalism. Asimakopoulos (2009) describes a world SSA based on global segmentation of labour. Wallace and Brady (2010), as mentioned earlier, base the new SSA on the spatialisation of labour control. Tabb (2012) argues that financialisation is the most important element of the current SSA. Robinson (2012) contends that globalisation is a qualitatively new epoch in world capitalism. Kotz (2015) interprets the current SSA as neoliberal capitalism, arguing that, while globalisation and financialisation are important features of this SSA, neoliberalism is its defining character. He argues that globalisation was accelerating well before the start of this SSA, while financialisation was released and gradually gained momentum following the triumph of neoliberal ideas and the passage of financial deregulation bills by the US Congress. Victor Lippit (2014) and David Jaffee (2019) also identify this period as the neoliberal SSA.

Both David Kotz (2010) and Duncan Foley (2012) use an analysis of the recent SSA and its crisis to categorise different kinds of structural crises. Kotz distinguishes between the crises that end a regulated form of SSA and those that end a liberal SSA: the latter are more severe, less easily resolved, and more system-threatening. He contends that latter kind of crisis is what we are facing today. Foley draws a distinction between crises caused by falling profitability and those caused by rising exploitation and that, because the current crisis is of the latter type, solving a severe shortfall in demand is the precondition for emerging from it.

While a solid body of theory and applications has been established within the SSA framework, there are some tasks which remain pressing. First, there has been relatively little discussion of the philosophy of social science underlying SSA theory. Other Marxian approaches to capitalist stage theory have implicitly assumed a traditional dialectical materialism or an Althusserian approach. Since the SSA approach proposes an intermediate level of structure between the conjuncture and the totality of capitalist history, this suggests an underlying depth ontology with layered social structures operating at multiple levels. One direction in which to pursue this would be within the critical realist philosophy founded by British philosopher Roy Bhaskar. The establishment of a depth ontology for stages of capitalism will involve the examination of actual determinative structures at play on several levels of abstraction and at the temporalities of capitalist history in total, the capitalist stage, and the conjuncture. Such an analysis must ask whether a realist depth ontology serves to clarify the multi-leveled expression of social structures in a periodised capitalist history, thus serving as an under-labourer for stage theory.

The study of institutions is a second aspect of SSA analysis that would benefit from further development. The current conception of institutions within the SSA framework is borrowed from the Veblenian tradition of institutional economics. As such, it is a rough and ready, partially empirical notion revolving around customs, habits, practices, rules and laws. These institutions are then regarded within the SSA framework as the crystallisation of the balance of class forces at a particular point in time. The SSA framework would benefit by integrating sociological discussions of structure into its conception of institutions. The sociological tradition has a rich discussion of the origin of structural relations within society. While this discussion is more centred on the concept of agency than a Marxist approach would warrant, further consideration of this tradition could deepen the SSA theory's approach.

INTERPRETING THE CURRENT POLITICAL ECONOMIC SITUATION

SSA theory is useful not only for interpreting the past. It also provides a framework for assessing current political-economic conditions and identifying possible near-future directions of change. According to SSA theory, US and global capitalism are still mired in an economic crisis that began in 2008. As of 2020, the elite response to the crisis consisted primarily of attempted intensifications of neoliberalism. SSA theory indicates that this is an intensification of the institutional structure that led to the crisis in the first place and thus is highly unlikely to constitute a successful response. As this becomes clear, other possible resolutions can be expected to come to the fore. These resolutions are likely to be either major restructurings of institutions within capitalism or initiatives designed to take human society beyond the capitalist pattern of alternating periods of long-run growth and crisis.

The severe financial crisis and Great Recession of 2008–09 took mainstream analysts by surprise, but it was predictable when seen in an SSA framework (Kotz 2008). The same institutions of the neoliberal SSA that fostered some 25 years of long economic expansions after the early 1980s created long-run trends that were unsustainable. Steadily rising household and financial sector debt, the introduction of complex and highly risky new securities, and huge asset bubbles underpinned the growth machine of neoliberal capitalism, but they also led to the collapse of that growth machine in 2008.

The SSA framework views the continuing crisis of global capitalism as rooted in the inability of the neoliberal SSA since 2008 to any longer promote accumulation. When the financial crisis and Great Recession broke out in 2008, it provoked a brief Keynesian response with fiscal and monetary expansion and bailouts of failing institutions. However, in 2010 the longstanding strictures of neoliberal capitalism returned, in the guise of austerity. The result has been a severe stagnation of the major European economies since the immediate recovery from the 2008 financial crisis and Great Recession. The US economy expanded steadily from 2009 to 2019 but at the slow average rate of 2.3 per cent per year.

A stagnation literature arose among mainstream US economists based on neoclassical growth theory (Gordon 2016) or Keynesian theory (Summers 2014). Kotz and Basu (2019) applied SSA theory to explain the long stagnation in the US economy. They found econometric evidence that the entry of the US economy into the crisis phase of the neoliberal SSA undermined the usual positive relation between the rate of profit and the rate of accumulation, explaining the puzzle of sluggish accumulation amidst a high profit rate.

An SSA crisis is expected to continue until a new SSA emerges from the actions and struggles of various groups and classes. Since around 2016, two possible directions of institutional restructuring have appeared. One is rooted in the rise of authoritarian nationalist governments, parties and leaders, in such places as Turkey, India, Poland, Hungary, France, Italy, Austria and the USA. The anti-democratic character of this development shocked mainstream analysts, who had assumed that the liberal democratic state faced no challenge since the end of the Cold War and demise of Communist Party rule in most of the world. However, this anti-democratic development can be understood as the product of a period of severe structural crisis that cannot be resolved within the existing institutional framework. The long stagnation, along with the continuing retrograde trends of neoliberal capitalism, intensified the oppression and insecurity of working people and small business owners, undermining their support for the current political arrangements. This created an opening for demagogues striving for authoritarian power. The programme of such figures can be understood as a possible new SSA to replace neoliberalism.

An authoritarian nationalist restructuring could create a new statist SSA but, unlike the post-war SSA, there would be no capital–labour compromise. The core institutions of an authoritarian nationalist SSA could include the following: (1) continuing domination of labour by capital, aided by a repressive state; (2) growing state spending on infrastructure and the military; (3) a retreat from globalisation and its replacement with bilateral deals between individual countries and limits on trade and capital movements; (4) state intervention in the location decisions of large corporations; (5) nationalist ideology as the glue to hold a cross-class alliance together. Weak trade unions would assure high profits, while expanding state spending would keep demand rising despite stagnating wages. Infrastructure spending, in addition to bringing growing aggregate demand, would aid the profitability of private capital, which depends on the systems of transportation, power and communication.

However, such an SSA would prevent action to counter disastrous global climate change. It would also carry the danger of inter-state conflict or war. Moreover, it would result in increasingly repressive regimes in developed capitalist countries. There are obstacles to consolidating such an SSA in the developed capitalist countries, including continuing support from big business for global economic integration, widespread opposition to the racism and retrograde social policy of such a regime, and popular resistance to the overall politics of authoritarian nationalism.

A second possible direction of restructuring that could lead to a new SSA is that of 'green social democracy'. Growing realisation that global climate change will bring disaster for the future of humankind has galvanised a growing movement around the world, demanding immediate action to restructure domestic and global economies to achieve environmental sustainability. At the same time, the crisis of neoliberal capitalism has stimulated growing support for progressive reform of capitalism in a number of countries in recent years, although, as we will note below, as of 2020 none led to more than brief political success. In Greece, Syriza unexpectedly took office in 2015. That same year the rank and file of the British Labour Party handed the leadership to the unreconstructed left-wing social democrat Jeremy Corbyn. In the USA, Senator Bernie Sanders, an open advocate of social democracy, came close to winning the Democratic Party presidential nomination in 2016 and made a strong showing again in the primary elections in 2020.

Green social democracy could potentially form the basis of a new SSA. The core institutions of a green social democratic SSA would include the following: (1) a new capital–labour compromise that provided wages that grew in step with labour productivity; (2) a shift from private to public provision of healthcare and higher education; (3) a big government infrastructure spending programme aimed both at transition to a green (sustainable) economy and at creating well-paying jobs; (4) expanded social programmes to assure that basic needs for food and shelter are satisfied; (5) global cooperation aimed at green transformation; (6) a revised global system of trade and finance that discourages a race to the bottom and allows space for progressive economic and social change within countries; (7) an ideology of cooperation, collective responsibility for the welfare of all, economic and racial justice, and peaceful relations among states. Rising corporate profits can potentially be consistent with such a regime if it brings rising labour productivity over time and a high level of capacity utilisation resulting from robust growth of demand for output. It is notable that, in the USA, the highest rate of profit since the end of the Second World War was reached, not during the neoliberal SSA, but in 1966 under the post-war SSA.

The viability of a green social democratic SSA would be challenged by the difficulty of stopping, or even slowing, global climate change within a regime that gives rise to relatively rapid economic growth. Social democracy, as a form of capitalism, requires relatively rapid economic growth so that wages and profits can both rise over time. Preventing disastrous global climate change might in the end not be compatible with any form of capitalism, because of its powerful accumulation drive that leads to ever-increasing production of commodities independent of human need. The biggest obstacle to establishing a green social democratic SSA is the relatively weak position of the trade union movement around the world, together with the relatively weak state of the organised left. The last SSA based on a capital–labour compromise, the post-war SSA, emerged in a period when the labour movement was powerful and socialist and communist parties were contending for power, or were already in office, in many countries. A social democratic restructuring may be possible only if the trade union movement and the political left gain sufficient strength to pressure big business into accepting such a transformation.

Each of the three previously mentioned recent examples of growing support for a social democratic direction ended in political defeat. In Greece, Syriza was unable to overcome the opposition to its programme from a powerful Germany that was demanding continued austerity. In the UK, Labour lost the 2019 election to the Conservatives despite widespread support for its domestic economic platform, as the Brexit issue dominated the vote. In the USA, Bernie Sanders was defeated by the centrist Joe Biden despite the popularity of his economic programme. However, the Coronavirus pandemic and associated deep economic depression appear so far to be increasing public support for a green social democratic transformation, which may form the basis for a new SSA.

FUTURE PROSPECTS

SSA theory was originated by Marxist economists who favoured not just progressive, pro-worker reform of capitalism, but a transition beyond capitalism to some form of socialist system. Early Marxism predicted that capitalism would increasingly empower its own grave-diggers, the proletariat, a class that would soon bring socialism to the most developed capitalist countries. The failure of that prediction was a motivation behind the development of SSA theory, which sought to explain the ways in which capitalism, when in difficulty, has been able to periodically restructure itself so as to forestall a challenge to capitalism itself, while resuming economic expansion. Thus, SSA theory has been a theory of the periodic reform of capitalism.

However, no previous socio-economic system has lasted forever, and capitalism may in the end encounter a challenge that it cannot surmount. SSA theory suggests that a transition beyond capitalism might occur in a crisis that cannot be resolved within capitalism itself. Each of the two emerging possible directions of restructuring today has serious flaws as a way forward. Authoritarian nationalism would be likely to bring repression, growing global con-flict, and environmental catastrophe. The emergence of a green social democratic SSA might be blocked by the resistance of capital to such a change in direction. Even if it does emerge, it might not be sufficient or timely enough to forestall a worsening environmental disaster.

A transition beyond capitalism may come onto the agenda as a possible direction of restruc-turing. That direction would leave behind the pursuit of profit for a small wealthy class as the driving force of economic decision-making and install in its place a system of production aimed at satisfying human wants and needs in an environmentally sustainable manner. SSA theory suggests that such a transition, while unlikely at this time, might emerge if neither of the two potentially viable new SSAs can emerge, or if one of the two emerges but in the end cannot forestall a final crisis of capitalism in the next period as the contradictions of that SSA mount.

NOTES

1. For useful collections of articles explaining, reviewing, and applying the SSA approach, see Kotz et al. (1994) and McDonough et al. (2010, 2014).
2. Kotz (2015: ch. 6) suggests that a decade-long liberal SSA emerged in the USA after the First World War and that the Great Depression that began in 1929 emerged from that SSA.
3. Sophisticated presentations of Keynesian economics, often termed post-Keynesian economics, allowed for a period in which cost-push pressures would lead to inflation even in the midst of sig-nificant unemployment. However, this was not emphasised in the simpler versions of 'neoclassical synthesis' Keynesian economics.
4. In much of Europe, the crisis of the late nineteenth century involved a sharp reduction in the rate of accumulation much like that of the 1930s, leading historians to refer to the Great Depression of the late nineteenth century for Europe. However, that term does not easily fit the US economic history. As a late developer, US capitalism experienced a crisis in the late nineteenth century, but it was one

of severe business cycle recessions and long-term deflation, not a slowdown in economic growth or long-run capital accumulation.

5.   Over time, the SSA literature has proposed several ways to understand exactly what happens to an SSA that leads to the crisis phase. At first the concept of 'collapse' of the SSA was suggested. In the later literature it was observed that, while some institutions of an SSA collapse or disappear, many others remain, which suggests that the SSA remains in place but no longer promotes accumulation. The latter conception is similar to the historical materialist claim in relation to the transitions between modes of production: a period of transition begins when the social relations of production shift from promoting the development of the forces of production to obstructing their further development.

6.   A later edition of that book (published in 1990) added a fourth buttress: limited inter-capitalist competition.

REFERENCES

Aglietta, M. (1979) *A Theory of Capitalist Regulation: The US Experience*, London: New Left Books.

Asimakopoulos, J. (2009) 'Globally Segmented Labor Markets: The Coming of the Greatest Boom and Bust, Without the Boom', *Critical Sociology*, **35** (2), pp. 175–98.

Baran, P.A. and Sweezy, P.M. (1966) *Monopoly Capital*, New York: Monthly Review Press.

Barlow, D.E., Barlow, M.H. and Chiricos, T.G. (1993) 'Long Economic Cycles and the Criminal Justice System in the US', *Crime, Law and Social Change*, **19** (2), pp. 143–69.

Bowles, S. and Edwards, R. (1985) *Understanding Capitalism: Competition, Command, and Change*, New York: Harper and Row.

Bowles, S., Gordon, D.M. and Weisskopf, T.E. (1983) *Beyond the Wasteland: A Democratic Alternative to Economic Decline*, Garden City, NY: Anchor Press/Doubleday.

Bowles, S., Gordon, D.M. and Weisskopf, T.E. (1986) 'Power and Profits: The Social Structure of Accumulation and the Profitability of the Postwar US Economy', *Review of Radical Political Economics*, **18** (1–2), pp. 132–67.

Bowles, S., Gordon, D.M. and Weisskopf, T.E. (1989) 'Business Ascendancy and Economic Impasse: A Structural Retrospective on Conservative Economics, 1979–87', *Journal of Economic Perspectives*, **3** (1), pp. 107–34.

Boyer, R. and Saillard, Y. (2002) *Regulation Theory: The State of the Art*, New York: Routledge.

Bukharin, N. ([1915] 1973) *Imperialism and World Economy*, New York: Monthly Review Press.

Foley, D.K. (2012) 'The Political Economy of Postcrisis Global Capitalism', *South Atlantic Quarterly*, **111** (2), pp. 251–63.

Goldstein, J.P. (1999) 'The Existence, Endogeneity, and Synchronization of Long Waves: Structural Time Series Model Estimates', *Review of Radical Political Economics*, **31** (4), pp. 61–101.

Gordon, D.M. (1978) 'Up and Down the Long Roller Coaster', in Crisis Reader Editorial Collective (ed.), *U.S. Capitalism in Crisis*, New York: Union for Radical Political Economics, pp. 22–35.

Gordon, D.M. (1980) 'Stages of Accumulation and Long Economic Cycles', in Hopkins, T.K. and Wallerstein, I. (eds), *Processes of the World-System*, Beverley Hills, CA: Sage Publications, pp. 9–45.

Gordon, D.M., Edwards, R. and Reich, M (1982) 'Long Swings and Stages of Capitalism', in *Segmented Work, Divided Workers: The Historical Transformation of Labor in the United States*, Cambridge: Cambridge University Press, pp. 18–47.

Gordon, R. J. (2016) *The Rise and Fall of American Growth*, Princeton, NJ: Princeton University Press.

Hall, C.A.S. and Klitgaard, K.A. (2012) *Energy and the Wealth of Nations: Understanding the Biophysical Economy*, New York: Springer.

Harriss-White, B. (2003) *India Working: Essays on Society and Economy*, Cambridge: Cambridge University Press.

Heintz, J. (2002) 'Political Conflict and the Social Structure of Accumulation: The Case of South African Apartheid', *Review of Radical Political Economics*, **34** (3), pp. 319–26.

Hilferding, R. ([1910] 1980) *Finance Capital*, London: Routledge & Kegan Paul.

Jaffee, D. (2019) 'The Current Crisis of Neoliberal Capitalism and Prospects for a New Social Structure of Accumulation', *Review of Radical Political Economics*, **51** (2), pp. 1–18.

Jeong, S. (1997) 'The Social Structure of Accumulation in South Korea: Upgrading or Crumbling?', *Review of Radical Political Economics*, **29** (4), pp. 92–112.

Jessop, B. (2001) *Regulation Theory and the Crisis of Capitalism, Volumes 1–5*, Cheltenham, UK and Northampton, MA, USA: Edward Elgar Publishing.

Klitgaard, K.A. and Krall, L. (2012) 'Ecological Economics, Degrowth, and Institutional Change', *Ecological Economics*, **84**, pp. 247–53.

Kotz, D.M. (1987) 'Long Waves and Social Structures of Accumulation: A Critique and Reinterpretation', *Review of Radical Political Economics*, **19** (4), pp. 16–38.

Kotz, D.M. (2008) 'Contradictions of Economic Growth in the Neoliberal Era: Accumulation and Crisis in the Contemporary U.S. Economy', *Review of Radical Political Economics*, **40** (2), pp. 174–88.

Kotz, D.M. (2010) 'The Final Conflict: What Can Cause a System-Threatening Crisis of Capitalism?', *Science and Society*, **74** (3), pp. 362–79.

Kotz, D.M. (2015) *The Rise and Fall of Neoliberal Capitalism*, Cambridge, MA: Harvard University Press.

Kotz, D.M. and Basu, D. (2019) 'Stagnation and Institutional Structures', *Review of Radical Political Economics*, **51** (1), pp. 5–30.

Kotz, D.M. and McDonough, T. (2010) 'Global Neoliberalism and the Contemporary Social Structure of Accumulation', in McDonough, T., Reich, M. and Kotz, D.M. (eds), *Contemporary Capitalism and Its Crises*, Cambridge: Cambridge University Press, pp. 93–120.

Kotz, D.M., McDonough, T. and Reich, M. (1994) *Social Structures of Accumulation: The Political Economy of Growth and Crisis*, Cambridge: Cambridge University Press.

Lenin, V.I. ([1917] 1969) *Imperialism, the Highest Stage of Capitalism*, New York: International Publishers.

Li, M., Xiao, F. and Zhu, A. (2007) 'Long Waves, Institutional Changes, and Historical Trends: A Study of the Long-Term Movement of the Profit Rate in the Capitalist World-Economy', *Journal of World-Systems Research*, **13** (1), pp. 33–54.

Lippit, V.D. (2014) 'The Neoliberal Era and the Financial Crisis in the Light of SSA Theory', *Review of Radical Political Economics*, **46** (2), pp. 141–61.

Mandel, E. (1970) *Marxist Economic Theory*, New York: Monthly Review Press.

Mandel, E. (1978) *Late Capitalism*, London: Verso.

Mandel, E. (1980) *Long Waves of Capitalist Development*, Cambridge: Cambridge University Press.

McDonough, T. (1994) 'Social Structures of Accumulation, Contingent History, and Stages of Capitalism', in *Social Structures of Accumulation: The Political Economy of Growth and Crisis*, Cambridge: Cambridge University Press, pp. 72–84.

McDonough, T., Kotz, D.M. and Reich, M. (2014) *Social Structure of Accumulation Theory*, Vols. 1 and 2, Cheltenham, UK and Northampton, MA, USA: Edward Elgar Publishing.

McDonough, T., Reich, M. and Kotz, D.M. (2010) *Contemporary Capitalism and Its Crises*, Cambridge: Cambridge University Press.

Michalowski, R.J. and Carlson, S.M. (2000) 'Crime, Punishment, and Social Structures of Accumulation: Toward a New and Much Needed Political-Economy of Justice', *Journal of Contemporary Criminal Justice*, **16** (3), pp. 272–92.

Mihail, D.M. (1993) 'Modelling Profits and Industrial Investment in Postwar Greece', *International Review of Applied Economics*, **7** (3), pp. 290–310.

O'Hara, P.A. (1995) 'Household Labor, the Family, and Macro-economic Instability in the United States: 1940s–1990s', *Review of Social Economy*, **53** (1), pp. 89–120.

Nattrass, N. (1992) 'Profitability: The Soft Underbelly of South African Regulationist/SSA Analysis,' *Review of Radical Political Economics*, **24** (1), pp. 31–51.

Prechel, H. (2000) *Big Business and the State: Historical Transitions and Corporate Transformation, 1880s–1990s*, Albany: State University of New York Press.

Ranganathan, S. and Prechel, H. (2007) 'Political Capitalism, Neoliberalism, and Globalization in India: Redefining Foreign Property Rights and Facilitating Corporate Ownership, 1991–2005', in Prechel, H. (ed.), *Politics and Neoliberalism: Structure, Process and Outcome: Research in Political Sociology, Vol. 16*, Amsterdam: JAI Press/Elsevier Ltd, pp. 201–43.

Reich, M. (1997) 'Social Structure of Accumulation Theory: Retrospect and Prospect', *Review of Radical Political Economics*, **29** (3), pp. 1–10.

Robinson, W.I. (2003) *Transnational Conflicts: Central America, Social Change, and Globalization*, London: Verso.

Robinson, W.I. (2004) *A Theory of Global Capitalism: Production, Class, and State in a Transnational World*, Baltimore, MD: Johns Hopkins University Press.

Robinson, W.I. (2008) *Latin America and Global Capitalism: A Critical Globalization Perspective*, Baltimore, MD: Johns Hopkins University Press.

Robinson, W.I. (2012) 'Global Capitalism Theory and the Emergence of Transnational Elites', *Critical Sociology*, **38** (3), pp. 349–63.

Summers, L. (2014) 'U.S. Economic Prospects: Secular Stagnation, Hysteresis, and the Zero Lower Bound', *Business Economics*, **49** (2) pp. 65–73.

Sweezy, P. (1968) *The Theory of Capitalist Development*, New York: Monthly Review Press.

Tabb, W.K. (2012) *The Restructuring of Capitalism in Our Time*, New York: Columbia University Press.

Valdes, F. and Cho, S. (2011) 'Critical Race Materialism: Theorizing Justice in the Wake of Global Neoliberalism', *Connecticut Law Review*, **43** (5), pp. 1513–72.

Wallace, M. and Brady, D. (2010) 'Globalization or Spatialization? The Worldwide Spatial Restructuring of the Labor Process,' in McDonough T., Reich, M. and Kotz, D.M. (eds), *Contemporary Capitalism and Its Crises: Social Structure of Accumulation Theory for the 21st Century*, Cambridge: Cambridge University Press, pp. 121–44.

Weisskopf, T.E., Bowles, S. and Gordon, D.M. (1983) 'Hearts and Minds: A Social Model of US Productivity Growth', *Brookings Papers on Economic Activity*, **2**, pp. 381–441.

Wolfson, M.H. (2013) 'An Institutional Theory of Financial Crisis', in Wolfson, M.H. and Epstein, G.A. (eds), *The Handbook of the Political Economy of Financial Crises*, New York: Oxford University Press, pp. 172–90.

14. Capital as power

Tim Di Muzio and Matt Dow

What is capital and how is it accumulated are fundamental questions in political economy. Does capital comprise the machines used in production, as the neoclassical economists tell us, or is it 'unpaid surplus labour' embodied in commodities for sale on the market, as Marxists suggest? A third view that has emerged over the last few decades seems more convincing on these important questions. This conceives of capital as social power represented in the monetary capitalisation of income-generating assets. This is the approach to the political economy of capitalism taken by the school of thought called capital as power.

This chapter explores this relatively new approach to political economy and argues that it is an insightful and important perspective that can be used to investigate and understand a variety of political-economic problems associated with the accumulation of capital, such as the inequality of wealth, climate change and planned obsolescence. We begin by examining the dominant process within capitalist societies: the ownership and capitalisation of income-generating assets. We discuss why this process developed, and how it flourished in the 1990s with the revolution in shareholder value and accounting changes related to the valuation of the largest corporations – those that accumulate the most money – in the global economy. Having established a clear understanding of the importance of capitalisation, we contrast the capital as power approach with neoclassical economics and Marxist political economy, before moving on to discuss some of the key innovations and debates arising from this school of thought. We conclude our exploration of the capital as power approach with discussion of its limitations and some avenues for future research.

THE SPECTRE OF CAPITAL ACCUMULATION IN POLITICAL ECONOMY

We know that the desire to accumulate money in a capitalist economy embodies a *structural logic*. This is reflected in the fact that no investor or businessperson takes risks with their money or their enterprise in order to lose money or their business. It is how the profits or surpluses (both measured in money) are created or accumulated in capitalist economies that underpins the big divisions between neoclassical economics, Marxism and the capital as power approaches to political economy. There is much at stake in answering the questions about what capital is and how capitalism functions. This is especially the case for those social forces that would like to transform global society towards well-being, equality and the logic of livelihood rather than the accumulation of profit and power. Therefore, to understand the origins and distinctive characteristics of the capital as power approach, we must first probe more deeply into the two dominant schools of political economy thought, neoclassical economics and Marxism, and their competing analytical definitions of 'capital'.

For neoclassical economists, capital is a material entity typically called 'capital goods' that represents the tools, equipment and sometimes technology that workers use during the labour process to provide goods and services to consumers. Capital is also understood as an entity that contributes to economic output (Mankiw 2009: 47ff.). Since 'capital', in this school of thought, is defined as capital goods (such as the machines, tools and equipment that workers use in the production process), it follows that the accumulation of capital means the increasing ownership of ever more capital goods, though neoclassicists also associate this with increasing 'utils' or pleasure (Nitzan and Bichler 2009; Di Muzio and Dow 2017). Importantly, they argue that profit is the reward capitalists receive for their contribution to economic output, just as workers receive wages or salaries for their contribution to the production process. In mainstream economics, this relates to the *production function*, showing the economic output of any given productive enterprise as a function of the amount of labour and capital that is used (Clark [1899] 1908). Therefore, if we have knowledge of what individual contributions labourers and capital goods make to the overall 'economic pie' produced, then we can know how to divide the pie. For example, if we know that workers contributed 30 per cent to output and capitalists the other 70 per cent, then if the market value of that economic output is $100, workers should get $30 and the capitalists $70. While this seems simple enough, the problem confronted by the production function is that you must know the contributions of each factor of production (labour and capital) *before* you know the value of the economic output. The nature of this problem can be considered in terms of a simple example, such as a bakery with an oven for baking bread. The oven is the capital good. Its present value, calculated according to standard financial practice, is calculated as:

Present Value = Expected Future Profit/Interest Rate +1

Now suppose the *expected* future profit arising from the use of the capital good is $100 and the rate of interest is 5 per cent. The calculation would be:

Present Value = 100/1.05 = $95.24

However, if the actual profit turns out to be $200, then:

Present Value = 200/1.05 = $190.48

What this suggests is that the same oven can have two (or multiple) values depending on the actual profit. The present value of the oven is based on the expected future profit it will yield. However, since we cannot know the actual profit in advance – and the production function tells us we must know the value of capital in advance – the attempt to justify capitalist profits breaks down. What this means is that the distribution of economic output between workers and capitalists cannot be the result of their individual contributions to economic output. Indeed, 'capital' may not be a tangible material entity after all.

Does the Marxist analysis of capital and its accumulation fare any better? In Marx's vast volumes and during the intellectual stages of his writing, he used the word capital in three slightly different ways. Sometimes it refers to the capitalist class, those who own the means of production. Sometimes it signified a social relation between the owners of the means of production and waged workers. Sometimes capital is viewed through the exploitation of waged workers involved in the production of commodities during the working day. In this third usage, unpaid labour is deemed to be retained by the capitalist owner as profit with a view to reinvesting in material production, thereby expanding the magnitude of money accumulated over time.

To measure how profits are made off the backs of labour, Marx relied on a labour theory of value. He argued that during the production process of commodities, workers are paid less than the full value of their labour power. Capital, in his view, is 'unpaid surplus labour' and is thus a *specific form* of exploitation (commonly represented as M → C → LP/MP → C' → M').[1] It follows that, if the full value of the labour power expended during the working day were remunerated, there would be no profit for the capitalist to take and no relationship of exploitation.

Here, it is useful to make a distinction between what exploitation means in common parlance and what Marx means by exploitation. The word exploitation entered the English language from French and originally meant to gain an advantage or profit from some activity at the expense of nature or someone else. When applied to workers, we would all be familiar with observing that workers are 'exploited' if they are paid below subsistence wages, intimidated by their employer or a manager, work in environmentally hazardous or generally unsafe environments, or are threatened with the sack or physical violence. But Marx means something more specific when he theorises exploitation – that the workers are not paid the full value of their contribution to the production of commodities. Part of their labour power exerted during the production process is exploited as profit for the capitalist. Another way of putting it is that the capitalist's profit is equal to the unpaid surplus labour of his or her employees.

It is one thing to say that the exploitation of labour is the source of all profit and quite another thing to demonstrate it empirically. This is where Marx's labour theory of value breaks down – a difficulty known as the 'transformation problem'. As anyone who has had a job knows, wages are paid in a certain currency unit (such as dollars and cents), whereas labour expended is measured in minutes and hours – the two measures are not commensurable units. So, to demonstrate the correctness of the Marxian theory, it would have to be shown how the exploitation of labour time gets converted into prices. This has never been convincingly done (Nitzan and Bichler 2009; Kliman et al. 2011; Cockshott et al. 2014; Bichler and Nitzan 2015a). In short, Marx and most Marxists define 'capital' abstractly as 'unpaid surplus labour' embodied in commodities. There are also additional empirical problems that have been left unanswered by Marxists who maintain that capitalism is just a mode of production and that capital is the surplus value produced of the work by industrial wage-labour after the produced commodities are sold by the capitalists. First, Marxists cannot quantifiably or empirically measure, nor differentiate between productive and unproductive labour, especially when it comes to generating surplus value because '[t]here is no objective way to separate "production" in general – and the sphere of "capitalist production" in particular – from other forms of social reproduction' (Nitzan and Bichler 2009: 121). Second, Marxist political economy has never been able to demonstrate that all capitalists or the earnings of firms are from simply producing commodities. This is not to say that waged-labour exploitation is not important or real: rather, all *forms* of labour discrimination and exploitation are important to commodity prices and thereby the profitability of firms, because commodities are priced by the cost of producing them plus their mark-up. Wages are just one part of a commodity's cost of production. Therefore, the central ontology of the capitalist regime of profits and prices cannot simply be rooted in the exploitation of waged labour. To argue that the labour theory of value still holds because unpaid surplus labour is hidden or embodied within commodities tells us very little of how capitalists and firms generate *all* their earnings in the capitalist world economy.

So, while both neoclassical economics and Marxist political economy provide frameworks for study of particular aspects of capitalism, we argue that their understandings of capital are flawed. A more convincing theory is provided by the capital as power approach introduced into critical political economy by Nitzan and Bichler (2009). This approach follows the original conception of the term capital as a set of funds invested in an income-generating asset (Cannan 1921; see also Braudel 1983: 232ff.; Muldrew 1998: 2ff.). As Cannan argues, it was Adam Smith who redefined capital as material goods used in production, thereby making a 'very serious departure from the conception of capital which had hitherto prevailed. Instead of making the capital a sum of money that is to be invested or has already been invested in certain things, *Smith makes it the things themselves*' (1921: 480, emphasis added). This conceptual error and historical departure was not only passed on to both Marx and neoclassical economics, but it has misled scholars and practitioners into believing capitalists want to accumulate machines or unpaid labour time because their earnings and profits are entirely dependent on them. Rather, the drive is to increase social power, which is at the very heart of capitalism (Di Muzio and Dow 2017).

THE LINEAGE AND KEY CONCEPTS OF CAPITAL AS POWER

The capital as power theory was primarily born of a frustration with neoclassical economics being the dominant ideology in the discipline and in university economics departments in North America, Israel and Western Europe; and from disquiet about the usual constructions of classical Marxism (Bichler and Nitzan 2015a, 2015b, 2020).

As an alternative perspective, the capital as power approach shares some affinities with the work of Kalecki ([1943] 1971) and the Monopoly Capital school of neo-Marxist political economy, both of which investigated the rise of monopoly capitalism and the importance of power to accumulation. For example, Kalecki's concept of the *degree of monopoly* was 'a quantitative proxy for economic power whose effect is registered on the profit markup', as well as his theory that structures of power in capitalism were 'linked to the class distribution of income – and from there to broad patterns of consumption, investment, the business cycle and economic policy' (Nitzan and Bichler 2009: 50–51). The later work of Baran and Sweezy, giving rise to the Monopoly Capital school, empirically demonstrated that structures of capitalism shifted from so-called competitive to monopolistic by the late nineteenth and early twentieth centuries – as the result of a new class structure of financiers, business executives, industrial owners and government officials who allied to become the primary social force in the making and remaking of monopoly capitalism (Baran and Sweezy 1966).

The fundamental difference between the capital as power approach and Monopoly Capital school is that the latter has maintained three key assumptions from Marx. First is the labour theory of value, seeing labour as the primary source of surplus value: all other forms of profit a corporation makes, outside of the production process, are called *economic surplus*. Second, the monopolistic era is treated as an anomaly, not capitalism proper. Third, industrial capital is regarded as 'productive', while finance capital is 'parasitic' and 'fictitious'. In contrast, the capital as power approach does not theorise capitalists by sectors (such as finance or industrial sectors). Instead, it draws on the insights of C. Wright Mills ([1956] 2000) and Matthew Josephson (1934) who emphasised the interwoven business and government power elites and networks that closely cooperate with each other if it results in more profits and power.

Exponents of the capital as power approach also argue that the unnecessary separation between finance and industry has led Marxist political economy towards a fabricated distinction – between what is considered as real and fictitious capital. The former is said to arise from production of actual goods and services that, when sold at a profit, create an increase in capital. This is the process of M–C–M', using the notation previous explained in note 1. In other words, 'capital exists as *commodities* – means of production, work in progress and commodity money whose prices are governed by labour time, whether historical or current' (Nitzan and Bichler 2009: 167). Fictitious capital, on the other hand, arises from the circulation of money in processes of buying and selling, i.e. M–M'. Fictitious capital is defined as 'ownership claims on earnings whose price is the present value of those earnings'; and the primary reason it is fictitious is it distorts, absorbs or parasitically lives off all surpluses generated in the production process (Nitzan and Bichler 2009: 168ff.; see also Marx [1883] 1993; Hilferding [1910] 1981).

Some contemporary Marxists have also adopted Hyman Minsky's (1982) *financial instability hypothesis* which shows '... credit and fictitious capital as oscillating around the util-denominated "capital stock" publicised by the national accounts' (Nitzan and Bichler 2009: 170). This has further led them to mistakenly see finance or fictitious capital as the 'manifestation of capitalism running out of breath' (Durand 2017: 12). Together, these features have led modern Marxist and neo-Marxist political economy to a narrow conception of capital accumulation that hinges on commodity production alone.

To build a more comprehensive view of capital and capital accumulation, the capital as power approach draws from Veblen's ([1923] 1967) conception that capitalists are now largely *absentee owners*, which means they are 'investors of "funds", absentee owners of pecuniary wealth with no direct industrial dealings' (Nitzan and Bichler 2009: 230). As Bichler and Nitzan state,

[t]he ultimate owners of these assets, whether big or small, exercise little voice in the management of the underlying production processes. For the most part, they merely buy and sell shares of these assets and collect the flow of dividends. Often, their diversification is so extensive that they don't know exactly what they own. And that characterization is by no means limited to portfolio owners. Many of the largest direct investors – including the capitalist dons whose names populate the Forbes listing of the superrich – are equally removed from any industrial dealings. (2009: 230)

The capital as power approach is also indebted to Veblen for his distinction between 'business' and 'industry'. Industry has always existed in human societies insofar that it depends on human creativity, cooperation, integration and synchronisation that aims to enhance community and overall human well-being. On the other hand, business is 'an institution of power. It exists to control human industry for profit, not production, and therefore bears a negative relationship to industry' (Di Muzio 2013: xv). Drawing on this distinction, Veblen ([1923] 1967) saw capitalists not as contributors to industry but as controllers of it for profitable ends. This is seen in how capitalists or business owners sabotage or restrict industry's capacity to innovate and produce, the creation of planned obsolescence, and the protection of private property rights (Noble 1977; Slade 2007; Cutler and Gill 2014). The primary aim of capitalists is to attempt to control or limit global human society's capacities to socially reproduce and innovate outside of capitalist social relations and the price system writ large (Nitzan and Bichler 2009).

While influenced by Veblen, it should be noted that there are some significant differences between the capital as power approach and Veblen's political economy (see Bichler and Nitzan 2019). The two most important distinctions are that the capital as power approach, methodologically, is dialectical and, politically, it seeks to move away from capitalism. The original critical institutionalists, like Veblen, understood history and change through an evolutionary lens. Yet more starkly, the more modern new institutionalist school, influenced by neoclassical economics, has abandoned the critique of capitalism (Bichler and Nitzan 2020).

Research agendas are usually informed by key concepts that form the heart of a theoretical perspective. In the capital as power approach to political economy, there are three key concepts: capitalisation, differential accumulation, and dominant capital. Each needs to be understood in relation to its historical context.

Capitalisation is the most fundamental of the three concepts. Especially during the 1990s, economists and financial investors debated how to value corporations (and other investments) (Edwards 1989; Krier 2009). An initial attempt at valuing the modern corporation argued that the value of a firm's outstanding shares should reflect the physical assets it owns, so that the value of shares should only go up or down if the firm increased or decreased its physical assets (Roy 1997; Krier 2005, 2009). Another attempt at valuation looked to the dividend payout or yield corporations issued to their shareholders (Krier 2005, 2009). Challenging these models of capitalist accounting was a different type of model, growing in prominence since the 1990s and now ubiquitous among investors – the capitalisation model (Baskin and Miranti 1997). This contends that the value of a corporation reflects the expectations that investors have about its future earnings (Krier 2009). The future is not foreseeable and therefore involves risk. Because money in the hand today is worth more than the prospect of receiving it in the future, investors discount future flows of income into a present-day money value equivalent. The monetary value of the shares that corporations trade on the stock markets of the world is known as their market capitalisation. To find the market capitalisation of a firm, all one needs to do is multiply the monetary value of one share at any one time with the number of shares outstanding on the market. Thus, a company with 10 outstanding shares valued at US$10 would have a market capitalisation or value of US$100.

According to the World Bank, the total market capitalisation of all publicly listed corporations at the end of 2018 was US$68 trillion.[2] Simultaneously, if we consider the world's governments, we find that total world public debt is about US$60 trillion, with the United States and Japan accounting for about half of this total.[3] The value of these shares and government bonds represent their capitalisation, and thus any theory of political economy that takes capitalism seriously should start with capitalisation. For example, we might be willing to pay US$10 dollars for a share today if we expect our investment to be valued at US$20 in the future. We would be very bad investors if we thought the reverse: paying more money today and getting less monetary value as a future return. With this in mind, we can define capitalisation as the process of discounting a future flow of income into a present value adjusted by some factor of risk.

Differential accumulation, a term coined by Bichler and Nitzan (1995), is the second key concept in the capital as power approach. It brings our attention to the fact that capitalist investors achieve different rates of return on their investments because they have different investment strategies and portfolios. To gauge their performance, investors typically rely on a benchmark or average rate of return such as the S&P 500 or the MSCI's Global Investable Market Index. The goal is not to meet the desired benchmark rate of return but to beat it. What this means is that accumulation is *always* differential – some accumulate more than others do and at a faster rate.

The third building block is the concept of dominant capital. It typically means the one hundred largest corporations by market capitalisation, since these are the firms that are price makers and largely shape and reshape the terrain of social reproduction through their business and political activities (Nitzan and Bichler 2009; Di Muzio 2013, 2015a, 2015b). The precise definition of dominant capital – whether focused on the top one hundred corporations or more or less – can be determined by the researcher. The key point of the dominant capital concept is to recognise the huge difference between firms such as Google, Amazon and Exxon Mobil in comparison with small- and medium-sized firms. The smaller enterprises can often play an important role in the local and sometimes global economy, but they have far less power over the lives of people than the large firms that dominate the world economy.

Having defined these concepts, we can consider examples of how the capital as power approach interprets capitalism.

KEY CONTRIBUTIONS AND DEBATES

The capital as power approach understands capitalism, not as a mode of production or exchange, but as a mode of power that prioritises the role of organised power over everyday life in a market economy. In this conception, there is absolutely no separation or distinction between economics and politics, insofar that the nation state and all branches of government are entirely interwoven and inseparable from capital accumulation, the market economy and social reproduction. The capital as power approach expands and deepens the concept of what capitalism is by emphasising what capitalists themselves largely care about: the institution of ownership and the capitalisation of income-generating assets, be they shares in corporations, government bonds or other instruments generating a rate of monetary return.

This is seen in how famously wealthy capitalists, such as Warren Buffet (Berkshire Hathaway), Bill Gates (Microsoft), Jeff Bezos (Amazon), and Mark Zuckerberg (Facebook), make most of their fortune – primarily from income generated by their ownership of corporate stock, not just from labour exploitation in their companies (Nitzan and Bichler 2009; Di Muzio 2015b). The prices of corporate stock are not solely contingent on labour exploitation but, rather, depend on a wide variety of social, natural, and political-economic issues and events (Nitzan and Bichler 2009; Krier 2009; Bichler and Nitzan 2018; Cochrane 2020). For example, Bezos's wealth increased after the onset of the Covid-19 pandemic – reportedly increasing by an average of US$13 billion per day – largely because the value of Amazon shares skyrocketed. This was due to the anticipation by investors that Amazon would be making record earnings throughout the crisis, reflecting Amazon's power and position in the global marketplace and its unique capacity to deliver in such a crisis (Pitcher 2020). So, a key research agenda for the capital as power approach would be to investigate how a corporation like Amazon generates its earnings. What we would find is rising and falling earnings are not simply generated from retail and other services that Amazon provides, but also by corporate lobbying, litigation, filing for patents to protect against competition, key investments in other firms, putting rivals out of business and various tax avoidance schemes – to name just some of the firm's many activities that have an effect on its profit (Nitzan and Bichler 2009; Bichler and Nitzan 2017b; Swartz 2019; Veblen [1904] 1975; Zucman 2015).

The capital as power approach argues that what is actually being capitalised by investors is the institutional power of corporations or governments to generate an income stream by shaping the terrain of social reproduction in their favour. In this view, the accumulation of capital is not a narrow offshoot of production. Rather, it involves a broad power process where many factors can bear on revenues or earnings (such as legislation, lawsuits, industrial accidents, corporate espionage, etc.). Therefore, capital accumulation is theorised as commodified differential power measured in money, not socially abstract labour time or utils (units of pleasure or satisfaction). In other words, the differential accumulation of capital in this framework translates into rising capitalisation of owned income-generating assets represented in money. Capital is theorised as 'commodified' because ownership claims to income generating assets can be bought and sold (for example, you can buy shares in Microsoft one day, then sell them another day and buy shares in Apple). Also, since money can be thought of as a claim on people and natural resources, the more money someone has access to, the more power they potentially have over people and natural resources. The income stream for firms is the revenue generated primarily by the sale of goods and services from which they derive profit, whereas the income stream for governments stems from taxes, fines and fees on a given population and revenue from the privatisation of public assets. Those firms and governments with the largest capitalisation are deemed to be the most powerful as they can shape and affect the social process more effectively than their rivals or counterparts.

The capital as power approach not only focuses on the differential capitalisation of firms (i.e. their market value as determined daily by investors relative to other firms) and states (i.e. their budgets) but also on how these institutions exert power over a broad social field to generate revenue (by using bribes, lobbying, mercenaries, disinformation campaigns, union busting, etc.). Looking from this viewpoint, capitalism is a politico-economic system premised on

> the social property relations between hierarchically arranged owners and non-owners whereby income-generating assets are differentially capitalized based on the institutional power of business and governments to generate income streams by shaping and reshaping the landscape of social reproduction through the market and price system. (Di Muzio and Dow 2017: 9)

By social reproduction here, 'we mean the way any society produces, consumes and reproduces its lifestyles, how it conceives of these lifestyles and how it defends them juridically or through the application of violence' (Di Muzio and Dow 2017: 9).

What of capitalism's origins? These have been extensively debated elsewhere (see Brenner 1977; Wood 2002; Anievas and Nişancıoğlu 2015; Lafrance and Post 2019). Suffice to say here that, from the capital as power perspective, finding the origins of capitalism must come through locating the practice of capitalisation, not just state-reinforced market-led commodity production rooted in waged-labour exploitation (Nitzan and Bichler 2009: 147ff.; Di Muzio 2018). Therefore, the capital as power approach loosely follows Fernand Braudel's (1981, 1983, 1984) historicism on European capitalism, which locates the European origins of capitalism starting in the thirteenth century in European financial centres: Venice (1250–1510), Antwerp (1500–1569), Genoa (1557–1627), Amsterdam (1627–1733), and London (1733–1896). The capital as power approach, however, also acknowledges the criticism of Braudel's view of the market economy as being reminiscent of Adam Smith's 'invisible hand': both tend to see the market as ahistorical and a 'pure sphere of exchange' relatively untouched by political or corporate power (Teschke 2003: 129ff.). That said, commodity production, wage workers, finance and markets have existed to some extent throughout human history (Bloch 1962; Braudel 1983; Wallerstein [1983] 2003; Nitzan and Bichler 2009; Harari 2011; Mann [1986] 2012, [1993] 2012; Neal and Williamson 2014; Di Muzio 2015a). As Braudel carefully reminds us, capitalism did not invent 'hierarchies, any more than it invented the market, or production, or consumption; it merely uses them' (1977: 75). As a result, the capital as power approach seeks to uncover both the present and historical social power relations that have contributed to the intensified influence of monetisation and ownership over everyday life.

Exponents of the capital as power approach agree, to a certain extent, that the origins of capitalism are connected to Marx's insight, in which he stated that '[n]ational debts, i.e. the alienation of the state – whether despotic, constitutional or republican – marked with its stamp the capitalist era ... Public credit becomes the credo of capital' (Marx [1867] 1976: 919). In other words, when investors buy government securities, they are not only looking to get a return on their investment but are capitalising the state's official power to tax and discipline populations and potentially to wage war, to shape the terrain of social reproduction for capital accumulation (Nitzan and Bichler 2009; Di Muzio and Robbins 2016; Hager 2016; Di Muzio and Dow 2017). On the other hand, they disagree with what has become known as *Political Marxism* or the *Capital-Centric* conception of the origins of capitalism as emerging in the English countryside sometime during 1380 to 1520 (Dimmock 2014; Lafrance and Post 2019; McNally 2020). The Political Marxist approach 'freezes capitalism's history' in England, reducing the origins of capitalism to a singular causality such as domestic class struggle through agrarian enclosure movements (Lafrance and Post 2019). Political Marxists are also criticised for promoting a form of Eurocentrism because they largely downplay or ignore the geopolitical origins of capitalist modernity from England and Europe's interactions with Eastern Empires (e.g. Mongol and Ottoman), African and Indigenous slavery and colonisation, and so on (Anievas and Nişancıoğlu 2015; Di Muzio 2015a; Di Muzio and Dow 2017). Di Muzio and Dow (2017) have critiqued both Political Marxists and Anievas and Nişancıoğlu's uneven and combined development approach to the study of the origins of capitalism, by drawing from the capital as power approach. They highlight that neither approach provides an adequate definition of capital and capitalism and that they have at least three important historical omissions with respect to the rise of capitalism in England: the financial revolution and the Bank of England; the transition to coal energy; and the capitalisation of state power as it relates to war, colonialism and slavery.

The empirical characteristics of the capital as power approach as a means of understanding modern capitalism are also distinctive. For example, one of Bichler and Nitzan's contributions has been their identification of what they labelled 'the Weapondollar–Petrodollar Coalition' (WPC). The WPC describes how armament firms, oil companies and producing countries (with the collaboration of the US government) have become dependent on energy conflicts in the Middle East to boost oil prices in order to beat the average rate of return. From their empirical work it seems that, without energy conflicts, the returns made by oil companies fail to meet the benchmark rate of return posted by the S&P 500 (Bichler and Nitzan 1995, 2015c, 2018). The other side of the relationship is that most major oil-producing nations are in the Middle East and usually acquire, with their increased revenue, more military equipment (usually from the USA) whose stated need is for national defence and potentially initiating the next energy conflict. This has been a dynamic trend in global capitalism until recently, helping to explain why the turmoil associated with the 'Arab Springs', Syrian and Libyan Civil Wars, the rise of ISIS, and the instability in Iraq, Iran, Lebanon, Venezuela and Crimea region have failed to raise the price of oil (Bichler and Nitzan 2017a, 2018). Bichler and Nitzan posit that a new global dominant coalition has potentially replaced the WPC, at least for now. They call it the Technodollar Coalition, which is representative of Fortune 500 technology companies, such as Apple, Microsoft and Alphabet Inc. (Bichler and Nitzan 2017a).

Investigating this coalition, Bichler and Nitzan demonstrate that neither neoclassical economics nor Marxist political economy can adequately explain how capital or corporate stock is measured, how commodity prices form, and the ongoing *collusion* between governments, corporate competitors and allied industries. Neoclassical economics argues that a corporation's 'capital stock' is measured in its util-generating capacity, while Marxists would say it is equal to the socially necessary abstract labour time (SNALT) it would take to reproduce it (Bichler and Nitzan 2015c, 2018). But utils are totally subjective and incapable of being measured (Keen [2001] 2011; Bichler and Nitzan 2015c, 2018). SNALT is also unobservable and unmeasurable: if capital stock is reflected by it, then why does Microsoft's (or Exxon Mobil's) stock value and market capitalisation end up greater than General Motors, even though General Motors has a far larger exploitable workforce and owns more machines, factories and other factors of production than either Microsoft or Exxon Mobil (Nitzan and Bichler 2009: 173)?

In the capital as power approach, the capital stock or value of a corporation like Exxon Mobil is not merely contingent on its ownership of oil reserves and oil prices. Rather, a wide range of factors bear on its earnings, including the confidence of investors, structural power and income-generating assets from refineries, transportation, advertising, labour laws, physical and intellectual property rights protection, taxation and environmental standards (or their lack of), and the effect of wars in the Middle East (Bichler and Nitzan 1995, 2018; Di Muzio 2015a). Exxon Mobil's market capitalisation, which is the preferred way to measure the power of a corporation in the capital as power perspective, hinges on the corporation's capacity to shape and reshape the terrain of social reproduction with the intention of generating higher earnings (and thereby bigger dividends and rising share prices) than their rivals in the corporate universe.

These insights from the capital as power school contrast with the difficulties neoclassical and Marxist economists evidently have in explaining why the price of oil went up or down during energy conflicts in the Middle East. Neoclassical economics believe commodity prices only go up when demand outpaces the supply or down when supply outpaces demand. This basic theory of supply and demand was disproved by Piero Sraffa's (1960) work (see also Keen [2001] 2011). Three fundamental problems are that: (1) perfect competition cannot exist because of 'market distortions' (government interference) and oligopolies; (2) capitalists create consumer wants (through advertising, creating artificial scarcity and planned obsolescence); and (3) supply and demand theory cannot empirically explain or measure the desires of buyers or sellers nor abundance or scarcity (Bichler and Nitzan 2015c). Marxists, on the other hand, focus on the cost of producing oil: for example, did the cost of the factors in the production of oil (labour, rent or royalties, machines) go up or down (Bina 1988; Labban 2008)? Eco-Marxist Anna Zalik (2010) attempted to explain price by arguing that oil is priced by its use value (which cannot be measured in prices objectively) with exchange value (measured in abstract labour time) based on supply and demand.

Proponents of the capital as power approach argue that both these perspectives largely ignore speculation in commodity stock exchanges, geopolitics and state intervention; and that they therefore fail to problematise how oil is priced (Bichler and Nitzan 2015c; see also Dicker 2011). Moreover, in this view, the price of oil (or any commodity) is the outcome of either a single corporation or an oligopoly (such as OPEC) using its power to engineer the price (Tarbell 1904; Sampson 1975; see also Veblen [1921] 2001). As economist M.A. Adelman stated during the first OPEC energy crisis: '[t]he world "energy crisis" or "energy shortage" is a fiction ... *But belief in the fiction is a fact. It makes people accept higher oil prices as imposed by nature, when they are really fixed by collusion*' (1972–73: 73, emphasis added). In other words, there are dominant capital blocs that are not entirely anchored to being alliances to their host nations (unless it benefits them) but to the pursuit of power and profits. As seen in the WPC, dominant armaments, energy and financial firms, as well as various governments are all willing to create regional instability if that helps them to exceed the average rate of return on capital. In the case of the first OPEC energy crisis, the fallout was a major factor that led to both the debt crisis in the global South and stagflation in the global North. Both developments contributed to the adoption of more neoliberal policies, favouring investors, corporations and creditors over labour (Nitzan and Bichler 2009; Bichler and Nitzan 2015c, 2018; Di Muzio 2015a; Di Muzio and Robbins 2016).

CONCLUSIONS: LIMITATIONS AND FUTURE RESEARCH

The capital as power approach is still developing, whereas more established currents of analysis such as neoclassical economics and Marxian political economy have been around for well over a century. A growing number of scholars deploying the capital as power framework have made significant contributions, ranging from the analysis of capital as a form of 'operational symbolism' and differential capitalisation as a form of 'calculable order' (Martin 2010) to new research into South Korea's political economy (Park 2016). There has also been research looking at De Beers as a global diamond cartel (Cochrane 2015), the relation between hierarchy and energy consumption/production (Fix 2015), the Hollywood industry's control of social creativity (McMahon 2013), the ownership of US public debt (Hager 2016), and the financialisation of the global food industry (Baines 2015). Other research work by one of the current authors has shown the applicability of the capital as power perspective to a wide range of contemporary issues: the prevalence of debt, the creation of money, capitalism's dependence on fossil fuel energy, and investigating the prevalence and persistence of global inequality (Di Muzio 2015a, 2015b; Di Muzio and Robbins 2016, 2017). The primary aims have been to question, challenge and overcome the limitations of the existing schools of political economy.[4]

While these advances are significant, other important topics remain under-researched. For example, capital as power researchers have yet to take seriously the gender and racial dimensions of capital accumulation, although Di Muzio (2015a) demonstrates the importance of both slavery and colonialism to the making of British and American global capitalism. There are also deeper conceptual challenges relating to the question of power itself. Samuel Knafo et al. (2013) have pointed out the somewhat circular logic of capital accumulation when seen from the capital as power perspective – insofar that a capitalist needs to have social power in the first place in order to get more social power. Nitzan and Bichler's (2009) suggestion that social power is being accumulated and possessed may require greater empirical detail by examining more specific cases. The capital as power approach has no difficulty in accepting Antonio Gramsci's (1971) insights into the nature and sources of *state hegemony* (a mixture of consensual and coercive social power) or how social power creates its own resistance (Marx's material dialectics) (Lukes [1974] 2005; Gill 2008; Martin 2010), but there too more applied research is indicated.

Examining the connections between increasing inequalities and environmental stresses is a field of inquiry where the capital as power approach has obvious relevance. Capital accumulation is primarily about the accumulation of money, and since money is a claim on society and resources, the more you have of it, the greater your potential power over society and resources. For example, the 1 per cent of wealth owners have built a separate economy for themselves and consume at far higher levels than their poorer counterparts, contributing disproportionately to global climate change relative to their numbers (Di Muzio 2015b; Kenner 2019). This lifeworld is not simply about 'billionaire playgrounds' (such as Monaco and Dubai) or other elements of the lifestyles of the rich and famous. These planetary capitalist elites are even trying to colonise outer space and Mars (e.g. SpaceX) (Piper 2018). Studying phenomena like these, the capital as power perspective focuses on social power relations that are embedded in ownership and finance and examines how the global capitalist/owners shape and reshape the terrain of social reproduction in their interests at the expense of both the biosphere and the rest of humanity (Di Muzio 2015b).

Researchers taking the capital as power perspective are always looking to build research networks, and create new dialogues and debates with other paradigms of political economy. The future of capital as power as a research agenda is, of course, up to researchers. There are still many questions, debates and contributions to be made from the capital as power perspective. For example, what powerful coalitions exist in global capitalism? How can we most effectively investigate the power of privately owned corporations? What are the origins of strategic sabotage? What does the future of capitalism look like? What are some alternatives to capitalist money, debt and finance? How can we transition out of capitalism peacefully? How does nature or the environment fit into the capital as power framework? How can gender and race be incorporated into the framework? These are just some of the important questions that can be addressed from the capital as power perspective.

NOTES

1. M represents money, C represents constant capital, and LP is labour power, MP is machine power, which would transform constant capital into the commodity C′ that, when sold in the market, generates the increased capital M′. The amount by which M is increased in this process is the surplus value.
2. See https://data.worldbank.org/indicator/CM.MKT.LCAP.CD (accessed 30/4/2020).
3. See https://www.economist.com/content/global_debt_clock (accessed 30/4/2020).
4. For a survey of Nitzan and Bichler's work, as well as that by other critical political economists using the capital as power method, readers can browse Nitzan and Bichler's archives at: https://bnarchives .yorku.ca/ and the capital as power website: https://capitalaspower.com/.

REFERENCES

Adelman, M.A. (1972–73) 'Is the oil shortage real? Oil Companies as OPEC Tax-Collectors', *Foreign Policy*, **9**, pp. 69–107.
Anievas, A. and Nişancıoğlu, K. (2015) *How the West Came to Rule: The Geopolitical Origins of Capitalism*, London: Pluto Press.
Baines, J. (2015) 'Fuel, Feed and the Corporate Restructuring of the Food Regime', *The Journal of Peasant Studies*, **42** (2), pp. 1–27.
Baran, P.A. and Sweezy, P.M. (1966) *Monopoly Capital: An Essay on the American Economic and Social Order*, New York: Modern Reader Paperbacks.

Baskin, J.B. and Miranti, P.J. (1997) *A History of Corporate Finance*, Cambridge: Cambridge University Press.

Bloch, M. (1962) *Feudal Society Vol. 1: The Growth of Ties of Dependence*, trans. L.A. Manyon, London: Routledge.

Bichler, S. and Nitzan, J. (1995) 'Bringing Capital Accumulation Back In: The Weapondollar-Petrodollar Coalition Military Contractors, Oil Companies and Middle East "Energy Conflicts"', *Review of International Political Economy*, **2** (3), pp. 446–515.

Bichler, S. and Nitzan, J. (2015a) *The Scientists and the Church*, World Economic Association, accessed 19/8/2021 at: http://bnarchives.yorku.ca/440/22/bn_tsatc_2015_wea.pdf.

Bichler, S. and Nitzan, J. (2015b) 'The CasP Project: Past, Present, Future', *Working Papers on Capital as Power*, No. 2015/04, December, pp. 1–29, accessed 19/8/2021 at: http://bnarchives.yorku.ca/466/.

Bichler, S. and Nitzan, J. (2015c) 'Still about Oil?' *Real-world Economics Review*, **70**, pp. 49–79, accessed 19/8/2021 at: http://bnarchives.yorku.ca/432/2/20150200_bn_still_about_oil_rwer.pdf.

Bichler, S. and J. Nitzan. (2017a) 'Oil and Blood in the Orient, Redux', *Research Note on Capital as Power*, accessed 19/8/2021 at: http://bnarchives.yorku.ca/525/2/20171200_bn_blood_and_oil_in_the _orient_redux.pdf.

Bichler, S. and Nitzan, J. (2017b) 'Growing through Sabotage Energizing Hierarchical Power', *Working Papers on Capital as Power*: accessed 19/8/2021 at: http://bnarchives.yorku.ca/512/2/20170700_bn _growing_through_sabotage_wpcasp.pdf.

Bichler, S. and Nitzan, J. (2018) 'Arms and Oil in the Middle East: A Biography of Research', *Rethinking Marxism*, **30** (3), pp. 418–40.

Bichler, S. and Nitzan, J. (2019) 'CasP's "Differential Accumulation" versus Veblen's "Differential Advantage"' (revised and expanded), *Working Papers on Capital as Power*, accessed 19/8/2021 at: http://bnarchives.yorku.ca/583/2/20190100_bn_casp_da_vs_veblen_da_revised_expanded_wpcasp .pdf.

Bichler, S. and Nitzan, J. (2020) 'The Capital as Power Approach: an Invited-then-Rejected Interview with Shimshon Bichler and Jonathan Nitzan', *Working Papers on Capital as Power*, accessed 19/8/2021 at: https://capitalaspower.com/wp-content/uploads/2020/06/20200600_bn_the_casp _approach_invited_then_rejected_interview_plus_epilogue.pdf.

Bina, C. (1988) 'Internationalization of the Oil Industry: Simple Oil Shocks or Structural Crisis?' *Review*, **11** (3), pp. 329–70.

Braudel, F. (1977) *Afterthoughts on Material Civilisation and Capitalism*, trans. Patricia Ranum, Baltimore, MD: Johns Hopkins University Press.

Braudel, F. (1981) *The Structures of Everyday Life: The Limits of the Possible. Civilization and Capitalism 15th to 18th Century*, trans. Sian Reynolds, London: William Collins Sons.

Braudel, F. (1983) *The Wheels of Commerce: Civilization and Capitalism 15th to 18th Century,* trans. Sian Reynolds, London: William Collins Sons.

Braudel, F. (1984) *The Perspective of the World: Civilization and Capitalism 15th to 18th Century*, trans. Sian Reynolds, London: William Collins Sons.

Brenner, R. (1977) 'The Origins of Capitalist Development: A Critique of Neo-Smithian Marxism', *New Left Review*, **104**, pp. 25–92.

Cannan, E. (1921) 'Early History of the Term Capital', *Quarterly Journal of Economics*, **35** (3), pp. 469–81.

Clark, J.B. ([1899] 1908) *The Distribution of Wealth: A Theory of Wages, Interest and Profits*, 3rd edn, New York: Macmillan.

Cochrane, D.T. (2015) 'What's Love Got to Do with It? Diamonds and the Accumulation of De Beers, 1935–55', unpublished PhD dissertation, Department of Political Science, York University.

Cockshott, P., Cottrell, A. and Alejandro, V.B. (2014) 'The Empirics of the Labour Theory of Value: Reply to Nitzan and Bichler', *Investigación Económica*, **73** (287), pp. 115–34.

Cochrane, D.T. (2020) 'Disobedient Things: The Deepwater Horizon Oil Spill and Accounting for Disaster', *Valuations Studies*, **7** (1), pp. 3–32.

Cutler, C.A. and Gill, S. (eds) (2014) *New Constitutionalism and World Order*, London: Cambridge University Press.

Di Muzio, T (ed.) (2013) *The Capitalist Mode of Power: Engaging the Power Theory of Value*, London and New York: Routledge.

Di Muzio, T. (2015a) *Carbon Capitalism: Energy, Social Reproduction and World Order*, London: Rowman and Littlefield.

Di Muzio, T. (2015b) *The 1% and the Rest of Us: A Political Economy of Dominant Ownership*, London: Zed Books.

Di Muzio, T. and Dow, M. (2017) 'Uneven and Combined Confusion: On the Geopolitical Origins of Capitalism and the Rise of the West', *Cambridge Review of International Affairs*, **30** (1), pp. 3–22.

Di Muzio, T. and Robbins, R. (2016) *Debt as Power*, London: Bloomsbury.

Di Muzio, T. and Robbins, R. (2017) *An Anthropology of Money: A Critical Introduction*, New York: Routledge.

Dicker, D. (2011) *Oil's Endless Bid: Taming the Unreliable Price of Oil to Secure the Economy*, Hoboken, NJ: John Wiley and Sons.

Dimmock, S. (2014) *The Origin of Capitalism in England, 1400–1600*, Leiden: Brill.

Durand, C. (2017) *Fictitious Capital: How Finance is Appropriating Our Future*, London: Verso.

Edwards, J.R. (1989) *A History of Financial Accounting*, London: Routledge.

Fix, B. (2015) 'Putting Power Back into Growth Theory', *Review of Capital as Power*, **2** (1): pp. 1–37.

Gill, S. (2008) *Power and Resistance in the New World Order*, 2nd edn, London: Palgrave Macmillan.

Gramsci, A. (1971) *Selections from the Prison Notebooks*, New York: International Publishers.

Hager, S.B. (2016) *Public Debt, Inequality and Power: The Making of the Modern Debt State*, Berkeley: University of California Press.

Harari, Y.N. (2011) *Sapiens: A Brief History of Humankind*, New York: Harper.

Hilferding, R. ([1910] 1981) *Finance Capital: A Study of the Latest Phase of Capitalist Development*, ed. T. Bottomore, London: Routledge.

Josephson, M. (1934) *The Robber Barons: The Great American Capitalists, 1861–1901*, New York: Harcourt, Brace and Co.

Kalecki, M. ([1943] 1971) *Selected Essays on the Dynamics of the Capitalist Economy 1933–1970*, Cambridge: Cambridge University Press.

Keen, S. ([2001] 2011) *Debunking Economics: The Naked Emperor Dethroned?*, revised and expanded edition, London: Zed Books.

Kenner, D. (2019) *Carbon Inequality: The Role of the Richest in Climate Change*, London: Routledge.

Kliman, A., Bichler, S. and Nitzan, J. (2011) 'Systemic Crisis, Systemic Fear: An Exchange', *Journal of Critical Globalization Studies*, **4**, pp. 61–118.

Knafo, S., Hughes, M. and Wyn-Jones, S. (2013) 'Differential Accumulation and the Political Economy of Power', in Di Muzio, T. (ed.) (2013), *The Capitalist Mode of Power: Engaging the Power Theory of Value*, London and New York: Routledge, pp. 134–51.

Krier, D. (2005) *Speculative Management*, Albany: State University of New York Press.

Krier, D. (2009) 'Finance Capital, Neo-Liberalism and Critical Institutionalism', *Critical Sociology*, **35** (3), pp. 395–416.

Labban, M. (2008) *Space, Oil and Capital*, London: Routledge.

Lafrance, X. and Post, C. (eds) (2019) *Case Studies in the Origins of Capitalism*, London: Palgrave Macmillan.

Lukes, S. ([1974] 2005) *Power: A Radical View*, 2nd edn, London: Palgrave Macmillan.

Mankiw, G. (2009) *Macroeconomics*, 9th edn, New York: Worth Publishers.

Mann, M. ([1986] 2012) *The Sources of Social Paper: A History of Power from the Beginning to AD 1760*, Volume 1, Cambridge: Cambridge University Press.

Mann, M. ([1993] 2012) *The Sources of Social Paper: The Rise of Classes and Nation-states, 1760–1914*, Volume 2, Cambridge: Cambridge University Press.

Martin, U. (2010) 'Rational Control and the Magma of Reality', paper presented at Eastern Economic Association Annual Conference, 26–8 February, Philadelphia.

Marx, K. ([1867] 1976) *Capital: A Critique of Political Economy, Volume One*, trans. Ben Fowkes, Toronto: Penguin.

Marx, K. ([1883] 1993) *Capital: A Critique of Political Economy, Volume Three: The Process of Capitalist Production as a Whole*, trans. David Fernbach, Toronto: Penguin.

McMahon, J. (2013) 'The Rise of a Confident Hollywood: Risk and the Capitalization of Cinema', *Review of Capital as Power*, **1** (1): pp. 23–40.

McNally, D. (2020) *Blood and Money: War, Slavery, Finance, and Empire*, Chicago, IL: Haymarket Books.

Mills, C.W. ([1956] 2000) *The Power Elite*, Oxford: Oxford University Press.

Muldrew, C. (1998) *The Economy of Obligation: The Culture of Credit and Social Relations in Early Modern England*, London: Macmillan.

Neal, L. and Williamson, J.G. (2014) *The Rise of Capitalism: From Ancient Origins to 1848, Volume 1*, London: Cambridge University Press.

Nitzan, J, and Bichler, S. (2009) *Capital as Power: A Study of Order and Creorder*, London: Routledge.

Noble, D.F. (1977) *America by Design; Science, Technology, and the Rise of Corporate Capitalism*, New York: Knopf.

Park, H.-J. (2016) 'Korea's Post-1997 Restructuring: An Analysis of Capital as Power', *Review of Radical Political Economics*, **48** (2), pp. 287–309.

Piper, K. (2018) 'The Case against Colonizing Space to Save Humanity', *Vox*, accessed 19/8/2021 at: https://www.vox.com/future-perfect/2018/10/22/17991736/jeff-bezos-elon-musk-colonizing-mars -moon-space-blue-origin-spacex.

Pitcher, J. (2020) 'Jeff Bezos Adds Record $13 Billion in Single Day to Fortune', *Bloomberg*, 20 July, accessed 19/8//2021 at: https://www.bloomberg.com/news/articles/2020–07–20/jeff-bezos-adds -record-13-billion-in-single-day-to-his-fortune.

Roy, W.G. (1997) *Socializing Capital: The Rise of the Large Industrial Corporations in America*, Princeton, NJ: Princeton University Press.

Sampson, A. (1975) *The Seven Sisters: The Great Oil Companies and the World They Made*, New York: Viking Press.

Slade, G. (2007) *Made to Break: Technology and Obsolescence in America*, Boston, MA: Harvard University Press.

Sraffa, P. (1960) *Production of Commodities by Means of Commodities: Prelude to a Critique of Economic Theory*, Cambridge: Cambridge University Press.

Schwartz, H.M. (2019) 'American Hegemony: Intellectual Property Rights, Money, and Infrastructural Power', *Review of International Political Economy*, **26** (3), pp. 490–519.

Tarbell, I. (1904) *The History of the Standard Oil Company*, New York: McClure, Philips and Co.

Teschke, B. (2003) *The Myth of 1648: Class, Geopolitics, and the Making of Modern International Relations*, London: Verso.

Veblen, T. ([1904] 1975) *The Theory of Business Enterprise*, New York: Scribner.

Veblen, T. ([1921] 2001) *The Engineers and the Price System*, Kitchener: Batoche Books.

Veblen, T. ([1923] 1967) *Absentee Ownership and Business Enterprise in Recent Times: The Case of America*, Boston, MA: Beacon Press.

Wallerstein, I. ([1983] 2003) *Historical Capitalism with Capitalist Civilization*, London: Verso.

Wood, E. M. (2002) *The Origin of Capitalism: A Longer View*, London: Verso.

Zalik, A. (2010) 'Oil Futures: Shell's Scenarios and the Social Constitution of the Global Oil Market', *Geoforum*, **41** (4), pp. 553–64.

Zucman, G. (2015) *The Hidden Wealth of Nations: The Scourge of Tax Havens*, Chicago, IL: University of Chicago Press.

15. Foundations of modern money theory

L. Randall Wray

Modern money theory, sometimes called Modern Monetary Theory or simply MMT, synthesises several traditions from heterodox economics. Its focus is on describing monetary and fiscal operations in nations that issue a sovereign currency.[1] MMT emphasises the difference between a sovereign currency *issuer* and a sovereign currency *user* with respect to issues such as fiscal and monetary policy space, ability to make all payments as they come due, credit worthiness, and insolvency. However, MMT acknowledges some similarities between sovereign and non-sovereign issues of liabilities, hence integrates a credit theory of money (or, endogenous money theory as it is usually termed by Post Keynesians) with state money theory. MMT uses this integration in policy analysis to address issues such as exchange rate regimes, full employment policy, financial and economic stability, and the current challenges facing modern economies: rising inequality, climate change, ageing of the population, tendency towards secular stagnation, and uneven development. This chapter traces its origins and heterodox underpinnings, and its theoretical and policy implications.

ORIGINS

MMT arose from an online discussion group of the 1990s, called Post Keynesian Thought (PKT). Warren Mosler, a hedge fund manager, joined the PKT group in January 1996. He had drafted a paper (Mosler 1996) and outlined the basic principles of a sovereign currency: taxes create demand for the sovereign's currency; bond sales by the sovereign are not a borrowing operation but, rather, they are used to drain excess reserves from the banking system; the sovereign cannot exhaust its own currency; and government should provide jobs at minimum wages to fight unemployment. While many PKT participants were hostile to these ideas, some recognised the heterodox economic foundations for these arguments. Supporters included Basil Moore (developer of the 'horizontalist' wing of endogenous money), Paul Davidson (among the 'fundamentalist' Keynesians), Bill Mitchell (who had developed a 'buffer-stock' approach to unemployment), Mat Forstater (who would act as our economic historian and historian of economic thought, and whose student, Pavlina Tcherneva, wrote a review of Warren's paper), and me.

Soon after this initial introduction, Warren and Pavlina organised a conference held at Bretton Woods in June 1996. Basil, Charles Goodhart, and I joined Warren and financial markets participants (and a few regulators) to propagate a new framework for macro policy analysis. Warren provided financial support for me to lay the foundations in a new book (Wray 1998a). Two research centres were soon set up: Bill Mitchell created the Centre of Full Employment and Equity (CofFEE) at the University of Newcastle, Australia; and Warren, Mat and I created the Center for Full Employment and Price Stability (CFEPS) at the Levy Institute in America. Later, Bill opened a European branch of CofFEE in Maastricht. Conferences and seminars were held at CofFEE, Levy and CFEPS over the years to refine our analysis and locate the foundations of MMT in heterodox traditions.

Here I outline the 'Kansas City' approach developed at the Levy Institute and University of Missouri–Kansas City (UMKC).[2] The parallel development of the 'Newcastle' approach was similar but began from different heterodox foundations, as did Warren Mosler's original creation that relied on real-world observations of sovereign bond markets. Focusing on the path to MMT in America does not privilege this strand, as we were in frequent contact and our different backgrounds allowed us to quickly progress. From Warren's first posts in 1996, a handful of researchers founded a new approach to macroeconomics by mid-1998. Barely 20 years later, MMT had achieved something rare for heterodox economics: getting in the headlines around the world. In quick succession, it was denounced by all respectable policy-makers, politicians and economists; and then suddenly embraced as the obvious and necessary response to a global pandemic.[3]

CHARTALISM–STATE MONEY THEORY

I was first exposed to Georg Friedrich Knapp's State Money Theory (Knapp [1924] 1973) through Keynes's *Treatise on Money* ([1930] 1976) in 1986 while writing my dissertation with Jan Kregel in Italy (later published as Wray 1990). I incorporated the Knapp–Keynes approach, as well as surveying Islamic banking, the rise of banking in Western Europe, the development of modern banking in England, and the logic imposed by the use of money in a capitalist system. The rest of the manuscript focused on developing an endogenous money approach to private banking. Still, I was intrigued by the link between the state and money and began to read speculations on the origins of money.

In April 1997, I presented a narrative of the origins of money in my presidential address at the Association for Institutional Thought, stressing links to authorities. I revisited Chartalism in *Understanding Modern Money* (1998a), written between the summer of 1996 and the autumn of 1997. By that time, we were working at the Levy Institute and had discovered the 1913 article by A. Mitchell Innes (Innes 1913; Wray 2004). He clearly laid out the origins and nature of money, and the links between the state's money and private credit money. We also discovered that Keynes had reviewed the article in the *Economic Journal* (Keynes 1914): it is probable that this is what led to his 'Babylonian madness' (Ingham 2000) a half decade later.

Mat Forstater found substantial evidence to support Warren's thesis that 'taxes drive money' through his study of colonial Africa (as well as colonial America) and also via well-known examples such as cowry shell 'commodity money'. As Mat demonstrated (Forstater 2004, 2005), colonial governors understood imposition of taxes was the way to monetise the colony. As Innes insisted, there are no examples of commodity money – the value of even a gold coin is established by the need to pay taxes. Mat showed that this was also true of cowry shell money and as well the 'stone wheel money' of the Yap Islands. All the tropes of the econo-mist's story about Robinson Crusoe and Friday choosing a medium of exchange to eliminate transaction costs were false. Money was not an invention of individuals, but, rather, was an instrument of, and created by, the authorities. My 1998 book goes through a variety of his-torical examples – Adam Smith's study of eighteenth-century money and banking; Keynes's explications in the Treatise and Volume XXVIII of his *Collected Works*; Innes on tally sticks in Medieval Europe; Colonial America (also taken up by Smith); and the disparate experiences of the North and South during America's Civil War. The evidence for the state's role in the creation and evolution of money is overwhelming.

Finally, Mat brought Abba Lerner's 'money is a creature of the state' argument: '[W]hatever may have been the history of gold, at the present time, in a normally well-working economy, money is a creature of the state. Its general acceptability, which is its all-important attribute, stands or falls by its acceptability by the state' (Lerner 1947: 313). Lerner argues the state can make anything acceptable as money by declaring it will 'accept the proposed money in payment and other obligations to itself', which ensures that even non-convertible paper money (often called 'fiat money') will be generally accepted even by those without obligations to the state 'because they know that the taxpayers, etc., will accept them in turn' (Lerner 1947: 313). Succinctly put, 'taxes drive money'.

Goodhart argued that the 'Chartalist school sees the power to create money as intimately bound up with the stable existence of government in general and its ability to raise money through taxation in particular, and consequently has no difficulty explaining or predicting the almost universal empirical observation of 'one government, one money' (Goodhart 1998). As Wynne Godley had put it in 1992:

> It needs to be emphasised at the start that the establishment of a single currency in the EC would indeed bring to an end the sovereignty of its component nations and their power to take independent action on major issues ... the power to issue its own money, to make drafts on its own central bank, is the main thing which defines national independence. If a country gives up or loses this power, it acquires the status of a local authority or colony (Godley 1992).

This is why, from the very beginning, MMT was skeptical of the Euro experiment. (See Wray 1998a: 91ff.)

Minsky had warned me not to do 'Genesis' (origin stories) in my doctoral dissertation for which he was the supervisor, but he had explained in the classroom that the reason we accept the state's money is because we have obligations such as taxes that have to be paid in currency. He extended the analogy to bank money: we accept it because we must repay loans to banks. In his own words:

> In an economy where government debt is a major asset on the books of the deposit-issuing banks, the fact that taxes need to be paid gives value to the money of the economy ... [T]he need to pay taxes means that people work and produce in order to get that in which taxes can be paid. (Minsky 1986: 231)

Following Knapp, Innes, Minsky, Mosler, Goodhart (and our own investigations of historical experience), we summarised our view as: *MMT insists that the usual case has been that each nation state chooses its own money of account, issues currency denominated in that money of account, and imposes obligations (such as taxes) payable in the currency.* This is the succinct view of money from the Chartalist view.

CREDIT MONEY: THE MONETARY CIRCUIT AND ENDOGENOUS MONEY

Over the course of the 1980s, Post Keynesians embraced an endogenous money approach. Basil Moore (1988) developed horizontalism, which viewed both money supply and reserves as horizontal at an exogenously set interest rate. This was contrasted with the monetarist 'verticalist' approach that saw the money supply as exogenous (set by the central bank) and the interest rate as endogenously determined by the market. Furthermore, Marc Lavoie helped to revive a circuit approach to money based on earlier work by French economists: this became the Franco-Italian *circuitiste* approach. It recalled the real bills doctrine (money is created to finance the production process) and was consistent with the monetary theory of production (production begins with money to produce commodities to sell for more money) adopted by Marx, Veblen and Keynes. This 1980s Post Keynesian scholarship rejected the textbook deposit multiplier story, instead insisting that money is created *ex nihilo* ('out of thin air'). Central banks provide money *reserves*. These reserves are used by banks for clearing (and, in the horizontalist story, they must always accommodate demand to hit their overnight interest rate target).

In both Post Keynesian approaches (horizontalism and the circuit), the government's role is downplayed. Augusto Graziani, the leading proponent of the circuit approach, insisted that government is like any other user of money and subject to the same rules: it has no 'seigniorage' rights and cannot settle its debts using its own liabilities. Most expositions of the circuit approach do not even include a government, which is similarly excluded from most horizontalist discussions – and the central bank's role is generally limited to setting the overnight interest rate target and fully accommodating bank demand for reserves. Some horizontalists have been among the most vehement heterodox critics of MMT. However, not all: Basil Moore participated in the earliest discussions with Mosler on PKT and was among the first to understand the latter's claim that government bond sales are a 'reserve drain', not a borrowing operation.

In Wray (1990), I explored the history of the endogenous money approach from the banking school/currency school debates (1830s–1840s), through Marx, Keynes and Schumpeter. I argued that, while endogenous money views were common or even dominant until Keynes's *General Theory* ([1936] 1964), both the 'neoclassical synthesis Keynesians' and the monetarists of the post-war period adopted the exogenous money and deposit multiplier approaches. A revival of endogenous money can be traced from the Post Keynesian Nicholas Kaldor and the Radcliffe Committee, the work of Gurley and Shaw in the late 1950s, Tobin, and Minsky (from the late 1950s).

Moore and other horizontalists interpret Keynes's treatment of money in the *General Theory* as exogenous (fixed by the central bank) and claim that his liquidity preference theory is inconsistent with endogenous money. In my 1990 book and elsewhere, I integrated Keynes's liquidity preference theory (from chapter 17 of the *General Theory*) with his *endogenous* money approach (outlined in his *Treatise on Money*). I argued that while chapters 13 and 15 of the *General Theory* can be interpreted along the lines that led to the orthodox IS–LM analysis (with an exogenous money supply), Keynes's approach to asset pricing in chapter 17 provides a rigorous exposition of his liquidity preference theory,[4] and this is perfectly consistent with endogenous money.

In my dissertation and its later book incarnation, I provided a close institutional analysis of the practices of modern banking, including discussion of the rise of 'nonbank banking' (later called shadow banking) and the increasing use of off-balance-sheet operations by banks. I showed that, by 1986, direct lending by banks had already declined to just 18 per cent of the increase of debt issued by nonfinancial corporations. I warned of the new trend to securitisation and use of derivatives that appeared to hedge risks but, due to the 'interdependence of on-balance sheet and off-balance sheet commitments, a covariance of shocks could lead to the transmission of shocks throughout the system' (Wray 1990: 215–16). I also argued that credit risk was becoming more concentrated among fewer behemoth institutions, and that this would return to haunt the Federal Reserve as it would eventually have to act as lender of last resort to cover even the off-balance-sheet items. That is precisely what happened in the global financial crisis almost two decades later, as the Federal Reserve was forced to spend and lend a total of $29 trillion to save the global financial system.

In all of this, I followed Minsky's view that 'everyone can create money, the problem is to get it accepted' (Minsky 1986: 228; see also Wray 2016). I used Minsky's notion of a 'hierarchy of monies' (1986), with the most acceptable government liabilities at the top, then chartered bank liabilities, 'nonbank bank' liabilities, nonfinancial corporate obligations, and finally the debts of small firms and households at the bottom. This pyramid reflects acceptability and liquidity, with entities lower in the pyramid using liabilities higher in the pyramid for payments. Minsky's understanding of money and banking was much deeper than that of the developers and followers of the horizontalist or *circuitiste* approaches, which focused on an outdated 'real bills' view of commercial banks. Minsky was among the first to fully recognise the importance of securitisation, arguing in 1987: 'that which can be securitized, will be securitized'. He proceeded to analyse the tremendous changes to the financial system that followed innovations of the 1980s in myriad papers and conferences at the Levy Institute from the early 1990s. Minsky's research programme at Levy tackled reform to 'reconstitute the financial system to promote the capital development of the economy' and has subsequently been expanded since his death. For example, I warned of the financial speculation that would lead to collapse beginning as early as 1998 and up to the global financial crisis of 2007. (For an early warning, see Wray 1998b; and for one of the first analyses of the crash of US real estate markets, see Wray 2007.)

Some critics have wrongly tried to claim that MMT leaves out the private financial system. Nothing could be further from the truth. The Kansas City/Levy proponents of MMT have been in the forefront of the analysis of the evolution of the financial system, standing on the shoulders of Minsky.

THE NATURE OF MONEY

In addition to the 1913 article by Innes mentioned above, we were also influenced by his second article on the same topic (Innes 1914). Not only does Innes provide the clearest exposition of state money, he includes state money as a category of credit money, posing a universal law of debt: the issuer of a debt must accept it back in payment. This applies equally to government, to banks, and to nonbank entities—not disregarding the different degrees of acceptability discussed above. Innes called this redemption: when a taxpayer returns to the government its currency in payment of taxes, both the taxpayer and the government are redeemed: the taxpayer is no longer in tax debt, and the government's obligation to accept its own currency is also fulfilled. Quadruple entry bookkeeping shows that two assets and two liabilities are simultaneously struck from the balance sheets.

What, then, is the nature of money? First, there is the money of account, the unit of measurement in which records are kept. Second, there is the record itself. Keynes ([1930] 1976) distinguishes between the two, calling money of account the 'name or description' and the record itself 'the thing': 'The State, therefore, comes in first of all as the authority of law which enforces the payment of the thing which corresponds to the name or description in the contracts.' This has been the case for 'some four thousand years at least'.[5] This is why MMT begins with the state's money – unlike the circuit approach that begins with private banks, or horizontalism that ignores the important role played by the state in choosing the money of account, issuing the liabilities at the pyramid's top, and enforcing money-denominated private contracts.

During the writing of my 1998 book, we discovered the work of Grierson – a foremost numismatologist (a collector and student of money) who speculated on money's origins in a short book (Grierson 1977), providing a convincing alternative. He argued that the notion of measuring debt in a unit of account originated from the tribal practice of Wergild. While Wergild 'fines' were measured in-kind, with the evolution to civilisation, public assemblies that imposed fines might have settled on a unit of account (such as the barley grain unit) to measure debts.

This leads nicely into Michael Hudson's (2004) story that locates money's origins in the record-keeping of Mesopotamia's temples. That also explains the close connection to religion of many terms having to do with money and debt, such as 'redemption' and 'debt jubilee', and why debt and sin are synonymous (for a thorough and entertaining account, see Atwood 2008). Money did not rise out of the search for a transactions cost-reducing medium of exchange, but rather emerged out of debt, a social relationship. While all human societies have recognised debts to one another (as do many other animals), it was a huge jump to 'monetise' debts with a single measuring unit. As Grierson (1977) insists, this is much more difficult than coming up with a convenient measure for length, weight, or volume – although each of those would also have required social consensus. Moreover, while there might be a small number of examples of private institutions creating moneys of account (such as the Giro money of Northern Europe discussed by Knapp and in my 1990 book), as emphasised by Keynes and Goodhart, the rule has been a money of account chosen by authorities.

Along the way we included the work of many others who emphasised the social-debt nature of money, including Geoff Ingham (2000). The principle of redemption was best illustrated by Grubb (2015) in relatively recent work on Colonial American paper currency (as opposed to earlier work undertaken by Adam Smith on the same subject). Because colonies were prohibited from issuing coins and forced to rely on an insufficient supply of British currency, they hit on the idea of issuing paper money. Colonies passed laws authorising the issuing of a specific number of notes for spending, simultaneously passing a tax law expected to raise an amount of revenue equal to the value of the notes issued. As tax revenue came in, the notes were burned. The taxes were called 'redemption taxes', acknowledging the recognised purpose: taxes are for redemption, not to finance spending – the spending had already been financed through notes, so the purpose of taxes was to create a demand for the notes. Once redeemed, the 'revenue' served no purpose. The term 'revenue', itself, was derived from early French (borrowed into English) meaning 'return to'. Tax revenue returns to the issuer the currency that has already been spent – this is the redemption phase.

Economists have long focused on the intrinsic value of coins, leading to a commodity money view that initially seems to support the barter story of money's origins. Abandoning gold has been viewed as the path to inflation as money's value became unmoored and reduced to 'trust' in irresponsible government. However, careful study demonstrates that money preceded metallic coins by thousands of years; and that the value of coins usually has not been determined by precious metal content. The first coins were produced under Pheidon of Argos in the seventh century BC (Wray 1990: 7). While use of precious metals in coins remained common, they were too valuable to be used in everyday commerce. As in Mesopotamia, most commerce took place using credit, recorded as 'chalk on slate' tallies with debts settled once a year at harvest, or even less frequently (see McIntosh 1988 for a study of London during the period 1300–1600). European kings relied largely on tally sticks – records of debt – as Innes argued. In any event, coins mostly circulated at a nominal value well above the commodity value of the coin.

The nominal value was set at the 'public pay houses' – at the announced value in payment of liabilities to the authority. This value could be changed by announcement – sending the town crier to 'cry down' the value – which was accepted as an appropriate way to increase the tax burden, so long as it was not carried too far. ('Crying down the coin' is the phrase used by historians, although an economist might get confused because the lower coin value means taxes have risen in terms of the currency.) Roman law proclaimed that courts would enforce only a coin's nominal value – not its 'real' precious metal value. I have linked continued use of precious metals in coin through the 'age of conquest' to the need to make payments outside the jurisdiction of the coin's issuer – in particular to hire and provision mercenaries (Wray 1998a). The high value of coins made them particularly useful for paying 'soldiers and sailors' – with infrequent large lump sums – and once issued, they would be redeemed in taxes ('Coinage was probably invented in order that a large number of state payments might be made in a convenient form … . Once issued, coinage was demanded back by the state in payment of taxes': Crawford 1970: 46). As they could be far from home, the embodied precious metal assured they would retain some value abroad, even if the issuer lost the war (see Wray 1998a: ch. 3; 2004: 252–4).

BALANCE SHEET CONSOLIDATION AND COORDINATION: HOW GOVERNMENT SPENDS

Like Post Keynesians, MMT recognises that central banks target overnight rates. The US Fed directly sets the discount rate (the ceiling at which it lends) and targets the fed funds rate for interbank lending. Before the global financial crisis, the Fed did not pay interest on reserves, but now uses that rate to set a floor. Central banks have discretion in determining how much the 'market' rate deviates from target (and in the range between the target rate but above the rate paid on reserves). All of this is consistent with endogenous money and horizontalist viewpoints.

What Mosler introduced was the view of Treasury bond sales as part of monetary policy, that is, as a reserve drain instead of a borrowing operation. Treasury spending credits bank reserves, with the receiving bank then crediting the deposit account of the recipient of government's spending. In a fractional reserve system, this creates excess reserves. Before the Fed paid interest on reserves, systemic excess reserves would push down the fed funds rate and if that were not relieved it could fall towards zero; now it falls to the floor rate. Bond sales debit bank reserves, relieving that pressure.

Warren's insight was that this is true whether the sale is by the Treasury (new issues) or by the central bank (open market sales) – in either case, the function is the same. Stephanie Bell (now Kelton) and I studied money and banking with John Ranlett at California State University Sacramento and had been schooled in the workings of the T-accounts, so immediately recognised that Warren was correct. Government spending adds reserves, while taxing and bond sales remove them. Why would we call one a fiscal borrowing operation and the other a monetary policy operation? In retrospect, this was completely missed by horizontalism: there is no discussion of the fiscal impact on reserves even though that is orders of magnitude greater than the impacts of 'monetary policy' operations.

Real-world operations are more complicated, involving several steps and institutional participants including dealer banks, tax and loan accounts at special deposit banks, and Treasury accounts at the central bank. For simple expositions MMT consolidates the Treasury and central bank into a 'government balance sheet', eliminating internal operations between them. This has led to erroneous complaints that accuse MMT of oversimplification. However, MMT has sought to fully expose all the operational details – to a degree that had never been attempted by academic economists (certainly not by Post Keynesians). This research began when I was writing my 1998 book, with the details of coordination amplified by Stephanie Bell (2000) and later by Scott Fullwiler (2011) and Eric Tymoigne (2016) for the USA, and Felipe Rezende (2009) for Brazil. However, a key point in all this research is that the 'consolidation' of the simplified model does not mislead: the final balances remain the same no matter how deeply one goes into the intermediate steps.

While orthodoxy (and some heterodoxy) argues that government faces a budget constraint similar to those faced by households and firms, MMT argues that the issuer of a currency faces no budget constraint (other than the budget and rules adopted by legislators). The typical exposition presents the constraint as: $G = T + dB + dHPM$, where G is government spending plus interest payments on debt, T is tax revenues (less transfers), dB is new bond issues, and dHPM is 'printing' of high-powered money (new issues of cash plus reserves). Further, the finance method is seen as a choice – government chooses whether to use taxes, borrowing, or money printing. Borrowing can push up interest rates and crowd out private spending; beyond some point it increases default risk and can lead to insolvency. Money printing causes inflation.

MMT objects that the so-called budget constraint is an ex post identity, not an ex ante constraint (Mitchell et al. 2019). Further, the 'financing' always takes the form of a credit to bank reserves (and a credit by a private bank to the recipient's account) – government doesn't 'choose' whether to use taxes, money or bonds. Indeed, spending normally involves all three even if the budget ends up 'balanced' or in surplus at the end of the accounting period. This is due to self-imposed procedures adopted by the treasury and central bank. There is no special 'deficit financing' – government is 'financed' as it spends, with a deficit recorded only ex post. If the central bank pays interest on reserves, then it can choose whether to leave excess reserves in the banking system or to drain them through bond sales. Only in that sense can one say that there is a choice whether to 'use' bonds as 'money' – but that choice is made *after* the spending occurs. Further, tax receipts are endogenously determined (and highly pro-cyclical) – they are not a discretionary choice used as a means of financing spending.

Government deficits do not drive interest rates up; all else equal they lead to net credits of reserves, pushing rates down. This was Mosler's original insight: bond sales drain excess reserves to help keep interest rates from dropping below target. It could be true that, if the Treasury chooses to issue bonds of a maturity unwanted by markets, this could push up rates of that maturity. But that is a 'debt management' mistake, not an inevitable outcome of deficits.

Bonds may be needed because of operational procedures – for example, the prohibition against central bank overdrafts for the Treasury. In that case, Treasury sells new issues before spending – which requires that the central bank ensures banks have the reserves needed to purchase them. This is accomplished by lending reserves or open market purchases coordinated with the Treasury's new issue. However, the central bank can always remove new bonds from markets (through, for example, 'quantitative easing' (QE)).

After multiple rounds of trillions of dollars of QE, it should now be obvious that, so far as inflation goes, there is no difference between leaving reserves in banks or draining them through bond sales. Reserves remain within the banking system and cannot cause inflation havoc – all excess reserves do is push the overnight rate to zero (or the support rate paid by the central bank). This does not mean that government spending cannot be too large, or misdirected. But if so, it is the (net) spending that causes inflation – not the 'choice' between 'borrowing' or 'money printing'. Too much private spending would similarly cause inflation pressures: as Stephanie Kelton points out, 'cash registers don't discriminate'. The danger is 'too much spending', not 'too much money'.

SECTORAL BALANCES

Wynne Godley arrived at the Levy Institute in the early 1990s to build a model of the US economy using his sectoral balance approach. His first Levy publications came in 1995, warning of a growing deficit in the US private sector – what he would later highlight as one of 'Seven Unsustainable Processes' (Godley 1999). MMT had already recognised that government deficits produce surpluses for nongovernment sectors, and government debt represents net financial wealth for these sectors. This observation was a major point of Minsky's 'Big Government' approach. What Godley provided was a stock-flow consistent model that included the foreign sector and used the flow of funds accounts. This was soon added to MMT. Wynne and I collaborated on some op-ed pieces in the *Financial Times* and on a Levy Policy Note (Godley and Wray 1999) warning about the coming collapse of the Goldilocks economy. Stephanie Bell (Kelton) applied Wynne's scepticism about the precarious future of the Euro project to her own work, and I included a section in my 1998 book. Stephanie and Ed Nell organised a conference at the New School on the Euro, and Warren helped to organise one in London.[6]

The most important take-away from all this is that the balances must balance, meaning that we cannot think about the government's budgetary outcome independently of the other two balances. It is not possible to reduce government's deficit by reducing spending or raising taxes unless the private sector's and/or the foreign sector's surplus declines. Policy has uncertain impacts on these balances as each is complexly determined and linked in complicated ways to one another.

Generally, robust US growth is associated with a declining private sector surplus but a rising foreign sector surplus. The net result is a reduction of the leakages (domestic private saving and net imports), allowing the government's injection (a deficit) to fall. But those movements of the balances also set off countervailing forces: the reduction of the private sector surplus increases debt ratios (one of Godley's unsustainable processes, and also highlighted by Minsky in his financial instability hypothesis) even as the co-movement of the government's budget towards surplus and the current account towards bigger deficits takes demand out of the economy. Once a breaking point is reached (a 'Minsky moment'), a financial crisis is triggered and the fall-out is accompanied by slow growth, a rising private sector surplus, falling current account deficit, and rising government deficit.

Deficit hawks who want balanced budgets must explain how they are going to control private and foreign balances to produce them. MMT posits that the government's balance should play the stabilising role by putting in place automatic stabilisers, such as pro-cyclical taxes and counter-cyclical spending. A deficit can certainly be too big – potentially fuelling inflation. US evidence suggests that federal taxes are already sufficiently pro-cyclical; however, if anything, federal spending is not sufficiently counter cyclical, so the focus should be placed on creating a stronger movement of spending against the cycle (see Wray 2019 for Congressional Testimony). It would also be helpful to address the inherent tendency towards financial instability in the private sector.

FINANCIAL INSTABILITY

Minsky is the most important contributor to our understanding of the inherent tendency of modern capitalism to evolve toward financial fragility. His financial instability hypothesis was developed between the late 1950s and the mid-1970s. He claimed to extend Keynes's 'investment theory of the cycle' by adding the 'financial theory of investment'. Minsky's understanding of banking and finance integrated the 'banker as the ephor of capitalism' view of his dissertation advisor (Schumpeter) with the broad approach to money and banking of Gurley and Shaw, who recognised the importance of what we called 'nonbank banks' until Paul McCulley renamed them 'shadow banks'. (See Mazzucato and Wray 2015 for an integration of the approaches of Keynes, Schumpeter and Minsky and a discussion of the role played by banks in financing the capital development of the economy.)

Minsky also had a good understanding of Ritter's integration of cash flows and balance sheets to produce a flow of funds matrix. He argued that every economic entity can be analysed as a 'bank' that issues liabilities to take positions in assets. He further argued that anyone can issue 'money' (a liability denominated in the money of account); the problem is to get it 'accepted'. And he not only kept up with financial innovations but recognised how they stretched liquidity and increased potential for fragility. In all these respects, he pushed the generalisation of money and banking as he analysed all economic units as financing positions in assets by issuing liabilities.

Minsky recognised the importance of New Deal and early post-war reforms that produced an unprecedented period of prosperity and financial tranquility, but he began to warn even in the 1950s that this would change behaviour of households, firms and financial institutions in ways that would threaten the system's stability. He argued that while institutions can potentially constrain instability, the inherent nature of market processes, particularly ongoing innovation and entrepreneurship, reduces their efficacy. Unlike most analyses of economic cycles, Minsky's view was that the 'invisible hand of the market' is destabilising, while the 'visible hand' of institutions (including, prominently, the visible hand of government) can produce a semblance of stability. But 'stability is destabilising'.

When he moved to the Levy Institute in 1990, his focus turned to analysis of the transformation of the financial system over the past century, identifying several stages of capitalism, each associated with a particular type of financial system. Minsky always joked about '57 varieties of capitalism' (from the Heinz pickles slogan), but this work focused on the rise of 'money manager capitalism' after 1980. In his view, this stage was like the era of 'finance capitalism' that crashed into the Great Depression. He worried this might 'happen again'. At the Levy

Institute he created the long-running annual 'Minsky Conference' to formulate proposals to 'reconstitute' the financial system. In his view, the key to a successful capitalist economy is ongoing reform of finance, because he viewed capitalism as a 'financial system' – and as the financial system evolved, capitalism did also (Tymoigne and Wray 2014).

Minsky's framework was always part of the Kansas City/Levy approach to MMT. When I first arrived at the University of Denver in 1987, I began to teach a course on Minsky that continued at UMKC and now at Bard and Levy. Minsky's views of banking and financial markets, his views of the nature of money and the role of the government in the monetary system, his recognition that the market is naturally unstable, and his policy reforms have always been part of our approach to theory and to how policy can be used to reform the system.

While Minsky was influenced by the Keynesian–Lerner approach to demand management, he rejected fine-tuning. For Minsky, the most dangerous tendency in the post-war economy is towards run-away euphoric booms originating in the finance sector – not the general collapse in aggregate demand in the economy as a whole. Indeed, for Minsky, it is the widespread recognition in the post-war period that government will likely prop up demand and intervene in a financial crisis that poses the greatest danger. This was apparent in his criticism of the Kennedy–Johnson War on Poverty (see Bell and Wray 2004). Sure, he argued, government can boost demand and move the economy closer to full employment – with some jobs trickling down to the poor – but this would unleash inflation and exacerbate financial instability so that full employment could not be maintained. It could never resolve the poverty and unemployment problem, he warned. For Minsky, getting to full employment would be easy, but remaining there would be difficult. Further, he criticised welfare as a 'conservative rebuttal' to the radical's claim that poverty and unemployment represent *failures* of the capitalism *system*. He argued that charity should not be the basis of a government's response to those failures.

The Levy Institute collected a number of his writings from the 1960s and 1970s that exposed the problems of trying to pursue full employment through the mainstream neoclassical Keynesian approach of 'aggregate demand management' (Minsky 2013). Instead, he preferred direct job creation through the employer of last resort (what MMT calls the job guarantee). MMT follows Minsky in rejecting general 'pump priming' to 'fine-tune' the economy because it will not produce sustainable full employment as it is prone to inflation and financial instability. In this, MMT reaches conclusions about Keynesian fine-tuning similar to those reached by Marxist critics (such as Baran and Sweezy, and Kalecki).

In chapter 24 of the *General Theory*, Keynes had warned of the two great faults of capitalism: the failure to operate at full employment and excessive inequality. Minsky added a third: the inherent tendency to financial instability, which could be fuelled by policy to address the other faults.

In retrospect, Minsky's earliest writing was remarkably prescient. The War on Poverty did fail. Financial instability did return, with a vengeance. The concern with inflation in the late 1960s helped to fuel the return of pre-Keynesian neoclassical economics, and later to the rise of neoliberalism that destroyed organised labour and ramped up inequality, while helping to undermine the neoclassical synthesis Keynesianism and ushering in the return of the 'New Classical' economics. President Clinton later ended 'welfare as we know it', putting the final nail in the War on Poverty's coffin. Minsky's alternative approach to stabilising the economy with a targeted jobs programme was always part of my Minsky course and became the most important policy pushed by MMT.

CONCLUSION: MMT AND POLICY

MMT describes how sovereign currency 'works' and identifies the policy space open to a sovereign currency issuer. MMT's developers are largely progressive but have sought to explain how the monetary system in place works with a view to exposing fallacies held by both the right and the left. The descriptive part of MMT largely can be separated from policies advocated by MMT's proponents. However, we see three policies as following directly from MMT: the job guarantee, flexible exchange rates, and interest rate targeting.

All the developers of the MMT approach have included the jobs guarantee (JG) as one of the fundamental policies. As discussed, MMT argues that 'taxes drive money' as obligations create demand for currency, but its value is determined by what one must do to obtain it. If one must work for one hour to obtain $15, that establishes that one hour of labour equals $15. With a JG programme, the sovereign government acts as price-setter and quantity-taker. As in Minsky's approach, the JG is a stabiliser of employment, wages, aggregate demand and prices. Setting the base wage and operating a buffer stock of labour helps to directly stabilise wages and prices more effectively than simply trying to rely on aggregate demand stabilisation (see Minsky 2013; Tcherneva 2020; see also Mitchell et al. 2019).

Flexible exchange rates maximise policy space and eliminate the danger of forced default by government on domestic currency obligations. A country that pegs its currency must have access to the metal or foreign currency, since its currency and bonds are effectively claims on reserves. To ensure it can meet those claims, its domestic policy must be shaped by the need to maintain adequate reserves. This generally means austerity policy to run current account surpluses and/or to please suppliers of the reserves through the capital account. MMT proponents do not claim that every country's currency should float: they simply argue that domestic policy advantages of issuing a sovereign currency are not available to a nation that doesn't float. In some cases, pegging or managing an exchange rate might be the best policy for an individual nation. For many or most, floating is best so that domestic policy can pursue full employment and other goals.

MMT accepts the horizontalist view that central banks set the overnight interest rate and then accommodate reserve demands – a view that is now accepted by central bankers. In contrast to conventional views (and those of some followers of horizontalism), however, MMT does not support use of interest rates to manage demand (and indirectly to manage inflation). First, there is little evidence that spending is sufficiently interest-elastic to influence aggregate demand within the normal range of interest rate targets. Second, there is little evidence that central bank rate policy (or even the non-traditional policies of quantitative easing and negative interest rates over the past decade) has been able to move inflation rates in desired directions. Third, while sharp increases to high interest rates (such as those produced by Volcker's monetarism after 1979) can break a speculative bubble, they do so by present value reversals, insolvencies, bankruptcies and financial crises. The costs of these episodes are great, and credit controls as well as tighter regulation of financial institutions would be more effective. For these reasons, MMT proposes greater reliance on fiscal policy as well as more focus on quantitative and qualitative control of financial institutions rather than manipulation of interest rates (see Wray 1993).

Keynes advocated 'euthanasia of the rentier' through eliminating interest on risk-free debt. Interest would be a reward only for taking risk – a recommendation for permanent Zero Interest Rate Policy – and it has been adopted by MMT proponents such as Bill Mitchell,

Warren Mosler and Mat Forstater. While I agree with this as a general policy, I can also see a public interest in offering risk-free savings bonds to individuals, pension funds and insurance companies. Only qualifying buyers would be allowed to hold them (with income and wealth caps for individuals and conditions placed on institutional holders) and the interest rate would be set by Congress or Parliament.

With the onset of the global Covid-19 pandemic, policymakers around the world embraced what they understood to be MMT – interpreted as 'money printing' to finance an array of monetary and fiscal policy initiatives. We have argued against many of these policies, and object to the characterisation of MMT as a policy of 'helicopter money'. We hope that the panoply of challenges that go well beyond Covid – climate change, inequality, racism, secular stagnation, a runaway financial system and the return of global fascism – will force a turn away from neoliberalism and back to a foundation based on the theoretical building blocks addressed in this chapter.

NOTES

1. For an introductory text on MMT, see Wray (2015); for a college textbook treatment, see Mitchell et al. (2019).
2. Our approach was called Chartalist and often labelled the 'Kansas City' approach in the Americas (an unfair designation that left out the contributions in Australia). The term Modern Money Theory did not arise until later, even though I had used the term 'modern money' in the title of the first academic monograph.
3. For responses to MMT before the pandemic, see, for example, the view in Japan in Nikkei Staff Writers (2019). In the USA, Kenneth Rogoff (2019) labelled MMT 'nonsense'; Larry Fink, CEO of BlackRock, called it 'garbage' (Collins 2019); Paul Krugman (2019) said its claims were 'obviously untrue'; and Larry Summers (2019) called it 'voodoo economics'. For links and a considered response to each of these attacks, see Montier (2019).
4. What sets the 'fundamentalist' Post Keynesians (such as Davidson, Minsky and Kregel) apart is their emphasis on the liquidity preference theory of asset pricing in chapter 17 of the *General Theory* – so I was following them in my attempt to integrate that with endogenous money.
5. This is the source of the term 'modern money' – which applies only to the 'modern' period, the past 'four thousand years at least' (Keynes [1930] 1976: 4). I chose to include this in the title of the first monograph on our new approach (*Understanding Modern Money*, Wray 1998a) as an inside joke. According to Bill Mitchell, a commentator on his blog was the first to use MMT as the name of our approach – we had usually called it 'Chartalism', following Knapp.
6. C-FEPS-sponsored conference on 'The Launching of the Euro' in London, May 1998: papers published in *The Launching of the Euro: A Conference on the European Economic and Monetary Union*, Annandale-on-Hudson, NY: The Bard Center; see also Godley (1997) and Mosler (2001).

REFERENCES

Atwood, M. (2008) *Payback: Debt and the Shadow Side of Wealth*, Toronto, ON: House of Anansi Press.
Bell, S. (2000) 'Do Taxes and Bonds Finance Government Spending?', *Journal of Economic Issues*, **34**, pp. 603–20.
Bell, S. and Wray, L.R. (2004) 'The War on Poverty after 40 Years: A Minskyan Assessment', *Public Policy Brief*, 78, The Levy Economics Institute of Bard College.
Collins, P. (2019) 'BlackRock CEO Larry Fink Says Modern Monetary Theory Is Garbage', Bloomberg, 7 March, accessed 3.8.2021 at: https://www.bloomberg.com/news/articles/2019–03–07/blackrock-s-ceo-fink-says-modern-monetary-theory-is-garbage.

Crawford, M. (1970) 'Money and Exchange in the Roman World', *Journal of Roman Studies*, **60**, pp. 40–48.

Forstater, M. (2004) 'Tax-Driven Money: Additional Evidence from the History of Thought, Economic History, and Economic Policy', Working Paper No. 35, August, Center for Full Employment and Price Stability, University of Kansas City Missouri.

Forstater, M. (2005) 'Taxation and Primitive Accumulation: The Case of Colonial Africa; The Capitalist State and Its Economy: Democracy in Socialism', *Research in Political Economy*, **22**, pp. 51–65.

Fullwiler, S. (2011) 'Treasury Debt Operations: An Analysis Integrating Social Fabric Matrix and Social Accounting Matrix Methodologies', accessed 3.8.2021 at: http:papers.ssrn.com/sol3/papers.cfm ?abstract_id=1825303.

Godley, W. (1997) 'Curried Emu: The Meal that Fails to Nourish', *The Observer*, London, 31 August.

Godley, W. (1999) 'Seven Unsustainable Processes', accessed 3.8.2021 at: http://www.levyinstitute.org/ publications/seven-unsustainable-processes.

Godley, W. and Wray, L.R. (1999) 'Can Goldilocks Survive?' Levy Economics Institute Policy Note 1999/4, April, accessed 3.8.2021 at: http://www.levyinstitute.org/publications/can-goldilocks -survive.

Goodhart, C.A.E. (1998) 'Two Concepts of Money: Implications for the Analysis of Optimal Currency Areas', *European Journal of Political Economy*, **14**, pp. 407–32.

Grierson, P. (1977) *The Origins of Money*, London: The Athlone Press.

Grubb, F. (2015) 'Colonial Virginia's Paper Money Regime, 1755–1774: A Forensic Accounting Reconstruction of the Data', Working Paper No. 2015–11, Alfred Lerner College of Business and Economics, University of Delaware.

Hudson, M, (2004) 'The Archeology of Money: Debt versus Barter Theories of Money's Origin,' in Wray, L.R. (ed.), *Credit and State Theories of Money*, Cheltenham, UK and Northampton, MA, USA: Edward Elgar Publishing, pp. 99–127.

Ingham, G. (2000) '"Babylonian Madness": On the Historical and Sociological Origins of Money', in Smithin, J. (ed.), *What is Money*, London and New York: Routledge, pp. 16–41.

Innes, A.M. (1913) 'What is Money?', *Banking Law Journal*, May, pp. 377–408.

Innes, A.M. (1914) 'The Credit Theory of Money', *Banking Law Journal*, December/January, pp. 151–68.

Keynes, J.M. (1914) 'What is Money?' *The Economic Journal*, **24** (95), pp. 419–21.

Keynes, J.M. ([1930] 1976) *A Treatise on Money*, Volumes I and II, New York: Harcourt, Brace and Co.

Keynes, J.M. ([1936] 1964) *The General Theory of Interest, Employment and Money*, New York: Harcourt Brace Jovanovich.

Knapp, G.F. ([1924] 1973) *The State Theory of Money*, Clifton, NY: Augustus M. Kelley.

Krugman, P. (2019) 'Running on MMT (Wonkish): Trying to Get this Debate beyond Calvinball', *The New York Times*, 25 Feb.

Lerner, A.P. (1947) 'Money as a Creature of the State', *American Economic Review*, **37** (2), pp. 312–17.

Mazzucato, M. and Wray, L.R. (2015) 'Financing the Capital Development of the Economy: A Keynes-Schumpeter-Minsky Synthesis', Working Paper No. 837, Levy Economics Institute of Bard College, Annandale-on-Hudson, NY.

Mcintosh, M.K. (1988) 'Money Lending on the Periphery of London, 1300–1600', *Albion*, **20** (4), pp. 557–71.

Minsky, H. (1986) *Stabilizing an Unstable Economy*, New Haven, CT: Yale University Press.

Minsky, H. (1987) 'Securitization', mimeo, September, Washington University, accessed 3.8.2021 at: http://www.levyinstitute.org/publications/securitization.

Minsky, H. (2013) *Ending Poverty: Jobs, not Welfare*, Annandale-on-Hudson, NY: Levy Economics Institute.

Mitchell, W., Randall Wray, L. and Watts, M. (2019) *Macroeconomics*, London: Red Globe Press.

Montier, J. (2019) 'Why Does Everyone Hate MMT? Groupthink In Economics', GMO Viewpoints, March, accessed 3.8.2021 at: https://www.gmo.com/americas/research-library/why-does-everyone -hate-mmt/.

Moore, B.J. (1988) *Horizontalists and Verticalists: The Macroeconomics of Credit Money*, Cambridge: Cambridge University Press.

Mosler, W. (1996) *Soft Currency Economics*, West Palm Beach, FA [updated version available at http://moslereconomics.com/wp-content/uploads/2018/04/Soft-Curency-Economics-paper.pdf].

Mosler, W. (2001) 'Rites of Passage', 1 May, accessed 3.8.2012 at: http://moslereconomics.com/wp-content/uploads/2018/04/Rites-of-Passage.pdf.

Nikkei Staff Writers (2019) 'BOJ Policy Board Member Yutaka Harada Kept up the Attack on MMT. The Approach Proposed by MMT will "cause [runaway] inflation for sure"', accessed 3.8.2021 at: https://asia.nikkei.com/Economy/Growing-Modern-Monetary-Theory-debate-rattles-Japan-officials.

Rezende, F. de (2009) 'The Nature of Government Finance in Brazil', *International Journal of Political Economy*, **38** (1), pp. 81–104.

Rogoff, K. (2019) 'Modern Monetary Nonsense', *Project Syndicate*, 4 March, available at: https://www.project-syndicate.org/commentary/federal-reserve-modern-monetary-theory-dangers-by-kenneth-rogoff-2019–03?barrier=accesspaylog.

Summers, L. (2019) 'The Left's Embrace of Modern Monetary Theory is a Recipe for Disaster', *The Washington Post*, 4 March.

Tcherneva, P. (2020) *The Case for a Job Guarantee*, Cambridge: Polity Press.

Tymoigne, E. (2016) 'Government Monetary and Fiscal Operations: Generalizing the Endogenous Money Approach', *Cambridge Journal of Economics*, **40** (5), pp. 1317–32.

Tymoigne, E. and Wray, L.R. (2014) *The Rise and Fall of Money Manager Capitalism: Minsky's Half Century from World War Two to the Great Recession*, London: Routledge.

Wray, L.R. (1990) *Money and Credit in Capitalist Economies: The Endogenous Money Approach*, Aldershot, UK and Brookfield, VT, USA: Edward Elgar Publishing.

Wray, L.R (1992) 'Alternative Theories of the Rate of Interest', *Cambridge Journal of Economics*, **16**, pp. 69–89.

Wray, L.R. (1993) 'Money, Interest Rates, and Monetarist Policy: Some More Unpleasant Monetarist Arithmetic?', *Journal of Post Keynesian Economics*, **15** (4), pp. 541–69.

Wray, L.R. (1998a) *Understanding Modern Money: The Key to Full Employment and Price Stability*, Cheltenham, UK and Northampton, MA, USA: Edward Elgar Publishing.

Wray, L.R. (1998b) 'Goldilocks and the Three Bears', available at: http://www.levyinstitute.org/publications/goldilocks-and-the-three-bears.

Wray, L.R. (ed.) (2004) *Credit and State Theories of Money: The Contributions of A. Mitchell Innes*, Cheltenham, UK and Northampton, MA, USA: Edward Elgar Publishing.

Wray, L.R. (2007) 'Lessons from the Subprime Meltdown', available at: http://www.levyinstitute.org/publications/lessons-from-the-subprime-meltdown.

Wray, L.R. (2015) *Modern Money Theory: A Primer on Macroeconomics for Sovereign Monetary Systems*, New York: Palgrave Macmillan.

Wray, L.R. (2016) *Why Minsky Matters: An Introduction to the Work of a Maverick Economist*, Princeton, NJ and Oxford: Princeton University Press.

Wray, L.R. (2019) 'Reexamining the Economic Costs of Debt', Statement of Senior Scholar L. Randall Wray to the House Budget Committee, *US House of Representatives*, November, available at: http://www.levyinstitute.org/publications/statement-of-senior-scholar-l-randall-wray-to-the-house-budget-committee.

16. The Austrian school of economics

Peter J. Boettke, Rosolino Candela, Karras J. Lambert and Dillon Tauzin

The foundational work of the Austrian school of economics, Carl Menger's *Grundsätze der Volkswirtschaftslehre* (*Principles of Economics*), celebrated its 150th anniversary in 2021. Menger's subjectivist approach to explaining value and cost, as well as his examination of individual choice on the margin, were eventually heralded as revolutionary throughout the international scientific community of economists and placed him as one of the co-founders of the marginalist revolution that gradually spread across the world in the late nineteenth and early twentieth centuries. Menger dedicated his work to Wilhelm Roscher, the leading representative of what was referred to as the German Historical school of economic thought. In Germany, however, Menger's work was met with scorn by members of the younger Historical school, who denied the existence of universal economic laws in favour of historically constrained empirical induction to explain social phenomena. In fact, the label 'Austrian school of economics' was created as a term of derision in the midst of the *Methodenstreit*, or 'battle over methods,' waged between Menger and his followers on one side and the German economists of the Historical school on the other. The fortunes of the Austrian school have both ebbed and flowed in the years since, attaining wide recognition in the scientific economics community by the 1930s, only to fall into near oblivion by the 1950s before a resurgence would begin in the 1970s that is still ongoing today.

From the start, Menger was concerned with investigating the causal laws of social phenomena and he therefore makes value-free scientific claims about necessary features of reality. Followers of Menger in the generations since his pathbreaking work have in large measure simply built upon and clarified the foundations laid by this extraordinary thinker, maintaining the focus on explaining the implications of purposive human action and interaction in the real world characterised by ineluctable scarcity. In recent decades, the monikers 'genetic-causal' and 'causal-realist' have been used to describe this 'Austrian' approach towards economic science as passed down since the founding efforts of Carl Menger.

The Austrian school is distinguished by its history of grand debates in political economy, such as Menger's dispute with the German Historical school, Böhm-Bawerk's rejection of Marxism, Ludwig von Mises's clash with the socialist economists, and F.A. Hayek's challenge to Keynes. Nevertheless, it is important to emphasise that the positions taken by the Austrians during these controversies were always grounded in uniquely Austrian contributions to economic *science*, not normative political philosophy. Today, the Austrian school is known for its strong methodological criticism of not just the historicism and old-style institutionalism of the late nineteenth century but also the two methodological trends that shaped economic science in the second half of the twentieth century: formalism and positivism. The Austrian economists challenged both the rise of mathematical modelling in economic theory and the emphasis on statistical significance as the appropriate scientific procedure to empirically adjudicate competing theoretical claims. This involvement in major debates in political economy and social philosophy, combined with scepticism towards the consensus among scientific markers in the discipline, has resulted in the unusual position in which economists working within the Austrian tradition find themselves in today's economic profession. Since they are at odds with significant portions of the profession at methodological, analytical and ideological levels, Austrian contributions to economic science reflect as much an alternative conversation as a voice within a consensus-seeking professional conversation.

As this chapter appears in a handbook dedicated to alternative approaches to political economy, our major aims are twofold. First, we seek to emphasise the categorical distinction between economics, a value-free positive science concerned with necessary causal laws of human action, and libertarianism, a normative political and legal philosophy concerned with the justified use of force in society. We also seek to show why it is not a mere coincidence that the economics of the Austrian school has recurrently been intertwined sociologically with European liberalism and American libertarianism throughout its history. To accomplish these two goals, we first provide a brief overview of some of the major scientific tenets of the Austrian school and describe the early context in which these ideas were developed in Vienna.[1] The remainder of the chapter then covers, in broad strokes, the future developments of the Austrian school following its migration to the United States, including the historical associations between economists of the Austrian school and the broader free market libertarian movement. This sheds light on the driving forces behind the ongoing research in Austrian economics today.[2]

AUSTRIAN ECONOMICS IN ONE SECTION

The 'Austrian' understanding of economics begins with the principles of *methodological individualism* and *methodological singularism*, which recognise that the analysis of social phenomena must ultimately be traced back to the concrete actions of individual human beings. Thus, economics as a science is concerned with the ends or goals individuals wish to attain and the means they choose to adopt in pursuit of these ends. *Value freedom* refers to the fact that economic analysis takes ends as given and only scientifically investigates the suitability of the various possible means that might be adopted in pursuit of those ends. Economic *goods* are those objects that individuals perceive as capable of serving as means for the attainment of their ends. The *value* of a good is derived from the subjective appraisal of the acting individual regarding the suitability of the good in removing felt uneasiness, a principle known as *methodological subjectivism*. All action involves a taking and a setting aside, a decision to adopt 'this' means rather than 'that' one. The potential satisfaction from the highest valued perceived opportunity forgone is the *cost* of an action, and can be roughly compared by an individual to the satisfaction ultimately attained by the action pursued to determine whether one experienced a *profit* or a *loss*. While such concepts and logical relations are useful in examining even the actions of a single individual removed from society, the existence of additional human actors and, consequently, exchange opportunities make more important the consideration of how social cooperation is possible, conflict is minimised, and wealth-generating activities can be undertaken without fear of aggressive interference.

Once individuals perceive the benefits of exchange with others, it becomes clear that one can acquire goods one values more highly by exchanging with others the goods one values less highly. Exchange reveals a double *inequality* in valuation, such that one party to a voluntary exchange may prefer good A to good B while the other party may prefer good B to good A. Preference is strictly ordinal, meaning economists can only say that one party preferred A to B at the moment of exchange and the other preferred B to A, not *how much* in quantitative units each party preferred one good to the other. *Prices* are the exchange ratios of the goods changing hands.

Barter exchange faces the problem of a 'double coincidence of wants', which requires one to find a counterpart that both has what you want and wants what you have. Perceptive individuals will seek to carry out exchanges not only for goods that are directly serviceable for the attainment of their ends but also those that one believes other individuals are more likely to value than what one already possesses. As *indirect* exchange proceeds in such a way, some goods are gradually recognised to be more *saleable* than others and are therefore desired for their superior ability to serve as a *medium of exchange*. The generally accepted medium of exchange is known as *money*.

While 'profit' and 'loss' could previously only be perceived in psychic terms by each individual actor, now *economic calculation* can occur, using money prices as a single common denominator. *Entrepreneurs* attempt to anticipate future market conditions, including consumer preferences and resource availability, and purchase an array of goods *now* with the expectation of then selling these goods, often following a productive transformation, *later*. Basic accounting can now inform the entrepreneur if he or she earned a *monetary profit* or a *monetary loss*.

To rise from subsistence levels of poverty, individuals must save (i.e. refrain from full present consumption) and engage in *production*. Production necessarily occurs through time, such that inputs are gradually transformed into valued outputs that can then be consumed or employed again within the *structure of production*. *Time-preference* refers to the degree to which one prefers the satisfaction of a good *sooner* versus the same satisfaction *later* and determines the proportion of consumption to investment as well as the pure ('originary') rate of interest. Following the emergence of money, it is possible to sum up the market values of the array of *producer goods* into a monetary sum simply called *capital*. Producer goods are those goods which do not service human wants directly as *consumer goods* but only indirectly in combination with additional factors of production. Thus, they are subjectively valued according to their perceived suitability for serving as 'way stations' to the eventual consumer goods.

Entrepreneurs can access economy-wide savings through *capital markets* and, according to their understanding of the past and appraisal of future market conditions, assign heterogeneous producer goods into particular production processes in anticipation that the eventual time-discounted proceeds from sale of the finished goods will surpass production costs, thus earning entrepreneurial profit. Alternatively, they will suffer entrepreneurial loss if their forecasts prove to be incorrect and revenues do not at least match costs.

The market economy, then, is the process of individuals, in their capacities as buyers and sellers, pursuing mutually beneficial exchanges to improve their self-perceived situations. By pursuing those production processes that they believe will yield output that consumers ultimately value, entrepreneurs profit by offering others what they want. Individuals who wish to consume must first produce, either by assuming risk of loss as an entrepreneur or contracting for a predetermined wage salary as an employee, thereby driving the process of wealth creation. Under the market economy characterised by social cooperation and capital-intensive production, the voluntary actions of all are oriented towards the benefit of others throughout society as a whole.

UNDERSTANDING THE AFFINITY BETWEEN AUSTRIAN ECONOMICS AND LIBERTARIANISM

Our purpose in describing the core ideas of the Austrian school in the previous section is twofold. First, it should be clear that value judgements do not enter into the systematic edifice of economic theory. To say that refraining from present consumption through saving and investing in roundabout production processes is the only way to attain meaningfully higher standards of living is not to say that the attainment of a higher standard of living is *ethically good* or *should be pursued* relative to other possible ends. Rather, economic reasoning allows us to say that *if* one wishes to live in a society experiencing a progressively general higher standard of living through increased material wealth, the most effective way is through capital accumulation and social cooperation under the division of labour. The economic calculation argument put forth by Mises and Hayek in debate with market socialists throughout their respective careers has nothing to do with the moral assessment of an individualist or collectivist society. The feasibility or non-feasibility of a command economy in which private property *and* residual claimancy for producer goods (factors of production) are abolished is solely a matter of means–ends analysis and not dependent on the value judgements over ends. The logical implications of this conclusion have arguably been difficult to accept for many as it puts parameters on their dreams for a better world.

Second, it should be noted that the state – the organisation of legitimatised compulsion in society – is perhaps conspicuous in its absence throughout the preceding section. This observation arguably goes a long way in helping us understand the historical affinity between Austrian economics and libertarianism. The state is not a *deus ex machina* that serves as a corrective for all perceived social ills. While the state must be accounted for and its role most be critically examined, it cannot be assumed that the state is populated by benevolent, omniscient and omnipotent beings who, guided by economic experts, who can simply select from a menu of pre-determined social goals.

That is not to say that all, or even most, members of the Austrian school were historically political anarchists. As will become clear in the following section, all the Viennese Austrian economists, despite holding classically liberal learnings to varying extents, assigned to the state certain key functions. Many later Austrian economists, too, maintain that the state is necessary to maintain the environment where the market process described above can occur. Others, meanwhile, have taken the more radical position that the state is unnecessary at best and a positive danger at worst to peaceful social cooperation and wealth generation.

Left implicit throughout the preceding section are the *institutional requirements* of the market economy, particularly *private property* and the *rule of law*. While economists subscribing to the tenets of the Austrian school share a recognition of the need for private property to enable the exchange and pricing of all goods and the rule of law to serve as a neutral standard by which competing property rights claims may be adjudicated, disagreement is possible concerning the conditions under which such institutions can emerge and persist. Some Austrian economists, such as Ludwig von Mises, saw the state as playing an essential role in using its monopoly on legitimised force to punish criminals who disturb the otherwise peaceful social order. Others influenced by Mises, such as Murray Rothbard, argued that policing and judicial services can be provided on the market just like any other goods or services. Others still, such as Friedrich Hayek, believed the state could assume additional functions while still preserving a stable market order characterised by private property and the rule of law. Despite sharing an understanding of the core tenets of economic science, each of these three thinkers nevertheless held distinct positions concerning the role of the state in society. Thus, Austrians share an understanding of the importance of private property in (positive) economic science, but justifications and conditions for the existence of property might differ. The pluralism we are suggesting here would mostly be at the level either of normative ethics (whether any intervention into voluntary action is immoral) or empirical generalisations (whether or not societies in which the state has a legal monopoly on police services will tend to safeguard property better than those that don't).

While the preceding section presents a high-level overview of some of the more important concepts held by economists of the Austrian school, it tells only half of the story, particularly that of an economy operating in the absence of intervention. This understanding of the 'unhampered' market serves as a baseline from which the consequences of particular interventions can then be analysed through economic reasoning. Many economists of the Austrian school, from Mises (1929) to Rothbard (1970) and Kirzner (1978) to Ikeda (1996) and Coyne (2013), have paid particular attention to the consequences of interventionism into otherwise voluntary market exchange.

To illustrate how intervention into natural market outcomes often produces consequences at variance with the stated ends of the intervention, Mises ([1979] 2006: 42–6) described the case of a price control imposed on a good regarded as essential, such as milk. In the attempt to allow poorer consumers to purchase milk at lower prices, the government may enact a price ceiling, or maximum price, making it illegal to sell a certain quantity of milk at any price higher than what is designated by the state. Milk will indeed now be sold at lower prices, but what are other consequences of this targeted intervention?

On the demand side of the market, consumers are now able to purchase more milk than before and, all else equal, will wish to do so. On the supply side of the market, however, marginal producers, or producers who faced the highest costs of production while still previously able to earn a profit, are driven out of the market. They suffer losses if the imposed maximum price of milk no longer exceeds their costs of production and entrepreneurs cannot suffer losses indefinitely and remain solvent. Furthermore, owners of cows now face lower profit margins in employing their cows towards milk production relative to other opportunities such as the production of cheese or beef. The net result is a decrease in the quantity of milk supplied on the market, coupled with an increase in the quantity demanded, causing a shortage. All who wish to buy milk cannot do so and the market price is not allowed to adjust to reflect extant supply and demand conditions. Rationing by some mechanism will follow, either on a first-come, first-served basis (perhaps resulting in long queues) or according to non-pecuniary motives (perhaps according to a manager's preference or government dictate).

While most mainstream economists will also carry the analysis of price controls this far, Austrians tend to next consider the logical implications of a situation where the government is committed to maintaining the imposed maximum price at the same quantity of milk produced as before. To do so, an intelligent bureaucrat may grasp the economic analysis of the preceding paragraph and realise that the costs of milk producers are now too high to produce the same quantity of milk. Since the fodder for cows accounts for part of this cost, the government may then place a price ceiling on fodder, instigating the same process yet again now for producers of fodder. Given the interconnectedness of all market phenomena, a government truly committed to its initial aims to lower the price of milk without affecting quantity supplied will end up abolishing market pricing for all goods, including all factors of production, in favour of government dictate.

Socialism, in the sense of all production decisions being brought under the discretion of the singular will of those working within the state apparatus, is the logical terminus of this initial goal to simply lower the price of milk. Yet as Mises ([1920] 1975) demonstrated a century ago, such a central planner lacks the ability to *economise*, or know the cost of pursuing one line of production relative to another. Without private ownership in the means of production and voluntary exchange, prices corresponding to the relative valuations of individuals cannot emerge. Without these prices, one cannot compare the costs of alternative production decisions under a single common denominator, nor can one compare the objective exchange values of inputs expended and outputs attained through whatever production process is ultimately chosen. In that sense, to have rational economic calculation under socialism is impossible and all production decisions will be arbitrarily groping in the dark. The gradual liquidation of accumulated capital and the virtual obliteration of the productive capacities of society would soon follow.

Of course, government need not pursue such a course of action to this conclusion. The initial controls may remain and, without further interference, the logic of intervention would not be pursued to its ultimate end. Shortages are eventually accepted and the market process continues, albeit in hampered form. Nevertheless, assuming the initial goal was to allow consumers to purchase the same amount of milk at lower prices without affecting other sectors of the economy, economic reasoning demonstrates that the means of imposing a price ceiling on milk are unsuitable for achieving the end desired. As the famous saying in economics goes, 'there is no such thing as a free lunch'. The ideas of the Austrian school, focused squarely on understanding real world phenomena, helps us see this lesson in every instance of intervention into voluntary exchanges.

For deontological libertarians who oppose any act of coercion that interferes with voluntary social relations on principle, the conclusion of the foregoing chain of reasoning is naturally alluring. Likewise, those who understand the teachings of the Austrian school and wish for a world of social harmony and increased wealth may then arrive at a broadly libertarian political position through consequentialist justification. Nevertheless, Austrian economists consistently maintain that the body of knowledge that comprises economic science is categorically separate from normative political philosophy. One could attain a complete intellectual grasp of the entire body of work produced by economists of the Austrian school yet still *desire* the consequences of particular interventions into the market order. To repeat once more, economists working within the tradition of the Austrian school, in their capacities solely as economists, treat the ends of individuals as given and can only make meaningful *economic* statements concerning the suitability of the means chosen in light of those given ends. It is perhaps more than a happy coincidence to those who identify both as economists of the Austrian school and political libertarians that there seems to be no fundamental clash between normative libertarian values and positive scientific understanding.

ECONOMIC SCIENCE AND POLITICAL LIBERALISM

Having attempted to justify why there tends to be a close association between the Austrian school of economics and libertarianism, we can now turn to consideration of how the nature of this association has manifested in the scientific contributions of some of the major personalities in the Austrian school since its formation until today.[3]

The Austrian school got its start in Vienna in the late nineteenth century, where many of the key figures in the early history of the school would remain until the 1930s. A number of them would later find their way to the United States in the midst of the Second World War and the eventual German annexation of Austria in 1938, but would retain the distinctive 'Austrian' character in their economics work and pass this on to a new generation of students in the United States.

As described at the beginning of this chapter, the Austrian school owes its existence to the work of Carl Menger. His first book, *Principles of Economics* (1871), laid the foundations from which each generation of Austrian school economists have since been elaborating and clarifying. In fact, nearly all of the concepts described in the theory-focused section of this chapter were already either explicitly or implicitly contained within this founding text of the Austrian school.

First working as an economic journalist, Menger studied the formation and daily movement of prices, and he noticed a discrepancy between what he observed and the teachings of major economics textbooks coming out of Germany at the time. The principal aim of his first major work was to trace the formation of actual market prices back to their original source in the subjective valuations of purposive human actors. However, Menger also laid the groundwork for both capital theory and monetary theory in the course of explaining capital accumulation and showing the progressive expansion of the structure of production to be the most significant mechanism driving economic growth.

Menger earnestly wished to advance the German tradition of economic science, but the tepid reception of his first volume compelled him to investigate more deeply the methodological underpinnings of economics. The results of his efforts appeared 12 years later in the form of his *Untersuchungen über die Methode der Socialwissenschaften und der Politischen Oekonomie insbesondere* (*Investigations into the Method of the Social Sciences with Special Reference to Economics*). Rather than simply being ignored, this time Menger's work launched a controversy over the proper method of economics that has still not been resolved to this day. While some historians of economic thought believe this controversy produced more heat than light, economists of the Austrian school tend to disagree and, ever since then, they have maintained an interest in clarifying the proper epistemological foundations and method of economics.

Among those Austrian economists joining Menger in the battle over method were Eugen von Böhm-Bawerk and Friedrich von Wieser. Böhm-Bawerk devoted much of his theoretical effort to capital and interest theory (1890, 1891, 1903) and dealt a devastating theoretical blow to the Marxian economic system ([1896] 1898); while Wieser (1927) is most widely remembered within the canon of the Austrian school for coining the phrase 'marginal utility' and for his efforts to further develop value and cost theory.

Politically, Menger was a liberal activist in his youth and was later appointed tutor to Crown Prince Rudolf of Austria. His 1876 lectures to the Crown Prince have survived and reflect his deep familiarity with the work of Adam Smith (Streissler and Streissler 1994). Nevertheless,

Menger maintained strict value freedom in his scientific economics work, setting an example for all future members of the Austrian school. Böhm-Bawerk shared Menger's liberalism and his influence was exerted through his considerable presence in the Austrian finance ministry, serving stints as Minister of Finance as an unwavering advocate of sound monetary policy and fiscal responsibility.[4] Wieser, meanwhile, was more sympathetic to a version of Fabian socialism and found interest in constructing mental experiments of a Communistic society. Wieser's chair at the University of Vienna passed to Hans Mayer, who infamously accommodated the National Socialist regime in Austria. This unfortunate episode perhaps demonstrates more than anything that a scientific understanding of the ideas of the Austrian school need not translate into political libertarianism.

Böhm-Bawerk's academic seminar in Vienna attracted a number of bright students, including Joseph Schumpeter and Ludwig von Mises. Schumpeter took primary inspiration from Wieser and Leon Walras, however, and would leave Austria in 1925 to assume an academic position in Bonn, Germany, which he would hold until leaving for Harvard University in 1932. Although he undoubtedly went on to a stellar career in economics, Schumpeter had little to do with future developments of the Austrian school and his work is rarely considered as fitting comfortably within the canon of the Austrian school, due primarily to methodological considerations. Mises, meanwhile, proceeded firmly from the foundations laid by Menger and soon contributed a substantial work in monetary theory titled *The Theory of Money and Credit*. Originally published in 1912, Mises successfully applied the principles of marginal utility to money and set forth the 'regression theorem', which recognises that people value money in the present because they expect the money to have a certain purchasing power in the future based on its purchasing power in the recent past. This logic can then be pushed backwards in time to the point when the commodity first began to serve as money, before which the commodity was valued subjectively by individuals just like any other good. Mises also describes the economy-wide effects of malinvestment and overconsumption due to expansion of 'fiduciary media' or unbacked bank notes. This phenomenon is now known as the Austrian Business Cycle Theory.

Mises surpassed his predecessors in his commitment to political liberalism, advocating a completely unhampered market economy outside whatever taxation is necessary to maintain police services, law courts and national defence. It is believed that such 'extreme' views, alongside his Jewish heritage and his reputation for not 'suffering fools gladly' in debate, contributed to his ultimate denial of a professorship in Austria. Whatever the reason, Mises earned a living at the Vienna Chamber of Commerce while writing his contributions to theoretical economics on the side.[5] Still, Mises was able to serve as an unsalaried *Privatdozent* and held a bimonthly seminar in his Chamber of Commerce office that welcomed the next, and arguably final, generation of Austrian economists actually born and trained in Austria.

This 'fourth' generation of Austrian economists included Fritz Machlup, Oskar Morgenstern, Gottfried Haberler and Friedrich Hayek. Since internal university politics made it difficult for Mises to obtain a position as full-time professor, most of this fourth generation spent their formative years under the instruction of Mayer and Othmar Spahn, only later joining Mises's seminar for discussion on topics in economics and philosophy, among various other disciplines.[6]

Hayek worked closely with Mises, serving as Director of the Austrian Institute for Trade Cycle Research from its founding in 1927 until his departure for London in 1931, at which time Morgenstern assumed directorial duties until Morgenstern's own emigration to the

United States in 1938 in the midst of the National Socialist takeover of Austria. Hayek quickly produced writings on business cycle theory and later took the side of Mises in the 'socialist calculation debate' concerning the impossibility of rational economic planning under a socialist economic system that prohibits private property in the means of production.[7]

In 1934, Mises accepted a position as professor at the Graduate Institute of International Studies in Geneva, Switzerland and remained there until 1940. During that time, he devoted his time and intellectual energies into completing a comprehensive treatise on economic theory titled *Nationalökonomie*. Finally integrating his advances in monetary theory, value theory, and epistemology within a systematic theoretical structure, Mises may have had high hopes for the impact his treatise might have on the field of economics. However, it was largely released to silence amidst the frenzy of the Second World War.

Given the turmoil in Europe at that time, it became politically impossible for Mises to remain in Geneva and his apartment in Vienna had already been ransacked by National Socialists. After a harrowing journey, Mises arrived in New York in 1940, carrying with him hopes for the survival of the ideas of the Austrian school. Hayek's later move from London to Chicago in 1945 reinforced the changing centre of gravity for the Austrian school from Europe to the United States. Meanwhile, Hayek's fourth-generation Austrian school contemporaries found academic homes at prestigious universities such as Harvard (Haberler), Johns Hopkins (Machlup), and Princeton (Morgenstern). While never losing sight of their Austrian roots, they incorporated other influences and were not, except for Machlup during a stint at New York University (NYU) in the 1970s, actively involved in fostering a new generation of distinctly 'Austrian school' economists in the United States. As a result, the Austrian school as it exists today largely followed the paradigms set forth by Mises and Hayek.

Although Mises arrived in New York as a stranger in a strange land, he would find a champion in Henry Hazlitt, who was then working on the editorial staff of the *New York Times*. Mises first took a position at the National Bureau of Economic Research and published two works, *Bureaucracy* (1944a) and *Omnipotent Government* (1944b), before moving to NYU that same year. He remained at NYU until 1969, just four years before his death at the age of 92.

In addition to Hazlitt, Mises found another close ally in Leonard Read, who went on to establish the Foundation for Economic Education (FEE) in Irvington-on-Hudson, New York City. Mises, Hazlitt, and later F.A. ('Baldy') Harper, among many others of note, were involved with educational and publishing initiatives at FEE; and Harper later founded the Institute for Humane Studies (IHS), which is now associated with George Mason University. As such, the institutional environment for the study of Austrian school ideas that we now recognise today was already taking shape.

Despite the prestige of the Austrian school reaching something of a nadir during and immediately following the Second World War years, Mises and Hayek would nevertheless produce some of their most important works during the 1940s. In addition to the two aforementioned volumes published in 1944, Mises expanded his earlier *Nationalökonomie* (1940) into the English-language treatise *Human Action* (1949). This work would serve, like Menger's *Principles*, as the foundation from which the Austrian school would again grow.

Hayek, meanwhile, wrote *The Road to Serfdom* (1944) while still in London. In that work, Hayek argued that comprehensive economic planning is inconsistent with the rule of law and democracy. Hayek was not addressing his book to the advocates of communism in Soviet Russia or the advocates of the total state in Nazi Germany but to his colleagues in Britain who believed they could combine socialist economic planning with liberal democratic institutions such as the rule of law and individual freedom. The suppression of individual freedom and the erosion of democratic institutions that Hayek envisioned as the logical outcome of efforts to substitute comprehensive economic planning for the market economy was a stark warning to his colleagues that their vision of a rational economic order would result in a political nightmare from their own point of view, as the rule of law and democracy would prove to be incompatible with the organisational logic of economic planning.

Though it was meant primarily for an academic audience, the commercial success of *The Road to Serfdom* took even Hayek by surprise. Before the end of the decade, Hayek also formed the Mont Pelerin Society, which held its inaugural meeting in 1947 with the intention to bring together scholars across a range of disciplines who were committed to defending the idea of a liberal society. He also published a collection of earlier essays in *Individualism and Economic Order* (1948) that have proven influential since the subsequent rebirth of the Austrian school.

At NYU, Mises re-started his seminar, this time predominately with American students. He once again found bright and eager students in Israel Kirzner and Murray Rothbard. Kirzner formally completed his dissertation *The Economic Point of View* (1960) under Mises and would soon make contributions in capital theory (1966) and entrepreneurship (1973) while himself a faculty member at NYU. Kirzner would go on to oversee the formation of a pro-gramme dedicated to the study and advancement of the Austrian school paradigm.

Rothbard was already a doctoral student at Columbia University upon discovering Mises's work but would play an active role in Mises's NYU seminar. Since Mises's *Human Action* assumed a high level of contemporary scientific literacy on the part of its readers, Rothbard was drafted by the Volker Fund to condense Mises's work into an accessible textbook. Rothbard's effort instead resulted in another full-blown treatise in the form of *Man, Economy, and State* (1962a).

While Kirzner would fix his focus primarily on academic scholarship, Rothbard split his attention between economic theory and libertarian thought and drove the formation of much of the liberty-oriented institutional infrastructure that exists today. He was personally involved in the 1970s and 1980s with founding the Libertarian Party, the Cato Institute and the Ludwig von Mises Institute. His works, such as *Power and Market* (1970) and *For a New Liberty* ([1973] 2006), attracted scores of eager young minds to think hard about economic and polit-ical freedom and, in particular, to give a fresh hearing to the ideas of the Austrian school of economics. Rothbard also wrote notable works in history, both economic (1962b, 1963) and otherwise ([1975] 2011).

Hans Sennholz, a German-born Austrian economist and Mises's first doctoral student, took a teaching position at Grove City College in 1956, retiring in 1992 to assume the role of President of FEE. Sennholz, like so many Austrian school economists before and after him, tried to make a positive difference both within an academic institution, primarily through his instruction of college students, and through articles intended for the public in periodicals like *The Freeman*. Sennholz wrote some shorter works on the importance of sound money and the causes of business cycles (Sennholz 1985, 1988), making Mises's ideas more accessible to lay readers.

Mises and Hayek also continued to publish during this time, with Mises (1957, 1962) focus-ing on the epistemological foundations of economics; and Hayek (1960, 1973, 1976, 1979) investigating the institutional framework required for peaceful social cooperation to flourish.

Meanwhile, the 'rebirth' of the Austrian school as a sociological entity is usually attributed to the year 1974 for two reasons. First, Hayek was co-awarded the 'Sveriges Riksbank Prize in Economic Sciences in Memory of Alfred Nobel' in that year, galvanising the youthful cadre of emerging Austrian economists inspired by the work of Mises, Hayek, Rothbard and Kirzner. Second, the IHS held the first of three consecutive annual conferences intended to foster the scientific development of the Austrian school, gathering a number of geographically disparate scholars committed to preserving and furthering the Austrian school tradition.[8]

These years also saw the return of Ludwig M. Lachmann into the scientific discourse community of the Austrian school. Lachmann, a student of Hayek's from the London School of Economics, published an influential work on capital theory (1956) before entering university administration at the University of the Witwatersrand in South Africa. He attended the South Royalton conference in 1974 and lectured alongside Rothbard and Kirzner, resuming scholarly output on topics such as macroeconomics (1973) and expectations (1977). Kirzner would arrange for Lachmann to spend part of each year from 1974 to 1987 supervising doctoral students at NYU, where he influenced the next generation of Austrian school economists coming out of that programme.

CONCLUSION

Today, the Austrian school is still considered 'heterodox' relative to the 'mainstream' of the economics profession, but has continued to grow since the seeds were planted by the migration of Mises and Hayek to the United States in the 1940s and 1950s.[9] There have been too many recent works published by economists associated with Austrian school ideas in recent decades to list, but they cover a wide range of topics, including monetary theory (White 1984, 1999; Salerno 2010); capital theory (Lewin [1999] 2011); comparative economic systems (Lavoie 1985a, 1985b); business cycle theory (Garrison 2000); entrepreneurship (Klein 2010); economic development (Powell 2014); foreign intervention (Coyne 2008, 2013); and private governance (Leeson 2014; Stringham 2015).[10] Austrian school economists are positioned on economics faculties around the world and books in the Austrian tradition are now being published by university presses such as Oxford University Press, Stanford University Press, and Cambridge University Press, while scholarly journals such as the *Review of Austrian Economics* and the *Quarterly Journal of Austrian Economics* give space for academics to engage with and further the ideas of the Austrian school. It thus seems little stretch to say that the future prospects of the Austrian school are at least as, if not more, bright as compared with any other time in its history.

NOTES

1. It is beyond the scope of this chapter to do full justice to either the nuances of economic theory from the Austrian perspective or the historical connections between Austrian economics and libertarian thought. Readers interested in further exploring the former may consult recent primers on the major ideas of the Austrian school such as Coyne and Boettke (2020) or Holcombe (2014). For more recent academic developments in Austrian economics, see Boettke and Coyne (2015).

2. For further exploration of the connections between Austrian economics and classical liberalism, both in Vienna and the United States, see Dekker (2016) and Doherty (2008), respectively. See also

Boettke et al. (2016) for more on the scientific development of the Austrian school in the United States after the Second World War.

3. For additional biographical details of many of the scholars associated with the Austrian school along with their major theoretical innovations, see the entries in Holcombe (1999).

4. At the time of this writing, the Austrian 100 schilling bank note bears Böhm-Bawerk's visage in recognition of his achievements in both economic science and state policy.

5. See Mises ([1922] 1951, [1927] 1985, [1960] 2003) for translations of some of his major works produced during his time in Vienna. Hülsmann (2008) provides a detailed look at Mises's life and accomplishments.

6. Despite his lack of a full-time professorship, Mises's seminar was famous worldwide and attracted such eminent economists as Lionel Robbins of the London School of Economics and Frank Knight of the University of Chicago as visiting guests.

7. On Hayek's contributions to business cycle theory, see Hayek ([1929] 1933, [1935] 1967); and see Hayek (1935a) for some of his writing during the socialist calculation debate.

8. Lectures and papers presented at the first two conferences are collected in Dolan (1976) and Spadaro (1978), respectively.

9. For a discussion of the distinction between the 'mainstream' versus the 'mainline' of economic thinking, see Boettke (2012).

10. For a comprehensive overview of the contemporary Austrian school of economics, we refer the reader to *The Oxford Handbook of Austrian Economics* (Boettke and Coyne 2015). Not only does this volume discuss the fields of research listed above, but it also contrasts the Austrian school with other contending perspectives in political economy, such as Ordo-Liberalism and Constitutional Political Economy.

REFERENCES

Boettke, P.J. (2012) *Living Economics: Yesterday, Today, and Tomorrow*, Oakland, CA: Independent Institute.

Boettke, P.J. and Coyne, C.J. (eds) (2015) *The Oxford Handbook of Austrian Economics*, Oxford: Oxford University Press.

Boettke, P.J., Coyne, C.J. and Newman, P. (2016) 'The History of a Tradition: Austrian Economics from 1871 to 2016', *Research in the History of Economic Thought and Methodology*, **34** (a), pp. 199–243.

Böhm-Bawerk, E. von (1890) *Capital and Interest: A Critical History of Economical Theory*, trans. William Smart, London: Macmillan.

Böhm-Bawerk, E. von ([1891] 1930) *The Positive Theory of Capital*, trans. William Smart, New York: G.E. Stechart.

Böhm-Bawerk, E. von ([1896] 1898) *Karl Marx and the Close of his System: A Criticism*, trans. Alice M. Macdonald, London: T. Fisher Unwin.

Böhm-Bawerk, E. von (1903) *Recent Literature on Interest (1884–1899)*, trans. William A. Scott and Siegmund Feilbogen, London: Macmillan & Co.

Coyne, C.J. (2008) *After War: The Political Economy of Exporting Democracy*, Stanford, CA: Stanford University Press.

Coyne, C.J. (2013) *Doing Bad by Doing Good: Why Humanitarian Action Fails*, Stanford, CA: Stanford University Press.

Coyne, C.J. and Boettke, P.J. (2020) *The Essential Austrian Economics*, Vancouver: Fraser Institute.

Dekker, E. (2016) *The Viennese Students of Civilization: The Meaning and Context of Austrian Economics Reconsidered*, Cambridge: Cambridge University Press.

Doherty, B. (2008) *Radicals for Capitalism: A Freewheeling History of the Modern American Libertarian Movement*, New York: Public Affairs.

Dolan, E.G. (ed.) (1976) *The Foundations of Modern Austrian Economics*, Kansas City, MO: Sheed and Ward.

Garrison, R.W. (2000) *Time and Money: The Macroeconomics of Capital Structure*, London: Routledge.

Hayek, F.A. ([1929] 1933) *Monetary Theory and the Trade Cycle*, trans. N. Kaldor and H. M. Croome, New York: Sentry Press.
Hayek, F.A. (ed) (1935a), *Collectivist Economic Planning: Critical Studies on the Possibilities of Socialism*, London: Routledge and Kegan Paul.
Hayek, F.A. ([1935] 1967) *Prices and Production*, 2nd edn, New York: Augustus M. Kelly.
Hayek, F.A. (1944) *The Road to Serfdom*, Chicago, IL: University of Chicago Press.
Hayek, F.A. (1948) *Individualism and Economic Order*, Chicago, IL: University of Chicago Press.
Hayek, F.A. (1960) *The Constitution of Liberty*, Chicago, IL: University of Chicago Press.
Hayek, F.A. (1973) *Law, Legislation and Liberty, Volume 1: Rules and Order*, Chicago, IL: University of Chicago Press.
Hayek, F.A. (1976) *Law, Legislation and Liberty, Volume 2: The Mirage of Social Justice*, Chicago, IL: University of Chicago Press.
Hayek, F.A. (1979) *Law, Legislation and Liberty, Volume 3: The Political Order of a Free People*, Chicago, IL: University of Chicago Press.
Holcombe, R.G. (ed.) (1999) *15 Great Austrian Economists*, Auburn, AL: Ludwig von Mises Institute.
Holcombe, R.G. (2014) *Advanced Introduction to the Austrian School of Economics*, Cheltenham, UK and Northampton, MA, USA: Edward Elgar Publishing.
Hülsmann, J.G. (2007) *Mises: The Last Knight of Liberalism*, Auburn, AL: Ludwig von Mises Institute.
Ikeda, S. (1996) *Dynamics of the Mixed Economy: Toward a Theory of Interventionism*, London: Routledge.
Kirzner, I.M. (1960) *The Economic Point of View: An Essay in the History of Economic Theory*, Kansas City, MO: Sheed and Ward.
Kirzner, I.M. (1966) *An Essay on Capital*, New York: Augustus M. Kelley.
Kirzner, I.M. (1973) *Competition and Entrepreneurship*, Chicago, IL: University of Chicago Press.
Kirzner, I.M. (1978) *The Perils of Regulation: A Market-Process Approach*, Coral Gables: Law and Economics Center, University of Miami.
Klein, P.G. (2010) *The Capitalist and The Entrepreneur: Essays on Organizations & Markets*, Auburn, AL: Ludwig von Mises Institute.
Lachmann, L.M. (1956) *Capital and Its Structure*, London: G. Bell and Sons.
Lachmann, L.M. (1973) *Macro-economic Thinking and the Market Economy: An Essay on the Neglect of the Micro-Foundations and its Consequences*, London: The Institute of Economic Affairs.
Lachmann, L.M. (1977) *Capital, Expectations, and the Market Process: Essays on the Theory of the Market Economy*, Kansas City, MO: Sheed Andrews and McMeel.
Lavoie, D. (1985a) *Rivalry and Central Planning: The Socialist Calculation Debate Reconsidered*, New York: Cambridge University Press.
Lavoie, D. (1985b) *National Economic Planning: What is Left?* Cambridge: Ballinger Publishing.
Leeson, P.T. (2014) *Anarchy Unbound: Why Self-Governance Works Better than You Think*, New York: Cambridge University Press.
Lewin, P. ([1999] 2011) *Capital in Disequilibrium: The Role of Capital in a Changing World*, 2nd edn, Auburn: Ludwig von Mises Institute.
Menger, C. ([1871] 2007) *Principles of Economics*, trans. James Dingwall and Bert F. Hoselitz, Auburn, AL: Ludwig von Mises Institute.
Menger, C. ([1883] 1985) *Investigations into the Method of the Social Sciences with Special Reference to Economics*, trans. Francis J. Nock, New York: New York University Press.
Menger, C. (2020) 'Errors of Historicism', ed. Karen Horn and Stefan Kolev, trans. Network for Constitutional Economics and Social Philosophy (NOUS), *Econ Journal Watch*, **17** (2), pp. 461–507.
Mises, L. von ([1912] 1953) *The Theory of Money and Credit*, New Haven, CT: Yale University Press.
Mises, L. von. ([1920] 1975) 'Economic Calculation in the Socialist Commonwealth', in Hayek, F.A. (ed.) *Collectivist Economic Planning*, Clifton, NJ: Augustus M. Kelley, pp. 87–130.
Mises, L. von ([1922] 1951) *Socialism: A Sociological and Economic Analysis*, trans. J. Kahane, New Haven, CT: Yale University Press.
Mises, L. von ([1927] 1985) *Liberalism in the Classical Tradition*, trans. Ralph Raico, San Francisco, CA: Cobden Press.
Mises, L. von (1929) *Kritik des Interventionismus: Untersuchungen zur Wirtschaftspolitik und Wirtschaftsideologie der Gegenwart*, Jena: Gustav Fischer.

Mises, L. von (1940) *Nationalökonomie: Theorie des Handelns und Wirtschaftens*, Geneva: Editions Union.

Mises, L. von (1944a) *Bureaucracy*, New Haven, CT: Yale University Press.

Mises, L. von (1944b) *Omnipotent Government*, New Haven, CT: Yale University Press.

Mises, L. von (1949) *Human Action: A Treatise on Economics*, New Haven, CT: Yale University Press.

Mises, L. von (1957) *Theory and History: An Interpretation of Social and Economic Evolution*, New Haven, CT: Yale University Press.

Mises, L. von ([1960] 2003) *Epistemological Problems of Economics*, 3rd edn, trans. George Reisman, Auburn, AL: Ludwig von Mises Institute.

Mises, L. von (1962) *The Ultimate Foundation of Economic Science: An Essay on Method*, Princeton, NJ: D. Van Nostrand Company.

Mises, L. von ([1979] 2006) *Economic Policy: Thoughts for Today and Tomorrow*, 3rd edn, Auburn, AL: Ludwig von Mises Institute.

Powell, B. (2014) *Out of Poverty: Sweatshops in the Global Economy*, New York: Cambridge University Press.

Rothbard, M.N. (1962a) *Man, Economy, and State: A Treatise on Economic Principles*, Princeton, NJ: D. Van Nostrand Company.

Rothbard, M.N. (1962b) *The Panic of 1819: Reactions and Policies*, New York: Columbia University Press.

Rothbard, M.N. (1963) *America's Great Depression*, Princeton, NJ: D. Van Nostrand Company.

Rothbard, M.N. (1970) *Power & Market: Government and the Economy*, Menlo Park, CA: Institute for Humane Studies.

Rothbard, M.N. ([1973] 2006) *For a New Liberty: The Libertarian Manifesto*, 2nd edn, Auburn, AL: Ludwig von Mises Institute.

Rothbard, M.N. ([1975] 2011) *Conceived in Liberty*, Auburn, AL: Ludwig von Mises Institute.

Salerno, J.T. (2010) *Money: Sound & Unsound*, Auburn, AL: Ludwig von Mises Institute.

Sennholz, H.F. (1985) *Money and Freedom*, Spring Mills: Libertarian Press.

Sennholz, H.F. (1988) *The Great Depression: Will We Repeat It?* Spring Mills, PA: Libertarian Press.

Spadaro, L.M. (ed.) (1978) *New Directions in Austrian Economics*, Kansas City, MO: Sheed Andrews and McMeel.

Streissler, E.W. and Streissler, M. (eds) (1994) *Carl Menger's Lectures to Crown Prince Rudolf of Austria*, trans. Monika Streissler and David F. Good, Cheltenham, UK and Northampton, MA, USA: Edward Elgar Publishing.

Stringham, E.P. (2015) *Private Governance: Creating Order in Economic and Social Life*, Oxford: Oxford University Press.

White, L.H. (1984) *Free Banking in Britain: Theory, Experience, and Debate, 1800–1845*, New York: Cambridge University Press.

White, L.H. (1999) *The Theory of Monetary Institutions*, Malden, MA: Blackwell.

Wieser, F. von (1927) *Social Economics*, trans. A. Ford Heinrichs, New York: Adelphi Company.

PART IV

EXPLORING THE SOCIO-ECOLOGICAL FOUNDATIONS OF ECONOMIC SYSTEMS

17. Polanyian political economy
Joy Paton

We live in an age where the meaning of 'economy' and how it works is seemingly self-evident in popular consciousness. The influence of neoliberalism has imparted an apparent truth status to mainstream economics, despite the ongoing crises in global capitalism. International economic and financial turbulence, together with enduring human and environmental crises that stem from ongoing policies of de/re-regulation and marketisation, have been hallmarks of neoliberalism in practice. Yet the notion of a 'free market' best governed by the law of supply and demand continues to drive such policies in a seemingly endless cycle of 'curative causation', with policy prescriptions invoking 'more of the same'. Thankfully, counter tendencies exist. The embrace of multiple economic perspectives in contemporary political economy provides much-needed respite from the economic orthodoxy, offering alternative platforms for analysing contemporary economic issues and policies. Amongst these different currents, the work of Karl Polanyi and his followers has attracted substantial attention in a wide range of disciplines and is now highly cited in the social sciences.

Both celebrated and critiqued, Polanyi's commonly referenced work, *The Great Transformation* (*TGT*) ([1944] 2001) appeals to diverse audiences across the political spectrum, including scholars, activists, journalists, business leaders and politicians. Identifying Polanyi as one of the first theorists to provide a moral critique of the 'self-regulating market', Frankel (2020: 44, 46) suggests his work is now currently marshalled to substantiate a wide range of 'antithetical policies and contradictory social objectives'. A multi-disciplinary scholar with interests in philosophy, politics, anthropology and history, Polanyi's economics has diverse conceptual links, including to the works of Adam Smith, Karl Marx and Carl Menger. His articulation of an institutional understanding of economy that is quite distinct from that of neoclassical economics contributes a basis upon which the notion of 'economy' itself can be contested. This holds out the promise of an alternative conceptual lens through which to understand contemporary economic issues during this protracted period of neoliberalism.

This chapter is primarily concerned with explaining Polanyi's economic thinking, as presented in and beyond *TGT*, locating his contributions within the parameters of an institutional approach (see Stanfield 1980; Paton 2011b; Maucourant and Plociniczak 2013). It begins with an introduction to *TGT*, followed by discussion of some of the key points of interest and scholarly debate emanating from the book in recent decades. The second half of the chapter considers Polanyi's thinking in relation to economic orthodoxy, exploring his institutionalism as this emerges after *TGT*. It also links the theoretical achievements of Polanyi's later work back to *TGT*, as therein lies the opportunity for developing a distinctive Polanyian perspective on the institutional organisation of capitalism. Along the way, critical observations and subsequent developments are considered, aiming to show the evolution, influence and status of Polanyian ideas.

INTRODUCTION TO *THE GREAT TRANSFORMATION*

The historical context of a nineteenth-century industrialising Britain preoccupied Karl Polanyi's analysis in his now classic 1944 text, *TGT*. The book aimed to influence the arguments and agendas that would shape the international system of political economy in the aftermath of the Second World War. Polanyi linked the Great Depression and rise of fascism in the interwar period back to the 'great age of *laissez faire*'. Key for Polanyi was the attempt by nineteenth-century proponents of *laissez faire* to institute a self-regulating international market system whereby the factors of production (land, labour, money) would ultimately be priced (governed) through the international gold standard. He believed there were crucial lessons to be learned from this history in terms of reconstructing the post-war international political economic architecture. Although the work lacked widespread influence at the time, it now ranks as a canon of twentieth-century social science (Block 2003: 275), holding significant resonance for the critics of contemporary 'market fundamentalism'.

In *TGT* is both an acknowledgement of the devastation unleashed in the name of *laissez faire* by the forces of liberalisation and a strong challenge to inherited ideas about *laissez faire* itself. Polanyi portrays a picture of nineteenth-century British market society (capitalism) as one that arose out of very specific actions intent on structural change. Creating a labour market was the vital, if 'repugnant' (Dow 2006: 137), step in establishing a market economy where the processes of production and distribution could be 'controlled, regulated, and directed by market prices', thereby entrusting economic *and* social order to a 'self-regulating price mechanism' (Polanyi 2001: 71). However, in one of the most memorable passages from *TGT*, Polanyi (2001: 145) points out 'free markets' were a political construction, arguing that '*laissez faire* itself was enforced by the state … free markets could never have come into being merely by allowing things to take their course […] [it] required an enormous increase in continuous, centrally organized and controlled interventionism' (Polanyi 2001: 146). The evident contrast to the small government rhetoric and free market ideology of neoliberalism has made *TGT* a go-to book for people seeking an alternative way of understanding capitalism and an alternative basis for public policies.

In 1979, Fred Block and Margaret Somers first made their case for the significance of Karl Polanyi's work and, since that time, the interest in Polanyi has grown significantly within academia and beyond (Somers and Block 2021). In the early decades of neoliberalism, Polanyi was seen to provide the intellectual foundations for a counter movement against the neoliberal dismantling of post-war welfare systems (Mendell 2001). Polanyian perspectives are evident in the writings of economic sociologists (Block and Somers 1984, 2014), feminist theorists (Fraser 2014), institutional economists (Stanfield 1980; Waller and Jennings 1991) and international political economy (IPE) scholars (Dale 2010), all utilising Polanyi to enrich the field of work challenging economic orthodoxy. Meanwhile, O'Connor (1998: 159) acknowledged his intellectual debt to Polanyi for the development of the 'second contradiction of capitalism' thesis that is at the core of his ecological Marxism. Similarly, Paton (2011a) and Prudham (2013) utilise Polanyi in their respective ecological and radical green political economic perspectives. More recently, Peck (2013, 2020) has extended the engagement with Polanyi in the field of economic geography.

These examples are suggestive, but by no means exhaustive, of the range of scholarly domains where an interest in the work of Polanyi can be found. At its best, Polanyi's approach points to an alternative way of framing economic processes to that posited by the 'iron law of the market'. It offers the promise of understanding markets as socially embedded rather than separate from social and political processes; economies as socially constructed and maintained rather than natural and self-regulating; and states as integral rather than marginal to such processes. However, the invoking of ideas articulated by Polanyi in *TGT* is sometimes polemical and metaphorical in nature. This reflects the character of the book itself which is both admired for its prescient turns of phrase and criticised for its inconsistencies and confusions (Hodgson 2017), historical inaccuracies (Halperin 2004; Frankel 2020) and the absence of a coherent and systematic theoretical framework. Such endeavours of critical engagement are a necessary part of developing Polanyian political economy as a scholarly tradition in the twenty-first century.

METAPHOR AND MEANING: DEBATES ARISING FROM *THE GREAT TRANSFORMATION*

Even strident critics of *TGT* acknowledge that the book 'contains illuminating insights'; and that Polanyi 'is to be admired for seeking to explain the devasting impacts of capitalist markets and the political forces constructing and sustaining market societies' (Frankel 2020: 47). These contributions appeal to critics of neoliberalism and market fundamentalism who observe that governments can remain unaccountable to their citizens for the consequences of market activity because of the view that markets are separate from the state. Block and Evans (2005: 506) suggest that this failure of accountability derives from the absence of adequate understanding of the social construction of states and markets and their 'mutually constituting' roles. Polanyi is clearly a voice against that sort of misunderstanding of state and market as separate spheres. However, critics indicate that Polanyi (2001: 71, 146) reproduces the state–market binary in using the language of 'self-regulation' and 'interventionism' with respect to market processes.

Block (2020) suggests that, while Polanyi is vulnerable to the criticism of sometimes reproducing such a binary, he nevertheless provides the basis for an alternative framework for understanding the state–economy relation in capitalism. While *TGT* might be confusing in language at times, Polanyi's intent is clear. He (2001: 69–73) wrote that the attempt to institute a self-regulating system was 'utopian' and unsustainable. It was incomplete as it was essentially an abstraction borne of the equally abstract price theory of neoclassical economics that could not be fully applied in the real world without devastating impacts. Indeed, one of the most quoted passages from *TGT* speaks directly to this. Polanyi (1944: 73) explains that turning land and labour into (fictitious) commodities[1] for sale in markets is 'essential' to a market economy (one defined as integrated through price-making markets); but that 'no society could stand the effects of such a system of crude fictions [...] unless its human and natural substance [...] was protected'.

Polanyi's idea of 'embeddedness' which speaks directly to the non-binary conception of state and market, is one of the concepts attracting significant attention in *TGT*. Embeddedness points to the social, political and environmental fabric within which economic activity is held and upon which it depends. In Polanyi's (1957: 250) words: '[t]he human economy [...] is embedded and enmeshed in institutions, economic and non-economic [...] religion or government may be as important for the structure and functioning of the economy as monetary institutions or the availability of tools and machines'. It is unsurprising that the idea of embeddedness appeals to contemporary commentators because it so evidently contrasts to the neglect of these factors in orthodox economics. Moreover, it directly challenges the neoliberal binary of state and market whereby government is deemed external to the capitalist economy and any interventions are considered 'unnatural' and 'distorting' (Jones 1984: 54).

However, the idea of embeddedness has also generated much critical debate (see Krippner and Alvarez 2007). Gemici (2008: 7) claims that Polanyi's work articulates two contradictory meanings of embeddedness: one that asserts 'all economic systems are embedded in social relations and institutions' and another that argues 'markets and the market economy are disembedded'. Polanyi seems to have referred to market society (capitalism) as one characterised by a disembedded self-regulating market, at the same time as he suggests a self-regulating market was a utopian idea, imagined and unrealised. Block (2003: 275) argues that Polanyi only 'glimpsed' the idea of the embedded economy at the time of writing *TGT*. Indeed, the word 'embedded' is used on just two occasions, with Polanyi elsewhere substituting synonyms such as 'absorbed', 'submerged', 'enmeshed', embodied' and 'intertwined' (Barber 1995: 401; Olofsson 1999: 45). Nevertheless, these confusions raise the question of how the idea of the 'always embedded market economy' (Block 2003: 275) can hold veracity if market society functions with a self-regulating or disembedded economy.

At issue here is what Polanyi meant by *dis*-embeddedness and whether this can be reconciled with the proposition that 'all economies are embedded' (Barber 1995; Block 2001: xxvi). In Ruggie's (1982: 385) articulation of post-Second World War 'embedded liberalism', he directly attributes to Polanyi the idea that the economic liberalism of the historical gold standard instituted a disembedded system of economy. Similarly, Blyth (2002: 5) argues that a 'second great transformation' occurred during the 1970s and the 1980s, whereby the neoliberal phenomenon is represented as a countermovement that attempts to 'disembed' the 'embedding' of the post-war era. However, the use of disembeddedness as a counter-metaphor misconstrues Polanyi's work. It suggests that self-regulation was possible and present at some point, which is a claim Polanyi (2001: 143–6) sought to reject. In practice, the free market was never a disembedded or unregulated economic system in the sense suggested by these uses of the term, even at its so-called peak in nineteenth-century *laissez faire*.

The idea of non-intervention by government in the nineteenth century – that the major economic decisions should be made by unregulated markets – was widely challenged in practice (Grampp 1965: 74; Polanyi 2001: 145). Grampp's (1965: 107) analysis of English parliamentary records demonstrated that support for *laissez faire* was by no means consistent. Rather, Polanyi (2001: 79) described this period as one characterised by an expanding *laissez faire* with respect to 'genuine commodities', and a constraining countermovement with respect to 'fictitious commodities' (land, labour, money). He (2001: 79) coined the term 'double movement' to capture this process of the (organised) forces of economic liberalism being met with resistance by a countermovement (spontaneous and uncoordinated) seeking protection from its harmful effects. However, these were coterminous processes that point to the always embedded economy, rather than discrete events that marked off a *laissez faire* period from an interventionist one. The concept of the double movement is thereby an expression of embeddeness, not disembeddedness: it points to the impossibility of a self-regulating free market economy and to the contingent character of its institutional foundations.

In these examples can be seen the common (mis)reading of Polanyi as referring to pre/non-capitalist economies as embedded, and (industrial) capitalism – or market society, as he commonly called it – as disembedded. In this binary, capitalism features a self-regulating market system that needs legislative re-embedding to transcend its status as a disembedded form of economy. Alternatively, Fraser (2011: 141) has suggested that Polanyi's distinction is 'better grasped as a difference in degree than as a difference in kind. While markets can never be fully disembedded, they can be more or less embedded.' This does speak more intuitively to the kinds of de/re-regulation practices of the neoliberal era. However, whether binary or spectrum, both approaches misrepresent Polanyi who used the term disembedded in relation to the *motives* of economic action deriving from the (embedded) structures of economy, rather than to the structures per se (Paton 2011b: 229). Similarly, Clark (2014: 62) suggests neo-Polanyian scholars have erred in conflating embeddedness with *institutedness*, thereby overlooking the significance of Polanyi's use of disembedded and (mis)locating it in the 'push and pull between regulation and deregulation', subject to policy fashion.

Rephrasing Block's (2003) interpretation, Clark (2014: 70) instead points to the 'always instituted economy', suggesting that, while the self-regulating market mechanism in capitalism *is* embedded in social institutions, the particular institutional arrangements dis-embed the motives for economic behaviour, destroying the 'ethical foundations of community'. Historically, under the specific social-property relations of capitalism, the motives driving the processes of production are 'freed' from social status and the religious/political imperatives evident under feudalism. Instead, they are driven by immediate 'economic' motives facilitated by contract between individuals of 'equal citizenship' (Polanyi 1977: 48). It is only in this sense of *motives* that a separation of economic and political can be understood to exist. Rather than direct political coercion, the 'fear of hunger' (labour) and 'hope of gain' (capitalist) are the motives driving an economic process integrated through market discipline (Polanyi 1977: 48; 1947: 63). Polanyi's ideas here are consistent with Marxian historiography that argues compulsion in capitalism is exercised indirectly through the dictates of the market but is nevertheless politically instituted by the coercive apparatus of the state (Wood 1984: 80).

This sampling of debates emanating from Polanyi's work is indicative of the diverse perspectives brought to the reading of *TGT*, as well as the ecumenical character of Polanyi's own intellectual interests. As Somers and Block (2021: 418) suggest, Polanyi's work is 'multidimensional and subject to different interpretations'. However, both supporters and critics of Polanyian perspectives often neglect Polanyi's later efforts to develop his ideas more fully. As I have argued elsewhere, embeddedness in *TGT* is best understood as a metaphor standing in for what Polanyi (1957, 1977) would later systematise in his general theory of (substantive) economy (Paton 2011a: 30). There, the idea of embeddedness is given substance as expressing the socially instituted character of economic processes and motives. Polanyi himself wrote in the Preface to *Livelihood* (1977: xxxix) that the book was intended to complete the project begun in *TGT* of developing new conceptual foundations to support a 'realistic view of the place occupied by the economy in human society'. It is therefore necessary to explore Polanyi's general theory of economy; and the place to begin is with a consideration of his relationship to neoclassical economic theory. This was the direct motivator underpinning his post-*TGT* conceptual endeavours.

THE SUBSTANTIVE CRITIQUE OF FORMALISM: LIMITATIONS OF NEOCLASSICAL THEORY

Polanyi had an ambivalent relationship to neoclassical theory and its 'mathematical study of exchange' in capitalist economies (Nelson 1993: 24). On the one hand, he (1971: 18) acknowledged what he described as 'the brilliant and formidable achievements of price theory opened up by Menger' and his respect for the logic and coherency of neoclassical price theory led him to suggest that critics not argue against it on its own terms. However, the neoclassical preoccupation with exchange and the belief that the price mechanism and its articulation in the marginal theory of utility 'could explain everything' was highly problematic for Polanyi (1971: 21) in terms of understanding real or 'substantive' economies, both historically and comparatively. For Polanyi, economy in its empirical sense was far too complex and diverse – over time and through space – to be captured in the formal abstractions of neoclassical theory. Polanyi noted that Menger himself believed price theory, as articulated in his *Principles of Economics* ([1871] 1950), lacked explanatory power and he therefore worked on a more general theory that was eventually published posthumously in 1923 as a second edition.[2]

Polanyi (1971) was strongly influenced by that second edition of *Principles* (1923), wherein Menger makes a distinction between the sphere of exchange and the sphere of production. The *economising* sphere of exchange was based on the principle of scarcity while the *technical* sphere of *production* was based on the principle of subsistence. Polanyi (1971: 17) noted that this distinction disappeared over time and that the subsistence and scarcity meanings are 'fused' in neoclassical economics. He (1977: xi) argued the term 'economic' was thereby 'bedevilled with ambiguities' that had significant practical implications for the social sciences generally and a 'confusing' influence on the study of non-market economies specifically. For Polanyi (1957: 244; 1971: 17), this rendered formal neoclassical theory irrelevant for comparative analysis between economic systems, because the economising behaviours it assumed were not universal. To utilise neoclassical theory as a frame of reference in these contexts commits what Polanyi (1977: 5) referred to as the 'economistic fallacy'.

These insights propelled Polanyi into the key disciplinary debates in economic anthropology during the 1950s and 1960s. Underpinned by methodological individualism, and with 'choice' as the unit of analysis, the 'formalist' school extrapolated neoclassical theory to other cultural contexts, promoting the idea that microeconomic models were universal (Schneider 1974: 9). In contrast, the 'substantivist' school cohering around Polanyi held that economic life was firmly located within its broader social and political context, noting that even where an interest centres on 'decisions and choices' these cannot be understood 'without close attention to the contexts in which they are made' (Carrier 2005: 13). According to Hann (2018: 13), this debate between formalists and substantivists 'enabled the theoretical flowering of the ethnographic method' so central to anthropology and, as a result, the confrontation 'continues in new guises'. Ultimately, with the rise of neoclassical thinking as economic orthodoxy within the academy, the formalist school triumphed in the struggle for intellectual hegemony and laid the basis for a similar orthodoxy in economic anthropology.

Nevertheless, Polanyi remained critical of the formal abstractions of economic theory because of their obfuscatory effect on the empirical understanding of economy in human society, which was the central preoccupation of substantivists. He (1957: 243; 1977: 19) famously declared the two approaches 'had nothing in common', with formalism being derived from logic and substantivism from 'fact' emerging from the human need for a sustaining physical environment. This does not deny that exchange plays an important role in the capitalist economy. Indeed, Polanyi (1977: 43) acknowledged the market exchange system is the 'principal [but not only] organising mechanism' for economic processes under capitalism. Yet the way in which such activities are theorised and understood in formal economic theory abstracts from, and makes invisible, substantive economic processes while making individual choice the *raison d'être* of theory.

The assumptions of formal economic analysis – including the laws of property and contract, commodification of all production inputs and optimal means–ends behaviours – permit economy to be understood as a set of interconnected and self-regulating markets distinct from other social spheres. Polanyi (1977: 14) rejected the idea that the price-regulated market form and 'rational' economising attributes of 'economic man' were universal, as implied in formal economic theory. Rather, they are socially instituted: the economising imperative only exists where access to subsistence is mediated through market exchange. Polanyi is not unique in noting the neoclassical theorists' preoccupation with exchange in price-making markets reveals little compared to that which it renders invisible: the human relations, ecological processes and much of the institutional matrix determining economic activities. Formal theory cannot account for the structures that shape production, distribution and consumption because these are not always evident in the 'surface behaviours' of individuals participating in exchange (Halperin 1994: 4).

Polanyi's intellectual endeavours therefore continued in the direction of substantivism where he (1957, 1977) developed a general theory of economy that could be utilised in historical and cross-cultural contexts (Halperin 1994). However, this anthropological work, maturing in the (posthumous) publication of *Livelihood* (1977), was not an endeavour disconnected from his earlier engagement with capitalism (market society). Indeed, folding this later work back into the preoccupations that featured in *TGT* provides a distinct contribution to economic theorising about capitalism that, while congruent with the work of Classical Political Economy, nevertheless provides a distinctive set of concepts and original framework of analysis. What then does Polanyi's theoretical vision of substantive economy look like and what relevance might such a general theory have for our understanding of contemporary capitalism?

THE FORMALISATION OF SUBSTANTIVISM: POLANYI'S GENERAL ECONOMIC THEORY

> The economy as an instituted process of interaction serving the satisfaction of material wants forms a vital part of every human community. Without an economy in this sense, no society could exist for any length of time. (Polanyi 1977: 31)

According to Polanyi (1971: 22), an institutional approach to the economy implies the substantive meaning of economic rather than the formal market meaning which, he argued, had relevance only to neoclassical economic analysis. Polanyi's general economic theory was derived in part from Marx and in part from anthropological research (Halperin 1994: 34).[3] As expressed in *Trade and Market in the early Empires* (1957) and *Livelihood of Man* (1977), there are two key elements. First, the model of *substantive economy* attempts to provide a general model of the economic process common to all social systems. It has its basis in the idea that all economies consist of socially organised processes of production and distribution geared towards material-means provisioning (Polanyi 1957: 241; 1977: 31). Second, the accompanying *forms of integration* 'designate the institutionalised movements through which the elements of the economic process […] are connected' (1977: 35). The *forms* represent the identifiable institutional structures such processes may take in any given society (Polanyi 1957: 250; 1977: 35). Together, these two aspects – the *substantive economy* and the *forms of integration* – comprise the formal model that Polanyi (1957: 245) claimed would provide a 'universal' frame of reference for understanding empirical economies.

During the mid-twentieth century, Polanyi's substantivism was influential within the disciplines of anthropology and ancient history and, according to Hann (2018: 14), Polanyi remains central to the canon of economic anthropology where 'his insights continue to exert an immense influence'. However, Polanyi's general economic theory has not gained traction in the field of economics where an emergent 'sociality' (such as the 'new institutional economics') has not fully broken from the (individualist) ontological and methodological underpinnings of the neoclassical paradigm (Paton and Cahill 2020: 43). Polanyi's model has been criticised on various fronts.[4] It is said to be static and functionalist, yet also evolutionary, despite his (1947: 43) own caution that it did not imply stages of development; and its ideal types accused of being so broad as to miss 'crucial differences' in the empirical contexts from which they were derived (Dale 2010: 120). Yet, there are also a range of thinkers, both Polanyians and critics of his model, that consider it 'fertile and suggestive' (Dale 2010: 123). It is therefore useful to consider a more detailed elaboration of Polanyi's substantivism.

To begin, the substantive economy was, according to Polanyi (1977: 31), 'an instituted process' of production and distribution designed to ensure the 'ordered advance of all material means towards the consumption stage of livelihood' (Polanyi 1957: 248; 1977: 32). To grasp the model, it is useful to first unpack his perspective on 'process'. Polanyi (1977: 32) identified two elements in the economic *process*: the 'locational' and 'appropriational' movements.[5] These represent the interactions between humans and their surroundings as they go about producing and reproducing their social existence (Polanyi 1957: 243). The *locational* movements refer to the spatial movements involved in production, including the necessary technical elements, whether ecological, technological, or human/social (Polanyi 1977: 32). The *appropriational* movements refer to distribution, and represent changes, fully or partially, in the rights of disposal over the elements of production and the output it generates (Polanyi 1977: 31). These movements articulate 'the shifts in the property sphere' that accompany the locational movements (Polanyi 1977: 32).

For Polanyi (1947: 32–4), while the locational and appropriational movements constitute the 'economy as process', it is the 'institutional vestment' that gives them coherence. The locational and appropriational movements are *instituted* – given order and predictability – so that the substantive economic process (social provisioning) can be secured and reproduced over time. The general model therefore also comprises the social structures that give 'unity and stability, structure and function' to the movements constituting the economic process (Polanyi 1977: 34). These structures – the *forms of integration* – both impel and integrate the locational and appropriational movements. They organise the physical aspects of production and distribution, but they also organise the political aspects – the 'appropriational power' – underpinning such movements (Pearson 1977: xxxii). This includes the social property relations that give order to the rights and obligations determining which individuals/groups/classes may own/control/access the physical elements of production, and on what basis they do so.

Polanyi (1957: 250; 1977: 35) identified three main patterns of movement of which reciprocity and redistribution had historically been 'the more significant forms' noted by anthropologists (Hann 2018: 7). *Reciprocity* entails movement between corresponding points of a symmetrical arrangement and requires a structure of two or more symmetrically placed groups, while *redistribution* involves movement towards and out of a central point of allocation, thereby requiring an established centre (Polanyi 1977: 36). Polanyi's third pattern was *exchange*, representing a movement between any two dispersed or random points and requiring a market system to function as a form of integration (Polanyi 1977: 37). Polanyi (1977: 38) explains: 'only in the presence of markets instituted to that purpose will the bartering attitude of individuals result in prices that integrate the economic activities of the community'. In other words, individual behaviour (barter) must be rendered an *imperative* by the institutional matrix (market system) for the pattern of movement (exchange) to have an integrative effect (Polanyi 1957: 249; 1977: 37).

Polanyi (1977: 35) also suggested that, in securing the economic process, one or some combination of the three forms of integration might organise the economic process within a given social context. However, where there was co-existence, he (1977: 42) argued one form was generally dominant, with others playing a subordinate role. For Polanyi, the crucial factor here was the form that organises productive forces. He (1957: 255) identified the dominant form of integration with 'the degree to which it comprises land and labour in society'. Although there may be independent instances of production and distribution evident, in Polanyi it is the mobilisation of land and labour on a social scale that is key to understanding the economic process of a given society. This emphasis on land and labour in economic integration provides an important link between Polanyi's general theory for the study of comparative economic systems and the earlier work of *TGT* centred on the rise and fall of nineteenth-century market society. The concept of *fictitious commodities*, first introduced in *TGT*, offers a reconciliation of these intellectual preoccupations (Paton 2010: 79).

In *TGT*, market society (capitalism) was one defined by the commodity status of land and labour, but Polanyi (1944: 73) also pointed to the problems of such commodification, arguing that '[n]ature would be reduced to its elements, neighbourhoods and landscapes defiled, rivers polluted [...] the power to produce food and raw materials destroyed'. Similarly, he pointed to the precarious situation of labouring bodies that require a market income to survive while demand for their services could not be guaranteed (1944: 73). Although land and labour are crucial elements in an economic process integrated through a commodity exchange system, Polanyi observed that they also embody purpose and value independently of markets. For this reason, he (1944: 69–73) argued that 'no society could stand the effects of such a system of crude fictions [...] unless its human and natural substance [...] was protected' to avoid the 'demolition of society'.

While Polanyi's moral urgings are noteworthy, there is also a structural dimension to the fictitious commodities: they are both means and ends. Nature is source and sink, while humans are producer and consumer. However, the abstract categories bought and sold in markets cannot be separated from their source: labour power remains attached to the labouring body (Pateman 1988: 150) and land remains attached to ecological processes. This dual character places them in a position of precarity, as they are necessarily within the economic process and, at the same time, within the matrix of structures needed to secure reproduction of that process. For Polanyi (1944: 69–73; 1947: 59), persistence of self-regulation in respect of land and labour jeopardised the very conditions necessary for the reproduction of social existence. As Fraser (2014: 548) puts it, the 'tendency of unregulated markets to destroy their own conditions of possibility' invokes protective regulation. Yet, if such is the case, the price-making market system cannot be a self-regulating mechanism as the advocates of nineteenth-century *laissez faire* proposed.

Fraser (2011: 142) has argued Polanyi did not translate the strong moral tone of the *TGT* 'into theoretical terms'. However, with the development of the general model of substantive economy a basis is laid for the theoretical significance of the fictitious commodities and the structural contradictions they invoke (Paton 2010: 79). The logic of the substantive model suggests that, if the market form of integration is unable to reproduce itself without degrading the conditions needed for its reproduction, it must then be an insufficient means for integrating the processes of social provisioning. It follows that an institutional matrix beyond that system is required to secure the conditions (land and labour) necessary for the market to function as the dominant form of integration under capitalism (Paton 2010: 85). Drawing on Polanyi's proposition that there could be co-existence amongst the forms of integration, the state and household can be understood as key sites of redistribution (and regulation) sitting alongside exchange in the market system. The former is necessary to sustain the integrity of the latter because of the dual character of land and labour as fictional commodities.

Although the state and household are not generally associated with economic production, the lens of the Polanyian general theory allows them to be seen as necessary adjuncts to the substantive economic process in capitalism. Examples are: state appropriation of taxes and their redistribution for the purpose of securing the conditions necessary for social/labour reproduction; and the household consumption of goods and services as well as redistribution of wages for reproduction of both waged and non-waged members. State and household are also regulatory institutions: the state guarantees and regulates social property relations and the rules governing ecological, social, economic and political engagement, while households are an important site of socialisation and acculturation. On the basis of the general model, both forms of integration – exchange and redistribution – are thus deemed connected in the integration of substantive capitalist economies.

What then of the charge of a static functionalism in Polanyi's approach – how might his model fit with the empirical realities of diversity and change evident in actually existing market societies? Fraser (2011: 143) suggests that, in embracing social actors and their 'collisions' in *TGT*, as evidenced in the idea of the 'double movement', Polanyi's work 'points beyond functionalism'. I would argue similarly regarding the general theory. Polanyi (1977: 35) viewed the institutions and interaction (movements) involved in any particular substantive economy as ultimately determined by their relation 'to the political and cultural spheres of society at large'. This means the forms of integration in capitalism (predominantly redistribution and exchange) are logical possibilities contingent on the presenting (and changing) material and ideological conditions. This contextual element shifts the focus from the forms of integration to the 'norms of integration' (Paton 2011a: 36) where 'values, motives and policy' (Polanyi 1957: 250) are pivotal in shaping the economic process through time.[6] Polanyi did not flesh out this aspect of the model, but it does signal that the always embedded (or instituted) economy is subject to change.

The presence of stability *and* change in Polanyi's model is linked to the question of crises. Fraser (2011: 143) suggests Polanyi's approach in *TGT* highlights the role of human agency and effectively 'jettisoned the orthodox view of crisis as an objective "system breakdown", conceiv[ing] it instead as an intersubjective process'. This is consistent with the later proposition in the general theory that agents bearing 'values, motives and policy' create the empirical realties of economic life. While providing 'unity and structure' on the one hand, institutional arrangements are also transient due to the periodic crises and tensions thrown up by the fictitious commodities.[7] These are 'resolved' in culturally and historically specific ways which, through the lens of substantivism, can be seen in the changing emphases given to the forms of integration over time. The growing significance of state redistribution in capitalism during the period after the Second World War is one example, while the more recent shift to increased personal responsibility under neoliberalism has heightened the importance of the family (household) and community in substantive economic processes.

The general theory suggests that capitalism's substantive economy emerges out of the evolving dialectics of the economic process, its institutional environment and prevailing ideological norms. Where *TGT* provides a moral basis underpinning protective movements against practices of deepening and extending the realms of fictitious commodification, the general theory provides a theoretical basis for this as well as for the structural necessity of redistribution. Drawing on the models of the general theory, together with the *TGT* insights about market society, suggests there is a systemic requirement to redistribute and regulate for the sustainability of land and labour if the market form of integration is to be made compatible with social provisioning and reproduction over time. The current neoliberal context raises the spectre of an ongoing struggle for social protectionists against 'the wanton disembedding promoted by neoliberals' (Fraser 2011: 143). Are we left then, with the proposition implied by Fraser (2011: 141) of 'more or less' regulation (and by implication, more or less redistribution) stemming from the balance of vested interests and economic crises at any given point in market society?

Certainly, there is a strong tradition of humane social democracy in Polanyian scholarship. Fred Block has been particularly influential in this regard. The dominant reading of Polanyi's concepts, especially in *TGT*, supports a regulated form of welfare capitalism. This 'regulatory Polanyi' is central to the majority of Polanyian scholarship. However, alternative views attribute more radical implications to Polanyi's work. Clark (2014), for example, draws on Polanyi's substantivism to suggest that the double movement compromises that are described in *TGT*, and by implication later compromises such as the post-war *Pax Americana* (Lacher 1999), are themselves not sustainable. Clark (2014) begins from the premise that Polanyi's use of dis-embedded refers to the economic motives propelling production and consumption in capitalism. From this, he (2014: 80) contends that Polanyi's (1947) notion that the self-regulating utopia and its 'market mentality' were 'obsolete' goes much further than simply suggesting markets in the fictitious commodities need protective legislation. Rather, Clark (2014: 80) argues that Polanyi's intent was for the 'abolition of the status of land, labour and money as commodities' – land, labour and money needed to be removed from the market sphere and re-embedded within *social motives*. This reading implies a quite radical transformation of capitalist economic structures.

CONCLUSION

Polanyi's legacy – whether 'regulatory' or 'radical' – continues to provide a rich source of material for those exploring alternative approaches to economic issues in our time. The early decades of neoliberalism, with its transformation of post-war welfare state regimes, generated a period of growing interest in Polanyi's work, most particularly *TGT*. Now a second wave of interest has emerged and grown in the years following the global financial crisis of 2007–08. This 'neo-Polanyian' scholarship builds on and extends elements of Polanyi's work to conduct analyses and develop policy recommendations for an array of contemporary settings. However, the need to further develop the Polanyian tradition of *political economy* persists, and this must necessarily be based in a systematic and critical engagement with Polanyi's works including, indeed most especially, his work beyond *TGT*.

In many ways, that now classic tome is both an opportunity and a limitation. On the one hand, the book's wide-ranging historical narrative and inspirational polemical flourishes have left an enduring legacy with contemporary resonance, influencing scholars, activists and politicians. However, *TGT* has also attracted criticism for its inconsistencies and absence of systematic theory. This has been explained by Fred Block (2003: 275) as stemming from both the hastiness of seeking publication in time to influence post-war reconstruction, but also as the result of Polanyi's own changing relationship to theory, specifically that of Marx. The book's currency continues to attract attention across the spectrum – from uncritical acceptance to dismissive critique – but often leaving neglected a serious engagement with Polanyi's subsequent work. Yet, therein lies the more considered articulation of the embryonic ideas first expressed in *TGT*, thereby providing fruitful prospects for contemporary neo-Polanyian scholarship.

NOTES

1. See Fraser (2014) for a useful articulation of money as Polanyi's third fictitious commodity.
2. According to Polanyi (1971: 21), the second (1923) edition was not well received by economists who thought a general theory was unnecessary and it remained untranslated and neglected as a result.
3. Polanyi (1947: 134) expressed admiration for the 'societal approach personified by Marx [but rejected what he believed was] the economistic element inherited from the classics', specifically Ricardo.
4. See Dale (2010: 124–5) for detailed articulation and critique of the formalist response to the publication of *Trade* (1957) which portrayed Polanyi's substantivism as unscientific because inductive; as ideological because romanticising or idealising non-market economies; as irrelevant because of the expanding dominance of the global market-system; and as relativist because rejecting the universality of economic imperatives.
5. Halperin (1994: 44) has suggested that the locational/appropriational categories are analogous to Marx's forces and relations of production.
6. Historically, witness the markedly different (and changing) nature of labour and environment institutions in the Scandinavian countries compared with the United States, for example.
7. Fraser (2014: 1) suggests that Polanyi's commodity fictions form the basis 'for an integrated structural analysis' connecting 'three aspects of [capitalist] crisis in the twenty-first century: the ecological, the social and the financial'.

REFERENCES

Barber, B. (1995) 'All Economies are "Embedded": The Career of a Concept, and Beyond', *Social Research*, **62** (2), pp. 387–413.
Block, F. (ed.) (2001) 'Introduction', in *The Great Transformation: The Political and Economic Origins of our Time*, 2nd edition, Boston, MA: Beacon Press.
Block, F. (2003) 'Karl Polanyi and the Writing of "The Great Transformation"', *Theory and Society*, **32** (3), pp. 275–306.
Block, F. (2020) 'Persistent problems in the Polanyian critique of the market', in Berndt, C., Peck, J. and Rantisi, N. (eds), *Market/Place: Exploring Spaces of Exchange*, Newcastle upon Tyne: Agenda Publishing.
Block, F. and Evans, P. (2005) 'The State and the Economy', in Smelser, N.J. and Swedberg, R. (eds), *The Handbook of Economic Sociology*, 2nd edition, Princeton, NJ: Princeton University Press.
Block, F. and Somers, M. (1984) 'Beyond the Economistic Fallacy: The Holistic Social Science of Karl Polanyi', in Skocpol, T. (ed.), *Vision and Method in Historical Sociology*, Cambridge: Cambridge University Press.

Block, F. and Somers, M. (2014) *The Power of Market Fundamentalism*, Cambridge, MA: Harvard University Press.

Blyth, M. (2002) *Great Transformations: Economic Ideas and Institutional Change in the Twentieth Century*, Cambridge: Cambridge University Press.

Carrier, J.G. (2005) 'Introduction', in Carrier, J.G. (ed.), *A Handbook of Economic Anthropology*, Cheltenham, UK and Northampton, MA, USA: Edward Elgar Publishing.

Clark, T. D. (2014) 'Reclaiming Karl Polanyi, Socialist Intellectual', *Studies in Political Economy*, **94**, Autumn, pp. 61–84.

Dale, G. (2010) *Karl Polanyi: The Limits of the Market*, Cambridge: Polity Press.

Dow, G. (2006) 'The Labour Market and Labour Market "Reform"', *Journal of Australian Political Economy*, **57**, pp. 137–54.

Frankel, B. (2020) *Capitalism versus Democracy: Rethinking Politics in the Age of Environmental Crisis*, Melbourne: Greenmeadows.

Fraser, N. (2011) 'Marketization, Social Protection, Emancipation: Toward a Neo-Polanyian Conception of Capitalist Crisis', in Calhoun, C. and Derluguian, G. (eds), *Business as Usual: The Roots of the Global Financial Meltdown*, New York: NYU Press.

Fraser, N. (2014) 'Can Society Be Commodities All the Way Down? Post-Polanyian Reflections on Capitalist Crisis', *Economy and Society*, **43** (4), pp. 541–58.

Gemici, K. (2008) 'Karl Polanyi and the Antinomies of Embeddedness', *Socio-Economic Review*, **6**, pp. 5–33.

Grampp, W.D. (1965) *Economic Liberalism: Volume 1, The Beginnings*, New York: Random House.

Halperin, R.H. (1994) *Cultural Economies Past and Present*, Austin: University of Texas Press.

Halperin, S. (2004) *War and Social Change in Modern Europe: The Great Transformation Revisited*, Cambridge: Cambridge University Press.

Hann, C. (2018) 'Economic Anthropology', in Callan, H. (ed.), *The International Encyclopedia of Anthropology*, London: John Wiley & Sons.

Hodgson, G.M. (2017) 'Karl Polanyi on Economy and Society: A Critical Analysis of Core Concepts', *Review of Social Economy*, **75** (1), pp. 1–25.

Jones, E. (1984) 'Government Intervention', *Journal of Australian Political Economy*, **17**, pp. 53–60.

Krippner, G.R. and Alvarez A.S. (2007) 'Embeddedness and the Intellectual Projects of Economic Sociology', *Annual Review of Sociology*, **33** pp. 219–40.

Lacher, H. (1999) 'Embedded Liberalism, Disembedded Markets: Reconceptualising the *Pax Americana*', *New Political Economy*, **4** (3), pp. 343–60.

Maucourant, J. and Plociniczak, S. (2013) 'The Institution, the Economy and the Market: Karl Polanyi's Institutional Thought for Economists', *Review of Political Economy*, **25** (3), pp. 512–31.

Mendell, M. (2001) 'A Karl Polanyi Revival', *Canadian Dimension*, **35** (2), p. 48.

Menger, C. ([1871] 1950) *The Principles of Economics: First, General Part*, ed. and trans. Dingwall, J. and Hoselitz, B.F., Glencoe, IL: The Free Press.

Nelson, J.A. (1993) 'The Study of Choice or the Study of Provisioning: Gender and the Definition of Economics', in Ferber, M.A. and Nelson, J.A. (eds), *Beyond Economic Man: Feminist Theory and Economics*, Chicago, IL: Chicago University Press.

O'Connor, J. (1998) *Natural Causes: Essays in Ecological Marxism*, New York: Guilford Press.

Olofsson, G. (1999) 'Embeddedness and Integration', in Gough, I. and Olofsson, G. (eds), *Capitalism and Social Cohesion: Essays on Exclusion and Integration*, London: Macmillan Press, pp. 38–60.

Pateman, C. (1988) *The Sexual Contract*, Oxford: Polity Press.

Paton, J. (2010) 'Labour as a (Fictitious) Commodity: Polanyi and the Capitalist "Market Economy"', *The Economic and Labour Relations Review*, **21** (1), pp. 77–88.

Paton, J. (2011a) *Seeking Sustainability: On the Prospect of an Ecological Liberalism*, Abingdon: Routledge.

Paton, J. (2011b) 'Theorising "Economy" – Reclaiming Karl Polanyi as an Institutionalist', in Chester, L., Johnston, M. and Kriesler, P. (eds), *Heterodox Economics: Ten Years and Growing Stronger*, Sydney: Society of Heterodox Economists.

Paton, J. and Cahill, D. (2020) 'Thinking Socially and Spatially about Markets', in Berndt, C., Peck, J. and Rantisi, N. (eds), *Market/Place: Exploring Spaces of Exchange*, Newcastle upon Tyne: Agenda Publishing.

Pearson, H.W. (1977) 'Editor's Introduction', in Polanyi, K., *The Livelihood of Man*, ed. H.W. Pearson, New York: Academic Press, pp. xxv–xxxvi.

Peck, J. (2013) 'For Polanyian Economic Geographies', *Environment and Planning A*, **45**, pp. 1545–68.

Peck, J. (2020) 'Where are Markets?', in Berndt, C., Peck, J. and Rantisi, N. (eds), *Market/Place: Exploring Spaces of Exchange*, Newcastle upon Tyne: Agenda Publishing.

Polanyi, K. (1944) *The Great Transformation*, New York: Farrar & Rinehart.

Polanyi, K. ([1947] 1968) 'Our Obsolete Market Mentality', in Dalton, G. (ed.), *Primitive, Archaic, and Modern Economies: Essays of Karl Polanyi*, New York: Doubleday & Company.

Polanyi, K. (1957) 'The Economy as Instituted Process', in Polanyi, K., Arensberg, C.M. and Pearson, H.W. (eds), *Trade and Market in the Early Empires: Economies in History and Theory*, New York: The Free Press.

Polanyi, K. (1971) 'Carl Menger's Two Meanings of "Economic"', in Dalton, G. (ed.), *Studies in Economic Anthropology*, Washington, DC: American Anthropological Association.

Polanyi, K. (1977) *The Livelihood of Man*, ed. H.W. Pearson, New York: Academic Press.

Polanyi, K. (2001) *The Great Transformation: The Political and Economic Origins of our Time*, 2nd edition, Boston, MA: Beacon Press.

Prudham, S. (2013) 'Men and Things: Karl Polanyi, Primitive Accumulation, and their Relevance to a Radical Green Political Economy', *Environment and Planning A*, **45** (7), pp. 1569–87.

Ruggie, J.G. (1982) 'International Regimes, Transactions, and Change: Embedded Liberalism in the Postwar Economic Order', *International Organization*, **36** (2), pp. 379–415.

Schneider, H.K. (1974) *Economic Man*, New York: Free Press.

Somers, M. and Block, F. (2021) 'Against Polanyian orthodoxy: A Reply to Hannes Lacher', *Theory and Society*, **50**, pp. 417–41.

Stanfield, J.R. (1980) 'The Institutional Economics of Karl Polanyi', *Journal of Economic Issues*, **14** (3), pp. 593–614.

Waller, W. and Jennings, A. (1991) 'A Feminist Institutionalist Reconsideration of Karl Polanyi', *Journal of Economic Issues*, **25** (2), pp. 485–97.

Wood, N. (1984) *John Locke and Agrarian Capitalism*, Berkeley: University of California Press.

18. Georgist political economy

Franklin Obeng-Odoom

Humanity faces multiple challenges. Economic uncertainty, health and environmental crises, inequality, systemic racism and segmentation are a few examples. Mainstream economics tends to marginalise these concerns because its economic models, built on assumptions of certainty and stability, put it out of kilter with reality. Political economy seeks a way out of the fog. To be a more formidable alternative, however, it needs to draw on some other currents of thought that have been accorded insufficient attention. Georgist political economy (GPE) is one. Originating from the writing and teaching of Henry George in the late nineteenth century, GPE provides a critique of, and an alternative to, classical and neoclassical ways of interpreting economic issues (George [1883] 1966, 1885, [1898] 1992). The practitioners of 'occult science', as George called the orthodoxy (George [1898] 1992: 205), did not welcome this alternative and have deliberately marginalised its study ever since (Gaffney 1994; Harrison 2016, 2021). However, contemporary concerns with growing concentration of economic wealth and power, enclosure of the commons, and socio-spatial injustice make renewed consideration of Georgist ideas important within modern political economy.

In recent years, proponents of the Georgist perspective have made significant progress in developing new explanations, identifying impediments to progress, and offering prescriptive pathways to a more inclusive, safer and cleaner world (see, for example, Haila 2016; Ryan-Collins et al. 2017). Yet, GPE still receives relatively little attention. As shown by Michael Hudson's (2008) extensive survey of the various criticisms levelled at this school of thought, the continuing obscurity is due to GPE's presumed singular focus on land, assumed exclusive emphasis on one policy (land value taxation) and the uninspiring nature of its reformist prescriptions.

Countering these caricatures, it is pertinent to show how GPE can be applied to current political economic and socio-ecological problems and how it may be developed further as a major school and influence within political economy. This chapter addresses these issues in three sections. The first clarifies the basic principles of GPE; the second explains how the 'housing question' is addressed in GPE; and the third considers some weaknesses of GPE and suggests how they may be addressed by, among other things, incorporating insights from the new sub-field of stratification economics, thereby strengthening GPE's contribution to modern political economy.

HENRY GEORGE'S POLITICAL ECONOMY

Many schools of thought existed during GPE's apogee, the Gilded Age in the United States at the end of the nineteenth century. Among the prevailing ideas, Henry George's systematic probing of the political economy of land stood out as a particularly powerful explanation of the coexistence of great wealth and deep poverty. Because it took courage to offend the landed aristocracy and, more generally, all existing large landowners, most of those who theorised about rent did so apolitically. David Ricardo, for example, emphasised the effects of differential soil fertility and location (Ricardo [1810] 2001). Other political economists, failing to distinguish adequately between land and capital, accorded little or no attention to landed property: the dominant focus on the relationship between capital and labour subsumed land under capital. The French Physiocrats had taken a detour from this main road, but they only ended up on the farm, searching for answers to agrarian questions. In general, key concepts in political economy (such as 'value in use' and 'value in exchange') were discussed without systematic reference to land (George [1898] 1992: 182–99). When land was explicitly analysed, its study was usually restricted to its quality and positioning within rural areas, rather than considering its wider political economic significance.

GPE emerged to confront and correct this neglect. As the universities were largely complicit in protecting landed interests (Jorgensen 1925), GPE found no place for itself in such scholarly environments. Challenging the older 'scholastic political economy' and mainstream 'occult science', Henry George set out to develop what he claimed to be a true science of the people. He had no formal higher education: rather, he related to his subject personally, driven by his own meagre economic circumstances and by the poverty of other people that he observed. Mass poverty in an already wealthy America taught him that it was not the behaviour of individuals that caused poverty. His observations of the struggle of migrants also showed him that migration was one of many posited 'solutions' to poverty that could worsen the problem.

George's historical reflections on the effects of privation, progress and plunder in ancient Egypt also revealed to him that poverty was not just a feature of so-called 'backward' civilisations (George 1884). Egypt had been the beacon of global civilisation, but it was also the cathedral of oppression and structural inequality. Because these problems predated the capitalist economic system, they could not all be attributed to capitalism. George argued that socialism could not be relied on to redress these serious problems either (George [1883] 1966: 176–8, 191; George and Hyndman [1885] 1914). Rather, the key was to be found in an analysis of land in relation to both labour and capital; and the remedy for ongoing poverty among plenty would need to address the land question in a specifically Georgist way.

George's broad aim was to explain systemic poverty as an outcome of *structural* inequality and its corrosive effects. Seen in this light, land may be regarded as both a problem and a solution. Processes of land transformation interact with labour and capital, shaping the forms that poverty and inequality take. George's analysis of these processes was infused with three fundamental principles. First, '[t]hat all men have equal rights to the use and enjoyment of the elements provided by Nature [and second] ... that each man has an exclusive right to the use and enjoyment of what is produced by his own labor' (George [1886] 1991: 280). Third, that wealth arises from the exertion of labour on matter used for the satisfaction of human need. Therefore, increase in wealth does not entirely come from capital, but also from labour, and from general social processes (George [1892] 1981; George [1883] 1981). The taxation of real labour is one poverty-creating channel. Because no one individual creates rents, the private appropriation of socially created increasing rent by landed interests is held to be another means by which wealth becomes more concentrated.

Following from these diagnoses, Georgists (such as Cleveland 2020; Harrison 2020; Rybeck 2020) typically propose three solutions to the problems of poverty and inequality. First, untaxing labour incomes and the products of labour to ensure that workers have more income, pay lower prices for goods and services, and thus get a fuller reward for their produce. Promotion of a labour-based, anti-monopoly system of production ensures that tax reductions filter through to ordinary workers. Second, keeping land as commons or, if land is already privatised, taxing away the rents generated by technological change, speculation, population growth and social investments in infrastructure that increase land values. Third, investing the resulting revenues in comprehensive social and public policies.

The building blocks of GPE can be found in George's best-known work, *Progress and Poverty* ([1897] 1935), and in *The Science of Political Economy* ([1898] 1992), which was his last book before his death. Interpretations of the nature of his contributions vary. Phillip Bryson (2011: 1–24), for example, seeks to show that, although George was not as lettered as his contemporaries, he was familiar with their theories and largely used the same tools as other economists at that time, namely: induction, deduction and experimentation. Other writers (such as Stilwell 2011a) acknowledge that George used concepts such as value, wealth, distribution and growth that were part of the wider classical political economy of the time but emphasise that he was critical of various aspects of these established concepts and reformulated them in distinctive ways.

While George used the *same names* for the principal concepts in classical political economy, he gave them *distinctive meanings*. Consider value, for example (George [1898] 1992: chs 10–14). George appreciated the classical and Marxist labour theories of value but, for him, labour was the source of *some*, *but* not *all*, value. He argued that land value does not solely arise from labour: other important drivers are speculation, population growth and public investment. Even without the application of labour to improve it, land can still gain in value.

Another example concerns the notions of 'use value' and 'exchange value', commonly used in political economy, particularly by Marxists (see, for example, Harvey [1973] 2009: ch. 5). George regarded the distinction between the two as forced (because each contains elements of the other) and considered the sequence of how they relate to exchange to be problematic (George [1898] 1992: ch. 10). For George, exchangeability follows value: value does not follow exchange. He preferred the analysis of value to be restricted to exchange only, although recognising that at the heart of this exchange value was use value. It is from this line of reasoning that George's distinctive preference for land value taxation arose, because no tax can fall on land with only use value, as would be the case for land set aside from market relations such as areas reserved for use by Indigenous peoples or as national parks.

Although working primarily with the (sometimes modified) tools of classical political economy, George also introduced some new concepts, such as *value in production* and *value in obligation* (George [1898] 1992: ch. 20). The former refers to the contribution of labour, to which George argued no tax should apply. The latter refers to value increases arising from imposed exertion, indebtedness, slavery and bondage, these being oppressive extractions that make no contribution to production per se and to which tax therefore should be applied.

Wealth is the subject of distinctive analysis, too. The standard political economic approach is to distinguish wealth, which is a stock, from income, which is a flow (Stilwell 2019: ch. 2). Land, therefore, is usually considered to be 'wealth'. In GPE, however, wealth is anything produced by labour. The focus on wealth is not so much on how it is distinct from income but, rather, on how its generation, purpose and distribution are distinct from land (George [1898] 1992: chs 15–20). Some wealth is capital, which is produced by labour. The rest is *improved* land. Therefore, capital is clearly distinct from land, as is labour, and their production processes are different.

Their roles and respective rewards are also different. Whether public or private, common or concentrated, wealth must satisfy *desires* (George [1898] 1995: ch. 11), an idea introduced by George to collapse the artificial distinction between 'needs' and 'wants'. For this reason, wealth must be widely diffused. However, George did not advocate the imposition of a *wealth tax* – as is often canvassed in other schools of political economy. Instead, a more appropriate policy would be reconstruction of the role of land and landed relations in the economy (George [1897] 1935: 328–30).

For all these reasons, land – its rent, features, forms and functions – is clearly the most crucial and distinctive factor in GPE. Accordingly, what land means to Georgists must be clarified. In *A Perplexed Philosopher* (George 1892), George states:

> Land – to us the one solid, natural element; our all-producing, all-supporting mother, from whose bosom our very frames are drawn, and to which they return again; our standing-place; our workshop; our granary; our reservoir and substratum and nexus of media and forces; the element from which all we can produce must be drawn; without which we cannot breathe the air or enjoy the light; the element prerequisite to all human life and action. (George [1892] 1981: 140)

Land is distinct from capital and governed by special rules.

The principle of equal rights is key to George's thinking. To quote George again:

> When men [*sic*] have equal rights to a thing, as for instance, to the rooms and appurtenances of a club of which they are members, each has a right to use all or any part of the thing that no other one of them is using. ... But where men have joint rights to a thing, as for instance, to a sum of money held to their joint credit, then the consent of all the others is required for the use of the thing or of any part of it, by any one of them. Now, the rights of men to the use of land are not joint rights; they are equal rights. (George [1892] 1981: 30–31)

These principles also apply to Indigenous land. As George said:

> Although within generally vague territorial limits each tribe may claim the right to exclude other tribes, yet the idea is not that of property in the land, but of that sort of separation which took place between Lot and Abraham, and the relation of the members to the land is not that of joint ownership but of equal right to use such regulations as in the earlier stages become necessary, being merely those which secure this equality in use. (George [1892] 1981: fn. 21)

The significance of this principle is that of sharing the earth. Consent is needed when land is reduced in supply but, at every point, land value is the preserve of the entire community.

Land rent, then, requires special attention. As George wrote:

> The term rent, in its economic sense – that is, when used, as I am using it, to distinguish that part of the produce which accrues to the owners of land or other natural capabilities by virtue of their ownership – differs in meaning from the word rent as commonly used. (George [1897] 1935: 165)

Conferred by the privilege to control land used in the creation of wealth, rent is determined not so much by fertility or even location, but by monopoly power. George again:

> Rent, in short, is the share in the wealth produced which the exclusive right to the use of natural capabilities gives to the owner. Wherever land has an exchange value there is rent in the economic meaning of the term. Wherever land having a value is used, either by owner or hirer, there is rent actual; wherever it is not used, but still has a value, there is rent potential. It is this capacity of yielding rent which gives value to land. Until its ownership will confer some advantage, land has no value. (George [1897] 1935: 166)

Rent can be enhanced by location, by productivity, or by exertion. More fundamentally, rent is conditioned by general progress within society.

Rent has been widely discussed in political economy, including an authoritative review by Nicholas Kaldor (see Kaldor 1956), but to understand rent in Georgist terms it is crucial to take account of the importance of 'marginal land'. 'George makes it quite clear that marginal land is not unproductive land, but merely the least productive land available at a particular time and place' (Cleveland 2020: 564). This marginal land, or 'extensive margin', is the floor below which neither rent nor wage can be set. The extensive margin is important in GPE because it sets the conditions for the determination of wages and rents, both of which are tied to land.[1] However, even more fundamental is the privilege of individual control that creates and sustains land rent. Without private appropriation of land, there is no rent. According to George: 'Rent, in short, is the price of monopoly, arising from the reduction to individual ownership of natural elements which human exertion can neither produce nor increase' (George [1897] 1935: 167). This price for the individual power to control land when capitalised or aggregated becomes land value. It can be actual or residual: so, rent also arises when landlords hoard land, use it solely for their own needs, or purport to develop land banking for social purposes (Yau and Cheung 2021). Because socially created rent tends to increase with wealth, its private appropriation usually constitutes a brake on the rewards of both labour and capital.

While in Marxian thought rent is a subset of surplus value, a Georgist perspective would regard 'surplus value'[2] as a sub-set of rent. What limited quantitative evidence exists on the relative size of these two – rent and surplus value – shows that rent is larger than surplus value (Giles 2019: 29). Landlords, then, can be, and often are, even more powerful than capitalists. Unlike capitalists, however, landlords make no direct contribution to the process of wealth creation. Rather, they absorb and privately retain the fruits of progress, while they externalise poverty to the masses. No matter what policy is implemented, the owners of land capture its gains. It is this dynamic that, according to Georgists, explains the co-existence of progress and privation and why greater prosperity increases poverty.

Land value and economic rent are, therefore, fundamental to the analytical foundations of GPE. George himself was at pains to distinguish economic rent (the focus of GPE) from 'rent' as used in general conversation. One distinction is that, while 'rent' used in common conversation does not refer to 'latent or potential' rent, economic rent also refers to residual value. The essence of his distinction is that economic rent arises not so much from individual human exertion or from the effort of landlords, but from land *ownership*. Other uses of the term refer to the products of human exertion such as buildings (such as rent paid because of ongoing services provided by a house builder). In cities, however, these two notions of rent tend to be interlocking, as apartment rents strongly reflect factors unrelated to the apartment owners' efforts (George [1897] 1935: 165–72).

What is called 'economic rent' in GPE is equivalent to 'net product'. According to George: 'Net product is really better terminology than rent, as not being so liable to confusion with a word in constant use in another sense' (George [1898] 1992: 150). More fundamentally, greater societal prosperity increases rent, variously referred to by George ([1898] 1992) as land power, *produit net*, net product, the unearned increment, or economic rent that accrues to landlords. This dynamic also makes the economic system prone to structural inequality, because of the structural monopoly position of the landowners who need exert no effort while gaining an increasing share of the fruits of general economic progress.

These were the breakthrough propositions and arguments in Henry George's *Progress and Poverty* ([1897] 1935) and *The Science of Political Economy* ([1898] 1992). Complementing these books were two other more methodological texts: *A Perplexed Philosopher* ([1892] 1981) and *Moses* (1884). The former provided the scaffolding for *The Science of Political Economy* ([1898] 1992) and the latter provided the springboard for *Progress and Poverty* ([1897] 1935). Other, more recent, writing in or about the Georgist tradition extends the exposition and shows the continuing relevance of GPE.[3]

Overall, the Georgist argument is that the root source of social problems is to be found in unequal access to land, the private appropriation of socially created rent, and the deprivation of workers' rights through taking away or reducing what is due to labour. While other factors might be named as 'causes', they are derived from these fundamental contradictions and hence are symptoms of deeper causal influences (George [1883] 1981). It is a position that is analytical, as shown by the way in which George described his approach in *The Science of Political Economy*:

> if political economy can be called science at all, it must as a science, that is to say from the moment the laws of nature on which it depends are discovered, follow the deductive method of examination, using induction only to test the conclusions thus obtained [...] Thus, in the main, the science of political economy resorts to the deductive method, using induction for its tests. (George [1898] 1992: 98, 100)

Beyond deductive and inductive reasoning, George called for 'imaginative experiment', seeking to 'separate, combine or eliminate conditions in our own imaginations, and thus test the working of known principles' (George [1898] 1992: 100). Contemporary political economists influenced by Georgism have applied this approach to various social problems: housing (Stilwell and Jordan 2004; Ryan-Collins et al. 2017); poverty and inequality (Stilwell 2019; Obeng-Odoom 2020a); sustainability (Stilwell 2011b); and trade (Obeng-Odoom 2020a). The *American Journal of Economics and Sociology* is the principal scholarly journal providing a dedicated outlet for GPE.

LAND AND HOUSING

Perhaps the most obvious application of GPE in modern capitalism is in explaining the roots of the seemingly intractable problems of housing that bedevil so many countries. Of course, housing affordability has always been a problem for the poor, but now even middle-income earners also struggle with this affordability challenge. In Marxist political economy, questions of (land) rent, rentierism and 'rent-based capitalism' are considered. Yet, land is not a primary concern in such analysis. Land is not given a special explanatory place in the 'circuit of capital', either. Indeed, in this circuit, land is subsumed in the concept of capital, consistent with the typical Marxist emphasis on capital and labour. Land is of secondary importance, usually considered separately in programmes of (land) nationalisation. In the George–Hyndman debate (see George and Hyndman [1885] 1914), Henry George made these distinctions clear, emphasising the fundamental differences between Marxist-socialists and Georgists with respect to 'socialism and rent-appropriation'. For Georgists, the analysis of rent, as we saw in the previous section of this chapter (see also Harrison 2021), is conceptualised differently from Marxist thinking and is primarily focused on land. Georgists seek to socialise land rent, whereas Marxists wish to remove rent. For Georgists, the inequalities of incomes and wealth are themselves caused by how land is treated, particularly through individual private property rights. Both inequality and problems of housing affordability have their roots in the political economy of land.

GPE indicates that the housing problem is compounded if socially created rent and value are privatised. Housing provision, in those circumstances, generates indebtedness, uncertainty, and insecurity. Crucially, social and transport stresses are also exacerbated as housing is developed on marginal land, often farther away from the city centre. More fundamentally, as the privatisation process generates inequality – and inequality lies at the heart of ecological crisis (Agyeman 2008; Obeng-Odoom 2021) – it makes the tendency to ecological damage yet more entrenched.

From a GPE perspective, therefore, economic rents that attach to land value should not be appropriated by landlords alone. Privatising land enables the perverse dynamic we have already identified to occur and recur, fuelling speculation and making the housing problem ever more complex and intractable. The only solution, from a Georgist perspective, is to socialise rents and use that revenue to provide comprehensive social protection, while seeking liberty for individuals. It is this blend of concerns with liberty and redressing societal problems that is characteristic of the Georgist paradigm.

Analyses of housing from a GPE perspective have yielded significant positive insights in many countries. For instance, they have shown how the growing privatisation of land and land rent in Ghana continues to worsen the housing problem (Obeng-Odoom 2020b). GPE scholars have been able to predict global crises (Harrison 1983; Gaffney 2015), and GPE has been the basis of a new theorising of the commons (Obeng-Odoom 2021). In terms of concrete policy, GPE analysis has also successfully shown how Georgist policy options, even in modest and modified forms, have been helpful in mitigating the housing problem in Singapore (Haila 2016). In Australia, Georgist organisations, such as Prosper Australia, made vigorous submissions to the 2008–10 national inquiry into the tax system, known locally as the 'Henry Tax Review', showcasing the ongoing engagement Georgists have with the policymaking process.

CRITICISMS AND DEVELOPMENTS

Like all schools of political economy, GPE has its critics. Michael Hudson (2008) has documented the twelve most common types of criticism, ranging from GPE's apparently unconditional support for free trade to its history of popularity 'on the streets' rather than in academic circles. Critics of GPE typically represent it as too narrowly focused because of its central concern with the land question. Henry George himself was confronted with this charge. He developed a systematic response in many publications, including *Protection or Free Trade* (George [1886] 1991). However, in 'The Crime of Poverty', he illustrated his position with an anecdote, based on a conversation between two people, one of whom considered the 'money question' more fundamental:

> The money question is […] a more important question than the land question. You give me all the money, and you can take all the land […] [Responding to this, his] friend said: Well, suppose you had all the money in the world and I had all the land in the world. What would you do if I were to give you notice to quit? (George 1885)

Modern Georgists tend to respond to criticisms of their focus on land by diagnosing the source of the critique, and probing whether it arises from ignorance, vested interest or institutional bias. In response, they typically offer clarification or a counter punch. However, whether such responses have been effective is an open question.

A more inclusive approach is to consider how GPE may be reconstructed to become more applicable to contemporary challenges. Even in its analysis of housing problems and policies – surely one of its most significant applications – GPE tends to neglect some pressing concerns. There is a tendency to overlook race, oversimplify the changing role of the state, and over-state the benefits of economic policy solutions such as tax reform (Beck 2012; Pullen 2014; Obeng-Odoom 2020a). These concerns and limitations deserve attention because, in each respect, redress is needed if further progress is to be made in the development and application of GPE.

First, on the matter of race, it must be said that Henry George's original analysis had racist characteristics (England 2015; O'Donnell 2015). George himself moved away from this approach, however, and he subsequently came to consider his earlier work unscientific in this respect. As we now know, human beings are 99.9 per cent the same genetically regardless of their race (Bangura and Stavenhagen 2005: 4). Yet, dealing with race by de-emphasising it and proposing a so-called race-neutral economic policy is also problematic. Indeed, it may be said that overlooking the *colour* of rent is a fundamental weakness of GPE, comparable to similar oversights in other currents of political economic thought. Race shapes economic processes and filters economic outcomes. Implicit assumptions about race have formed the basis of much economic theorising (as noted by MacLean 2017; Darity and Mullen 2020; Darity 2021). Whether by John Locke or James Buchanan, theories of property were carefully crafted to privilege a predominantly white landed elite and to keep racial minorities, especially black people, in their place. The global history of slavery, Jim Crow in the USA, and the development of modern capitalism across cities and nations illustrate the point (Hamilton 2018; Darity and Mullen 2020).

The question of the state also needs more attention in the development and application of Georgist analysis. Much is required of the state in redressing the social inequalities and crises that result from the failure to adequately address solutions to the land question. Yet, state theorising is notably underdeveloped in GPE. If states are to be the vehicle for radical reform by introducing comprehensive land value taxation, perhaps even replacing other taxes on incomes going to labour and capital, this asks much of them, both in the global North and the global South. Do they have the requisite will and capacity to engage in comprehensive fiscal reform? Even if a state has both, it is unclear in what ways it would be possible to confront the kinds of resistance the class of landlords are likely to put up. Can all these concerns be addressed by a better developed Georgist theory of the state (Petrella 1984)? In addressing this challenge, it is also pertinent to note that the modern state is typically an avenue where *institutional racism* can be transmitted through the assessment and execution of land value tax, as well as through the provision of public services (Bangura and Stavenhagen 2005; Bangura 2006). This implies a different structure to GPE's generally *assumed* social state. State institutions, like colonial programmes, that shape where migrants settle, also tend to be overlooked or over-simplified in GPE. Nor does GPE consider the implications of the hierarchy of states in the global order (England 2015: 134–5), which is a significant weakness.

Finally, there is the question of whether the characteristic Georgist policy prescriptions are too narrowly economic in character. GPE's traditionally strong emphasis on land and tax – in particular, the oft-posited ideal 'single tax' on land to replace taxes on labour, capital and processes of exchange – can be criticised for its over-reliance on economic policy instruments as the key to social progress more generally. Certainly, it is important to remove economic impediments to progress, such as tax arrangements that foster inefficiency and inequality. However, it is misleading to expect that to be a panacea for all the political economic challenges in the modern world. Engagement of GPE with the emerging sub-field of stratification economics (Darity and Mullen 2020; Darity 2021) could be useful in this respect. The latter forms a new and flourishing field of political economy centred on the study of long-term, inter-group inequalities. The further development of empirical studies bridging the two approaches could help to ensure that research is grounded in the practical political economic challenges of the current era.

CONCLUSION

Social problems in the world have metastasised into socio-ecological crises. This chapter has sought to clarify the approach of Georgist political economy, showing how it can be applied to a range of such contemporary concerns, particularly but not exclusively those relating to land, housing and cities. Fundamentally different from both mainstream economics and other schools of thought in political economy, GPE offers an alternative approach to understanding and transcending social problems. The centrality of land to the approach is unmatched in any other school of political economy. Having said that, GPE also has important limitations, such as its failure to probe *structural* racism, its limited theorising of the state and its tendency to overstate the efficacy of economic policy instruments for solving social problems. Redressing these weaknesses requires further development of GPE through forging stronger connections with other schools of political economy and social science that recognise the deep-seated and complex character of social inequalities and injustices.

NOTES

1. In neoclassical economics, the concept of extensive margin has been abandoned. What is usually analysed is the intensive margin or landlord investment in landed property (which is regarded in Marxist political economy as differential rent II). What about rent in the extensive margin? Is it 'free' or 'frontier', as colonists and land grabbers claim? Marxists introduced absolute rent to analyse such a situation, but the GPE approach to existing rent analysis is *sui generis*, among others, in linking rent to persistent and prevalent long-term inequalities (Haila 2016: 46–8; Cleveland 2020: 564–7).
2. There is no concept of 'surplus value' in GPE per se. I use the concept here only to show the contrast between GPE and Marxian political economy.
3. For example, Bryson (2011); Pullen (2014); O'Donnell (2015); Haila (2016); Ryan-Collins et al. (2017); Giles (2019); Cleveland (2020); Rybeck (2020); Harrison (2021).

REFERENCES

Agyeman, J. (2008) 'Toward a "Just" Sustainability?', *Continuum*, **22** (6), pp. 751–6.

Bangura, Y. (ed.) (2006) *Ethnic Inequalities and Public Sector Governance*, New York and Geneva: Palgrave/UNRISD.

Bangura, Y. and Stavenhagen, R. (eds) (2005) *Racism and Public Policy*, New York and Geneva: Palgrave/UNRISD.

Beck, J.H. (2012) 'Henry George and Immigration', *American Journal of Economics and Sociology*, **71** (4), pp. 966–87.

Bryson, P.J. (2011) *The Economics of Henry George: History's Rehabilitation of America's Greatest Early Economist*, New York: Palgrave Macmillan.

Cleveland, M. (2020) 'Homelessness and Inequality', *American Journal of Economics and Sociology*, **79** (2), pp. 559–90.

Darity, W.A. (2021) 'Reconsidering the Economics of Identity: Position, Power, and Property', T.W. Schultz Memorial Lecture, Agricultural and Applied Economics Association, 3.1.2021.

Darity, W.A. Jr. and Mullen, K. (2020) *From Here to Equality: Reparations for Black Americans in the Twenty-First Century*, Chapel Hill: University of North Carolina Press.

England, C.W. (2015) 'Land and Liberty: Henry George, the Single Tax Movement, and the Origins of 20th Century Liberalism', PhD dissertation, Graduate School of Arts and Sciences, Georgetown University.

Gaffney, M. (1994) 'Neo-Classical Economics as a Strategem Against Henry George', in Harrison, F. (ed.), *The Corruption of Economics*, London: Shepheard-Walwyn, pp. 29–163.

Gaffney, M. (2015) 'A Real-Assets Model of Economic Crises: Will China Crash in 2015?', *American Journal of Economics and Sociology*, **74** (2), pp. 325–60.

George, H. ([1883] 1966) *Social Problems*, New York: Robert Schalkenbach Foundation.

George, H. ([1883] 1981) *Social Problems*, New York: Robert Schalkenbach Foundation.

George, H. (1884) *Moses*, London: The United Committee for Taxation of Land Values.

George, H. (1885) 'The Crime of Poverty', Robert Schalkenbach Foundation, accessed 14.6.2021 at: http://schalkenbach.org/library/henry-george/hg-speeches/the-crime-of-poverty.html.

George, H. ([1886] 1991) *Protection or Free Trade*, New York: Robert Schalkenbach Foundation.

George, H. ([1892] 1981) *A Perplexed Philosopher*, New York: Robert Schalkenbach Foundation.

George, H. ([1897] 1935) *Progress and Poverty*, 50th anniversary edition, New York: Robert Schalkenbach Foundation.

George, H. ([1898] 1992) *The Science of Political Economy*, London: Kegan Paul, Trench, Trubnerand.

George, H and Hyndman, H.M. ([1885] 1914) 'Socialism and Rent-Appropriation', *Land Values*, May, pp. 530–34.

Giles, R.L. (2019) *An Exploration of the Growth of Economic Insanity: An Indictment of the Economics Profession*, Sydney: Association for Good Government.

Haila, A. (2016) *Urban Land Rent: Singapore as a Property State*, Chichester: Wiley-Blackwell.

Hamilton, T.G. (2018) *Immigration and the Remaking of Black America*, New York: Russell Sage Foundation.

Harrison, F. (1983) *The Power in the Land*, London: Shepheard-Walwyn.

Harrison, F. (ed.) (2016) *Rent Unmasked: How to Save the Global Economy and Build a Sustainable Future: Essays in Honour of Mason Gaffney*, London: Shepheard-Walwyn.

Harrison, F. (2020) 'Cyclical Housing Markets and Homelessness', *American Journal of Economics and Sociology*, **79** (2), pp. 591–612.

Harrison, F. (2021) *We Are Rent: Book 1 – Capitalism, Cannibalism, and How We Must Outlaw Free Riding*, London: Land Research Trust.

Harvey, D. ([1973] 2009) *Social Justice and the City*, revised edition, Athens and London: University of Georgia Press.

Hudson, M. (2008) 'Henry George and His Critics', *American Journal of Economics and Sociology*, **67** (1), pp. 1–45.

Jorgensen, E.O. (1925) *False Education in Our Schools and Colleges*, Chicago, IL: Manufacturers and Merchants Federal Tax League.

Kaldor, N. (1956) 'Alternative Theories of Distribution', *Review of Economic Studies*, **23** (2), pp. 83–100.

MacLean, N. (2017) *Democracy in Chains: The Deep History of the Radical Right's Stealth Plan for America*, New York: Penguin.

O'Donnell, E.T. (2015) *Henry George and the Crisis of Inequality*, New York: Columbia University Press.

Obeng-Odoom, F. (2020a) *Property, Institutions, and Social Stratification in Africa*, Cambridge: Cambridge University Press.

Obeng-Odoom, F. (2020b) 'Urban Political Economy', in Dunn B. (ed.), *Research Agenda for Critical Political Economy*, Cheltenham, UK and Northampton, MA, USA: Edward Elgar Publishing, pp. 181–93.

Obeng-Odoom, F. (2021) *The Commons in an Age of Uncertainty: Decolonizing Nature, Economy, and Society*, Toronto: University of Toronto Press.

Petrella, F. (1984) 'Henry George's Theory of State's Agenda: The Origins of His Ideas on Economic Policy in Adam Smith's Moral Theory', *American Journal of Economics and Sociology*, **43** (3), pp. 269–86.

Pullen, J. (2014) *Nature's Gifts: The Australian Lectures of Henry George on the Ownership of Land and Other Natural Resources*, Sydney: Desert Pea Press.

Ricardo, D. ([1810] 2001) *The Principles of Political Economy and Taxation*, Ontario: Batoche Books.

Ryan-Collins, J., Lloyd, T. and MacFarlane, L. (2017) *Rethinking the Economics of Land and Housing*, London: Zed Books.

Rybeck, R. (2020) 'Gentrification and Blight: Relationship to Involuntary Displacement', *American Journal of Economics and Sociology*, **79** (2), pp. 541–57.

Stilwell, F. (2011a) *The Condition of Labour, Capital and Land*, Sydney: Association for Good Government.

Stilwell, F. (2011b) *Land, Social Justice and Sustainability*, Inaugural Clyde Cameron Lecture, Canberra: Association for Good Government.

Stilwell, F. (2019) *The Political Economy of Inequality*, Cambridge: Polity Press.

Stilwell, F. and Jordan, K. (2004) 'The Political Economy of Land: Putting Henry George in His Place', *Journal of Australian Political Economy*, **54**, pp. 119–34.

Yau, Y. and Cheung, T.C. (2021) 'Revisiting the Concept of the Property State: Private Landowners and Suburban Development in Hong Kong', *American Journal of Economics and Sociology*, **80** (2), pp. 427–64.

19. Ecological economics
Neil Perry

Ecological economics started as a fundamental critique of capitalism and neoclassical economics, including standard macroeconomics. It was an intellectual, political and ideological movement grounded in a dissatisfaction with the way in which mainstream economics incorporated the environment, in ontological, ethical and epistemological terms. As ecological economics has evolved and matured, tension has arisen between those who hold to the radical origins of the field and those who offer technical, social and policy solutions that have little or no grounding in political reality and larger systematic and structural forces. This tension also reflects different opinions about the best way to achieve effective change.

Neoclassical economists incorporating ecological variables into their economic models and ecologists dabbling in economic policy often produce analyses that fit within the current political economic institutions and policy settings, apparently acting on a belief that more profound change is not required or not possible. Because the political environment and power relations are not explicitly considered, their proposed policy solutions are unlikely to work. Indeed, in practice, such actions tend to create opposite reactions that result in toothless policy prescriptions. The consequences are minor manipulations of policy, a continuing rhetoric of 'jobs versus the environment', and internal adjustments in industries and firms that produce little environmental improvement while the owners and managers of capital continue to prioritise their pursuit of profit.

Arguments for more systemic change come from the heterodox economic (or political economy) wing of ecological economics. However, few remedies to systemic environmental threats have occurred since ecological economics commenced: climate change is not being adequately addressed, biodiversity continues to decline, and water resources are not being used sustainably. Meanwhile, the distribution of income has become more unequal. Taking account of this distressing reality, ecological economics needs to develop stronger analyses of social and political transition. Otherwise, great ideas merely become hoped-for technical solutions with no grounding in political reality and thus little prospect of success. This chapter provides support for these claims by considering the principal political economic insights and theoretical innovations of ecological economics, its key debates and its limitations, concluding with proposals for further development of its research agenda.

POLITICAL ECONOMIC INSIGHTS AND THEORETICAL INNOVATIONS

Ecological economics rejects the concept of an economy independent from nature. The economy is viewed as interdependent with the natural environment, embedded within and coevolving with ecosystems through time and space (Norgaard 1994; Costanza et al. 1997; Kallis and Norgaard 2010). A key theoretical underpinning of this perspective is found in Georgescu-Roegen's (1971) classic essay on the entropy law and economic process. Echoing earlier work by Boulding (1966) on the 'spaceship economy' that sees the earth as an (almost) closed system, Georgescu-Roegen draws upon scientific principles to situate the economy within a fundamentally limited energy and material system. According to the second law of thermodynamics, energy continually degrades into unusable states; and Georgescu-Roegen argues that matter is similarly subject to entropic degradation (see also Georgescu-Roegen 1986). Matter and energy cannot be created or destroyed but only used, and such use transforms matter and energy from a usable to an unusable state. Whilst the planet receives a significant amount of energy from the sun, the economy is nonetheless restricted by this physical reality and simply cannot grow without limit.

The recognition of limits to growth (Meadows et al. 1972; Meadows et al. 1992) leads to proposals for a 'steady state' economy (Daly 1991), a notion which had earlier, but rather different, roots in the work of classical economists such as John Stuart Mill. Recycling and new technology can help overcome limits, but each requires the use of further energy and materials. As such, recycling and new technology merely reduce the use of energy and material per unit of consumption; that is, they decouple the economy from nature in a *relative* rather than absolute way. As the economy continues to expand through growth in population and consumption per person, the aggregate resource use grows, and therefore *absolute* decoupling does not and cannot occur (Ward et al. 2016). Thus, a system such as capitalism that is based on the pursuit of profits and growth is intrinsically unsustainable. While the classical economists viewed the steady state or stationary state as a natural end point of the capitalist economy, Daly's advocacy of a steady state requires an active political agenda to change from the current economic arrangements that are based on throughput, population growth and inequality.

As an openly ideological and political discipline (Spash 2013: 352), the roots of ecological economics lie in the realisations that orthodox economics promotes unsustainable economies and that environmental thresholds were being reached. Daly (2005) makes the distinction between 'empty world' and 'full world' economics. He posits that, during the formative years of economics, human well-being was limited by human capital constraints, so the focus of economics was on enhancing well-being through the accumulation of human capital. Then, as the economy grew within the non-growing natural ecosystem, the limits to well-being became natural capital but the economic paradigm did not change. Therefore, a new 'full world' economic paradigm is now needed, one that recognises the interdependence of the economy and environment. Ecological economics aims to be that paradigm.

Recognising that the economy and nature are interdependent, environmental thresholds are being breached, and that the pursuit of growth is unsustainable, a new theoretical framework based on non-linear, dynamic and uncertain systems is required. H.T. Odum (1971), who had a great deal to do with the entropy law, also worked (along with his brother E.P. Odum 1953) on systems theory and ecosystem ecology, raising questions that still concern ecological economists today, such as how human and natural systems interact (Costanza et al. 1997: 62). Holling's (1987) work on the resilience of complex adaptive systems is also formative in this regard. In contrast to standard perspectives on ecosystem dynamics, focused on the exploitation and conservation phases and on convergence to a single equilibrium, Holling explained that ecosystems cycle through longer dynamic processes. He showed that the conservation phase has increasing complexity and connectedness that leads to a disturbance and release of resources and a subsequent renewal or reorganisation phase, which becomes the source of the next exploitation stage. Holling's work led to a new understanding of resilience in natural systems where multiple equilibria exist and disturbance can flip a system from one stable state to another. With such non-linearity and complexity in the system, fundamental uncertainty rather than probabilistic risk becomes the more relevant concept.

Orthodox economics does not model fundamental uncertainty because it is impossible to make rational decisions when the outcome of those decisions cannot be known (Arrow 1962: 615): hence its usual focus on calculable risk, expected utility and probabilities when modelling decision-making under uncertainty. In contrast, the political economy wing of ecological economics does seek to take account of the fundamental uncertainty due to the inherent complexity in ecological-economic systems. This is reflected in its emphasis on decision-making frameworks such as the precautionary principle and minimising the maximum loss (or regret). The precautionary principle states that a lack of knowledge regarding the environmental (or health) implications of a decision should not be a reason for delaying action to halt adverse environmental impacts (Convention on Biological Diversity 1992). Recognising that proof of environmental impacts before the fact is difficult to find in complex, ecological-economic systems, the precautionary principle suggests that this should not be used as a reason to halt development or establish mitigation measures. Minimising the maximum loss (or regret) is a way to operationalise the principle (Gardiner 2006: 45; Aldred 2012: 10). Thus, in a 'development versus preservation' decision where uncertainty prevails, the right decision is the one that minimises the maximum loss or the alternative with the least damaging 'worst-case' outcome. The precautionary principle implies a stewardship role for humans over the environment or future generations; and a different ethical framework focused on duties rather than the consequentialist utilitarianism of orthodox economics (Perry and Primrose 2015).

In a similar vein, ecological economics can challenge conventional human-centred, monetary valuation of environmental attributes. This type of valuation is common in cost–benefit analysis and throughout mainstream economics. Challenging its appropriateness aligns ecological economics with the substantive rationality of Weber and Polanyi and Kapp's substantive economics (Berger 2008a, 2008b; Gerber and Scheidel 2018). 'Substantive rationality' refers to 'the degree in which needs are met through economic activity' as opposed to 'formal rationality' which refers to 'the degree in which activities can be calculated in monetary terms' (Gerber and Scheidel 2018: 187). The former has more affinity with ecological economics where the concern is the real material conditions of society (Berger 2008b) rather than a single end goal of efficiency or GDP. Ecological economists attempt to point out that economic actions have substantive, material impacts on nature and that these impacts feed back onto the economic system through various mechanisms, including the physical – such as pollution and climate change – and the metaphysical – such as mental health, learning, meaning and well-being. Nature also has an intrinsic value which again implies a stewardship role for humans. These values are incommensurate but weakly comparable (Martinez Alier et al. 1998); and substantively rational choices can be made using multi-criteria analysis. Or, following Kapp's (1978) logic, a system of social and ecological minima can be established from which decisions can be supported or rejected according to their impact on the various social and ecological indicators.

Orthodox economics is regarded as part of the problem by those in the political economy wing of ecological economics who argue that the recourse to formal rationality facilitates neoclassical analysis being used to legitimate the neoliberal, capitalist system. Furthermore, the neoclassical theory of the firm is predicated on the business enterprise focusing exclusively on monetary outcomes and pushing costs onto others wherever possible. The mainstream's focus is on a narrow and uncritical perspective on markets that all too easily can be used to benefit the powerful and bestow legitimacy on undesirable and unviable economic, social and environmental arrangements. The marginalisation of concerns with inequality is a further concern. Willingness to pay and capacity to pay are often either implicitly or explicitly conflated within orthodox economics; but the lack of purchasing power among poorer members of society – and other natural species – results in their well-being counting for little, thereby limiting their ability to flourish. Indeed, in the absence of wealth and income equality, it is impossible to achieve any morally defensible definition of efficiency with a market-based price system (Berger 2008b). Any defensible definition must incorporate satisfaction of the higher values associated with a substantive rationality, such as social and ecological equality.

Consideration by ecological economists of the multitude of incommensurable values associated with ecological economics implies an affinity with post Keynesian and institutional economics (Holt et al. 2009; Perry and Primrose 2015). In contrast to orthodox economics, these political economy approaches regard preferences as lexicographic, where fundamental values cannot be traded off with each other or against commodity production or income (Georgescu-Roegen 1954; Gowdy 1992; Spash and Hanley 1995; Lavoie 2009). There is also a different conception of social costs, compared with the treatment of 'externalities' in orthodox environmental economics. To Kapp and Polanyi, cost shifting is a systemic problem, written into the formal rationality of economics and the capitalist system rather than an '*unintended* or *incidental* by-product of some otherwise legitimate activity' (Mishan 1971: 2, emphasis·in original; see also Baumol and Oates 1988: 17).

In contrast with orthodox economics, ecological economics has always been considered both transdisciplinary and methodologically pluralist: it is a broad church (Norgaard 1989; Costanza et al. 1997). There are many theoretical frameworks used for recognising the interdependence of economy and nature. Practitioners adapt heterodox and/or orthodox economic theory in new ways, join ecological and economic models, and bring insights from anthropology, environmental sociology, philosophy and cultural studies to achieve some of the broad aims and understandings discussed in this section. This plurality creates tensions, and in some cases can be seen as inherently contradictory and even undermining the founding principles of ecological economics, as discussed in the following section.

THE KEY DEBATES

Debates within ecological economics reflect a plurality of views and ideologies associated with the different theoretical positions. Spash (2013) identifies three types of ecological economists – social ecological economists, new environmental pragmatists and new resource economists. An understanding of each helps to show the basis of the positions they characteristically take in the principal debates.

Social ecological economists are the most relevant in the context of this book because they identify with the heterodox economics tradition, including evolutionary and institutional economics. They argue for a paradigm shift in economic theory because the ontological and ethical foundations of orthodox economics are incapable of modelling environment–economy interactions. They regard the atomistic nature of orthodox economics as ill-suited to the analysis of complex social and ecological systems. Moreover, they see orthodox economics as operating in a political vacuum which therefore cannot address the root causes of environmental degradation which is an economic system based on the pursuit of profits and growth at any cost. Social ecological economists seek to present a more comprehensive, system-wide analysis.

New environmental pragmatists include many environmental scientists who utilise any social science approach they believe to be politically acceptable (Spash 2013: 354). Rigorous assessment of the appropriate social science method is absent; and the result tends to 'buy into the methodology and ideology of commodifying, quantifying and pricing Nature' (Spash 2013: 354). In practice, there is a focus on market-based solutions, such as biodiversity offset schemes and pricing ecosystem services, which are seen as politically acceptable and more likely to be adopted than direct regulation of environmentally damaging activities.

New resource economists comprise a third group, applying orthodox economic analysis, associating environmental problems with 'externalities' and proposing solutions based on markets and 'getting the prices right'. While they may engage with ecological theory, they do so by using ecological models – such as population dynamics, maximum sustainable yield or predator–prey relationships – in combination with orthodox economics models of optimising behaviour, for example, in modelling the 'optimal harvest' of an environmental resource. Mathematical models of species extinction may be derived; and price-based policies may be advocated as means to maximise economic welfare, as it is understood in orthodox economics.

It is the contest of ideas and influence between these three groups that shapes modern ecological economics. While ecological economics had its origins as a political and ideological movement opposed to orthodox economics, the impact of the new environmental pragmatists and new resource economists has been to strengthen the influence of mainstream economics and to put emphasis on technical fixes that are apolitical, exemplify closed system thinking and limit the field (Spash 2011: 343–4). The different approaches are evident in many debates that reflect the deep theoretical and ideological differences.

One longstanding difference has centred on the distinction between *weak and strong sustainability*. While largely played out between ecological economists and orthodox economists, the debate is worth revisiting due to the currently strong influence of neoclassical economics within the ecological economics literature. Weak sustainability can be understood in terms of the 'Hartwick rule' where human and natural capital are substitutable. This rule holds that whenever resource rents (profits) from the exploitation of non-renewable resources are invested in human-made capital, the total capital stock is maintained (in the absence of depreciation) and there is a non-declining consumption level through time (Hartwick 1977). Such an economy is held to be sustainable, in the Brundtland Commission sense that future generations have the same aggregate level of opportunities as the current generation (World Commission on Environment and Development 1987). Ecological economics rejects such a notion of sustainability, pointing to the important nonlinearities, thresholds and irreversibility in nature. Its alternative view is that, due to those nonlinearities, reductions in natural capital are non-substitutable, or at least many elements of nature cannot be degraded beyond certain limits if future generations are to be as well off as the current generation.

Daly (1990) sets down the 'rules' for *strong sustainability*. First, for renewable resources such as forests and fish stocks, the rate of harvest should be less than the rate of regeneration. Second, rates of waste generation from the economy must be less that the assimilative capacity of the environment, where the assimilative capacity is viewed as an aspect of natural capital. Third, for non-renewable resources, such as coal and oil, depletion should be accompanied by comparable development of renewable substitutes, such as solar and wind power. Clearly, these rules have not been put in place around the world. Doing so would require genuine democratic control of the political and economic processes by a properly informed electorate, but this does not occur and is very unlikely to emerge in neoliberal capitalism. Of course, many countries have incentives for renewable energy development, but these have come too late to stop global warming and often work alongside existing subsidies for fossil fuels.

New resource economists generally adhere to the *weak sustainability* agenda because the theoretical framework they use is atomistic, linear and formally rational. As such, the elements within the models, such as the value of species and the value of harvest, are substitutable. Constraints can be added, such as sustainable maximum yields, in an attempt to meet Daly's renewable-resource rule. However, given uncertainty and the complexity of ecological-economic systems, maintaining the natural capital stock can never be guaranteed once it is traded off with economic output within a formally rational system. Moreover, political economic issues do not enter the models. For example, the political agencies and vested interests behind the setting of maximum sustainable yields are not discussed, while the monitoring and enforcement of harvest limits is taken as given but, in practice, it is always imperfect and subject to compromise. There is a yet more fundamental methodological problem too: the inherent contradiction in using a theoretical framework with an atomistic ontology within a field of research that preaches the non-substitutability of environmental attributes.

A second debate revolves around the *use of markets to solve environmental problems*, including setting resource harvest limits. This policy approach is openly promoted by both new environmental pragmatists and new resource economists but usually opposed by those in the social ecological economics camp. Orthodox economics generally regards environmental markets and other, incentive-based policies as being more efficient than direct regulation. Because it is impossible to know marginal abatement cost curves for individual polluters, setting direct limits for each polluter will not equalise marginal abatement cost, which is a requirement for achieving the environmental aim at minimum cost. But this conclusion derives from a model devoid of political and economic power relations. In reality, when a market-based policy is proposed and implemented, the vested interests in the existing system can be expected to manipulate it to their own advantage, reducing the policy's impact to merely tinkering around the edges.

Polluters are not static agents and are incentivised by the formally rational capitalist system to shift costs and find ways around the policy. This was seen in both the EU and Australian carbon markets. In the EU, the biggest polluters reaped windfall gains from the free permits they received (Martinez and Neuhoff 2005; Grubb and Neuhoff 2006; Hepburn et al. 2006; Spash 2010). In Australia, the biggest polluters used the 'jobs will flow overseas' rhetoric to secure up to 97 per cent of their permits for free, although the cost structures of the polluting businesses relative to international competitors could have easily accommodated a price on carbon (Perry 2012). Firms using their economic and political power to get around the policy ensured that the result would be little improvement in environmental outcomes and, ultimately, abandonment of any substantial climate change policy.

Australia's brief era of carbon pricing provides a particularly stark example of the dedication to market solutions. The policy's intention was to cover 500 firms who were the biggest polluters in the country, collectively producing 60 per cent of Australia's emissions, with just 50 of those firms producing 75 per cent of those emissions (Department of Climate Change and Energy Efficiency 2011: 21; Minister for Climate Change and Energy Efficiency 2012: 1). Thus, the complexity and expense of creating an artificial market was ultimately targeting the 50 firms who collectively produced 45 per cent of Australia's carbon emissions. It would have been far easier and less costly to directly regulate the targeted firms, nationalise them, or work collaboratively with them to reduce emissions. Such an approach would be more aligned with the heterodox economic tradition of social ecological economics and more attuned to the practical political economy of decision-making.

The problem with market-based policies at an ontological level is evident with biodiversity markets, which are being established and expanding around the world (Madsen et al. 2010) at the behest of new environmental pragmatists and new resource economists. Biodiversity markets allow land clearing for agriculture or development when suitable offsets can be found. In theory, offsets must be like-for-like to ensure no net loss in biodiversity. However, the neat picture that comes to mind – with one area cleared and a nearby barren area reforested – is never the case. Because every patch of forest, every part of biodiversity, is different and can never be replaced, a pure market arrangement cannot function. There could only ever be one buyer or one seller for a biodiversity credit that is attached to a particular area. Thus, the like-for-like rule must be relaxed, in the name of 'making the market work'. The primary concern of this orthodox economic reasoning, one may infer, is to establish a *formally rational* solution rather than dealing with the actual problem where many incommensurable social, ecological and economic values cannot be traded off and reconciled within a market process.

In a biodiversity market, three political economic and cost-shifting events occur. First, the existence of an offset option reduces activity in the rest of the mitigation hierarchy. The mitigation hierarchy proceeds from first avoiding biodiversity impacts to mitigating the impact on biodiversity and lastly to offsetting any remaining impact. As developers are inherently incentivised to shift costs, they tend not to avoid or mitigate because offsetting the biodiversity impacts is less costly. Thus, the existence of the offset market can be expected to worsen the biodiversity impact of development projects. Second, to make the market work, 'averted loss' offsets are allowed (Maron et al. 2012). A long-term stewardship agreement over land with existing biodiversity is said to avert future loss and is considered equivalent to forest regeneration, given some exchange ratio based on biodiversity attributes. However, in this situation there is no additionality to the biodiversity created and, in many cases, there was never any intention or likelihood that the biodiversity in question was going to be disturbed in the future. Third, to make the market work, there must be many buyers and sellers of credits, so the like-for-like rules are relaxed using new exchange ratios between plant community types or other biodiversity indicators.

Of course, it is sometimes argued by environmental pragmatists that any policy is better than no policy. However, Spash (2013) makes the point that such an argument reflects a lack of proper questioning of the methodological underpinnings of policy. In the case of biodiversity markets, the existing formally rational economic system is being reinforced; and it is this system that is the cause of the ecological problems and biodiversity loss that we face. By commodifying nature through markets, we are undermining the very values we are trying to protect.

More generally, the issue of value monism separates social ecological economists from new environmental pragmatists and new resource economists. Non-market valuation is often seen as a way of making powerful arguments in support of preservation or conservation and there have been some positive outcomes from this approach. For example, when a new gold mine was proposed in the exclusion zone around Australia's World Heritage listed Kakadu National Park, a contingent valuation study revealed that the willingness to pay to avoid the environmental damage was greater than the economic benefits of the mine. The mine proposal was rejected, although the main reason stated was due to concerns for Aboriginal heritage values (Carson et al. 1994). Nonetheless, non-market valuation can be seen as useful in cost–benefit analysis, which is increasingly being used in government decision-making. As above, the argument against non-market valuation is that it undermines the very pluralist values we are trying to protect and it is unnecessary if we accept the basic tenets of ecological economics. That is, if the economy is embedded within nature and if we rely on nature for our survival, or if we have a stewardship role in relation to the environment, or if natural capital is non-substitutable, non-market valuation becomes irrelevant. The idea of trading off a World Heritage listed national park for a mine is irrational from a substantive economics perspective.

Non-market valuation approaches are also unable to capture the non-linearities inherent in the social ecological economics understanding of the world. Non-market valuation is generally applied to marginal changes to the environment. In cost–benefit analysis, for example, it is applied to a small change to a forest or an impact on a population of an endangered species. However, if there are many such marginal losses, we eventually reach thresholds where an entire species or forest is lost, and this does not enter the values provided in stated or revealed preference approaches to non-market valuation. More generally, ignorance regarding the value of nature and biodiversity reduces the values in stated preference methods of non-market valuation (Spash and Hanley 1995).

Many other methods have been proposed and used for valuing the environment non-monetarily. The obvious choice for a theory based on entropy is to use some form of an energy theory of value. However, Georgescu-Roegen (1986) rejects this approach on the basis that it simply substitutes one type of singular value for another. On the other hand, there does not seem to be the same objection to using measures of biodiversity, such as species richness or taxonomic diversity, in a cost-effectiveness framework. Kapp refers to achieving social and ecological indicators at minimum cost (Berger 2008b: 250); and measures of biodiversity allow for the fact that there are multiple values for biodiversity. Similarly, such non-monetary values or measures can be used when applying the precautionary principle or minmax loss decision-making rule; and there is a long tradition of applying multi-criteria analysis in ecological economics, which is in accordance with a weak comparability of pluralist values (Martinez-Alier et al. 1998).

There is also continuing debate about the need for *an end to economic growth*, defined as growth in GDP and more specifically GDP per capita. The anti-growth arguments, extending Daly's (1991, 1996) critique of the dominant growth paradigm, rest on two basic tenets. First, resource limits and the entropy law imply that the economy simply cannot continue to grow. Second, GDP growth is not necessarily associated with increased levels of well-being. On the first of these tenets, the debate turns on the ability of the economy to achieve *absolute decoupling* from material and energy throughput. Optimists argue that decoupling is possible through relatively minor changes to the economy, such as carbon pricing, technology-specific policies, and flexible work arrangements (van den Bergh 2011). Modern 'green growth' proposals and proponents of ecological modernisation also occupy the optimistic camp (United Nations Conference on Sustainable Development 2012), positing that technical change and substitutions can create the conditions for an absolute decoupling while GDP growth continues to increase (Hickel and Kallis 2020). Those in the more pessimistic camp argue for *degrowth* because absolute decoupling is not possible without radical institutional change (Kallis 2011).

The range of policies and institutional changes required for degrowth – or the 'socially sustainable process of downscaling society's metabolism and throughput' (Kallis 2011: 875)

– is daunting, especially in the current neoliberal political environment. Degrowth requires, amongst other things, a reduction in working hours (such as the proposal for a 21-hour work week), a basic income policy, redistributive taxation to ensure an equitable transition, capping salaries, growth in the health and education sectors where human labour creates value, institutions guaranteeing minimum health, reductions in international capital flows and internal banking institutions, a strengthening of local economies, taxes on environmental damage and carbon dioxide, and regulatory bans on resource extraction and advertising (Kallis 2011). Many of these suggestions are also prevalent in other currents within heterodox economics. They speak to substantive rationality and a different way of understanding what growth or progress is, emphasising the importance of the qualitative aspects of growth (Perry 2013). However, they also point to the limitations of ecological economics in terms of the problems associated with operationalising these policies in the current political environment.

Consideration of how changes to the system will come about has tended to be quite problematic within ecological economics. There is often reluctance to engage with the difficult political economic questions of vested interests and how to overcome the impact of those vested interests on policymaking and natural resource decisions. Instead, the principal focus has been on proposing alternative, democratic decision-making processes, but without addressing the underlying reasons for their current absence. Topics have included deliberative democracy and participatory approaches to governance; value-articulating institutions; going beyond cost–benefit analysis and monetary valuation to incorporate multi-criteria analysis and weakly comparable values; and the role that citizens' juries could play in decision-making (Jacobs 1997; Martinez-Alier et al. 1998; Söderholm 2001; Vatn 2005). While a participatory approach to governance could well allow myriad values to enter the decision-making process, analysis of how such a democratic arrangement would arise is generally lacking.

LIMITATIONS

A major limitation in much ecological economics arises from the inherent contradiction of using a formally rational theoretical framework, such as neoclassical economics, to analyse issues concerning substantive rationality or the real societal circumstances and material conditions of people and the environment. Ontologically, neoclassical economics assumes linearity and atomism which is ill-suited to analysing complex socio-ecological systems where the whole is greater than the sum of the parts and where fundamental uncertainty pervades. The failure of orthodox economics – and therefore new resource economists – to consider the influence of economic power is also a recurrent limitation. Environmental pragmatists, too, are firmly situated within the current political environment and they have rarely, if ever, engaged with the economic ontology, ethics or epistemology of the policies they propose. Consequently, they cannot see the 'importance of social, political, ethical and institutional factors' (Spash 2011: 364).

Spash (2013) argues that a solution can be found in a social ecological economics grounded in heterodox economic theory. Perry and Primrose (2015) also argue that heterodox economics is more suited to analysing environmental issues, such as the biodiversity crisis, for ethical and ontological reasons. On ethics, heterodox economics is not so intrinsically tied to utilitarian/consequentialist ethics and is more able to incorporate Kantian, deontological, duty-based ethics required for a stewardship role over the environment. Yet social ecological economics may also be criticised because power and inequality are under-theorised (Kallis and Norgaard 2010: 697), and its policy proposals often lack analysis of political power. For example, Daly's 'rules' for a sustainable society have not been implemented – and it is hard to believe that they ever could be – because the vested interests that benefit from the status quo cannot be readily replaced by more progressive bases of power. Daly (1991) argues for political institutions to adopt policies for a steady state economy, such as population controls and maximum limits on income and wealth, but how these changes are to occur is not modelled or analysed. The requirements for degrowth (Kallis 2011) have a similarly unrealistic character because of the certain opposition to them by vested interests.

Having roots in the study of biophysical processes, ecological economics of all forms tends to lack a theoretical framework that engages with social change and the political and corporate power preventing socio-economic adjustment to a sustainable future. The predominant emphasis is on identifying technical solutions that focus on singular goals within the current, formally rational system and are devised within a model of the economy that lacks political and corporate power. As Spash (2011: 363) points out, policies that are analysed within an analytical framework that does not account for vested interests are sure to play into the hands of the very same vested interests. As explained earlier, problems like these have been evident within carbon emission trading schemes. Biodiversity markets are even more susceptible to such problems and have a clear track record of regularly justifying and perversely incentivising the destruction of biodiversity for unlimited 'development'. Moreover, simply linking ecological and economic models is unlikely to be adequate because neither type of model usually allows for economic power relations.

Consideration of political and corporate power is not wholly lacking in social ecological economics, however, and there has been some discussion of how change can occur. For example, Kallis and Martinez Alier (2010) discuss the political process for degrowth and particularly how to introduce caps on resource use. Their argument is that institutional change is a monumental task, given the influence of neoliberalism in democratic societies, the lack of a global enforcement mechanism, and the potential for manipulation of the caps in authoritarian regimes to enhance existing power relations. Buch-Hansen explains that the prerequisites for a socio-economic paradigm shift to a degrowth society are

> a deep crisis that cannot be solved by the institutional arrangements to which the currently prevailing political project has given shape (prerequisite 1); one or more alternative political projects that show the ways out of the crisis (prerequisite 2); organic intellectuals and a comprehensive alliance of social forces promoting the project in political struggles (prerequisite 3); and broad-based consent, or at least passive consent, for the political project (prerequisite 4). (Buch-Hansen 2018: 159)

While prerequisites 1 and 2 are clearly met, prerequisites 3 and particularly 4 have not yet been met and there is scope for a properly conceived ecological economics to assist in meeting these prerequisites.

DEVELOPING THE RESEARCH AGENDA

To address the limitations reviewed in the preceding section, an extended research agenda is required. Ecological economics must analyse means of overcoming the vested interests that currently stop the last two of Buch-Hansen's (2018) prerequisites from being met. New resource economists and environmental pragmatists, although both subject to criticisms in this chapter, could contribute in at least four specific ways. First, they could model the political process, vested interests and cost shifting that occurs during and after the implementation of their technical solutions, such as carbon pricing. Game theory models could be suitable for this purpose, helping to predict how entrepreneurs will react and dynamically respond when environmental policies are proposed. Second, they could engage with the mainstream economic 'theory of the second best' (Lipsey and Lancaster 1956) and not model the economy 'as if' it is structured along the lines of zero transaction costs, perfect information, and perfect competition. Such analyses are likely to demonstrate that direct action, 'green procurement' practices by governments and cooperative regulation are preferable to market-based solutions on both cost and effectiveness grounds. Third, the models of orthodox economics could be turned to analysing the network or ecosystem of vested interests. This would seem to be a natural area of interest for economists modelling ecosystems (Finnoff and Tschirhart 2003a, 2003b) or economic processes using ecosystem dynamics (Brock and Xepapadeas 2003; Tilman et al. 2005). Fourth, modelling could show the empirical link between profits and environmental degradation, revealing the extent to which the profits of retailers, manufacturers and banks are grounded in dirty industries: that would be useful information for participants in the bottom-up social change required for a sustainable future.

Social ecological economists could assist by analysing how economics can be changed. This is a tall order, of course. Not even prerequisite 1 of Buch-Hansen's (2018) prerequisites (the acknowledgement of crisis in current arrangements) is usually met because most mainstream economists do not currently admit to a crisis that their theories cannot address. However, social ecological economists engaging in analysis of political and corporate power and social change (Green 2016) can seek to actively create the organic intellectuals and the bottom-up alliance of social forces needed for Buch-Hansen's (2018) prerequisites 3 and 4. For example, there would appear to be merit in pursuing a research agenda based on J.K. Galbraith's notion of *countervailing power* to control corporate interests (Galbraith 1952; Dunn and Pressman 2006). While Galbraith focused on the use of countervailing power in remedying other problems of social and economic imbalance, a countervailing power is needed now to drive the institutional changes required for a sustainable society. In the area of environment–economy interactions, the development of that countervailing power could take the form of a coalition of social and environmental non-government organisations, but these organisations currently compete for funds and lack a coordinating institution (Perry 2013). Social ecological economists could model the countervailing power requirements and actively seek to create the coalition.

Finally, engagement with environmental sociology is required from all camps within ecological economics. Bourdieu's (1989) concepts of *field* and *habitus* show one example of potentially useful application. Fields are the 'network of objective social relations' that we inherit and that maintain the logic of specific forms of capital (Glenna 1996: 24). The forms of capital refer to the social, cultural and economic resources that can be used to wield power and maintain dominant positions in relationships. Habitus is then the internalisation of the system of logic in a field, which agents continually recreate. For example, instrumental rationality and a focus on profits, wealth, superannuation and the efficient use of resources is the dominant habitus as this allows members of the field to wield power. However, while difficult, change to the habitus and field is possible. The habitus is not a closed loop and agents can reason upon different structures, relationships and objects (Glenna 1996). As field and habitus relate to the norms and conventions of institutional economics, social ecological economists may be well suited to analysing the changes needed in society via the changes in field and habitus.

For all ecological economists, putting greater emphasis on the analysis of power and its distribution in contemporary economies and societies would facilitate a shift to a substantive economics and the realisation of the critically important goals of ecological economics. The potential is as yet under-realised. A search of the journal *Ecological Economics*, which is the key journal for ecological economists of all types, reveals little engagement with issues of corporate power, vested interests, habitus or countervailing power. For example, in the 30 years of the journal there are a mere nine articles referencing 'corporate power', nine referencing 'habitus', five mentioning 'countervailing power', and 24 mentioning 'vested interest'. This seems inadequate for a movement aiming to create comprehensive change in social and economic institutions. Ecological economics can and should go beyond merely offering technical solutions that tinker around the edges of the major ecological challenges, which is the characteristic approach of new environmental pragmatists and new resource economists. It needs to emphasise fundamentally changing the capitalist system and the influence of mainstream economics, as social ecological economists have sought to do, but for this purpose it needs to also engage, both theoretically and practically, with the vested interests that obstruct the attainment of those goals. Thus, if ecological economics is to have long-lasting impact it must engage with the corporate and political power that perpetuates unsustainable systems.

REFERENCES

Aldred, J. (2012) 'Climate change uncertainty, irreversibility and the precautionary principle', *Cambridge Journal of Economics*, **36** (5), pp. 1051–72.

Arrow, K.J. (1962) 'Economic welfare and the allocation of resources for invention', in National Bureau of Economic Research (ed.), *The Rate and Direction of Inventive Activity*, Princeton, NJ: Princeton University Press.

Baumol, W.J. and Oates, W.E. (1988) *The Theory of Environmental Policy*, Cambridge: Cambridge University Press.

Berger, S. (2008a) 'Karl Polanyi's and Karl William Kapp's substantive economics: important insights from the Kapp–Polanyi correspondence', *Review of Social Economy*, **66** (3), pp. 381–96.

Berger, S. (2008b) 'K. William Kapp's theory of social costs and environmental policy: towards political ecological economics', *Ecological Economics*, **67** (2), pp. 244–52.

Boulding, K.E. (1996) 'The economics of the coming spaceship earth', in Jarrett, H. (ed.), *Environmental Quality in a Growing Economy*, Baltimore, MD: Resources for the Future/Johns Hopkins University Press, pp. 3–14.

Bourdieu, P. (1989) 'Social space and symbolic power', *Sociological Theory*, **7**, pp. 14–25.

Brock, W. and Xepapadeas, A. (2003) 'Valuing biodiversity from an economic perspective: a unified economic, ecological, and genetic approach', *The American Economic Review*, **93** (5), pp. 1597–614.

Buch-Hansen, H. (2018) 'The prerequisites for a degrowth paradigm shift: insights from critical political economy', *Ecological Economics*, **146**, pp. 157–63.

Carson, R.T., Wilkes, L. and Imber, D. (1994) 'Valuing the preservation of Australia's Kakadu conservation zone', *Oxford Economic Papers*, **46**, pp. 727–49.

Convention on Biological Diversity (1992) United Nations, accessed 1.4.2012 at: http://www.biodiv.org/doc/legal/cbd-en.pdf.

Costanza, R., Cumberland, J., Daly, H., Goodland, R. and Norgaard, R. (1997) *An Introduction to Ecological Economics*, Boca Raton, FL: St. Lucie Press.

Daly, H. E. (1990) 'Toward some operational principles of sustainable development', *Ecological Economics*, **2**, pp. 1–6.

Daly, H.E. (1991) *Steady-State Economics*, 2nd edition, Washington, DC: Island Press.

Daly, H.E. (1996) *Beyond Growth: The Economics of Sustainable Development*, Boston, MA: Beacon Press.

Daly, H.E. (2005) 'Economics in a full world', *Scientific American*, **293**, pp. 100–107.

Department of Climate Change and Energy Efficiency (2011) *Securing a Clean Energy Future: The Australian Government's Climate Change Plan*, Canberra: Commonwealth of Australia, accessed 10.8.2021 at: https://webarchive.nla.gov.au/awa/20110709072631/http://pandora.nla.gov.au/pan/127961/20120509–0039/www.cleanenergyfuture.gov.au/wp-content/uploads/2011/07/Consolidated-Final.pdf.

Dunn, S.P. and Pressman S. (2006) 'The lasting economic contributions of John Kenneth Galbraith, 1908–2006', *Journal of Post Keynesian Economics*, **29** (2), pp. 179–90.

Finnoff, D. and Tschirhart, J. (2003a) 'Protecting an endangered species while harvesting its prey in a general equilibrium ecosystem model', *Land Economics*, **79** (2), pp. 160–80.

Finnoff, D. and Tschirhart, J. (2003b) 'Harvesting in an eight-species ecosystem', *Journal of Environmental Economics and Management*, **45** (3), pp. 589–611.

Galbraith, J.K. (1952) *American Capitalism: The Concept of Countervailing Power*, Boston, MA: Houghton Mifflin.

Gardiner, S.M. (2006) 'A core precautionary principle', *Journal of Political Philosophy*, **14** (1), pp. 33–60.

Georgescu-Roegen, N. (1954) 'Choice, expectation and measurability', *Quarterly Journal of Economics*, 68, pp. 503–34.

Georgescu-Roegen, N. (1971) *The Entropy Law and the Economic Process*, Cambridge, MA: Harvard University Press.

Georgescu-Roegen, N. (1986) 'The entropy law and the economic process revisited', *Eastern Economic Journal*, **12** (1), pp. 3–25.

Gerber, J.-F. and Scheidel, A. (2018) 'In search of substantive economics: comparing today's two major socio-metabolic approaches to the economy – MEFA and MuSIASEM', *Ecological Economics*, 144, pp. 186–94.

Glenna, L.L. (1996) 'Rationality, habitus, and agricultural landscapes: ethnographic case studies in landscape sociology', *Agriculture and Human Values*, **13**, pp. 21–38.

Gowdy, J. (1992) 'Georgescu-Roegen's utility theory applied to environmental economics', in Dragan, J.C., Demetrescu, M. and Seifert, M. (eds), *Entropy and Bioeconomics*, Milan: Nagard Publishers.

Green, D. (2016) *How Change Happens*, New York: Oxford University Press.

Grubb, M. and Neuhoff, K. (2006) 'Allocation and competitiveness in the EU emissions trading scheme: policy overview', *Climate Policy*, **6** (1), pp. 7–30.

Holt, R.P.F., Pressman, S. and Spash, C.L. (eds) (2009) *Post Keynesian and Ecological Economics: Confronting Environmental Challenges*, Cheltenham, UK and Northampton, MA, USA: Edward Elgar Publishing.

Hartwick, J.M. (1977) 'Intergenerational equity and the investment of rents from exhaustible resources', *American Economic Review*, **67**, pp. 972–4.

Hepburn, C., Grubb, M., Neuhoff, K., Matthes, F. and Tse, M. (2006) 'Auctioning of EU ETS phase II allowances: how and why?', *Climate Policy*, **6** (1), pp. 137–60.

Hickel, J. and Kallis, G. (2020) 'Is green growth possible?' *New Political Economy*, **25** (4), pp. 469–86.

Holling, C.S. (1987) 'Simplifying the complex: the paradigms of ecological function and structure', *European Journal of Operational Research*, 30, pp. 139–46.

Jacobs, M., (1997) 'Environmental valuation, deliberative democracy and public decision-making institutions', in Foster, J. (ed.), *Valuing Nature? Economics, Ethics and Environment*, London and New York: Routledge, pp. 211–31.

Kallis, G. (2011) 'In defence of degrowth', *Ecological Economics*, **70** (5), pp. 873–80.

Kallis, G. and Martinez-Alier, J. (2010) 'Caps yes, but how? A response to Alcott', *Journal of Cleaner Production*, **18**, pp. 1568–71.

Kallis, G. and Norgaard, R.B. (2010) 'Coevolutionary ecological economics', *Ecological Economics*, **69**, pp. 690–99.

Kapp, K.W. (1978) *The Social Costs of Business Enterprise*, revised and extended edition, Nottingham: Spokesman University Paperback.

Lavoie, M. (2009) 'Post Keynesian consumer choice theory and ecological economics', in Holt, R.P.F., Pressman, S. and Spash, C.L. (eds), *Post Keynesian and Ecological Economics: Confronting Environmental Issues*, Cheltenham, UK and Northampton, MA, USA: Edward Elgar Publishing.

Lipsey, R. and Lancaster, K. (1956) 'The general theory of the second best', *Review of Economic Studies*, **2**, pp. 11–32.

Madsen, B., Carroll, N. and Moore Brands, K. (2010) *State of Biodiversity Markets Report: Offset and Compensation Programs Worldwide*, Washington, DC: Ecosystem Marketplace, accessed 10.8.2021 at: https://www.ecosystemmarketplace.com/wp-content/uploads/2015/09/sbdmr.pdf.

Maron, M., Hobbs, R.J., Moilanen, A., Matthews, J.W., Christie, K., Gardner, T.A., Keith, D.A., Lindenmayer, D.B. and McAlpine, C.A. (2012) 'Faustian bargains? Restoration realities in the context of biodiversity offset policies', *Biological Conservation*, **155**, pp. 141–8.

Martinez, K.K. and Neuhoff, K. (2005) 'Allocation of carbon emission certificates in the power sector: how generators profit from grandfathered rights', *Climate Policy*, **5** (1), pp. 61–78.

Martinez-Alier, J., Munda, G. and O'Neill, J. (1998) 'Weak comparability of values as a foundation for ecological economics', *Ecological Economics*, **26**, pp. 277–86.

Meadows, D.H, Meadows, D.L. and Randers, J. (1992) *Beyond the Limits: Global Collapse or a Sustainable Future*, London: Earthscan.

Meadows, D.H, Meadows, D.L., Randers, J. and Behrens III, W.W. (1972) *The Limits to Growth*, London: Earth Island.

Minister for Climate Change and Energy Efficiency (2012) *Securing a Clean Energy Future: Implementing the Australian Government's Climate Change Plan*, Commonwealth of Australia, accessed 10.8.2021 at: https://archive.budget.gov.au/2012–13/ministerial_statements/ms_climate _change.pdf.

Mishan, E.J. (1971) 'The postwar literature on externalities: an interpretative essay', *Journal of Economic Literature*, **9** (1), pp. 1–28.

Norgaard, R.B. (1989) 'The case for methodological pluralism', *Ecological Economics*, **1**, pp. 37–57.

Norgaard, R.B. (1994) *Development Betrayed: The End of Progress and a Coevolutionary Revisioning of the Future*, London: Routledge.

Odum, E. P. (1953) *Fundamentals of Ecology*, Philadelphia, PA: Saunders.

Odum, H. T. (1971) *Environment, Power and Society*, New York: John Wiley.

Perry, N. (2012) 'A post-Keynesian perspective on industry assistance and Australia's carbon pricing policy', *Economic and Labour Relations Review*, **23** (1), pp. 47–66.

Perry, N. (2013) 'Environmental economics and policy', in Harcourt, G.C. and Kriesler, P. (eds), *The Oxford Handbook of Post-Keynesian Economics, Volume 2: Critiques and Methodology*, New York: Oxford University Press.

Perry, N. and Primrose, D. (2015) 'Heterodox economics and the biodiversity crisis', *Journal of Australian Political Economy*, **75**, pp. 11–31.

Söderholm, P. (2001) 'The deliberative approach in environmental valuation', *Journal of Economic Issues*, **35** (2), pp. 487–95.

Spash, C.L. (2010) 'The brave new world of carbon trading', *New Political Economy*, **15** (2), pp. 169–95.

Spash, C.L. (2011) 'Social ecological economics: understanding the past to see the future', *American Journal of Economics and Sociology*, **70** (2), pp. 340–75.

Spash, C.L. (2013) 'The shallow or the deep ecological economics movement?', *Ecological Economics*, **93**, pp. 351–62.

Spash, C.L. and Hanley, N.D. (1995) 'Preferences, information, and biodiversity preservation', *Ecological Economics*, **12**, pp. 191–208.

Tilman, D., Polasky, S. and Lehman, C. (2005) 'Diversity, productivity and temporal stability in the economies of humans and nature', *Journal of Environmental Economics and Management*, **49** (3), pp. 405–26.

United Nations Conference on Sustainable Development (2012) *The Future We Want*, United Nations, accessed 10.8.2021 at: https://sustainabledevelopment.un.org/content/documents/733FutureWeWant .pdf.

van den Bergh, J.C.J.M. (2011) 'Environment versus growth—a criticism of "degrowth" and a plea for "a-growth"', *Ecological Economics*, **70** (5), pp. 881–90.

Vatn, A. (2005) 'Rationality, institutions and environmental policy', *Ecological Economics*, **55** (2), pp. 203–17.

Ward, J.D., Sutton, P.C., Werner, A.D., Costanza, R., Mohr, S.H. and Simmons, C.T. (2016) 'Is decoupling GDP growth from environmental impact possible?', *PLoS ONE*, **11** (10), e0164733.

World Commission on Environment and Development (1987) *Our Common Future*, Oxford: Oxford University Press.

20. Social economics

John B. Davis

Social economics is distinguished from classical political economy and contemporary neoclassical and mainstream economics – and, indeed, from most other political economic approaches – by its goal of explaining and premising the concept of 'social' in economics. Its main organising principle is that the economy is embedded in human society rather than vice versa. Market processes are consequently understood as conditioned by social relationships, with the latter not reducible to economic relations. Thus, human economic behaviour involves a wide range of motivations and concerns that cannot be reduced to explanations of market behaviour alone.

This chapter explores the evolution of this school of thought and its contribution to modern political economy. First, it briefly reviews the origins and early history of social economics, discusses recent post-war social economics, and then identifies new themes in social economics' current research agenda. Second, the chapter discusses social economists' understanding of economic policy and their views about the relationship between ethics and economics, both of which concern the embeddedness relationship between society and markets. Their understanding of policy has two main dimensions: (i) the 'moral limits of markets' approach, regarding some domains of social life as 'off limits' to markets and behaviour driven by self-interest; and (ii) the 'taming the market' approach, aiming to use economic policy to improve social well-being by modifying how markets operate in society. Social economists' views of the relationship between ethics and economics include an alternative vision of the place of ethics in economics, and arguments regarding how this relation may evolve in an interdisciplinary way in the future.

Having considered these ethical issues, the chapter moves on to methodological matters, including the social economics critique of the positive–normative distinction in mainstream economics and the positivist view that economics should practise value-neutrality in order to be a science. It reviews the origins of these views in Hume's is–ought distinction and outlines Putnam's 'entanglement' thesis in response to Hume. It then links mainstream positivism to its understanding of the individual seen as *Homo economicus*, before arguing that the view of economics as inherently value-laden provides an important foundation for disciplinary pluralism that differs from other heterodox arguments for pluralism. Finally, the chapter discusses the goals and values in social economics, identifying its three main subjects of investigation and its three corresponding areas of normative concern: the nature of well-being, values in economic relationships, and the moral status of the person in economic life.

THE ORIGINS AND HISTORICAL DEVELOPMENT OF SOCIAL ECONOMICS

Social economics, as a distinct theoretical approach within political economy, has two main connected histories. The first has its origins and initial development in eighteenth-century

European 'third way' cooperative movements – particularly in France, Belgium, Netherlands, Germany, Italy, and Britain, where early modern capitalism was ascendant. The literature arising from these movements grappled with explaining non-market, local types of economic relationships in broad social system terms. The second, more recent history involves the emergence and development of a professional academic social economics society and scholarly journals in the United States and Canada in the second half of the twentieth century through to the new millennium. The resulting literature focuses on confronting and resisting the market-centric economic analysis that has dominated economics since 1950, while advancing alternative foundations for a more humanistic economics. Social economics thought in this century has subsequently taken on new issues, normative concerns and voices, including from outside Europe and North America, as capitalism has globalised.

'The First 200 Years'

The eighteenth- and nineteenth-century development of social economics in Europe emerged in connection with investigation of the 'social economy' or what has come to be called the 'third way' or 'third sector' of modern capitalist market economies – the *l'économie sociale*, *Gemeinschaft* or *Sozialoekonomie*. These are understood primarily as associational and cooperative forms of community-based economic activities (Nitsch 1987, 1990; Lutz 1999). The state and market had become the dominant forms of economic activity in emerging capitalist economies. Yet, distinct from and intermediate between these two forms, there also existed a wide variety of different kinds of local economic activity that operated neither in terms of market-driven self-interest nor state-based broad national goals, instead focusing on advancing local concerns. Early examples were craft and artisan guilds, farmers' cooperatives, and mutual-aid societies. If the market and modern state were distinctive of post-feudal, national capitalist economies, what became the third sector following their emergence also had its antecedents in transitional pre-capitalist economies, as well as in feudalism when most economic activity remained local.

Thus, whereas (classical) political economy developed primarily around the two more dominant forms of economic activity characterising capitalism – market and state – social economics simultaneously developed around a third form – community-based arrangements. Nitsch (1987) distinguishes three strands of this social economic thought as it developed in Europe over the next two centuries: secular-positive, secular-normative and religious-normative. Seeking an alternative conception of economic systems, this literature was often highly philosophical. Nitsch includes as leading early figures Quesnay, J.S. Mill, Sismondi and Proudhon, and as later influential contributors Walras, Weber, Cassel, Wieser and Pigou. An important non-European figure in this later tradition was the early twentieth-century American J.M. Clark. All were critics, to varying degrees, of the development of classical political economy along the lines of a natural science following Smith, Ricardo and others, with its 'mechanical or mechanistic approach' that 'runs in terms of equilibria and gravitational movements' (Nitsch 1990: 74). All adopted as a guiding principle the idea that economic life is based on human relationships and direct association and social interaction between people. Thus, contrary to political economy's epistemology, social values are deemed fundamental in economic life and economics – not only for explanations of local economic activity, but also for comprehending the economy as a whole.

If market- and state-based forms of economic activity are inherently impersonal in nature, because people interact at 'arm's length' with people they generally do not know, community-based economic activities are inherently more personal, because everyone more or less knows everyone else. Recognising this key difference, in turn, entails comprehending the divergent social values informing each economic activity. Markets and the state give precedence to reciprocity, justice and freedom, because these values apply to people irrespective of who they are. Conversely, when communities emphasise social provisioning, mutuality and dignity, it is because these values apply to people *because* of who they are. Whereas thinking in terms of markets and the state means improving how markets work and compensating people when they fail, cooperative, community-based economic organisations concern themselves with local needs as determined by fraternal groups, family ties, churches, and craft affiliations (see Waters 1984).

Social economic thinking, then, still accepts liberal values in its respect and concern for individuals, since communities are also embedded in larger societies and economies. Yet, in conceiving individuals as primarily members of communities, it simultaneously expands the range of social values needed to explain economic life. People are not abstract, atomistic *Homo economicus* beings; but are who they are by virtue of their places, roles and positions in particular communities. Early debates among advocates of social economics as a distinctive way of thinking thus focused on the relationships between liberal values and those social values grounded in community relationships between people. These fundamental concerns with value remain important to current social economics, albeit thinking about the social values associated with being part of a community has developed as the character of communities themselves has evolved.

Social Economics' Twentieth-century Development

Voluntary, cooperative associations grew and evolved in Europe through the decades that followed the First World War, and social economic thought continued to provide conceptual foundations for this movement. An important dimension of this was the development in the Polanyian tradition of social enterprises that rely on cooperative pacts based on norms of reciprocity (Sacchetti et al. 2021). After 1945, social economics acquired an additional mode of expression and development within a burgeoning US and Canadian academic economics that distanced itself from the newly dominant, market-centric neoclassical approach. It was still influenced by its earlier European origins and association with cooperativism. Indeed, twentieth-century North America had itself seen considerable growth in cooperative associations, including civic organisations, charitable activities, church groups, labour unions, credit unions, women's movements, rural alliances, business and industry trade organisations, fraternal societies, children's clubs and youth movements (Putnam and Garrett 2020: ch. 4).

An additional source of 'third way' thinking arose in reaction to the post-war US economic profession's turn towards a strong defence of markets. Whereas earlier social economists had seen themselves as offering an alternative to classical political economy, post-war social economists in the USA and Canada saw themselves as offering an alternative to US neoclassical economics (see Lutz 1990; Waters 1990, 1993). Central to this development, in institutional terms, was the formation of a professional association of academic social economists. Initially from American Catholic universities, in 1941 these economists created the Catholic Economic Association (CEA), and founded what became the leading journal in social economics, the

Review of Social Economy.[1] From the beginning, however, CEA membership was open to economists with different backgrounds and beliefs and included a diverse variety of theoretical approaches. Catholic social economists advocated solidarism, and drew especially on the writings of the German economist, Heinrich Pesch.[2] Institutional economists in the Veblenian and Ayres traditions were particularly influential, since they emphasised the diversity of institutional arrangements underlying markets.[3] Similarly, Marxist economists demonstrated that class conflict, not economic harmony, was fundamental to the social organisation of capitalist economies.[4] There were also communitarians, Keynesians, Kantians, public policy advocates, and others committed to making ethics central to economics.

Over time, the CEA gradually dissociated itself from its Catholic origins and became an explicitly pluralist organisation. In 1970, at a time of social upheaval in the USA associated with the Vietnam War and counter-cultural youth movements, the CEA changed its name to the Association for Social Economics (ASE) to reflect its more diverse nature and actively opened its membership to heterodox economists. Two developments reflected further changes in the ASE in the years approaching the new millennium.

First, during the 1990s, there was briefly debate within the ASE over whether its pluralism should accommodate neoclassicism. However, that debate died out as most neoclassical economists ultimately left the association, thus affirming the ASE's rejection of neoclassicism as foundational to social economics. Second, men had long dominated the ASE, with women's importance in economics and the economy concomitantly neglected. Feminist economists, however, began to publish in the *Review* in the late 1980s and 1990s (e.g. Ferber and Sander 1989; Ferber and Berg 1991; Emami 1993; Nelson 1993; Figart 2005), which further extended the scope of association social values to include the rejection of patriarchy. One reflection of this change was that the editorial team of the *Review* commencing in 2005 was balanced with two women – Deborah Figart and Martha Starr – and two men – Wilfrid Dolfsma and Robert McMaster. That principle has continued with subsequent editorships of the journal.

Broadly, then, social justice and human dignity became unifying social values for the diverse range of approaches within the association, such that social economics could be characterised as a 'humanistic economics' (Lutz and Lux 1988; Lutz 1999) or a 'real-life' economics (Ekins and Max-Neef 1992). Yet, at this stage, little significant attention was accorded to questions of race, or to the significant divide between rich and poor nations in the global economy.

One factor that would eventually begin to influence the latter was the change in how the *Review* was published. From its origins, it had always been self-published by the CEA/ASE. However, in 1995, Routledge commenced publishing the journal and consequently promoted its international circulation (especially through networks of libraries and institutions). If submissions were still slow to come from the developing world, there was nonetheless increasing attention to international development and worldwide poverty. This gradually became a new dimension to social economics, whose origins and history had been framed by countries' domestic economies.

Social Economics at the New Millennium

Broadly, three factors united most social economists in the second half of the twentieth century, as reflected by what was published in ASE journals, in ASE membership, and in ASE conference presentations.[5]

First, they accept Karl Polanyi's argument that the economy is embedded in human society rather than vice versa (Polanyi 1944; see also Stanfield 1989). Markets do not function independently of social relationships and people are not simply self-interested economic agents. The latter do not 'behave or decide as atoms outside a social context, nor do they adhere slavishly to a script written for them by the particular intersection of social categories that they happen to occupy'. Instead, they are 'embedded in concrete, ongoing systems of social relations' (Granovetter 1985: 487).

Second, social economists thus reject the strong version of Chicago school neoclassicism that explicitly reduces social relationships to market relationships and is built around extending the rational actor model. That view is well represented by Gary Becker's application of this model to non-market domains of social life – such as his economics of the family, which treats children as investment goods and explains marriage according to comparative advantage (Becker 1981). In contrast, social economists argue that economics needs to prioritise the human person. This implies that the utility maximisation model of individuals as essentially self-interested should be abandoned, and a fuller conception of the person in economic life be developed in its place. Combined with Polanyi's embeddedness view, this involves explaining how individuals are socially embedded beings rather than disembedded, atomistic individuals – a *Homo socialis* or *Homo socioeconomicus* rather than *Homo economicus* (O'Boyle 1998; Danner 2002; Davis 2003).

Third, social economists are also united in rejecting the increasingly strident positivism of post-war mainstream economics. For social economists, economics is inherently value-laden, because it is built around values regarding how economic life contributes to social life. Indeed, the mainstream market-centric view of the economy depends on emphasising certain values and excluding others. Seeing the economy as embedded thus requires economic life be explained in terms of the full range of values operating in society.

Social Economics for the Twenty-first Century

The history of social economics since the turn of the millennium is still yet to be written (though see Davis 2009; Davis and Dolfsma 2015; Dolfsma et al. 2016). While social economics has historically explained economic relationships in terms of how communities organise economic life on a local level, the increasing integration of the world economy has meant that social economists have begun to operate with a more complex understanding of community. On this view, communities can extend across great distances, different cultures, and national boundaries when people see themselves sharing common experiences and circumstances. This has increased the importance of poverty and inequality, as well as sustainability and the environment, as important issues for social economists, because these issues particularly affect local communities throughout the world. Communities, then, are still local in regard to people's most immediate and familiar social relationships, but the well-being of people at this level around the world adds a second layer to how community is understood.

Consequently, in addition to more traditional types of community, new types of long-distance community relationships have also emerged between people connected to one another by shared social values. One important manifestation of this particular concern to social economists is the growth and increasing reach of myriad non-profit, non-governmental organisations (NGOs) – such as the International Red Cross, Greenpeace, Médecins Sans Frontières, Save the Children – which have brought together people in NGOs and local populations in a new type of community. If the third sector was formerly associated with national economies, this interaction has produced a new type of international third sector with relationships to markets and states differing from those characterising national third sector organisations.

One prominent example of this new expression of community is a United Nations organisation dedicated to promoting the well-being of the poorest people throughout the world: the United Nations Development Programme (UNDP). This third sector – transcending markets and states – effectively places people from many geographical locations in a single community under the manner of redressing global poverty. Specifically, the Human Development Index (HDI) of the UNDP has made the basic capabilities of people everywhere a matter of international concern and made it possible to design development strategies oriented towards their improvement. From a social values perspective, this elevates justice and dignity as social values for many social economists due to their universal meaning. A global social economics thus redefines the concept of a community to internationalise the social values inherent in local communities.

POLICIES TOWARDS MARKETS AND THE RELATIONSHIP BETWEEN ETHICS AND ECONOMICS

Two primary, interconnected, practical issues divide social economics and most mainstream economics: what policies ought to exist towards markets, and what is the relationship between ethics and economics? The first concerns the nature and status of markets in society; the second reflects on the nature and status of ethics in relation to an economics primarily formulated around how markets work. Both issues can be understood in terms of whether the economy is embedded in society or society is embedded in the economy.

Policies Towards Markets

The first issue dates back to the origins of social economic thinking and is no less important to contemporary social economics. For contrast, consider the standard neoclassical view of policies towards markets to which most mainstream economists adhere. If one believes that society is embedded in the economy, and that one ought to model social relationships on economic relationships, then one is likely to understand policies towards markets solely in terms what would make the latter operate efficiently. Further, if one believes that all social relationships are ultimately economic relationships, one may also hold that markets operate efficiently most of the time, and that when they do not it is only because an 'external' factor (usually government) has interfered with their operation. Policies towards markets in mainstream economics, therefore, are essentially aimed at freeing markets from social interference. A more moderate mainstream position is that markets themselves sometimes fail on their own, and that policies should additionally be designed to deal with market failure. Still, the goal is to make markets operate efficiently.

Conversely, the social economic view denies that all social relationships are ultimately economic relationships and should be modelled as such. Social economists do not favour the complete elimination of market relationships; instead, positing that society should determine the extent and character of the market. On the one hand, where appropriate, this entails promotion and extension of the distinctive and valuable features of human life characterising non-market social relationships. On the other hand, it means resisting and reversing the erosion of these relationships due to the augmentation of markets.

The social economic view of policies towards markets is, thus, concerned with setting boundaries on markets and influencing how they work. There are two primary ways in which this programme has been pursued (see Davis 2019): (i) the 'moral limits of markets' view, and (ii) the 'taming the market' view. Both strategies utilise social values that go well beyond mainstream economics' utilitarian welfarist thinking and employ broader conceptions of human well-being.

The *moral limits of markets* view argues that normative principles cannot be modelled on the logic of market processes, that doing so is often 'morally repugnant' (Roth 2007), and that markets often 'crowd out' normative principles. Thus, there are certain domains of social life that should simply be 'off limits' to markets. In effect, some things in life are 'priceless'.

We can distinguish two versions of this view. The first argues that market processes conflict with and are destructive of normative principles. Michael Sandel (2012) has made this argument in holding that there are some things that 'money can't buy' – exemplified by the practice of slavery in directly placing a price on human life, despite most societies regarding this as morally repugnant. Equally, the commodification of life-saving drugs provided by large pharmaceutical companies may price them out of reach of those most needing them. The second variety of this view posits that, if we allow that normative principles operate in markets, we should be concerned when these 'crowd out' and preclude other, equally valuable normative principles. For example, one might argue that market processes exhibit commutative justice (justice in exchange), but markets typically do not address distributive justice (socially equitable distributions of goods).

The *taming the market* view focuses on how markets themselves work and how they ought to be transformed to be socially acceptable. If the 'off limits' view aims to preserve ethical principles in a distinctive, independent part of human life, this approach aims to make existing markets function in an ethically acceptable way. To do so, proponents favour using economic policy, not to make markets work more efficiently according to their own logic, but to modify how they work to serve ethical goals. For example, ensuring that housing is non-discriminatory makes housing markets work in an ethically more acceptable way. Thus, if mainstream accounts hold that economic policy should be judged only on the basis of its efficiency, the 'taming' view prioritises consideration of which values ought to prevail and in what ways.

Two different strategies may be delineated here: one aiming at intervening in how market outcomes are produced (a direct strategy) and the other seeking to change the underlying conditions affecting market outcomes (an indirect strategy). The former employs interventions such as price controls – for example, price floors in the case of minimum wages and price ceilings in the case of rent controls – and also quantity controls, such as when air and water quality is protected by capping industrial pollutants or when regulations in workplaces exist for worker safety. The indirect strategy aims to influence the underlying conditions in particular markets though such measures as taxes and subsidies, along with those conditions affecting markets generally such as public expenditure and production of social goods. In effect, in the direct strategy markets are 'tamed' from within, while the indirect strategy 'tames' them from without. For most social economists, both strategies are motivated by the goals of improving social well-being, reducing the effects of social stratification, promoting equality irrespective of race, gender, sexual orientation, age, and religion, and sustaining democracy.

The Relationship Between Ethics and Economics

The second broad issue, the relationship between ethics and economics, is especially associated with the more recent development of social economics in reaction to post-war neoclassical positivism. Social economics has not been alone in addressing the relationship between ethics and economics, since other heterodox economics approaches share this concern – indeed, the status of ethics is a key consideration across the social sciences. Neoclassical positivism is addressed in the next section, while here the focus is placed on, first, what status ethics has in relation to economics and, second, how this relationship has been understood in terms of interdisciplinarity.

Regarding the status of ethics and economics, the post-war professionalisation of science and academic research has sharpened and institutionalised differences between different disciplines, as they have come to possess their own research outlets, social structures and standards for individual advancement. In practice, this has tended to fragment intellectual work, especially in social science. Working against this is the trend toward greater interconnectedness between different kinds of social scientific investigations, as well as between descriptive and normative economics.

In this context, one method to explain the current distance between ethics and economics is to identify the different roles historically fulfilled by economics, and then argue that increasing specialisation within science has led economics to largely adopt one role to the exclusion of others. Amartya Sen (1987) articulated this form of argument, distinguishing in the history of economics an engineering role concerned with how to achieve one's ends, and a politics and ethics role addressing what ends people seek to achieve. For Sen, mainstream economics has settled almost exclusively on the former, but ought to reincorporate the latter. Others have subsequently elaborated on his plea for economics to adopt a new, broader identity, particularly in connection with the capabilities approach and its deeper conception of the person (see DeMartino 1999; van Staveren 2001; Crespo 2013).

The relationship between ethics and economics may also be explained through examining how different disciplines relate to one another and recommending alternative relationships between them. In this vein, Mark White (2018) has argued that economics and ethics is a cross-disciplinary field of investigation in which each, as separate disciplines, borrows from the other to serve independent disciplinary goals. Thus, there are actually two economics and ethics fields: one in economics and another in philosophy. Focusing on the former, White argues that, because economics itself is divided between mainstream and heterodox approaches, the development of economics and ethics as a field in economics also follows two opposite paths. The path charted by heterodox economists rejects how the mainstream incorporates ethical concepts and normative reasoning into economics. Conversely, the path trailed by mainstream economists – which he labels 'accommodationist' – works to transform those concepts and reasoning so that they accord with the goals of standard theory, thereby distorting them and sustaining a strong divide between economics and philosophy. For White, reappraising the nature of ethical concepts and normative reasoning within economics would change this.

Might the relationship between ethics and economics change in the future? Since the emergence of behavioural, experimental, and other new schools, economics has moved away from its post-war trajectory as a highly autonomous discipline to increasingly draw on other social sciences – a 'mainstream pluralism' (Davis 2006, 2008). Though there is considerable debate regarding the effects of this on mainstream economics, particularly on rational choice theory, a case can be made that economics will become more interdisciplinary in the future. For social economics, this development is important in that it may move economics towards a more serious appraisal of ethical concepts and normative reasoning, as well as a revaluation of the relationship between ethics and economics. Might the alternative vision of ethics and economics promoted by Sen or the re-appraisal strategy of White provide the more influential pathway forward? The next section turns to some of the main methodological issues that would need to be addressed in each case.

METHODOLOGICAL ISSUES: POSITIVISM VERSUS 'ENTANGLEMENT'

The 'accommodationist' stance of mainstream economics towards ethics and economics has foundations in the assumption that all social relationships are ultimately economic ones. However, David Hume's (1739) famous thesis that 'ought' statements cannot be derived from 'is' statements also provides a basis for the mainstream's positivist understanding of economics as a value-free science. While Hume's view was about the nature of language, mainstream economics extends it to the nature of science. This is questionable for at least two reasons.

First, economics is also a policy science, so adopting the Hume thesis suggests that there is an unbridgeable gulf between positive and normative economics. The position of mainstream economics is that policymakers can use the results of economic analysis as they choose – and that the analysis implies nothing about what policies *ought* to be adopted. However, this misrepresents the close connection between economic analysis, formulated in terms of the efficient operation of free, competitive markets, and Pareto efficiency policy recommendations. Contrary to the idea that policy is carried out independently of economic analysis, standard economic analysis implies those Pareto recommendations.

Second, standard economic formulations centred on the behaviour of atomistic *Homo economicus* economic agents reduce all social relationships to isolated interactions between self-regarding individuals. Social economists recognise many types of interaction and relations between people who can be other-regarding, caring and altruistic, as well as self-regarding. What the purportedly positive standard economics does, then, is determine what type of social world people *ought* to occupy – specifically, a neoliberal world – which depends on a particular set of values.

On both counts, the standard mainstream economic claim to be a value-free science is a masquerade because of its distinctive value-laden view of the economic world. Simultaneously, while asserting itself to be value-free, the mainstream charges that alternative approaches that are explicit about their value foundations fall short as science because they are value-laden.

Social economists argue that not only is economics a value-laden science but – as Myrdal (1958), Boulding (1969) and many others have noted – a scientific stance towards economic practice requires being explicit about the value assumptions informing one's explanations. That economics is intrinsically value-laden was argued by philosopher Hilary Putnam (2002), based on a critique of Hume's 'is–ought' distinction regarding language. Putnam demonstrated that 'is' statements often contain implicit value claims, so that, though they may appear to simply describe the world and avoid value terms, language-users are often well aware of these implicit meanings. Rather than being value-free, then, our 'is' statements are often 'entangled' with 'ought' statements. His famous example is: 'The Roman emperor Nero was cruel.' While, on the surface this is a value-free statement, understanding its meaning depends on comprehending the values people associate with 'cruel' as a description of Nero. For Putnam, mainstream economics is consequently highly 'entangled' with values it promotes at the expense of others it suppresses (see Davis 2015).

Social economists seek to make this explicit and to open economics to examination of the 'entanglement' of values and economic life. Doing so changes the nature of economic analysis itself, since how economists explain economic life differs according to their own 'entanglement' with values. Indeed, social economists' original interest in a third sector of the economy – where people interact in cooperative ways, show trust for one another, and exhibit care towards others – was motivated by their belief that the values underlying these activities were important and often neglected or discouraged by the development of capitalism. The same is true of contemporary social economists interested in cooperative relationships in a global world economy.

Furthermore, if we suppose that people are diverse and occupy very different social circumstances, then there are also many different value foundations in economics and, correspondingly, myriad ways to conduct economic analysis. This contrasts with the 'one-size-fits-all' approach of mainstream economics, which assumes that people essentially correspond to rational individuals and that there is only one truly 'scientific' economics (thereby implicitly endorsing one set of values). Yet, economics is intrinsically a pluralistic science in virtue of its value-ladenness. Thus, while defences of pluralism along methodological lines emphasise different theoretical commitments in economics (see Dow 1997), social economics stresses the links between those commitments and different economists' normative allegiances.

THE NORMATIVE GOALS AND SOCIAL VALUES OF SOCIAL ECONOMICS

Three main subjects of investigation in social economics can be distinguished: how economic life supports people's livelihoods, the nature of social relationships in economic settings, and what the person is in economic life. These subjects, in turn, point towards three primary areas of normative concern for social economists: the nature of well-being, values in economic relationships, and the moral status of the person in economic life.

The Nature of Well-being in Economic Life

On the Polanyian embeddedness view discussed above, economic life is a means to maintaining and improving people's well-being, not the purpose of life itself. While mainstream economics conceives of economic life in narrow terms as constrained by scarcity, social economists follow a long tradition in economics that frames economic life in terms of abundance (Peach and Dugger 2006; Dugger and Peach 2009). From this perspective, the economy is a means of social provisioning – or a means of producing – not what people can afford, but what they need to live their lives both in and outside markets by drawing on the technologies and level of knowledge available at any given time. That is, the economy ought to promote not just better living standards and reductions in poverty and inequality: it should promote full human flourishing (Figart 2007).

At first glance, this conception of social provisioning may appear no different from mainstream economics' concept of welfare. However, there is a fundamental difference. The latter concept is formulated as the satisfaction of individual preferences, which are defined as isolated individuals' private, subjective tastes. In contrast, the concept of social provisioning is based on comprehending people as social beings whose well-being transcends their private tastes, and includes the nature of their social relationships, concern for others, and their existence in communities in which they live. By comparison, the mainstream welfare concept only calls for markets to work optimally as if people's lives are fully represented by their involvement in markets.

The mainstream representation of welfare in terms of private preferences is also a basis for declaring that economics should be value-free, since those preferences are individual tastes, not social values. As a normative concept, welfare is extremely narrow: essentially limited to the libertarian notion that people should be free to pursue their own goals. This opens the door to malevolent and socially harmful tastes, which the concept of taste as private does not prohibit. It also forecloses encompassing within our understanding of well-being the diverse social values that people share. In contrast, social provisioning potentially encompasses all ideas about well-being and is therefore able to evolve in what it values as social priorities also change.

It is difficult, then, to state simply what social provisioning means in normative terms. One powerful principle which emphasises the centrality of community suggests that it entails promoting the common good (Lutz 1999), as open-ended as that can be. We might, however, resist searching for a single idea to capture what social provisioning involves if we wish to emphasise that communities themselves determine what they value. Sen (2005) has made this point in resisting Martha Nussbaum's (2000) recommendation that we should identify a specific list of capabilities that together constitute the social good. This is supported by the fact that the HDI used by the UNDP to measure capabilities has changed and evolved since its original adoption to reflect both issues of measurement and developing perceptions of what is socially valuable.

Values in Economic Relationships

In mainstream economics, the only values exhibited by social relationships are market values because the former are assumed to be ultimately reducible to their market form. For social economists, market relationships are only a sub-set of broader social relationships which exhibit a much wider range of social values. For instance, if a key social value promoted by market relationships is economic freedom – or that only an individual is 'free to choose' (Friedman 1962) – freedom in a wider social sense also means being free from coercion and compulsion of all kinds and having the capacity to act freely regardless of one's circumstances. Similarly, while market relationships may promote justice in exchange, or commutative justice, social economics also posits the centrality of distributive and procedural justice – that is, whether resources, well-being, and opportunities in life are fairly and equitably distributed across people. Justice, in this latter sense, is indeed a precondition of commutative justice.

Thus, while social interactions in markets are understood in mainstream economics as exchanges between equals, since goods are exchanged at a single price, these 'equal exchanges' can be unequal when the circumstances of the people involved are markedly different. This produces two sets of social values promoted by social economists, associated with the two interpretations of social policy towards markets distinguished above: the 'off limits' and 'taming the market' views. For the first, if inequality in exchange is severe from a distributive justice perspective – as when exchanges are exploitive – markets should not be allowed to exist. For the second, when inequality in exchange is remediable, the functioning of markets should be changed to prevent this – either directly through such mechanisms as price controls, or indirectly by modifying the underlying conditions affecting markets through policies such as the redistribution of wealth.

At the level of human motivation, social economists associate social values with how people orient towards one another in ways that transcend the 'equals for equals' principle of exchange. If that principle enforces a reciprocal relation between people, social economists also examine how people are motivated to act in a unidirectional manner toward others through caring (Davis and McMaster 2017) and gift relationships (Cedrini and Marchionatti 2017). Caring evokes the value of altruistic concern for others, while gift relationships are built around values that create trust between people. Both reflect ways in which people directly interact with each other beyond systems of isolated market interactions.

The Moral Status of the Person in Economic Life

Defences of economic freedom are often coupled with defences of the legal rights that people need to participate effectively in markets. The wider sense of freedom defended by social economists entails a broader set of rights – human rights – that people need to secure their economic well-being in and beyond markets. Human rights accrue to people on the same basis as narrower legal rights do – that people are entitled to pursue their livelihoods as best they can while not causing harm to others. Human rights, in this sense, are pre-eminently individual rights; but social economists also defend community rights, because they see the inexorable interrelation between people's well-being as individuals and their lives in communities.

Defences of human rights are motivated by a deep social value: namely, that people have inherent value and are entitled to respect simply by virtue of being human. Social economists make this the central, anchoring value of life – economic and otherwise – and refer to it as the dignity of the person. In Kantian philosophy, people are ends in themselves, have intrinsic worth, and ought never be a means to others' purposes (White 2011). This means that ethics and economic policy should always be organised around reducing human vulnerability and promoting people's choices in life to the extent that this avoids causing harm to others (DeMartino 2019).

Respect for others as human beings also means respecting others' choices in the expectation that people's choices and lives can be diverse. That is, the value of human dignity involves valuing human diversity and differences between people. This is a shared human value in that what people have in common is not some single characteristic, but that people are all uniquely different from one another. What people have in common, that is, is their diversity.

Overall, social economists' social values are a reflection of, and a normative foundation for, their analysis of economic life lived in close interaction with others – whether in local or more far-reaching communities. Shared life with others not only invests all people with essential human dignity, but calls for an open, pluralist economic analysis. In this respect, social economics elevates and prioritises the 'social' in economic life and human life more broadly, and thereby offers a humanistic, real-life alternative to mainstream economics.

NOTES

1. In 1971, the ASE started a second journal, the *Forum for Social Economics*. A third social economics journal, the *International Journal of Social Economics* was also founded in the UK in 1974. See Showler (1974) in the inaugural issue of the latter for a statement of the meaning and content of social economics that characterises it as a 'new' approach with earlier antecedents.
2. Pesch's famous work was his *Lehrbuch* (Pesch 1904–23; see Mulcahy 1952; Mueller 1977).
3. For a radical institutionalist expression of this current, see Dugger and Waller (1996).
4. See the special issues of the *Review of Social Economy* devoted to Marx's thinking (Waters 1979), especially the lead paper by Elliott (1979) and that on analytical Marxism by Elliott and Davis (1989).
5. It should be noted that the CEA joined the re-organised Allied Social Science Associations (ASSA) in 1951 (Clary 2008) and, accordingly, there is a long history of CEA/ASE conference presentations at the annual ASSA meetings.

REFERENCES

Becker, G. (1981) *A Treatise on the Family*, Cambridge, MA: Harvard University Press.
Boulding, K. (1969) 'Economics as a Moral Science', *American Economic Review*, **59** (1), pp. 1–12.
Cedrini, M. and Marchionatti, R. (2017) 'Theoretical and Practical Relevance of the Concept of the Gift to the Development of a Non-Imperialist Economics', *Review of Radical Political Economics*, **49** (4), pp. 633–49.
Clary, B.J. (2008) 'The Evolution of the Allied Social Science Associations', *American Journal of Economics and Sociology*, **67** (5), pp. 985–1005.
Crespo, R. (2013) *Philosophy of the Economy: An Aristotelian Approach*, Basingstoke: Palgrave Macmillan.
Danner, P. (2002) *The Economic Person: Acting and Analyzing*, Lanham, MD: Rowman and Littlefield.
Davis, J. (2003) *The Theory of the Individual in Economics*, London: Routledge.
Davis, J. (2006) 'The Turn in Economics: Neoclassical Dominance to Mainstream Pluralism?' *Journal of Institutional Economics*, **2** (1), pp. 1–20.
Davis, J. (2008) 'The Turn in Recent Economics and Return of Orthodoxy', *Cambridge Journal of Economics*, **32** (3), pp. 349–66.
Davis, J. (2009) *Global Social Economy: Development, Work and Policy*, London: Routledge.
Davis, J. (2015) 'Economists' Odd Stand on the Positive-Normative Distinction: A Behavioral Economics View', in DeMartino, G. and McCloskey, D. (eds), *The Oxford Handbook of Professional Economic Ethics: Views from the Economics Profession and Beyond*, Oxford: Oxford University Press, pp. 200–18.
Davis, J. (2019) 'Ethics and Economics: A Complex Systems Approach', in White, M. (ed.), *Oxford Handbook on Ethics and Economics*, Oxford: Oxford University Press, pp. 208–28.
Davis, J. and Dolfsma, W. (eds) (2015) *The Elgar Companion to Social Economics*, 2nd edition, Cheltenham, UK and Northampton, MA, USA: Edward Elgar Publishing.
Davis, J. and McMaster, R. (2017) *Health Care Economics*, London: Routledge.
DeMartino, G. (1999) *Global Economy, Global Justice: Theoretical Objections and Policy Alternatives to Neoliberalism*, London: Routledge.
DeMartino, G. (2019) 'Econogenic Harm and the Case for "Economy Harm Profile" Analysis', *New Political Economy*, **24** (6), pp. 798–815.
Dolfsma, W., Figart, D., McMaster, R., Mutari, E. and White, M. (eds) (2016) *Social Economics*, Critical Concepts in Economics Series, London: Routledge.
Dow, S.C. (1997) 'Methodological Pluralism and Pluralism of Method', in Salanti, A. and Screpanti, E. (eds), *Pluralism in Economics: Theory, History and Methodology*, Cheltenham, UK and Northampton, MA, USA: Edward Elgar Publishing, pp. 89–99.
Dugger, W. and Peach, J. (2009) *Economic Abundance: An Introduction*, London: Routledge.

Dugger, W. and Waller, W. (1996) 'Radical Institutionalism: From Technological to Democratic Instrumentalism', *Review of Social Economy*, **54** (2), pp. 169–90.

Ekins, P. and Max-Neef, M. (eds) (1992) *Real-Life Economics: Understanding Wealth Creation*, London: Routledge.

Elliott, J.E. (1979) 'Social and Institutional Dimensions of Marx's Theory of Capitalism', *Review of Social Economy*, **37** (3), pp. 261–74.

Elliott, J.E. and Davis, J. (eds) (1989) 'Issues in Contemporary Marxism', *Review of Social Economy*, **47** (4), pp. 338–436.

Emami, Z. (1993) 'Challenges Facing Social Economics in the Twenty-First Century: A Feminist Perspective', *Review of Social Economy*, **51** (4), pp. 416–25.

Ferber, M. and Berg, H. (1991) 'Labor Force Participation of Women and the Sex Ratio: A Cross-Country Analysis', *Review of Social Economy*, **49** (1), pp. 2–19.

Ferber, M. and Sander, W. (1989) 'Of Women, Men, and Divorce: Not by Economics Alone', *Review of Social Economy*, **47** (1), pp. 15–26.

Figart, D. (2005) 'Gender as More than a Dummy Variable: Feminist Approaches to Discrimination', *Review of Social Economy*, **58** (3), pp. 509–36.

Figart, D. (2007) 'Social Responsibility for Living Standards', *Review of Social Economy*, **65** (4), pp. 391–405.

Friedman, M. (1962) *Capitalism and Freedom*, Chicago, IL: University of Chicago Press.

Granovetter, M. (1985) 'Economic Action and Social Structure: The Problem of Embeddedness', *American Journal of Sociology*, **91** (3), pp. 481–510.

Hume, D. (1739) *A Treatise of Human Nature*, ed. Selby-Bigge, L.A; 2nd edition, revised by Nidditch, P.H., Oxford: Clarendon Press, 1978.

Lutz, M. (1990) 'Emphasizing the Social: Social Economics and Socio-Economics', *Review of Social Economy*, **48** (3), pp. 303–20.

Lutz, M. (1999) *Economics for the Common Good: Two Centuries of Social Economic Thought in the Humanistic Tradition*, London: Routledge.

Lutz, M. and Lux, K. (1988) *Humanistic Economics: The New Challenge*, New York: Bootstrap Press.

Mueller, F. (1977) 'Social Economics: The Perspective of Pesch and Solidarism', *Review of Social Economy*, **35** (3), pp. 293–7.

Mulcahy, R. (1952) *The Economics of Heinrich Pesch*, New York: Henry Holt.

Myrdal, G. (1958) *Value in Social Theory*, London: Routledge.

Nelson, J. (1993) 'Gender and Economic Ideologies', *Review of Social Economy*, **51** (3), pp. 287–301.

Nitsch, T. (1987) 'Social Economics: From Search for Identity to Quest for Roots', *International Journal of Social Economics*, **14** (3–5), pp. 70–90.

Nitsch, T. (1990) 'Social Economics: The First 200 Years', in Lutz, M. (ed.), *Social Economics: Retrospect and Prospect*, Boston, MA, Dordrecht and London: Kluwer, pp. 5–90.

Nussbaum, M. (2000) *Women and Human Development: The Capabilities Approach*, Cambridge: Cambridge University Press.

O'Boyle, E.J. (1998) *Personalist Economics: Moral Convictions, Economic Realities, and Social Action*, Basingstoke: Palgrave.

Peach, J. and Dugger, W. (2006) 'An Intellectual History of Abundance', *Journal of Economic Issues*, **40** (3), pp. 693–706.

Pesch, H. (1904–23) *Lehrbuch der Nationalökonomie*, 5 volumes, Freiburg im Breisgau: Herder.

Polanyi, K. (1944) *The Great Transformation*, Boston, MA: Beacon Press.

Putnam, H. (2002) *The Collapse of the Fact/Value Dichotomy and Other Essays*, Cambridge, MA: Harvard University Press.

Putnam, R., with Garrett, S. (2020) *The Upswing: How America Came Together a Century Ago and How We can Do It Again*, New York: Simon Schuster.

Roth, A.E. (2007) 'Repugnance as a Constraint on Markets', *Journal of Economic Perspectives*, **21** (3), pp. 37–58.

Sacchetti, S., Borzaga, C. and Tortia, E. (2021) 'The Institutions of Livelihood and Social Enterprise Systems', *Forum for Social Economics*, http://doi.org/10.1080/07360932.2021.1927792.

Sandel, M. (2012) *What Money Can't Buy: The Moral Limits of Markets*, New York: Farrar, Straus and Giroux.

Sen, A. (1987) *On Ethics and Economics*, Oxford: Basil Blackwell.

Sen, A. (2005) 'Human Rights and Capabilities', *Journal of Human Development*, **6** (2), pp. 151–66.

Stanfield, J.R. (1989) 'Karl Polanyi and Contemporary Economic Thought', *Review of Social Economy*, **47** (3), pp. 266–92.

van Staveren, I. (2001) *The Values of Economics: An Aristotelian Perspective*, London: Routledge.

Waters, W. (ed.) (1979) 'Karl Marx, Social Economist', *Review of Social Economy*, **37** (3), pp. 261–387.

Waters, W. (ed.) (1984) 'Community Dimensions of Economic Enterprise', *Review of Social Economy*, **42** (3), pp. 219–438.

Waters, W. (1990) 'Evolution of Social Economics in America', in Lutz, M. (ed.), *Social Economics: Retrospect and Prospect*, Boston, MA, Dordrecht and London: Kluwer, pp. 91–117.

Waters, W. (1993) 'A Review of the Troops: Social Economics in the Twentieth Century', *Review of Social Economy*, **51** (3), pp. 262–86.

White, M. (2011) *Kantian Ethics and Economics: Autonomy, Dignity, and Character*, Stanford, CA: Stanford University Press.

White, M. (2018) 'On the Relationship between Economics and Ethics', *Annals of the Fondazione Luigi Einaudi*, **52** (1), pp. 47–57.

21. A social property relations approach to class, gender, race

Andreas Bieler and Adam David Morton

A dualist framing of history recurs in mainstream international studies. Distinct spheres – such as 'agents' and 'structures', 'politics' and 'economics', or 'states' and 'markets' – are identified as separate entities in a relationship of *ontological exteriority* (Morton 2013: 139–43). By taking the separate appearance of the state and market as their starting point of analysis, they fail to acknowledge the historical specificity of the current capitalist period. Hence, there is the need for a historical materialist moment, in which it is asked why it is that the state and market, the political and the economic, appear as separate in the first place (Bieler and Morton 2018: 3–23). This assertion is attached to a *philosophy of internal relations*, which implies that the character of capital is considered as a social relation in such a way that the internal ties between the relations of production, state–civil society, and conditions of class struggle can be realised (Ollman 1976: 48). On the basis of such a philosophy of internal relations, it can then be comprehended that it is the specific ways in which capitalist social relations of production are organised that makes the state and market appear as separate spheres.

This chapter provides an introduction to (and an example of) this particular political economic perspective, developing a historical materialist analysis with an emphasis on social property relations. It is an approach that draws on Marx but also on more recent contributions by Bertell Ollman, Ellen Meiksins Wood and Robert Brenner, which we have previously applied in our own writing on global political economy (such as Bieler and Morton 2018). In this current chapter our particular focus is to explain the dialectical matrix of class, gender and race. This is significant because historical materialist perspectives are often accused of economic reductionism, focusing on class but tending to neglect other factors such as gender and race. In this chapter, we engage with recent feminist and post-colonial scholarship in order to show how an emphasis on the internal relations between class, gender and race can be accomplished through an analytical focus on class struggle within a historical materialist perspective.

In the next section, we discuss how a historical materialist approach is able to define capitalism in a way that acknowledges its historical specificity. Subsequently, our attention turns towards the way the internal relations between class and gender can be incorporated in such an analysis, emphasising capitalist dynamics around exploitation, resistance and struggle. This is followed by a section that does the same for the internal relations between class and race, emphasising the legacy of colonialism and how racism shapes capitalist development. The conclusion points towards a recentring of historical materialism around the dialectical matrix of class, race and gender.

THE HISTORICAL EMERGENCE OF CAPITALISM

Historically, capitalism emerged in England in the sixteenth century when, against the background of the enclosures of the commons, new social property relations were established around the private ownership of land and agricultural wage labour. Once established in England, capitalism then expanded outward within an already existing international system of absolutist states along lines of uneven and combined development. Thus, it is the particular way production is organised that is the key characteristic of capitalism. Due to the spatially expansive drive of capitalist competition and its crisis tendencies, it is structurally conditioned to seek relentlessly ever greater forms of surplus value.

Based on wage labour and the private ownership of the means of production, the extraction of surplus labour is not directly politically enforced, unlike in feudalism, because those who do not own the means of production are 'free' to sell their labour power (Wood 1995: 29, 34). Strictly speaking, nobody is forced to work for a particular employer. However, without owning one's means of production, people are indirectly forced to look for paid employment. They are compelled to sell their labour power in order to reproduce themselves. Thus, to understand inequality and exploitation in capitalism, we need to investigate the 'hidden abode of production, on whose threshold there hangs the notice "No admittance except on business". Here we shall see, not only how capital produces, but how capital is itself produced. The secret of profit-making must at last be laid bare' (Marx [1867] 1990: 279–80).

Under capitalism, the sole purpose of capital is to accumulate surplus value, not in order to satisfy any needs, but as a goal in itself. Instead of private consumption, profits constantly have to be re-invested in order to generate yet further surplus value and, thus, for capitalists to stay ahead under competitive pressures. The type of production in which capital is invested does not much matter: whatever offers the prospect of the highest rate of return is preferred. Surplus value is then used to generate yet more surplus value in an ongoing process. Yet the question remains: where does this relentless pressure towards constantly increasing accumulation of surplus value come from? The answer depends on how capitalism and its emergence as the globally dominant mode of production is understood.

From the perspective of world-systems analysis, capitalism is understood as 'production for sale in a market in which the object is to realise the maximum profit' (Wallerstein 1979: 15). So, the origins of capitalism are linked to an expanding world market as 'a capitalist mode is one in which production is for exchange; that is, it is determined by its profitability on a market' (Wallerstein 1979: 159). Similarly, processes of state formation and the emergence of an international states system are closely linked to the emergence of capitalism. As Wallerstein argues, 'the development of strong states in the core areas of the European world was an essential component of the development of modern capitalism' (Wallerstein 1974: 134). State formation and capitalism are regarded as two sides of the same coin.

Nevertheless, by basing its argument on a commercialisation model of market exchange relations, this definition of capitalism assumes that the outward expansion of capitalism arises from individual greed (Teschke 2003: 140). Like neoclassical economics and its understanding of the utility-maximising *Homo economicus*, world-systems analysis overlooks the systemic compulsion to constant outward expansion, which goes far beyond the satisfaction of individual pleasures. As Marx had already pointed out, 'the idea that accumulation is achieved at the expense of consumption … is an illusion that contradicts the essence of capitalist production, in as much as it assumes that the purpose and driving motive of this is consumption, and not the grabbing of surplus-value and its capitalisation, i.e. accumulation' (Marx [1884] 1978: 579). Unsurprisingly, the feminist Marxist Silvia Federici, who also relies on a commercialisation definition of capitalism as a 500-year-long phenomenon based on a world market, is unable to conceptualise and explore the spatially uneven developmental conditions of capitalist expansion. 'How can we account', she wonders, 'for the fact that after five hundred years of relentless exploitation of workers across the planet, the capitalist class in its different embodiments still needs to pauperise multitudes of people worldwide?' (Federici 2019: 19).

Contrasting with world-system analysis is the social property relations approach, developed by Robert Brenner (1986), Ellen Meiksins Wood (1995) and others, which we adapt in our definition of capitalism. Through a detailed analysis of variances in social property relations, Brenner argues that it was in medieval England that a specific set of social property relations, based on a landlord/capitalist tenant/wage-labourer structure, was established (Brenner 1985: 46–9). As a result of the enclosures of the commons, peasants were driven from the land and thereby separated from their means of subsistence. This then led to a situation in which both the capitalist tenants and the wage-labourers depended on the market for their social reproduction. Each capitalist tenant was in competition with other capitalist tenants for market share, while peasants competed with each other for wage labour as the only way to ensure their survival. Importantly, the specificity of this development was not facilitated by the emerging world market and the growing trade in luxury goods for the elites, but the development of a unique domestic economy based on a growing mass market for cheap basic goods such as foodstuffs and cotton cloth (Brenner 2001: 233; Wood 2002b: 82). To quote Wood: 'This system was unique in its dependence on intensive as distinct from extensive expansion, on the extraction of surplus value created in production as distinct from profit in the sphere of circulation, on economic growth based on increasing productivity and competition within a single market, in other words, on capitalism' (Wood 2002a: 23). While Brenner asserts the importance of the emergence of agrarian capitalism in England in the sixteenth century as a result of the enclosures, he also demonstrates how this was a rather specific development, very different from agricultural development in France, where peasant ownership of the land continued, or Eastern Europe that was characterised by the 're-feudalisation' of the peasantry.

This definition of capitalism based on the social property relations approach has important implications for the question of the relation between the emergence of capitalism and state formation. In the historically peculiar case of state formation in England, the development of capitalism and the state was intertwined. Thus, in England,

> state formation took the form of a cooperative project, a kind of division of labour between political and economic power, between the monarchical state and the aristocratic ruling class, between a central political power that enjoyed a virtual monopoly of coercive force [...] and an economic power based on private property in land more concentrated than elsewhere in Europe. (Wood 2002a: 172)

In contrast to world-systems analysis, however, in different places across continental Europe, capitalism was 'born into' the prior system-of-states (Wood 1991: 26). It was propelled through an anterior states system configured by conditions of uneven and combined development as a structuring principle of 'the international' (Teschke 2003; Lacher 2006). The differentiation of the moment of appropriation through market imperatives from the moment of coercion in the state, in so doing, allocated two distinct complementary spheres, with capital having a unique capacity for spatial expansion (Wood 2002a: 177–8). The spatially fragmented order of multiple states has nevertheless remained an assiduous feature of the uneven development of capitalism, with global capital advancing rather than dissolving the unevenness of state territoriality and political space (Wood 2002a: 180–1; Wood 2006: 25–6).

Due to the way in which capitalist social relations of production are organised around wage labour and the private ownership or control of the means of production, capitalism is characterised by a set of key structuring conditions of uneven development (Bieler and Morton 2018: 38–41). First, because not only labour but also capital has to reproduce itself through the market, the compulsion of competitiveness makes capitalism such a dynamic mode of production. At the same time, however, capitalism is also crisis-ridden. This is the second structuring condition, arising from regular 'crises of overaccumulation' when surpluses of both capital and labour can no longer be brought together in a productive way within capitalist social relations of production (Harvey 1985: 132).

To overcome these crises, capital has a number of strategies at its disposal. As Marx and Engels already pointed out in the Communist Manifesto (Marx and Engels [1848] 1998: 18), capital can increase exploitation of the existing workforce through salary cuts and harsher working conditions. Alternatively, it can engage in 'creative destruction' of existing production capacities. Thus, for example, two companies in the same sector may merge and shut down part of their production lines. Additionally, however, as the third structuring condition, there is also the relentless pressure to expand outward in the attempt to overcome crises. Rosa Luxemburg had already pointed to 'the inherent contradiction between the unlimited expansive capacity of the productive forces and the limited expansive capacity of social consumption under conditions of capitalist distribution' (Luxemburg [1913] 2003: 323; see also Bieler et. al. 2016). These crises, she argued, cannot be solved within capitalism itself. Instead, new markets have to be opened or expanded elsewhere. 'The decisive fact is that the surplus value cannot be realised by sale either to workers or to capitalists, but only if it is sold to such social organisations or strata whose own mode of production is not capitalistic' (Luxemburg [1913] 2003: 332). One example is Britain's opening up of China and India for the export of textile goods amongst other commodities during the nineteenth century, supported by brute force if necessary, leading to the Opium Wars with China in 1839 to 1842 and 1856 to 1860. Equally important, though, is outward expansion in the search for cheaper labour. Dutch capitalism in the seventeenth century depended on access to cheap labour in Asia (Anievas and Nişancıoğlu 2015: 226–7). More recently, the overcoming of the worldwide recession during the 1970s relied on transferring labour-intensive production to selective locations in the global South.

Expansion, therefore, does not only imply capitalist expansion into non-capitalist space, but can equally take place through a re-organisation of existing centre–periphery relations within global capitalism. The latest re-organisation of this type is reflected in the rolling out of an expanded free-trade regime, extending beyond the trade in goods to trade in services, public procurement and including investment measures and intellectual property rights (Bieler and Morton 2014: 40–42). Finally, expansion can also be internally related through processes of commodification of areas not yet commodified or which had previously been de-commodified (Harvey 2006: 44–50).

Starting political economic analysis through a focus on social property relations (or relations of production), also allows the identification of key collective agency. Due to the way production is organised around the private ownership or control of the means of production and wage labour, two main classes oppose each other. Capital, on one hand, owning the means of production; and labour, on the other hand, being 'free' to sell its labour power. Analytically, these two classes can then be further divided into different fractions of capital and labour, depending on the particular scale of production (e.g. national versus transnational capital and labour) or orientation of production (e.g. producing predominantly for the domestic market or being internationally, export-oriented) (Bieler 2000: 10–11; Bieler 2006: 32–5). In order to grasp both structure and agency and their internal relations within the analysis, the focus has to be on class struggle as the heuristic device to investigate key dynamics underpinning struggles in the global political economy (Bieler and Morton 2018: 49–50).

However, this focus on the social relations of production implies the danger that the main emphasis is placed on workers, narrowly defined, as a privileged agent of transformation, making the workplace the main location of struggle. Indeed, due to trade unions' prominent role in the political economies of advanced capitalist countries after the Second World War, scholarship on resistance, including historical materialist research, often reduced class struggle to conflicts at the workplace and to struggles between workers and employers or trade unions and employers' associations as the respective institutional expressions (Barker 2013: 52). In order to avoid this tendency, as a first step, we need to define 'labour' more broadly, going beyond the capitalist workplace, and understand that there will be organisations different from trade unions that are also involved in class struggle. Moreover, as Camfield (2002: 42) notes, 'Here it is very important to heed the feminist insistence that work is much more than what is done for wages. Much human labour is unpaid, including the unpaid domestic labour, largely carried out by women.'

CONCEPTUALISING THE INTERNALITY OF CLASS AND GENDER

How are the internal relations between class and gender conceptualised within a historical materialist perspective? This needs careful consideration. Some feminists have criticised the often-exclusive focus by historical materialist approaches on the sphere of production and confrontations between employers and workers. Thus: 'Large swathes of historical-materialist analysis have failed to understand and emphasise the interdependence between relations of production and reproduction, or to capture the role of gender and sexuality in forms and struc-tures of oppression that shape capitalism's social matrix in terms of both material conditions and ideologies (Ferguson et al. 2016: 28–9). How then can we more adequately conceptualise the internal relations between class and gender? Ellen Meiksins Wood has argued that 'if cap-italism derives advantages from racism or sexism, it is not because of any structural tendency in capitalism toward racial inequality or gender oppression, but on the contrary because they disguise the structural realities of the capitalist system and because they divide the working class' (Wood 2002c: 279). Yet our argument is that, whereas it is entirely fitting to articulate that 'the disappearance of class inequalities [...] is by definition incompatible with capitalism' (Wood 1995: 259), there is a set of much more problematic assertions buried within this topog-raphy of social identities, human emancipation and capitalism.

It may seem reasonable to contend that capitalism is 'uniquely indifferent' to the social identities of the people it exploits (Wood 1995: 266). This stance, after all, finds wider support elsewhere, focusing on capitalists' indifference to how production unfolds. For example, William Clare Roberts highlights the case of Mary Anne Walkley in the chapter on the working day from *Capital, Volume I*. The suffering and death of Mary Anne Walkley, he argues, did not result from her own individuality but rather from the circumstances that attended her labours, ensuing from capitalist exploitation and her role qua labourer. Hence the reassertion that 'the aim of capital – the realisation of surplus value – is indifferent to the particular aim of the labour on which it depends' (Roberts 2017: 126). With a similar echo, Moishe Postone (1993: 281, emphasis added) has argued that 'Marx's analysis of the process of production seen as a process of creating value provides an initial logical determination of the *indifference, structurally implicit in capitalism*, toward the production of specific products.'

Nevertheless, demanding more Marxist Feminist curiosity into the historical and contemporary racialised and patriarchal ordering of the political economy of race and gender is surely required here, because it is incorrect to enforce the monochromatic viewpoint that, whereas class is constitutive of capitalism, wider gender and racial inequalities are not (Wood 1995: 259). In fact, racial domination and gender oppression are central constitutive underpinnings in the making of capitalism, and a Marxist Feminist curiosity would immediately and easily reveal the specification of such relations of power as class relations.

Indeed, returning to Marx, the death of Mary Anne Walkley in 1863 from 'simple over-work' should be revisited. For doing so would reveal a much more complex intertwining of expropriative practices of concrete labour power. Not all labourers are alike, for Mary Anne Walkley is presented as a *white slave*, officially deceased due to apoplexy, but whose labouring for more than 26 hours was due as much to garment-making for the guests at a ball given by the Princess of Wales; as the gendered working conditions of consumption, undernourishment and malnutrition; as the forced supply of alcohol to her and other women to sustain their failing labour-power; as the demand for needlewomen (over men) to 'conjure up magnificent dresses for the noble ladies', rather than simply over-work and overcrowding within the capitalist specificities of the millinery industry (Marx [1867] 1990: 364–5). This alternative reading starts to reveal 'the coercive underbelly of capitalist value creation' and violence without the cost of gender-blindness (Ferguson 2019: 121). Equally it is meaningful that Marx was attuned to the role of unpaid labour in this way. 'In England', he argued

> women are still occasionally used instead of horses for hauling barges, because the labour required to produce horses and machines is an accurately known quantity, while that required to maintain the women of the surplus population is beneath all calculation. Hence we nowhere find a more shameless squandering of human labour-power for despicable purposes than in England, the land of machinery. (Marx [1867] 1990: 517)

Hence, to hold that there is no specific *structural necessity* for gender oppression in capitalism – or to evade the structural ways that capitalism has specific racialised antagonisms and ruptures – would reinforce an impoverished attendance to conditions of class struggle.

Silvia Federici makes the important claim that the medieval witch-hunt across Europe constituted part of the processes of primitive accumulation, preparing the ground for the emergence of capitalism. While the enclosures put an end to people's access to the commons, the witch-hunt resulted in the loss of women's control over their bodies. In other words, the witch-hunt was an essential aspect of the establishment of capitalist social relations of production (Federici [1998] 2014: 75). Federici's analysis of the witch-hunt across Europe assumes primitive accumulation in the form of the enclosures of the countryside and the commons as a uniform process throughout Europe. What is neglected is the spatially uneven development of dispossession and expropriation in the unfolding of capitalism and the differentiated and variegated role of witch-hunts within that history. Rather than being part of the emergence of capitalism and some kind of primitive accumulation, perhaps the witch-hunt should be understood as a response to the crisis of feudalism from within feudalism. As Federici outlines herself, the Black Death of the mid-fourteenth century had decimated population numbers across Europe. As a result of the subsequent shortages of people, peasants became empowered. 'For a broad section of the western European peasantry, and for urban workers, the fifteenth-century was a period of unprecedented power', writes Federici. 'Not only did the scarcity of labour give them the upper hand, but the spectacle of employers competing for their services strengthened their sense of self-value, and erased centuries of degradation and subservience' (Federici [1998] 2014: 46–7). Emboldened by their new-found strength, the common people started to challenge the nobility's power. Heretic movements sprang up, indicating paths of development beyond feudalism. 'Throughout Europe, vast communal-istic social movements and rebellions against feudalism had offered the promise of a new egalitarian society built on social equality and cooperation' (Federici [1998] 2014: 61). The foundations of feudalist social relations of production were shaken to the core. Thus, while the witch-hunts were not part of the emergence of capitalism (in most parts of Europe and elsewhere they preceded it), capitalism emerged into a pre-existing system of patriarchal rela-tionships enforced through the witch-hunt. Thus, Maria Mies ([1986] 2014: 13) understands 'patriarchal civilisation as a system, of which capitalism constitutes the most recent and most universal manifestation'.

In other words, from the very beginning, patriarchy has been part and parcel of capitalist exploitation and throughout history has also been re-shaped by it. In contrast to the social property relations approach, Mies ([1986] 2014: 38) continues:

> it is my thesis that capitalism cannot function without patriarchy, that the goal of this system, namely the never-ending process of capital accumulation, cannot be achieved unless patriarchal man-woman relations are maintained or newly created. We could, therefore, also speak of neo-patriarchy. Patriarchy thus constitutes the mostly invisible underground of the visible capitalist system. As capitalism is necessarily patriarchal it would be misleading to talk of two separate systems, as some feminists do.

In more concrete terms, '"capitalism" as a simple abstraction does not actually exist. There is only concretely racialised, patriarchal, colonial capitalism, wherein class is conceived as a unity of the diverse relations that produce not simply profit or capital, but capitalism' (Ferguson 2016: 47).

This idea of patriarchy being a part of capitalism has been picked up by Marxist Feminist social reproduction theory, especially. Here, it is pointed out that the reproduction of workers depends not only on wage labour but, equally importantly, on unpaid labour in the sphere of social reproduction. Workers need to earn a wage in order to buy the goods necessary for their survival, but they also need someone to cook meals, look after children, wash and mend clothes. Hence, capitalist accumulation must be understood as a social system including both the spheres of production and social reproduction. As Tithi Bhattacharya (2017a: 2) writes, 'The relations between labour dispensed to produce commodities and labour dispensed to produce people [are] part of the systematic totality of capitalism.' Struggles between capital and labour, therefore, are not only taking place at the workplace, but equally within the sphere of social reproduction. Thus, 'struggles for access to abortion, childcare, better wages, and healthy drinking water', for example (Ferguson 2016: 52), are to be conceptualised as class struggle similar to struggles over pensions, salary levels and working conditions in the work-place. As Bhattacharya (2017b: 92) argues:

Let us rethink the theoretical import of extra-workplace struggles, such as those for cleaner air, for better schools, against water privatisation, against climate change, or for fairer housing policies. These reflect, I submit, those social needs of the working class that are essential for its social reproduction. They also are an effort by the class to demand its 'share of civilisation'. In this, they are also class struggles.

In sum, when analysing capitalist dynamics around exploitation and resistance, class and gender can be conceptualised as internally related through a focus on class struggle (Bieler and Morton 2021).

RACIAL CAPITALISM AND THE LEGACY OF COLONIALISM

The relationship of race to capitalism, like that of gender to capitalism, also needs careful analysis from a social property relations perspective. Is capitalism structurally indifferent to race, as implied by the logic of Wood's argument? Or is it more helpful to regard capitalism as unfolding within already existing racialised forms of oppression, rather similar to the way capitalism emerged within existing patriarchal relations of oppression?

In line with the separation of the economic and the political, colonialism is often separated from capitalism. Thus: 'Given that colonialism is represented as a political phenomenon, it is presented as analytically distinct from capitalist relations whose development it may facilitate, but with which it has only a contingent relation' (Bhambra and Holmwood 2018: 576). As Matthew Watson (2018) points out, Robinson Crusoe is often taken as the ideal '*Homo economicus*'. Crusoe, maximising his own gains in a supposedly untouched state of nature, is taken as the ideal starting point in some standard economics textbooks. From a historical materialist perspective, too, a narrow focus on exploitation at the (capitalist) workplace can result in overlooking the racialised implications of capitalist accumulation. Nevertheless, as capitalism emerged within a pre-existing system of patriarchy, so too did it also emerge within a pre-existing system of racialised relations.

We need to remember that capitalism as a mode of production will always include forms of exploitation other than wage labour. As Marx argued, developed capitalism depends on the dominance of wage labour, but this does not exclude the contemporary existence of other forms of oppression and domination (Marx [1884] 1978: 554). Thus, historical capitalism is not some kind of abstract, pure form of social relations of production and any definition of capitalism as an abstract mode of production risks overlooking the historical forms through which capitalism emerged. 'The externalisation of "extra-economic" forms of exploitation and oppression from capitalism ultimately leads Political Marxists [i.e. the social property relations approach] to exclude the histories of colonialism and slavery from the inner workings of the capitalist production mode' (Anievas and Nişancıoğlu 2015: 31).

British capitalism in the eighteenth century, for example, was not only characterised by wage labour and the production of commodities in Britain, but also dependent on slave labour in the production of, for example, cotton in the colonies. 'In the late eighteenth century, income from colonial properties in the Americas was equal to approximately 50 per cent of British gross investment. Since much of this would have been reinvested in British industries, it provided a significant input into British industrialisation' (Anievas and Nişancıoğlu 2015: 164). In turn, slave labour in the Americas was only possible on the basis of the Atlantic slave trade, in which Britain was heavily involved and the receipts of which also directly fuelled the industrial revolution from the late eighteenth century onwards. As Marx said: 'Liverpool grew fat on the basis of the slave trade. This was its method of primitive accumulation' (Marx [1867] 1990: 924). In other words, the full establishment of the capitalist mode of production in Britain was dependent on the slave trade as well as slave labour. 'The English Industrial Revolution would have been virtually impossible without cotton and the expropriation of populations and the land in Africa and the Americas with which the empire of cotton was built. The origin of the age of capital was thus intimately bound to a racialised system of accumulation' (Foster and Clark 2018: 12). For example, Quarry Bank Mill, owned by the Samuel Gregg family, near Manchester (or Cottonopolis) retained wealth based on the Hillsborough Estate, a profitable sugar plantation on the Caribbean island of Dominica, which had its roots in the violent appropriation of territory and slave labour linked to the imperial British state. In short, capitalism has been from the very beginning racialised and needs to be understood as such.

As much as capitalism's own conjunctural coming into being, it is also as important to recognise the view of Frantz Fanon ([1952] 1970: 144) that capitalist society is 'only accidentally white'. The racial order of capitalism – or racial capitalism – became permeated with racist social structures and property relations as a material force (Robinson [1983] 2000: 2). Extending this focus on racial capitalism, Gargi Bhattarcharyya makes an important advance:

> Racial capitalism is not an account of how capitalism treats 'racial groups', but it is an account of how the world made through racism shapes patterns of capitalist development. In this, racial capitalism is better understood as a variety of racecraft in the economic realm (Bhattarcharyya 2018: 103)

Racecraft can therefore be akin to witchcraft as a mobilising force of difference-making – based here, though, on racialisation processes that take on a specific form within capitalism (see also Fields and Fields 2012). Nancy Fraser also provides a way to understand the importance of racial capitalism to ongoing accumulation, both historically and in present-day forms. 'Even "mature" capitalism relies on regular infusions of commandeered capacities and resources, especially from racialised subjects, in both the periphery and core', she says. 'Historically, accordingly, expropriation has always been entwined with exploitation in capitalist society – just as capitalism has always been entangled with racial oppression' (Fraser 2016: 167). Thus, capitalist exploitation not only depends on exploitation of surplus labour in the workplace: it also relies on expropriation in the way that primitive accumulation is an ongoing process, lowering production costs by relying on cheap and 'free' inputs. 'The expropriation of racialised "others" constitutes a necessary background condition for the exploitation of "workers"' (Fraser 2016: 168). Expropriated people, in the process, never become formally 'free labour', exploited in the production process (Dawson 2016: 151). In the twenty-first century, a conservative estimate is that there are more than 21 million people living in conditions of forced labour, or modern slavery, including sex-trafficking and human-trafficking, subjected to direct coercion as a source of value creation, which has highly racialised manifestations.

CONCLUSION

At first blush, it may seem reasonable to contend that capitalism is 'uniquely indifferent' to the social identities of the people it exploits. 'Capitalism could survive the eradication of all oppressions specific to women as women', Wood argues, 'while it would not, by definition, survive the eradication of class exploitation' (Wood 1995: 270). Nevertheless, as we have argued in this chapter, analyses of the historical emergence of capitalism as well as its contemporary manifestations reveal that racial domination and gender oppression are central constitutive underpinnings in the making of capitalism. This can lead to them acquiring a structural necessity. As Ferguson puts it, 'The continuity of women's oppression across different historical junctures and locations is thus explained by the specifically capitalist differentiation between reproductive and productive labour, and its impulse to privatise the former' (Ferguson 2016: 50). We, therefore, need to remember that capitalism has always relied on forms of exploitation other than wage labour, be it the unpaid work of women in the sphere of social reproduction, the receipts from trade with slaves, or the oppression of slaves in the production of raw materials such as cotton in the colonies. As Marx ([1867] 1990: 414) reminds us, 'Labour in a white skin cannot emancipate itself where it is branded in a black skin.'

Evidently, capitalism is not indifferent to gender and race. As Angela Davis subtly remarks on the internality or dialectical matrix of class, gender and race:

> Expediency governed the slaveholders' posture toward female slaves: when it was profitable to exploit them as if they were men, they were regarded, in effect, as genderless, but when they could be exploited, punished and repressed in ways suited only for women, they were locked into their exclusively female role. (Davis [1981] 2019: 4)

It is a focus on class struggle from a historical materialist perspective that allows us not only to conceptualise the internal relations of class agency and capitalist restructuring conditions but also to see how different forms of oppression around class, gender and race are entwined in capital's relentless quest for ever more surplus-value.

This form of political economic analysis shows how capitalism's relentless spatial expansion results from how the production of commodities is shaped by the ownership and control of the means of production and by wage labour, which is the dominant form of exploitation in capitalism. It is by extending the analysis to consider the connections between class, gender and race that a social property relations approach to political economy can most effectively illuminate capitalist societies and their internal power relationships. Importantly, previous work in the social property relations approach needs to be amended and extended to consider how these various forms of exploitation have shaped the emergence and development of capitalism and continue to shape its character and effects today. Like any other school of thought in political economy, the ultimate test is whether the analysis provides adequate understanding of historical experiences and helps to form useful responses to current political economic conditions, including the redress of inequalities based on class, gender and race.

REFERENCES

Anievas, A. and Nişancıoğlu, K. (2015) *How the West Came to Rule: The Geopolitical Origins of Capitalism*, London: Pluto Press.

Barker, C. (2013) 'Class Struggle and Social Movements', in Barker, C., Cox, L., Krinsky, J. and Nilsen, A.G. (eds) *Marxism and Social Movements,* Leiden: Brill, pp. 41–61.

Bhambra, G.K. and Holmwood, J. (2018) 'Colonialism, Postcolonialism and the Liberal Welfare State', *New Political Economy*, **23** (5), pp. 574–87.

Bhattacharya, T. (2017a) 'Introduction: Mapping Social Reproduction Theory', in Bhattacharya, T. (ed.), *Social Reproduction Theory: Remapping Class, Recentering Oppression*, London: Pluto Press, pp. 1–20.

Bhattacharya, T. (2017b) 'How Not to Skip Class: Social Reproduction of Labour and the Global Working Class', in Bhattacharya, T. (ed.), *Social Reproduction Theory: Remapping Class, Recentering Oppression*, London: Pluto Press, pp. 68–93.

Bhattarcharyya, G. (2018) *Rethinking Racial Capitalism: Questions of Reproduction and Survival*, London: Rowman & Littlefield International.

Bieler, A. (2000) *Globalisation and EU Enlargement: Austrian and Swedish Social Forces in the Struggle over Membership*, London: Routledge.

Bieler, A. (2006) *The Struggle for a Social Europe: Trade Unions and EMU in Times of Global Restructuring*, Manchester: Manchester University Press.

Bieler, A. and Morton, A.D. (2014) 'Uneven and Combined Development and Unequal Exchange: The Second Wind of Neoliberal "Free Trade"?', *Globalizations*, **11** (1), pp. 35–45.

Bieler, A. and Morton, A.D. (2018) *Global Capitalism, Global War, Global Crisis*, Cambridge: Cambridge University Press.

Bieler, A. and Morton, A.D. (2021) 'Is Capitalism Structurally Indifferent to Gender? Routes to a Value Theory of Reproductive Labour', *Environment and Planning A: Economy and Space*, **53** (7), pp. 1749–69.

Bieler, A., Bozkurt, S., Crook, M., Cruttenden, P., Erol, E., Morton, A.D., Tansel, C.B and Uzgören, E. (2016) 'The Enduring Relevance of Rosa Luxemburg's *The Accumulation of Capital*', *Journal of International Relations and Development*, **19** (3), pp. 420–47.

Brenner, R. (1985) 'Agrarian Class Structure and Economic Development in Pre-Industrial Europe', in Aston, T.H. and Philpin, C.H.E. (eds), *The Brenner Debate: Agrarian Class Structure and Economic Development in Pre-Industrial Europe*, Cambridge: Cambridge University Press, pp. 10–63.

Brenner, R. (1986) 'The Social Basis of Economic Development', in Roemer, J. (ed.), *Analytical Marxism*, Cambridge: Cambridge University Press, pp. 23–53.

Brenner, R. (2001) 'The Low Countries in the Transition to Capitalism', *Journal of Agrarian Change*, **1** (2), pp. 169–241.

Camfield, D. (2002) 'Beyond Adding on Gender and Class: Revisiting Feminism and Marxism', *Studies in Political Economy*, **68**, pp. 37–54.

Dawson, M.C. (2016) 'Hidden in Plain Sight: A Note on Legitimation Crises and the Racial Order', *Critical Historical Studies*, **3** (1), pp. 143–61.

Davis, A.Y. ([1981] 2019) *Women, Race and Class*, London: Penguin.

Fanon, F. ([1952] 1970) *Black Skin, White Masks*, translated by C. L. Markmann, London: Paladin.

Federici, S. ([1998] 2014) *Caliban and the Witch: Women, the Body and Primitive Accumulation*, Brooklyn, NY: Autonomedia.

Federici, S. (2019) *Re-enchanting the World: Feminism and the Politics of the Commons*, Oakland, VA: PM Press.

Ferguson, S. (2016) 'Intersectionality and Social-Reproduction Feminisms Toward an Integrative Ontology', *Historical Materialism*, **24** (2), pp. 38–60.

Ferguson, S., Le Baron, G., Dimitrakaki, A. and Farris, S.R. (2016) 'Special Issue on Social Reproduction: Introduction', *Historical Materialism*, **24** (2), pp. 25–37.

Fields, K.E. and Fields, B.J. (2012) *Racecraft: The Soul of Inequality in American Life*, London: Verso.

Foster, J.B. and Clark, C. (2018) 'The Expropriation of Nature', *Monthly Review*, **69** (10), pp. 1–28.

Fraser, N. (2016) 'Expropriation and Exploitation in Racialised Capitalism: A Reply to Michael Dawson', *Critical Historical Studies*, **3** (1), pp. 163–78.

Harvey, D. (1985) 'The Geopolitics of Capitalism', in Gregory, D. and Urry, J. (eds), *Social Relations and Spatial Structures*, London: Macmillan, pp. 128–63.

Harvey, D. (2006) 'Neoliberalism and the Restoration of Class Power', in Harvey D. (ed.), *Spaces of Global Capitalism: Towards a Theory of Uneven Geographical Development*, London: Verso, pp. 7–68.

Lacher, H. (2006) *Beyond Globalization: Capitalism, Territoriality and the International Relations of Modernity*, London: Routledge.

Luxemburg, R. ([1913] 2003) *The Accumulation of Capital*, translated by A. Schwarzschild, London: Routledge.

Marx, K. ([1867] 1990) *Capital, Volume I*, introduction by E. Mandel, translated by B. Fowkes, London: Penguin.

Marx, K. ([1884] 1978) *Capital: A Critique of Political Economy, Volume II*, translated by D. Fernbach, London: Penguin Books.

Marx, K. and Engels, F. ([1848] 1998) 'Manifesto of the Communist Party', in Cowling, M. (ed.), *The Communist Manifesto: New Interpretations*, Edinburgh: Edinburgh University Press, pp. 14–37.

Mies, M. ([1986] 2014) *Patriarchy and Accumulation on a World Scale: Women in the International Division of Labour*, London: Zed Books.

Morton, A.D. (2013) 'The Limits of Sociological Marxism?', *Historical Materialism*, 21 (1), pp. 129–58.

Ollman, B. (1976) *Alienation: Marx's Conception of Man in Capitalist Society*, 2nd edition, Cambridge: Cambridge University Press.

Postone, M. (1993) *Time, Labor and Social Domination: A Reinterpretation of Marx's Critical Theory*, Cambridge: Cambridge University Press.

Roberts, W.C. (2017) *Marx's Inferno: The Political Theory of* Capital, Princeton, NJ: Princeton University Press.

Robinson, C.J. ([1983] 2000) *Black Marxism: The Making of the Black Radical Tradition*, Chapel Hill: University of North Carolina Press.

Teschke, B. (2003) *The Myth of 1648: Class, Geopolitics and the Making of Modern International Relations*, London: Verso.

Wallerstein, I. (1974) *The Modern World-System I: Capitalist Agriculture and the Origins of the European World-Economy in the Sixteenth Century*, London: Academic Press.

Wallerstein, I. (1979) *The Capitalist World-Economy*, Cambridge: Cambridge University Press.

Watson, M. (2018) 'Crusoe, Friday and the Raced Market Frame of Orthodox Economics Textbooks', *New Political Economy*, 23 (5), pp. 544–59.

Wood, E.M. (1991) *The Pristine Culture of Capitalism: An Historical Essay on Old Regimes and Modern States*, London: Verso.

Wood, E.M. (1995) *Democracy Against Capitalism: Renewing Historical Materialism*, Cambridge: Cambridge University Press.

Wood, E.M. (2002a) *The Origin of Capitalism: A Longer View*, London: Verso.

Wood, E.M. (2002b) 'The Question of Market Dependence', *Journal of Agrarian Change*, 2 (1), pp. 50–87.

Wood, E.M. (2002c) 'Capitalism and Human Emancipation: Race, Gender, and Democracy', in Holmstrom, N. (ed.), *The Socialist Feminist Project: A Contemporary Reader in Theory and Politics*, New York: Monthly Review Press, pp. 277–92.

Wood, E.M. (2006) 'Logics of Power: A Conversation with David Harvey', *Historical Materialism*, 14 (4), pp. 9–34.

22. The Systems of Provision approach

Robin Chang

Most people around the world secure access to use-values that satisfy their material needs through consumption of goods and services clothed in the commodity form. Frequently, this is a matter of attaining the food, clothing and shelter enabling their mere subsistence. In industrialised countries, higher levels of consumption, including myriad luxury goods, are commonplace, creating markedly different living standards and defining their lifestyles. Concurrently, because consumption is the most direct way in which many engage with capitalism as a system, it informs their attitudes towards it – whether enabling their well-being through purchase of goods and services or locking them into dependency and debt. More broadly, the way in which consumption is organised and structured is central to myriad problems in contemporary global capitalism, ranging from coexistence of mass hunger and mass obesity, extreme exploitation of textile workers in developing countries, high levels of mortgage stress, inequality and uneven development within and between countries, and the persistence of ecologically unsustainable socio-economic practices (Hudson and Hudson 2021). Critical reflection on the operation of the commodity form is, therefore, an integral part of a comprehensive grasp of the dynamics of contemporary capitalism.

Not surprisingly, consumption has become an increasingly prominent field of study across the social sciences, particularly since the 1970s (Macinnis and Folkes 2009; Pietrykowski 2009). While such research has demonstrated the complex range of factors determining consumption – from sociological variables such as social status and psychological variables such as attitudes and habits to cultural variables such as taste and meaning – it has been largely compartmentalised by academic disciplines. Psychology, for example, focusing on the individual, studies the way in which consumers process information about products and make decisions that are to a greater or lesser extent deliberate. Sociology has highlighted the symbolic content of consumption items and their role in affirming the status or social position of various classes or social groups. Mainstream economics has focused on the influence of market prices on patterns of consumption, centring on the empirical study of demand elasticities for individual products. These forms of research, while interesting in their own fields, have largely failed to promote interdisciplinary dialogue (Fine and Leopold 1993; Fine 2002).

This chapter explores how the 'Systems of Provision' (SoP) approach within political economy, pioneered by Ben Fine and his colleagues, has sought to promote such a dialogue and new research directions. The SoP approach is concerned with analysis of consumption processes in a holistic, interdisciplinary framework, explicitly connecting structural features in the provision of commodities to important cultural characteristics. It explores how individual goods or services have their own unique political economies, including all the processes and relations involved in creating, distributing, consuming and disposing of them – from physical resource extraction to labour processes, transportation, and the cultural meanings associated with consumption practices. It thus explores the material production and cultural significance of different types of consumption as an integral part of a series of interlinked and overlapping social processes.

The chapter engages with the SoP approach in five steps. First, it outlines three schools of thought against which the SoP practitioners define their concerns and considers the more positive connection with Marxian political economy. Second, it considers the general features of the SoP approach. Third, it examines its key conceptual features when applied to different commodities. Fourth, it considers some empirical applications of the SoP approach to the United Kingdom (UK) where most SoP research has been focused to date. Finally, the SoP approach is considered in relation to other currents in political economy and interdisciplinary social science.

CONTENDING APPROACHES TO STUDYING CONSUMPTION

A 'productivist' bias has frequently been identified in the social sciences, particularly in mainstream economics but also in much of political economy (Ritzer and Slater 2001; Santos et al. 2014). This may be said to have followed from the 'analytical categories, nomenclature and concepts forged by the "founding fathers" of the social sciences in the late nineteenth century and early twentieth century, who sought mainly to deal with the problems and consequences of production and the social organisation of an emerging industrial order'. Consumption was analysed as 'the endpoint of a production sequence […], rather than as integrally intertwined with social-material processes' (Cook et al. 2011: 1–2). The discipline of sociology has also tended to favour the study of production and distribution, relegating the study of consumption to specific fields such as culture, gender, family and inequality (Evans 2019).

Concern with the social relations underpinning production and a rejection of the fetishism of technology were drivers for the emergence of the SoP approach. The approach was originally articulated by Fine and Leopold (1993) as a means of addressing the perceived limitations of prevailing theories of consumption across the social sciences, particularly as evident in neoclassical economics, but also institutional political economy and postmodernism. In a manner influenced by Marx (1973), the pioneering SoP theorists argued that production, distribution, exchange and consumption must be analysed together if we are to fully comprehend provisioning processes. While neoclassical, institutional and postmodern approaches to consumption may employ the same terms as SoP – production, distribution, exchange and consumption – their approaches are partial, not seeing all parts of the chain nor the complex and variegated interconnections that shape provisioning processes. Moreover, their use differs from the theoretical project of the SoP proponents, who seek to connect analysis of capitalist consumption processes with classical Marxian value theory (Bayliss et al. 2013). This pre-analytical commitment determines how agency, structure, process, relation and material culture are translated into concrete terms to facilitate applications of the SoP approach to empirical research.

Table 22.1 summarises the main conceptual and methodological differences between these four schools of thought in their analyses of consumption. This typology provides an organising framework for further exploration of how the SoP approach seeks to transcend the limitations of the first three approaches and build fruitful connections with the fourth. These alternative starting points are distinguished by their theories of value and are presented as ideal types rather than comprehensive literature summaries.

Table 22.1   Major alternative starting points for the study of consumption

	Neoclassical economics	Institutionalist political economy	Postmodernist criticism	Marxian political economy
Theory of value	Subjective preference	Cost of production	Social constructivist	Abstract labour
Logical structure	Deductive	Inductive	Varies	Systems
Key actors	Maximising individuals	Organisations and structures	Subjectivities; traditions	Social classes
Key sphere	Exchange	Distribution	Consumption	Production
Explanatory strategy	Math models of perfect and imperfect competition and rational choice theory; econometrics	Typologies: organisation and systems theories and ideologies	Discourse analyses	Historical materialist logical reconstruction
Decision-making	Supply and demand equilibrium	Power negotiations	Dominant discourse	Capitalist dynamics and class struggle
Leverage points	Privatisation	Developmental state	Varies	Capitalist state
Causation	Methodological individualism	Organisational bargaining	Constructivist	Mutual conditioning
Provisioning	Consumer sovereignty	Producer sovereignty	Power relation	Capitalist social-property relations

Exchange: Neoclassical Economic Theory

Economists of the neoclassical tradition have directed explanatory effort into consumption as part of a distinctively narrow orthodoxy. The focus is on the sphere of *exchange*, in which individuals are assumed to meet voluntarily in markets to trade goods and services for money, making interpersonal transactions and agreeing to a range of other contractual obligations. Concomitantly, neoclassical analysis depends on an economic logic connecting consumers' individual preferences to production decisions by firms, operating in markets governed by equilibrating forces. In other words, production processes are held to be 'harmoniously and efficiently linked through the free play of the market mechanism' (Fine and Leopold 1993: 20); individual utility simultaneously constitutes a determining explanatory factor and desirable consequence engendering consumer sovereignty; and production systems adjust to respond to consumer demands. Thus,

> [t]he system of production responds as a servant to the needs and wishes of consumers subject to the availability of resources. In this sense, consumption can be traced back from the individual, through exchange, to act as a determining moment upon production – even if allowance can also be made for distortions in efficiency and competitiveness along the way. (Fine and Leopold 1993: 20)

From the perspective of neoclassical economics, real-world economic systems are generally conceived as a departure from an idealised equilibrium. Essentially, the starting point is a pro-market position, with markets for specific goods being examined in terms of their 'market imperfections'. This approach is built on a raft of unrealistic assumptions, taking as its model the perfectly competitive industry with well-informed consumers, each of whom has fixed preferences, and where goods have straightforward meanings in and of themselves and to the consumers. The goods being exchanged in the market are effectively defined by their physical properties and are 'subjectively' enjoyed. Thus, neoclassical economics holds that the free market – driven by rational, utility-maximising individuals – operates as a means of enhancing individual and collective economic welfare.

Yet, while the study of consumption for this school may initially appear as a 'simple matter of more or less structured supply and demand within a particular sector', once 'we begin to investigate what is provided, how and to whom, and with what meanings to its participants, it becomes a matter of unravelling a whole series of complex but interconnected issues' (Fine and Bayliss 2021: 41). On this basis, Fine (2016: 39–40) posits eight reasons for rejecting the neoclassical approach to consumption. First, its focus on individual choice treats consumers as having very limited motivation and capacities. Second, to focus only on the limited act of purchase, as opposed to the processes attached to consumption from expectation through to disposal, misconstrues the consumption process as a whole and allows consumers to be unrealistically regarded as sovereign. Third, the failure to specify the nature of consumption goods themselves reflects the subjectivism of its utility theory of value. Fourth, it fails to take account of social influences and context. Fifth, it does not recognise the inherently social nature of consumption – its spatial and temporal dimensions, the interdependence between individuals, and the significance of social categories such as gender, class, race and nationality. Sixth, neoclassical microeconomic theory is grounded in mathematical modelling, using axiomatic and deductive methods focused on optimisation, despite the aggregation problems and limited empirical applicability. Seventh, the applied econometrics used 'is often as clumsy and arbitrary as the theory' (Fine 2016: 45). Eighth, because economists do not engage with the insights of other social sciences, except to 'colonise' their fields (Fine 2016: 40), the 'traditional treatments of consumption across other disciplines have been more analytical in content' (see also Fine and Milonakis 2009).

Distribution: Institutional Political Economy

What about looking at consumption through the lens of institutional economics? For as long as neoclassical economics has existed, institutionalists have rejected the dominant marginal utility theory and proffered alternative ways of understanding consumption (Fine and Milonakis 2009). Indeed, Fine's list of criticisms overlaps substantially with those levelled at neoclassicism by heterodox economists for many decades (Hodgson 2008). From an institutional economics perspective, the main agents in the economy are large organisations, including corporations, labour unions, governments and non-governmental organisations, not individual consumers. Because the relations between these organisations feature substantial power imbalances, questions of distributional inequalities are ever present. Also, institutionalists recognise the intertwining of economic and social factors shaping consumption. From Veblen ([1899] 2012) onwards, they have been concerned with social emulation and other social influences on the levels and patterns of consumer spending. These features are prominent throughout John Kenneth Galbraith's alternative 'multi-centric organisational' model of contemporary capitalism (Miller 2018), including analysis of the effects of commercial advertising, the 'revised sequence' of consumption and production, and the replacement of consumer sovereignty by producer sovereignty (Galbraith 1998).

Also notable in recent decades has been the wide-ranging influence of sociologist Gosta Esping-Andersen's Welfare Regime Approach (WRA) to comparative political economy, spawning a large literature on consumption practices in industrialised countries. The approach combines different traditions of institutional analysis, drawing on rational choice, sociological and historical variants, to fill perceived gaps in classical political economy by centring analysis on decommodification as a key area of social contestation (Esping-Andersen 1990). While conceding that this engages with worthy issues, however, SoP proponents have been generally unimpressed. As Fine and Bayliss (2021: 78) write: 'whatever validity as it emerged, Esping-Andersen's approach had been very much the creation of the post-war boom period, seeking to distinguish different systems of welfare provision in (Keynesian-style) contexts that were already being discarded [...] when the WRA was first put forward'. Hence their view that, 'social policy is anchored in empirically grounded study of differentiated analyses by sector and by country and, most recently, within the context of globalised, financialised and neoliberalised provision' (Fine and Bayliss 2021: 78). The focus on the forms of state-centred social provision with which Esping-Anderson's analysis is primarily concerned is different from SoP's primary focus on private consumption, although the influence of neoliberalism has resonated in both fields by reconfiguring state–market relations, affecting the distribution of income and therefore impacting on who gets what.

Consumption: Postmodernist Criticism

The critique of postmodernism's influence on the study of consumption differs from the critique of neoclassical economics and the limitations of institutionalism. It acknowledges that the effect of the rise of postmodern scholarship, emerging during the 1980s because of frustration with the shortcomings of extant critical social theory, was to shift the analytical focus from production and producers to consumption and consumers (Fine 2002). Especially with its application to consumption within cultural studies by French philosopher Jean Baudrillard, postmodernism sought to interpret 'the meanings of the consumed to consumers and the corresponding constructions of their individual identities' (Fine and Bayliss 2021: 3). Specifically, postmodern analyses rearticulated consumers as subjectively flexible and inventive – able to construct their own meanings autonomously and independently of the meanings intended by the industry or any other hegemonic structure. Seen in this way, consumers are largely unbound by their own material circumstances and those of the goods and services consumed. From this perspective, rather than promoting uniformity, consumption acts as a source of creativity and social innovation. According to Schor (2007: 19–20):

> The 'postmodern' consumer is a playful and adventurous individual, putting on and taking off roles like costumes from her or his eclectic closet, shunning conventional (upscale) status aspiration [...] the 'good life' is no longer a matter of acquiring a well-defined set of consensual status symbols but is a project of individual self-creation. Studies of subcultures also rejected the trickle-down model on the basis of a growing tendency for consumer innovation to come from the social margins, as trends in fashion, music, art, and language were originating among poor inner city youths, rather than the wealthy.

Postmodernism's popularity has waned considerably since the 1990s as criticisms of the approach have grown. For Fine and Bayliss, the subjectivism of postmodernism may be regarded as veering towards a form of methodological individualism in which the liberal, isolated individual subjectivity gets recreated as the key agent. It also assumes that acquisition of consumer goods – and the plurality of meanings associated with this – does contribute to increasing individual well-being. Consumption is implied to belong to the intimate sphere of the individual seat of consciousness, understood as individuated, isolated and hedonistic, devoid of political content and thus exempt from critical assessment. This perspective, thereby, hinders consideration of the socio-economic factors relevant to an analysis of consumption (Santos et al. 2014). Consequently, as Fine and Bayliss (2021: 4) say, 'in the intervening years since consumer studies took off [...] there has been something of a reaction against the postmodernist approach' – less 'to set aside an understanding of the cultures of consumption but more to root them in, and through interaction with, the material practices to which they are attached'.

Production: Marxian Political Economy

One might expect SoP proponents to also be critical of much Marxian political economy (MPE) because of its primary focus on the sphere of production. As Marx famously argued, that is where the creation of value, critical to his theory of surplus value, takes place. A long tradition of Marxian political economy, stretching back to nineteenth-century classical political economy, takes this as its point of departure. SoP proponent Ben Fine himself had been an important leader in the 1970s revitalisation of Marxian political economy, engaging in still ongoing theoretical debates on the theory of value, crisis and state expenditures (Fine and Harris 1979; Fine and Saad-Filho 2016). Yet, it is by relating the analysis of production to the analysis of consumption that a path to further progress occurs because this makes the social and political content of social reproduction more visible.

Fine and Bayliss (2021: 32) make clear that, 'from its beginnings, then, the SoP approach focused upon consumption derived from private commodity production and, as a result, was heavily influenced by the theory of commodity production to which it is generally acknowledged, even if often critically, that Marx himself, and MPE are major contributors'. Further, 'the SoP approach builds on this MPE interrogation of the commodity and the social relations that underpin production not just because of their social implications but also because the production processes underpin and interact with what is consumed and how.' Thus, 'value and how it is conceived in MPE,' is 'of particular significance' for the SoP approach. Especially, the SoP approach draws on 'value theory's qualitative insights into commodity production', where in a capitalist society, 'the means of production (capitalist firms) are generally privately owned and their products are distributed through market exchange.' Finally, 'because products are exchanged through the market in what are more or less impersonal relations, they appear as commodities primarily disassociated by their purchasers/consumers from the production processes (and other processes) by which they have been brought to the market' (Fine and Bayliss 2021: 32). Evidently, the relationship between the SoP approach and a Marxist political economy is regarded as fruitful, if not essential.

STRUCTURE OF ANALYSIS

The most general premise of the SoP approach is that a 'vertical' approach to studying consumption needs to replace the 'horizontal' approach that has been a feature of most previous theories. Neoclassical economics is an extreme example of the latter because it presumes that a general theory of utility-maximising behaviour is applicable to understanding consumption outcomes for all types of goods and services. But all discipline-specific approaches have this 'horizontal' tendency because of their characteristic themes and interests. By contrast, a vertical approach focuses on the analysis of specific commodities – whether food, clothing, housing, or whatever – and explores whatever is the relevant chain of horizontal factors influencing the consumption processes and outcomes relating to the commodity being studied. This results in an integrated analysis of production, distribution, retailing, consumption, and material culture that is relevant and specific to each commodity.

Each consumption good, such as a pair of designer jeans, is treated as potentially having its own unique system of provision. The factors shaping patterns of consumption, such as the social, cultural and economic factors that led to the spread of denim trousers around the world and the emergence of fast fashion manufacturing and retail, then become the focus of detailed study. Of course, there may be common elements – the influence of financialisation in the current era on how a wide range of goods are produced and consumed is a case in point – but differences always arise in how those general influences interact with the specific features pertaining to each commodity. These specific influences are revealed only by detailed study of each specific system of provision.

What makes the SoP approach so appealing from a critical political economic perspective is the engagement with historical materialism and especially the production of value. Understating the 'jeans' system of provision' means charting how denim trousers have become a popular choice of clothing for millions of people and explaining where and how different processes are undertaken to make jeans into a commodity. Rather than forensically detailing the journey of the same cotton bolls from farm gate to retail floor, related processes are discussed to give the bigger picture. Indeed, materials pass around the world and, as cotton threads are woven into denim and that denim is cut and sewn into denim pants, the commodities gather and attract value. As political economists, however, we must look beyond the fetishism of the thing and the market to understand how value is socially constructed.

According to Fine and Bayliss, the abstract notion central to the SoP approach is the focus, for any good or service, on an 'integral unity of the economic and social factors that go into both its creation and its use' (Fine and Bayliss 2021: 29). Each SoP is distinct and, for analytical purposes, independent because 'different areas of provisioning are seen as forming separate but integral social entities that are themselves constituted out of the chains of activities that are involved, from production through to consumption or, more generally, use or application' (2021: 29).

Fine and Bayliss also point out that each reflects, 'social, political, economic, geographical and historical' factors defining the character of its production, distribution, exchange, and consumption modes (2021: 29). Accordingly, 'the SoP approach examines the system as a whole even if the focus of interest, for research or policy purposes, might be on one aspect of the SoP alone' (Fine and Bayliss 2021: 29–30). Figure 22.1 illustrates these features of any SoP in the most abstract of terms.

However, for this approach, the idea of a merely linear chain can be misleading (Hudson and Hudson 2021: 18). One reason is that, while each SoP is specific to a particular commodity, they frequently interact with other systems of provision. Moreover, as Fine and Bayliss (2021: 29) suggest, 'we should not think of one element in the system, without connecting and relating it to others in the chain of structured activities, which can reach across local, national, regional, and global sites and influences.'

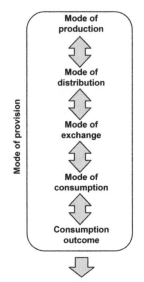

Input into social reproduction for capitalist production

Figure 22.1   Features of Systems of Provision approach

METHODS OF INQUIRY

For Fine and Bayliss (2021: 38), the SoP approach is 'open to a large degree regarding methodologies' while incorporating 'certain core elements which have long been used widely across the social sciences'. This contrasts with mainstream economics where such openness is rare because it 'is dominated by reductionism to a market/non-market dualism based on individual optimisation on the basis of given utility functions' (2021: 38). Nevertheless, SoP does have its own form of meta-method, arising from the categorical building blocks on which SoP research is conducted, and its proponents are explicit about this. Specifically, within the chain of activities – production, distribution, exchange, and consumption – they point to 'agents, structures, processes, relations, and material cultures' (Fine and Bayliss 2021: 41). Such categories are simultaneously general and overlapping and may feature in research in varying ways depending on the object of inquiry – whether 'grand and global or highly specific and local in content' (Fine and Bayliss 2021: 38).

On this basis, SoP's research method may be understood as consisting of three phases – which, for the purposes of this chapter, are labelled 'selection', 'research' and 'recalibration' – comprising a total of seven different steps. Figure 22.2 presents a flow diagram reflecting this interpretation of the SoP method, depicting how the steps follow one another in a logical fashion.

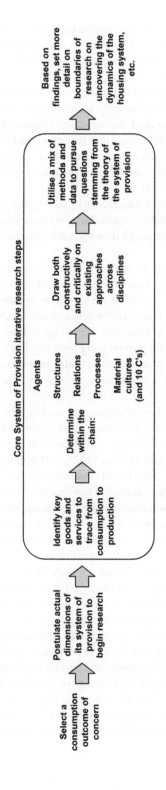

Figure 22.2   Three-phase Systems of Provision research method

Moving from left to right, phase one, *selection*, begins the research process with the identification of a consumption outcome to study. This may be, for instance, housing, nutritional or medical. This outcome is the human act that connects it with some set of goods and services which valorises its cultural significance.

Next, during phase two (which comprises the 'boxed' parts of Figure 22.2), *research* is an iterative process, in which 'there is not necessarily an initial research question or hypothesis to be tested but rather an identifiable area of investigation' (Fine and Bayliss 2021: 43). It is 'not a matter of taking an ideal type off the shelf that is deemed to fit best, nor does it involve applying a predetermined template'; rather, 'it is a reasoned dialogue between theory and evidence in light of purpose, ranging over the chain of provision, its broader determinants, its material culture and its context' (2021: 43).

Finally, in phase three, *recalibration*, is the process of sorting out the research findings and presenting them in a systematic and coherent form. Therein lies a recurrent conundrum – how much order should be retrospectively imposed on a research process that is essentially inductive and open-ended in nature.

Particular attention should be given to the categories of agents, structures, processes, relations, and material cultures, because Fine and Bayliss (2021: 157) posit that these can be 'unpacked' further to increase precision in SoP analysis. These are the elements that appear in Figure 22.2 at the centre of the second stage. We briefly consider each in turn.

The *agents* (and agencies) relevant to each SoP, according to Fine and Bayliss (2021: 38), are 'determined by the participants in the provisioning system'. They are 'those who produce and those who consume but also wider bodies such as trade unions, consumer groups, the state and those who affect delivery of finance, investment, technology, and so on', and within each category there are sub-categories.

The *structures* may be organisational, institutional and social, formal or informal. Fine and Bayliss (2021: 38) hold that, 'at the grand theoretical level, there is the structuring of capitalism itself in terms of production and exchange and for profit or not, often termed economic reproduction'. In their research, Fine and Bayliss (2021: 39) point out that, 'at the level of specific SoPs, in time, place and sector, such broad structures are more concrete, although they may be complex with extensive potential scope'. They include 'vertical structures of provisioning themselves (across not only production but also financing, marketing, state regulation, and so on) [which] will interact with horizontal factors'. Finally, 'levels of income, and all the structured variables of economic and social status such as race and gender' are also critically important considerations to be included in any SoP application.

The *processes* relevant to each SoP are shaped not only by *who* does what but *how* it is done as a structured sequence of activities. To explain, Fine and Bayliss say that 'processes can be understood both in systemic and abstract terms such as globalisation and privatisation, as well as in specific activities within the SoP (the labour process, advertising, and so on) and around the SoP (gendering, etc.)' (2021: 39). Furthermore, although 'processes are engaged in everyday life […] these are much more broadly situated in social processes […] not least for privatisation […] as it changes both the structures and agencies in provisioning as well as how the consumer engages with provisioning both in terms of how consumption is accessed but also how it is perceived'. Fine and Bayliss (2021: 40) add that: 'the SoP approach in practice most recently has laid considerable emphasis upon globalisation, neoliberalism and financialisation as influential processes with clear implications for consumption, although each of these is highly contested in terms of meaning and content across the literature, and how they give rise to variegated outcomes.'

Relations must also be identified. As Fine and Bayliss (2021: 4) say, 'SoPs are constituted upon and, in turn, constitute and reproduce relations of class, gender, race, caste, etc., contingent upon who exercises power, and how, and with what purpose (and meaning to participants) and, as such, are open to contestation and conflict.' Moreover, 'the relations upon which SoPs are founded are differentiated by the roles of capital (or state as employer) and labour in production and other commercial (or non-commercial) operations through to the relational norms and implicit codes of practice that are attached to levels and meanings of consumption.' Summing up, Fine and Bayliss categorise relations under three headings: 'how are relations structured; how are positions in those structures occupied by different agencies; and what are the processes by which the SoP is reproduced or transformed'.

Finally, there is the need to identify the relevant *material cultures*. These may have different meanings for those who are involved in various aspects of the SoPs, whether as workers, citizens, consumers, policymakers, or in the media. For Fine and Bayliss (2021: 41), 'a crucial part of the SoP approach is to emphasise that there is an integral relation between each SoP and the cultures that are attached to or, more accurately, interact with it.' However, they claim to be cognisant that 'more generally, study of the relationship between the material and cultural worlds is highly controversial and, the SoP approach seeks to finesse these controversies in the ways in which it frames material culture as a product of, and contributing factor to, SoPs themselves.'

A further distinctive feature of the analysis of material cultures is what has come to be known as the '10 Cs', described by Fine and Bayliss (2021: 63) as 'part and parcel of understanding material cultures in applying the SoP approach'. These are ten adjectives starting with the letter 'C' that describe the ontological features constituting the mode of material culture that shapes the lived experience in SoPs. They are: Constructed, Construed, Commodified, Conforming, Contextual, Contradictory, Chaotic, Closed, Contested, and Collective. As Fine and Bayliss note, this framing is compatible with different approaches and methodologies (in common with the SoP approach more broadly) and is applicable to a range of subject matter (not just consumption). They say that 'the aim is to provide a useful checklist for interrogating material cultures of specific provisionings' while also noting that 'not every "C" will be equally relevant in all cases' (2021: 63).

Class may be thought a notable omission from the 10 Cs, given the close affinity between SoP and Marxist political economy, but Fine and Bayliss (2021: 63) say 'this should not be privileged [...] any more than gender, ethnicity or whatever even though these may be vital determinants.' Yet, they continue, 'as consumption is driven by the commodity form, it is the capacity and willingness to pay that is the most important proximate quantitative determinant [and] income and lifestyle do have some correspondence to class position'. Clarifying further, while class is 'an important determinant of consumption and is part of the SoP [...] it is not inevitably a proximate determinant of corresponding cultural systems, and its presence can be filtered through the other 10 Cs, possibly overtly through the Collective, the Construed, and the Contested for example' (2021: 63).

Drawing all these elements together, the general claim is that 'applying this framework draws attention to the systemic factors that determine who gets what, not just in terms of end consumption but also how value is distributed in the chain of provisioning' (Fine and Bayliss 2021: ix). Moreover, 'SoPs work through multifarious channels, from policy design and practice through production, financing and commercial operations, through sale and use (and disposal in some cases).' Hence, each SoP gives rise to 'distinct, commodity-specific cultures of consumption, and so inform the patterns of practices, ideas and meanings that shape consumption configurations' (2021: ix). The general social norms of consumption are relevant in this context alongside – and interacting with – the social influences on the consumption of specific goods and services. Commercial advertising is a significant factor in both respects.

EMPIRICAL APPLICATIONS

The SoP approach has been applied to both industrialised and industrialising societies (Fine and Bayliss 2021) but the principal focus of empirical studies to date has been the UK. Table 22.2 displays some, more recent, key contributions.

Table 22.2   Selected United Kingdom Systems of Provision research

Provisioning system	Countries	Reference
Housing	England	Robertson (2016)
Clothing	England	Brooks (2015)
Water	England and Wales	Bayliss et al. (2018)
Health services	England	Fine and Bayliss (2021)
Food	England	Fine and Bayliss (2021)

The list of provisioning systems in the first column of Table 22.2 is not surprising, given the centrality to sustaining human livelihoods of items such as housing, clothing and food, together with clean water and medical care. These are fields of consumption where the SoP approach has appropriately focused. Moreover, under capitalism, what happens in these fields is far more than the mere results of individual choices over goods and services: the material cultures in which these consumptive social practices are embedded are indicative of the contradictions that capitalist social relations generate in social reproduction.

Take housing as a primary example. The form of its provision has a major bearing not only on affordability but also on the spatial forms of settlement, social mobility, individual and social attitudes to public and private property, and much else besides. Michael Ball's work on housing in the UK decades ago led the way for housing studies with this character (for example, Ball 1983). More recently, looking at housing through an explicitly SoP lens, Mary Robertson (2016) has made further innovative use of several Marxian concepts. She applies Marx's theory of rent and Fine's Marxist approach to financialisation[1] to the UK housing system in order to contextualise it historically within neoliberalism, arguing that: 'a deeper understanding of the manifold problems confronting housing in Britain can be attained once it is seen that both housing consumption and production are increasingly organised around attempts to appropriate ground rent on residential land, which has been heavily inflated by the expansion of the financial sector' (Robertson 2016: 8–9). She traces extant housing patterns to the shift in housing tenure engendered by policies implemented by the Thatcher government in the 1980s and shows that the burgeoning inequality in access to, and provision of, housing is correlated with the subsequent extension of owner-occupation and mortgaging as well as the decline of social housing. Robertson (2016: 8–9) argues that the role of finance in the UK housing system is bound up with the centrality of land to housing and, in particular, its ability to generate rent. Mortgage lending is a form of credit creation – it not only directs value in circulation in the economy towards residential land but also expands the total amount of value in circulation.

Because increased mortgage lending caused a greater share of value circulating in the economy to be accumulated into land, 'finance has become a source of generalised (though differentiated) ground rent' (Robertson 2016: 8–9). Furthermore, 'increased availability of mortgage credit, by expanding effective demand for housing, drives up the general component of ground rent on residential land [and] this ground rent is based on credit, it is very volatile – hence the cyclicality of land and housing prices and their proneness to speculative bubbles' (2016: 8–9). Consequently, substantial profits were possible from land speculation due to the way finance has channelled value into residential land and propelled ground rents upward. In turn, land, and particularly residential land, has increasingly come to resemble a financial asset.

Turning from housing to clothing, other important empirical work has been undertaken by Andrew Brooks (2015). His research into the UK clothing SoP shows that clothing is 'constructed through a web of relationships which draw upon and reproduce positions of power and dependency emerging from decades, even centuries, of uneven development' (Fine and Bayliss 2021: 94). In the case of apparel, Brooks extends the general criticism of institutional political economists that 'consumer preferences are directly and indirectly shaped by producers' (Fine and Bayliss 2021: 95). Specifically, 'fast fashion' is responsible for the 'overconsumption' of clothing in the UK, as reflected in the vast surplus that is donated to charity. Simultaneously, intense consumer demand for 'cheap but quality clothing has led to the migration of industries to the less expensive South and the depression of wage rates for many workers' (2021: 95).

It is to be expected that the SoP approach will be applied to an increasingly wide array of goods and services. Because the essence of the approach is the focus on specific cases and unique contexts, a case study approach is in-built in the method. Yet, therein also lie some distinctive challenges about how research is undertaken and how its results are written up. One issue is the treatment of agency and contingency, which can be a significant feature in SoP research, given that consumption is regarded as both a cause and a consequence of social actions and social reproduction. This creates challenges for SoP researchers since the specific effects of agency and contingency must be discovered through empirical study, provision system by provision system. As Fine and Bayliss (2021: 73–4) say, 'where the difficulty does occur is where to begin in deploying these elements in an overview of SoP applied research. Is it with production or consumption, with culture or norms of provision, is it with the agents or the processes, and so on? [...] [T]his conundrum, in turn, reflects a more general issue – the distinction between the order of investigation (by SoP researchers) and the order of presentation (to others)'. Fine and Bayliss (2021: 73–4) add that, 'in retrospect, it is easy to realise in our own work, and presume this is true of others, that before we present a SoP, we have spent considerable time investigating what it is, why and how, and then come to a view on how best to explain this to others, and this is liable to be in a way that does not coincide with how the investigation occurred'.

CONCLUSIONS

In wrapping up this chapter, it is pertinent to reflect generally on the SoP approach and its relationship to other currents within political economy and the social sciences. SoP's emphasis on the interconnections between consumption and production (and potentially waste, too) for each specific commodity, and between the economic, social and cultural factors that operate in mutually shaping ways, has the appeal of providing in-depth political economic analysis. There is clear recognition of the need for 'understanding of the processes by which the consumed was created [because] consumption items do not come from thin air and the act of consuming is to participate in a potentially contested chain of activities connected to production' (Fine and Bayliss 2021: 34). Moreover, some claim to cohesion comes from SoP's underpinnings in Marxian value theory. As Fine and Bayliss say, 'to understand consumption, both quantitatively and qualitatively, we have to delve beyond the exchange relations by which individual consumption is proximately derived, and penetrate into what goes on beforehand in the (concealed, possibly misrepresented) activities that precede exchange and consumption' (2021: 34).

The potential benefits of this approach for political economic scholarship are substantial. To quote Fine and Bayliss (2021: xi) again: 'when the SoP approach lifts the lid on the production system, and its connections to consumption, the ways that agents are competing to capture value in the system are revealed. Outcomes emerge from contested social relations embedded in longstanding structures and processes.' In this way, the approach 'goes beyond the simple tracking of value chains and agents, to consider how these interact and how the state is involved in promoting specific outcomes'. The recognition of mutual interdependence between materiality and culture, rather than a linear causation from the former to the latter, is also distinctive.

So, what are the prospects for the SoP approach within political economy? These may be considered in relation to two ongoing, broader conversations in the social sciences: the increasing popularity of 'social provisioning' as a theoretical organising concept (Power 2004) and developments in interdisciplinary social science (ISS).

The former theme is particularly prominent in feminist political economy. Marilyn Power (2004: 3) uses the term '"social provisioning" to describe [an] emerging methodology' among feminists which has five main components: incorporation of caring and unpaid labour as fundamental economic activities; use of well-being as a measure of economic success; analysis of economic, political, and social processes and power relations; inclusion of ethical goals and values as an intrinsic part of the analysis; and interrogation of differences by class, race-ethnicity, and other factors. Her goal in synthesising the feminist literature that employs these themes is 'to encourage explorations in this alternative methodology' because 'social provisioning is a fruitful beginning for an *economic analysis* that has at its core a concern with human well-being, with the empowerment of subordinated groups, and to return to [...] the fulfillment of human potential in all its dimensions – for each and everyone' (Power 2004: 13). While a focus on social provisioning is not synonymous with a Systems of Provision approach, the element of convergence may be considered encouraging, indicating a basis for close cooperation, including analysis of the role of SoP in social reproduction (see Fine 2020).

What of SoP's contribution from the viewpoint of ISS? The field is expanding greatly and, according to Miller (2020), has produced three types of approaches: multi-disciplinary, cross-disciplinary, and trans-disciplinary. Multi-disciplinary approaches are those characteristically 'juxtaposing parts of several conventional disciplines'; while cross-disciplinary approaches 'involve real interaction across the conventional disciplines'; and trans-disciplinary approaches 'involve articulated conceptual frameworks that seek to transcend the more limited world views of the specialized disciplines [and are] holistic in intent' (Miller 2020: 18). Seen in terms of this taxonomy, SoP is a transdisciplinary approach. While it reflects the influence of Marxism, it goes beyond Marxism's traditional concerns in the critique of political economy (and economics). Hence, the SoP approach might be more appropriately viewed as a contribution to ISS rather than heterodox economics.

Seen from this perspective, the conundrum for SoP researchers that was noted earlier in this chapter – the tension between the order in which the research is undertaken and the form in which results are presented – can be better understood. Methods of inquiry and research investigations are notoriously hard to match throughout ISS studies (Miller 2020). Hence, the challenges arising in how empirical work is structured seem quite normal, pervading all research that is inductive rather than deductive in method. Seen in this light, the conundrum of research design and reporting does not reflect negatively on the SoP approach: rather, it comes with the trans-disciplinary territory.

NOTE

1. For alternatives to Fine's particular conception, see Marois (2012).

REFERENCES

Ball, M. (1983) *Housing Policy and Economic Power: The Political Economy of Owner Occupation*, New York: Routledge.

Bayliss, K., Fine, B. and Robertson, M. (2013) 'From Financialisation to Consumption: The Systems of Provision Approach Applied to Housing and Water', Financialisation, Economy, Society and Sustainable Development Working Paper Series No. 2.

Bayliss, K., Fine, B. and Robertson, M. (2018) 'The Systems of Provision Approach to Understanding Consumption', in Kravets, O., Maclaren, P., Miles, S. and Venkatesh, A. (eds), *The SAGE Handbook of Consumer Culture*, London: Sage, pp. 27–42.

Brooks, A. (2015) *Clothing Poverty: The Hidden World of Fast Fashion and Second-Hand Clothes*, London: Zed Books.

Cook, D.T., Miller, L.J., Schor, J.B. and Stillerman, J. (2011) 'Section Proposal: The Sociology of Consumers and Consumption', *American Sociological Association*, accessed 22.6.2021 at: https://asaconsumers.files.wordpress.com/2013/09/consumers-consumption_asa_section_proposal.pdf.

Esping-Andersen, G. (1990) *The Three Words of Welfare Capitalism*, Cambridge: Polity Press.

Evans, D.M. (2019) 'What is Consumption, Where Has it Been Going, and Does it Still Matter?', *The Sociological Review*, **67** (3), pp. 499–517.

Fine, B. (2002) *The World of Consumption: The Material and Cultural Revisited*, London: Routledge.

Fine, B. (2016) *Microeconomics: A Critical Companion*, London: Pluto Press.

Fine, B. (2020) 'Framing Social Reproduction in the Age of Financialisation', in Santos, A. and Teles, N. (eds), *Financialisation in the European Periphery: Work and Social Reproduction in Portugal*, London: Routledge, pp. 257–72.

Fine, B. and Bayliss, K. (2021) *A Guide to the Systems of Provision Approach: Who Gets What, How and Why*, Basingstoke: Palgrave Macmillan.

Fine, B. and Harris, L. (1979) *Rereading Capital*, London: Macmillan.

Fine, B. and Leopold, E. (1993) *The World of Consumption*, 1st edition, London: Routledge.

Fine, B. and Milonakis, D. (2009) *From Political Economy to Economics*, London: Routledge.

Fine, B. and Saad-Filho, A. (2016) *Marx's* Capital, 6th edition, London: Pluto Press.

Galbraith, J.K. (1998) *The Affluent Society*, New York: Houghton Mifflin.

Hodgson, G. (2008) 'An Institutional and Evolutionary Perspective on Health Economics', *Cambridge Journal of Economics*, **32**, pp. 235–56.

Hudson, I. and Hudson, M. (2021) *Consumption*, Cambridge: Polity Press.

Macinnis, D.J. and Folkes, V.S. (2009) 'The Disciplinary Status of Consumer Behavior: A Sociology of Science Perspective on Key Controversies', *Journal of Consumer Research*, **36**, pp. 899–914.

Marois, T. (2012) 'Finance, Finance Capital, and Financialization', in Fine, B., Saad-Filho, A. and Boffo, M. (eds), *The Elgar Companion to Marxist Economics*, Cheltenham, UK and Northampton, MA, USA: Edward Elgar Publishing, pp. 138–43.

Marx, K. (1973) 'Introduction', *The Grundrisse*, trans. Martin Nicolau, London: Verso.

Miller, R.C. (2018) *International Political Economy: Contrasting World Views*, 2nd edition, London: Routledge.

Miller, R.C. (2020) 'Interdisciplinarity: Its Meaning and Consequences', *Oxford Research Encyclopaedia of International Studies*, accessed online 1.9.2020 at: https://oxfordre.com/internationalstudies/view/10.1093/acrefore/9780190846626.001.0001/acrefore-9780190846626-e-92.

Pietrykowski, B. (2009) *The Political Economy of Consumer Behavior: Contesting Consumption*, London: Routledge.

Power, M. (2004) 'Social Provisioning as a Starting Point for Feminist Economics', *Feminist Economics*, **10** (3), pp. 3–19.

Ritzer, G. and Slater, D. (2001) 'Editorial', *Journal of Consumer Culture*, **1**, pp. 5–8.

Robertson, M. (2016) 'The Great British Housing Crisis', *Capital and Class*, **41** (2), pp. 195–215.

Santos, A.C., Costa, V. and Teles, N. (2014) 'The Political Economy of Consumption and Household Debt: An Interdisciplinary Contribution', *RCCS Annual Review*, **6** (October), pp. 55–82.

Schor, J. (2007) 'In Defense of Consumer Critique: Revisiting the Consumption Debates of the Twentieth Century', *The Annals of the American Academy of Political and Social Science*, **611** (1), pp. 16–30.

Veblen, T. ([1899] 2012) *The Theory of the Leisure Class*, New York: Dover Publications.

23. The diverse economies approach

Jenny Cameron and J.K. Gibson-Graham

The approach to political economy outlined in this chapter is one that self-consciously places thinking in the service of making other worlds possible. The grounds of this Diverse Economies approach are squarely located in nineteenth- and twentieth-century Marxian and feminist theory, but its genealogy has been shaped by important epistemological and ontological ruptures within these traditions. For all of us interested in alternative theories of political economy, the famous Marxist adage that we seek to understand the world in order to change it remains a driving motivation. Yet, *how* we understand and what understanding *produces* is where our approach offers a distinctive stance, one that we characterise in this chapter as a *political economy of possibility*.

In the mid-1990s, the joint authorial presence of J.K. Gibson-Graham was fed up with 'waiting for the revolution' – the strategic dead end in which Marxian political economy appeared to be mired. The piercing vision of capitalism that had been so meticulously theorised by critical scholars (and to which Gibson-Graham had contributed) had erected an edifice that was ever-inventive and all-encompassing. Leftist thinkers all appeared to agree that there was no 'outside' to capitalism. This was presented as an unfortunate, undeniable, toe-stubbing fact. In *The End of Capitalism (As We Knew It): A Feminist Critique of Political Economy* (1996), Gibson-Graham proposed that capitalist dominance was not a fact, but the product of a hegemonic 'capitalocentric' discourse that was strangling any attempt to imagine and enact other economies. To make this argument, they drew on anti-essentialist Marxian political economy and feminist poststructuralist thinking and, in doing so, rejected epistemological realism and the essentialist ontology of structural determinism. By naming this hegemonic discourse 'capitalocentrism', they shed critical light on the way that 'Big C' Capitalism had become the only model of what an economy was and could be. In its capitalist guise, the 'economy' was represented as having an insatiable need for growth and an inherent resilience to crisis. All other forms of economy were rendered inadequate or non-viable in comparison to Capitalism. Although capitalocentric discourse seemed to endow the radical theorist with superior powers of insight into the structures of economy and society, it had politically disabling effects.

Rather than waiting for the revolution, Gibson-Graham set out to challenge the dominant capitalocentric discourse that had the performative effect of limiting possibility. Focusing on radical heterogeneity and difference rather than dominance, they proposed a *diverse economy*. This was a language of economy that was more inclusive of the wide range of practices that make and support livelihoods, create and distribute wealth, marshal and steward resources, make infrastructures and shape futures. They argued there was a need to broaden the scope of who might act to reshape economies and, thus, who was the 'subject of economy'. They also proposed starting right now with what is already at hand by engaging in collective action to build ethical *community (not capitalist) economies*.

A collective of scholars and practitioners working with Gibson-Graham and each other have subsequently identified their performative intellectual stance as a form of ontological politics

(Gibson-Graham et al. 2015). For the Community Economies Collective, ethical economic practices already exist in abundance (Gibson-Graham et al. 2021). Determining just how these practices might connect and cohere to build a different world is the current task for a political economy of possibility. New kinds of economies are not there to be 'discovered': they must be performed and experimented with. This is a materialist argument that recognises that a different economy cannot be thought into existence; rather, it must be enacted and made durable by multiple means, including infrastructures, subjects, ecologies *and* theories.

This chapter briefly introduces the principal theoretical contributors to the Diverse Economies approach, namely: anti-essentialist Marxian political economy and feminist post-structuralism. It concludes with a discussion of the ever-evolving practice of making community economies and some research directions for a political economy of possibility.

A DIVERSE ECONOMY OF CLASS PROCESSES

Theorising diverse economies started by challenging the singularity of economic identity with a reading of Marxian political economy that emphasised difference, not dominance (Gibson-Graham 2020). These readings were inspired by the anti-essentialist analysis of Marxian political economy developed by Stephen Resnick and Richard Wolff (1987). The two components of Resnick and Wolff's work that have been particularly important in developing the Diverse Economies approach are their class analysis and their introduction of Louis Althusser's theory of overdetermination into political economy.

The distinctive reading of Marx offered by Resnick and Wolff draws attention to the use of class as a verb to describe the *process* of producing, appropriating and distributing surplus labour, in contrast to the more familiar use of class as a noun to describe groups of people defined by their structural location with respect to the mode of production. The class process points to the particular role of human labour in creating new wealth (often in concert with exploitation of nature) and to the legally and extra-legally regulated mechanisms with their varying degrees of agreement or coercion that govern how new wealth is generated and apportioned.

In *Capital: A Critique of Political Economy*, Marx ([1867] 1976) distinguished the capitalist class process from other historical forms of class. The capitalist class process is one in which workers produce surplus labour that is then appropriated (or taken) by the capitalist as surplus value and distributed in ways that might benefit the latter. The market price paid for waged labour masks this process of wealth appropriation. Marx theorised this hidden transaction as a form of theft from the producers, the rightful owners of this wealth. Marx identified other class processes. In the feudal class process, lords directly appropriate peasants' surplus labour in-kind in the form of products such as grain or livestock. Traditionally, this arrangement was underpinned by the lord's commitment to protect the peasants, and the peasants' right to access land. In the collective (or cooperative) class process, the workers jointly own the surplus labour that they produce together. In the self-appropriative class process, a single producer owns what she or he produces. And in the slave class process, the master owns not just all that the slaves produce, but the slaves themselves. This arrangement is frequently intertwined with an ideology of racial hierarchy which means that slaves are subject to multiple and ever-present abuses.

Resnick and Wolff's anti-essentialist Marxism opened up 'the economy' to diversity by pointing to the continued coexistence of these different class processes. Their analysis also pointed to the prevalence of class processes in a range of sites, not just in industrial enterprises or mines, but also in households, farms, schools, universities and churches (for example, Gibson-Graham et al. 2000; Gibson-Graham et al. 2001). It brought to light how, in a modern so-called 'capitalist' economy, a large number of people's livelihoods are maintained by participating in non-capitalist class processes, whether it be in their own small business or farm, a coercive feudal household, an employee-owned business or worker-owned cooperative, or a slave enterprise. Furthermore, all of us are involved in multiple class processes (at work, at home and in the community) and, therefore, occupy multiple economic subject positions.

This reframing has major implications for how we think about economic determination, that is, what causes economic restructuring and social transformation. The anti-essentialist approach advanced by Resnick and Wolff drew inspiration from Louis Althusser's concept of overdetermination (Althusser 1968). Simply put, this means acknowledging the myriad dynamics and relationships at work in a world in which things are multiply determined. No one dynamic (such as the appropriative moment of the class process or the drive to accumulate) is necessarily more efficacious than any other. In a world understood as being comprised of multiple coexisting determinations it is up to us as thinkers, writers and researchers to make decisions about how we proceed with making sense of the world. Resnick and Wolff explain this in terms of using an 'entry point' (1987: 25–30). Their entry point for analysis is class understood as a process. Selecting an entry point is itself an overdetermined process and the outcome of a host of interactions, as Resnick and Wolff (1987: 27) describe:

> We would [...] point to the variety of political, cultural, and economic processes whose interaction overdetermined our deployment of the class process as our conceptual entry point. Among them would be certain educational and political processes in which we have participated, as well as certain imaginative processes in which we conjured up visions of a future society that we might like to see, as well as certain economic processes in which we were constrained to participate, and so on.

Entry points are the culmination of our pasts as well as our projections for the type of world we want to live in and that we think might be feasible. This signals the end of the authoritative all-knowing theorist who has the 'correct' analysis, ushering in a more pragmatic, humble, self-consciously performative and, thus, political thinker.

The entry point for analysis in a Diverse Economies approach is ethical economic action and practice, with the aim of expanding opportunities for collective actions that might help produce a more just and more livable world. Class as a process provides one lens for helping do this because of how it sheds light on different ways of appropriating surplus labour that are less exploitative and different ways of distributing surplus value that will contribute to the well-being of people and the planet. As we discuss below, other lenses used in the Diverse Economies approach focus on different forms of work and ways of remunerating labour; different types of transactions and ways of establishing or bypassing commensurability; different forms of property and how these might be used to benefit people and the planet; and different forms of finance and ways of investing in futures.

In terms of ways of appropriating surplus labour, one strategy is to ensure that workers receive adequate remuneration for their labours (and that they work in safe conditions). This political intervention, typically the focus of leftist political struggles, targets exploitation and the appropriative moment of the class process. Another strategy, also focused on the appropriative moment, is for workers to become the appropriators of their own surplus labour through setting up worker-owned cooperatives or through employee buyout schemes. Struggles such as Argentina's *recuperadas por sus trabajadores* (or worker-recuperated enterprises) movement have helped to make this type of intervention more visible by showing how capitalist enterprises can be transformed into worker cooperatives (Heras and Vieta 2020).

In terms of ways of distributing surplus labour, there are a range of strategies that can contribute to well-being. In a stereotypical capitalist class process, the priority is to maximise profits, for example, by distributing surplus value to managers who can pressure workers to work faster; to accountants who will devise ways to minimise tax payments; and to marketing firms to increase product sales. But surplus is a potentiating force that can be used to generate well-being both within and beyond the firm. For example, some of the worker cooperatives in Argentina take the view that the surplus labour they produce does not belong to them but to the wider community in which their enterprises are located (Gibson-Graham et al. 2013). These cooperatives make significant distributions to schools, healthcare centres, libraries and the like. Simultaneously, workers in these cooperatives pay themselves a living wage, rather than an extravagant one, to ensure that they generate surplus that can be distributed. In the Mondragon cooperatives in the Basque region of Spain, surplus is sometimes distributed across the network of cooperatives. For example, during times of economic crisis, workers in one cooperative may be paid to re-train (via a distribution of surplus generated by others in the network) so they can shift to working in another cooperative. In social enterprises, especially those with a non-profit legal form, surplus is distributed back into the enterprise to help generate more job opportunities for those who are often marginalised from employment options.

Importantly, one consequence of the anti-essentialism that characterises the Diverse Economies approach is that it does not assume that capitalist enterprises are necessarily destructive (Cameron 2020). Capitalist enterprises *can* appropriate surplus labour from workers in ways that are non-exploitative (for example, by providing safe working conditions and high levels of remuneration for workers, and by incorporating workers in decision-making). Capitalist enterprises *can* distribute surplus value in ways that will benefit communities and environments (and in the next section we provide some examples of how this is happening in the manufacturing sector).

A second consequence of the anti-essentialism of the Diverse Economies approach is that it provides a starting point for dislodging 'Big C' Capitalism. In place of discussion of the capitalist system or the capitalist context or Capitalism, the focus is on ways of producing, appropriating and distributing surplus labour in a capitalist class process. Our ontological entry point is that we live in a radically heterogeneous economic world in which there are multiple economic actions, practices and possibilities. It makes no sense to ask about how Capitalism operates or how Capitalism swallows up other economic systems or how Capitalism is aided and abetted by neoliberalism. These types of questions reflect a capitalocentric framing and what we have elsewhere discussed as instances of 'strong theory' (Gibson-Graham 2006, 2020; Cameron 2020). Instead, in a Diverse Economies approach, the focus is on interrogating specific examples and instances without assuming in advance the determinants that may or may not be at work, deploying what we have elsewhere discussed as 'weak theory' (Gibson-Graham 2006, 2020). This does not preclude taking a hard, critical look at the power of certain capitalists and capitalist businesses to, for example, squander wealth, corrupt processes of public regulation, pervert justice and enrol racist practices to suit their accumulation goals. In a diverse economy, however, competition and private interest are exercised in many different ways. And, in an overdetermined economy, a range of non-class actions affects whether society's wealth is pooled or dispersed equitably, or not. Regarding class as a process offers one lens for contributing to ethical economic actions and practices because of how it opens a plethora of avenues for tracing flows of wealth and economic power and, importantly, proposing new mechanisms by which these flows can be directed to building a more livable world.

EXPANDING THE DIVERSE ECONOMY

The work of feminist economists and feminist poststructuralist thinkers plays a significant role in expanding the conception of a Diverse Economy to include all those 'other' activities and practices that contribute to livelihoods but that mainstream economics ignores, silences or renders invisible. The empirical work of feminist economists has been crucial in documenting the scale of what was excluded from 'the economy' in both neoclassical economics and most other traditions in political economy. The philosophical approach of feminist poststructuralists helped to expose how capitalocentric discourse worked to subordinate the power of these other economic realms. Deconstruction and queering provided techniques for further challenging the singularity of economic identity and the essentialism of structural determination.

Marilyn Waring's (1988) documentation of the extent to which women's unpaid labour contributed to a national economy was a major eye-opener. Feminist scholars documented the significant amount of time that women spent doing unpaid work and non-market-oriented activities such as housework, volunteering, child-rearing, and care for the elderly and infirmed (see Folbre 2001). The revelation that this women's work was uncounted and unvalued severely undermined economists' claims to neutral coverage of what constituted an economy. Women's work was positioned as having no determining effect on economic fortunes. It was important but subordinate to the work that generated wealth, transacted commodities and made investments.

The empirical research of feminist economists had a parallel in the work of social scientists concerned with the 'developing' or majority world. Economic anthropologists and informal economy scholars pointed to the quantitative dominance of workers involved in subsistence and self-employment in functioning economies that were, nevertheless, regarded as backward, stagnant and not dynamic enough to raise people out of poverty, as did capitalist economic activity (for example, Hart 1985; Ostrom 1990; Gudeman 2001; see also Gibson et al. 2018). Others have pointed to the global geographic spread of economic practices such as cooperativism and community-based financing by diasporic communities (for example, Hossein 2019). It seemed that there were a great many practices that contributed to livelihoods but did not contribute to 'the economy' as it was conventionally understood.

The diversity of all these economic activities was captured in the simple representation of the economy as an iceberg (Figure 23.1). Visible above the waterline are the capitalist businesses, the commodity exchange markets and the paid workforce that constitute what is seen as the legitimate economy. Below the waterline are the myriad additional activities and practices that people are involved in and that help to keep them alive. This image by J.K. Gibson-Graham and the Community Economies Collective took off as a tool for undermining capitalist dominance, shifting to a language of the diverse economy, and enacting a more inclusive vision of economy in which people made multiple contributions in different class and non-class processes, and in a variety of settings, not just the formal workplace.

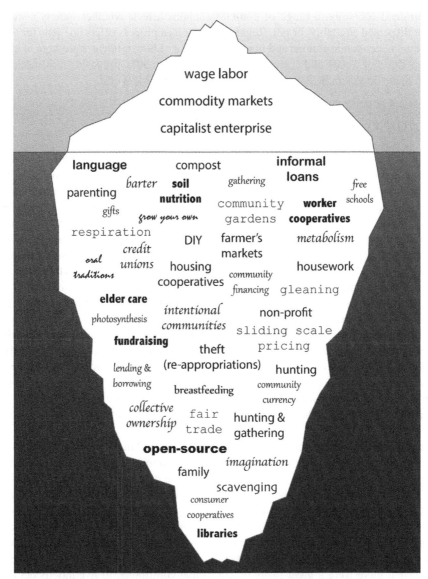

Figure 23.1   *Diverse Economies Iceberg*

The inventory work that went into elaborating the Diverse Economies approach was accompanied by a critique of the knowledge/power nexus by which unpaid labour and informal economic practices are subordinated within capitalocentric discourse. Feminist poststructuralists (also employing an anti-essentialist epistemology) used Derrida's method of deconstruction to unpick the binary structures central to Enlightenment knowledge and show that meaning is always in process and incomplete. Contrary to the common misunderstanding that deconstruction refers to the act of breaking something down and demolishing meaning, this way of seeing highlights moments of contradiction and undecidability in what appears to be neatly conceived structures or text; and it pinpoints the decisions and arbitrary violence intrinsic to all attempts to fix meaning. The effect of fixing the meaning of Capitalism (the tip of the iceberg) as opposed to non-capitalism (everything under the waterline), and then of conflating Capitalism with the idea of 'an economy' was, Gibson-Graham (1996) argued, to violently make less credible a whole swathe of economic activities (in addition to class processes) that have kept the world afloat for millennia.

It was the poststructuralist feminist critique of phallogocentrism – that is, systems of knowledge that privileged the masculinised dominant term in any binary – that inspired Gibson-Graham (1996) to propose that economic theory was capitalocentric and that capitalocentrism was standing in the way of imagining and enacting 'other' economies. Capitalocentrism positions all economic activities in relation to a set of capitalist practices (namely, waged labour, market exchange of commodities and privately accumulating business), as either the same as, a complement to, the opposite of, or existing within the container of capitalism. There is no distinctive identity or independent dynamism granted to a wide range of activities that include, for example, caring labour, reciprocal exchange of labour, worker-owned cooperatives, sole proprietorships, ritual gifting and sharing with natural ecologies or other species. The consequences of this discursive violence are only just now becoming widely recognised.

A political economy of possibility accepts that we can never escape the undecidability of meaning. What constitutes the economy will never be settled definitively. But herein lies the political moment of *political* economy – the moment when a decision is made to fix meaning (temporarily, at least) because of the effect it might perform, the actions it might inform and the worlds that this might make possible. Once a diverse economy of radical heterogeneity is sketched out, the political moment of stepping into the fray and performing new meanings presents itself. This includes identifying the diversity of activities, unravelling the various logics or determinations that impel the activities (for example, care, service, stewardship, survival), and recognising that these things are overdetermined (not just by familiar socio-legal formations, but by ways of seeing and knowing with which we are unacquainted). In the Diverse Economies approach, decisions about which elements and alignments to bring to the fore involve both a calculation and a leap of faith about ways that economic activities and practices might be reshaped to service people and the planet. This is not to 'wish away' embedded relations of power but to acknowledge that there are always openings and opportunities. As discussed above, as thinkers, writers and researchers we make decisions about our entry points, and this includes deciding on the extent to which we focus on what seems to be constantly obstructing change or whether we seek out those moments that reveal how things might be otherwise, with a view to strengthening these possibilities.

Developing new ways of researching determination frequently comes up against the assumptions of connection that are part of a dominant knowledge system. Here the strategy of queering as suggested by queer politics of the 1980s and 1990s has been useful. Queering destabilised meanings that were once viewed as essentially locked together, unravelling the clear lining-up of the male/female binary in terms of biology, socialisation, cultural roles, desire, sex and gender (for example, Butler 1990; Sedgwick 1993). If elements of personal identity could be queered, so too could elements of economic identity. In place of a Capitalist whole comprised of entangled capitalist enterprises, commodified transactions and wage-labour relations, the Diverse Economies approach delinks these elements, such that they are regarded as nothing more than one way of running an enterprise, one way of transacting goods and services and one way of remunerating work. Furthermore, there are no necessary logics driving these elements: capitalist enterprises need not be governed by profit-making to the exclusion of other considerations; markets need not operate on a basis of price-taking; and wage-labour relations need not be cornered in an unending tussle between employer and employee.

Returning to the industrial heartland of political economy, a Diverse Economies approach has been used to study an emerging cluster of manufacturers in a way that illustrates this delinking of elements. The study focuses on manufacturers who are guided by a commitment to generating better employment outcomes (including for those who are marginalised from employment options) and to manufacturing in ways that will reduce adverse environmental impacts (Gibson et al. 2019). The manufacturers include cooperatives, social enterprises *and* capitalist enterprises (in public and private ownership). Their shared commitment to better social and environmental outcomes shapes how these diverse forms of the firm are appropriating surplus labour (in a way that prioritises workers' rights for fair wages and safe working conditions) and distributing surplus value (to transform their production processes and reduce environmental impacts). Capitalist enterprises are taking their place alongside social enterprises and cooperatives to problem-solve ways in which manufacturing can redress social and environmental harms, including by fostering novel transactions. As part of this study, the researchers have stepped into the fray by engaging with politicians and policymakers to make visible the new culture of manufacturing that these firms are building (Cameron and Gibson 2020).

In locking together a set of practices as Capitalism, 'the state' has been seen by some political economists as inescapably interwoven into the whole, with the latest neoliberal iteration of the state serving to protect and advance the interests of capitalists (for example, Harvey 2007; Brenner et al. 2010). For others, there is some hope that the vestiges of a social democratic welfare orientation can be worked with (for example, Eskelinen et al. 2020). Recognising that the state is a complex and diverse set of entities, the Diverse Economy approach theorises a diversity of state practices, refusing to line them up into any pre-determined structure (see also Ferguson 2010; Mazzucato 2013), leaving it possible to use a queer logic to be creative about economic change. The role of state payments to citizens in a diverse economy is a case in point. Feminists have not been reticent in commandeering the state to enact changes that benefit the lives of women and children. The fight for equal pay in the paid workplace is one agenda that has been championed at the national state level, but so too have struggles to get wealth distributed to carers, to childcare, and to people with disabilities and the aged who seek to live independent and dignified lives. These state payments are *investments* in economies of care, which are supplemented by vast contributions of unpaid, gifted and volunteer labour largely done by women. Current interest in a Universal Basic Income signals another strategy by which state redistribution to guarantee a livable income is a way of investing in economies in which people are free to work on generative projects of environmental repair, creative art, social connection, innovative care, waste management, renewable technologies, sustainable travel and so on (Cameron 2017).

The diversifying of the economy that feminism helped make possible, the deconstructing of the economy that poststructuralist feminism enabled, and the queering of the economy that queer theorists and activists provoked has not just opened up the scope of political economy interventions. There are also implications for how the subjects of economies are conceived.

For example, in the emerging economic landscape of just and sustainable manufacturing, the meaning of 'worker' and 'employer' is shifting. A hybrid economic subject emerges as a maker, a social justice producer and an environmental carer. This subject is positioned not in antagonism to the capitalist, but in antagonism to unscrupulous competitors, neglectful regulators and unthinking consumers. Providing a Universal Basic Income defuses the notion of the 'unemployed', 'unproductive' and dependent citizen; and it activates new economic subjects, potentially as direct subsistence providers, community builders, cultural producers and extended family carers.

PERFORMING MORE ETHICAL ECONOMIES

So far, we have presented the Diverse Economies approach as one that reframes the economy as radically heterogeneous and as populated by myriad diverse economic activities. Many of these activities exploit people and the planet – but not all. A diverse economy includes economic activities that are conducted in other ways, some perhaps recognising ethical interdependence and honouring reciprocity, others purposefully striving for equitable sustainability. The foundational anti-essentialism of the Diverse Economies approach opens up the economy as a space of possibility. Yet this discursive opening up does not guarantee concrete change. If more ethical economies are to be realised, they must be imagined, enacted and made durable. This work is not wish-fulfillment, but involves pragmatic and strategic steps about how to use what is at hand in order to help make other worlds possible.

A starting point for Diverse Economies researchers is to develop inventories of different forms of work and ways of remunerating labour; different forms of enterprise and ways of appropriating and distributing surplus; different types of transactions and ways of establishing or bypassing commensurability; different forms of property and ways of accessing and benefiting from these; and different forms of finance and ways of investing in futures. Scholars from a variety of disciplines are taking this work into a range of directions, as illustrated by entries in *The Handbook of Diverse Economies* (Gibson-Graham and Dombroski 2020).

J.K. Gibson-Graham and members of the Community Economies Collective are interested in those practices that enact ethical concern for the fortunes of the 'other' and the 'whole'. We are particularly interested in bringing to visibility those that enact an ethic of care for: (a) surviving well (by people and the planet); (b) distributing surplus to grow social and environmental well-being; (c) encountering others (human and non-human) responsibly; (d) making, sharing and caring for commonly held and common pool resources; (e) investing in equitable and flourishing futures; and (f) consuming sustainably. The contours of a theory of *community economies* have developed out of inventorying real live cases of ethical economic action around these six concerns (Gibson-Graham 2006; Gibson-Graham et al. 2013).

Following Jean-Luc Nancy (1991), we theorise community as always in the process of becoming, as not presuming sameness and, following new developments in ecological humanities, as not only 'human'. Although community is usually associated with groups of people, we challenge ourselves to envision community as a process of enactment with earth others as well as humans. We re-centre the idea of community on the making of more-than-human ecological livelihoods (Miller 2019) involving the participation of plants, animals, atmospheres, soils, humans, bacteria and more. A political economy of possibility shifts focus away from a sole interest in the capitalocentric concerns of paid work, capitalist business, market exchange, private property and market finance with their associated 'driving motivations' of individualism, personal gain, private ownership, competition and growth. This political economy involves stepping into the mess to activate and support ethical action around care for the ecological basis of life, and for the well-being of people and the planet (Gibson-Graham et al. 2013).

In a series of place-based experiments, we have engaged citizen researchers to test out new ways of making community economies possible. In the resource region of the Latrobe Valley in south-eastern Australia, the Community Partnering Project used poststructuralist partici- patory action research to develop an economic pathway based on the 'assets' of those most marginalised by restructuring in the region, following the downsizing and privatisation of its local state-owned coal mines and power stations (Cameron and Gibson 2005). What came to the fore was the diversity of people's creative outlets. The project saw citizen-led initiation of three social enterprises, a community garden, a Santa's Workshop making Christmas decorations, and a woodworking and repair shed. The attempt to reframe people rather than coal as the 'resource' at the centre of the Latrobe Valley economy had a large impact on those involved, but it did not gain the needed support of local government. Caught up in political jockeying, the community-based initiatives that were started during the period of research continued for several years (in the case of Santa's Workshop, for a decade) but eventually fizzled out.

In so many resource extraction regions in Australia and around the world, an antagonistic 'jobs versus environment' discourse corrals thinking. For the *ecological* health and well-being of the Latrobe Valley to be placed on an equal footing with that of *human* health and well-being was a long way off at the turn of the millennium when the Community Partnering Project was running. In Australia's resource regions, that shift is yet to be embraced, but small steps are being made. In recent years, the Valley has suffered major environmental challenges from a prolonged mine fire caused by company negligence. There has been increasing com- munity recognition of the extent of damage to the health of people and ecologies wrought by decades of brown coal mining and electricity generation, and there is greater preparedness to act on social and environmental harms. In this context, a combined union and environmental movement initiative, Earthworker Cooperative, is putting the well-being of people and the environment at the heart of its operations. Government support is uneven and, once again, the necessary institutional backing that this venture requires is not easy to find. The Latrobe Valley is, however, an important test site for making community economies possible. There is an appetite for change and the availability of people willing to shift their old economic identity and embrace new commitments to environmental care and collective business. The power of a discourse of capitalist extractivism as the ultimate provider of material wealth is being undermined by its impact on embodied well-being but, without a supportive infrastructure of laws, regulations and education, experiments in a renewable future are vulnerable.

One of the conditions of bringing community economies into existence is metrics that can clearly demonstrate their benefit. To measure is to make real in our metricised society. Feminist economists used this insight to great effect and have now influenced national gov- ernments to regularly collect data on unpaid caring and household labour. The imputed value of this labour is equal to if not more than the value created in the commoditised economy (Ironmonger 1996). A political economy of possibility can extend this success and begin to measure the return on investment that care affords, or how environmental repair and change of habits can reduce ecological footprint impacts.

In a different place-based project in suburban Paris, we have used quantitative tools to document the value of commoning and to make the case, in terms that resonate with policymakers, for why there should be support for community-based initiatives founded on social and environmental justice (Petrescu et al. 2021). R-Urban was an urban commons project initiated in 2011 by the activist architecture practice atelier d'architecture autogérée (aaa) on unused urban land in Colombes, a multicultural municipality on the outskirts of Paris where residents have incomes below the national average and where social housing towers are interspersed with single-family dwellings. The project was centred on community food production, materials recycling and activities for transitioning to a smaller urban environmental footprint. It included a micro-farm, family garden plots, cafe, teaching space, compost school and a self-constructed community recycling and eco-construction centre with workshop space, materials storage, a design studio and an apartment. The researchers adapted the Community Economy Return on Investment (CEROI) developed by Gibson-Graham et al. (2013) and presented the community economies accounts for one year (2015) for R-Urban. The accounts documented the direct financial revenues generated by R-Urban (such as sales from the resident-run cafe), the value of unpaid volunteer labour inputs, the value of increased individual capacity (including the value of skills that were developed that led to employment outcomes), and the costs saved (including the costs saved for individuals and households, the state and the planet). According to these calculations, in 2015 the Community Economy Investment of €1.2 million resulted in a Community Economy Return on Investment of 180 per cent. However, these outcomes, even framed in terms of their return on investment, were not sufficient to sway a new right-wing municipal administration, and the project was subsequently evicted and replaced by a parking lot. Nevertheless, this is not the end of the story. The R-Urban model has been replicated in three other urban areas of Paris (in Gennevilliers, Nanterre and Bagneux, by aaa) and in two areas of London (in Hackney Wick and Poplar, by PublicWorks), and in these locations there has been funding support from local municipalities. Using a tool based on the idea of return on investment may seem to be ceding to the dominant economisation of lifeworlds. If a political economy of possibility is to proceed, though, tools are needed to track inputs and outputs of money, labour, care, conviviality and experimentation, making these inputs and outputs more visible and helping to add to the infrastructure that might support the shift to more renewable futures.

The research in the Latrobe Valley and Paris are just two examples of the ways that members of the Community Economies Collective have used the Diverse Economies approach to enact a political economy of possibility. The work starts with the economic diversity that is already at hand and mobilises this diversity for more ethical economies.

WHERE TO FOR A POLITICAL ECONOMY OF POSSIBILITY?

The Diverse Economies approach has been shaped by some of the significant epistemological and ontological ruptures within the traditions of Marxian and feminist thought and practice. What has resulted is an embrace of performativity and anti-essentialism as the basis for progressing a political economy of possibility. The performative understanding means that in a Diverse Economies approach, theory and research are a means for building worlds. How and what we think matters. Theorising economic diversity outside of a capitalocentric framing supports research to make more visible the multitude of possibilities that abound and that might be acted on. Using an anti-essentialist understanding means that there is a willingness to trace rather than assume identity and alignments, and to use empirical description to unravel potential pathways and connections. Thus, for example, relations of power or actions of 'the state' are to be investigated rather than presumed. There are many entry-points into researching the radical heterogeneity of diverse economies. Our thinking and our political commitments are directed towards fostering ethically oriented community economies.

Like so many others, Diverse Economies researchers are grappling with how to respond to what has been called 'The Great Acceleration' (Steffen et al. 2015): the speeding up of both human activity and human planetary impact since the mid-twentieth century. One promising avenue involves the radical rethinking of what it means to be human, with implications for the distinction between economy, society and environment (Miller 2019). The idea of the more-than-human has been crucial for demonstrating how the human body is not a bounded entity, but part of the worlds of microbes, other entities, flows, relations and energies. These worlds encompass multiple beings that are engaged in entangled practices of sustenance and securing livelihoods (Miller 2020). Thus, it makes no sense to distinguish between economies, societies and environments; instead, we might imagine a multiplicity of interdependent livelihood practices which involve humans to varying degrees. Where this might take us is an open question. However, as a first step, we might start to trace out some of the lesser-known livelihood practices to which humans could play supporting roles.

Here we are also learning from important scholarship on Indigenous and black economic practices that sheds light on how livelihoods have been shaped for millennia by different cosmologies, including many that are still operating today (for example, Bargh 2012; Hossein 2019). This is not a matter of appropriating these practices, but to further deepen understandings of the prevalence of past and current economic diversity, the types of discourses, relationships and ethics that sustain those practices, and what opportunities there are for a political economy of possibility to be extended.

REFERENCES

Althusser, L. (1968) *For Marx*, trans. Brewster, B. (1970), New York: Vintage.
Bargh, M. (2012) 'Rethinking and re-shaping indigenous economies: Māori geothermal energy enterprises', *Journal of Enterprising Communities: People and Places in the Global Economy*, **6** (3), pp. 271–83.
Brenner, N., Peck, J. and Theodore, N. (2010) 'After neoliberalization?', *Globalizations*, **7** (3), pp. 327–45.
Butler, J. (1990) *Gender Trouble: Feminism and the Subversion of Identity*, New York: Routledge.
Cameron, J. (ed.) (2017) 'Book review symposium – James Ferguson's "Give a Man a Fish: Reflections on the New Politics of Distribution"', *Antipode Online*, 1 February, accessed 24.4.2022 at: https://antipodeonline.org/2017/02/01/give-a-man-a-fish/.
Cameron, J. (2020) 'Framing essay: the diversity of enterprise', in Gibson-Graham, J.K. and Dombroski, K. (eds), *The Handbook of Diverse Economies*, Cheltenham, UK and Northampton, MA, USA: Edward Elgar Publishing, pp. 26–39.
Cameron, J. and Gibson, K. (2005) 'Participatory action research in a poststructuralist vein', *Geoforum*, **36** (3), pp. 315–31.
Cameron, J. and Gibson, K. (2020) 'Action research for diverse economies', in Gibson-Graham, J.K. and Dombroski, K. (eds), *The Handbook of Diverse Economies*, Cheltenham, UK and Northampton, MA, USA: Edward Elgar Publishing, pp. 511–19.

Eskelinen, T., Hirvilammi, T. and Venäläinen, J. (eds) (2020) *Enacting Community Economies Within a Welfare State*, MayFly Books: http://mayflybooks.org/.

Ferguson, J. (2010) 'The uses of neoliberalism', *Antipode*, **41** (s1), pp. 166–84.

Folbre, N. (2001) *The Invisible Heart: Economics and Family Values*, New York: New Press.

Gibson, K., Hill, A. and Law, L. (2018) 'Community economies in Southeast Asia: a hidden economic geography', in McGregor, A., Law, L. and Miller, F. (eds), *Routledge Handbook of Southeast Asian Development*, London: Routledge, pp. 131–41.

Gibson, K., Cameron, J., Healy, S. and McNeill, J. (2019) *Beyond Business as Usual: A 21st Century Culture of Manufacturing in Australia*, Sydney: Institute for Culture and Society, Western Sydney University, accessed 1.4.2021 at: http://www.communityeconomies.org/publications/reports/beyond-business-usual-21st-century-culture-manufacturing-australia.

Gibson-Graham, J.K. (1996) *The End of Capitalism (As We Knew It): A Feminist Critique of Political Economy*, Oxford: Blackwell.

Gibson-Graham, J.K. (2006) *A Postcapitalist Politics*, Minnesota: University of Minneapolis Press.

Gibson-Graham, J.K. (2020) 'Reading for difference', in Gibson-Graham, J.K. and Dombroski, K. (eds), *The Handbook of Diverse Economies*, Cheltenham, UK and Northampton, MA, USA: Edward Elgar Publishing, pp. 476–87.

Gibson-Graham, J.K. and Dombroski, K. (eds) (2020) *The Handbook of Diverse Economies*, Cheltenham, UK and Northampton, MA, USA: Edward Elgar Publishing.

Gibson-Graham, J.K., Cameron, J. and Healy, S. (2013) *Take Back the Economy: An Ethical Guide to Transforming our Communities*, Minneapolis: University of Minnesota Press.

Gibson-Graham, J.K., Resnick, S. and Wolff, R. (eds) (2000) *Class and Its Others*, Minneapolis: University of Minnesota Press.

Gibson-Graham, J.K., Resnick, S. and Wolff, R. (eds) (2001) *Re/presenting Class: Essays in Postmodern Marxism*, Durham, NC: Duke University Press.

Gibson-Graham, J.K., Roelvink, G. and St Martin, K. (eds) (2015) *Making Other Worlds Possible: Performing Diverse Economies*, Minneapolis: University of Minnesota Press.

Gibson-Graham, J.K., Cameron, J., Dombroski, K., Healy, S., Miller, E. and The Community Economies Collective (2021) 'Cultivating community economies: tools for building a liveable world', in Speth, J. and Courrier, K. (eds), *The New Systems Reader: Alternatives to a Failed Economy*, New York: Routledge, pp. 410–32.

Gudeman, S. (2001) *The Anthropology of Economy: Commodity, Market, and Culture*, Oxford: Blackwell.

Hart, K. (1985) 'The informal economy', *The Cambridge Journal of Anthropology*, **10** (2), pp. 54–8.

Harvey, D. (2007) *A Brief History of Neoliberalism*, Oxford: Oxford University Press.

Heras, A.I. and Vieta, M. (2020) 'Self-managed enterprise: worker-recuperated cooperatives in Argentina and Latin America', in Gibson-Graham, J.K. and Dombroski, K. (eds), *The Handbook of Diverse Economies*, Cheltenham, UK and Northampton, MA, USA: Edward Elgar Publishing, pp. 48–56.

Hossein, C.S. (2019) 'A black epistemology for the social and solidarity economy: the black social economy', *The Review of Black Political Economy*, **46** (3), pp. 209–29.

Ironmonger, D. (1996) 'Counting outputs, capital inputs and caring labor: estimating gross household product', *Feminist Economics*, **2** (3), pp. 37–64.

Marx, K. ([1867] 1976) *Capital: A Critique of Political Economy*, trans. Fowkes, B., Harmondsworth: Penguin Books in association with New Left Review.

Mazzucato, M. (2013) *The Entrepreneurial State: Debunking Public vs. Private Sector Myths*, London: Anthem Press.

Miller, E. (2019) *Reimagining Livelihoods: Life Beyond Economy, Society, and Environment*, Minneapolis: University of Minnesota Press.

Miller, E. (2020) 'More-than-human agency: from the human economy to ecological livelihoods', in Gibson-Graham, J.K. and Dombroski, K. (eds), *The Handbook of Diverse Economies*, Cheltenham, UK and Northampton, MA, USA: Edward Elgar Publishing, pp. 402–10.

Nancy, J.-L. (1991) *The Inoperative Community*, Minneapolis: University of Minnesota Press.

Ostrom, E. (1990) *Governing the Commons: The Evolution of Institutions for Collective Action*, Cambridge: Cambridge University Press.

Petrescu, D., Petcou, C., Safri, M. and Gibson, K. (2021) 'Calculating the value of the commons: generating resilient urban futures', *Environmental Policy and Governance*, **31** (3), pp. 159–74.

Resnick, S. and Wolff, R. (1987) *Knowledge and Class: A Marxian Critique of Political Economy*, Chicago, IL and London: University of Chicago Press.

Sedgwick, E. (1993) *Tendencies*, Durham, NC: Duke University Press.

Steffen, W., Broadgate, W., Deutsch, L., Gaffney, O. and Ludwig, C. (2015) 'The trajectory of the Anthropocene: the great acceleration', *The Anthropocene Review*, **2** (1), pp. 81–98.

Waring, M. (1988) *Counting for Nothing: What Men Value and What Women are Worth*, Sydney: Allen and Unwin.

PART V

EXTENDING POLITICAL ECONOMY THROUGH INTERDISCIPLINARITY

24. Spatial political economy

Brett Christophers

The importance of the spatial dimension in political economy can be illustrated in various ways. Consider, for example, the events of 2016, a genuine *annus horribilis* for the Anglo-American liberal establishment which was left reeling by the savage one-two punch of the Brexit vote in the UK's referendum on membership of the European Union, swiftly followed by Donald's Trump's victory in the US presidential election. Pious orthodoxies about a rising post-1970s tide of prosperity having lifted all boats – albeit having encountered distinctly choppy waters in 2007–09 before a period of apparent becalming – were rapidly, if not universally, shelved. For what became unarguable in the wake of the Brexit and Trump victories was that those victories were driven substantially, although certainly not only, by the dissatisfactions of a large class of economically left-behind voters. In short, liberal commentators accepted what had for many years been obvious to those less compromised by ideological blinders: that neoliberalism produces vast swathes of losers as well as winners.

And there was more. The commentators also noticed that the left-behind people who voted for Trump and Brexit shared something more than their lowly socio-economic status – a distinctive geographical pattern. They were concentrated in parts of the USA and UK – most notably the Midwest in the former and the north-east in the latter – that historically had featured thriving industrial economies, but which had seen those industrial formations radically hollowed out during the neoliberal era, to be replaced not so much by different economic formations as by economic vacuums. The left-behind shared, in other words, an economic geography. The *Financial Times* spoke for the liberal commentariat more generally when its economics editor, Chris Giles (2016), in discussing the UK case specifically, conceded that 'we' – and the 'we' spoke volumes – 'have to recognise that geography matters'. Warming to the theme, Giles's colleague, Martin Sandbu (2016), subsequently argued in his own column that the evident importance of geography warranted the formulation of what he referred to as an 'economics of place'.

The premises of this would-be economics of place appeared to be twofold. First, geography mattered in the straightforward sense that economic outcomes differed from place to place. Far from a rising tide equally lifting all boats, some boats remained at a distinctly low ebb, and others were marooned, having seemingly not even left shore. Second, geography mattered as a starting condition. The reason that different places experienced different economic outcomes, Giles and Sandbu ventured, was that they were initially endowed with different propensities to succeed. 'Towns located close to coal seams or the seaside were perfect for industry and respite 100 years ago', wrote Giles (2016), 'but not today. Britain can choose to pump in welfare, but this is not compensation for lost relevance. We can build infrastructure, but this is not sufficient to overcome locational disadvantage.'

Meanwhile, commentators from further to the left (e.g. Hazeldine 2017) offered a very different reading. True enough, they said, the votes for Brexit and Trump emanated disproportionately from regions suffering deep-seated economic distress. But to put such distress down to 'locational disadvantage' was a crude and ill-informed spatial determinism. A considerably more serious and credulous 'economics of place' was required to come to grips with the travails of such regions and the political sentiments that those travails fomented. Such an economics would need to recognise, at the very least, that the US Midwest and England's north-east had for several decades been inserted into the globalising circuits of the capitalist world market in markedly different ways than, say, California or the City of London, respectively. It would also need to recognise that the experiences of California and the US Midwest or of the City of London and England's north-east were not just different from one another but connected *to* each other; and, thus, that understanding their differences required elucidating those connections.

After all, two decades earlier, no less an establishment figure than Eddie George, the then Governor of the Bank of England, had offered a striking acknowledgement of such connections, or at least of how the Bank – in its own peculiarly mechanical way – believed those connections to work. At a lunch held in London for regional newspaper executives, George suggested that job losses in the north of the UK were 'an acceptable price to pay' for curbing inflation in the south (BBC News 1998). This explicitly spatial rendering of the famous Phillips curve, positing an inverse relationship between rates of unemployment and corresponding rates of price rise, was assuredly a gross simplification of existing UK economic-geographic realities. Nonetheless, it conveyed an essential truth, and one inaccessible to the myopic 'economics of place' ventured in 2016 by the *Financial Times*: namely, that one place's success is connected to, even predicated upon, another's relative failure. Such socio-spatial insights are the fundament of the school of thought with which this chapter is concerned, which, for want of a better label, we can name 'spatial political economy'.

WHAT'S IN A NAME?

'Spatial political economy' is itself a seldom-used label (cf. Morton 2017), as is its sibling, 'geographical political economy' (cf. Sheppard 2011). This may seem unimportant, but it is not. Paradoxically, understanding *why* such labels are rarely used can help us to a deeper appreciation of what spatial (or geographical) political economy is all about.

The first thing to say is that spatial political economy differs from political economy as it is predominantly conceived and practised today in mainstream economics or political science. In the former field (see, for example, the work of someone like Daron Acemoglu), what is called political economy is essentially orthodox economics, but making more than a mere nod to the role political institutions play in shaping economic processes and outcomes; it is concerned with how politics, in the most formal, institutional of senses, shapes economics. Within political science, meantime, the direction of interest is essentially reversed: what is studied is how economics shapes politics (such as in the work of Allan Drazen). The quintessential example of political economy in this latter guise is public choice theory, which conceives political agents – voters, politicians, bureaucrats – as the self-interested actors of neoclassical economic lore, and which examines and understands their interactions accordingly. Treating political life *as* economic life, political economy à la political science uses the theory and methods of mainstream economics to explore its objects of study.

Spatial political economy exists within an entirely different intellectual tradition. Its lineage is traceable instead to so-called 'classical' political economy or, more simply, 'classical economics' – which is to say, economics as it was practised before the shift to neoclassicism that occurred toward the end of the nineteenth century, and in which the very distinction between realms of 'politics' and 'economics' would have been considered wrongheaded because the economy was understood to be irreducibly political, being conflict-ridden and shot through with relations of power.

We can be more specific still. Spatial political economy bears the indelible imprint of Marx and his critique of the pre-Marxian political economy of Adam Smith and David Ricardo. This is not to say that all practitioners of spatial political economy are classical Marxists and mobilise Marx's ideas in the same way. They are not, and do not. Consider the substantive differences, for example, between David Harvey and Doreen Massey, two of the most influential exponents of spatial political economy. Harvey's is a spatial political economy of abstraction – theorised at a high level of generalisation – and one that is enacted via an ongoing critical dialogue with Marx himself, whose voice is powerfully present in Harvey's writings. Now tragically passed, Massey was concerned with three main elements within capitalism: accumulation, the relation between capital and labour, and space. Those concerns have been shared by Harvey and other spatial political economists but how Massey put those elements together was quite different from Harvey's approach. Despite her socialism and the deep influence of Marx, she generally shunned using Marx's texts in her own writing. Also, unlike Harvey, she made her argument primarily through empirical cases, particularly examples drawn from the massive industrial restructuring taking place in England during the 1970s and 1980s – and which would contribute to the Brexit vote decades later.

Or consider, yet more distant from Harvey, the work of J.K. Gibson-Graham, also deeply influential in spatial political economy. Gibson-Graham has been a trenchant critic of spatial political economy in the classical Marxian mould that Harvey arguably epitomises, and indeed would likely baulk at the label 'spatial political economy', having consistently railed against what she perceives as the tendency for political economy ('spatial' or otherwise) both to explain everything in terms of economic logics, which she describes as 'capitalocentrism', and to do so in a manner of unjustifiable confidence and certainty. Yet as Eric Sheppard (2011) points out, even Gibson-Graham's work remains 'haunted' by Marx. Certainly, it is deeply influenced by feminism, postcolonialism and poststructuralism. But, rather than throwing away Marx's basic insights about exploitation and accumulation, it would be truer to say that Gibson-Graham grafts them onto the insights that feminism, postcolonialism and poststructuralism have, in turn, enabled her to provide. Gibson-Graham's scholarship is post-Marxist – and political economic – not in the sense that it has left Marx behind, but rather in the sense that it inhabits an epistemological milieu that has clearly progressed beyond Marx, but which was irrevocably coloured by his intervention.

It is in any event noteworthy that all three of the aforementioned luminaries of spatial political economy – Massey, Harvey and Gibson-Graham – are or were economic geographers. While spatial political economy has always spilled over the boundaries of Geography as an institutionalised discipline, with some of the most important works of spatial political economy being produced by sociologists, historians and heterodox economists, economic geography has long been its heartland. Spatial political economy, in turn, has long been economic geography's bedrock. The writer John Lanchester (2016) recalled a revealing anecdote:

> I once asked Danny Dorling [a professor of geography at Oxford] why, when I was at school, geography was about the shapes of rivers, but now all the best-known geographers seem to be Marxists. He said it's because when you look at a map and see that the people on one side of some line are rich and healthy and long-lived and the people on the other side are poor and sick and die young, you start

to wonder why, and that turns you towards deep-causal explanations, which then lead in the direction of Marxism.

Spatial political economy, then, is less a discipline or field itself, than an approach to understanding the world that is found principally, though not exclusively, in economic geography. This is one reason that the label spatial political economy is rarely used. But it is not the only reason, and probably not the main one. For those convinced by the basic axioms of spatial political economy – that capitalism not only produces socio-spatial inequality, but that uneven geographical development is part of capitalism's DNA – the very label 'spatial political economy' is, in quite a profound sense, problematic. The prefix 'spatial' (or 'geographical') suggests that there can and perhaps even should be a form of political economy that is *not* spatial, to which geographical insights can be usefully appended. This goes against the entire grain of the narrative that spatial political economists have for several decades now rehearsed, which is that political economy must *always* be spatial, and historical materialism must always be – in Harvey's coining – historical-geographical materialism. Bringing Marx and his critique of liberal political economy into the geographical mainstream, Massey and Harvey were (and in Harvey's case, still is) just as much concerned with bringing space into Marxist political economy – *not* as an optional add-on, but as something integrated into the very marrow of theoretical understanding.

ON HIDDEN ABODES

As is the case with classical political economy of both Marxian and non-Marxian variants, spatial political economy prioritises the issue of commodity production. It begins, as Sheppard (2011: 324) has written,

> with the actions of capitalists setting aside capital to finance the production of commodities, rather than at the moment of exchange. Commodity production entails the transformation of "natural resources" (themselves a social construction) into other material and immaterial objects, whose production and exchange are believed to be profitable. Production is thus entangled with biophysical, social, political and cultural processes and presupposes the commodification of nature.

So far, arguably, so unremarkable: Marx himself discussed at length, for example, the fact that nature is indeed enrolled alongside human labour power in capitalist commodity production. But, as Sheppard goes on to say, *spatial* political economy tells us much more: 'Processes of commodity production and the realisation of profits create complex, shifting geographies as commodity chains assemble materials for production and humans mobilise to seek work. Production occurs in (and transforms) various places: farms, factories, offices, stores, cities, regions and nations.' Meanwhile, the 'market' is, in reality, nothing like neoclassicism's 'abstract space' occupied by autonomous actors – individual or corporate – with equal opportunities to benefit from exchange. Firms are themselves 'unequally positioned […] in terms of location, economic and political power, strategic acumen, ruthlessness and know-how'; in competing with one another, they 'co-evolve with places and territorial economies, are embedded in multi-scalar corporate and governance hierarchies, and stretch their relations across space through polyvalent networks'. Moreover, as Sheppard further notes, struggles over the distribution of the fruits of commodity production – for shares in Marx's surplus value – not only reflect but '*are shaped by* the complex, co-evolving, geographies of social class – geographies that immensely complexify Marx's "workers versus capitalists" narrative' (Sheppard 2011: 325–6; emphasis added).

In introducing and rationalising his own sortie into the territory of commodity production – he did not get there until the seventh chapter of the first volume of *Capital* – Marx ([1867] 1990: 279–80) explained that it was crucial to understand how labour-power was not just bought and sold but *consumed*, which, he said, occurred 'as in the case of every other commodity, outside the market or the sphere of circulation'. The benefit of doing so was that it was in the realm of commodity production – such production being 'at the same time' the consumption of labour-power – that we would come to see 'not only how capital produces, but how capital is itself produced [and thus] the secret of profit-making'. Marx famously called the space of production a 'hidden abode'. He did so partly because it *was* hidden (on its threshold, Marx wrote, 'there hangs the notice "No admittance except on business"'), and partly because what he called the 'vulgar economists' – the likes of Thomas Malthus, Nassau Senior and John Stuart Mill – helped *keep* it hidden by concentrating their own analysis on the space of market exchange, 'this noisy sphere, where everything takes place on the surface and in full view of everyone'.

What is particularly striking about spatial political economy is that, in the course of carrying out its own incursions into the realm of commodity production, it has simultaneously helped to prise open any number of other hidden abodes – abodes often hidden, moreover, within other variants of political economy, not least 'classical' Marxian political economy itself. It is as if 'space' has served as a productive conceptual wedge: once inserted into the struts of existing Marxist understanding, the effect of this insertion has been to bring out of the woodwork – if not automatically then certainly by logical, deductive extension – the acute significance of other hitherto-neglected dimensions of social and economic life.

The point can be illustrated, beginning with the seminal work of Doreen Massey. Massey (1984) conceived capital accumulation as a set of distinct rounds of investment unfolding over time. The product of each round of investment was what she referred to as a distinctive 'spatial division of labour'. The original idea of the division of labour was, of course, an old one, going back to Adam Smith who described how industrial production was predicated on a high degree of worker specialisation, a division of labour in which each labourer undertook a different specific work task. Massey's concept of the *spatial* division of labour referred to the fact that worker specialisations are geographically as well as socially distinct, and buttress different local regimes of accumulation. Some places, for example, get investment in iron and steel furnaces; their spatial division of labour is that of heavy industry. Other places accrue investment in, say, car assembly plants; their spatial division of labour is manufacturing automobiles.

As a geographer practising spatial political economy, Massey paid particular attention to the local micro-sites of accumulation. One of her favourite examples concerned South Wales in the UK. For at least a century up until the 1970s, South Wales experienced a particular form of accumulation – a particular spatial division of labour – associated with heavy industry, coal mining, and iron and steel production. Massey found that this type of industry was associated with a particular form and configuration of socio-spatial relationships: left-wing politically active communities allied with unions and to the British Labour party; tight-knit social and cultural solidarity reinforced by Methodist chapel-going; and, last but not least, a masculinist patriarchal culture in which men worked in factories or mines while women were expected to stay at home, and to work – but not for money – there. Massey saw the crucial importance of domestic space to the accumulation regime: local industry prospered to the extent that women's unpaid work at home enabled men to work outside it. While production had been a 'hidden abode' in nineteenth-century vulgar economics, *reproduction* had been no less hidden in much twentieth-century political economy, and it was Massey's attention to the different spaces of work that led her to shed new light on that abode. She considered it so important that, to refer to the process whereby investment in value-producing labour generates economic growth, she ultimately preferred 'social reproduction' to Marx's 'accumulation'.

Massey's analysis of subsequent, post-1970s, rounds of investment in South Wales demonstrates especially well the unique power of her distinctive spatial political economic approach to social reproduction. Towards the end of the 1970s, foreign-owned electronics firms were beginning to invest in the region, and they did so, she argued, *because* the existing spatial division of labour – heavy industry – encouraged it. Historic industrial investment in the context of entrenched patriarchy had (inadvertently) produced a pool of women who were now a perfect potential labour force for electronics firms. Many women in the region had never worked in the formal economy before, had never been unionised, and thus tended to be relatively pliable, especially under male supervision. Being expected to continue to provide domestic labour at home, they were also a captive labour market unable to seek out jobs extra-locally. As the state – then the principal employer of male workers in coal mining and iron and steel – began withdrawing investment from South Wales's heavy industry, following the logic of neoliberalism introduced by Margaret Thatcher's post-1979 Tory government, the resulting protracted miner's strike (1984–85) also pushed women to work in the electronics industry to increase family income. One spatial division of labour, in short, had helped seed the next.

Whereas Massey's attention to the space of the home was a waystation to the hidden abode of reproduction, Harvey's attention to the space of the city – and to the processes of urbanisation whereby cities are built and rebuilt – has for him long been a waystation to altogether different hidden abodes: those of exchange and rent. Though in the 1990s and beyond Harvey has made a name for himself as a general interpreter of Marx, he had originally established his scholarly reputation in the 1970s and 1980s with a series of highly influential interventions at the interface of Marxism and urban theory. It is this work that contains many of his most enduring contributions to spatial political economy.

One issue that especially fascinated Harvey was the relationship between industrialisation and urbanisation. It seemed to him that, in the nineteenth century, urbanisation represented in significant part a response to the demand that industrial expansion created for unprecedented geographical concentrations of fixed capital and labour-power. Surveying the twentieth century from the vantage point of the 1970s, by contrast, one thing Harvey noted was that major capitalist crises tended to be preceded by construction booms – city (re)building – that increasingly bore no reasonable relationship to levels of demand. Evidently, money was not flowing to the urban built environment even though demand for more buildings – commercial or residential, still less industrial – dictated that it should. Rather, something else seemed to be going on.

To resolve this conundrum, Harvey (1978) turned, as he so often would, to the work of the French Marxist, Henri Lefebvre. From Lefebvre he took the idea that, in moments when capitalist crisis tendencies intensify, capital might 'switch' from the production of goods and services – that is, of 'commodities', material or immaterial – into the production of the built environment. It is particularly apt to do so when the economy is suffering from a lack of effective demand. When capitalists are faced with a shortage of opportunities for the profitable reinvestment of surplus capital in commodity production (a scenario Harvey refers to as 'overaccumulation' in the sense that too much capital has been accumulated relative to opportunities to put it back into productive circulation), they can invest it instead in the built environment, where the turnover time of capital is much longer. Theorised thus, some (but not all) construction booms can be seen as episodes of frenzied surplus capital absorption that precede, delay, and displace economic crises, but never wholly avert them.

Capital switching is one of a series of capitalist responses to crisis tendencies that Harvey would ultimately lump together under the general category 'spatial fix'. What he meant by this term was that the production and reproduction of different economic-geographic formations – from export markets to free-trade zones and to transportation and communications infrastructures – is an integral part of the process whereby capital attempts, always imperfectly and transitorily, to 'fix' the crises that capitalism itself inevitably generates.

The spatial fix is of interest to us here less because of the theory per se than because it emphasises the materiality – at least, as Harvey sees it – of exchange relations. Most approving interpreters of Marx have played down the importance of markets. In fact, they have effectively reversed the bias of the 'vulgar' economists: whereas the latter were preoccupied with the 'noisy sphere' of exchange and kept production hidden, political economists working in the Marxian tradition have typically prioritised production to the extent of effectively neglecting exchange. For Harvey, that is simply wrong (and, he says, a misreading of Marx to boot). To be sure, it is in production that labour is exploited and, as a result, that value and surplus value are created. However, unless such value can be successfully realised through market exchange – which under conditions of over-accumulation, it cannot – it is for nothing. Thus, exchange matters. It was Harvey's deep and abiding interest, as a spatial political economist, in urbanisation and spatial fixes more generally that brought him to this conclusion and convinced him of its veracity.

Consider, Harvey says, by way of example, the question of competition. In a response to one of the most ardent critics of his insistence on taking seriously markets and exchange relations, Harvey (2018) wrote:

> Marx's account over struggles over the working day and the forces that drive technological and organizational changes in the search for relative surplus value all depend upon the 'coercive laws of competition'. That term comes up at various key points in Marx's argument throughout *Capital*. Where is this force mobilized and most clearly felt? In the market of course! We cannot understand what goes on in the realm of production (or social reproduction for that matter) without market forces playing their part. It is the coercive laws of competition in the market that mandate capitalist reinvestment and the lengthening of the working day etc.

Harvey is right: understanding the spatial political economy of capitalism requires attention not just to production *or* markets but to the dynamic relationship between them. This includes, as he says, understanding the role of competition in mediating that relationship (cf. Christophers 2016).

Harvey also has been critical of much political economic analysis conducted in Marx's name and spirit that regards rent as peripheral – another analytical hidden abode. Although Marx did discuss rent and advanced on Ricardian rent theory, it was still something of a quandary for him. Ultimately, he could not bring himself to assign more than a relatively minor role to the rentier – who, in his account, was specifically the land rentier. A landed-property class having a significant role in society and economy was something that Marx associated with feudalism.

In the brave new world of industrial capitalism, by contrast, the landowner was what Marx once dismissed derisively as a 'useless superfetation', serving – so far as Marx could see – no useful purpose. Thus, expecting the land rentier eventually to pass quietly into the night, much as Keynes would later prophesise the euthanasia of the financial rentier, Marx treated the said rentier as essentially a residual actor in the unfolding capitalist drama.

Time would prove Marx's expectations on this score – and Keynes's parallel prognosis – to be fundamentally flawed. Landowners not only retained their importance as capitalism developed but, arguably, grew in importance. 'Capitalism has taken possession of the land', Lefebvre observed in 1974, 'and mobilized it to the point where this sector is fast becoming central' (Lefebvre [1974] 1994: 335). Yet, many political economists indebted to Marx have continued – both before Lefebvre and after him – to treat land, land rent and the land rentier as one more hidden abode, paying it scant attention. 'The power of land and resource owners has been much under-estimated', Harvey has noted, 'as has the role of land and resource asset values and rents in relation to the overall circulation and accumulation of capital' (Harvey 2010: 183). No such under-estimation, however, characterises Harvey's own work. Just as he has sought to peer into the black box of exchange, so too, his concern with cities has led him to take the lid off the rent 'box' and to show just how pivotal land and land rentierism are to contemporary capitalism, particularly urban capitalism. Land and the money to be made from owning, developing, and letting it – money which flows in astronomical proportions in dense global cities such as Hong Kong, London and New York – today shapes more general processes of capital accumulation and corresponding transformations of class relations in profound ways.

Indeed, in the context of the wider concerns of the present chapter, Harvey goes further still. As already noted, he says political economy should always be spatial political economy, and historical materialism always historical-geographical materialism. Yet more fundamentally, he claims that land and land rent are, respectively, the real-world phenomena and the conceptual counterpart that are most essential to *making* political economy spatial. The power of the landowner is, he maintains, the 'singular principal power [lurking behind] all the contingencies and the uncertainties involved in the perpetual making and remaking of capitalism's geography'. It follows that 'rent and land value are the theoretical categories whereby political economy integrates geography, space and the relation to nature into the understanding of capitalism' (Harvey 2010: 180, 183). While not all economic geographers would necessarily go as far as Harvey on this point, it would be hard to disagree with his proposition that relegating rent and land value to a hidden abode is entirely unwarranted.

This leads to the more general point that I want to make about the work of the trailblazers of spatial political economy such as Massey and Harvey. This is that their opening up of political economy's hidden abodes is not merely incidental or contingent – a happenstance by-product of the analytical exercise of rendering political economy geographical. Rather, it is a *defining feature* of spatial political economy. When he was in the relatively early stages of his encounter with Marxism, Harvey (1985: 141) observed that the incorporation of space and geography into any social theory tends to have what he described as a 'numbing effect' upon the central propositions of such a theory – propositions such as, in the case of Marxian theory, that production is paramount (legitimating the neglect of the spheres of both reproduction and exchange) and that land ownership and land values are little more than residual concerns. Writing of theorists' grappling with space and geography, Harvey says: 'Microeconomists working with a theory of perfect competition encounter spatial monopolies, macroeconomists find as many economies as there are central banks and a peculiar flux of exchange relations between them, and Marxists looking to class relations find neighbourhoods, communities, regions and nations.' Those Marxists also find, among other things, unpaid domestic labour, crises of effective demand, and speculation in land value gains. It is therefore no accident that the cutting edges of research in spatial political economy today are all concerned in one way or another with the elucidation of political economy's hidden abodes and of their spatialities.

A few examples can illustrate this. First, an enormous amount of political-economic research has been conducted in recent years with a view to building on Massey's (and others') early insights into the relationship between household and wider spatial divisions of labour, thus allying a better understanding of social reproduction to that of capitalist commodity production. One study with this focus by Karin Schwiter, Kendra Strauss and Kim England (2018) provides a flavour of current lines of enquiry. The authors examined migration and labour regimes established by government bodies in the UK, Canada, Austria and Switzerland to facilitate the supply of immigrant workers to provide paid live-in care in the homes of global North households. The study asks: what have been the consequences for the social reproduction of the workers in question? Challenging what the authors describe as 'assumptions of migrant care workers as victims and always "forced" to live-in', the research found that, notwithstanding 'significant, multi-dimensional barriers and constraints', the government schemes did nonetheless 'allow the workers to continue their care for themselves, their children, spouses or other family members – even if temporally and geographically removed – when they are in paid care work'.

A second example is the burgeoning of research into the geographies of markets. While much of this research has eschewed political economy, instead using the tools of science and technology studies to unpick the minutiae of market formation (e.g. Berndt and Boeckler 2011), spatial political economists have nevertheless been active in exploring the relationship between exchange and production highlighted by Harvey. Shaina Potts (2020), for example, has written about cross-border payment transactions, which are so often taken for granted but which, being constitutive of transnational markets, represent the spine of global capitalism. Potts shows that, far from being the frictionless and continuous phenomena they are typically presumed to be, global payment flows are divided into discrete spatial segments whose arrangement has become the focal point of wider struggles between creditor and debtor institutions. Those struggles evidence the fact that the sphere of circulation is no more – to use Marx's ([1867] 1990: 280) term – 'a very Eden of the innate rights of man [characterised by] Freedom, Equality, Property and Bentham' than is the sphere of production. Rather, it is saturated with relations of power that are exercised – in the specific case of major cross-border payment transactions – via the law (especially US common law) and litigation around contracts and their interpretation.

A third example relates to spatial political economists' research into the significance of land values and rents to the overall circulation and accumulation of capital in the early twenty-first century. While much of this work focuses, understandably, on the city (e.g. Gillespie 2016), not all does. In a recent study of transformations in property access regimes in rural Maine in the north-eastern USA, for instance, Kelly Kay (2017) illustrates the increasing importance of land rents to patterns of accumulation, showing the effects of the timber industry being restructured from vertically integrated forest products companies towards individual and institutional investor-owners. The latter, through using lease lots and working forest conservation easements, have succeeded in enclosing lands with previously long-standing rights of common access, enhancing their ability to extract monopoly rents.

Indeed, it is not only geographically, across rural and urban regions, that rents have proliferated. Spatial political economists have described how colossal rents are now being earned on innumerable *types* of scarce assets: in other words, land is far from being the contemporary rentier's sole source of income generation. So central have multiple proprietary asset forms and the associated rents become that they now dominate many Western economies and societies, giving rise to a new era of 'rentier capitalism' (Christophers 2020). Alongside land rentiers, who would have been reasonably familiar to Marx (even as he would have been shocked by the flourishing of this ostensibly residual class), there are categories of rentier whose materialisation and prominence he could scarcely have imagined. These include natural-resource rentiers (Purcell 2017), intellectual property rentiers (Zeller 2007), digital platform rentiers (Meier and Manzerolle 2019) and infrastructure rentiers (Ashton et al. 2016), to name the most prominent examples.

These examples of recent work relating to social reproduction, markets, and asset rents within the capacious research terrain of spatial political economy barely scratch the surface of the wider body of work currently being conducted. They are merely indicative of the central point I have been making: that a principal, significant thrust of this research field has been – and remains – the analysis of capitalist abodes rendered marginal within much of what stands for political economy more generally. If, as Harvey suggested, incorporating space tends to have a numbing effect on 'traditional' social theory, including 'traditional' political economic theory, then political economic theorisation of the various abodes hidden within such theory but opened by explicit spatialisation is positively enlivening.

CONCLUSION

We have come a long way, in this relatively short chapter, from the anaemic 'economics of place' toward which the *Financial Times* gestured in attempting to come to terms with the Trump and Brexit victories of 2016. Certainly, 'geography matters', as Chris Giles put it in that newspaper – but it matters in ways far more complex than the mere imprint of locational advantage or disadvantage. Giles presumably did not know it, but 'geography matters' had actually long been the rallying cry of the then recently deceased Doreen Massey. Along with innumerable other spatial political economists, Massey has done much to elucidate the main *ways* in which geography matters – to processes of capital accumulation and circulation and to the social relations that mediate, and are in turn shaped by, those processes.

Spatial political economy does not exist in glorious isolation, however. It would be wrong to imply that the topics broached, still less the theoretical ideas mobilised, are altogether different from those found in other sub-fields of political economy. They are not: there are important overlaps with – and currents of cross-fertilisation between – many of the other political economic traditions surveyed in this book. Some spatial political economists would regard themselves as institutionalists; others as regulationists; some, not least Massey herself, have been deeply influenced by feminist political economy and have made substantive contributions to it; some owe debts to Polanyi that are as deep as those to Marx; and so on. Nevertheless, if you add spatial political economy's integral geographical sensibilities to its no less integral commitment to uncovering and illuminating capitalism's hidden abodes, the totality represents, I think, a distinctive and vital sub-field in and of itself.

REFERENCES

Ashton, P., Doussard, M. and Weber, R. (2016) 'Reconstituting the state: city powers and exposures in Chicago's infrastructure leases', *Urban Studies*, **53** (7), pp. 1384–400.

BBC News (1998) 'Governor tries to douse north's fire', 22 October.

Berndt, C. and Boeckler, M. (2011) 'Geographies of markets: materials, morals and monsters in motion', *Progress in Human Geography*, **35** (4), pp. 559–67.

Christophers, B. (2016) *The Great Leveler: Capitalism and Competition in the Court of Law*, Cambridge, MA: Harvard University Press.

Christophers, B. (2020) *Rentier Capitalism: Who Owns the Economy, and Who Pays for it?* London: Verso.

Giles, C. (2016) 'The poor suffer while Britain avoids straight-talking', *Financial Times*, 14 December.

Gillespie, T. (2016) 'Accumulation by urban dispossession: struggles over urban space in Accra, Ghana', *Transactions of the Institute of British Geographers*, **41** (1), pp. 66–77.

Harvey, D. (1978) 'The urban process under capitalism: a framework for analysis', *International Journal of Urban and Regional Research*, **2** (1–3), pp. 101–31.

Harvey, D. (1985) 'The geopolitics of capitalism', in Gregory, D. and Urry, J. (eds), *Social Relations and Spatial Structures*, Basingstoke: Macmillan, pp. 128–63.

Harvey, D. (2010) *The Enigma of Capital and the Crises of Capitalism*, London: Profile Books.

Harvey, D. (2018) 'The misunderstandings of Michael Roberts', accessed 15.5. 2021 at: thenextrecession.wordpress.com.

Hazeldine, T. (2017) 'Revolt of the rustbelt', *New Left Review*, **105**, pp. 51–79.

Kay, K. (2017) 'Rural rentierism and the financial enclosure of Maine's open lands tradition', *Annals of the American Association of Geographers*, **107** (6), pp. 1407–23.

Lanchester, J. (2016) 'Brexit blues', *London Review of Books*, 28 July.

Lefebvre, H. ([1974] 1994) *The Production of Space*, Oxford: Blackwell.

Marx, K. ([1867] 1990) *Capital: Volume 1*, Harmondsworth: Penguin.

Massey, D. (1984) *Spatial Divisions of Labour: Social Structures and the Geography of Production*, Basingstoke: Macmillan.

Meier, L.M. and Manzerolle, V.R. (2019) 'Rising tides? Data capture, platform accumulation, and new monopolies in the digital music economy', *New Media and Society*, **21** (3), pp. 543–61.

Morton, A.D. (2017) 'Spatial political economy', *The Journal of Australian Political Economy*, **79**, pp. 21–38.

Potts, S. (2020) '(Re-) writing markets: law and contested payment geographies', *Environment and Planning A: Economy and Space*, **52** (1), pp. 46–65.

Purcell, T.F. (2017) 'The political economy of rentier capitalism and the limits to agrarian transformation in Venezuela', *Journal of Agrarian Change*, **17** (2), pp. 296–312.

Sandbu, M. (2016) 'Place and prosperity', *Financial Times*, 16 December.

Schwiter, K., Strauss, K. and England, K. (2018) 'At home with the boss: migrant live-in caregivers, social reproduction and constrained agency in the UK, Canada, Austria and Switzerland', *Transactions of the Institute of British Geographers*, **43** (3), pp. 462–76.

Sheppard, E. (2011) 'Geographical political economy', *Journal of Economic Geography*, **11**, pp. 319–31.

Zeller, C. (2007) 'From the gene to the globe: extracting rents based on intellectual property monopolies', *Review of International Political Economy*, **15** (1), pp. 86–115.

25. Cultural political economy

Bob Jessop and Ngai-Ling Sum

Cultural political economy (CPE) is a distinctive approach in evolutionary and institutional political economy that is pre-disciplinary in inspiration, trans-disciplinary in perspiration, and post-disciplinary in aspiration. In short, CPE takes the cultural turn seriously in political economy. It is not just concerned with the political economy of culture (e.g. the economics of art, theatre, or intellectual property rights) or with taking discourse as an optional methodological entry-point. Instead, it takes culture (semiosis, or sense- and meaning-making) as co-foundational to political economy (including social relations with nature).

Semiosis is one of the ways in which agents reduce complexity to 'go on' in the world. CPE posits that the real world is far too complex to be understood in all its complexity in real time (if ever) and that social agents attribute sense and meaning to certain features of the real world so that they can act towards it (see Sum and Jessop 2013). The raison d'être of CPE is to address the problems of complexity reduction in an evolutionary and institutional context. It draws in part on post-structural and post-foundational approaches to social science and, while it originated in a critique of the regulationist approach in heterodox political economy (see Boyer 1990; Jessop 1990; Jessop and Sum 2006), can be applied elsewhere in political economy. The gap in conventional political economy that CPE seeks to fill is a systematic neglect of sense- and meaning-making as a co-foundational ontological feature of political economy that exists alongside analysis of its institutional forms and economic conduct. Its emphasis on critical semiotic analysis suggests a performative approach, which CPE nonetheless criticises for its ideational tendencies. Examining four selectivities and their contribution to selection and retention of discourses shows the limits to a purely discursive approach to performativity, just as it reveals the limits of a purely materialist analysis (see below).

The other dimension of complexity reduction is structuration. We define this as the practices that set limits to action repertoires and their covariation in time-space. It also attempts to articulate different forms of structural configuration. CPE studies semiosis and structuration as essential and potentially complementary mechanisms of complexity reduction in the field of political economy, but they can also be contrary or become disconnected. This approach can be generalised to all social relations.

SEMIOSIS AND STRUCTURATION AS MEANS OF COMPLEXITY REDUCTION

For social agents to 'go on' in the world, they must reduce complexity by selectively attributing meaning to some of its features rather than others and they must impose limits to the covariation of sets of social relations through structuration. Thus actors (and observers) must focus selectively on some aspects of the world as the basis for becoming active participants therein and/or for describing and interpreting it as disinterested observers. These 'aspects' are not objectively pre-given in the real world, nor are they subjectively pre-scripted by hard-wired cognitive capacities. Instead, they depend for their selective (mis)recognition largely on the currently prevailing meaning systems of relevant actors and observers. In turn, meaning-making helps to shape the overall constitution of the natural and social world insofar as it guides a critical mass of self-confirming, path-shaping actions that diagnose the scope for the world to be different and thereby contribute to realising what was previously only potentially there.

An illustration of the importance of complexity reduction (and its limitations) is the confession by Alan Greenspan, Chair of the US Federal Reserve (1987–2006). Asked by Representative Henry Waxman whether he thought that his ideology had pushed him into making decisions that he had since come to regret in the light of the continuing financial crisis, he replied:

> remember what an ideology is: a conceptual framework for people to deal with reality. Everyone has one. You have to – to exist, you need an ideology. The question is whether it is accurate or not [...] I've found a flaw. I don't know how significant or permanent it is. But I've been very distressed by that fact [...] A flaw in the model that I perceived as the critical functioning structure that defines how the world works, so to speak. (US Congressional Hearing, 23.10.2008)

This ideology was the 'efficient market hypothesis', a key element in neoclassical economics, and the basis of his conviction that markets could and, indeed, should be left to manage themselves. If necessary, the state would step in later to clear up any problems (on the impact of this approach in expanding neoliberal financialisation, see Konings 2018). Of course, there are many other economic 'ideologies' – or, as we prefer to call them, 'imaginaries' – that simplify economic relations in different ways. An imaginary is a semiotic ensemble that frames individual subjects' lived experience of a complex world and/or guides collective calculation about that world. There are many such imaginaries and they are involved in complex and tangled relations at different sites and scales of action. As noted above, without them, individuals cannot 'go on' in the world and collective actors (such as firms or organisations) could not relate to their environments, make decisions, or pursue more or less coherent and successful strategies in a complex, often deeply complex, environment. In this sense, as Greenspan observed, everyone needs an ideology. There are countless other ways of reducing complexity through sense-making that attribute meaning to other aspects of the natural and social world, construing them in one way or another.

But, while all social *construals* are equal (insofar as all social agents must engage in meaning-making in order to be able to 'go on' in the world), some interpretations are more equal than others in their impact on the social *construction* of the social world (Sayer 2000: 40, 53, 61). The role of semiosis in social construction requires identifying and exploring the extra-semiotic conditions that enable meaning-making and influence practical action. This highlights the role of variation, selection and retention in the development and consolidation of some construals rather than others and in their embodiment and embedding in practices that transform the natural and social world. This is an area where CPE's interest in the conditions that shape the selection of imaginaries contributes to the evolutionary dimension of political economy. In this sense, it goes beyond a purely ideational concern with the constructive performativity of discourses (for a critique of performativity in economic analysis, see Brisset 2017). For, as one moves from variation through selection to retention, extra-semiotic factors linked to specific communication channels and broader social configurations play an increasing role in determining which discourses or imaginaries are translated into durable social constructions. They also shape actors' personal and social identities, promote certain social dispositions and routines, get enacted in organisational routines, or become institutionalised in various ways. Inquiring into such processes is especially important where meaning systems have become so sedimented (taken-for-granted or naturalised) that their socially contingent nature goes unremarked. One role of CPE is to critique accepted understandings and practices. Another intriguing question concerns the relation between micro-social diversity and stable macro-social configurations, which is another area where structuration enters the investigation.

Structuration establishes possible connections and sequences of social interaction (including interaction with natural worlds) that facilitate routine actions and set limits to path-shaping strategic actions. While *structuration* refers to a complex, contingent and tendential process that is mediated through action but produces results that no actors can be said to have completely willed, *structure* refers to the contingently necessary outcome of diverse structuration efforts. With its mix of constrained opportunities, recursive reflection, redundancy and flexibility, structuration facilitates social reproduction somewhere between an impossible stasis and the edge of chaos. Reproduction is not automatic but is mediated through situated social action that occurs in more or less structured contexts. Structural constraints operate selectively: they are not absolute and unconditional but are always temporally, spatially, agency- and strategy-specific. Conversely, where agents are reflexive, can reformulate within limits their own identities and interests, and able to engage in strategic calculation about their current situation, they may be able to alter these selectivities.

Where semiosis and structuration complement each other, they transform meaningless and unstructured complexity into sets of meaningful and structured complexity. In terms of societal configurations, this involves hegemonic imaginaries and institutional and spatio-temporal fixes that, together, produce zones of relative stability based on active or, more likely, passive consent and structured coherence. This illustrates the synthesis of semiosis and materiality that is at the core of CPE. The social and natural world becomes relatively meaningful and orderly for actors (and observers) insofar as not all *possible* social interactions are *compossible* (can durably co-exist) in a given time-space envelope. This excludes many other meanings and many other possible social worlds. This does not prevent competing imaginaries of different fields of social action or, indeed, rival principles of societal organisation. For, in a social world characterised by exploitation, oppression and exclusion, there are many possible standpoints for construing the world and many sources of social disruption. How relatively stable social orders emerge in particular time-space matrices in the face of such complexity is an enduring challenge in the social sciences.

LIVED EXPERIENCE, SOCIAL IMAGINARIES AND IDEOLOGIES

Imaginaries may be thought of as 'the ways people imagine their social existence, how they fit together with others, how things go on between them and their fellows, the expectations that are normally met, and the deeper normative notions and images that underlie these expectations' (Taylor 2003: 23). While some social imaginaries are organised around (oriented to, help to construct) specific systems of action (for example, economy, law, science, education, politics, health, religion and art), others are more concerned with different spheres of life, the 'lifeworld' (broadly interpreted) or 'civil society'. The latter kind of imaginaries may nonetheless acquire system-relevance through their articulation into the operation of system logics (for example, the use of gender to segment the labour force, the mobilisation of 'racial' identities to justify educational or political exclusion). System-relevant and lifeworld imaginaries provide the basis for identities and interests, whether individual, group, movement or organisational. Agents normally have multiple identities, privileging some over others in different contexts. This has prompted the recent interest in 'intersectionality' – in other words, the study of the effects of different mixes of system-relevant and 'lifeworld' identities.

While everyone engages in social construal, not everyone makes an equal contribution to the social construction of social relations. Some individuals and/or collective intellectuals (such as political parties and old and new social movements) are particularly active in bridging different systems and spheres of life, attempting to create hegemonic meaning systems or to develop sub- or counter-hegemonic imaginaries. And, of course, increasingly, semiosis is heavily 'mediatised', that is, influenced by mass media and social media. Given the diversity of systems and the plurality of identities in the 'lifeworld', one should not assume that one type of social actor will be the leading force in semiosis in general or in hegemony-making in particular. Nor is there any guarantee that one principle of structuration will dominate the others.

While there is usually wide scope for variation in individual transactions, the medium- to long-term semiotic and material reproduction demands of meso-complexes and macro-social orders narrow this scope considerably. This is another limit on a purely performative reading of a linguistic account of social relations. In a complex world there are many sites and scales on which such processes operate. For present purposes, what matters is how local sites and scales come to be articulated to form more encompassing sites and scales and how the latter in turn frame, constrain and enable local possibilities. If these are not to be random, unpredictable and chaotic, possible connections and sequences of action must be limited. This poses intriguing questions about the articulation of micro-social diversity to produce relatively stable macro-social configurations (Foucault 1979; Wickham 1983; Bourdieu 1990; Luhmann 1992, 1996; Jessop 2007b; Konings 2018).

FOUR MODES OF SELECTIVITY IN SOCIAL RELATIONS

In synthesising Marx, Gramsci and Foucault, CPE looks more carefully at four kinds of selectivity to clarify how social relations are understood in terms of semiosis and structuration (see Table 25.1 and Sum and Jessop 2013: 214–24). *Structural selectivity* is a short-hand term for structurally inscribed strategic selectivity and denotes the asymmetrical configuration of constraints and opportunities on social forces as they pursue particular projects. This selectivity is reproduced through social practices and can be altered through time, through cumulative molecular changes and/or more deliberate attempts to transform the pattern of constraints and opportunities. Whether these attempts succeed or not, they are likely to have path-dependent legacies.

Discursive selectivity is also asymmetrical. The primary aspect and principal stake are the asymmetrical constraints and opportunities inscribed in particular genres, styles and discourses (or, more generally, particular forms of discourse) both in terms of what can be enunciated, who is authorised to enunciate, and how enunciations enter intertextual, interdiscursive and contextual fields. In other words, discursive selectivity concerns how different discourses (whether 'everyday' or specialised) enable some rather than other enunciations to be made within the limits of particular languages and the forms of discourse that exist within them (cf.

de Saussure [1916] 2013 on *parole* and *langue*, or Foucault 1970 on discursive configurations). A related set of selectivities concerns the extent and grounds that make some discursive forms more or less accessible to some agents rather than others because of their respective sense- and meaning-making competences and their discursive competences (in relation to everyday interactions or more specialised discourses such as law, medicine, and engineering). Regarding spatio-temporal selectivities, different languages have different ways of expressing temporality and spatiality, privileging some spatio-temporal horizons.

Discursive selectivity is not purely discursive. It derives from the differential articulation and co-evolution of the discursive and extra-discursive moments of social processes and practices and their conjoint impact in specific contexts and conjunctures. The primary aspect of discursive selectivity (that is, the asymmetries inscribed in language as a repertoire of discursive possibilities) is overdetermined by the media of communication used in enunciations (its technological mediation and the biases these contain) and by the linguistic and communicative competences of particular agents (its agential mediation). Semiotic constructions are neither independent nor neutral: they derive meanings as a part of a network of statements and social practices in the inter-discursive fields. Foucauldian discourse analysis has much to offer here in terms of conceptual architectures and semantic fields (Foucault 1970); and critical discourse analysis clarifies how discursive selectivity operates in terms of its lexical, semantic and pragmatic features and their relation to modes of expression, forms of discourse, genre chains, framing and so forth (see especially Fairclough 2003).

Technological selectivities can be considered, paradoxically, both too broadly and too narrowly. In the broader sense, they include the full range of forces of production and technical and social relations of production involved in the social division of labour. Nonetheless these are often studied in narrowly technological terms. Michel Foucault was more concerned to examine the social technologies involved in constituting objects, creating subject positions and recruiting subjects and, particularly in this context, in creating relations of power/knowledge and shaping the possibilities of governmentalisation. The latter term refers to the mode of governance and rationality involved in sovereignty, discipline, and the code of conduct (e.g. Foucault 1991, 2008). These technological selectivities can be studied in strategic-relational terms along (neo-)Foucauldian lines (see Table 25.1). At stake here are the asymmetries inscribed in how technologies produce objects and subject positions. As for regimes of truth, their apparatuses and strategic logics may selectively limit choice and regulate bodies, thoughts and conduct. These limit the scope for developing alternatives and opposition to possibilities that are inscribed in, or imaginable within, the logic. At best this allows for proposals to reform the existing order rather than to radically transform it, let alone to challenge the basic principles on which it is founded.

Agential selectivity is the theoretically necessary (but empirically contingent) complement to structural and discursive selectivities. Specifically, it denotes the differential capacity of agents to engage in structurally oriented strategic calculation – whether in regard to structurally inscribed or discursively inscribed strategic selectivities – not only in abstract terms but also in relation to specific conjunctures. Agents can make a difference thanks to their different capacities to persuade, read particular conjunctures, displace opponents, and re-articulate in timely fashion discourses and imaginaries. This is always overdetermined by discursive and technological selectivities. Ultimately, agential selectivity depends on the difference that specific actors (or social forces) make in particular conjunctures.

Table 25.1   Four modes of strategic selectivity in CPE

Modes	Grounded in	Effects
Structural	Contested reproduction of basic social forms (e.g. capital relation, nature–society relations, patriarchy, racism), their specific instantiations in institutional orders and organisational forms, and in specific interaction contexts.	Structures favour certain interests, identities, agents, spatio-temporal horizons, strategies and tactics over others. Focuses on how path-dependency limits scope for path-shaping. Selectivities are always relative and relational – structure is not an absolute constraint that applies equally to all actors – it is necessarily asymmetrical.
Discursive	Semiosis as meaning-making grounded in enforced selection in the face of complexity. Operates at all scales from the micropores of everyday life to self-descriptions of world society.	Semiosis provides and articulates elements of meaning-making and thereby shapes perception and social communication. Discursive-inscribed selectivity frames and limits possible imaginaries, discourses, genre chains, arguments, subjectivities, social and personal identities, and the scope for hegemony, sub-hegemonies and counter-hegemonies.
Technological	Technologies regarded as assemblages of information and categories, disciplinary and governmental rationalities, sites and mechanisms of calculated intervention, and social relations for appropriating and transforming nature and/or governing social relations.	These involve specific objectivation, subjectivation, knowledging technologies, interwoven dispositives, and social coordination. In addition to their differential capacities to transform nature, technologies also shape social relations through (1) horizontal and vertical divisions of labour and knowledge, (2) their material effects (e.g. the built environment or anatomo- and biopolitics), and (3) their epistemological effects ('truth regimes'). Technologies shape choices, capacities to act, distribute resources and harms, and convey legitimacy through technical rationality and effectivity.
Agential	Specific capacities of specific social agents (or sets of agents) to 'make a difference' in particular conjunctures thanks to their idiosyncratic abilities to exploit structural, discursive, and technological selectivities.	'Agents make their own history but not in circumstances of their own choosing'. Making a difference depends on abilities to (1) read conjunctures and identify potentials for action; (2) re-politicise sedimented discourses and re-articulate them; (3) invent new social technologies or recombine extant technologies; (4) deploy strategies and tactics to shift the balance of forces in space-time.

Source: Adapted from Sum and Jessop (2013: 218–19), re-printed with permission of Edward Elgar Publishing.

The four selectivities in Table 25.1 are presented in general terms on two grounds. First, they derive from a synthesis of approaches that employ sometimes radically different vocabularies (e.g. Gramsci, Marx, Foucault, various old and new institutionalisms, critical discourse analysis, actor-network theory, and conjunctural analysis). Second, they must be reinterpreted and re-specified as the analysis moves from abstract or general reflections to more concrete and particular cases.

POLITICAL ECONOMY

The distinctive feature of CPE is its approach to semiosis. It can be combined with different kinds of political economy. Our version is inspired by the first generation of the Parisian regulation approach and transnational historical materialism as significant developments of

Marx's claim that 'capital is not a thing but a social relation between people, established by the instrumentality of things' (Marx 1996: 753). We emphasise the formal features of capitalist social relations of production, the contradictions associated with different social forms, the strategic dilemmas entailed by contradictions, and how social relations are mediated through imaginaries and agents' choices linked to strategic dilemmas. We accept that capital accumulation presupposes the world market and that the latter is also an effect of capital accumulation. But the world market is not yet complete – neoliberalism can be seen as a class project of world market completion.

Marx distinguished between the conditions that create the abstract possibility of crises and the historical conditions that produce specific forms and types of crises (Marx 1969: 515). Crisis tendencies are inherent in the capital relation but their specific form needs explaining, as do the attempts to defer and displace crisis symptoms and resolve crisis tendencies in one way or another. Accumulation regimes have different ways of dealing with contradictions and therefore different kinds of crisis tendencies. Within the world market, different varieties of capitalism are intertwined, so one should not study individual varieties in isolation. Nor can one posit a world systems perspective that treats the logic of global accumulation as prior to the interactive dynamics of varieties of capitalism in a variegated capitalism that is often organised in the shadow of one dominant form.

From this perspective, neoliberalisation can be understood as a process that one-sidedly emphasises the exchange-value aspect of the contradictions in social relations. Thus, it prioritises the wage as a cost of production rather than a source of demand, capital as value in motion rather than a stock of specific assets that need to be valorised in a specific time-place, money as international currency rather than a national money, land as a source of rents rather than gift of nature, knowledge as source of intellectual property rights rather than common intelligence, and so on. Neoliberalisation takes different forms in different social formations and changes as its contradictions need resolving (see Jessop 2012).

CRISES

Crisis is an inherently *temporal concept* with spatial connotations. It implies that time unfolds *unevenly*, with continuities and discontinuities, transition points and ruptures, with scope for irreversible change rather than simple iteration – hence scope for path-shaping alongside path-dependence. '[T]ime moves faster in periods of crisis, and stagnates in times of regression' (Debray 1971: 90). This indicates an important uncertainty in the crisis concept: is it a *single event* (and, if so, how would one identify its beginning and its conclusion), a *contingent series of events distributed in time and space* that are connected, if at all, because of earlier crisis responses that could have taken a different turn with different effects, or a series of events with an underlying tendential logic that therefore unfolds as *a relatively predictable process* (if only from the perspective of informed observers)?

It is useful to classify crises on two dimensions. The first concerns their causation. On the one hand, some crises appear 'accidental', that is, are readily (if sometimes inappropriately) attributed to natural or 'external' forces (for example, a volcanic eruption, tsunami, crop failure, invasion). When these have significant effects, they may be termed '*disasters*'. This distinguishes them from crises that are rooted in crisis tendencies, or antagonisms grounded in specific structural forms (for example, those of profit-oriented, market-mediated capitalism).

In other words, they result from the inherent crisis potentials and crisis tendencies of a given social form and may have corresponding patterns of crisis management. This distinction does not imply that accidental crises lack causes – it is just that these are so varied, individually or in their interaction, that they are hard to show in a systematic manner. This said, external, coincidental or incidental causes may trigger structural or systemic crises by working 'through the intermediary of the internal, structural, essential causes that constitute the determining element in society's crises' (Debray 1971: 101–2). In this regard, they have a primary causal mechanism that is expressed in very diverse ways.

The second dimension concerns the significance of crises in terms of their potential impact on the relevant 'order' or 'system', including its typical modes of reproduction, its conditions of existence, and its relative embedding in a wider social formation. Such reproduction in the social world depends on the reproduction of the social relations that support the relevant 'order' or 'system' – relations that can be contradictory, conflictual or antagonistic (the capitalist mode of production is an obvious example). On the one hand, crises '*in*' are normal (expected). They occur within the parameters of a given natural environment and/or set of social arrangements. There are also well-developed routines for dealing with accidental crises. Indeed, repeated observation of 'normal' disasters, accidents and crises, learning *about* and *from* recurrent crises may encourage monitoring, risk management, disaster education and preparedness, rehabilitation, and the sharing of best practice. Instead, the basic features of disturbed arrangements are routinely restored through internal adjustments and/or shift crisis effects into the future, elsewhere, or onto marginal and vulnerable groups. This is shown in alternating phases of unemployment and inflation in the post-war advanced capitalist economies and their treatment through counter-cyclical economic policies.

Crises '*of*' are less common. They occur when there is a crisis of crisis management (that is, normal responses no longer work) and efforts to defer or displace crises encounter growing resistance. 'Crisis of crisis management' is a term introduced by Claus Offe (1984), a German political sociologist, to denote potential second-order effects of economic crisis management routines, manifested in the displacement of crisis tendencies from the economic into extra-economic spheres (e.g. fiscal crisis, administrative crisis). This implies that crisis tendencies remain incompressible but have different forms of appearance linked to different institutional and spatio-temporal fixes and to different crisis management routines. This is a heuristically insightful notion and deserves broader use in dealing with crisis dynamics. For example, crises of crisis management may shift the balance of forces and intensify crisis tendencies by weakening or resisting established modes of crisis management.

One reason that crises of crisis management occur is that previously successful crisis management routines may no longer work in new circumstances. For, given the particular features of any given set of crisis tendencies associated with a specific type of crisis, no algorithm would be cognitively adequate for the *singularity* of the crisis, which, therefore, remains subjectively indeterminate.

Crises of crisis management are more disorienting than crises 'in' specific structures or systems, indicating the breakdown of previous regularities and an inability to 'go on managing crises in the old way'. In certain regards, one might consider these as crises in/of crisis management. The prepositional ambivalence of 'in/of' reflects the prospective, as opposed to retroductive, character of crisis construal, with the latter more suited to scientific analysis, the former more dependent on speculative bets about the future and, a fortiori, whether crisis management routines are irretrievably broken or open to piecemeal reform. This creates space for strategic interventions to significantly redirect the course of events rather than 'muddling through' until the crisis is eventually resolved or hoping that the 'business as usual' can be restored through emergency measures. This poses a whole series of epistemological problems about crisis construal and the asymmetry between explanation and prediction. More generally, crises of crisis management can cause social stasis or regression, attempts to restore the old system by *force majeure*, fraud or corruption; efforts at more radical social innovation for good or ill, leading in some cases to temporary states of emergency or more enduring exceptional regimes (for example, military dictatorship, fascism); or to efforts to break the power of such regimes.

A crisis is never a purely objective, extra-semiotic event or process that automatically produces a definite response or outcome. The objective moment of crisis becomes socially and historically relevant through the moment of subjective indeterminacy. For there is no algorithm that unambiguously identifies a self-evident way to restore reproduction or to move smoothly to another stable 'order' or 'system'. The subjectively indeterminate response set includes non-decision or non-intervention – which, given the objective nature of crisis, also has system-relevant effects and is therefore a mode of decision and intervention. Ideas and imaginaries shape the interpretation. A rigorous analysis of crises, crisis construals and crisis management must be able to distinguish these alternatives or else fall into a simplistic form of constructivism.

Crises do not generate their own resolution, even where trusted crisis management routines exist. On the contrary, crises *of* given sets of social relations, especially where form-determined, often need relatively long, discursively, institutionally, technologically and agentially mediated search processes before a new, relatively durable order based on new institutional and spatio-temporal fixes allows movement beyond such a crisis. Without subjective indeterminacy, there is no crisis – merely chaos, disaster or catastrophe and, perhaps, fatalism or stoicism in the face of the inevitable. In this sense, crises are a potential moment of decisive intervention, where, rather than muddling through, resolute action may repair broken social relations, promote piecemeal adaptation, or produce radical transformation.

CONSTRUING SYMPTOMS

The dual character of crisis means that struggles over crisis construal shape the nature and relative success, if any, of efforts at crisis management, depending on whether the construals are substantively adequate to dealing satisfactorily with complex crises. This typically involves providing suitable ways of reducing their complexity as a basis for taking decisive action for at least some key actors affected by the crisis rather than waiting for more information about its nature at the risk of things getting worse. This depends in part on the nature of learning in, through and from crisis, whether from previous crises, which might guide adequate responses to current crises, or during current crises in real time with possible lessons for future crisis events or processes.

While crises become visible through symptoms, the latter have no one-to-one relation to crisis tendencies and specific conjunctures. There are competing schools and interpretive paradigms to construe crisis symptoms. This explains the subjective indeterminacy that attends the objective overdetermination of crisis and why crises are moments of profound cognitive and strategic disorientation. They disturb inherited expectations and practices; challenge dominant paradigms and produce radical uncertainty; undermine faith in past lessons and ways of learning; open space for new lessons and ways of learning; and provide the context for struggles over the right way forward.

Crises can be seen as stratified. They are generated by real mechanisms, they are actual events or processes, and they have evidential symptoms. This invites the question: *what must the real world be like for this event to have occurred and/or these symptoms to exist?* Thus, the challenge is to relate the empirical symptoms, actual crisis, and underlying mechanisms as a basis for possible decisive interventions.

Crisis construals can be assessed in three ways (Jessop 2018). The first is in terms of their *scientific validity* (i.e. their conformity with prevailing scientific procedures and rules of evaluation). This depends on specific protocols of investigation and acknowledges that conclusions may be fallible. Even the origins of the Great Depression in the 1920s and 1930s are still contested within and between theoretical paradigms. The second way is in terms of the *narrative plausibility* of a given construal in identifying and explaining the (symptoms of) crisis relative to the prevailing discourses in circulation among relevant social forces. Narrative plausibility depends on rules of argumentation oriented to persuasion. In this context, while scientific argument also has rhetorical features, these should be subordinate to scientific analysis; conversely, the plausibility of crisis narratives may be enhanced by reference to facts, but these are chosen to lend credibility to the overall narrative so that the factual elements are less rigorous and often screen out inconvenient details. The third way concerns the *pragmatic correctness* of construals, namely, their ability to read a conjuncture, discern potential futures, provide a plausible narrative, and guide action that transforms the conjuncture (Lecercle 2006). Pragmatically correct construals are epistemologically different from scientific accounts and plausible narratives because they involve what currently exists (if at all) only *potentially*, may never be actualised, and cannot therefore be analysed in the same ways as the past and present.

At stake here, then, is the distinction between the *explanation* of past and present events, processes or conjunctures, and the *prediction* of the future of *open systems* where development depends on the strategic and tactical choices of diverse actors and social forces. Here prediction is related not just to the objective indeterminacy of the future but also – crucially – to agents' differential capacity to shape their future through appropriate actions and inactions.

Narrative Plausibility

Narratives employ selected past events and forces in terms of a temporal sequence with a beginning, middle and end in the form of a story that embodies causal and moral lessons. The plausibility of narratives and other construals and their associated crisis management solutions (including inaction) depends on their resonance with (or capacity to reinterpret and mobilise) key social forces. For example, neoliberals narrated how trade union power and the welfare state undermined economic growth in the 1970s and called for more market, less state. The Tea Party and Occupy Wall Street movements offered different narratives about the recent crisis and reached radically different conclusions. Narratives play a key role in strategic action because they can simplify complex problems, identify simple solutions, connect to common sense, and mobilise popular support. To be effective in the long run, however, they should correspond to the objective conditions and the real possibilities of action. Yet strategies based on 'inorganic' narratives, however, can have adverse path-shaping effects, making recovery from a crisis harder or shifting its forms and consequences.

Although many plausible narratives may be advanced, their narrators will not be equally effective in conveying their messages and securing support for the proposed solutions. All narratives are selective, appropriate some arguments, and combine them in specific ways. So, we must also consider what goes unstated or silent, repressed or suppressed, in specific discourses. Interpretive power depends on the 'web of interlocution' (Somers 1994) in different fields and its discursive selectivities, the organisation and operation of the mass media, the role of intellectuals in public life, and the structural biases and strategically selective operations of various public and private apparatuses of economic, political and ideological domination. This is mainly an issue of political contestation, broadly interpreted.

Pragmatic Correctness

Whereas scientific validity concerns the genealogy of the crisis as an event and/or continuing process, pragmatic correctness is judged in the light of future developments, including counterfactual analysis, and depends on social agents' ability to read present and future conjunctures in terms of what exists *in potentia* and how it might be realised. Plausible narratives are typically an important moment of pragmatic correctness. This is mediated through language as well as through social practices and institutions beyond language. Indeed, since the development of print media at least, crisis construal is heavily mediatised, depending on specific forms of visualisation and media representations, which nowadays typically vary across popular, serious and specialist media. Pragmatic correctness depends on: (1) the strategically selective limits to action set by the objectively overdetermined form of a crisis conjuncture; (2) the interpretive and mobilising power of crisis construals and strategic perspectives – notably its ready communicability to relevant audiences – which affects the capacities of strategic forces to win hegemony; and (3) the balance of forces associated with different construals or, at least, the ability of some forces to impose their preferred construals, crisis management options, and exit solutions (Debray 1971: 106–7; Lecercle 2006: 40–41; and, on the first limit, Patomäki 2008).

Considered in these terms, to paraphrase Gramsci, 'there is a world of difference between conjunctural analyses [he writes of ideologies] that are arbitrary, rationalistic, and willed and those that are organic' (Gramsci 1971: 376–7). The former analyses misconstrue the crisis – minimising or exaggerating its scale and scope and its system-threatening qualities – and misidentify necessary or feasible solutions. An organic analysis is an at least minimally adequate analysis of the objective dimensions of the crisis and its manageability or transformability. This is judged in terms of a possible attenuation of crisis symptoms, muddling through, displacement or deferral, and so forth, and in terms of the correlation of forces and the strategic horizons of action of the social forces whose ideal and material interests it represents. This raises the key issue of the (always limited and provisional) fit between imaginaries and real, or potentially realisable, sets of material interdependencies in the real world. Proposed crisis strategies and policies must be (or seen to be) effective within the spatio-temporal horizons of relevant social forces in a given social order.

In all cases, how a crisis is managed has path-shaping effects on how subsequent crises will develop. A 'correct' reading creates its own 'truth-effects' and may then be *retained* thanks to its capacity to shape reality. Getting consensus on an interpretation about which aspects of a crisis or, alternatively, which of several interlocking crises matters is to have framed the problem (variation). Nonetheless this consensus must be translated into a coherent, coordinated policy approach and solutions that match objective dimensions of the crisis (selection). Effective policies adapt crisis management routines and/or discover new routines through experimentation and can be consolidated as the basis of new forms of governance, meta-governance and institutionalised compromise (retention). Only crisis construals that grasp key emergent extra-semiotic features of the social world as well as mind-independent features of the natural world are likely to be *selected* and *retained*. Effective construals, therefore, also have constructive force and produce changes in the extra-semiotic features of the world and in related tendential real mechanisms and social logics.

Often, wider ideational and institutional innovation going beyond the economy narrowly conceived is needed, promoted and supported by political, intellectual and moral leadership. Indeed, as Milton Friedman put it hyperbolically but tellingly: '[o]nly a crisis produces real change. When that crisis occurs, the actions that are taken depend on the ideas that are lying around' (1965: 32). It follows that preparing the ground for crisis-induced strategic interventions helps to shape the nature and outcome of crisis management and crisis responses. Inadequate preparation (for whatever cause) makes it harder to influence struggles over crisis construal and crisis management, even if the eventual crisis construal is 'organic'.

COMPARISON WITH FICTIONAL EXPECTATIONS

CPE can be compared with the analysis offered by Jens Beckert, a German economic sociologist, of the role of fictional expectations in dealing with uncertain futures. For him, 'fictional expectations allow actors to create a representation of future events, making them capable of acting purposefully with reference to this pretended future, even though this future is indeed unknown and therefore unpredictable' (Beckert 2011: 6). The term refers to the images actors form as they consider future states of the world, the way they visualise causal relations, and the ways they perceive their actions influencing outcomes (Beckert 2016: 9). 'While the expectations formed from within these cognitive frames are oriented towards the future, the frames themselves are strongly influenced by the past, in the form of the distribution of resources, historically shaped cultural norms, social networks, and the use of historical information' (Beckert 2016: 14). Fictional expectations provide insights into the micro-foundations of the dynamics of capitalism, regarding four domains: money and credit, investment decisions, innovation processes, and consumption choices (2016: 12).

In addition to analysing the dynamics of capitalism in these four domains, Beckert also explores the role of forecasting practices as coordination devices for the actions that produce the future and their role in shaping the contested politics of expectations and guiding creative destruction (2016: 242). Theories and methods also have an important technological role in capitalist dynamics. Indeed, this 'depends on the creativity and imaginary power of actors, which sometimes articulates itself as resistance to capitalism itself. But in the end, none of that creativity ever sweeps away the principle of accumulation itself. Ultimately, imagined futures are all reincorporated into the inner logic of capitalism' (2016: 285).

CPE and the theory of fictional expectations share some assumptions but also differ. They stress the ontological nature of speculations about the future that are based in part on past behaviour and anchored in institutions. They reject the rational foundations and knowledge of future states of neoclassical economics and adopt an evolutionary and institutional political economy. They reject the invisible hand of the market as the main steering mechanism of capitalist dynamics, emphasising competition to establish the credibility of projected futures and attribute symbolic meaning to commodities (2016: 173). They agree on the role of more or less powerful agents (firms, politicians, experts, the media, and so on) and governmental practices (Beckert cites Foucault gesturally in this regard, e.g. 2016: 262) in shaping the selection of imaginaries. The approaches also differ in terms of CPE's fourfold analysis of selectivities, with Beckert emphasising discursive and agential selectivity and CPE according equal analytical weight to all four (see Table 25.1). CPE also has stronger institutional foundations in a form-analytical critique of the capital relation, gives more explicit recognition to the contradictions and strategic dilemmas of capitalist social formations, deploys a typology of crises as objectively overdetermined, subjectively indeterminate events and processes, and distinguishes scientific investigation, narrative plausibility and pragmatic correctness. In contrast, Beckert's fictional expectations tend to emphasise the discursive, imaginative aspects of political economy at the expense of structuration and lack the more detailed analysis of genre chains and related knowledging technologies that shape and limit evolutionary and institutional dynamics (Sum and Jessop 2013: 221–2). He is too concerned to show the ontological basis of the dynamics of capitalism in fictional expectations and to emphasise their imaginative mediation, assuming that data and methods are correct (Konings 2018: 15). In this respect, CPE can absorb his analysis and provide a more profound dialectical analysis of capitalist dynamics.

CONCLUSIONS

The key theoretical debates between different advocates of CPE concern which techniques of semiosis to adopt and its limitations in understanding political economy. As a heuristic approach, CPE integrates research on sense- and meaning-making into the analysis of the basic features of capital accumulation, including its contradictions, crisis-tendencies and crisis dynamics. But its general approach to the differential articulation of semiosis and structuration can be applied far beyond the critique of political economy. The present authors' own work uses the heuristic differently. Bob Jessop tends to focus on crisis dynamics as objectively overdetermined but subjectively indeterminate, and to consider the contestation of rival construals as attempts to explain crises and their alternative solutions (see Jessop 2007a, 2018). Ngai-Ling Sum focuses more on the development of new political economic imaginaries and their performative effects (e.g. the BRIC imaginaries, the emergence of subaltern subjects in China, and the 'One Belt, One Road', since relabelled the 'Belt Road Initiative': see Sum 2013, 2016, 2019). In both cases, we consider the four selectivities that are involved in shaping the variation, selection and retention of different imaginaries and construals. This highlights the choice for CPE theorists in analysing political economy.

The cultural turn can be employed with different accounts of political economy and also applied within the social sciences more generally. We interpret the cultural turn as ontological, emphasising that semiosis is co-foundational with structuration, and distinguish this version of the cultural turn from thematic and methodological cultural turns. A thematic turn simply chooses cultural aspects of the economic to thematise, and otherwise uses normal analytical techniques. This is evident in Gary Becker's use of rational utility maximisation applied to the family, crime, drug addiction and suicide (see, for example, Becker 1991). A methodological turn chooses semiosis as an optional analytical method, but does not consider semiosis as ontologically co-foundational to political economy. Thematic and methodological turns can be combined. This is shown in Viviana Zelizer's work, combining a 'connected lives' approach to the intersection of economic activity and personal relations to explain 'how people integrate economic activity into the wider range of their social relations, and with what consequences for those social relations' (2011: 359). She shows that the market is a cultural and not just an economic structure, but notes that reducing the market to an abstract set of meanings excludes the material, institutional, and social reality of economic life. She concludes that the cultural approach needs a better connection to class systems, family structure, gender, age, and other such structural factors (2011: 375). We believe that an ontological turn that treats semiosis as co-foundational in political economy – and hence as a co-substantial analytical focus – enriches political economic and social analysis. It takes us beyond thematic and methodological cultural turns and provides the basis for a serious evolutionary and institutional economics.

The version of CPE we have presented in this chapter and developed in our other writing synthesises the work of Marx, Gramsci and Foucault to produce an integrated micro–macro analysis. In effect, it seeks to Gramscianise Marx, Foucauldise Gramsci, and Marxianise Foucault. We take Marx's analysis of capital as a social relation as the material base of political economy but argue that he also practised critical semiotic analysis (Jessop and Sum 2018). We use Gramsci's vernacular materialism, based on his philological studies and interests, to expand the Marxian critique of the capital relation and state power (on vernacular materialism, see Ives 2004). Gramsci was more interested in hegemony as political, intellectual and moral leadership but, like Marx, he neglected the micro-disciplinary and governmental bases of class powers. Following Richard Marsden, whereas Marx explains *why* but cannot explain *how*, Foucault explains *how* but cannot explain *why*. He adds that 'to marry "why" and "how" it is necessary to explicate "what": to synthesise Marx's description of relations of production and Foucault's description of the mechanisms of disciplinary power' (Marsden 1999: 135). Accordingly, we use Foucault to explain key aspects of the *how* of exploitation, domination and hegemony. Foucault's analysis of governmentality can be complemented by Marxian and Gramscian insights into the *why* and *what* of political economy. Whether this specific interpretation of capitalist dynamics that we adopt in our approach to CPE is correct or not is a secondary issue compared with the overall power of critical semiotic analysis as part of modern political economy.

REFERENCES

Becker, G.S. (1991) *A Treatise on the Family*, enlarged edition, Cambridge, MA: Harvard University Press.

Beckert, J. (2011) *Imagined Futures: Fictionality in Economic Action*, Köln: MPIfG Discussion Paper 11/08.

Beckert, J. (2016) *Imagined Futures: Fictional Expectations and Capitalist Dynamics*, Cambridge, MA: Harvard University Press.

Bourdieu, P. (1990) *The Logic of Practice*, Cambridge: Polity.

Boyer, R. (1990) *The Regulation School: A Critical Introduction*, New York: Columbia University Press (first published in French 1986).

Brisset, N. (2017) 'The future of performativity', *Oeconomia*, **7** (3), pp. 439–52.

de Saussure, F. ([1916] 2013) *Course in General Linguistics*, trans. and ed. R. Harris, London: Bloomsbury.

Debray, R. (1971) 'Time and politics', *Prison Writings*, London: Allen Lane, pp. 87–160.

Fairclough, N. (2003) *Analysing Discourse*, London: Routledge.

Foucault, M. (1970) *The Order of Things: An Archaeology of the Human Sciences*, London: Tavistock.

Foucault, M. (1979) *History of Sexuality: Volume 1: Introduction*, trans. R. Hurley, London: Allen Lane.

Foucault, M. (1991) 'Governmentality', in Burchell, G., Gordon, C. and Miller, P. (eds), *The Foucault Effect: Studies in Governmentality*, Hemel Hempstead: Harvester Wheatsheaf, pp. 87–104.

Foucault, M. (2008) *The Birth of Biopolitics: Lectures at the Collège de France, 1978–1979*, trans. G. Burchell, Basingstoke: Palgrave Macmillan.

Friedman, M. (1965) *Capitalism and Freedom*, Chicago, IL: University of Chicago Press.

Gramsci, A. (1971) *Selections from the Prison Notebooks*, London: Lawrence & Wishart and New York: International Publishers.

Greenspan, A. (2008) 'Evidence given on 23 October 2008', Washington, DC: House Committee on Oversight and Government Reform.

Ives, P. (2004) *Language and Hegemony in Gramsci*, London: Pluto Press.

Jessop, B. (1990) 'The regulation approach in retrospect and prospect', *Economy and Society*, **19** (2), pp. 153–216.

Jessop, B. (2007a) 'Knowledge as a fictitious commodity: insights and limits of a Polanyian analysis', in A. Buğra and K. Ağartan (eds), *Reading Karl Polanyi for the 21st Century: Market Economy as a Political Project*, Basingstoke: Palgrave, pp. 115–34.

Jessop, B. (2007b) *State Power: A Strategic-Relational Analysis*, Cambridge: Polity.

Jessop, B. (2012) 'Neoliberalism', in G. Ritzer (ed.), *The Wiley-Blackwell Encyclopedia of Globalization*, vol. 3, Chichester: Wiley-Blackwell, pp. 1513–21.

Jessop, B. (2018) 'Valid construals or correct readings? On the symptomatology of crises', in B. Jessop and K. Knio (eds), *The Pedagogy of Economic, Political and Social Crises*, London: Routledge, pp. 49–72.

Jessop, B. and Sum, N.L. (2006) *Beyond the Regulation Approach: Putting Political Economy in its Place*, Cheltenham, UK and Northampton, MA, USA: Edward Elgar Publishing.

Jessop, B. and Sum, N.L. (2018) 'Language and critique: some prefigurations of critical discourse studies in Marx's work', *Critical Discourse Studies*, **15** (4), pp. 325–37.

Konings, M. (2018) *Capital and Time: For a New Critique of Neoliberal Reason*, Stanford, CA: Stanford University Press.

Lecercle, J.J. (2006) *A Marxist Philosophy of Language*, trans. G. Elliott, Leiden and Boston: Brill.

Luhmann, N. (1992) *Social Systems*, trans. J. Bednarz with D. Baecker, Stanford, CA: Stanford University Press.

Luhmann, N. (1996) 'Politics and economics', *Thesis Eleven*, **53**, pp. 1–9.

Marsden, R. (1999) *The Nature of Capital: Marx After Foucault*, London: Routledge.

Marx, K. (1969) *Theories of Surplus Value, Volume 2*, London: Lawrence and Wishart and New York: International Publishers.

Marx, K. (1996) *Capital, Volume I*, Marx–Engels Collected Works, vol. 35, London: Lawrence and Wishart and New York: International Publishers.

Offe, C. (1984) *Contradictions of the Welfare State*, in J.R. Keane (ed.), London: Hutchinson and Boston, MA: MIT Press.

Patomäki, H. (2008) *The Political Economy of Global Security: War, Future Crises and Changes in Global Governance*, London: Routledge.

Sayer, A. (2000) *Realism and Social Science*, London and Thousand Oaks, CA: Sage.

Somers, M. (1994) 'The narrative constitution of identity: a relational and network approach', *Theory and Society*, **23** (5), pp. 605–49.

Sum, N.L. (2013) 'A cultural political economy of crisis recovery: (trans-)national imaginaries of "BRIC" and subaltern groups in China', *Economy and Society*, **42** (4), pp. 543–70.

Sum, N.L. (2016) 'The makings of subaltern subjects: embodiment, contradictory consciousness, and re-hegemonization of Diaosi in China', *Globalizations*, **14** (2), pp. 298–312.

Sum, N.L. (2019) 'The intertwined geopolitics and geoeconomics of hopes/fears: China's triple economic bubbles and the "One-Belt-One-Road" imaginary', *Territory, Politics, Governance*, **7** (4), pp. 528–52.

Sum, N.L. and Jessop, B. (2013) *Towards a Cultural Political Economy: Putting Culture in its Place in Political Economy*, Cheltenham, UK and Northampton, MA, USA: Edward Elgar Publishing.

Taylor, C. (2003) *Modern Social Imaginaries*, Durham, NC and London: Duke University Press.

Wickham, G. (1983) 'Power and power analysis: beyond Foucault?', *Economy and Society*, **14** (4), pp. 468–98.

Zelizer, V.A. (2011) *Economic Lives: How Culture Shapes the Economy*, Princeton, NJ: Princeton University Press.

26. Postcolonial and poststructural political economy

Penny Griffin

This chapter reflects on the relationship between postcolonial and poststructural traditions of thought in analysing the studies and practices of political economy. It discusses some of the significant questions raised in the synergies between postcolonial and poststructural approaches, and the ideas and practices that, together, contribute to knowledge of and about the contemporary global political economy. To do this, it argues that gender scholarship that draws on postcolonial and poststructural traditions provides the closest, most productive, reading of the uneven constitution and effects of the global political economy. Drawing specifically on postcolonial and poststructural feminisms, the chapter focuses at the global level to describe and engage questions of imperialism, race and gender in the contemporary global political economy. It shows that postcolonial feminist contributions to political economy, using poststructural ideas and strategies, pose especially probing, challenging questions about the nature and practices of power, knowledge and change in the global political economy, questions that are worth reflecting on in some detail.

This chapter does not argue that, as terms, 'postcolonial' and 'poststructural' are, or ought to be, interchangeable. Moreover, while the postcolonial and poststructural approaches discussed here are highlighted in conversation with each other, this is not to underestimate the differences between scholarly traditions of thought, to undo the significance of their embodied spaces and locations, or to insist on any uniformity across ways of thinking about the world. Postcolonialism and poststructuralism have developed from different epistemological, geographical and colonial histories and life experiences. Hopeful not to inflict any unwarranted generalisations, the chapter argues that there are important examples of powerful and incisive scholarship that pay close attention to academic practices of racialised and gendered knowledge production, while successfully building knowledge across the traditions.

Such a project is, of course, a work in progress, and to show how this is being achieved, the chapter locates three specific ways in which postcolonial and poststructural approaches, together, create and challenge political economy knowledge. The first concerns postcolonial and poststructural political economy's rejection of economism. The second relates to a postcolonial, poststructural feminist commitment to deconstructing imperial, racialised and gendered hierarchies. The third involves the ways in which postcolonial and poststructural traditions highlight contested realities across the global political economy and, therein, the possibilities for subverting imperial, racialised and gendered sites and practices.

DECOLONIAL, POSTCOLONIAL AND POSTSTRUCTURAL POLITICAL ECONOMY

There is much to be said in the meeting grounds between postcolonial thought, poststructuralism and political economy research. This section outlines an understanding, and use, of the terms 'postcolonial' and 'poststructural' as they relate to political economy. This serves as a precursor to consideration of the intersections of these thought projects in the chapter's subsequent sections.

This chapter uses 'postcolonial' scholarship as a general, catch-all term, to refer to a form of 'social inquiry in general' that 'foregrounds the centrality of colonialism to the making of the modern world' (Gruffydd Jones 2013: 49). Postcolonial scholars have interrogated the hierarchical and racialising European philosophies on which unequal capitalist practices have been built (Inayatullah and Blaney 2010, 2018). They have critiqued (and destabilised) colonial centres of knowledge across discourses and practices of world-building, acknowledging difference *within* as much as between (see Parashar 2016). Rejecting the idea that the 'Western canon' of knowledge (Grosfoguel 2011) provides the answers, they have highlighted discursive colonialism and actively built anti-imperialism into political economy scholarship and practice. Especially through analysis and understandings of the material and discursive locations of gendered, sexualised bodies, postcolonial feminist scholars have deconstructed, challenged and subverted the violence embedded in postcolonial apparatuses, and have decolonised the sites of the global political economy and the practices of disciplinary political economy work itself.

It is worth noting that both *postcolonial* and *decolonial* traditions of thought have long and diverse histories, and both can be argued to have emerged as distinct intellectual movements. Bhambra (2014) articulates these variances in terms of disciplinary, time-based and geographic differences. For Bhambra, postcolonial and decolonial approaches both constitute 'developments within the broader politics of knowledge production', and 'both emerge out of political developments contesting the colonial world order established by European empires, albeit in relation to different time periods and different geographical orientations' (2014: 119). Postcolonial studies, she argues, have developed as an intellectual movement from the writing of (often) diasporic scholars from the Middle East and South Asia, such as Edward Saïd, Homi K. Bhaba and Gayatri Chakravorty Spivak. While postcolonial work has directly addressed issues of the material and the socio-economic, it has also tended to focus on the 'realm of the cultural' (Bhambra 2014: 115).

Decolonial approaches have emerged, on the other hand, in the form of engagements with the modernity/coloniality project, from the fifteenth century onwards, and as embodied in the work of diasporic Latin American scholars such as Anibal Quijano, María Lugones and Walter Mignolo (Bhambra 2014: 115; see also Grosfoguel 2011). Notions of materiality and socio-economic status lie at the heart of decolonial approaches, wherein uneven development and global economic inequality can only fully be understood in reference to the capitalist asymmetries unleashed by European colonialism. Led by Latin American scholars' multifaceted engagements with the colonial and neocolonial structures of world order and knowledge creation that have privileged European/Western knowledges and practices, decolonial inquiry is perhaps most evident in *dependista* and world-systems theorising. Decolonial perspectives have been especially concerned, as Grosfoguel notes, with de-privileging the Eurocentric thinkers on which postcolonial studies have often relied (figures such as Foucault, Derrida and Gramsci). Rather than using Western poststructuralists to present 'a Eurocentric critique of Eurocentrism', decolonial writers have sought to generate 'a critique of Eurocentrism from subalternised and silenced knowledges' (Grosfoguel 2011: 3–4). An insight of particular and ongoing impact across decolonial critiques has been their concern, as Roy articulates, 'with the relationship between place, knowledge and power' (2016: 205). Decolonising knowledge requires taking seriously 'the epistemic perspectives/cosmologies/insights of critical thinkers from the global South thinking from and within subalternised racial/ethnic/sexual spaces and bodies' (Grosfoguel 2011: 4). Decolonial critiques have thus sought to engender 'subaltern' knowledges, challenging, as Bhambra suggests, 'the insularity of historical narratives and historiographical traditions emanating from Europe (2014: 115).

It can be argued that postcolonial studies, as understood distinctly from decolonial research, have tended not to focus particularly on economic questions (see Kayatekin 2009; Charusheela 2011), but also that studies in political economy have not taken on board the challenges offered by the postcolonial critique either extensively or profoundly (Grosfoguel 2011: 7–8; Rao 2000: 165–6; Haag 2020: 4). While decolonialism has been, by nature, rooted in a critique of global capitalism and so exists already in political economy form, commentators have noted that postcolonial studies and political economy tend not to speak to each other, at least not as often as they should (see, for example, Kayatekin 2009 and Haag 2020). Studies of global financial and trade relations rarely, for example, scrutinise colonial patterns or render colonial discourse central to their research agendas (Haag 2020: 4), while colonialism, slavery and race 'form a major gap' in work on the global political economy (Gruffydd Jones 2013: 49). Studies in political economy 'still continue to produce knowledge from the Western man "point zero" god-eye view' (Grosfoguel 2011: 7–8). Furthermore, the constitutive role of colonised, raced women in the construction of global economic orders remains, for most political economy, entirely invisible. As Sheila Nair writes, while there is an argument to be made that postcolonial theory has become much more influential, and thus less marginalised, in the social sciences academy in recent years, as far as political economy is concerned, postcolonial feminism is still 'significantly understudied' and much less widely known, and engaged with, than 'for example, Marxist feminist accounts' (2018: 50).

For the sake of clarity, I use in this chapter the framing of 'postcoloniality' to refer to questions relevant to political economy raised by *both* postcolonial and decolonial traditions, acknowledging that not all scholars use these terms interchangeably. Both postcolonial and decolonial analysis are relevant to conceptualising, and reconceptualising, capitalism as a global or world system, and the postcolonial analysis discussed here includes the work of decolonial scholars, such as Grosfoguel, who are committed both to decolonising political economy paradigms themselves, and to proposing 'alternative decolonial conceptualisation[s] of the world-system' (2011: 4). In socio-economic terms, decolonial and postcolonial perspectives both critique and challenge the foundations of, and value hierarchies implicit in, the 'modernisation' project of Western development, especially 'the parochial character of arguments about the endogenous European origins of modernity' (Bhambra 2014: 115). Both perspectives emphasise 'the necessity of considering the emergence of the modern world in the broader histories of colonialism, empire, and enslavement' (Bhambra 2014: 115).

Both decolonial and postcolonial approaches reveal the 'colonial matrix of power' that underscores ongoing global inequalities (Bhambra 2014: 119). Both necessitate understanding global, socio-economic questions of race and racism, the legacies of colonialism, empire and imperialism, and ongoing questions of dependency, ethnocentrism and the denial of agency, theoretically and pragmatically, to people outside Europe. Where, traditionally, postcolonial studies have been a little less interested in economic questions than they might have been, the 'frame of postcoloniality' remains, nonetheless, an important mechanism for rethinking political economy, not least because of 'the recognition that the transformations in the world economy that have taken place in the course of the past 30 years or so have left no country in the world outside their loop' (Venn 2006: 123).

Poststructural political economy emerges as a distinctive critique of the production of knowledge in and about the global political economy as part of a broader, critical project of resisting the 'objective pursuit of cumulative knowledge', as practised by mainstream political economy and economics approaches (De Goede 2006: 21). Poststructuralism is anti-foundationalist in ontology and deconstructive in method, which makes it critical of approaches to social science wherein a 'foundation' of knowledge supplies particular and universal claims (about, for example, who acts and in what ways in the global political economy, see Griffin 2013: 209–11). Economic theory provides some good examples here, because economists only rarely consider that the models they draw, the calculations they make, and the knowledge they produce about the world are culturally specific in any way. This includes the assumed propitiousness of economic liberalisation, the inevitability of economic globalisation, or the inexorable logic of economic growth. These are each presented as universal truths in a globally applicable system of rational expectations and economic 'common sense', which is founded on the assumed reliability of economic theory's hypothetical person, Economic Man (*homo economicus*), and the predictability of his supposedly rational and rent-seeking behaviour. Such 'truths' are, of course, ideas about economic practice reproduced from centuries of cultural, historical, gendered and racialised assumptions about what people are, what they do, and who holds, or should hold, authority. As Grapard has so eloquently described, the 'self-sufficiency' of *homo economicus* 'conceals the labour of others', particularly the racialised and gendered labour of others (Grapard 1995: 33; see also Grapard and Hewitson 2012). That the cultural conditions of possibility of (neo)liberal economic ideas have been obscured so successfully, and over enough time, that they appear universal is testament both to Western economic theory's enduring grip on global policy, and to its power to reproduce as inevitable knowledge that is contingent and conditioned by the historical, cultural production of racialised, gendered inequalities.

Rejecting rationalism, poststructural analyses seek to challenge and unsettle established forms of knowledge and social science practice by exploring and deconstructing dominant Western discourses, looking for the less obvious meanings, and undermining the hierarchical, binary systems of meaning and knowledge reproduction through which they make sense of the world. Poststructuralism highlights the dependence of much Western political and economic thought and practice on centred, fixed meanings that exist somehow beyond debate, which, through careful analysis, can be shown to be highly historically and culturally contingent. Western capitalism's dependence, for example, on the 'natural', given, nature of private property, or liberal democratic assumptions of the essential character of autonomy, freedom and the market, can be deconstructed to show how they have been socially constructed, through histories of imperialism, social disenfranchisement and the establishment of powerful and punitive systems of social regulation and control, such as mass slavery, the enforced landlessness of the working classes and the deprivileging of women throughout history. Poststructuralists often use the concept of 'governmentality' to describe the ways in which human bodies become key elements of discursive regulation (biopolitics), so that regulatory, disciplinary technologies (of political representation, healthcare, education, crime and justice, economic development, and so on) are enforced, and enforceable, across people's lives and their bodies. Postcolonial scholars have frequently drawn on poststructuralists (for example, Derrida on deconstruction, as in Spivak's writing; Foucault on discourse and relations of power, as in Edward Saïd's work), although it should not be assumed that poststructural and postcolonial approaches are consistently complementary.

While poststructural approaches are generally well embedded across the social sciences, poststructural interventions in political economy have been somewhat sporadic (Langley 2009: 133). As De Goede (2006) argues, political economy has often been resistant to post-structural work (see also Peterson 2006; Zalewski 2006), while poststructuralism has been rather regularly dismissed 'as obscurantist, relativist and morally vacuous' (Griffin 2011: 46). Approaches that, as Zalewski describes, favour deconstructive, poststructural ways of thinking are frequently described as having 'little or indeed no use' in understanding material conditions, and are considered incapable of alleviating them (2006: 25–6). This is most likely because poststructural analyses reject the rationalism of mainstream approaches but also critique some of the economistic intractability and emancipatory certainty of non-mainstream, materialist paradigms in global political economy, rendering poststructuralism distasteful to an array of political economy traditions (for a fuller discussion, see Griffin 2018). On the other hand, postcolonial scholars have embraced poststructuralism's emphasis on understanding the social, cultural and historical conditions of power. Cognisant of political economy's rather longstanding 'blind spot' for race and colonialism (LeBaron et al. 2021: 287), and the 'epistemic privilege' often afforded European, and Eurocentric, thinkers across poststructural writing (Grosfoguel 2011: 2), postcolonial scholars have taken some of the key tools of post-structural critique to deconstruct all aspects of the 'material and ideological legacies of colonialism' (Kayatekin 2009: 1115). This has included, for example, challenging the desirability of 'development' itself (Omar 2012: 43) and the possibility of 'the economy' existing outside cultural relations (Charusheela 2011: 181).

SHARED SITES OF/FOR POSTCOLONIAL AND POSTSTRUCTURAL POLITICAL ECONOMIES

Without wishing to recentre Eurocentric forms of poststructural analysis or impose rigid boundaries around the theoretical practices of individual scholars, there are many places in the studies of political economy where postcolonial inquiry and poststructural ideas already intersect. Examples include the work of such scholars as Eiman O. Zein-Elabdin, Couze Venn, Stuart Hall, Arturo Escobar, Ilan Kapoor, S. Charusheela, Vinay Gidwani, Michael Shapiro, Dipesh Chakrabarty, Christine Sylvester, Ulla Grapard, Gillian Hewitson, Rob Aitken, Ash Amin, Shirin Rai, Nitasha Kaul and Marieke De Goede, among others. Much postcolonial theory has, as Nair (2018: 50) argues, embraced significant aspects of poststructuralism. Poststructural analytical strategies are well-embedded across postcolonial scholarship.

Indeed, one of the defining elements of both postcolonial and poststructural traditions has been their commitment to deconstructing modernism, decentring the modernist project that is so often embedded across the Western social sciences (in, for example, the theories and practices of neoclassical economics, development, feminism, institutionalism and historical materialism). Modernism, here, signals a project of replacing the 'traditional' with the 'modern' through scientism, secularism, individualism and progressivism. As a European/Western project, modernism embodies a concern to promote human freedom, justice and prosperity, but cannot be disassociated, as postcolonial scholars have made clear, from the many and varied legacies of empire and imperialism. Following Bhambra, and her discussion of Homi K. Bhabha's highly influential work, 'modernity' is not understood as a 'singular event' and 'there are no moderns', as in 'those who have lived through modernity' (2014: 116). Rather, modernity is a cultural thought construct that prioritises certain (European) historical moments, such as the French and industrial revolutions, while displacing the context of slavery, inequality and disenfranchisement on which dominant European/Western discourses have been built (Bhambra 2014: 116). Like poststructuralism, postcolonial theory challenges the modernism evident across 'different strands of feminist, post-Keynesian, institutionalist and a varied and long tradition of Marxist political economy' (Kayatekin 2009: 1114). Using poststructural tools to deconstruct 'the concept of the rational economic agent' as a 'pillar of neoclassical economic theory' and universalisable 'product of capitalist modernity' (Kayatekin 2009: 1114), postcolonial theory is a potential source of much inspiration for political economy research. Here, cultural abstraction and the recourse to universals, such as rationality, emancipation and equality, work at various levels to obscure – or indeed entirely eradicate – the privileging of certain (historical and cultural) types of human subjectivity.

What is called social sciences or humanities today 'have some of their roots in European history', as Kayatekin writes, but these roots also lie 'in colonial history' (2009: 1114). The colonial foundations and legacies of exploitation that mark the social sciences and humanities are worth scrutinising, steeped as they are in forms of 'naturalist modernism consonant with the West's 'encounter' of the other through the period of mercantilist colonialism' (Callari 2004: 115). The emergence of economics, for example, as a discipline in and of itself, is based on the centring of a progressive, 'enlightened' view of individual prosperity and accumulation, wherein the individual (white, male, European) subject is liberated from the chains of serfdom and feudal monopoly, as agrarian ('rude', to borrow Adam Smith's language) societies are reorganised to achieve the 'common good' of individual economic gain. Callari notes how classical political economy developed in the eighteenth century to reflect core beliefs of Western (European) superiority against the non-Western 'other', while Marxist political economy has often replicated colonial narratives and images of the 'deficient other' in its critique of capitalism (2004: 115–20). Similarly, Western feminisms have relied extensively on 'the discursive colonisation of Third World Women's lives and struggles' (Mohanty 2002: 501). Displaying 'ethnocentrism, ignorance, and condescension', Western feminism's reliance on 'individualism, equality, rights struggles, and identity politics' has proven 'insufficient in the light of women's more complicated positioning as citizens and subjects in both Western and non-Western contexts' (Sunder Rajan and Park 2005: 65–6).

Given, then, the multiple complementarities of postcolonial and poststructural approaches in deconstructing, challenging and creating political economy knowledge, the chapter turns now to consider some of the key places where these traditions of thought come together. For the sake of brevity, the chapter focuses on *three* postcolonial, poststructural intersections of knowledge, acknowledging that there are many more. The first concerns the efforts that postcolonial and poststructural approaches share in *rejecting economism*. The second lies in their commitment to *deconstructing imperial, racialised, gendered hierarchies*. The third resides in ongoing efforts to *highlight contested realities and the possibilities for subverting imperial, racialised and gendered sites and practices*, deconstructing and challenging the violence embedded in postcolonial apparatuses.

Rejecting Economism

The first way in which poststructural and postcolonial analysis combine to create and to challenge political economy knowledge lies in a shared rejection of economism. This is 'the view that economics is a distinct and technical science as opposed to an acknowledgement that it is inherently political' (Gradin 2016: 354).

When an approach, idea, discussion, policy, and so on, is described as 'economistic', it is at this point usually understood that social and political relations have somehow been subsumed to 'the economy'. Economism, in its simplest form, is the assumption that economics, rather than politics, is in command of society, and as a term, has most often been discussed in and across Marxist debates. Postcolonial and poststructural theories resist economism, both for the power it bestows on disciplinary economics, including its vice-like grip on contemporary policymaking and development 'common sense', and for the ways in which economic relations defined by dominant (neoclassical) economic theory have come to define the life chances of people everywhere. This is especially the case where 'development' has come to signal embedding the primacy of market rationality across societies, at all costs. Postcolonialism and poststructuralism are distinctly interpretive forms of intervention, which means they are approaches focused on understanding the meanings that humans attach to their environments, actions and to each other. For poststructural approaches, there is always an 'inescapable uncertainty, ambiguity, and inconstancy' that attaches to meanings, because meanings and identities are continuously renegotiated and recreated as material conditions are lived and transformed (Peterson 2006: 120). Economism is untenable, because, in an economistic analysis, there is no room for ambiguity and complexity, and all human, social life is reduced to the 'fact' of the economy and economic relations.

While postcolonial theory has grown 'in tandem with poststructuralism, postmodernism and feminism', economics has proven to be a discipline particularly 'resistant to change' (Kayatekin 2009: 1113). This is in large part because modern economics rarely reflects on its history, heritage and position of power within society, but also because economics does not often consider the role of culture in economic behaviour and decision-making (Zein-Elabdin 2009: 1153). An important part of the subversive project of postcolonial feminism in the global political economy has been the task of capturing – and challenging – the 'cultural hegemony' of the field of economics (Zein-Elabdin 2004: 36), and the gendered erasure of culture, history and the organisation of knowledge therein. As Charusheela and Zein-Elabdin note, 'economics has taken over from anthropology the role of drawing powerful worldviews that organize knowledge and inform policy in both domestic and international contexts' (2004: ii). Economic theory throughout the twentieth and twenty-first centuries has developed to emulate modern physics, through a 'scientific' model that assumes, as Venn articulates, 'necessary relationships and invariant correlations, much as Newtonian physics does' (Venn 2006: 15). It has thus become entirely legitimate for the discipline and practices of economics 'to proceed through the logic of abstraction that characterizes conventional Western science', as if the economy operates according to laws 'inherent in its nature' rather than 'humanly constituted and variable practices that work under quite specific conditions that are equally subject to human manipulation' (Venn 2006: 15). This has played out 'in the deployment of highly abstract frameworks and methods that may seem, on the surface, "value-neutral" because they have proved so effective at, figuratively and literally, removing any hint of the human body from economic analysis and practice' (Griffin 2018: 463).

For postcolonial and poststructural approaches, the rejection of economism is rooted in a rejection of economics' so-called value neutrality, as embedded in a highly ethnocentric discipline, built on, and reproducing, the knowledge produced by white men, for white men, and inflicted on the 'developing' world through various racialised and gendered processes of neoliberal development. While poststructural political economy does not doubt, in any sense, the discursive and material power of the 'economic', poststructuralists reject the assumption, as De Goede argues, that ideas and reality exist somehow separately to each other (2003: 80). There is no material economic 'reality' separate to our knowledge of the world, nor can the economic sphere be understood as existing independently in any sense from human life, in all its forms. Economic practices 'do not exist prior to, or independently from, ideas and beliefs about them' (De Goede 2003: 81). Denying the separation of discourse and materiality is not to affirm that poststructural political economy is ahistorical and anti-materialist, because it is not, and poststructural political economy has furnished powerful analyses of the constitution and effects of historical and material realities in the global political economy (Griffin 2018: 89). Rather, asserting that economic practices and ideas exist together and are mutually constitutive is to reaffirm only that the 'real and material existence of people' (Douglas 2001) matters. Asking how power operates requires focusing on how power and authority are produced, which in turn directs analytical attention 'to the consequences' of this (Peterson 2006: 120–1). Materiality always lies at the heart of feminist inquiry but, to paraphrase Zalewski (2006: 27–8), answering material questions requires political, discursive work.

'The economy' is, then, and as Venn articulates, a human construction; it is the 'result of the functioning of assemblages' and is 'the active and purposive combination of specific technologies of production', such as institutions, human individuals, organisations and geographies, 'put into place over the years to accomplish the goals relating to the production and distribution of the means of existence at determinate points in time and place' (Venn 2006: 15). There is no place where economics stands apart from its cultural conditions of possibility (except perhaps in its own imagination of itself). While economics labours to reproduce a vision of itself as ahistorical, acultural and objective, cultural factors, 'such as ideologies, values, and ways of being', play a huge part 'in determining what kinds of devices work and in what conditions' (Venn 2006: 15). The influence of culture on what works in what conditions is especially evident when considering concepts that are also 'things', such as 'money' and 'credit'. These are material, to varying degrees and in different ways, while being simultaneously social and discursive in nature. That is, concepts such as money, profit and capital 'exist' and are 'brought into being' by historically grounded, discursive practices, 'ideas and beliefs' (De Goede 2003: 79–81).

Rejecting economism, postcolonial and poststructural scholars have focused, instead, on querying practices and processes of 'cultural representation', 'discourse' and 'the ambiguity of political dissent' (De Goede 2006: 1–2). This leads poststructural political economy to interrogate the basis of power and knowledge in the global political economy, to ask questions about how abstract categories such as 'capital', 'finance' and 'risk' can be measured or known, or how the day-to-day realities of ordinary people might better be accounted for (Griffin 2011: 43–4).

Often deploying a deliberately and self-consciously genealogical, deconstructive strategy of analysis (see Kaul 2004, 2007; Charusheela 2010), postcolonial writing embodies a 'consciousness of resistance to the current cultural hegemony powerfully maintained in place by monopoly over economic resources as well as the discursive construction of what constitutes economy and economics' (Charusheela and Zein-Elabdin 2004: 6). Postcolonial theory rejects 'the common (mis)understanding of economy and economics' as 'an extra-cultural universally applicable rationality' or 'self-contained "science"', and instead reads 'development as an orientalist, colonial discourse rather than a culturally neutral, scientifically knowable path of an economy' (Zein-Elabdin 2011: 216–17). Postcolonial and poststructural approaches ask questions that are often overlooked by much mainstream and critical political economy. These might include, for example, asking how neoliberal governance strategies 'define "opportunities" according to models of economically appropriate/expected behaviour derived from privileging the experiences of white, western and elite men' (Griffin 2011: 43–4). There are, in fact, infinite questions to be asked – about identity, the reproduction of relations of power in the global political economy, the role of dominant, and dominating, practices of knowledge production, and the political, social and cultural implications of discourses of economic 'common sense', to name only a few.

Deconstructing Imperial, Racialised, Gendered Hierarchies

The second way in which postcolonial and poststructural analysis combine lies in postcolonial feminism's commitment to deconstructing imperial, racialised, gendered hierarchies in the global political economy.

Postcolonial theory's use of poststructural analytical strategies to deconstruct the binary, hierarchical thinking beloved of 'modern', European knowledges means that it plays a key role in revealing the artificiality of imperial, gendered binary oppositions, the hierarchies that they embody, and their social effects (including, for example, the marginalisation of women and people of colour in systems of governance predicated on public/private, liberal/illiberal, modern/traditional distinctions). It is worth noting, however, that much poststructural and postcolonial work excludes explicitly gendered engagements, and this chapter's focus on postcolonial feminism is not to disguise substantial gaps in postcolonial and poststructural traditions in this regard. It is also important to acknowledge that, while postcolonial theory's development in tandem with poststructuralism and feminism 'explains the obvious influence of the intellectual traditions it contains' (Kayatekin 2009: 1113–14), the relationship between postcolonial theory and Western disciplinary agendas, of which certain feminisms are undoubtedly a part, is complicated, and sometimes fractious. While important postcolonial feminist contributions have certainly used poststructural strategies to deconstruct prevailing racialised, gendered and sexualised hierarchies in the global political economy, postcolonial feminists have also extensively problematised the practices of othering on which Anglo/Northern feminisms have been built. They have interrogated at length and in comprehensive detail the racialised, discursive privilege embedded in Western feminist accounts of women in development and the Third World. Postcolonial feminists have extensively, and painstakingly, exposed the policing practices of the production of knowledge in the Global North as they regulate which bodies do and do not count in world politics, including the practices through which poststructural feminisms themselves have marginalised and othered non-Northern knowledges.

Postcolonial analysis, in its critique of the 'modern' centre that drives the cultural, exclusionary and racist production of European/Western knowledge, turns to poststructuralism to deconstruct the 'essentialist and totalising categories of "truth", "reality" and "reason"' (Haag 2020: 18) embodied in modernist epistemologies. For postcolonial and poststructural scholars, discourses configure social, political, cultural and economic spaces in physical and tangible ways, and through the discursive relations of power they reproduce. Discourses only make sense, and are only sensible, when their historical and material conditions of possibility are made legible. Postcolonial feminist analysis of the global political economy, in particular, is concerned with understanding the world both discursively and materially. Herein, intersections of race, gender and class are central to the formation and reproduction of identity in the global political economy. Inequality, power, identity, access to resources – each condition how, and where, human life is positioned. For postcolonial feminists, that positioning can best be grasped by understanding that marginality is always embedded in histories of imperialism and colonisation (Nair 2018: 50). As Mohanty has famously articulated, the processes of economic exchange at the heart of globalisation are intrinsically exploitative, such that the 'link between political economy and culture remains crucial to any form of feminist theorising' (2002: 509). The discursive constructions of economics are especially worth thinking about, as Charusheela argues, because of their pragmatic effects, shaping both the 'analytical and evaluative practices' of modern economic practice (2004: 47). Taking this point seriously means understanding that the outcomes of economic evaluations and the policies therein produced have taken shape in an environment *already* structured by, and biased according to, gendered, racialised assumptions and expectations. For postcolonial feminists, there is no part of capitalism and liberal democracy that can be separated from the centuries of racist oppression and exploitation through which they have been enabled.

Whereas poststructural approaches operate a 'relational and differential account' of language and society and have always stressed 'the context in which social actions occur and their meaning is produced' (Wullweber and Scherrer 2010), postcolonial feminist analysis has interrogated the social contexts shaped by the intersections of economic, political and racial marginalisation for women in both Global South and North. For postcolonial and poststructural feminists, the binding of knowledge and power impacts the ways in which actions, interests, identities become coherent and meaningful. Since knowledge is always partial and incomplete, the various legacies of colonialism are always revealing themselves in changing political, social and economic consequences. As conditions and historical practices shift over time, the transitions they engender are particularly significant for postcolonial feminists, for it is the constant nature of transition that permits decolonisation and the decentring of the 'West'.

In decentring the white, Western, Eurocentric perspective, postcolonial feminists look both to reclaim and decolonise knowledge and practice, and to create ways of being, lived experiences and forms of activism that undo some of the, ongoing, legacies of colonialism. This, in turn, requires some personal commitment from the researcher, part of which necessitates understanding and challenging the researcher's own position (positionality) and privilege. A core part of Gayatri Chakravorty Spivak's work, for example, has been concerned with the processes of 'unlearning' privilege, so that the speaking subject not only becomes 'able to listen' to less privileged constituencies, but 'learns to speak in such a way that [they] will be taken seriously by that constituency' (Harasym and Spivak 1990: 42).

Spivak has been perhaps one of the most celebrated writers of postcolonial, feminist deconstruction. In 'Can the Subaltern Speak?' (Spivak 1988), she famously combines discussion of gender, race and class to articulate a feminist, intellectual task of challenging racial appropriation and epistemic violence. Herein, Spivak considers, in particular, the constellations of meaning that the category 'gender' suggests and obscures. Part of Spivak's project has been to challenge the 'discourse of women as produced, as defined by men' that has dominated Western knowledge production, institutions and governance structures, by placing women in the position of the 'questioning subject' of theory/practice, not least because the 'position of the speaking subject within theory' has been so historically powerful (Harasym and Spivak 1990: 42). As she notes, women are not equally well-located to assert themselves, and so 'the women who can in fact begin to engage in this particular "winning back" of the position of the questioning subject are in very privileged positions in the geopolis today' (Harasym and Spivak 1990: 42).

Spivak is, of course, not alone in her problematisation of the privileges, exploitations and cooptations that characterise thinking about gendered bodies in the global political economy. Attuned to the legacy of colonisation that 'entwines with older, precolonial as well as postcolonial systems and relations of rule to produce multilayered and multiply-related matrices of power, constituting what we call today "world politics"' (Chowdhry and Ling 2010), postcolonial feminists have used poststructural analysis to deconstruct the global political economy, past and present, and to decentre its 'Euro-American colonial patriarchy'. Colonial and postcolonial systems are made powerful through discursive relations of power, such as ethnocentric practices of commerce, government, development or transnational production, while material structures, such as global capitalist relations, 'underwrite, mobilize, account for, signify, and reflect' this discursive matrix 'of domination and privilege' (Chowdhry and Ling 2010). It is here, in discourse but also in practice, that the conditions of struggle over material resources, politics, family life, medicine, the legacies of conflict, education, well-being and so on, are reproduced, including who decides how these are known and practised (Griffin 2018: 96–7).

Research into racialised, gendered privilege in the global political economy represents, this chapter argues, some of the most powerful, dynamic and revealing examples of the successful merging of postcolonial and poststructural traditions of thought in and across political economy. Postcolonial feminism, as Sunder Rajan and Park argue, 'cannot be regarded simply as a subset of postcolonial studies' and is a critical intervention 'that is changing the configuration of both postcolonial and feminist studies' (2005: 53). As Parashar asserts, postcolonialism 'offers feminism the conceptual tool box to see multiple sites of oppression and to reject universalisms around gendered experiences' (2016: 371). Just as Western feminists have deconstructed, as Mohanty suggests, the 'latent anthromorphism in Western discourse', so postcolonial feminists have offered a parallel strategy of 'uncovering the latent ethnocentrism' in writings on people in the Third World, especially writings on Third World women (2003: 42). Frequently (but not only) through recourse to the language of poststructuralism, postcolonial feminists have demonstrated 'how coloniality not only divides the world according to a particular racial logic', but 'creates specific understandings of gender that enable the disappearance of the colonial/raced woman from theoretical and political consideration' (Bhambra 2014: 119). They have revealed the dynamic and multifaceted operations of the 'colonial matrix of power' in all its gendered forms, including the ways in which colonialism and imperialism leave behind gendered, racialised legacies of power and identity, traceable across various discourses and practices of the global political economy (local, national and global) and evident in the everyday lives of people everywhere. These legacies can be seen across the organisation of economic activity and the neoliberal governance of development, for example, in assumptions about the value of types of 'rational' economic practice, in distinctions between productive and reproductive labour and the bodies that are disappeared in national systems of accounts, or the types of 'nimble', gendered bodies best suited to the transnational production structures of post-industrial capitalism.

Highlighting Contested Realities and the Possibilities for Subverting Imperial, Racialised and Gendered Sites and Practices

The third key way in which postcolonial and poststructural approaches combine to create and to challenge political economy knowledge exists in the form of highlighting contestation and encouraging subversion across the imperial, racialised and gendered global political economy.

Postcolonial and poststructural theories, as diverse as they are, interrogate what is otherwise taken for granted in the global political economy, questioning the basis of power, knowledge, representation and identity in politico-economic discourse and practice. In this they constitute a direct challenge to rationalistic and economistic accounts of what drives our socio-economic systems. Importantly, in their focus on the role of the politics of representation, postcolonial and poststructural approaches are highly attentive both to the repressive function of discourse in socio-economic life and to the transformative potential of discursive reconfiguration.

By concentrating on the role of political, social and cultural dissent, anti-imperial and anti-colonial approaches have developed powerful conceptualisations of resistance and its possibilities. A 'central unifying theme in postcolonial theory', argues Kayatekin, has been the 'analysis of constructions and representations of culture and subjectivity in and through colonial discourse(s)' (2009: 1114). As colonial and imperialist regimes have relied on particular representations of the 'conquered', positioning subject people and populations as fundamentally different (different especially to 'modern' Europeans), so the postcolonial project has challenged in radical ways these representations of the 'other', contesting in particular the primacy afforded the white, rational, European man in global political economy knowledge and practice. By 'conceptualising the historical and social context of these constructions', postcolonial approaches reveal the 'distinct notions of race, ethnicity, gender and class in their constitution', seeking to replace these with alternative notions and representations (Kayatekin 2009: 1114).

Postcolonial feminists frequently use poststructural strategies to engage with and subvert the ethnocentric reproduction of knowledge and socio-economic practice. Working tirelessly to reveal the intersecting nature of racialised, gendered oppression in the global political economy, postcolonial and poststructural feminists have revealed how the racialised feminisation of identities and practices effectively devalues them (Peterson 2006: 125). They have focused at length on the effects of the sex and gender binaries from which ethnocentric, neoliberal discourses have reproduced ideas about 'successful', 'rational' and 'predictable' economic behaviour (Griffin 2018: 97). They have revealed in careful detail how and where women, gender, sexuality, and race are presented, or obscured, as 'largely unexamined questions or non-contested categories of analysis' (Agathangelou and Turcotte 2010) in and across the global political economy.

Postcolonial and poststructural feminists are particularly interested in understanding how dominant discourses, such as the neoclassical economic theory at the heart of governance and development regimes, provide the limits of intelligibility to global, and local, practices and knowledges. In this vein, Agathangelou and Ling (2004 and 2009) articulate a 'postcolonial-feminist framework' that situates 'power relations and identities within historical constructions of race, gender, class, and culture', outlining a theory of the (violent and imperial) 'material and ideological struggles of historically situated agents in a neoliberal world economy' (Agathangelou and Ling 2004: 518). For Agathangelou and Ling, postcolonial theory offers rich resources for feminist political economy because it 'defictionalises liberalism's bordering of the "public" from the "private", "outside" from "inside" "group" from "individual", "East" from "'West"', and in this reveals how a nexus of class-race-gender is constantly exploited through elite discourse (such as that reproduced by MNCs, IFIs, the media and nation-states themselves) to enable the reproduction of neocolonial interest and privilege in global politics' (Agathangelou and Ling 2004: 518–19). Agathangelou and Ling's work, and that of many others, has illustrated the perniciousness of the racism, sexism and elitism reproduced by economic practices.

In contesting the 'truths' of neoliberal rationality, postcolonial and poststructural feminists thus also importantly generate space for doing political economy 'otherwise'. The importance of this space for confronting and subverting ethnocentric and gendered patterns of knowledge production and practice in the global political economy should not be underestimated. Only by appreciating how neoliberal economic theory has been built out of, and on, gendered, racialised hierarchies of imperial knowledge and practice does it become possible to challenge and subvert what Agathangelou and Ling (2004: 533) articulate as the 'political economy of exploitation and violence' that propels neoliberal, and neoliberalising, discourses of economic development and national security.

At the same time, then, as postcolonial and poststructural contributions to feminist political economy have centralised inquiry into the effects of technologies and practices of economic domination on gendered and racialised bodies, they have also fought to open space across global political economy research and practice for productive and relational engagements with questions of who is speaking, to and for whom. Understanding global governance, international institutions and/or economic practice as constituted by race, gender, class and sexuality, postcolonial and poststructural feminist approaches have both challenged oppressive regimes of truth in global political economy and have sought to generate new forms of listening and learning from others.

Following Spivak, the opening of space for contestation and subversion lies in the act of communication itself, and so postcolonial and poststructural feminist approaches have pushed political economy to honour the lives and voices of women and people of colour. The significance of generating dialogue is crucial to the longevity of the feminist project across the global political economy, and to future feminist successes therein. It speaks to the core of much contemporary feminist global political economy scholarship: of reflexively acknowledging and disclosing position and positionality; unlearning privilege; learning to speak appropriately to other constituents; and representing and analysing the texts of the oppressed. This reflexivity necessitates acknowledging, as per Sunder Rajan and Park (2005), the dominance of the 'metropole' in the writing and citational practices of political economy writing. This is equally the case for gendered political economy scholarship, which is certainly not immune to poor citational practices, and requires that Northern feminists 'abandon their unexamined ethnocentrism and the reproduction of orientalist categories of thought' (Sunder Rajan and Park 2005: 54). Northern feminists, argue Sunder Rajan and Park, must commit themselves to the 'hard work of uncovering and contesting global power relations' (2005: 54), while ensuring that they make space for neglected geographical voices, locations and empirical content.

Engaging with the imperial, racialised and gendered content of the global political economy requires not only the engendering of global political economy analyses themselves, but also, as Rai notes, a very 'close attention to issues of South/North inequalities' (2008: 19). There is, or should be, always a central role for understanding dialogue and subversion as practised through unequal discourses of race and gender, and a constant, if not always acknowledged, conversation persists between the parts of the political, social, economic and cultural binaries that continue to sustain imperial, neoliberal and capitalist world orders. Power is very much more than simple economic or military superiority, as Agathangelou and Ling describe, and can only fully be understood when 'power relations and identities' are placed 'within historical constructions of race, gender, class, and culture' (2004: 518). The links between coloniser and colonised, private and public, outsiders and insiders, and the micro-personal and the macro-structural cannot be undone, but these categories can be 'disassembled to help us understand and eventually transform the transnational forces that shape their formations in the first place' (Agathangelou and Ling 2009: 5). The concept of 'worldism', for Agathangelou and Ling, presents a potential alternative to the binary of 'self versus other' that characterises the global political economy under neoliberal imperialism. Agathangelou and Ling deliberately build on, and from, the 'postcolonial notion that *all* parties make history, albeit with unequal access to power', and, as such, 'our mutual embeddedness makes us mutually accountable' (2009: 85–6, emphasis in the original).

This 'multiple worlds' approach accounts for 'the context of social relations that make world politics what it is', encourages an openness to integrating 'languages, norms, institutions, practices, and political economies', and engenders a commitment to disrupting neoliberal imperialism's 'hegemonic ontology and its socio-political practices' (Agathangelou and Ling 2009: 1–2). This includes, for example, paying attention to the various material and ideological struggles of historically situated agents in the neoliberal global political economy, 'de-fictionalising' liberalism's hierarchical binaries (of public/private, outside/inside, group/individual and East/West); and acknowledging the 'savage intimacy' between coloniser and colonised that continues to bind households and empire to the global economy (Agathangelou and Ling 2004: 518–19). Only by adopting a politics of mutual accountability can we 'face the complicities (including our own) that sustain violence in the making of history, so that we may, as Marx extorted, change it' (Agathangelou and Ling 2009: 87).

Agathangelou and Ling use the language of poststructuralism to encourage the transformation of approaches to and actions within global politics. For Agathangelou and Ling, disrupting dominant practices creates space to change them. This emancipatory project also means that Agathangelou and Ling's work fits uneasily within the 'postmodern' orthodoxy that has arisen (especially in the US academy) over the last thirty to forty years (as Mohanty notes in her 2002 response to her 1984 essay, 'Under Western Eyes'). Theoretical eclecticism is, however, something that characterises much postcolonial feminist work, and it is this dynamism, and its refusal, ultimately, to be subsumed to restrictive theoretical orthodoxies, that embodies postcolonial, poststructural feminist global political economy scholarship with its potential subversiveness. Questions of power, and of relations of power, of the role of ethnocentric discourses as 'centred' systems of meaning, and of the mythical, binary truths created and sustained by racialised, gendered practices of representation and the production of knowledge animate poststructurally informed, postcolonial feminist engagements with the global political economy.

In particular, postcolonial feminist research often fuses poststructural language and analytical strategies with embedded, material accounts of political and economic structures, processes and practices and their everyday effects. Here, the neoliberal markets and the governance institutions at the heart of capitalist social relations are socially and materially embedded, productive of and dependent upon racialised, gendered 'cleavages of inequality' that condition access, competitiveness and efficiency (Rai 2008: 24). At the same time as postcolonial feminist work challenges the 'false universality' of Eurocentric discourses such as neoliberal economic development, it does so through a care for everyday life and 'local gendered contexts' (Mohanty 1984, 2002). Seeking, ultimately, to contribute to transforming the racialised, gendered inequalities of life in the global political economy, postcolonial feminists have paid significant attention to material structures, which are understood to involve multiple positionalities, assorted social and political relations, and numerous contingent realities (Chowdhry and Ling 2010).

This effort to ensure that theoretically sophisticated efforts to demystify and subvert imperial, gendered relations of power are grounded in practical engagements with everyday, material life in the global political economy is central to much feminist effort in this space. Postcolonial and poststructural feminist approaches have proved adept at moving beyond comprehension of intersectional dynamics towards a focus on transforming these dynamics, including through activist, policy, legal and civil society engagements (see, for example, Cho et al. 2013). Scholars such as Naila Kabeer (2000, 2017), Dina Siddiqi (2009), Dipti Tamang (2020) and Celeste Koens and Samanthi Gunawardana (2021), among others, have focused on the agency that women are able to bring to bear on their lives, and in conditions otherwise dismissed by Western scholars as simplistically patriarchal or universally oppressive.

For scholars such as Chandra Mohanty, the feminist project is one that is, and should be, both personal and collective and, as she writes in her 2003 monograph, the point should be to 'encourage both a personal and a larger, collective genealogy of feminist practice, which moves through the enforced boundaries of race, colour, nation, and class' (2003: 10). Mohanty contributes to a practical project of 'progressive, left, feminist, and anti-imperialist' scholarship, which is designed to contribute to certain intellectual and practical outcomes. These include demystifying power and decolonising and politicising knowledge so as to engender strategies of resistance across 'scholarship, pedagogy, grassroots movements, and academic institutions'; rethinking 'self and community through the practice of emancipatory education'; building 'an ethics of crossing cultural, sexual, national, class, and racial borders'; and theorising and practising 'anticapitalist and democratic critique in education, through collective struggle' (2003: 10). For Mohanty, the struggle to implement a transnational feminist practice of solidarity, organising women against global capitalism's exploitative, (re)colonising practices, is an urgent one, not least as neoliberal globalisation continues its ever-more brutal trajectory of exacerbating economic, racial and gender inequalities (Mohanty 1984, 2002, 2003).

CONCLUDING THOUGHTS

Acknowledging that the relationship between postcolonial inquiry and poststructural analysis has not always been harmonious, this chapter has shown how key questions for the studies and practices of the global political economy, which have often been and are often being eclipsed by the production of 'Anglo' disciplinary knowledge, entail the combined wisdom of postcolonial and poststructural approaches. Analysis that places questions of gender and sexuality in juxtaposition with those of race and empire is especially enabling, constituting some of the most significant examples of the integration of postcolonial and poststructural thinking in and across contemporary political economy. In their focus on deconstructing binary forms of knowledge, their efforts to understand and grapple with social relations of power, and their descriptions of identities and economic structures as mutable and constructed, postcolonial and poststructural feminists dissect and expand the global political economy, opening much-needed space for contestation and subversion. This chapter has sought to contribute further to existing feminist efforts in this space, advancing approaches to political economy that *begin with* the (messy, contradictory and sometimes unknowable) realities of people's lives and work their way up.

While feminists, of course, vary in approach and method, combining postcolonial and poststructural language to describe the world through the language of intersectionality, representation and power has enabled feminism to assemble powerful critiques of the constitution and effects of Eurocentrism, neocolonialism and imperialism in the global political economy. This chapter has focused on where postcolonial and poststructural ideas intersect to centralise the racialised, gendered practices of the global political economy in three ways. The first locates the role of postcolonial and poststructural feminism in deconstructing the discursive hegemony of disciplinary, neoclassical economics, and its enduring grip on contemporary governance and development discourse, as evidenced by the ongoing pervasiveness of economism. The second outlines postcolonial and poststructural feminist engagement with imperial, racialised and gendered hierarchies, and their constitutive role in ideas about and processes of economic exchange in the global political economy. The third examines how raced and gendered discourses, practices and realities in the global political economy can be shown to be contested, open to critique and possibly transformed. The chapter has argued that feminist approaches that use the strategies of postcolonial and poststructural analysis (but which ultimately resist neat classifications) constitute an ongoing project of deconstructing and decolonising the subject matter of political economy, revealing the imperialist legacies and tendencies of disciplinary political economy work itself.

Of all approaches to political economy, postcolonial and poststructural feminist analyses have most clearly recognised, centralised and deconstructed the significance of questions of colonialism, race, empire and the role of alternative epistemologies in the production of political economy knowledge. They have pushed these efforts to their fullest potential, interrogating the intersections of race and gender across the structures of knowledge production in and the everyday practices of the global political economy in all their forms.

REFERENCES

Agathangelou, A.M. and Ling, L.H.M. (2004) 'Power, Borders, Security, Wealth: Lessons of Violence and Desire from September 11', *International Studies Quarterly*, 48, pp. 517–38.
Agathangelou, A.M. and Ling, L.H.M. (2009) *Transforming World Politics: From Empire to Multiple Worlds*, London and New York: Routledge.
Agathangelou, A.M. and Turcotte, H. (2010) '"Feminist" Theoretical Inquiries and "IR"', in Denemark, R.A. (ed.), *The International Studies Encyclopedia*, Oxford: Wiley-Blackwell.
Bhambra, G.K. (2014) 'Postcolonial and Decolonial Dialogues', *Postcolonial Studies*, 17 (2), pp. 115–21.
Callari, A. (2004) 'Economics and the Postcolonial Other', in Charusheela, S. and Zein-Elabdin, E.O. (eds), *Postcolonialism Meets Economics*, London and New York: Routledge, pp. 113–29.

Charusheela, S. (2004) 'Postcolonial Thought, Postmodernism, and Economics: Questions of Ontology and Ethics', in Charusheela, S. and Zein-Elabdin, E.O. (eds), *Postcolonialism Meets Economics*, London and New York: Routledge, pp. 40–58.

Charusheela, S. (2010) 'Imagining Economics Otherwise: Encounters with Identity/Difference by Nitasha Kaul', *Feminist Economics*, **16** (2), pp. 141–6.

Charusheela, S. (2011) 'Where is the "Economy"? Cultural Studies and Narratives of Capitalism', in Smith, P. (ed.), *The Renewal of Cultural Studies*, Philadelphia: Temple University Press, pp. 177–87.

Charusheela, S. and Zein-Elabdin, E.O. (eds) (2004) *Postcolonialism Meets Economics*, London and New York: Routledge.

Cho, S., Kimberlé, W.C. and McCall, L. (2013) 'Toward a Field of Intersectionality Studies: Theory, Applications, and Praxis', *Signs: Journal of Women in Culture and Society*, **38** (4), pp. 785–810.

Chowdhry, G. and Ling, L.H.M. (2010) 'Race(ing) International Relations: A Critical Overview of Postcolonial Feminism in International Relations', in Denemark, R.A. (ed.), *The International Studies Encyclopedia*, Oxford: Wiley-Blackwell, accessed 5.8.2021 at: https://www.oxfordreference.com/view/10.1093/acref/9780191842665.001.0001/acref-9780191842665-e-0318?rskey=e7XXjr&result=362.

De Goede, M. (2003) 'Beyond Economism in International Political Economy', *Review of International Studies*, **29**, pp. 79–97.

De Goede, M. (2006) 'Introduction: International Political Economy and the Promises of Poststructuralism' and 'Part I: Poststructural Interventions', in De Goede, M. (ed.), *International Political Economy and Poststructural* Politics, Basingstoke: Palgrave, pp. 1–20 and pp. 21–4.

Douglas, I.R. (2001) 'Poststructuralism', accessed 5.8.2010 at: https://ianrobertdouglas.com/2001/06/01/poststructuralism/.

Gradin, S. (2016) 'Rethinking the Notion of "Value" in Global Value Chains Analysis: A Decolonial Political Economy Perspective', *Competition and Change*, **20** (5), pp. 353–67.

Grapard, U. (1995) 'Robinson Crusoe: The Quintessential Economic Man?', *Feminist Economics*, **1** (1), pp. 33–52.

Grapard, U. and Hewitson, G. (eds) (2012) *Robinson Crusoe's Economic Man: A Construction and Deconstruction*, London and New York: Routledge.

Griffin, P. (2013) 'Deconstruction as "Anti-Method"', in Shepherd, L.J. (ed.), *Critical Approaches to Security: An Introduction to Theories and Methods*, London and New York: Routledge, pp. 208–22.

Griffin, P. (2011) 'Poststructuralism in/and IPE', in Shields, S., Bruff, I. and Macartney, H. (eds), *Critical International Political Economy: Dialogue, Debate and Dissensus*, Basingstoke: Palgrave Macmillan, pp. 43–58.

Griffin, P. (2018) 'Gender, IPE and Poststructuralism: Problematising the Material/Discursive Divide', in Elias, J. and Roberts, A. (eds), *Handbook on the International Political Economy of Gender*, Cheltenham, UK and Northampton, MA, USA: Edward Elgar Publishing, pp. 86–101.

Grosfoguel, R. (2011) 'Decolonizing Post-Colonial Studies and Paradigms of Political Economy: Transmodernity, Decolonial Thinking, and Global Coloniality', *Transmodernity: Journal of Peripheral Cultural Production of the Luso-Hispanic World*, **1** (1), pp. 2–38.

Gruffydd Jones, B. (2013) 'Slavery, Finance and International Political Economy', in Seth, S. (ed.), *Postcolonial Theory and International Relations: A Critical Introduction*, London and New York: Routledge, pp. 49–69.

Haag, S. (2020) 'Bridging the Postcolonial Political-Economy Divide: Towards a Theoretical Framework', DPS Working Paper Series No. 7, April, pp. 1–28, accessed 5.8.2021 at: https://www.uni-kassel.de/fb05/fachgruppen/politikwissenschaft/entwicklungspolitik-und- postkoloniale-studien/dps-working-papers.html.

Harasym, S. and Spivak, G.C. (eds) (1990) *The Post-Colonial Critic: Interviews, Strategies, Dialogues*, London and New York: Routledge.

Inayatullah, N. and Blaney, D.L. (2010) *Savage Economics: Wealth, Poverty and the Temporal Walls of Capitalism*, London and New York: Routledge.

Inayatullah N. and Blaney, D.L. (2018) 'Race and Global Inequality', in Persaud, R.B. and Sajed, A. (eds), *Race, Gender, and Culture in International Relations: Postcolonial Perspectives*, London and New York: Routledge, pp. 116–34.

Kabeer, N. (2017) 'Economic Pathways to Women's Empowerment and Active Citizenship: What Does the Evidence from Bangladesh Tell Us?', *The Journal of Development Studies*, **53** (5), pp. 649–63.

Kabeer, N. (2000) *The Power to Choose: Bangladeshi Women and Labour Market Decisions in London and Dhaka*, London: Verso.

Kaul, N. (2004) 'Writing Economic Theory An*Other* Way', in Charusheela, S. and Zein-Elabdin, E.O. (eds), *Postcolonialism Meets Economics*, London and New York: Routledge, pp. 183–200.

Kaul, N. (2007) *Imagining Economics Otherwise: Encounters with Identity/Difference*, London and New York: Routledge.

Kayatekin, S.A. (2009) 'Between Political Economy and Postcolonial Theory: First Encounters', *Cambridge Journal of Economics*, **33** (6), pp. 1113–18.

Koens, C. and Gunawardana, S.J. (2021) 'A Continuum of Participation: Rethinking Tamil Women's Political Participation and Agency in Post-War Sri Lanka', *International Feminist Journal of Politics*, **23** (3), pp. 463–84.

Langley, P. (2009) 'Power-Knowledge Estranged: From Susan Strange to Poststructuralism in IPE', in Blyth, M. (ed.), *Routledge Handbook of International Political Economy: IPE as a Global Conversation*, Abingdon and New York: Routledge, pp. 126–39.

LeBaron, G., Mügge, D., Best, J. and Hay, C. (2021) 'Blind Spots in IPE: Marginalized Perspectives and Neglected Trends in Contemporary Capitalism', *Review of International Political Economy*, **28** (2), pp. 283–94.

Mohanty, C.T. (1984) 'Under Western Eyes: Feminist Scholarship and Colonial Discourses', *Boundary*, **12** (3)/**13** (1), pp. 333–58.

Mohanty, C.T. (2002) '"Under Western Eyes" Revisited: Feminist Solidarity Through Anticapitalist Struggles', *Signs: Journal of Women in Culture and Society*, **28** (2), pp. 499–535.

Mohanty, C.T. (2003) *Feminism Without Borders: Decolonising Theory, Practicing Solidarity*, Durham, NC and London: Duke University Press.

Nair, S. (2018) 'Postcolonial Feminism', in Elias, J. and Roberts, A. (eds), *Handbook on the International Political Economy of Gender*, Cheltenham, UK and Northampton, MA, USA: Edward Elgar Publishing, pp. 50–60.

Omar, S.M. (2012) 'Rethinking Development from a Postcolonial Perspective', *Journal of Conflictology*, **3** (1), pp. 42–9.

Parashar, S. (2016) 'Feminism and Postcolonialism: (En)Gendering Encounters', *Postcolonial Studies*, **19** (4), pp. 371–7.

Peterson, V.S. (2006) 'Getting Real: The Necessity of Critical Poststructuralism in Global Political Economy', in De Goede, M. (ed.), *International Political Economy and Poststructural Politics*, Basingstoke: Palgrave, pp. 19–138.

Rai, S.M. (2008) 'Analysing Global Governance', in Rai, S.M. and Waylen, G. (eds), *Global Governance: Feminist Perspectives*, Basingstoke: Palgrave, pp. 19–42.

Rao, N. (2000) '"Neocolonialism" or "Globalization"? Postcolonial Theory and the Demands of Political Economy', *Interdisciplinary Literary Studies*, **1** (2), pp. 165–84.

Roy, A. (2016) 'Who's Afraid of Postcolonial Theory?', *International Journal of Urban and Regional Research*, **40** (1), pp. 200–209.

Siddiqi, D. (2009) 'Do Bangladeshi Factory Workers Need Saving? Sisterhood in the Post-Sweatshop Era', *Feminist Review*, **91**, pp. 154–74.

Spivak, G.C. (1988) 'Can the Subaltern Speak?', in Nelson, C. and Grossberg, L. (eds), *Marxism and the Interpretation of Culture*, Champaign, IL: University of Illinois Press, pp. 271–316.

Sunder Rajan, R. and Park, Y.-M. (2005) 'Postcolonial Feminism/Postcolonialism and Feminism', in Schwarz, H. and Ray, S. (eds), *A Companion to Postcolonial Studies*, Oxford: Blackwell, pp. 53–71.

Tamang, D. (2020) 'Rethinking "Participation" in Women, Peace and Security Discourses: Engaging with "Non-Participant" Women's Movements in the Eastern Borderlands of India', *International Feminist Journal of Politics*, **22** (4), pp. 485–503.

Venn, C. (2006) *The Postcolonial Challenge: Towards Alternative Worlds*, London: Sage.

Wullweber, J. and Scherrer, C. (2010) 'Postmodern and Poststructural Political Economy', in Denemark, R.A. (ed.), *The International Studies Encyclopedia*, Oxford: Wiley-Blackwell, accessed 5.8.2021 at: https, p.//www-oxfordreference-com.wwwproxy1.library.unsw.edu.au/view/10.1093/acref/9780191842665.001.0001/acref-9780191842665-e-0442?rskey=vi2kpe&result=349.

Zalewski, M. (2006) 'Survival/Representation', in De Goede, M. (ed.), *International Political Economy and Poststructural Politics*, Basingstoke: Palgrave, pp. 25–42.

Zein-Elabdin, E.O. (2004) 'Articulating the Postcolonial (With Economics in Mind)', in Charusheela, S. and Zein-Elabdin, E.O. (eds), *Postcolonialism Meets Economics*, London and New York: Routledge, pp. 21–39.

Zein-Elabdin, E.O. (2009) 'Economics, Postcolonial Theory and the Problem of Culture: Institutional Analysis and Hybridity', *Cambridge Journal of Economics*, **33** (6), pp. 1153–67.

Zein-Elabdin, E.O. (2011) 'Postcoloniality and Development: Development as a Colonial Discourse' in Keita, L. (ed.), *Philosophy and African Development: Theory and Practice*, Oxford: African Books Collective, pp. 215–30.

27. Behavioural economics and neuroeconomics

David Primrose

The notion of 'rationality' enjoys near-unparalleled scrutiny within political economy (Zouboulakis 2014). Some researchers have explored its radical potential to address the 'irrationality' of capitalism and articulate more 'rational' socio-economic systems (e.g. Panayotakis 2011). More pervasively, it has been critically appraised as buttressing the conceptual and normative project of neoclassical economics. Myriad scholars have rebuffed its deductively determined, logically problematic and unrealistic representation of human rationality as 'hyper-rationality', whereby actors universally maximise (or minimise) an objective function according to particular constraints (Davis 2011).[1] Simultaneously, this essentialist understanding of the human subject – embodied in the avatar of *Homo economicus*, or 'economic man' (*sic*) – has been criticised for normatively equating 'free markets' with individual freedom: only hyper-rational actors left to exchange in freely operating markets will secure economic outcomes maximising individual and collective welfare (Sen 1977; Shaikh 2016).

Notwithstanding such reflections, the hyper-rationality axioms informing neoclassicism have resisted falsification. In part, this reflected increasing methodological formalism in the tradition since the mid-twentieth century – characterised by intensified deductive reasoning, abstraction and mathematical modelling, while retaining the axioms themselves as self-evident (Lawson 1997). Similarly, attacks on the hollowness of neoclassical assumptions have been dismissed through reference to Milton Friedman's (1953: 3–43) instrumentalist 'as if' methodological contention: the validity of a hypothesis depends on its predictive capacity, rather than realism of assumptions (Mäki 2012). However, during the last four decades, the hyper-rational presuppositions and formalist structure of neoclassicism have also been progressively challenged by empirical evidence. As Blaug (1992) demonstrates, anomalies arising from such evidence were initially rejected as random micro-level perturbations. Yet, particularly since the 1980s, neoclassicism has increasingly theorised individual deviations from predictions of hyper-rationality and the pertinence of socioeconomic institutions in shaping this behaviour and aggregate outcomes (Madra 2017).

The rise of behavioural economics and, later, neuroeconomics can be understood in this context. Modelling individual decision-making and behaviour based on 'more realistic assumptions' of human-beings' psychological and neurobiological underpinnings (Camerer and Lowenstein 2004: 3) both have sought greater theoretical sophistication, more rigorous predictions and enhanced policy guidance than neoclassicism. Rather than taking hyper-rationality as axiomatically given – without interpreting it as a property of individual actors – both employ interdisciplinary evidence from psychology and neuroscience, respectively, to develop more complex, empirically rich explanatory models. In some cases, such insights have demonstrated how 'real' subjects' cognitive processes are 'predictably irrational' (Ariely 2008: xviii). Behaviouralism and 'behavioural economics in the scanner' (Ross 2008) within neuroeconomics analyse how and why individuals systematically deviate from hyper-rationality by not consistently ordering preferences, poorly judging probabilities, failing to address risk 'rationally', committing multiple reasoning errors and, more generally, making decisions based on biases and habits. The project of 'neurocellular economics' has also constructed interdisciplinarity accounts of decision-making. Yet, it has *extended* hyper-rationality axioms to neuroscience to explain neuronal system and brain functioning.

This chapter surveys these features of behaviouralism and neuroeconomics. First, it briefly outlines neoclassical hyper-rationality as the axiomatic model against which the traditions have emerged. The following two sections survey key tenets of behaviouralism and neuroeconomics, highlight their similarities and disparities, and consider claims by proponents to have advanced the discipline. The chapter then posits that, despite their theoretical sophistication and methodological innovations, both traditions warrant critical scrutiny. The final section contends that other traditions – particularly 'old' institutionalism, Marxism and psychoanalytic political economy – offer more solid bases for conceptualising behaviour, decision-making and individual–society relations.

THE NEOCLASSICAL CONCEPTION OF *HOMO ECONOMICUS*

Neoclassical microeconomics proffers a positive theory that all individuals approach decision-making in a universally 'rational' manner, thereby engendering common responses – that is, making utility-maximising decisions (for a critical survey, see Fine 2016). Embodied in the subjective avatar of *Homo economicus*, individuals are assumed to possess stable, well-defined, coherent preference sets, manifesting in their choices. They are, thereby, not cognitively impeded in assessing given alternatives, nor hindered by problems of self-control that would impair the identification and pursuit of optimal choices (Hollis and Nell 1975; Davis 2011). Instead, individual preferences remain stable, while only factors constraining alternative actions are variable. Guided by narrow self-interest, choice depends on each individual's subjective preferences and the constraints they face, especially their income and the relative price of the alternatives under consideration. These attributes equip individuals to pursue and realise the best possible outcomes in market interactions – which, in turn, provide information and incentives to augment choices, thereby maximising individual utility and social welfare (the sum of individual utilities) (Sen 1977).

This formulation of *Homo economicus* reflects the apparent separation of neoclassicism from psychology (Sent 2004). While neoclassicism informally addresses individual 'preferences' as psychological phenomena, the term embodies a formal ordering relation fashioned to enable equilibrium analysis. Rational 'choices' depend on 'well-behaved' preferences, guaranteeing downward-sloping demand and upward-sloping supply curves. Reasoning is assumed to be instrumentally oriented, while individuals act *as if* drawing on mathematical logic: forming correct beliefs about their environment, along with their own and others' behaviour, and selecting actions satisfying their preferences (Davis 2011). Thus, rationality and individuality are co-defined according to the logical-mathematical properties of functioning markets.

BEHAVIOURAL ECONOMICS

Behaviouralism encompasses both 'old and 'new' strands (Sent 2004; Heukelom 2014). The former, pioneered by Herbert Simon (1955, 1956) and developed within the 'frugal heuristics' approach (Gigerenzer 2000, 2015), supplants atomistic hyper-rationality with holistic, evolutionary accounts of rationality and individuality. The 'new' school – arising from Amos Tversky and Daniel Kahneman (1973, 1974) – retains the atomistic neoclassical conception of individuals but revises it to embed agents within an ahistorical and non-developmental social ontology. This newer iteration constitutes the mainstream of behavioural research (Heukelom 2014) and is the most politically influential – manifest in the global institutionalisation of governmental 'nudge' research units (Whitehead et al. 2017). This chapter focuses on the 'new' strand to assess the extent to which this aspect of the nascent 'pluralist turn' within mainstream economics marks a genuine break with neoclassicism (Madra 2017).

Postulating that neoclassical models cannot capture 'real' human behaviour, behaviouralism seeks to 'increase the explanatory and predictive power of economic theory by providing it with more psychologically plausible foundations' (Angner and Loewenstein 2012: 642). Inspired by empirical evidence countering hyper-rationality axioms, alongside cognitive psychological comprehensions of the mind as an information-processing device, behaviouralism formulates more empirically realistic models, tests psychological predictions, and draws conclusions about decision-making processes (Heidl 2016). Specifically, demonstrating that neoclassicism fails to construct models based on realistic assumptions, nor adequately consider socio-cultural parameters affecting decision-making, behaviouralism identifies decision-making in practice that diverges from hyper-rationality (Angner 2019). While 'irrational' from the neoclassical perspective, such divergence is revealed as pervasive by empirical accounts of real-world decision-making (e.g. Henrich et al. 2005) and theorised as depending on psychological, cultural and biological considerations irrelevant to *Homo economicus*.

Two overlapping waves of behavioural research can be distinguished (Camerer et al. 2003: 1214–16). The first, beginning in the 1970s, empirically questioned and explained how economic behaviour diverges from *Homo economicus*. Experimental studies demonstrated particular divergences from neoclassical models and highlighted the significance of institutions in shaping individual decision-making and aggregate outcomes. The second wave, which gained particular momentum during the 1990s, has buttressed and formalised these empirical results through configuring them into models and predictions. Thus, contemporary behaviouralism incorporates psychological research to identify predictably recurring departures from hyper-rationality; demonstrates such deviations in diverse economic contexts; formalises these through constructing novel models of behaviour; and applies these models to areas such as economic policy and law.

How does the tradition develop its theory of economic behaviour? One regular entry-point is to conceptualise simultaneous 'dual processes' operating in the brain and shaping decision-making (see Grayot 2020). Actors' mental capacities are conceptualised as aligned with properties of two systems: one 'automatic' and one 'reflective' (Thaler and Sunstein 2008: 21). Decision-making is theorised as a process in which each system concentrates on addressing differing cognitive and deliberative tasks. As depicted in Table 27.1, the *automatic* system is formulated as rapid, instinctual and emotional and, thus, capable of managing straightforward precepts and stimulation beyond contemplation. Conversely, the *reflective* system better handles concepts and deliberative behaviours considered rule-bound, deductive and logical, as it is controlled, effortful and neutral. While neoclassicism assumes that decision-makers possess complete access to and utilise the latter, empirical evidence indicates that the former underpins decision-making in practice. Behaviouralism thereby conceptualises the biases, heuristics and framing effects that shape decision-making as grounded in information being simplified and distorted by the automatic system, leading actors to expedient, albeit not always prudent, choices (Kahneman 2003a).

Table 27.1   A simplified model of dual processes

	Automatic System	Reflective System
Processes	Fast	Slow
	Parallel	Serial
	Automatic	Controlled
	Effortless	Effortful
	Associative	Rule-governed
	Slow-learning	Flexible
	Emotional	Neutral

Source: Adapted from Kahneman (2003a: 1451).

Like neoclassicism, behavioural models utilising this heuristic assume individuals purposefully formulate optimal choices based on their preferences between available options (Laibson and List 2015). Yet, rather than a logico-deductive theory of choice engendering *Homo economicus*, individuals are described as *boundedly rational*. Initially proposed by Simon (1955, 1956), bounded rationality foundationally challenges hyper-rationality axioms. Rather than decision-making reflecting consistent application of knowledge, reflection and deliberation (the 'reflective system'), Simon contended that it stems from insufficient knowledge, sub-optimal cognitive practices and the imperative for regular hasty decision-making (Velupillai and Kao 2016). He utilised this conception to explain actors pursuing short-term over long-term objectives, making impulsive judgements, and allowing social norms and habits to influence decisions – that is, decision-making favouring the 'automatic system' (Kahneman 2003b). While such 'aberrations' transcended the neoclassical purview, Simon centred them as objects of analysis (Velupillai and Kao 2016).

The 'prospect theory' of Tversky and Kahneman (e.g. 1973, 1974; Kahneman and Tversky 1979) subsequently sought to deepen this conception by uncovering processes engendering bounded rationality. Utilising detailed empirical studies, they isolated various *heuristics* (or necessary shortcuts) as steering decision-making by rendering complex problems more manageable. Specifically, through streamlining matters of judgement (evaluating options, including estimating probabilities) and choice (selecting between those options), heuristics constitute context-specific rules of thumb that facilitate choices without thorough deliberation (Kahneman 2003b). These heuristics seem intuitively judicious to optimising individuals and enable practical strategies to manage given situations. Thus, 'a good heuristic provides fast, close to optimal, answers when time or cognitive capabilities are limited' (Camerer and Loewenstein 2004: 11). Yet, they simultaneously infuse systematic *biases* into decision-making and, consequently, engender sub-optimal outcomes relative to those of *Homo economicus*. Behaviouralism thereby presents individuals as lacking complete information and having recourse to biases and heuristics to enable swift and satisfactory decision-making.

Such insights would be relatively unproblematic for neoclassicism if behavioural deviations remained idiosyncratic and, on average, cancelled each other out. Yet, behaviouralism holds that utility maximisation is *universally* hindered by systematic biases and heuristics (Ariely 2008). As Sunstein and Thaler (2003: 176) explain:

> People do not exhibit rational expectations, fail to make forecasts that are consistent with Bayes' rule, use heuristics that lead them to make systematic blunders, exhibit preference reversals (that is, they prefer A to B and B to A) and make different choices depending on the wording of the problem.

That is, the nature of human cognitive processes inherently engenders 'irrationality'. In turn, as identified in DellaVigna (2009), behaviouralism posits three qualities in individuals diverging from *Homo economicus*. First, while neoclassicism assumes that individual preferences concerning future plans remain identical at different points in time, behaviouralism conceptualises *non-standard preferences*. For instance, it posits a systematic tendency toward present-biased preferences, disproportionately weighing present over future concerns, such as consuming income at any given moment despite committing to long-term savings plans (Benartzi and Thaler 2007). Second, subjects are conceptualised as holding *non-standard beliefs*. This may include systematic overconfidence, whereby subjects overestimate their capabilities and undervalue probabilities of adverse phenomena and the time required to accomplish projects, such as naïvely overestimating commitment to future gym attendance (Camerer and Lovallo 1999). Third, subjects are informed by *non-standard decision-making*. Rather than behaviour being determined by individuals' context-free preference orderings, individuals adopt inconsistent standpoints on objectively similar alternatives based on context-specific reference points that frame their choice (Tversky and Kahneman 1986, 1991), such as whether breakfast cereals are labelled '95% fat-free' or '5% fat'.

Behaviouralism thereby challenges neoclassical accounts of decision-making and offers an alternative, boundedly rational conception of subjects. The contrast is encapsulated by Thaler and Sunstein's (2008: 24) dichotomy between neoclassical 'econs' and real-world 'humans'. The former are hyper-rational utility maximisers replete with given utility functions, whereas the latter are shambolic in their decision-making – more akin to the Homer Simpson 'lurking somewhere in each of us' than to *Homo economicus*. Even when strategic and purposeful, behavioural subjects are not 'lightning calculator[s] of pleasures and pains' (Veblen 1898: 398–9); rather, they are influenced by external factors and may repeatedly miscalculate in pursuing objectives.

NEUROECONOMICS

Neuroeconomics develops these behavioural insights to construct alternative, more complex theories of decision-making. However, neuroeconomics reverses the causal chain. Behaviouralism focuses on behavioural *outcomes* of individual decision-making, with researchers reading back from these to model the internal processes leading to them. Conversely, neuroeconomics pries open the 'black box' of the *brain* itself – and the nervous system – to explain decision-making not based on its results, but through examining its purportedly *biological* causes (Camerer 2013; Krastev et al. 2016). Specifically, it endeavours to: (i) research the neuronal basis from which behaviour results; (ii) visualise neuronal activity corresponding with decision-making; and (iii) predict behavioural outcomes of neuronal regulation (Schmitz et al. 2015). Thus, it seeks more comprehensive explanations of decision-making processes through a better understanding of brain functioning.

Neuroeconomists argue that *Homo economicus* cannot capture the complex motivating factors driving decision-making. For Camerer et al. (2005), neoclassicism failed to theorise emotions and other factors endogenous to individuals driving these processes, partly due to scepticism about the possibility of studying human feelings beyond their *observable effects* on behaviour. William Stanley Jevons ([1874] 2013: 85) claimed that quantification of feeling was impossible: '[e]very mind is […] inscrutable to every other mind, and no common denominator of feeling seems to be possible'. Conversely, for neuroeconomists, recent developments in neuroscientific research and technologies enable examination of biological variables affecting behaviour previously 'considered inherently unobservable' (Camerer 2008: 45).

Specifically, neuroeconomists posit that sophisticated, non-invasive neuroscientific methods can measure the metabolic correlates of neural activity and produce algorithmic analyses of the 'physical mechanism of choice' (Glimcher and Fehr 2014: xxiv) – that is, *directly* measure thoughts, feelings and, hence, utility (Camerer 2007, 2013). Thus, neoclassical 'as if' axioms may be transcended by explanations informed by 'as is' reasoning (Crespo 2017: 91). Decision-making is modelled through amalgamating neuroscientific procedures such as functional Magnetic Resonance Imaging (fMRI) scanning (visualising blood flows diverging from the 'resting state' brain) and electroencephalography (EEG) technologies (measuring neural electrical impulses). Other experimental methods, such as questionnaires, game theory scenarios, pre- and post-test measurements, and visual stimuli, may also be used. Insights from economics and cognitive psychology can then be added to the mix (Serra 2019). Through such methods, neuroeconomists claim to overcome the deductive limitations of neoclassicism; instead, constructing more complex, empirically precise models and predictions, grounded in realistic assumptions about individual cognitive processes (Camerer et al. 2005; Glimcher and Fehr 2014). These insights have been applied to myriad social realms, such as the socio-ecology (Sawe 2019) and human health (DeStasio et al. 2019).

Based on this broad raison d'être, neuroeconomic contributions can be categorised into two distinct camps: behavioural economics in the scanner (BES) and neurocellular economics (NCE) (Vromen 2011).

Behavioural Economics in the Scanner

Arising from the work of Colin Camerer, BES focuses on evidence from brain scans to complete the research of behaviouralism: probing the *neurobiological* origins of 'irrational' decision-making. To understand behavioural deviations from *Homo economicus*, neuroscience is utilised to open-up the 'black box' of the brain to identify the neural bases of decisions (Camerer et al. 2005; Camerer 2007, 2008, 2013). Neuroscientific techniques reveal that brain organisation and functionality does not correspond to hyper-rationality: individuals do not possess well-ordered preferences or 'as if' utility functions (Davis 2016). That is, decision-making cannot be explained exclusively through reference to 'rational' deliberation processes based on relative values expressed by prices. Instead, research focuses on 'repeating protocols that [...] demonstrate human "irrationality" under neuroimaging'; and exploring 'how "anomalies" in rational choice have origins and explanations in framing effects that result from the computational processing architecture of the brain' (Harrison and Ross 2010: 187). Thus, contrary to the NCE tradition discussed below, BES argues that introducing neuroscience into economics may reshape the discipline – requiring key neoclassical axioms to be modified or, in the longer-term, even disbanded (Camerer et al. 2005).

Using insights from cognitive localisation theories, Camerer et al. (2005) associate particular cognitive functions with different fractions of the brain (see also Zak 2011). Mirroring behaviouralist dual-processes theory outlined above, BES conceptualises the correlation between decision-making and activation of two competing systems – the 'affective' (emotional) and 'cognitive' (rational) – with both allocated to distinct brain regions. That is, conscious, rational control is separated from unconscious, emotional regulation, with decision-making conceptualised as reflecting how these coalesce (Sanfey et al. 2003). For example, Bechara et al. (2019) contend that drug addicts are more prone than non-addicts to impulsiveness and favouring short-term satisfaction over future considerations ('temporal discounting'). Such irrationality arises from interactions between two competing decision systems: the 'impulsive' (in the limbic and paralimbic brain regions), which functions to obtain biologically important reinforcers; and 'executive' (in prefrontal cortices), which considers longer-term consequences. Drug addiction is thereby explained by the executive system being weakened and overwhelmed by a hyperactive impulsive system, with priority accorded to immediate gratification (temporal discounting).

BES correspondingly presents two primary insights contradicting hyper-rationality (Camerer et al. 2005). First, evidence from brain-scans demonstrates that 'automatic' processes are executed more quickly than conscious deliberation (Camerer et al. 2003). Arising to address problems of 'evolutionary importance rather than respect logical dicta' (Camerer et al. 2005: 11), the former determine default modes of behaviour, despite occurring without conscious awareness and intention. Conversely, by reducing 'rationality' to consciously controlled, cognitively-driven behaviour, neoclassicism cannot encompass the behavioural complexity revealed by neuroscience. Second, rather than the rational deliberation of *Homo economicus*, neuroscience demonstrates that decision-making is primarily driven by emotions stemming from the 'affective' system. Accordingly, using fMRI technology to study the brains of subjects in game-theoretic experiments, Sanfey et al. (2003) hold that subjects failed to behave as predicted because emotion prevailed over economic (rational) reasoning. Conceptualising competing processes of emotions and cognitive control thereby challenges hyper-rationality axioms (cf. McMaster and Novarese 2016).

Neurocellular Economics

Whereas BES mobilises neuroscience to reconfigure economic analysis, NCE does the opposite. Building on the research of Paul Glimcher and Don Ross, it *applies* neoclassicism (particularly, expected utility theory and game theory) to neuroscience to model the activation patterns of neural areas and, thus, explain decision-making (Glimcher 2003). NCE also diverges from BES by commencing from an alternative ontology of brain structure. As discussed, BES assumes a dualistic brain characterised by internal competition, whereby disparate evolutionary trajectories have produced distinct decision-making modules within different anatomical regions. NCE adopts a more monistic ontology: brain functioning constitutes a unitary neural structure that has evolved to cultivate a systemic behavioural pattern maximising reproductive success in given contexts (Schüll and Zaloom 2011; Vromen 2011). By supplying the evolutionary yardstick presumed necessary for survival of human and non-human species, neoclassicism effectively identifies the computational objective of the brain: expected utility maximisation (Glimcher 2003, 2011; Glimcher and Rustichini 2004). In turn, by developing algorithmic models of the neural mechanisms through which the brain values and compares multiple stimuli, NCE studies activity in brain areas concerned with decision-making to comprehend how individuals maximise utility (Ross 2011).

This has led to research focusing on two primary objects: the neural and psychological correlates of utility, and the apparatuses through which these are converted into choice (Glimcher 2011). For example, individual utility functions have been theorised as integral to a neural mechanism for choice – a form of 'neural utility' (Platt and Glimcher 1999; Glimcher

2011). That is, while neoclassicism assumes that decision-makers choose 'as-if' employing a common currency for valuing options, NCE offers a more literal interpretation whereby subjective value representations are *actually* integrated and computed in the brain: 'neural architecture actually does compute desirability for each available course of action' (Glimcher et al. 2005: 220). Harrison and Ross (2012: 87), for example, theorise that 'dopamine signals in the ventral striatum and medial prefrontal cortex constitute a "common currency" of reward that has many properties in common with the mainstream economist's concept of utility'.

Utility maximisation thus occurs at the neuronal level – a straight application of hyper-rationality to the internal logic of the brain (McMaster and Novarese 2016). To illustrate, Glimcher's (2003: 322) experimental research on monkeys' choice behaviour concludes that 'the behaviours of individual parietal neurons are well-described by [neoclassical] economic tools'. Evaluating the results of an experiment conducted with thirsty rhesus monkeys – rewarded when looking at the 'correct' spot on a screen – Platt and Glimcher (1999) assert the predictive virtues of extending neoclassicism to neuroscience. They contend that the monkeys' eye movements – and action potential and firing rates of neuronal clusters in the lateral intraparietal area of the posterior parietal cortex (area LIP) – corresponded with variations in, and probabilities of, reward. Thus, a theory of expected utility predicted observable choice behaviour *and* neural activity in area LIP (Glimcher 2003; Dorris and Glimcher 2004). Glimcher et al. (2005: 8) thereby assert that the brain literally processes expected utilities akin to a computer:

> Neoclassical theory has always made the famous *as if* argument: it is *as if* expected utility was computed by the brain [...] The available data suggest that the neural architecture actually does compute a desirability for each available course of action. This is a real physical computation, accomplished by neurons, that derives and encodes a real variable. The process of choice that operates on this variable then seems to be quite simple: it is the process of executing the action encoded as having the greatest desirability.

Analogously, Ross (2008: 473) utilises neuroscience to conceptualise (mammalian) brains as akin to neoclassical markets: 'massively distributed information-processing networks over which executive systems can exert only limited and imperfect governance'. This cognitive network regulates behaviour through progressively learning correlations between reward predictors and categories of actions. Accordingly, the brain network – like a market – constitutes an efficient parallel processor of information and valuations, able to be modelled via constrained maximisation game-theoretic experiments and simulations (Glimcher 2003, 2011). Further, Ross (2005) rejects anthropomorphism as necessary for analysis – that is, commencing with *human* agents. Instead, agency is located in the optimising *neuron* by taking the neuroscientific entry-point as the segmented brain structure and positing that this demonstrates how neurons and neural structures exhibit servosystematicity – the ability to maintain themselves as relatively autonomous entities (cf. McMaster and Novarese 2016). That is, the neoclassical conception of individuals optimising their utility functions is extended to 'collections of optimising sub-personal neural agents' – neurons, the neurotransmitter system, or the quasi-modular circuit – interacting symbiotically in coordination games internal to individuals (Davis 2011: 127).

LIMITATIONS FOR POLITICAL ECONOMY

Fundamental Continuities with Neoclassical Economics

Behaviouralism and neuroeconomics offer means of moving beyond the axiomatic form that *Homo economics* usually takes in neoclassical economics. In practice, however, they remain limited by their continued subsumption within neoclassicism. The potential of psychology and neuroscience to nourish interdisciplinary, non-neoclassical accounts of decision-making has been diverted to *buttressing*, rather than transcending, the orthodoxy. This is explicable by considering both traditions in the context of two epistemological trends within economics: 'economics imperialism' and 'reverse economics imperialism' (see Fine and Milonakis 2009; Crespo 2017). The former entails neoclassical 'colonisation' of other academic disciplines, inculcating an economistic calculus in social deliberation and establishing quasi-market social interactions in areas traditionally not conceptualised in such terms. This is exemplified by Gary Becker's application of 'human capital theory' to conceptualise behaviour within families, marriages and households (see Fine 1998; and Chapter 29 by Cedrini and Dagnes in this book). Conversely, the latter – reverse economics imperialism – involves neoclassicism bringing home 'booty' seized from other disciplines: utilising insights from psychology, neuroscience, sociology, politics and so forth to *bolster* itself (Madra 2017). In both cases, neoclassicism remains the key reference point: exporting axioms to other disciplines or importing interdisciplinary tools within its extant framework.

NCE exemplifies economics imperialism: extending unrealistic axioms of constrained optimisation to the internal logic of the brain, thereby analysing it and individuals as a cooperative game between utility-maximising neurons. For Ross et al. (2008: ix), 'claims by behavioural economists [including BES] that observed systematic "irrationality" in human behaviour "refutes" standard neoclassical theory should be rejected.' Instead, NCE relates evolutionary efficiencies to underlying mechanisms, with neoclassical utility theory offering 'the ultimate set of tools for describing these efficient solutions', evolutionary theory demarcating the field within which these mechanisms are optimised according to neoclassical constraints, psychology enabling investigation of empirical behaviour, and neurobiology according 'the tools for elucidating those mechanisms' (Glimcher et al. 2005: 253).

Behaviouralism and BES present more complicated cases. Many practitioners have labelled their interdisciplinarity as engendering disciplinary 'revolution' by enabling construction of more realistic accounts of decision-making and behaviour transcending deductive neoclassical analysis (e.g. Fehr and Camerer 2007; Camerer 2013; Angner 2019). However, outside the orthodoxy, they appear less ground-breaking. Both selectively utilise psychology and neuroscience to revise and augment, rather than transcend, neoclassicism. This reverse imperialism results in two primary shortcomings.

The first is *limited increases in descriptive realism*. Amalgamating psychology and neuroscience within neoclassicism undermines the posited objective of explaining empirical evidence deviating from hyper-rationality. Rather than necessitating 'wholesale rejection' of neoclassicism 'based on utility maximization, equilibrium, and efficiency' (Camerer and Loewenstein 2004: 3), behavioural anomalies discovered through experiments 'are used as inspiration to create alternative theories that generalise existing models' (Camerer and Loewenstein 2004: 7). That is, bolstering its psychological and neurobiological foundations will improve neoclassicism on its own terms through increasingly sophisticated theory, superior predictions, and more comprehensive policy recommendations (Rabin 2002; Camerer 2007, 2013).

The result is an incongruous methodology. Behaviouralism holds that psychological experimental results will advance economic analysis when filtered through models allowing for phenomena diverging from hyper-rationality. Yet, 'domesticating' (Davis 2008: 363) psychological insights within neoclassicism does not engender greater realism; instead, it generalises the axiom that all behaviour is oriented around constrained optimisation, while incorporating slight modifications to account for biases, dysfunctions and heuristics (White 2017). For example, social preferences theorists (e.g. Fehr and Schmidt 1999) affix parameters weighting individuals' concern for gaining relative to others to an otherwise-neoclassical utility function. Introducing such novel parameters merely produces more complex optimisation problems to solve. Thus, rather than conceptualising *actual* decision-making processes, behaviouralism remains dependent on Friedman's (1953) instrumentalist 'as-if' defence to justify *increasingly unrealistic* formulations. To produce sophisticated behavioural predictions, individuals are assumed to behave *as if* they are solving elaborate constrained optimisation problems (Berg and Gigerenzer 2010).

Similarly, BES employs neuroscience to formulate complex decision-making models that assume different preference orderings correspond to distinct brain states. Camerer (2007) thereby contends that neuroeconomics can engender progressively complete characterisations of human motivations and, thus, enable improved economic predictions. Yet, by retaining a deductive methodology focused on predicting behavioural field phenomena, neuroeconomic models also assume complete, unchanging preference orderings or other closure conditions for each brain state (Martins 2010). For instance, Bernheim and Rangel (2005) distinguish the preference ordering of a 'hot' (emotional) state from that of a 'cold' (rational) state. Rather than transcending neoclassicism, these modifications extend its extant methodology.

A second, related shortcoming entails interdisciplinary insights *normatively buttressing Homo economicus as the ideal economic subject*. While both traditions reject this hyper-rational subject as capturing the cognitive capacities of real human beings, it endures as the archetype for 'rational' cognition and behaviour, and a potentially realisable subject to be procured through policy (Infante et al. 2016). Specifically, both retain *Homo economicus* as a normative model of economic subjectivity because they remain within the foundational epistemological problematic of neoclassicism: investigating the conditions of possibility for functioning markets premised upon hyper-rational subjects – in this case, *given subjects are characterised by cognitive limitations in reality* (Primrose 2017). For neoclassicism, behaviour approximating *Homo economicus* provides the subjective micro-foundation for markets to function in reconciling individual and aggregate rationality in a Pareto equilibrium state (see Madra 2017). Behaviouralism and BES explain such predictions of functioning markets as failing due to individuals' restricted cognitive capacities relative to *Homo economicus* – whether due to psychological or neurophysiological factors – thereby engendering 'irrational' behaviour. That is, both accord the hyper-rational subject central ontological status as determining the economy as a whole, in that deviations are responsible for market imperfections. Behaviouralists Akerlof and Shiller (2015: 164), accordingly, analyse 'the role of markets when people have weaknesses, so markets are not efficient'. Similarly, BES theorists Camerer and Fehr (2006: 47) contend that behaviour deviating from hyper-rationality occludes welfare-maximising outcomes, while sufficient subjects approximating *Homo economicus* 'may cause aggregate outcomes to be close to the predictions of a [neoclassical] model that assumes that everyone is rational and self-regarding'. Remedial policies are therefore required to ensure that markets function better, fostering more hyper-rational individual behaviour (for fuller discussion, see Primrose 2017).

Consequently, while dismissing hyper-rationality 'as a positive or descriptive theory' (Angner and Loewenstein 2012: 668) because real individuals do not resemble *Homo economicus*, both traditions pathologise reality as 'anomalous' to or 'deviating' from this norm (e.g. Thaler 1987). The implicitly phallogocentric character of the 'dual processes' ontology exemplifies this pathologisation. Challenging the universalist presumptions of hyper-rationality and explicitly theorising emotional processes previously denigrated as 'feminine' or 'soft' appears to answer calls by feminist political economists for transcending the modernist reason-emotion dualism (Hewitson 1999). Rather than examining emotion and intuition to *understand* decision-making, however, these are denigrated relative to 'rational' qualities (Schmitz et al. 2015; Clouser 2016). Reliance on the automatic system leads to 'irrational' behaviour, as biases and heuristics engender 'faulty' perceptions about choice effects, preferences detrimental in the long term, or choosing damaging behaviour when 'rationally' preferring otherwise.

Consider how both traditions comprehend financial instability. Within behaviouralism, Thaler and Sunstein (2008), for example, attribute high household indebtedness and financial instability to individual self-control problems (favouring immediate gratification over the long-term costs of impulsiveness) and difficult-to-comprehend information, resulting in injudicious consumption and investment decisions. Similarly, neuroeconomic studies – such as that by Frydman and Camerer (2016) – hypothesise that financial instability stems from the reward system in greedy individuals' brains being relentlessly activated by prospects of short-term pecuniary gain and overwhelming more 'rational' segments. This leads to myopic and risky behaviour, such as excessive speculation. These forms of reasoning, whereby observed deviations from hyper-rationality are conceptualised as resulting from psychological and/or neurobiological deficiencies, effectively presupposes *Homo economicus* as normatively correct.

Limited Conceptions of Individual Agency

Behaviouralism and neuroeconomics also present *biologically deterministic* accounts of individual subjects. Both under-theorise social phenomena and their contribution to moulding behaviour. Instead, they proceed by recourse to universal characteristics deemed *intrinsic to human beings as individuals*: explaining 'irrational' behaviour as due to psychology and/or brain physiology. This generates impoverished conceptions of agency arising from biologically derived cognitive limitations.

Behavioural accounts of systemic 'irrationality' better represents real behaviour than *Homo economicus*. To contest the descriptive realism of hyper-rationality, behaviouralism employs insights from cognitive psychology – examining the functioning of the cognitive apparatus informing all human beings (Angner and Loewenstein 2012; for a survey, see Petracca 2017). In turn, it analyses common mistakes made by individuals *as members of the same species* when theorising systemic 'irrationality' (Frerichs 2019). That is, humans are deemed irrational and fallible *by nature*: '[t]hey are not *homo economicus* [sic]; they are *homo sapiens*' (Thaler and Sunstein 2008: 7, emphases added). Thus, 'irrationality' is determined by *psychologically determined 'processing errors'*: being prone to biases and judgemental 'faults', human cognitive processing capabilities are limited relative to *Homo economicus*, thereby engendering 'poor' decisions and sub-optimal behaviour (Pedwell 2017).

Yet, this formulation is not linked to a more holistic account of the psycho-social complexity of decision-making. Accepting cognitive 'limitations' as a priori hard-wired in humans, behaviouralism downplays the institutionally embedded character of 'irrationality' (Streeck 2010). For example, experimental research has established a bias termed the 'endowment effect', whereby individuals irrationally overvalue something they own – exhibiting reluctance to sell the good at its market value or offering a lower purchase price than they are willing to accept when selling (Reb and Connolly 2007). Nevertheless, behaviouralism underplays how ownership is institutionalised and why individuals internalise it. Because private property is institutionally constitutive of capitalism, the endowment effect arguably reflects prevailing notions of ownership (Screpanti 2001). Thus, behaviouralism exhibits a 'naturalist bias': it focuses on supposedly universal qualities of human nature while leaving unexplored the contingent psycho-social foundations of behaviour (Frerichs 2019).

Biological determinism is heightened further in neuroeconomics. To explain individual preferences, neuroeconomics assumes that choice utility is not determined by formal preference relationships, but by a complex neural mechanism (Camerer 2013). '*Homo neurobiologicus*' supplants *Homo economicus*, arising from a 'neurobiological development able to generate sentiments, beliefs, actions, and the capacity to make decisions' (Graziano 2013: 32). In practice, however, neuroeconomics articulates a 'modern neurodeterminism' (Schmitz et al. 2015): behaviour, rationality and emotion stem solely from brain structures and neuronal activation at a given point which, when comprehended, enables researchers to predict responses to different economic scenarios (Fehr and Rangal 2011). This determinism is distinct from considerations of whether brain structures and operations themselves are intrinsic to humans or stem from experience – so-called 'brain plasticity' (Pitts-Taylor 2010). Rather, by amalgamating behaviour and cognition with neurobiology, *Homo neurobiologicus* constitutes a 'cerebral subject': an anthropological figure in which the self is constituted by its brain (Vidal 2009). Neuroeconomics thereby largely eliminates human intent: amputating responsibility for positive and negative behaviour from subjects, attributing it instead to physiological brain qualities. Concomitantly, political, economic and social influences are downplayed in-favour of sterile, naturalistic accounts of decision-making – exemplified by Glimcher's (2003: 336) framing of economics as 'a biological science [...] the study of how humans choose'.

Such problems manifest in both neuroeconomic schools. For BES, the complexity of human psychology, emotion and affect collapse into the relation between brain activation in the process of conscious, rational control and unconscious, emotional regulation. In a striking example, Durante and Saad (2010) reduce the inexorably social notion of 'trust' to a mere expression of individual oxytocin levels (the hormone correlated with trust) – leading to the awkward hypothesis that ovulating women are particularly untrustworthy due to raised levels of progesterone inhibiting oxytocin uptake (Pykett 2016)![2] More broadly, BES accounts for 'irrational' decision-making through 'reward system' functioning in the centre of the brain and parts of the anterior lobe (e.g. Ruff and Fehr 2014; Krastev et al. 2016). By encoding the saliency of the reward associated with a given decision and processing the likelihood this decision will engender the desired outcome, this system motivates particular behaviour, albeit *remaining impartial to the direction of the decision*. Individual satisfaction, thus, largely depends on activating this system, which treats short-term gains – such as those associated with financial speculation (Frydman and Camerer 2016) and drug consumption (Bechara et al. 2019) – as most rewarding. That is, behaviour is determined by reward system reactions, even when engendering 'irrational' behavioural outcomes. Yet, even if accepting that this system reacts to particular stimuli in specific ways, decision-making is a complex psycho-social process that cannot be reduced to simple stimulus-response processes (Pykett 2016). Moreover, this logic disregards free and conscious decisions – rational or not – to privilege supposedly *biological causes* of behaviour (Crespo 2017: ch. 5).

NCE extends this determinism by reducing individuals to collections of sub-personal (neuronal) optimising agents. To illustrate, recall Glimcher et al's (2005) experiment involving monkeys, which purportedly proved that neoclassicism explained decision-making *and* that neurobiology produced this economic behaviour. This account disregards social scientific accounts of behaviour and consciousness (Pykett 2016) – such as holistic explanations that conceptualise individuals in relation to others in groups and institutions (Herrmann-Pillath 2009; Davis 2011). Instead, rejecting the putatively defeatist notion that 'irrational' behaviour constitutes a 'complex social syndrome' (Ross et al. 2008: 7), subjects are rendered biologically determined. In Glimcher's words: 'like all other known biological processes, consciousness is subject to *natural selection and follows the physical laws of the universe*' (Glimcher 2003: 344, emphasis added). By collapsing complex philosophical questions of free will and conscious decision-making into biology, NCE crowds out considerations of responsibility, ethics and political debate (Pykett 2016). Thus, Glimcher (2003: 342) states:

> Free will may simply be the name we give to probabilistic behaviours that are mixed solution strategies. Our subjective experience of deciding may be what we experience when a mixed strategy solution requires the activation of a lawful [biophysical] neuronal randomizer.

Limited Conception of the 'Social'

The traditions of behaviouralism and neuroeconomics are also vulnerable to criticism because of their limited insights into the broader context of individual decision-making.

Both *adopt a thin social ontology*. Proponents claim to complicate, or even transcend, the abstract methodological individualism of neoclassicism by conceptualising the sociality of individual decision-making. Behaviouralists have promulgated 'socially embedded' accounts of individuals (Davis 2015), whereby 'the degree of rationality bestowed to the agents depends on the context being studied' (Thaler 2000: 134). Framing effects and reference-dependence inform individual decision-making, reflecting the anchoring of choice in particular circumstances, thereby engendering hyperbolic time discounting (individuals tend to undervalue the future) (Tversky and Kahneman 1991). Similarly, BES proponents have sought to identify the physiological mechanisms informing choice behaviour and compliance with social norms (Fehr and Camerer 2007). For example, through experiments utilising transcranial direct current stimulation, Ruff et al. (2013) deduce that norm observance is independent of knowledge about the norms – the brain mechanism responsible for compliance is distinct from processes representing comprehension and beliefs about norms – and can be augmented by stimulating the lateral prefrontal cortex.

The corresponding notion of the 'social' in both of these variants is significantly circumscribed. First, there is a limited conception of *environment*, defined as individuals' immediate physical space. Second, there is a restricted conception of *social norms*, conceptualised quantitatively as how the majority of agents operate in a given context (Davis 2013; Leggett

2014). This tends to take the norms as given, rather than theorising their social construction. The result is a thin social ontology and an instrumental treatment of social phenomena, dealing with the latter only to the extent that they affect individual capacity to process information (Frerichs 2019). In turn, assuming economic conduct corresponds to essentialised conceptions of human nature – whether psychologically or neurobiologically determined – leaves subjectivity and preferences themselves largely unexplored (Davis 2011; White 2017).

Both traditions thereby exclude three rudimentary insights established in other social sciences (Leggett 2014). These lacunae may be illustrated by considering their manifestations in behavioural accounts of poverty (e.g. World Bank 2015). First, agents are not comprehended as unevenly distributed within extant social structures *prior* to decision-making (Frerichs 2019). Yet, myriad studies have demonstrated how class relations are constitutive of development processes (Selwyn 2017), while uneven distribution of economic, cultural and other forms of capital frame, constrain and enable decision-making by impoverished individuals (Fine et al. 2016). Second, while highlighting interfaces between subjects and their immediate environment, both traditions disregard the contingency of the latter on historical decisions, contestation and power relations (Strauss 2009). Contextualising poverty in the global South within the historical processes of uneven development and contemporary capitalist power relations highlights that smallholder farmers' capacity to escape poverty through agriculture is not reducible to individual strategies – themselves temporally and spatially abstracted (Selwyn 2017).

Neither tradition accords an ontologically thick account of social norms, conceptualised as the aggregation of individual choices. They consequently underplay how ideological structures prefigure and influence norms (Žižek 1989; Pedwell 2017), such as those manifest as traditional values. For example, public health messages concerning HIV/AIDS in sub-Saharan Africa are declared ineffective because individuals prioritise short-term pleasure from unsafe sex while discounting potential long-term costs from contracting HIV – due to prevailing social norms or myopia (De Walque et al. 2012). Yet, numerous studies (such as Johnston et al. 2018) demonstrate that ideology – manifest in religious or ethical positions concerning sexuality and gender – profoundly shapes community attitudes towards HIV.

Disregarding such lessons ignores the broader systemic features and psycho-social dynamics of capitalism when trying to comprehend the complex drivers of behaviour, and while formulating policies to reconfigure political economic processes (Fine et al. 2016).

This also engenders another limitation: *reductionist accounts of social phenomena.* Behaviouralism and neuroeconomics are underpinned by methodological individualism, reducing the study of political economic phenomena to formulating naturalistic explanations of individual cognitive processes through psychological or neurobiological reductionism. Behaviouralism condenses explanations of complex socio-ecological issues to an *economic problem* of 'irrational behaviour' engendered by individuals' limited capacity to comprehend and respond to economic incentives. Hence, when analysing obesity, myopic individuals are presumed to prioritise short-term pleasure derived from consuming junk-food over the long-term benefits of a balanced diet (Chance et al. 2016). Individual cognition is, thereby, pathologised as responsible for undesirable social outcomes, while naturalising structural determinants of ill health in global capitalism associated with class, inequality and corporate power (Guthman 2011).

This limitation is compounded in neuroeconomics' neurophysiological reductionism. BES, in particular, has reframed complex political economic problems as biophysical issues of hormone levels in the brain driving irrational behaviour. Huijsmans et al. (2019), for example, conceptualise poverty as constraining 'rational' decision-making by engendering a 'scarcity mindset', one that irrationally focuses on scarce resources over unrelated factors. This mindset is correlated with neural mechanisms associated with consumption decisions: increased orbitofrontal cortex activity (implicated in valuation processes) and decreased dorsolateral prefrontal cortex activity (associated with goal-directed choice). This leads impoverished actors to entrench their condition 'by exhibiting "irrational" behaviour through the non- or under-utilisation of available opportunities' (Huijsmans et al. 2019: 11699). Poverty is, thereby, attributed to the neurophysiology of the poor: focusing less on *why* individuals are impoverished than pinpointing the 'neural locus for a scarcity mindset' as underlying goal-directed decision-making. Thus, while accepting the impoverished face difficulties in making decisions under uncertain conditions, BES naturalises the perpetuation of poverty in neurophysiological deficiencies promulgating 'irrational', non-poverty-reducing behaviour (see Pitts-Taylor 2019).

CONCLUSION

Enormous energy has gone into developing behaviouralism and neuroeconomics. The effect – and, to a considerable extent, the motivation – has been to highlight the narrowness and deficiencies of conventional presumptions about hyper-rationality. However, these twin fields of inquiry have each taken two steps forward and two back in articulating alternative political economic projects. Both seemingly surpass neoclassicism by favouring greater 'realism' through analysis of the psychological and neurobiological foundations of choice behaviour by real-world individuals, exploring deviations from the behavioural norm of *Homo economicus*. Second, by combining economic analysis with insights from psychology and neuroscience, they give the appearance of a more interdisciplinary methodology. Yet, the potential advances created by the twin fields of inquiry remain limited by two highly restrictive factors: they remain subsumed within the neoclassical tradition and its axiomatic focus on individual hyper-rationality; and, accordingly, they fail to provide more holistic understandings of the psycho-social drivers of decision-making.

Some practitioners have developed their insights in more heterodox directions to ameliorate such problems. Within behaviouralism, the 'frugal heuristics' school has utilised Herbert Simon's earlier insights on bounded rationality to construct evolutionary, complex models of cognitive processes and their social environments, seeking to determine when and why heuristics are successful under uncertain conditions (for surveys, see Gigerenzer 2000, 2015; cf. Wade Hands 2014). Similarly, other contributors (Carsten Herrmann-Pillath 2012; Harbecke and Herrmann-Pillath 2020) have sought to integrate insights from other social sciences to construct relational neuroeconomic accounts of the neural processes of individuals within groups and institutions.

Such efforts to bolster the social foundations of behaviouralism and neuroeconomics indicate that, from a political economic perspective, the twin fields still have some potentially useful contributions. However, it is pertinent to question whether political economic research on behaviour and decision-making processes would, in fact, be better served by returning to insights *already* offered by other schools of thought. Rather than tinkering at the margins of the mainstream to develop more elaborate models of individual cognition deviating from

Homo economicus, might more be gained from considering other traditions positing entirely different epistemological projects? Two potential paths appear particularly useful in this regard. First, *'old' institutional political economy* (OIPE) fundamentally breaks with the tenets of neoclassicism when conceptualising the psychology of individual behaviour (Hermann 2020). Whereas neoclassicism and behaviouralism fail to explore the *source* of preferences, OIPE explores the inherently complex, evolving character of 'human nature'. Specifically, this facilitates research on how individual preferences are not given, but socially determined by institutions. Habits are conceptualised as *learned*, rather than being either 'rational' or 'irrational' and, thus, may be *either* advantageous or detrimental, depending on the motivations of those influencing cognition (Hodgson 2004).

Second, *Marxism* and *psychoanalytic political economy* enable more radical accounts of subjectivity. Contrary to the thin social ontology of behaviouralism and neuroeconomics, Marxism posits that comprehension of decision-making and behaviour is inseparable from the material dynamics of capitalism. For example, Marx's ([1844] 1964) analysis of commodity fetishism highlights how class antagonisms previously institutionalised through social force are, under capitalism, legitimised through the wage labour contract and entrenched in the commodity form. This condition is not reducible to individual cognition: it constitutes an 'objective illusion' constitutive of capitalist social relations (Arfken 2017). Equally, by accounting for how unconscious processes influence perception, belief and action in ways that elude conscious deliberation, psychoanalytic political economy explores the psychodynamic mechanisms animating the logic of capital accumulation (Madra and Özselçuk 2010; Kapoor 2020). Contrary to a hierarchical dualism between 'rationality' and 'emotion', psychoanalysis demonstrates that human passions are *constitutive* of, rather than supplementary to, social reality. Thus, while most subjects are aware of the deleterious socio-ecological effects of capitalism, psychoanalysis explores how the system secures libidinal attachment by sustaining them in a perpetual state of desire (McGowan 2016).

Re-engaging with and extending these traditions circumvents the foundational limitations of behaviouralism and neuroeconomics, while also opening windows to alternative, more critical political economic research on subjectivity and individual–society relations.

NOTES

1. In this chapter, the neoclassical conception of rationality will be termed 'hyper-rationality' to distinguish it from the philosophical principle of 'rationality' holding that actions and opinions should be grounded in reason (Shaikh 2016: 78). This step circumvents the neoclassical practice of juxtaposing hyper-rationality as 'perfect' and real-world cognition as 'imperfect'.
2. Similarly, Zak (2011) examines individual morality as biologically determined by oxytocin – the 'moral molecule'.

REFERENCES

Akerlof, G.A. and Shiller, R.J. (2015) *Phishing for Phools*, Princeton, NJ: Princeton University Press.

Angner, E. (2019) 'We're All Behavioural Economists Now', *Journal of Economic Methodology*, **26** (3), pp. 195–207.

Angner, E. and Loewenstein, G. (2012) 'Behavioral Economics', in Mäki, U. (ed.), *Handbook of the Philosophy of Science: Philosophy of Economics*, Amsterdam: Elsevier, pp. 641–90.

Arfken, M. (2017) 'Marxism as a Foundation for Critical Social Psychology', in Gough, B. (ed.), *The Palgrave Handbook of Critical Social Psychology*, Basingstoke: Palgrave Macmillan, pp. 37–58.

Ariely, D. (2008) *Predictably Irrational*, New York: HarperCollins.

Bechara, A., Berridge, K.C., Bickel, W.K., Morón, J.A., Williams, S.B. and Stein, J.S. (2019) 'A Neurobehavioral Approach to Addiction: Implications for the Opioid Epidemic and the Psychology of Addiction', *Psychological Science in the Public Interest*, **20** (2), pp. 96–127.

Benartzi, S. and Thaler, R. (2007) 'Heuristics and Biases in Retirement Savings Behavior', *The Journal of Economic Perspectives*, **21** (3), pp. 81–104.

Berg, N. and Gigerenzer, G. (2010) 'As-If Behavioral Economics: Neoclassical Economics in Disguise?', *History of Economic Ideas*, **18** (1), pp. 133–66.

Bernheim, B.D. and Rangel, A. (2007) 'Behavioral Public Economics: Welfare and Policy Analysis with Non-Standard Decision-Makers', in Diamond, P. and Vartiainen, H. (eds), *Behavioral Economics and its Applications*, Princeton, NJ: Princeton University Press, pp. 7–84.

Blaug, M. (1992) *The Methodology of Economics*, Cambridge: Cambridge University Press.

Camerer C.F. (2007) 'Neuroeconomics: Using Neuroscience to Make Economic Predictions', *Economic Journal*, **117** (519), pp. C26–C42.

Camerer, C.F. (2008) 'The Case of Mindful Economics', in Caplin, A. and Schotter, A. (eds), *Foundation of Positive and Normative Economics*, New York: Oxford University Press, pp. 43–69.

Camerer, C.F. (2013) 'Goals, Methods, and Progress in Neuroeconomics', *Annual Review of Economics*, **5** (1), pp. 16.1–16.31.

Camerer, C.F. and Fehr, E. (2006) 'When Does "Economic Man" Dominate Social Behavior?', *Science*, **311** (5757), pp. 47–52.

Camerer, C.F., Issacharoff, S., Loewenstein, G., O'Donoghue, T. and Rabin, M. (2003) 'Regulation for Conservatives: Behavioral Economics and the Case for "Asymmetric Paternalism"', *University of Pennsylvania Law Review*, **151** (1211), pp. 1211–54.

Camerer, C.F. and Loewenstein, G. (2004) 'Behavioral Economics: Past, Present, Future', in Camerer, C., Loewenstein, G. and Rabin, M. (eds), *Advances in Behavioral Economics*, Princeton, NJ: Princeton University Press, pp. 3–52.

Camerer, C.F., Loewenstein, G. and Prelec, D. (2005) 'Neuroeconomics: How Neuroscience Can Inform Economics', *Journal of Economic Literature*, **43** (1), pp. 9–64.

Camerer, C. and Lovallo, D. (1999) 'Overconfidence and Excess Entry: An Experimental Approach', *The American Economic Review*, **89** (1), pp. 306–18.

Chance, Z., Dhar, R., Hatzis, M. and Huskey, K. (2016) 'Nudging Individuals Toward Healthier Food Choices with the 4Ps Framework for Behavior Change', in Roberto, C.A. and Kawachi, I. (eds), *Behavioral Economics and Public Health*, New York: Oxford University Press, pp. 177–202.

Clouser, R. (2016) 'Nexus of Emotional and Development Geographies', *Geography Compass*, **10** (8), pp. 321–32.

Crespo, R.F. (2017) *Economics and Other Disciplines*, London and New York: Routledge.

Davis, J.B. (2008) 'The Turn in Recent Economics and Return of Orthodoxy', *Cambridge Journal of Economics*, **32** (3), pp. 349–66.

Davis, J.B. (2011) *Individuals and Identity in Economics*, Cambridge: Cambridge University Press.

Davis, J.B. (2013) 'Economics Imperialism under the Impact of Psychology: The Case of Behavioral Development Economics', *Oeconomica*, **3** (1), pp. 119–38.

Davis, J.B. (2015) 'Bounded Rationality and Bounded Individuality', *Research in the History of Economics and Methodology*, **33**, pp. 75–93.

Davis, J.B. (2016) 'Economics, Neuroeconomics, and the Problem of Identity', *Schmollers Jahrbuch*, **136** (1), pp. 15–31.

De Walque, D., Dow, W.H., Nathan, R. and Abdul, R. (2012b) 'Incentivising Safe Sex: A Randomised Trial of Conditional Cash Transfers for HIV and Sexually Transmitted Infection Prevention in Rural Tanzania', *BMJ Open*, **2**, pp. e000747.

Della Vigna, S. (2009) 'Psychology and Economics: Evidence from the Field', *Journal of Economic Literature*, **47** (2), pp. 315–72.

DeStasio, K.L., Clithero, J.A. and Berkman, E.T. (2019) 'Neuroeconomics, Health Psychology, and the Interdisciplinary Study of Preventative Health Behavior', *Social and Personality Psychology Compass*, **13** (10), pp. e12500.

Dorris, M.C. and Glimcher, P.W. (2004) 'Activity in Posterior Parietal Cortex is Correlated with the Relative Subjective Desirability of Action', *Neuron*, **44** (2), pp. 365–78.

Durante, K.M. and Saad, G. (2010) 'Ovulatory Shifts in Women's Social Motives and Behaviors: Implications for Corporate Organizations', in Stanton, A.A., Day, M. and Welpe, I.M. (eds), *Neuroeconomics and the Firm*, Cheltenham, UK and Northampton, MA, USA: Edward Elgar Publishing, pp. 116–30.

Fehr, E. and Camerer, C.F. (2007) 'Social Neuroeconomics: The Neural Circuitry of Social Preferences', *Trends in Cognitive Sciences*, **11** (10), pp. 419–26.

Fehr, E. and Rangel, A. (2011) 'Neuroeconomic Foundations of Economic Choice: Recent Advances', *Journal of Economic Perspectives*, **25** (4), pp. 3–30.

Fehr, E. and Schmidt, K. (1999) 'A Theory of Fairness, Competition, and Cooperation', *The Quarterly Journal of Economics*, **114** (3), pp. 817–68.

Fine, B. (1998) 'The Triumph of Economics; Or, "Rationality" Can Be Dangerous to Your Reasoning', in Carrier, J. and Miller, D. (eds), *Virtualism*, London and New York, Routledge, pp. 49–73.

Fine, B. (2016) *Microeconomics*, London: Pluto Press.

Fine, B., Johnston, D., Santos, A. and Van Waeyenberge, E. (2016) 'Nudging or Fudging: The World Development Report 2015', *Development and Change*, **47** (4), pp. 640–63.

Fine, B. and Milonakis, D. (2009) *From Economics Imperialism to Freakonomics*, London and New York: Routledge.

Frerichs, S. (2019) 'Bounded Sociality: Behavioural Economists' Truncated Understanding of the Social and its Implications for Politics', *Journal of Economic Methodology*, **26** (3), pp. 243–58.

Friedman, M. (1953) 'The Methodology of Positive Economics', in *Essays in Positive Economics*, Chicago, IL: University of Chicago Press.

Frydman, C. and Camerer, C.F. (2016) 'The Psychology and Neuroscience of Financial Decision Making', *Trends in Cognitive Sciences*, **20** (9), pp. 661–75.

Gigerenzer, G. (2000) *Adaptive Thinking*, New York: Oxford University Press.

Gigerenzer, G. (2015) *Simply Rational*, New York: Oxford University Press.

Glimcher, P. (2003) *Decisions, Uncertainty, and the Brain*, Cambridge, MA: MIT Press.

Glimcher, P. (2011) *Foundations of Neuroeconomic Analysis*, New York: Oxford University Press.

Glimcher, P., Dorris, M.C. and Bayer, H.M. (2005) 'Physiological Utility Theory and the Neuroeconomics of Choice', *Games and Economic Behaviour*, **52** (2), pp. 213–56.

Glimcher P. and Fehr, E. (2014) 'Introduction: A Brief History of Neuroeconomics', in Glimcher, P.W. and Fehr, E. (eds), *Neuroeconomics*, Amsterdam: Elsevier, pp. xvii–xxviii.

Glimcher, P. and Rustichini, A. (2004) 'Neuroeconomics: The Consilience of Brain and Decision', *Science*, **306** (5695), pp. 447–52.

Grayot, J.D. (2020) 'Dual Process Theories in Behavioral Economics and Neuroeconomics: A Critical Review', *Review of Philosophy and Psychology*, **11** (1), pp. 105–36.

Graziano, M. (2013) *Epistemology of Decision*, Dordrecht: Springer.

Guthman, J. (2011) *Weighing In*, Berkeley: University of California Press.

Harbecke, J. and Herrmann-Pillath, C. (eds) (2020) *Social Neuroeconomics*, London and New York: Routledge.

Harrison, G. and Ross, D. (2010) 'The Methodologies of Neuroeconomics', *Journal of Economic Methodology*, **17** (2), pp. 185–96.

Heidl, S. (2016) *Philosophical Problems of Behavioural Economics*, London: Routledge.

Henrich, J., Boyd, R., Bowles, S., Camerer, C., Fehr, E., Gintis, H., McElreath, R., Alvard, M., Barr, A., Ensminger, J., Henrich, N.S., Hill, K., Gil-White, F., Gurven, M., Marlowe, F.W., Patton, J.Q. and Tracer, D. (2005) '"Economic Man" in Cross-Cultural Perspective: Behavioral Experiments in 15 Small-Scale Societies', *Behavioral and Brain Sciences*, **28** (6), pp. 795–815.

Hermann, A. (2020) 'The Psychological Contributions of Pragmatism and of Original Institutional Economics and their Implications for Policy Action', *Economic Thought*, **9** (1), pp. 48–71.

Herrmann-Pillath, C. (2009) 'Elements of a Neo-Veblenian Theory of the Individual', *Journal of Economic Issues*, **43** (1), pp. 189–214.

Herrmann-Pillath, C. (2012) 'Towards an Externalist Neuroeconomics: Dual Selves, Signs, and Choice', *Journal of Neuroscience, Psychology, and Economics*, **5** (1), pp. 38–61.

Heukelom, F. (2014) *Behavioural Economics*, Cambridge: Cambridge University Press.

Hewitson, G. (1999) *Feminist Economics*, Cheltenham, UK and Northampton, MA, USA: Edward Elgar Publishing.

Hodgson, G.M. (2004) 'Reclaiming Habit for Institutional Economics', *Journal of Economic Psychology*, **25** (5), pp. 651–60.

Hollis, M. and Nell, E.J. (1975) *Rational Economic Man*, London: Cambridge University Press.

Huijsmans, I., Ma, I., Micheli, L., Civai, C., Stallen, M. and Sanfey, A.G. (2019) 'A Scarcity Mindset Alters Neural Processing Underlying Consumer Decision Making', *Proceedings of the National Academy of Sciences*, **116** (24), pp. 11699–704.

Infante, G., Lecouteux, G. and Sugden, R. (2016) 'Preference Purification and the Inner Rational Agent: A Critique of the Conventional Wisdom of Behavioural Welfare Economics', *Journal of Economic Methodology*, **23** (1), pp. 1–25.

Jevons, W.S. ([1871] 2013) *The Theory of Political Economy*, London and New York: Macmillan and Co.

Johnston, D., Deane, K. and Rizzo, M. (2018) *The Political Economy of HIV in Africa*, London and New York: Routledge.

Kahneman, D. (2003a) 'Maps of Bounded Rationality: Psychology for Behavioral Economics (Nobel Speech)', *American Economic Review*, **93** (5), pp. 1449–75.

Kahneman, D. (2003b) 'A Psychological Perspective on Economics', *American Economic Review*, 93 (2), pp. 162–8.

Kahneman, D. and Tversky, A. (1979) 'Prospect Theory: An Analysis of Decision Under Risk', *Econometrica*, **47** (2), pp. 263–91.

Kapoor, I. (2020) *Confronting Desire*, Ithaca, NY: Cornell University Press.

Krastev, S., McGuire, J.T., McNeney, D., Kable, J.W., Stolle, D., Gidengil, E. and Fellows, L.K. (2016) 'Do Political and Economic Choices Rely on Common Neural Substrates? A Systematic Review of the Emerging Neuropolitics Literature', *Frontiers in Psychology*, **7**, article 264.

Laibson, D.I. and List, J.A. (2015) 'Principles of (Behavioral) Economics', *American Economic Review*, **105** (5), pp. 385–90.

Lawson, T. (1997) *Economics and Reality*, London and New York: Routledge.

Leggett, W. (2014) 'The Politics of Behaviour Change: Nudge, Neoliberalism and the State', *Policy and Politics*, **42** (1), pp. 3–19.

Madra, Y.M. (2017) *Late Neoclassical Economics*, London and New York: Routledge.

Mäki, U. (2012) 'Realism and Antirealism About Economics', in Mäki, U., Woods, J., Gabbay, D.M. and Thagard, P. (eds), *Handbook of the Philosophy of Economics*, Oxford: Elsevier, pp. 3–24.

Martins, N.O. (2011) 'Can Neuroscience Inform Economics? Rationality, Emotions and Preference Formation', *Cambridge Journal of Economics*, **35** (2), pp. 251–67.

Marx, K. ([1844] 1964) *The Economic and Philosophical Manuscripts of 1844*, New York, International Publishers.

McGowan, T. (2016) *Capitalism and Desire*, New York: Columbia University Press.

McMaster, R. and Novarese, M. (2016) 'Neuroeconomics: Infeasible and Underdetermined', *Journal of Economic Issues*, **50** (4), pp. 963–83.

Özselçuk, C. and Madra, Y.M. (2010) 'Enjoyment as an Economic Factor: Reading Marx with Lacan', *Subjectivity*, **3**, pp. 323–47.

Panayotakis, C. (2011) *Remaking Scarcity*, London: Pluto Press.

Pedwell, C. (2017) 'Habit and the Politics of Social Change: A Comparison of Nudge Theory and Pragmatist Philosophy', *Body and Society*, **23** (4), pp. 59–94.

Petracca, E. (2017) 'A Cognition Paradigm Clash: Simon, *Situated Cognition* and the Interpretation of Bounded Rationality', *Journal of Economic Methodology*, **24** (1), pp. 20–40.

Pitts-Taylor, V. (2010) 'The Plastic Brain: Neoliberalism and the Neuronal Self', *Health*, **14** (6), pp. 635–52.

Pitts-Taylor, V. (2019) 'Neurobiologically Poor? Brain Phenotypes, Inequality, and Biosocial Determinism', *Science, Technology, & Human Values*, **44** (4), pp. 660–85.

Platt M.L. and Glimcher, P.W. (1999) 'Neural Correlates of Decision Variables in Parietal Cortex', *Nature*, **400** (6741), pp. 233–8.

Primrose, D. (2017) 'The Subjectification of *Homo Economicus* in Behavioural Economics', *Journal of Australian Political Economy*, **80**, pp. 88–128.

Pykett, J. (2016) 'From Global Economic Change to Neuromolecular Capitalism', in De Vos, J. and Pluth, E. (eds), *Neuroscience and Critique*, London and New York: Routledge, pp. 81–99.

Rabin, M. (2002) 'A Perspective on Psychology and Economics', *European Economic Review*, **46** (4), pp. 657–85.

Reb, J. and Connolly, T. (2007) 'Possession, Feelings of Ownership and the Endowment Effect', *Judgment and Decision Making*, **2** (2), pp. 107–14.

Ross, D. (2005) *Economic Theory and Cognitive Science*, Cambridge, MA: MIT Press.

Ross, D. (2008) 'Two Styles of Neuroeconomics', *Economics and Philosophy*, **24** (3), pp. 473–83.

Ross, D. (2011) 'Methodology for Experiments Should be Determined Empirically, Not Philosophically', *Journal of Economic Methodology*, **18** (2), pp. 189–93.

Ross, D., Sharp, C., Vuchinich, R.E. and Spurrett, D. (2008) *Midbrain Mutiny*, Cambridge, MA: MIT Press.

Ruff, C.C. and Fehr, E. (2014) 'The Neurobiology of Rewards and Values in Social Decision Making', *Nature Reviews Neuroscience*, **15**, pp. 549–62.

Ruff, C.C., Ugazio, G. and Fehr, E. (2013) 'Changing Social Norm Compliance with Noninvasive Brain Stimulation', *Science*, **342** (6157), pp. 482–4.

Sanfey, A.G., Rilling, J.K., Aronson, J.E., Nystrom, L.E. and Cohen, J.D (2003) 'The Neural Basis of Economic Decision-Making in the Ultimatum Game', *Science*, **300** (5626), pp. 1755–8.

Sawe, N. (2019) 'Adapting Neuroeconomics for Environmental and Energy Policy', *Behavioural Public Policy*, **3** (1), pp. 17–36.

Schmitz, S., Koeszegi, S.T., Enzenhofer, B. and Harrer, C. (2015) 'Quo Vadis Homo Economicus? References to Rationality/Emotionality in Neuroeconomic Discourses', *WP-2/2015*, TU Wien, Labor Science and Organization.

Schüll, N. and Zaloom, C. (2011) 'The Shortsighted Brain: Neuroeconomics and the Governance of Choice in Time', *Social Studies of Sciences*, **41** (4), pp. 515–38.

Screpanti, E. (2001) *The Fundamental Institutions of Capitalism*, London and New York: Routledge.

Selwyn, B. (2017) *The Struggle for Development*, Oxford: Polity.

Sen, A. (1977) 'Rational Fools: A Critique of the Behavioural Foundations of Economic Theory', *Philosophy and Public Affairs*, **6** (4), pp. 317–44.

Sent, E.-M. (2004) 'Behavioral Economics: How Psychology Made Its (Limited) Way Back into Economics', *History of Political Economy*, **36** (4), pp. 735–60.

Serra, D. (2019) 'Neuroeconomics and Modern Neuroscience', *CEE-M Working Paper 2019–12*, Montpellier, Centre for Environmental Economics.

Shaikh, A. (2016), *Capitalism*, New York: Oxford University Press.

Simon, H.A. (1955) 'A Behavioral Model of Rational Choice', *Quarterly Journal of Economics*, **69** (1), pp. 99–118.

Simon, H.A. (1956) 'Rational Choice and the Structure of the Environment', *Psychological Review*, **63** (2), pp. 129–38.

Strauss, K. (2009) 'Cognition, Context, and Multimethod Approaches to Economic Decision Making', *Environment and Planning A*, **41** (2), pp. 302–17.

Streeck, W. (2010) 'Does "Behavioural Economics" Offer an Alternative to the Neoclassical Paradigm?', *Socio-Economic Review*, **8** (2), pp. 387–97.

Sunstein, C.R. and Thaler, R. (2003) 'Libertarian Paternalism', *American Economic Review*, **93** (2), pp. 175–9.

Thaler, R. (1987) 'Anomalies: The January Effect', *Journal of Economic Perspectives*, **1** (1), pp. 197–201.

Thaler, R. (2000) 'From Homo Economics to Homo Sapiens', *Journal of Economic Perspectives*, **14** (1), pp. 133–41.

Thaler, R. and Sunstein, C.R. (2008) *Nudge*, New Haven, CT: Yale University Press.

Tversky, A. and Kahneman, D. (1973) 'Availability: A Heuristic for Judging Frequency and Probability', *Cognitive Psychology*, **5** (2), pp. 207–32.

Tversky, A. and Kahneman, D. (1974) 'Judgement Under Uncertainty: Heuristics and Biases', *Science*, **185** (4157), pp. 1124–31.

Tversky, A. and Kahneman, D. (1986) 'Rational Choice and the Framing of Decisions', *Journal of Business*, **59** (4), Part 2, pp. S251–S78.

Tversky, A. and Kahneman, D. (1991) 'Loss Aversion in Riskless Choice: A Reference-Dependent Model', *The Quarterly Journal of Economics*, **106** (4), pp. 1039–61.

Veblen, T. (1898) 'Why Is Economics Not an Evolutionary Science?', *The Quarterly Journal of Economics*, **12** (4), pp. 373–97.

Velupillai, V. and Kao, Y.F. (2016) 'Herbert Alexander Simon', in Faccarello, G. and Kurz, H. (eds), *Handbook of the History of Economic Analysis, Volume 1*, Cheltenham, UK and Northampton, MA, USA: Edward Elgar Publishing, pp. 669–74.

Vidal, F. (2009) 'Brainhood, Anthropological Figure of Modernity', *History of the Human Sciences*, **22** (19), pp. 5–36.

Vromen, J. (2011) 'Neuroeconomics: Two Camps Gradually Converging – What Can Economics Gain from It?', *International Review of Economics*, **58** (3), pp. 267–85.

Wade Hands, D. (2014) 'Normative Ecological Rationality: Normative Rationality in the Fast-and-Frugal-Heuristics Research Program', *Journal of Economic Methodology*, **21** (4), pp. 396–410.

White, M.D. (2017) 'Preferences All the Way Down': Questioning the Neoclassical Foundations of Behavioural Economics and Libertarian Paternalism', *Oeconomica*, **7** (3), pp. 353–73.

Whitehead, M., Jones, R., Lilley, R., Pykett, J. and Howell, R. (2017) *Neuroliberalism*, London and New York: Routledge.

World Bank (2015) *World Development Report 2015*, Washington, DC: World Bank.

Zak, P. (2011) 'The Physiology of Moral Sentiments', *Journal of Economic Behavior and Organization*, **77** (1), pp. 53–65.

Žižek, S. (1989) *The Sublime Object of Ideology*, London: Verso.

Zouboulakis, M. (2014) *The Varieties of Economic Rationality*, London and New York: Routledge.

PART VI

MAKING A DIFFERENCE

28. Pluralism in political economy
Tim B. Thornton

Economic pluralism asserts that multiple approaches to economics are valid and useful in building up our understanding of economic and social reality. No single approach is seen as having a monopoly of the truth (Dow 2007). Pluralism contrasts with monism, which asserts that a single and complete understanding is obtainable. Among political economists, there has been growing interest in pluralism. This is evident in developments such as the formation of the International Confederation for Pluralism in Economics. However, the concept is still ignored by most orthodox economists, presumably because it is seen as having little relevance to their professional practice. Even amongst some political economists, including those who are supportive of pluralism in principle, its meaning, boundaries and limits are still under active debate (see, for example, Davidson 2004; Hodgson 2019). This general context – comprising a mixture of ignorance, hostility and controversy – means that pluralism is something that needs to be explained and argued for.

This chapter presents an intellectual case for the pursuit of pluralism in political economy. This rests primarily on three arguments: that economic and social theory arises out of simplification; that economic and social reality exists as an open (rather than closed) system; and that values and purposes necessarily shape social and economic analysis. Different levels of pluralism are then discussed. The focus then turns to a discussion of available criteria for the evaluation of theory. Pluralism is also related to differing conceptions of what is scientific. Arguments concerning the political implications of pluralism are then discussed. The chapter concludes by arguing the pluralism is intrinsically connected to a political economy that seeks to better understand the world in order to improve it.[1] This book's Chapter 31 on strategies for educational reform is, in effect, a sequel, exploring how pluralism may actually be promoted in the curriculum.

DRIVERS OF PLURALISM

A key driver of pluralism is the inadequacy of any single theory to provide a truly adequate account of the reality it seeks to explain (Stretton 1969). To understand why this is so, it is helpful to consider how theory is constructed in the social sciences. While theory is a prerequisite for understanding the world, it is also a deliberate simplification. In other words, theory construction necessarily involves the *loss* of knowledge (Duesenbury 1958; Boulding 1970; Stilwell 2011). No matter how complicated an economic or social theory is, it cannot ever be as complicated as the world it seeks to explain. Theorists are always forced to make difficult and uncertain decisions about exactly how to safely simplify the world around them. The difficult decisions include making judgements – about what is central and what is peripheral to the matter under examination; about what can be simplified or stylised and what cannot; and about what is exogenous and what is endogenous. Purposes and values invariably influence this process (Stretton 1999). The result of all this simplification is a type of tunnel vision (of one sort or another), which is the necessary price we pay for avoiding total blindness (Leff 1974). Managing this situation requires us to understand what is illuminated, what is ignored, what might be actively obscured or distorted, in each particular 'tunnel vision' that is on offer. In some circumstances this may allow us to build up a composite knowledge of economic and social processes, or at least allow us to make a more informed choice between competing tunnel views.

The process of simplification through theory, although necessary, is always contestable. Many social scientists used to think that approaches such as logical positivism or Popperian falsificationism could provide some reliable and mechanical adjudication on whether one attempt at simplification was superior to another. This hope is now seen as misguided due to under-determination, the theory-laden nature of observations, the social nature of science, relativism, anti-foundationalism and naturalism that show the old rules-based approach as untenable (Pheby 1987; Hands 2001). In summary, if the very process of theory construction requires simplifications and abstractions, and there are no agreed rules for deciding which simplifications and abstractions are best, a multiplicity of theories will inexorably emerge. Some form of pluralism, on this reasoning, is inevitable. The only uncertainty is in the particular way that pluralism will manifest itself in any given context.

If theory construction were purely a process of simplification, one might expect – or at least hope – that the architects of any new theory would be aware of the simplifications they are making, and thus of the limitations of their theory. Deliberate choices must be made about the form of abstraction, the extent and nature of simplification and which variables should be set as either endogenous or exogenous. In doing so, the theoretical architects cannot help but be guided by their own particular values and purposes (Stretton 1969, 1999). Once their theory is constructed, other analysts who subsequently *apply* that theory may not know, or have no interest in understanding, what has guided its construction. Indeed, when presented in textbooks, theories are prone to be uncritically presented as singular and complete truths 'from above'. In other words, it is the disciples of a theory, rather than the original prophet, that are usually at most danger of deploying a theory uncritically and without due regard to its limitations and its appropriate domain of applicability.

A good example of the prophet–disciple disconnect is apparent in modern general equilibrium theory. Its original architects, such as Kenneth Arrow and Gerard Debreu, often stressed how little their work has to say directly about the real word, yet this has not prevented their theoretical contributions being adapted as a cornerstone of policy advice (Ackerman 1999). Consequently, rather ridiculous questions – which can amount to asking whether we 'can we afford the future?'– are answered through recourse to ridiculous models (Ackerman 2009). Nordhaus's macroeconomic modelling of climate change is an egregious instance of this (Keen 2020). As Blaug notes, analytical and expository convenience can be an excuse for various lines of theoretical simplification but 'the temptation to read more significance into the analysis than is inherent in the procedure is irresistible and most neoclassical writers have succumbed to it' (Blaug 1997: 692). Pluralism is an antidote to this bizarre tendency.

Another rationale for pluralism is that theories differ in what they seek to explain and predict. In other words, they differ in their explanatory focus. For example, orthodox economists, following Robbins (1932), usually regard economics as the study of the allocation of scarce resources between given ends. By contrast, institutional economists consider the origin and evolution of the ends themselves to be central issues that cry out for explanation. Another example is the focus of orthodox economics primarily on exchange, contrasting with other schools of thought, such as Marxism, that focus primarily on production (Robinson 1977).

Pluralism is also a corollary of historical specificity. Theories tend to be developed in, and for, particular historical terrain. As the world and the economy changes, so we have to change our theories (Dasgupta 1986). The economy is a human construction, not an entity like the natural world which is subject to physical laws such as gravity and thermodynamics. This issue of historical specificity can be usefully seen in relation to the neo-Kantian concepts of the idiographic and the nomothetic. A nomothetic approach is concerned with the study or discovery of underlying general laws that are assumed to lie below the surface. It is 'looking to establish the general law, principle, or theory. The fundamental assumption in the sciences is that behind all the blooming, buzzing confusion of the real world, there are patterns or processes of a more general sort, an understanding that enables prediction and explanation of the particulars' (Bates 2005: 9). A nomothetic approach pays little heed to the issue of historical specificity, other than perhaps as a source of statistical 'noise'. Orthodox economists have tended implicitly to adopt this nomothetic approach. To cite an extreme case, Lawrence Summers, in evangelical tone, has argued: 'spread the truth – the laws of economics are like the laws of engineering; one set of laws works everywhere' (cited in Klein 2007: 218).

Contrasting with a nomothetic approach, an idiographic approach stresses the unique context and processes that are decisive in understanding any given situation. It regards getting to know the specific circumstances as the cornerstone of building a genuine understanding. The result is 'a nuanced description and assessment of the unique facts of a situation or historical event, in which themes and tendencies may be discovered, but rarely any general laws' (Bates 2005: 9). An idiographic approach is highly supportive of historical specificity, and of context in general. If economic and social reality is inherently idiographic in nature, then economics needs to be inherently pluralist.

Another rationale for pluralism is the need for comparison. Even if a single theory is regarded as satisfactorily explaining a specific phenomenon, an actual process of comparison must be involved in order to arrive at such a conclusion. As Hodgson (2004) notes, this is equivalent to the Catholic Church's use of a 'devil's advocate' approach, whereby a priest is required to make the strongest possible arguments against Catholic doctrine in order to test and demonstrate its supposed strength. It is a process whereby even 'correct' theories become more persuasive via comparison with rival theories; and one that is also likely to promote clarification and refinement (Hodgson 2004: 21). This 'devil's advocate' rationale is consistent with John Stuart Mill's argument that one does not fully understand one's own argument unless one understands the arguments of those who criticise it. As Mill himself put it:

> he who knows only his own side of the case knows little of that. His reasons may be good, and no one may have been able to refute them. But if he is equally unable to refute the reasons on the opposite side, if he does not so much as know what they are, he has no ground for preferring either opinion. (Mill 1859: 104)

A final rationale for pluralism is that our values and purposes necessarily shape our analysis. In a society made up of individuals with different purposes and values, intellectual pluralism is inevitable. Orthodox economists (and some political economists) are wont to assert that values and purposes have *not* influenced their analysis. Such arguments ultimately rest on the use of 'Hume's guillotine' – the idea that we can and should separate 'what is' from 'what should be' (Hands 2012). While it is true that facts and values are not the same thing, we can never entirely excise values from analysis (Myrdal 1970; de Marchi and Blaug 1991; Stretton 1999). Consider, for example, the pervasive use of the assumption of individual rationality within so-called 'positive economics'. The use of this assumption is value-laden because it implies that we *should* be rational. Of course, we seldom are rational in the way neoclassical economics assumes (Ariely 2010). This cornerstone assumption of economic orthodoxy is heroically prescriptive rather than objectively descriptive. So, because different values and purposes pervade economic reasoning, a pluralist approach is the essential antidote to dogma.

DIFFERENT LEVELS OF PLURALISM

Having made the case for the desirability, even inevitability, of pluralism, it is also necessary to recognise that pluralism exists at a number of levels: in method, theory, epistemology, methodology and ontology (Dow 2007). Each needs to be carefully considered.

Pluralism of *method* occurs when there are multiple ways of 'doing economics'. In this context, questions of method are about *how* economists provide explanations and descriptions (Boumans et al. 2010) – that is, they pertain to the choice of techniques. Such techniques include differential calculus, interviews, econometrics, case studies, and so forth.

Theoretical pluralism exists whenever there are multiple possible explanations for particular phenomena. This is nearly always the case because many forms of description, explanation, prediction and prescription are available to economists (Dow 2007). Multiple theories can exist even within an overall school of thought. Within orthodox economics, for example, business cycle theory and the neoclassical synthesis provide rival explanations for, and prescriptions for reducing, macroeconomic instability.

Epistemological pluralism emphasises that there are multiple types of knowledge. The most obvious example is the long-standing debate concerning rationalism and empiricism as sources of knowledge. Within economics, the most famous manifestation of this dispute was in the *Methodenstreit* of the late nineteenth century – a contest between the German Historical school, which asserted the virtues of empirical and inductive pathways to knowledge, and the Austrian school, which asserted the virtues of rationalist and deductivist approaches (Pheby 1987).

Yet more fundamental – and probably the most confronting form of pluralism – is *methodological* pluralism. This exists whenever there is no single criterion, or set of criteria, by which a ruling can be made on which is the best theory. This is a pervasive feature in economics (Dow 2007). The concept of methodological pluralism may be seen as a corollary of the breakdown of the 'received view' in the philosophy of science and economic methodology. The 'naturalistic turn' and the rise of rhetorical and sociological approaches have led to the abandonment of a strict rule-based approach to methodology (Hands 2001; Boumans et al. 2010). However, it is pertinent to ask whether the acceptance of methodological pluralism is a bridge too far. Does it promote nihilism and a rejection of the idea of scientific progress? No, or at least, not quite. In practice, the proliferation of rival methodologies is limited by social forces, in that each methodology needs to be validated, accepted and practised by a particular scientific community to have any standing, influence or institutional support (Dow 2004). Indeed, a key argument from Kuhn, and the sociology of scientific knowledge in general, is that science is a social process (Hands 1998). One may have a view, but if you cannot *persuade* others of its merits, then it is unlikely that your view will gain traction and outlive you. This does not mean that the knotty issue of relativism is entirely resolved, but it does provide some counter to the claim that methodological pluralism can be directly equated with saying that 'anything goes' (Feyerabend 1988). Making a claim and being able to persuade others that it is intellectually warranted are not synonymous.

Ontological pluralism is the final level to be considered. As ontology in general concerns questions as to the nature of reality, so economic ontology is concerned with questions as to the *essential* nature of the economy and society (i.e. their essence). One's ontological viewpoint – what Schumpeter (1954) called the 'pre-analytic vision' – is of great importance to any analysis. Ontology is doubly important to the issue of pluralism because a person's ontological commitments can also heavily influence their stance towards pluralism at the levels of epistemology, methodology, theory, and method. As Dow has argued, 'the crucial point is to recognise the origins of theoretical approaches in methodological approaches and ultimately in conceptions of reality' (Dow 2007: 33).

OPEN VERSUS CLOSED SYSTEMS

The most central ontological difference is whether one presupposes that economic and social reality is an open or a closed system. An open system is one where

> not all the relevant variables can be identified, and where the external boundaries of the system are therefore not knowable. The system is subject to outside influences which cannot be accounted for in advance (where 'account for' includes knowledge that an outside influence, or relationship, is random). Further, within the system, there is scope for change in the relationships between variables which cannot be identified in advance, and indeed for change in the nature of the constituent variables themselves. Since the system in reality cannot be understood in terms of constituent parts of a fixed nature, it is pluralist. (Dow 2007: 28)

By contrast, a closed system is one where

> all the relevant variables can be identified, where the boundaries of the system are knowable, so that variables can be classified as endogenous or exogenous, and where the relationships between variables are knowable and unchanging (so that all change in the system can be accounted for). The constituent parts of the system are of a common, fixed nature, with an independent existence (as in atoms or rational individuals). (Dow 2007: 27–8)

In a closed system, the theorist can expect to find what Lawson (1997) would call 'event regularities' – if event 'A', then event 'B'. This creates the alluring prospect of finding 'laws of economics' – a distinctly nomothetic ambition. A closed-system reality is totally inconsistent with epistemological and methodological pluralism and is very limiting, if not totally limiting, on questions of method.

Different ontological presuppositions provide an important part of the explanation of why disagreements between economists are so often intractable. It may have less to do with them 'having no ears' (Keen 2001: 1) and more to do with the fact that they have built their world on a strikingly different conception of reality. On this basis, it may be futile to try to convince a mainstream economist of the merits of pluralism – whether of method, theory, methodology or epistemology – if they are knowingly (or, more likely, unknowingly) committed to a closed-system ontology. In circumstances like this, a mutual understanding of differing ontological presuppositions is a necessary, though probably not sufficient, basis for productive communication.

While the open-system versus closed-system conception of reality is important, it also needs to be conceded that all theory requires closure if it is to be operationally useful in practice. The key distinction then becomes whether theorists accept that they are overlaying a closed framework over an open system reality, or whether they are overlaying closed theory on top of what they presume is a closed-system reality. In the former case, the theorist would probably understand that he or she is engaging in a temporary and provisional closure (Lawson 2003). This self-awareness is often particularly important to keep in mind when provisional closure is invoked to allow the use of formal/mathematical methods. In all cases, formal or not, the theorist invoking provisional closure needs to be aware that something of importance might be missed, distorted, over-emphasised or under-emphasised. This means that researchers should be naturally modest, tentative and open to persuasion about their conclusions, recognising the difference between the provisionally closed system ontology of the theory and the open system nature of reality. By contrast, if a theorist is overlaying a closed system theory on what they assume is a closed-system reality, the theorist is in pursuit of (or feels they have obtained) a singular and immutable truth; in such an instance, the scope for intellectual discussion will inevitably be circumscribed.

ONTOLOGICAL COMMUNALITY WITH POLITICAL ECONOMY

There is a strong case for political economists to go beyond adopting an ontology that is either open versus closed, or even 'fully closed' versus 'provisionally closed'. We might think instead of fully connected systems versus partially connected systems. Potts (2000) argues that the ontology of mainstream economics not only presupposes a closed system, but a system where all the elements of the system are fully connected to one another. The assumptions of perfect information, perfect rationality, and instant and perfect adjustment (among many others) sit easily within such a system. Whilst a fully connected system like this can appear *complicated* (witness the many pages of equations in books and articles on general equilibrium theory, for example), the consistent nature of the connections between agents means that it is not *complex*. Indeed, beneath the surface it is really a simple system (Foster 2005). Its fully determined and connected nature means that it exhibits the type of event regularities that make it well suited for the deployment of mathematical methods to gain knowledge of the system's workings.

In contrast, political economy – and the social sciences in general – not only presuppose an open system, but also presuppose that the elements of the system are not usually fully connected with each other. The connections that do exist within the elements of the system are a result of path-dependent, historical time. Full information and full rationality are not possible if the elements of the system are not fully connected to one another. As a consequence, economic agents may be expected to act as rule-followers and as creatures of habit, adjusting and learning as they go along. Moreover, the system's connections can be expected to evolve under their own momentum and in response to variables such as learning and experimentation. Significantly, all the schools of political economy, even including libertarian-leaning Austrians, sit within the ontology just described. Just as significantly, all the other social sciences such as history, politics, anthropology and sociology can also sit inside it. The only area of knowledge that cannot be nested within it is orthodox (neoclassical) economics. This is a crucial point because, seeing orthodox economists as representing 'a strange and lost tribe' (Leijonhufvud 1973) that is often unable to engage in meaningful dialogue with political economists and other social scientists becomes far more understandable – and perhaps more manageable – once the fundamental differences are understood.

ANYTHING GOES?

Having narrow limits of how underlying economic realities are perceived and analysed meets the current preferences of many orthodox economists. Some may even think it a necessary defence against a potential slide into anarchy whereby 'anything goes'. However, the fear is not soundly grounded. Pluralism does have limits, even if they are sometimes not understood.

The most obvious limits to pluralism were noted in the earlier discussion of methodological pluralism. To recap, whilst various theories may emerge and proliferate, each faces the survival challenge of attracting and sustaining adherents. Aspiring prophets may be able to convince themselves of the correctness of their own beliefs, but unless others can be convinced, the beliefs probably just die with them. A proponent of original ideas does not a school of thought make.

A three-step process of Darwinian evolution of variety, retention and selection can help to make sense of what has just been described. Variety can expected to emerge, given that theory in economics – or any aspect of studying human behaviour – is necessarily selective and shaped by particular purposes and values. There are many variations on every theme. However, whether retention and selection also occur is far less certain and is highly dependent on a range of intellectual *and* social factors. Indeed, social as well as intellectual factors are likely to influence what forms of variety emerge in the first place. Given this, rather than being overly concerned with the possibility of 'anything goes', the pluralist political economist should instead take the closest interest in the intellectual and social forces that actually shape 'what grows'.

The next thing to consider in this context is that methodological pluralism is a by-product of a breakdown of an older, monist view of science and the absence of agreed criteria that can serve as judge, jury and executioner for any particular theory. In the absence of a simple rule-based methodology, a scientific community needs to exercise judgement. This term 'judgement' is understood here to be the use of practical reason and ordinary logic practised under the weight of uncertainty, drawing on a range of methods to arrive at a conclusion that is necessarily uncertain and provisional (Dow 2007). To exercise judgement sounds somewhat vague, yet it can be approached in a structured way, and there are concrete things we can do to improve the quality of our judgement.

First and foremost, judgement needs to be informed by the range of analyses and analytical frameworks. This requires understanding the strengths and weakness of the contending theories and methods (be they quantitative or qualitative) that are available to us. It also involves developing our knowledge of economic methodology, economic history, history of economic thought and political philosophy. A knowledge of other social sciences – and biophysical sciences, including psychology, too – is also beneficial. Such a menu of requirements recalls Keynes's daunting list of attributes required of the master economist:

[T]he master-economist must possess a rare combination of gifts. He must be mathematician, historian, statesman, philosopher – in some degree. He must understand symbols and speak in words. He must contemplate the particular in terms of the general, and touch abstract and concrete in the same flight of thought. He must study the present in the light of the past for the purposes of the future. No part of man's nature or his institutions must lie entirely outside his regard. He must be purposeful and disinterested in a simultaneous mood; as aloof and incorruptible as an artist, yet sometimes as near the earth as a politician. (Keynes [1933] 1963: 56)

We can also try to make our judgements in a structured way, by which is meant that there are lines of questioning which, while falling short of a rule-based methodology, offer demanding lines of investigation and are worth pursuing. A taxonomy for organising this process provides us with a good example of the structured lines of questioning and evaluation that are open to us (Table 28.1).

Table 28.1   Criteria for the evaluation of theory

Explanatory coherence
The number and quality of linkages in the explanatory chain
The number of unlinked elements in the explanation
The degree to which linkages stretch back to an organising concept
The elegance and clarity of the explanation
Explanatory power
Capacity to handle evidence
Degree of vulnerability to facts
Clarity on counter-factual tests
Number of special exceptions being canvassed
Explanatory reach
Range of issues covered
Scale and importance of matters ignored/unexplained
Degree of depth – status of unexplained independent variable
Degree to which, as range expands, coherence diminishes
Explanatory openness
Capacity to absorb new circumstances/new lines of research
Openness to articulation with additional lines of explanation
Degree to which that openness is compatible with original coherence
Openness to criticism and to self-reflection
Explanatory impact
The social consequences of applying its prescriptions
The pattern of winners and losers associated with its prescriptions
The interests privileged
The values structuring the approach

Source: Coates (2005: 267).

The first grouping of criteria in Table 28.1, *explanatory coherence*, demands that theory be internally consistent at the level of logic. It can be argued, rather strongly, that a theory can have no claim of offering knowledge about the world when it does not even make sense as a set of ideas. Specific failures of explanatory coherence in economics include problems of circularity (i.e. assuming what one seeks to explain) and logical inconsistency. A commonly noted example of the former problem is the neoclassical conception of 'capital' as used in standard aggregate production functions (Harcourt 1972). The requirement for explanatory coherence is usually regarded as a minimum requirement for a theory to be seen as legitimate, including amongst those who embrace the concept of pluralist political economy (Chick and Dow 2001; Hodgson 2001; King 2011). The general position on pluralism amongst such economists is that we should expect and accept the existence of contradictory ideas within the community of economists, but we should not accept contradictory ideas within particular theories or concepts (Hodgson 2001).

The next group of criteria, *explanatory power*, pertains to how a theory fits with evidence. A theory may be internally (logically) elegant, but externally irrelevant in that it cannot explain or predict real-world phenomena. Despite recognising the theory-laden nature of facts and the difficulties of empirically testing theory (Dow 2007; Boumans et al. 2010), it is important to care about empirical evidence that might assist in either corroborating or contradicting our theoretical assertions (Lavoie 2009; Blaug 2010). Theories that shy away from empirical evidence – like Dracula from a stake – should generally invoke concern.

The third cluster of criteria, *explanatory reach*, examines the scope or boundaries of explanation. A key consideration here is what is treated as exogenous (and thereby unexplained). One might initially think that the more a theory explains the better, but greater explanatory scope is not always a good thing. A few examples can illustrate the point. One is the 'economics imperialism' of Gary Becker, showing the dangers of over-reach (Harcourt 1979; Harcourt and Kerr 1982). Becker extends the rational choice framework to matters of marriage, crime, sleep and other social phenomena. Yet the flawed, indeed sometimes seemingly ludicrous, nature of some of this work (Nelson 1995; Varoufakis 1998) reveals that it has little claim to be a general theory of human behaviour (Nelson 1995). Furthermore, as Hodgson (2001) argues, the pursuit of excessive generality can result in the elimination of important features that are common to a particular sub-set of economic and social reality; in other words, the price of generality can be vacuousness (Bowles 2005). Different theories, resting on different methodological foundations, are often required to understand different phenomena.

The fourth category, *explanatory openness*, examines how brittle and inflexible a particular theoretical approach may be. Can it interact meaningfully with other approaches, or is it a self-enclosed 'package-deal' that cannot articulate with other approaches? Again, economics imperialism provides a relevant illustration of this problem of insularity: assumptions of full rationality and endogenous preferences severely limit economic orthodoxy's ability to interact with, and benefit from, other approaches in the social sciences. That its practitioners often see themselves as offering scientific salvation for their fellow social scientists further compounds the problem (for an unwitting example of this problem, see Lazear 2000).

The final group of criteria, *explanatory impact*, prompts us to consider how analysis can be closely intertwined with the interests of particular groups in society. Almost inexorably, certain groups of people will benefit or suffer as a consequence of how we choose to understand the working of the economy. Indeed, beliefs about the economy are themselves intrinsic working parts of the economy (Stretton 1999) and will advantage and disadvantage different social groups. Economics is, among other things, a conduit for the expression of social, economic and political interests (Halevi 2002). The popular currency of an idea or approach may have less to do with its explanatory merit than with its ability to serve the interests of particular social groups. This line of argument has long been used by Marxian and radical political economists to explain the continuing persistence of neoclassical economics as effectively serving an ideological role for a dominant capitalist class – including reassuring the capitalists themselves that a capitalist system inherently works for the broader public benefit (Heilbroner 1986) – rather than elucidating how capitalism actually works. This is unfortunate, given that 'only an economics that is critical of capitalism can be a guide to successful policy for capitalism' (Minsky 1986: 332).

It should be noted that that there are often, if not always, trade-offs between criteria such as those discussed here. For example, a theory that rates highly on explanatory coherence may rate poorly on explanatory openness. Similarly, depth and breadth may be in tension with one another. Values and purposes will likely influence how trade-offs are made between different criteria. Furthermore, social forces are also likely to come into play in deciding what criteria get precedence.

IS PLURALISM SCIENTIFIC?

Let us now relate the idea of pluralism to the history and philosophy of science. In doing so, the first thing to note is that there have been marked shifts on what is, and what is not considered scientific. Indeed, the issues have become less, rather than more, straightforward in recent times. Initially, it was hoped that a rules-based approach could be developed to distinguish the scientific from the non-scientific. For example, Whewell in the nineteenth century argued that: 'the philosophy of science [...] would imply nothing less than a complete insight into the essence and conditions of all real knowledge, and an exposition of the best methods for the discovery of new truths' (Whewell 1840). Such a view presents a very attractive vision of science – as a looking glass with which we shall be able to see the singular truth. An economic methodologist explains

> the Enlightenment view of scientific knowledge that has been handed down from Bacon, Descartes, and other philosophers. The view that knowledge of the causal structure of the world could be obtained with certainty if the proper method were followed, and even though philosophers have differed radically about what the proper method actually is, the idea that it – the scientific method – is the secret of epistemic success is common to all the various philosophical approaches. (Hands 2001: 4)

The logical positivists of the Vienna Circle, Popper's falsificationism and Friedman's instrumentalism are all good examples of this rule-based approach to scientific analysis. Although different in many respects, they have in common a rule-based approach that is consistent with the received view of science (Hands 1998). This view fits awkwardly, if it all, with the concept of pluralism: if there is a reliable rule-based methodology, then we should be able to identify the best theory from among the plurality of contenders.

While this 'received view of science' still has its adherents, the philosophy of science has moved on. Concerns about under-determination, theory-ladenness, the social nature of science, relativism, anti-foundationalism and naturalism have exposed the old rules-based approach as untenable (Hands 2001; Boumans et al. 2010). From such a perspective, the history of science looks less like a steady cumulative progression towards finding the rules and processes by which we can find the truth; and more like a history that is 'full of examples of prophets spurned, old truths forgotten or neglected, even older heresies enthusiastically embraced, and egregious errors pursued at great speed to the end of the of the appropriate cul-de-sac' (King 2002: 241–2). Furthermore, examining the history of science as practised (rather than as professed) shows that our understanding of scientific advance is closely connected with institutional success and social acceptance. This post-received view of science meshes well with the concept of pluralism: in the absence of a decisive rule-based methodology to decide between theories, we should be open to consideration of multiple theories and to a degree of eclecticism.

Political economists are usually quite aware, and often much concerned with, these contemporary debates in economic methodology and philosophy of science. By contrast, orthodox economists rarely show much active interest in, or even awareness of, debates in economic methodology and the philosophy of science (Lawson 1997, 2001; Fullbrook 2009; Davis 2019). Paul Samuelson famously asserted that 'those who can, do science; those who can't prattle about its methodology' (Samuelson 1992: 240). However, having no interest in methodology does not mean an absence of a methodological position: it just means that one does not care to examine, defend or compare the position that one holds.

Usually implicitly rather than explicitly, orthodox economists seem to hold to some (probably incoherent and normally superficial) blend of Popperian falsificationism and Friedmanesque instrumentalism. However, what is not usually recognised is that economists do not – and to an extent, cannot – practise the methodological principles they espouse (Hutchison 1960; Canterbury and Burkhardt 1983). To illustrate the point, John Quiggin's *Zombie Economics: How Dead Ideas Walk Among Us* (Quiggin 2010) laments the persistence of various orthodox economic theories despite their recurrent predictive failure and falsification by real-world events and experiences.

What matters even more deeply than the existence of methodological weaknesses in the work of orthodox economists is that such weaknesses are commonly unrecognised and ignored. Yet there is no obvious internal, institutional imperative to change. Being comfortable with, if not proud of, their methodological position is a practical stance for mainstream economists seeking to have their articles published in highly ranked journals, get jobs and promotions, and impress audiences of other economists and policymakers. Because mainstream economists currently hold the institutional power, they can largely ignore the critique of economic methodologists and philosophers of science. What all this means is that mainstream economics could potentially remain anchored, for quite some time, in an outdated and unconvincing view of science, largely impervious to criticism at this level.

The continuing dominance of the 'received' but misconceived view of science helps to explain the intolerance and persecution to which political economists have sometimes been subjected (for examples of this, see Lee 2012). If there is a valid rule-based methodology to determine science, and orthodox economists believe they follow such rules, then political economists are easily represented as dissenting from science itself. On that reasoning, the political economists *deserve* to be marginalised, if not altogether expunged, from the profession.

For all these reasons, the prospect of achieving genuine pluralism in economics is constrained by discredited notions of science (Negru 2009) and by the paucity of understanding that real science is pluralist (Fullbrook 2001). Certainly, mainstream economists have often been keen to claim a degree of consensus for their discipline. For example, Samuelson argued 'there is a scientific consensus about what comprises good economics – a core of foundational concepts, methods and propositions that is "accepted by all but a few extreme left-wing and right-wing writers"' (Samuelson 1967: 197–8).

Davis (2008) argues that the entire history of economic thought has been heavily shaped by a fear that pluralism endangers a scientific economics. He views the history of economics as an ongoing alternation between periods of pluralism and the dominance of a single approach.

Orthodoxy is understood to emerge out of heterodoxy in a core–periphery relationship that regularly reconstitutes itself. Thus, an economist may have licence to be eclectic in approach during a phase of high pluralism but will come to grief as the tide of pluralism recedes, leaving nothing but a rigid orthodoxy. The implication is that, if the mainstream research frontier is to progress, some part of the profession will have to actively destroy the standing of neoclassicism (Davis 2008: 350). Furthermore, this view may be taken to imply that, for political economy to be become more influential – even eventually dominant – it will need to become less plural and to coalesce into something approaching a unified whole. It is an interesting and controversial thesis that sits awkwardly with other claims that 'real science is pluralist' (Fullbrook 2001).

The relationship of the economics profession to its broader public audience also requires consideration. This is because a significant barrier to pluralism may arise from expectations among the general public for clear, simple and unambiguous answers to complex economic problems. Indeed, there is evidence of community frustration as to 'why can't economists be like *"proper"* scientists and agree amongst themselves?' (Dow 2002: 15, emphasis added). Thus, society in general also may struggle to see that rigorous science is pluralist. Consequently, political economists must be able to articulate why pluralism is intellectually valid – and do so not only to their colleagues but also in ways that resonate with policymakers and the public in general.

PLURALISM AND POLITICS

One final, but significant, matter is the *political* dimension inherent in intellectual pluralism. That pluralism is political is a logical consequence of values and purposes shaping analysis. This ties in to the argument that 'the problem of generating and protecting knowledge is a problem in politics, and, conversely, that the problem of political order always involves solutions to the problem of knowledge' (Shapin and Schaffer 1985: 21).

To support these claims, we can explore them via Shapin and Schaffer's most interesting analysis, the well-known scientific dispute that occurred between Thomas Hobbes and Robert Boyle in the 1660s and early 1670s. At the surface level, the dispute was about the scientific legitimacy of Boyle's air-pump experiments. These experiments involved a suction pump being attached to a replaceable glass bulb. The pump would evacuate the air, and thus create what in today's terms would be called a vacuum. However, back then, what exactly was created by the evacuation of the air was a matter of intense disagreement between Hobbes and Boyle, with Hobbes strongly attacking the significance and legitimacy of Boyle's work. Initially, Shapin and Schaffer make a point from the sociology of scientific knowledge, namely that *internal* social pressures from within a scientific community are important. Thus, 'the member who poses awkward questions about "what everybody knows" in the shared culture runs a real risk of being dealt with as a troublemaker or an idiot. Indeed, there are few more reliable ways of being expelled from a culture than continuing to seriously question its taken-for-granted intellectual framework' (Shapin and Schaffer 1985: 6). However, their analysis goes deeper, stressing how political philosophy and concerns about social order can exert a powerful influence over science.

Hobbes argued that the path to absolute certainty was via a deductive epistemology that utilised logic and geometry and recognised no boundaries between the natural, human and the social. It was a monist/non-pluralist approach that left no scope for dissent. Shapin and Schaffer argue that Hobbes's adoption of such a methodological position cannot be separated from his controversial views on social order, specifically his arguments concerning the desirability and legitimacy of a strong state (i.e. a Leviathan) to determine what is true and correct and what must be obeyed. Hobbes's particular method of knowledge production, and the supposed degree of certainty it could deliver, was seen as having profound implications for societal order. Shapin and Schaffer argue that, for Hobbes, it was a case of 'show men what knowledge is and you will show them the grounds of assent and social order' (Shapin and Schaffer 1985: 100). It was on this basis that Hobbes viewed Boyle's air-pump experiments, not as interesting scientific experiments that utilised empirical, inductive and probabilistic methods, but as misguided attempts at knowledge creation that provided a basis for civil war. Thus: 'the vacuism Hobbes attacked was not merely absurd and wrong, as it was in his physical texts; it was dangerous. Speech of a vacuum was associated with cultural resources that had been illegitimately used to subvert proper authority in the state' (Shapin and Schaffer 1985: 91). Shapin and Shafer point out that 'for Hobbes, the rejection of vacuum was the elimination of a space within which dissension could take place' (Shapin and Schaffer 1985: 109).

Boyle was also aware of the larger significance of his experimental methods. He realised that defending the air-pump experiments was about defending the legitimacy of an inductive and experimental approach to knowledge that relied on probabilistic reasoning. If this approach to knowledge creation could be defended, a political philosophy that recognised a pluralism of views could also be defended; for if our knowledge is only partial, a pluralism of views is valid. In other words, his 'adversary's civic philosophy and theology could be invalidated if it were shown that his physics was unsound' (Shapin and Schaffer 1985: 207). Hobbes's claim that there could be a leader who could determine what is correct and what must be obeyed would thus be robbed of its supposed intellectual basis (Shapin and Schaffer 1985: 24).

Shapin and Schaffer argue that the dispute between Boyle and Hobbes was afflicted with Kuhnian incommensurability: there was no common ground on which to settle the dispute (Jennings 1988). They also argue that Boyle's views prevailed because they were in keeping with the political tides of the time. For Shapin and Schaffer, this scientific debate was a case of 'he who has the most, and the most powerful, allies wins' (Shapin and Schaffer 1985: 342), and so accordingly, 'the form of life in which we make our scientific knowledge will stand or fall with the way we order our affairs of the state' (Shapin and Schaffer 1985: 344).

One may consider that, because intellectual pluralism is generally intellectually and socially desirable for the reasons set out earlier in this chapter, it would normally be a source of social stability. However, Shapin and Schaffer emphasise how it may be regarded as a vice. What is notable in their example is that it is not social inequality, nor lack of opportunity, that is the source of social disorder: rather, it is the erosion of mass belief in the existence of singular truths that we all must accept and be guided by. This is a deeply conservative and illiberal understanding of pluralism. Yet it seems to resonate in relation to modern economics, particularly the way it is usually taught, with a straitly constrained syllabus that inhibits students from too much free thinking or engaging with too many different ideas (Robinson 1980).

CONCLUSION

This chapter has sought to explain the nature and merits of economic pluralism. This has included an examination of its various levels: method, theory, methodology, epistemology, and ontology, with an open-system ontology providing the underlying foundation for pluralism in all its forms. It has been argued that a commitment to pluralism is not a commitment to the idea that 'anything goes'. Rather, it is a commitment to rigour, given that pluralism requires us to understand the strengths and weakness of different approaches to analysis and to weigh up these strengths and weakness in a structured and systematic way. This requires us to be self-aware enough to know how our own values and purposes will influence this weighing process. We also need to understand how political and social forces affect the sociology of knowledge in general. Our final analysis may then be guided by one preferred approach or by some eclectic combination or synthesis of approaches. In all cases, however, the analyst should be open to reviewing and justifying how they have decided to go about their analysis, given the inherently complex and changing nature of social and economic reality.

NOTE

1.   This chapter extends and updates analyses from Thornton (2013, 2017).

REFERENCES

Ackerman, F. (1999) 'Still Dead After All These Years: Interpreting the Failure of General Equilibrium Theory', Global Development and Environment Institute, Tufts University: Boston.
Ackerman, F. (2009) *Can We Afford the Future? The Economics of a Warming World*, London: Zed Books.
Ariely, D (2010) *Predictably Irrational*, New York: Harper Collins.
Bates, M.J. (2005) 'An Introduction to Metatheories, Theories, and Models', in Fisher, K.E., Erdelez, S. and McKechnie, L.E.F. (eds), *Theories of Information Behavior*, Medford: Information Today, pp. 1–24.
Blaug, M. (1997) *Economic Theory in Retrospect*, Cambridge: Cambridge University Press.
Blaug, M. (2010) 'Popper's Logic of Discovery', in Boumans, M. and Davis, J.B. (eds), *Economic Methodology: Understanding Economics as a Science*, Basingstoke: Palgrave Macmillan, pp. 84–91.
Boulding, K.E. (1970) *Economics as a Science*, New York: McGraw-Hill.
Boumans, M., Davis, J.B., Blaug, M., Maas, H. and Svorencik, A. (2010) *Economic Methodology: Understanding Economics as a Science*, Basingstoke: Palgrave Macmillan.
Bowles, S. (2005) *Microeconomics: Behavior, Institutions, and Evolution*, Princeton, NJ: Princeton University Press.
Canterbury, E.R. and Burkhardt, R.J. (1983) 'What Do We Mean By Asking "Is Economics s Science?",' in Eichner, A.S. (ed.), *Why Economics is Not Yet a Science*, London: Macmillan, pp. 15–40.
Chick, V.and Dow, S.C. (2001) 'Formalism, Logic and Reality: A Keynesian Analysis', *Cambridge Journal of Economics*, **25** (6), pp. 705–21.
Coates, D. (2005) *Varieties of Capitalism, Varieties of Approaches*', Basingstoke: Palgrave Macmillan.
Dasgupta, A.K. (1986) *Epochs of Economic Theory*, Delhi: Oxford University Press.
Davidson, P. (2004) 'A Response to King's Arguments for Pluralism', *Post-Autistic Economics Review*, **24** (March), pp. 1–5.
Davis, J.B. (2008) 'The Turn in Recent Economics and Return of Orthodoxy', *Cambridge Journal of Economics*, **32** (3), pp. 349–66.

Davis, J.B. (2019) 'Economics and Economic Methodology in a Core-Periphery Economic World', *Brazilian Journal of Political Economy*, **39**, pp. 408–26.

de Marchi, N.and Blaug, M. (1991) *Appraising Economic Theories: Studies in the Methodology of Research Programs*, Aldershot: Edward Elgar Publishing.

Dow, S.C. (2002) *Economic Methodology: An Inquiry*, Oxford: Oxford University Press.

Dow, S.C. (2004) 'Structured Pluralism', *Journal of Economic Methodology*, **11** (3), pp. 275–90.

Dow, S.C. (2007) 'Pluralism in Economics', in Groenewegen, J. (ed.), *Teaching Pluralism in Economics*, Cheltenham, UK and Northampton, MA, USA: Edward Elgar Publishing, pp. 22–39.

Duesenbury, J. (1958) *Business Cycles and Economic Growth*, New York: McGraw-Hill.

Feyerabend, P.K. (1988) *Against Method: Outline of an Anarchistic Theory of Knowledge*, London: Verso.

Foster, J. (2005) 'From Simplistic to Complex Systems in Economics', *Cambridge Journal of Economics*, **29** (6), pp. 873–92.

Fullbrook, E. (2001) 'Real Science is Pluralist', *Post-Autistic Economics Review*, **5** (March).

Fullbrook, E. (2009) (ed.) 'Ontology and economics: Tony Lawson and his critics', London: Routledge.

Halevi, J. (2002) 'High Priests and Run-of-the-Mill Practitioners', *Post-Autistic Economics Review*, **14** (June), http://www.paecon.net/PAEarticles/Fullbrook1.htm.

Hands, D.W. (1998) 'Sociology of Scientific Knowledge', in Davis, J.B., Hands, D.W. and Mäki, U. (eds), *The Handbook of Economic Methodology*, Lyme: Edward Elgar Publishing, pp. 474–7.

Hands, D.W. (2001) *Reflection Without Rules: Economic Methodology and Contemporary Science Theory*, Cambridge: Cambridge University Press.

Hands, D.W. (2012) 'The Positive-Normative Dichotomy and Economics', in Mäki, U. (ed.), *Philosophy of Economics*, Amsterdam: Elsevier, pp. 219–23.

Harcourt, G.C. (1972) *Some Cambridge Controversies in the Theory of Capital*, London: Cambridge University Press.

Harcourt, G.C. (1979) 'The Social Science Imperialists', *Politics*, **14** (2), pp. 243–51.

Harcourt, G.C. and Kerr, P. (1982) *The Social Science Imperialists: Selected Essays of G.C. Harcourt*, London: Routledge.

Heilbroner, R.L. (1986) *The Nature and Logic of Capitalism*, New York: W.W.Norton.

Hodgson, G. (2019) *Is There a Future for Heterodox Economics? Institutions, Ideology and a Scientific Community*, Cheltenham, UK and Northampton, MA, USA: Edward Elgar Publishing.

Hodgson, G.M. (2001) *How Economics Forgot History: The Problem of Historical Specificity in Social Science*, New York: Routledge.

Hodgson, G.M. (2004) 'Is it All in Keynes's General Theory?', *Post-Autistic Economics Review*, **25** (May), pp. 21–4.

Hutchison, T.W. (1960) *The Significance and Basic Postulates of Economic Theory*, New York: A.M. Kelley.

Jennings, R.C. (1988) 'Review Article: Leviathan and the Air-Pump', *The British Journal for the Philosophy of Science*, **39** (3), pp. 403–10.

Keen, S. (2001) 'Economists Have No Ears', *Post-Autistic Economics Review*, **7** (July), pp. 7–9.

Keen, S. (2020) 'The Appallingly Bad Neoclassical Economics of Climate Change', *Globalizations*, **18** (7), pp. 1149–77.

Keynes, J.M. ([1933] 1963) *Essays in Biography*, New York: Norton.

King, J.E. (2002) *A History of Post-Keynesian Economics Since 1936*, Cheltenham, UK and Northampton, MA, USA: Edward Elgar Publishing.

King, J.E. (2011) 'Arguments for Pluralism in Economics', in Stilwell, F. and Argyrous, G. (eds), *Readings in Political Economy: Economics as a Social Science*, Melbourne: Tilde University Press, pp. 54–6.

Klein, N. (2007) *The Shock Doctrine: The Rise of Disaster Capitalism*, Camberwell: Allen Lane.

Lavoie, M. (2009) 'After the Crisis: Perspectives for Post Keynesian Economics', Conference Paper Presented at *Encontro Internacional de Associação Keynesiana Brasileiro*, Porto Alegre.

Lawson, T. (1997) *Economics and Reality*, London: Routledge.

Lawson, T. (2001) 'Back to Reality', *Post-Autistic Economics Review*, **6** (May), http://www.paecon.net/PAEtexts/Lawson1.htm.

Lawson, T. (2003) *Reorienting Economics*, London: Routledge.

Lazear, E.P. (2000) 'Economic Imperialism', *Quarterly Journal of Economics*, **115** (1), pp. 99–146.

Lee, F.S. (2012) 'Heterodox Economics and its Critics', *Review of Political Economy*, **24** (2), pp. 337–51.

Leff, A. (1974) *Economic Analysis of Law: Some Realism About Nominalism*, New Haven, CT: Yale University Press.

Leijonhufvud, A. (1973) 'Life Among the Econ', *Economic Inquiry*, **11** (3), pp. 327–37.

Mill, J.S. (1859) *On Liberty*, London: John Parker and Son.

Minsky, H (1986) *Stabilizing and Unstable Economy*, New Haven, CT: Yale University Press.

Myrdal, G. (1970) *Objectivity in Social Research*, London: Gerald Duckworth.

Negru, I. (2009) 'Reflections on Pluralism in Economics', *International Journal of Pluralism and Economics*, **1** (1), pp. 7–21.

Nelson, J.A. (1995) 'Feminism and Economics', *Journal of Economic Perspectives*, **9** (2), pp. 131–48.

Pheby, J. (1987) *Methodology and Economics: A Critical Introduction*, Basingstoke: Macmillan.

Potts, J. (2000) *The New Evolutionary Microeconomics: Complexity, Competence, and Adaptive Behaviour*, Cheltenham, UK and Northampton, MA, USA: Edward Elgar Publishing.

Quiggin, J. (2010) *Zombie Economics: How Dead Ideas Still Walk Among Us*, Princeton, NJ: Princeton University Press.

Robbins, L. (1932) *An Essay on the Nature and Significance of Economic Science*, London: Macmillan.

Robinson, J. (1977) 'What Are the Questions?', *Journal of Economic Literature*, **15** (4), pp. 1318–39.

Robinson, J. (1980) *Collected Economic Papers*, Cambridge, MA: MIT Press.

Samuelson, P.A. (1967) *Economics*, New York: McGraw-Hill.

Samuelson, P.A. (1992) 'My Life Philosophy: Policy Credos and Working Ways', in Szenberg, M. (ed.), *Eminent Economists: Their Life Philosophies*, New York: Cambridge University Press, pp. 236–47.

Schumpeter, J.A. (1954) *History of Economic Analysis*, London: Allen and Unwin.

Shapin, S. and Schaffer, S. (1985) *Leviathan and the Air-pump: Hobbes, Boyle, and the Experimental Life: Including a Translation of Thomas Hobbes, Dialogus physicus de natura aeris by Simon Schaffer*, Princeton, NJ: Princeton University Press.

Stilwell, F. (2011) *Political Economy: The Contest of Economic Ideas*, 3rd edition, Melbourne: Oxford University Press.

Stretton, H. (1969) *The Political Sciences: General Principles of Selection in Social Science and History*, New York: Basic Books.

Stretton, H. (1999) *Economics: A New Introduction*, Sydney: UNSW Press.

Thornton, T.B. (2013) 'The Possibility of a Pluralist Economics Curriculum in Australian Universities: Historical Forces and Contemporary Strategies', PhD thesis, School of Economics, La Trobe University, Melbourne.

Thornton, T.B. (2017) *From Economics to Political Economy: The Promise, Problems and Solutions of Pluralist Economics*, London: Routledge.

Varoufakis, Y. (1998) *Foundations of Economics: A Beginner's Companion*, London: Routledge.

Whewell, W. (1840) *The Philosophy of the Inductive Science*, Cambridge: John W. Parker.

29. Economics imperialism and a transdisciplinary perspective

Mario Cedrini and Joselle Dagnes

This chapter deals with the evolution from political economy to economics imperialism and the possibility of developing a transdisciplinary perspective in social sciences. At issue is the difficulty, not so much of reaching a consensual view of the *historical* evolution of economics in relation to the social sciences, but of defining the evolving traits of *today*'s economics. While retaining a neoclassical core within the mainstream, the discipline has become more diverse in recent decades. If its unity is now 'flexible', it is also because non-theoretical, empirical work tends to prevail as a driver of knowledge progress in its non-core elements.

The first section of the chapter focuses on the birth of economics as a separate discipline among social sciences, resulting from the disintegration of political economy. In the second section, we reflect upon the origins and development of so-called 'economics imperialism' – on why and how economics became an 'imperial' science, one that is 'aggressive in addressing central problems in a considerable number of neighboring social disciplines and without any invitations' (Stigler 1984: 311). The next two sections look at economics 'from without': presenting a short history of 'economic sociology' in the third section and discussing the origins and evolution of that sub-discipline in reaction to economics imperialism in the fourth section. The latter section also considers the transformative impact that economic sociology can have on economics by invading the latter's traditional territory. In the fifth section, we propose a more general perspective on how the emerging 'complexity' view of the relationships between social science disciplines (here exemplified by that between economics and economic sociology) may lead to the establishment of a transdisciplinary behavioural science.

FROM POLITICAL ECONOMY TO ECONOMICS

The pursuit of a 'unified' approach has been a recurring theme in political economy and is evident in the variety of approaches presented in earlier chapters of this book. Awareness of the intrinsic and inescapable connections between individuals acting in an economy, the society and the public dimension of government and public policies, creating a view of 'the economy as part of a polity' (Mayntz 2019) profoundly shaped mercantilist thought. Then, with the institutionalisation of the field, largely in opposition to mercantilism itself, a similarly broad view of economy and society was taken by Smith, Ricardo and other writers in the tradition we now call classical political economy. From this originated two broad schools: one (from Marx to Marxists) focused on production and therefore class relations, equality and inequality, while the other ended up with unpacking nineteenth-century political economy into a series of distinct research fields. A logic of division of labour (Hargreaves Heap 2020) can be invoked to explain the shift towards social science disciplines that are narrower in scope and methods (with distinct ontological and epistemic premises), but the evolution is far from linear. Because the epoch when Marshall (and others) built neoclassical economics broadly coincided with the disintegration of political economy into a variety of (institutionalised) social science academic disciplines, one may infer that the technical apparatus developed by Marshall is part of the story that leads from political economy to economics imperialism. Yet, it is also true that there is nothing linear in this evolution, and that economists are responsible for the traits that their discipline assumed over time.

As Backhouse and Tribe (2018: 251) observe in their recent *The History of Economics* textbook (written 'for students and teachers'), 'economists often talk as though the Robbins definition of economics is obvious, leaving the reader to infer that it was accepted immediately. However, the reality is that it took around 30 years for the definition to be widely accepted', and that 'even then its acceptance was never universal'. Robbins's definition of economics as the science of instrumental rationality – human behaviour being seen 'as a relationship between ends and scarce means which have alternative uses' – is the one that, for a variety of reasons, finally triumphed over other candidates. It replaced Marshall's definition of economics as the 'study of mankind in the ordinary business of life' which examines 'that part of individual and social action which is most closely connected with the attainment and with the use of the material requisites of wellbeing'. With Robbins, economists could now occupy themselves with *any* possible choice that involves a trade-off, but their analysis loses in depth what it gains in breadth.

Discussing one of the subsequent theoretical frontiers of the dismal science, namely the 'economics of happiness', Pasinetti argued that classical economists had opted for material wealth, not happiness, as the central subject of the new discipline of political economy: taking a narrow but 'coherent and unambiguously defined subject of investigation' (Pasinetti 2003: 338), adequate room being left for the analysis of a 'vast range of factors connected with wealth, including non-economic factors'. Economics after Robbins is another discipline, with different foundations. It is economics after the marginalist revolution *and* after the neoclassical approach had conquered (to expand indefinitely with Robbins) the core of a discipline that had heretofore had a certain extent of internal pluralism. It is economics after the neoclassical approach had triumphed over Veblen's institutionalism and eliminated the residuals of (Marshall's) connections with the Classics. Colander (2000) famously defined (the original) neoclassical economics as focusing on (out-of-time) resource allocation and on marginal trade-offs, with (some variants of) utilitarianism as its underlying philosophy, an assumption of far-sighted rationality for economic agents, and adopting methodological individualism and the method of general equilibrium.

The rationality–individualism–equilibrium nexus (Davis 2013) is the essence of *orthodox economics* (meaning the theoretical neoclassical core of the discipline, whereas the sociological concept of 'mainstream' economics refers to the ideas that the elite of the profession finds acceptable). It presupposes a world of atomised individuals with given preferences, interacting purely through prices, underpinned by complete contracts and full information. This is confirmed, in the negative, by what non-orthodox economists concentrate upon: the nexus (to continue with Davis 2013) of institutions, history and social structure. With given preferences, in fact, there is no need to consider socialisation, culture and history, while complete and costless contracting implies no role for ethics (and trust). The hypothesis of full information and rationality rules out any need for learning and for institutions to manage uncertainty, as well as ability to dupe, deceive, manipulate and frame. Fine and Milonakis (2009) summarise all this by claiming that three reductionisms characterise the first stage of the evolution from political economy to economics. First, the ('representative') individual suppresses collective agents; second, social factors disappear from the scene; and third, economic analysis becomes divorced from history. The remarkable results are that market relations turn out to be the new central subject, and that, contra the hypothesis of a division of labour between social disciplines, if political economy could be once considered as 'a sort of a unified social science' (Fine and Milonakis 2009: 2), economics could now let other disciplines deepen the understanding of the 'social' and the 'history' from which economics had decoupled.

ECONOMICS IMPERIALISM

The move from political economy to Robbins's analytical definition has been portrayed as a one-way road which is given another name halfway down, from reductionism to expansionism (Fine and Milonakis 2009). Formalism, ethical neutrality and concentration on theoretical rather than empirical work – and the idea that all human behaviours, after Robbins, are susceptible to economic analysis – are among the elements one can invoke to explain the expansion of economics into new territories in the post-war period and particularly at the end of the 1960s.

There is nothing obvious in the development of this pugilistic attitude adopted by economics as against other social science disciplines, nor in the creation of 'economic' approaches to (traditionally believed to be) other-than-economic dimensions of human life and activity – the 'rational choice' approach in sociology, the 'public choice' approach in political science, the 'formalist' strand in anthropology, and Gary Becker's perspective concerning the family, addiction, law and punishment. In general, there is nothing illegitimate in scientific expansionism: provided certain constraints and norms of scientific inquiry are met, the ambition to expand the domain of phenomena explained by a given theory – let alone to come to a unity of science – is respectable and meaningful (see Mäki 2009). However, more surprising is the fact that a de-socialised, ahistorical discipline such as neoclassical economics, which focuses on market relations and employs a purely technical apparatus (a 'method', as implied in Robbins's definition), could aspire to become the 'universal grammar of social science', in Hirshleifer's (1985: 53) famous words.

The division of labour itself might have played a role here. The marginalist revolution and the launch of economics as a distinct discipline had left the 'non-economic' to other social sciences – the 'social' to be understood as the non-market and the non-rational. For sure, a de-socialised, ahistorical discipline is relatively easy to apply to the study of issues and facts that do not belong to the traditional domain of the discipline itself. A fundamental benefit ensured by reducing rationality to utility maximisation is the ease with which it then becomes possible to analyse the real world in terms of its anomalies with respect to (the beauty and rigour of) such a benchmark. In other words, it is all too easy to consider non-market environments as 'market imperfections'.

Yet, there is more: increasing confidence on the part of economists about the discipline's generality (Davis 2013) is accompanied by 'growing "economism" in society ... and the increasing reliance of policy making on economics expertise' (Mäki 2020). If problems typically addressed by other social scientists – those 'broader-thinking sociologists, anthropologists, and perhaps psychologists', who 'may be better at identifying issues, but worse at providing answers' (Lazear 2000: 99) – can be treated as economic problems, after Robbins, then

Gary Becker can extend the application of the economic approach to any 'social' problem. This he did – from *The Economics of Discrimination* in 1957 to *A Treatise on the Family* in 1981 – in the belief that

> human behavior is not compartmentalised, sometimes based on maximising, sometimes not, sometimes motivated by stable preferences, sometimes by volatile ones, sometimes resulting in an optimal accumulation of information, sometimes not. Rather, all human behavior can be viewed as involving participants who maximise their utility from a stable set of preferences and accumulate an optimal amount of information and other inputs in a variety of markets. (Becker 1976)

Since social problems were becoming a major concern of policymakers (see Backhouse and Tribe 2017), the economic approach was used to figure out a 'scientific' perspective with which to look at non-market decision-making. The 'public choice' approach developed in political science, with Anthony Downs's *An Economic Theory of Democracy* (1957), James Buchanan and Gordon Tullock's *The Calculus of Consent* (1965), and Mancur Olson's *The Logic of Collective Action* (1965) as cornerstones. Then came the economic analysis of law, and specifically Posner's and Calabresi's contributions.

The peculiarity of economics imperialism with respect to the generality of expansionism is therefore that 'the new types of explanandum phenomena are located in territories that are occupied by disciplines other than economics' (Mäki 2009: 360). It is a fact that supporters of economics imperialism typically feel the necessity to provide reasons in favour of this presumed superiority. Sometimes, however, shocking theses on social issues 'in an economic perspective', like Becker's argument about the (presumed) desirability of polygamy or Philipson and Posner's reasoning on the (presumed) damages of HIV tests, *are not* supported by empirical evidence in their favour, as Guala (2006) remarks. Economics imperialists are thus declaring the irrelevance of non-economic factors, or ignoring the 'theories, traditions, achievements, and practices of the discipline whose domain is being entered' (Mäki 2020: 112), rather expressly suppressing 'values held important from a human or cultural point of view'. When 'discipline-intrusive', economics imperialism can even come to 'replace or reshape theories and methods, cultures and conventions, rules and standards, projects and practices held and pursued in … recipient disciplines' (Mäki 2020: 112), while 'bad' economics imperialism makes economics appear 'as being in possession of superior theories and methods, thereby excluding rival theories and approaches from consideration' (Mäki 2009: 360).

ECONOMICS 'FROM WITHOUT': A SHORT HISTORY OF ECONOMIC SOCIOLOGY

While a final judgement on its precise nature has still to be reached, we believe that the discipline's imperialism presents an obstacle to the development of a non-reductionist perspective on those intrinsically complex human institutions 'founded on the unity of individual and society, freedom and obligation, self-interest and concern for others' (Hart 2007: 9). When a narrowly economic approach is taken, it is as if the multiple dimensions that permeate social interactions could be separated and human behaviour reduced to one and one only of such dimensions.

Paradoxically, given that the author of the *Theory of Moral Sentiments* was evidently well aware of the complexity of human nature, Adam Smith may have played a role in facilitating the advent of economics imperialism. At the dawn of political economy, to replace Hobbes's solution to the 'war of all against all' with the intrinsic rationality of the market system, Smith abuses the conjectural method. Instead of using the ethnographic sources that were available to him, Smith founded political economy, in the *Wealth of Nations*, on a sort of 'bartering savage' stereotype. Having portrayed primitive societies as the opposite of civilised societies, Smith was compelled by the fact that such societies are also the initial stage in human history, and therefore must contain modern societies *in fieri* (population growth and division of labour are key factors in the process), to postulate that exchange is natural. Market exchange (fully developed in modern societies) comes to be regarded as the last stage of this evolving (presumed) natural disposition (see Marchionatti and Cedrini 2017; Cedrini et al. 2020). Archaic societies are thus conjecturally reconstructed from the standpoint of civilised societies. In contrast, non-economists such as Marcel Mauss (in *The Gift*) will adopt a reverse logic and study the historical working of archaic societies with an emphasis on the possibility of a non-linear path towards modern market societies. A sort of original sin might therefore be invoked to explain the not-so-cooperative attitude of economics as a discipline within the milieu of social sciences and, in part at least, for the de-socialising of economics.

There are several reasons for focusing on economic sociology to highlight further possible lines of evolution in the relationships between political economy, economics, and a future transdisciplinary social science. Some of the most intriguing reflections on today's economics as a discipline have origins in sociology. Marion Fourcade narrates that,

> for a while in the 1980s and 1990s, every economic sociology article, on every topic, ran seething like this: it began by ritualistically presenting the view from economics, and then proceeded to pull it to pieces by showing that 'it is, in fact, much more complicated' than the play of interests and incentives. (Fourcade 2018: 1)

But now the situation has changed: first, sociologists 'started to free themselves from their inferiority complex and became more confident in their own contribution to the analysis of economic processes (some of which, like network analysis, has influenced recent economic research); second, they turned their analytic lens toward economics itself. They started to investigate the sources of the economists' authority and its complicated relationship to democratic politics; building on the contributions of historians of economics, they probed the discipline's development over time and its variability across nations, shattering the myth of a universal science; and they strove to make sense of what the expansion of economic technique means for the way we live our lives' (Fourcade 2018).

It has been argued that, in general, today's renaissance of political economy appears as 'a counter-movement to the progressive separation between the disciplines called economics, political science, and sociology' (Mayntz 2019: 5). Economic sociology provides a useful viewpoint on this, exactly because it originates as the attempt to elaborate a 'sociological perspective applied to economic phenomena' (Smelser and Swedberg 2010: 3). Its historical origins, between the end of the nineteenth century and the beginning of the twentieth century, largely correspond to the first phase of development of sociology *tout court*. In fact, many classical sociologists who we now consider founders of the discipline contributed to the analysis of the historically founded relationships between the economy and the society (e.g. Weber's study on the origins and transformations of modern Western capitalism), filling a space that was perceived as left vacant by neoclassical economics (conversely focusing on the general rules of efficient allocation of resources) (Trigilia 2002). It was during the post-war period that general sociology and economic sociology came to occupy their territories. The former acquired recognition from the formulation of highly generalised theories, such as Parsons's structural-functionalism (in which, despite references to classical thought, both relevance of actors and their motivations, à la Weber, are de facto abandoned). The latter, on the contrary, encountered greater difficulties, having to deal directly with the increasingly hegemonic orthodox economic approach (Swedberg 1990).

Thus, economic sociology finds itself squeezed, so to speak, between two disciplinary orientations that tend to compress its vital space. On the one hand, general sociologists' search for universal rules for the functioning of society, which evidently does not favour investigations about the reciprocal influences of the social and economic contexts. On the other hand, mainstream economists develop formalised models on the functioning of the market and provide policy suggestions which appear to have scientific bases. This latter aspect greatly contributed to the establishment of the primacy of economics over other social sciences, which are contrariwise unable to produce general 'laws' and to significantly influence public policies through them (Smelser and Swedberg 2010). Economic sociology felt thus compelled to rethink its role, and as a consequence had to give up the ambition to concentrate its work on advanced countries. It therefore occupied the residual spaces of institutional analysis which economists had left uncovered, relaunching its capacity to focus on the specific interrelations between economic and social action in other contexts. The 'sociology of development' then developed, with its focus on the modernisation of economically backward areas and comparative analysis of the role of political institutions in such processes (Kiely 2014). In this context, the approach of economic sociology came, somewhat paradoxically, close to that of political economy, which contributes considerably to defining hypotheses and analytical tools.

In sum, the central part of the twentieth century saw economic sociology facing serious difficulties in establishing itself as an autonomous discipline. Such difficulties persisted until the beginning of the 1970s, when a generalised condition of crisis in advanced economies both at the macro level – with the decline of the Keynesian welfare state and the impossibility of keeping the inflation rate at sustainable levels – and at the micro level – with the loss of hegemony of the Fordist production model – contributed to raise interest in the interrelationships between socio-political institutions, on one side, and institutions and forms of economic organisation on the other (Smelser and Swedberg 2010).

These circumstances literally produced new areas of investigation for economic sociologists. The international crisis that emerged in the 1970s disconfirmed the expectation that the economy could grow relentlessly while ensuring the desired levels of social cohesion. This changed scenario encouraged non-economists to investigate the causes and possible solutions to the crisis, paying renewed attention to the role of institutional factors and their variety in different national contexts. Thanks also to competencies acquired in analysing modernisation in developing countries, the sub-discipline of economic sociology appeared to be particularly well equipped, from an analytical point of view, to accomplish such new tasks (Hirsch and Goldthorpe 1978). An approach called New Comparative Political Economy thus developed: a 'macro' research perspective fundamentally relying on the comparison between different cases, through which it can bring out the peculiarities of different national models – in terms, for example, of social protection, interest representation and market regulation – as well as the role played by political-institutional factors (Lange and Regini 1990).

At the same time, the crisis of Fordism prompted a series of studies on the relationship between institutional factors and production models. A 'micro' research perspective was thus created, looking at new organisational paradigms centred on flexibility and innovation. From a theoretical point of view, these studies had strong continuity with the analysis of the forms of productive organisation carried out by institutional economics (Williamson 1988). In general, however, economic sociology started establishing relationships with non-neoclassical approaches in economics. A research programme then emerged within economic sociology during the 1970s and 1980s, exploring the plurality of organisational forms – and, more generally, of economic processes – outside a 'pursuing-efficiency' framework (albeit in conditions of bounded rationality à la Williamson). Rather, it concentrated on the autonomous role of cognitive, cultural, political-institutional and relational elements in shaping economic action (Trigilia 2002).

Dissatisfaction with the emphasis placed by 'new' institutional economics on institutions as seeking an 'efficient solution' to market failures is at the basis of so-called New Economic Sociology (or 'structural' approach), which originates from pioneering contributions by Mark Granovetter. Granovetter proposes a theory of economic action that steers away from both the hyper-socialised conception of agents in economics, and the functionalist hyper-socialised vision typical of the sociological field. Re-elaborating Karl Polanyi's concept of embeddedness, Granovetter highlights the social roots of economic action and focuses on the positioning of actors within social networks. In other words, the structural dimension of relationships – later referred to as 'social capital', although with various meanings – comes to define the system of constraints and opportunities that actors confront in the pursuit of their own interests (Granovetter 1985, 2017). Another approach, known as New Institutionalism in Sociology, further articulates the concept of embeddedness in relation to the processes of creation and reproduction of institutions, thereby coming to elaborate a multidimensional theory of action. The relational dimension is supported by cognitive, cultural and politico-institutional factors. The cognitive element recognises the existence of implicit interpretative schemes orienting individual and collective behaviour; the cultural element recognises the sharing, in spatially and socially bounded contexts, of such schemes; and politico-institutional factors are the regulatory and power dimension. Thus, the social embeddedness of action is accompanied by cultural embeddedness, which constitutes an autonomous factor of influence (Powell and DiMaggio 1991).

While marked by significant differences, these three approaches – New Comparative Political Economy, New Economic Sociology, and Sociological New Institutionalism – also exhibit remarkable points of convergence, which helps to explain why economic sociology takes its distance from economics. Attention devoted to contextual factors – at macro, meso and/or micro levels – implies abandoning the ambitions to generalisation that are typical of neoclassical economics, instead going towards the development of models of more limited scope, closer to Merton's middle-range theories (Trigilia 2002). The 'risk' of overlapping with economics, enhanced by the fading away of disciplines' (recent) specificities as concerns their objects of study, is thus avoided, provisionally at least, by the different capacity for generalisation exhibited by the two disciplines. By the way, this specific diversity inevitably favours economics in the public arena to the detriment of economic sociology (Hirsch et al. 1987).

The institutionalisation of economic sociology as it is known today – hence the use of the *contemporary economic sociology* label – has proven to be, from the very beginning, a process that has been strongly plural, with a variety of complementary, rather than alternative, approaches. This trend seems even more pronounced in recent years and has become the object of explicit reflection within the discipline. Increasing attention is devoted to the 'attempt to favor interaction between approaches that interpret the regulation of the economy in institutional terms (Political Economy and New Institutionalism), and those that place greater emphasis on the role of the social structure (New Economic Sociology)' (Barbera and Negri 2008: 141, our translation). That the concepts and tools of each approach pertain to different analytical levels can perhaps favour integration between them, supporting a convergence effort towards common local analysis models. Because contemporary economic sociology has blurred internal boundaries, it is not uncommon for scholars strongly rooted in one of the three above-mentioned approaches to make use of tools from other analytic traditions in their empirical research. The external boundaries of the discipline show greater rigidity, particularly those that separate economic sociology from economics. The hegemony of the latter in the scientific and public sphere – its 'superiority' (Fourcade et al. 2015) – is often perceived as a threat by economic sociologists (Smelser and Swedberg 2010).

NEW ECONOMICS IMPERIALISM, REVERSE IMPERIALISMS AND THE POSSIBILITY OF COOPERATION

What is the relevance of this phase of 'economics from without', represented by the advent of economic sociology, in the more general story of the relationships between economics and other social science disciplines, following the disintegration of political economy? Let's come back to economics imperialism à la Becker. Fine and Milonakis (2009) consider that the 1982 decision of the Swedish central bank to award its 'Nobel Prize' in economics to the arch economics imperialist Gary Becker was an exception to a generally more cautious attitude that had prevailed, even among (other) economics imperialists, up to the 1980s, to considering non-economic behaviour as reducible to such a narrow economic rationality. Even an 'old' imperialist like Stigler (1984: 309) thought that 'there remains a large class of social phenomena to which it is not apparent that presently available economic analysis can contribute significantly'. Limits were clearly perceived to the extent to which the 'social' (intended as the 'non-rational' and therefore 'non-economic') could be reduced to the individual and 'as if' market relations.

Then came a second phase in the history of economics imperialism, Fine and Milonakis (2009) argue, resulting from the development of the information-theoretic approach and new institutional economics. Research by Joseph Stiglitz and George Akerlof, among others, enabled economics to address the social and reintroduce the historical into the analysis (though in very limited forms). Economics could now 'appear more attractive to other social sciences', mainly because social entities, that is 'economic and social structures, institutions, customs, habits, culture, and apparently non-rational behavior, are explained as the rational, possibly collective, sometimes strategic, and often putatively path-dependent, responses to market imperfections'. They 'emerge as a result of, and a response to, the existence of market imperfections' (Fine and Milonakis 2009: 9).

As an illustration, consider Peter G. Klein's definition of the approach of new institutional economics (NIE) as an interdisciplinary enterprise combining economics, law, organisation theory, political science, sociology and anthropology to understand the institutions of social, political and commercial life. It borrows liberally from various social-science disciplines, but its primary language is economics. Its goal is to explain what institutions are, how they arise, what purposes they serve, how they change and how – if at all – they should be reformed. (Klein 2000: 456)

'New' economic sociology would thus be a reaction to the 'new' economics imperialism of 'new' institutional economics. As Fine and Milonakis (2009) maintain, the 'new' fields 'within and around economics' testify the extension of economics to previously neglected topics. But the case of economic sociology shows the possibility of exploring another path, one related to so-called 'reverse imperialisms' of other sciences, like psychology, that have evidently exerted a significant influence on economics since the 1980s.

A decisive role in shaping the discipline of economic sociology was played by defining 'who the enemy was', says Fligstein (2015: 305). 'That was easy: neoclassical economics. But the opposition to neoclassicism was produced by a set of criticisms, some of which originated in moral theory, some of which came from political economy, and others which had their origin in organisational theory. All of these perspectives shared the view that neoclassicism was wrong because it was wrong empirically, morally defective, and damaging when used to create a set of social policies. The goal of all the builders of organisational structures for economic sociology was to unite these critiques and to produce a broad tent under which scholars from many sub-fields in sociology and from other related disciplines in political science, business studies, law, public policy, and to some degree heterodox economics, could come together' (Fligstein 2015: 305). The ultimate ambition behind the establishment of economic sociology as discipline was to bring together 'scholars with varying research programs that were interested in pursuing economic issues and opposing the hegemony of economics as a discipline over our understanding of those issues' (Fligstein 2015: 305).

As Panther (2019) maintains, economics and sociology have developed as a 'pair tied to each other by othering each other'. In this view, 'old' economics imperialism broke the pact between the two disciplines. One might be induced to believe that the 'new' economics imperialism stemming from the information-theoretic approach and new institutional economics could have helped sociologists and economists fruitfully engage in conversation, despite the differences that separate these new approaches from 'new economic sociology'. Panther notes that, notwithstanding overlapping of topics and potential complementarities, sociology and economics developed the two fields, respectively, of economic sociology and social economics independently. The two disciplines thus end up by competing on very similar fields (if not the same) but, while mainstream economics can be said to address social phenomena using the method of economics, economic sociology can be said to investigate economic phenomena using the method of sociology. Concurrently, as Zafirowski (2016: 56) remarks: 'much of contemporary economics undergoes a certain trend toward economic sociology or socio-economics, in virtue of increasingly acknowledging and incorporating various sociological components and influences'. The evidence he finds in support of this claim includes the revival of economic sociology, the renewal of the economic sociology of the market, the return of socio-economic institutionalism, and the rediscovery of cultural factors in the economy and markets. Moreover, there would be sociological influences in contemporary economics that make it appear 'increasingly congruent with modern economic sociology rather than with sociological rational choice theory'. Thus, 'the renewal of economic sociology both within contemporary economics and sociology provides the fertile ground for interdisciplinary collaboration between economists and sociologists today' (Zafirowski 2016: 56).

In discussing economic sociology, Fine and Milonakis highlight two features. First, the naïvety wherewith Granovetter employed the term 'embeddedness' in launching the (potential) revolution of economic sociology, which is then considered 'symbolic of the extent to which the fledging new economic sociology discarded big questions and big theory' (2009: 89). Second, the weak structure of the new economic sociology, a reflection of economics and sociology 'othering' strategies. 'Inevitably', they argue, 'contributions tend to fall upon one or the other side of the disciplinary divide': economic sociology provides 'a broad umbrella in which both sociology and economics can contribute, adding elements from one another's frameworks or critically deploying their absence' (Fine and Milonakis 2009: 89; see also Zelizer 2007).

As Orléan (2005: pt. III) puts it, the development of new economic sociology as counterpart to economics imperialism allowed the new field 'to present itself as a competitor to economic theory on economic theory's own territory'. Remarkably, economics had by then become a 'contestable' field, but the 'aggression' – a reaction to economics imperialism – sees virtually all approaches in sociology that are notoriously critical of orthodox economics engaged in contributing under the 'broad umbrella' called 'economic sociology'. This also means that: 'the question of the unity of the social sciences under the authority of a general sociology, a unity defended in various forms by Durkheim, Pareto, Schumpeter, Veblen, and Weber, has completely disappeared from the contemporary theoretical agenda'. 'Granovetter never raises it', Orléan adds, and rather rejects the idea of reducing one of the two fields to the other one. After all, the end of the 'Pax Parsonia' (the original division of labour between economics and sociology) could result in two effects, as Zelizer (1988) made clear: it could induce economic sociologists to reinforce the boundaries separating it from economics for fear of field invasions, but it could also allow the opening of new spaces for making the two parent disciplines interact.

According to Fligstein (2015: 314), Granovetter would deserve the Nobel Prize in economics. 'We would all of sudden move from a troubled discipline (sociology) to a legitimate approach to understanding how the economy and society are connected', he states. Yet more specifically: 'Granovetter's contribution has pushed not just us, but also the economics profession to reconsider the role of social relationships in market structures'. In other terms, Granovetter had a transformative impact on the economics discipline, one that is admittedly independently from the ambition to 'reduce' economics to sociology, or to a 'grand social science' like political economy. The focus on economics sociology may thus help understand the recent evolution of economics as discipline. Or, better, the development of 'new economic sociology' is (*mutatis mutandis*) part of the more general story of economics as discipline.

THE (COMPLEX) ROAD TO A TRANSDISCIPLINARY SOCIAL SCIENCE

The economist Ronald Coase once maintained that economists will likely study other social systems 'not with the aim of contributing to law or political science, but because it is necessary if they are to understand the economic system itself' (Coase 1978: 210). This is where we are now. The current phase in the history of economics as a discipline has been aptly described as one of 'mainstream pluralism' (Davis 2006): mainstream economics is populated by a variety of research programmes (behavioural game theory, experimental economics, evolutionary economics, happiness economics, complexity economics, behavioural economics, and so on). These significantly deviate from the neoclassical core, are pursued by different, often separate communities of researchers, and have their origins outside economics (game theory came from mathematics, its behavioural version from biology; experimental economics from physical and natural sciences, evolutionary economics from Darwinian biology, happiness economics from ethics, complexity economics from computer science, behavioural economics from psychology, etc.: see Davis 2006; Cedrini and Fontana 2018). Other sciences, sometimes in cooperation with heterodox economics, have established colonies in the discipline in the form of research programmes whose core ideas, once adequately domesticated, have been authorised to enter the realm of mainstream economics.

It can be safely argued that mainstream economics is no longer all neoclassical, as Colander, Holt and Rosser (2004: 496) maintain – their examples include: 'evolutionary game theory is redefining how institutions are integrated into the analysis; ecological economics is redefining how nature and the economy are viewed as interrelating; psychological economics is redefining how rationality is treated; econometric work dealing with the limitations of classical statistics is redefining how economists think of empirical proof; complexity theory is offering a way of redefining how we conceive of general equilibrium; computer simulations are offering a way of redefining models and how they are used; experimental economics is changing the way economists think about empirical work'.

Mainstream pluralism is, more correctly, a plurality. It would only be truly 'pluralist' if it could exhibit some reasons in favour of the *desirability* of this state of affairs (see Mäki 1997): but it cannot, internally at least. If the term pluralism is used, therefore, it is mainly because it helps see things in perspective, and because there are 'pragmatic reasons supporting the plurality of approaches. As Davis (2007: 50) argues: 'the object of economics, the economy, is only becoming increasingly complex with a growing multitude of dimensions and aspects'. 'Not only', he continues, 'are new approaches to explaining different previously unrecognised aspects of the economy continually arising, but no single approach seems any longer to be sufficiently comprehensive to explain the economy in its diverse dimensions and aspects'. Another factor that plays a role here is specialisation in economics research. Specialisation has become an obliged individual response to the growing difficulty experienced in navigating an increasingly sophisticated economic theory, as well as the strategy to be implemented in order to reach the research frontier without being victim of the 'burden of knowledge' (Cedrini and Fontana 2018).

Economics would have thus become an 'immature' science, that is, a discipline whose once recognisable core, the neoclassical orthodoxy, is now one only of many research programmes, none of which can safely be omitted when trying to define the discipline itself. As Rodrik (2015) has recently remarked, 'economics is a collection of models that admits a wide variety of possibilities, rather than a set of prepackaged conclusions'. Standard accounts 'tend to miss the diversity that exists within the profession, and the many ideas that are being tried out'. 'One can be part of the mainstream and yet not necessarily hold "orthodox" ideas', he correctly concludes. These factors also explain the increase in inter-disciplinary relations across sciences, which evidently complicate matters – 'what economics is as a discipline can be investigated in terms of its relations to other disciplines since what makes it relatively distinct and different from other disciplines helps define its scope and nature'. But this means that 'disciplines cannot be defined in a purely internal manner without reference to other related disciplines' (Davis 2019: 410).

Based on the trading nation metaphor, that is, conceiving social science disciplines as nations in a global environment, Ambrosino, Cedrini and Davis (2021) show that this overall picture condemns the idea of a unified (social) science to remain only an ideal. They use Rodrik's well-known world political trilemma, whereby democracy, national sovereignty and global economic integration are mutually incompatible. In this case, the trilemma is self-determination of science, disciplines and disciplinary integration. Unity of social science as an ideal can be achieved either by bypassing disciplines – which would require (the utopia of) a radically different institutional environment for conducting scientific research – or by imposing frameworks for unification that use scientific imperialism as a method to suppress undesired developments (that is, those incompatible with the unified social science) in specific disciplines.

It is to be noted that economics imperialism is not without unintended consequences as regards inter-disciplinary relations. Consider Lazear's (2000) famous argument about the superiority of the economic approach. Lazear argued that 'by almost any market test, economics is the premier social science', because of its 'rigour, relevance, and generality'. In his words: 'our discipline has a rigorous language that allows complicated concepts to be written in relatively simple, abstract terms. The language permits economists to strip away complexity. Complexity may add to the richness of description, but it also prevents the analyst from seeing what is essential.' The most important market test usually exhibited by supporters of economics imperialism is the 'strong export surplus economics maintains in its trade in ideas and methods with the other social sciences' (Demsetz 1997: 1). The problem is that Lazear only considers trade flows, ignoring the possible effects on other disciplines of accompanying capital flows – here 'disciplinary capital' flows – that are required to compensate trade imbalances. Such disciplinary capital is what causes trade in ideas between disciplines to have a transformative impact on one another. Supporters of economics imperialism implicitly propose a vision of science wherein disciplines are autonomous one from another: they are somehow compelled to neglect capital flows, because otherwise they would have to admit that, by locating 'disciplinary capital' of their own within economics, psychology and other 'reverse imperialist' disciplines do have a transformative impact on economics itself (Ambrosino et al. 2020).

There is a third, non-reductionist way of conceiving the integration of social sciences, and thereby of discussing the possible re-creation of a sort of grand social science like political economy. It is a 'complexity' approach that combines disciplines and self-determination of science; and favours a horizontal pattern of integration. Disciplines tend to grow by deepening their specialisations, also because of the rising transaction costs of trespassing disciplinary boundaries. The same applies within disciplines, however, and internal specialisation favours exchange at the periphery with other disciplines. Foreign ideas can be 'domesticated' in the attempt to serve disciplinary goals, and in some cases, such imports have transformative effects on the importing discipline. This occurs especially when such exchanges are conducive to the establishment of new research programmes at the frontier. These tend to blur the boundaries between the disciplines, not least because they attract specialists also from the exporting disciplines. But then, cross-disciplinary ventures resulting from different disciplines drawing on one another to serve independent goals can finally develop into transdisciplinary research programmes.

The case of new economics sociology is illustrative and worthy of exploration because of the peculiar features it exhibits in relation to the line of reasoning proposed here. In general, there is nothing truly intentional in the logic of integration it seems destined to promote. At the origins of the economic sociology approach, we find the attempt to reduce, in effect, the impact of the separation of economics from political economy, and the ambition to investigate economic phenomena by means of a sociological perspective. Then, after a period of self-confinement into a political economy approach applied to the developmental issue and a multidimensional comeback during the decade of Western crisis, the attempt arose to distance itself from the new imperialism of the dismal science which reduces the non-economic to market imperfections. A whole series of 'otherings' – although not necessarily or not always with claims of superiority attached – actively encouraged continuous cross-disciplinary borrowings of the kind which, in a complexity vision of knowledge development, are the key drivers of integration.

Seen in this light, the development of a transdisciplinary perspective in social sciences appears less improbable. The main obstacle that prevents economics from participating in this venture is the discipline's core–periphery structure, which reflects the divide between the orthodox core and the heterodox periphery (Davis 2019). The enlargement of mainstream economics through increased internal variety and openness to external influences occurs at the expenses of the core. This suggests the need for a more pragmatic approach than those that have inspired some recent attempts (e.g. Gintis 2007; Colander et al. 2010; for a discussion, see Ambrosino et al. 2021) at elaborating theoretical frameworks for unifying behavioural sciences. At a time of unprecedented plurality in mainstream economics, it would be useful to give more consideration to the possibility of a 'complexity' path towards the renaissance of political economy.

REFERENCES

Ambrosino, A., Cedrini, M. and Davis, J.B. (2020) 'Economics Imperialism and Economic Imperialism: Two Sides of the Same Coin', mimeo.

Ambrosino, A., Cedrini, M. and Davis, J.B. (2021) 'The Unity of Science and the Disunity of Economics', *Cambridge Journal of Economics*, **45** (4), pp. 631–54.

Backhouse, R. and Tribe, K. (2017) *The History of Economics: A Course for Students and Teachers*, Newcastle upon Tyne: Agenda Publishing.

Barbera, F. and Negri, N. (2008) *Mercati, Reti Sociali, Istituzioni*, Bologna: Il Mulino.

Becker, G.S. (1957) *The Economics of Discrimination*, Chicago, IL: University of Chicago Press.

Becker, G.S. (1976) *The Economic Approach to Human Behavior*, Chicago, IL: University of Chicago Press.

Becker, G.S. (1981) *A Treatise on the Family*, Cambridge, MA: Harvard University Press.

Buchanan, J.M. and Tullock, G. (1965) *The Calculus of Consent: Logical Foundations of Constitutional Democracy*, Ann Arbor: University of Michigan Press.

Cedrini, M.A., Ambrosino, A., Marchionatti, R. and Caillé, A. (2020) 'Mauss's *The Gift*, or the Necessity of an Institutional Perspective in Economics', *Journal of Institutional Economics*, **16** (5), pp. 687–701.

Cedrini, M. and Fontana, M. (2018) 'Just Another Niche in the Wall? How Specialization Is Changing the Face of Mainstream Economics', *Cambridge Journal of Economics*, **42** (2), pp. 427–51.

Coase, R. (1978) 'Economics and Contiguous Disciplines', *Journal of Legal Studies*, **7** (2), pp. 201–11.

Colander, D. (2000) 'The Death of Neoclassical Economics', *Journal of the History of Economic Thought*, **22** (2), pp. 127–43.

Colander, D., Holt, R. and Rosser, Jr, B. (2004) 'The Changing Face of Mainstream Economics', *Review of Political Economy*, **16** (4), pp. 485–99.

Colander, D., Kupers, R., Lux, T. and Rothschild, C. (2010) 'Reintegrating the Social Sciences: The Dahlem Group', Middlebury College Economics, Discussion Paper No. 10–33.

Davis, J.B. (2006) 'The Turn in Economics: Neoclassical Dominance to Mainstream Pluralism?', *Journal of Institutional Economics*, **2** (1), pp. 1–20.

Davis, J.B. (2007) 'Why Is Economics Not Yet a Pluralistic Science?' *Post-Autistic Economics Review*, **43**, pp. 42–51.

Davis, J.B. (2013) 'Mäki on Economics Imperialism', in Lehtinen, A., Kuorikoski, J. and Ylikoski, P. (eds), *Economics for Real: Uskali Mäki and the Place of Truth in Economics*, London and New York: Routledge, pp. 217–34.

Davis, J.B. (2019) 'Economics and Economic Methodology in a Core-periphery Economic World', *Brazilian Journal of Political Economy*, **39** (3), pp. 408–26.

Demsetz, H. (1997) 'The Primacy of Economics: An Explanation of the Comparative Success of Economics in the Social Sciences', *Economic Inquiry*, **35** (1), pp. 1–11.

Downs, A. (1957) *An Economic Theory of Democracy*, New York: Harper and Brothers.

Fine, B. and Milonakis, D. (2009). *From Economics Imperialism to Freakonomics: The Shifting Boundaries between Economics and Other Social Sciences*, London and New York: Routledge.

Fligstein, N. (2015) 'What Kind of Re-Imagining Does Economic Sociology Need?', in Aspers, P. and Dodd, N. (eds), *Re-imagining Economic Sociology*, Oxford: Oxford University Press, pp. 301–16.

Fourcade, M. (2018) 'Economics: The View from Below', *Swiss Journal of Economics and Statistics*, **154** (5), pp. 1–9.

Fourcade, M., Ollion, E. and Algan, Y. (2015) 'The Superiority of Economists', *Journal of Economic Perspectives*, **29** (1), pp. 89–114.

Gintis, H. (2007) 'A Framework for the Unification of the Behavioral Sciences', *Behavioral and Brain Sciences*, **30** (1), pp. 1–61.

Granovetter, M. (1985) 'Economic Action and Social Structure: The Problem of Embeddedness', *American Journal of Sociology*, **91** (3), pp. 481–510.

Granovetter, M. (2017) *Society and Economy*, Cambridge, MA: Harvard University Press.

Guala, F. (2006), *Filosofia dell'economia: Modelli, causalità, previsione*, Bologna: Il Mulino.

Hargreaves Heap, S.P. (2020), 'Two Accounts of the Relation between Political Economy and Economics (and Why It Matters Which Account Is Better)', *Social Philosophy & Policy*, **37** (1), pp. 103–17.

Hart, K. (2007) 'Marcel Mauss: "In Pursuit of the Whole": A Review Essay', *Comparative Studies in Society and History*, **49** (2), pp. 473–85.

Hirsch, F. and Goldthorpe, J. (1978) *The Political Economy of Inflation*, London: Martin Robertson.

Hirsch, P., Michaels, S. and Friedman, R. (1987) '"Dirty Hands" versus "Clean Models": Is Sociology in Danger of Being Seduced by Economics?', *Theory and Society*, **16** (3), pp. 317–36.

Hirshleifer, J. (1985) 'The Expanding Domain of Economics', *The American Economic Review*, **75** (6), pp. 53–68.

Kiely, R. (2014) *The Sociology of Development: The Impasse and Beyond*, London: Routledge.

Klein, P.G. (2000) 'New Institutional Economics', accessed 5.9.2021 at: http://dx.doi.org/10.2139/ssrn .115811.

Lange P. and Regini M. (1990) *State, Market and Social Regulation*, Cambridge: Cambridge University Press.

Lazear, E.P. (2000) 'Economic Imperialism', *The Quarterly Journal of Economics*, **115** (1), pp. 99–146.

Mäki, U. (1997) 'The One World and the Many Theories', in Salanti, A. and Screpanti, E. (eds), *Pluralism in Economics: New Perspectives in History and Methodology*, Aldershot: Edward Elgar Publishing, pp. 37–47.

Mäki, U. (2009) 'Economics Imperialism: Concept and Constraints', *Philosophy of the Social Sciences*, **39** (3), pp. 351–80.

Mäki, U. (2020) 'Notes on Economics Imperialism and Norms of Scientific Inquiry', *Revue de Philosophie Economique*, **21** (1), pp. 95–127.

Marchionatti, R. and Cedrini, M. (2017) *Economics as Social Science: Economics Imperialism and the Challenge of Interdisciplinarity*, London and New York: Routledge.

Mayntz, R. (2019) 'Changing Perspectives in Political Economy', MPIfG Discussion Paper No. 19/6, Max Planck Institute for the Study of Societies: Cologne, accessed 5.9.2021 at: https://www.econstor .eu/bitstream/10419/201550/1/1670275116.pdf.

Olson, M. (1965) *The Logic of Collective Action: Public Goods and the Theory of Groups*, Cambridge, MA: Harvard University Press.

Orléan, A. (2005) 'Economic Sociology and the Question of the Unity of the Social Sciences', *L'Année Sociologique*, **55** (2), pp. 279–305.

Panther, S. (2019) 'What Can Teaching Critical Pluralist Economics Gain from "De-othering" Sociology?', in Decker, S., Elsner, W. and Flechtner, S. (eds), *Principles and Pluralist Approaches in Teaching Economics: Towards a Transformative Science*, London: Routledge, pp. 52–64.

Pasinetti, L. (2005) 'Paradoxes of Happiness in Economics', in Bruni, L. and Porta, P. L. (eds), *Economics and Happiness: Framing the Analysis*, Oxford: Oxford University Press, pp. 336–44.

Powell, W. and DiMaggio, P.J. (eds) (1991) *The New Institutionalism in Organizational Analysis*, Chicago, IL: University of Chicago Press.

Rodrik, D. (2015) *Economics Rules: The Rights and Wrongs of the Dismal Science*, New York: W.W. Norton and Company.

Smelser, N.J. and Swedberg R. (eds) (2010) *The Handbook of Economic Sociology*, Princeton, NJ: Princeton University Press.

Stigler, G.J. (1984) 'Economics: The Imperial Science?', *The Scandinavian Journal of Economics*, **86** (3), pp. 301–13.

Swedberg, R. (1990) *Economics and Sociology*, Princeton, NJ: Princeton University Press.

Trigilia, C. (2002) *Economic Sociology: State, Market, and Society in Modern Capitalism*, Oxford: Blackwell.

Williamson, O.E. (1988) 'Economics and Sociology of Organizations: Promoting a Dialogue', in Farkas, G. and England, P. (eds), *Industries, Firms, and Jobs: Sociological and Economic Approaches*, New York: Plenum Press, pp. 159–86.

Zafirovski, M. (2016) 'Toward Economic Sociology/Socio-economics? Sociological Components in Contemporary Economics and Implications for Sociology', *The American Sociologist*, **47** (1), pp. 56–80.

Zelizer V.A. (1988) 'Beyond the Polemics on the Market: Establishing a Theoretical and Empirical Agenda', *Sociological Forum*, **3** (4), pp. 614–34.

Zelizer, V.A. (2007) 'Pasts and Futures of Economic Sociology', *American Behavioral Scientist*, **50** (8), pp. 1056–69.

30. Approaches to, and measures of, progress

Pratistha Joshi Rajkarnikar

Conventional economic assumptions about growth and societal well-being have been subjected to strong challenges. An obvious target is the widespread presumption that a higher gross domestic product is always desirable, irrespective of *what* is being produced, *how* it is produced and *to whom* it is distributed. To challenge that presumption, however, we need clarity about alternative concepts and better measures for understanding what constitutes progress. This chapter looks at various possibilities and discusses their scope, strengths and limitations. These considerations are pertinent not only to the critique of mainstream economics but also to the development of alternative heterodox perspectives.

The foundational idea that guides the analysis and arguments here is that the purpose of economic activity is to promote human well-being (Ackerman et al. 2013; Goodwin et al. 2019: ch. 1). Here, the definition of well-being is based on the 'capabilities' approach developed by Amartya Sen and extended by Martha Nussbaum and others (Nussbaum 2000; Alexander 2008; Robeyns [2011] 2016). Sen defines development as the process of expanding human freedom, so that people have the ability to be and to do things that they have reason to value. This expansion in human freedom involves increasing human capabilities by enlarging the set of choices available to each individual to enable them to live the life of their choice (Sen 1999: 18). The capabilities approach focuses on human 'functionings' (people's ability to be and to do things) as being central to human life, instead of emphasising 'what resources people have' or 'how satisfied they are with their lives' (Nussbaum 2000: 230). Aspects that are important to human well-being include the ability to live a long, healthy and happy life, to acquire knowledge, to have political liberties, and to live in a society that is socially stable and environmentally sustainable. Accordingly, consideration of what should be included in evaluating social and economic progress needs to focus on these aspects that, by and large, improve the quality of life.

Having defined social and economic progress in these broad terms, we need to consider how to measure progress when more specific metrics are necessary. One approach is to assign monetary values to the various components of well-being and add them up. This approach, however, requires estimating monetary values for things that do not usually have a price tag attached. It also raises the question of whether we should combine the different aspects, such as health, education, environmental quality, life satisfaction and income levels, into a single index or keep them separate using a 'dashboard' approach. The latter may be preferred because multiple indicators do not always move in the same direction, making the overall change in well-being hard to determine.

This chapter considers these issues in relation to various alternative indicators of progress. It begins by discussing the standard measures of economic well-being that focus almost exclusively on income growth. Attention is then given to alternative indicators that focus on the broader aspects of, and influences on, well-being, showing how these have been used in international comparative studies. Moving towards an overall assessment of the options, the recommendations of the Commission on the Measurement of Economic Performance and

Social Progress are considered; and the final section presents concluding remarks on the possibilities for further progress.

STANDARD MEASURES OF ECONOMIC WELL-BEING

The metrics we use to measure economic and social progress are central to designing and assessing economic policies and programmes. Using indicators that do not accurately capture key aspects of human well-being can result in misguided policies. Consider, for example, the most common measurement of poverty based on a *headcount ratio*, showing the proportion of the population below a specific poverty threshold. This portrays poverty as a binary concept, failing to capture the *extent* to which people fall below the poverty line. Using the headcount ratio to guide poverty reduction programs may also lead to an operational problem – policy-makers seeking to lower the headcount ratio have an incentive to direct resources to the people closest to the poverty line who can be easily nudged above the threshold, rather than to those much further below it. Alternative measures, such as the poverty gap ratio, measuring the average income shortfall from the poverty line, or the Foster–Greer–Thorbecke (FGT) class of indices that account for distributional underpinnings of poverty, are better able to address such issues.[1] Moreover, it is important to recognise that, beyond the measurement problems, lie deep-seated biases in how peoples' economic well-being are framed and understood.

Utility and Social Welfare

Within mainstream economics, the neoclassical literature on economic well-being is largely based on the notion of 'utility maximisation', where utility is defined as satisfaction or pleasure. Early formulations of utility theory presumed that almost anything can provide utility, albeit with diminishing returns, and that individual utilities could be added up to obtain a measure of social welfare. However, there is no precise way to measure utility since individual satisfaction cannot be directly quantified. Also, because utility depends on individual preferences, which vary from person to person, interpersonal comparison and aggregation is difficult, if not impossible (Stanton 2007: 6). Traditional economics has dealt with this issue by inferring the value of utility from consumer behaviour. This 'revealed preference' approach assumes that the amount that an individual is willing to pay for something can be taken as a proxy for utility gained from it. For example, someone who prefers coffee over tea would gain higher utility from drinking coffee and would be willing to pay more for coffee than for tea. Using this approach, utility can be measured in purely mathematical terms and the utilities of individuals can be summed to derive the total utility of the society and obtain a measure of aggregate social welfare.

This way of seeing welfare underlies cost–benefit analysis (CBA), which is one of the most common approaches to assessing specific government policies and programs. CBA involves calculating the net present value of the future stream of costs and benefits of a proposed policy; and then implementing that policy if the benefits exceed the costs. The estimates of costs and benefits are often based on people's willingness-to-pay (WTP), that is, the maximum amount of money people are willing to pay for a good or service, especially when costs and benefits are associated with environmental or health outcomes that cannot be directly measured in monetary values.

While the CBA methodology is widely used to make policy decisions, there are several critical issues with using this assessment tool.[2] For example, in calculating the present value of all the future costs and benefits, an assumption must be made about the appropriate discount rate, which is the annual percentage rate at which future costs and benefits are discounted relative to current costs and benefits. The overall cost–benefit ratio depends crucially on the value selected for this discount rate, but there is an inherent element of arbitrariness in the rate that is selected, varying according to how much weight the researcher puts on future gains and losses. Additionally, because the CBA approach considers the costs and benefits at the aggregate level, it usually omits the question of distribution. It assumes that as long as the gains are higher than the losses, social welfare increases. However, if the costs and benefits are borne by different groups, then one group of people could be benefiting at the expense of another, resulting in social tensions. Inequality is also a substantial issue if costs and benefits are estimated according to people's WTP, which is directly affected by their ability to pay. Since the WTP for a wealthy individual is much higher than the WTP for a poorer individual, the aggregate WTP is problematic in the absence of an even distribution of income. Such critical problems must always be considered when CBA is used.

GDP as a Measure of Well-being

A yet more pervasive problem throughout mainstream economic analysis and policy prescription has been the widespread use of gross domestic product (GDP) to measure overall economic well-being. GDP is defined as the total market value of all final goods and services newly produced in a country over a specific period of time. As a monetary measure of the total level of market production, it allows the aggregation of diverse goods and services, such as cars, computers, haircuts, and healthcare services. Growth in real GDP is calculated as the rate of change in GDP adjusted for inflation or deflation, thus providing a real measure of change in production levels. GDP per capita (GDP/population) is the standard measure used to compare the average standard of living across different countries.

Arguments for using GDP per capita as the primary indicator of economic well-being include its close association with employment. The general presumption is that producers usually need more workers when the production level is increasing. Hence, employment as well as aggregate income levels in the economy can be expected to rise with an increase in GDP. Similarly, if an economy is in a downturn and GDP is declining, unemployment is expected to rise while income levels fall. This relationship is expressed by Okun's law, which suggests an inverse relationship between the unemployment rate and GDP growth, where a one percentage point fall in the unemployment rate is associated with an approximately three percentage point boost to real GDP. Of course, in the longer term, job-displacing technological change may reduce the ratio of labour to capital employed. However, that is typically not seen as problematic because growth in GDP is associated not just with lowering unemployment but also with economic development and improvement in human well-being more generally.

It should be noted, however, that GDP was never intended for the purpose of measuring human well-being. In the 1930s, Simon Kuznets, the original formulator of GDP, explicitly stated that it was designed to measure market activities, making it easier for policymakers to manage the national economy through financial crisis and wars, and that the welfare of a country cannot be inferred from a measurement of national income (Kuznets 1934). However, by the 1940s, the newly formed World Bank and International Monetary Fund quickly adopted the GDP for broader purposes, and it has subsequently come to be used as a proxy for well-being. Influential economic theories, such as Rostow's growth theory (1960) and the Harrod–Domar model, focused on increasing aggregate income and output as the key to development (Ghatak 2003). Economic growth remains the central consideration in macroeconomic policymaking in both developing and developed countries.

The relationship between economic well-being or development and GDP growth is, however, far from simple. Firstly, any measure of economic well-being must consider issues of social stability and environmental sustainability. Erosion of social relationships due to political conflicts, increased violence at the community or household level, or increased stress due to overwork could all have adverse impacts on well-being, but these are not accounted for by GDP. Similarly, access to cleaner air and water, ability to enjoy the natural environment, and greater stock of natural capital all contribute to human well-being, but these are also ignored by the GDP. Even though production of goods and services (and GDP growth) is heavily dependent on nature's ability to provide resources and assimilate waste, GDP ignores environmental costs and benefits. In fact, often things that are harmful to the environment or to social life show up as *additions* to GDP. For example, natural disasters cause a decline in well-being as people lose their homes, jobs, and their lives, but these show up as economic gains in GDP if money is spent on rebuilding from such disasters. Similarly, if a rise in crime rates results in increased spending on security measures, GDP rises while actual well-being in the society might decline.

Since GDP focuses entirely on market production, it leaves out the well-being enhancing production that takes place within households and communities. Gains in well-being from consuming a home-cooked meal, receiving care from a family member, helping a neighbour, or volunteering to build a community garden all go unaccounted for in GDP statistics. These activities are central to forming healthy family units, strengthening bonds of love and friendships, and forming a vibrant community, but these benefits are not counted in GDP. A study by economist Nancy Folbre (2015) estimates the value created from unpaid household work for the 27 highest income countries to be more than 25 per cent of a country's GDP, on average. The problem of accounting for unpaid work is especially acute in rural communities in poorer countries, where access to formal markets and to public services may be limited and where individuals rely more heavily on their family and community members to meet their livelihood needs.

Another critical problem with GDP is that it leaves out the question of income distribution. Average income levels in a country could be increasing even when most of the gains in income are going to a tiny group of wealthy individuals while income levels are declining for most of the people. GDP accounting also leaves out the issue of financial sustainability and fragility. Some of the rise in GDP might come from increased consumption based on high levels of borrowing. Having to repay these loans is a future burden, perhaps rendering the consumption unsustainable. The US housing crisis in 2008 was driven by such phenomena because the demand for houses was based on unsustainable levels of borrowing, causing a housing market crash that led to the wider global economic crisis.

There are also methodological issues associated with calculating GDP. For things that do not have exact market value, the method of imputation is used to estimate their contribution to GDP. The imputation method usually involves estimating the value of goods or services, either by using market value of similar products or by calculating the cost of inputs. For example, the estimated value of housing services provided by houses occupied by their owners is based on the cost of renting similar houses. This imputed rent makes up almost 10 per cent of US GDP (Fox 2012). More importantly, the value of public programmes, such as healthcare, education, public libraries and parks, is often based on the cost of inputs. While these programmes may create huge gains in well-being, especially for the relatively poor who may rely more heavily on public programmes, the value of these public services, measured by the cost of inputs, is unlikely to be accurately reflected in GDP.

Finally, GDP says nothing about the quality of life. Periods of high GDP are usually characterised by low unemployment rates, but this says nothing about the standard of living or the quality of work (i.e. whether workers are paid fairly, or if they are overworked). Income is only a *means* to achieve well-being goals. We need to look beyond income measures to understand if people succeed in using these means to achieve *ends* such as living a long, healthy and happy life and having the freedom to do and be things they value in life (as discussed in Sen's capability approach).

ALTERNATIVE MEASURES OF WELL-BEING

Given the problems just discussed, it is not surprising that there has been a growing interest in alternative indicators. Political economists – indeed all who are interested in the reform of economic analysis to make it more directly relevant to societal well-being – need to consider these alternatives carefully, identifying which aspects of well-being each of these indicators focus on, the unit(s) of measurement they use, and the possibility of combining multiple measures into a single numerical measure.

The Human Development Index

Influenced by Sen's capability approach, the concept of human development has been developed and promoted as a basis for evaluating social and economic progress. The Human Development Index (HDI), developed by the United Nations Development Programme (UNDP), focuses on three aspects of individual functioning – the ability to lead a long and healthy life, to acquire knowledge, and to achieve a decent standard of living. It measures social welfare by combining average measures of health (using life expectancy at birth), education (using mean years of schooling), and living standard (using per capita income). These three components are combined, with equal weight, to get a measure for the HDI. This index recognises that health and education are not simple functions of income per capita. For example, increases in income generally improve health and educational achievements but at a diminishing rate. Both health and education also have non-income dimensions and substantial public goods components (Stanton 2007: 20). In regions with greater public provision of these services, HDI value may be high even with low average income levels.

The HDI is one of the standard metrics published by the UNDP in its annual Human Development Report (HDR). The 2019 Report, including data for 189 countries, shows that countries in sub-Saharan Africa have the lowest HDI value, followed by South Asian countries. Most of the developed regions of the world, including the United States, Canada, Australia and countries of Western Europe, have very high levels of HDI – usually above 0.8 (Human Development Report, UNDP 2019a). The data show considerable variation between countries according to their GDP per capita and HDI. For example, in 2018, the HDI values for

Bolivia (0.703) and Panama (0.795) were similar, even though per capita income in Panama ($11,724) was more than four times higher than that in Bolivia ($2,560). Equatorial Guinea, with income per capita similar to Panama at $10,135, on the other hand, has a much lower HDI value (0.588) than Bolivia.[3] These differences can be explained by the higher value for health and education indicators for Bolivia (life expectancy of 71 years, mean years of schooling of 8.9 years, and expected years of schooling of 14 years) compared with Equatorial Guinea (life expectancy of 58.4 years, mean years of schooling of 5.5 years, and expected years of schooling of 9.3 years).

While the HDI goes some distance towards redressing shortcomings in income-based measure of economic progress, it also has limitations. First, because it is based on average measures of health, education and income across the population, it does not consider distributional issues. Inequality in each of the three components of HDI could have corrosive effects on social well-being through their association with decreasing social cohesion, or lowering environmental protection.[4] Inequality in income, health or education also affects other aspects of well-being. For example, the distribution of educational attainment may have a profound impact on the distribution of power in the society and on aspects such as political participation and access to public goods.[5] In fact, Sen argues that unequal distribution of opportunities have important impacts on human well-being that are not directly captured by income measures 'since what we can or cannot do, can or cannot achieve, does not depend just on our incomes but also on the variety of physical and social characteristics that affect our lives and make us what we are' (Sen 1995: 28).

Also, HDI focuses more on individual achievements than social and communal aspects of life. Yet, individuals acquire capabilities and make choices not in isolation but, as members of social groups – they cooperate and compete with each other and adapt to the attributes of others. Focusing on individual achievements may thus leave out well-being impacts of community life. The HDI has also been criticised for being limited to a narrow set of indicators, failing to account for many other aspects that are relevant for human well-being. Like GDP, it ignores aspects of social stability and environmental sustainability. The methodology of giving equal weight to each of the three dimensions has also been criticised (Deb 2015). Moreover, even though aggregate measures of health and education are included, HDI says nothing about the *quality* of health or education. Of course, the rationale for keeping the metric limited to a few objective functions of human well-being is to keep it simple and easy to measure, which is one reason why this indicator has been used so widely.

Recognising some of these concerns about the adequacy of HDI, the HDRs have developed additional measures of well-being. In 2010, three indices were launched to monitor poverty, inequality and gender empowerment across multiple human development dimensions. These are the Multidimensional Poverty Index (MPI), inequality-adjusted HDI (IHDI), and the Gender Inequality Index (GII). These three alternatives deserve comparable attention.

The MPI is similar to the HDI in that it includes data on living standards, education and health, but it uses a much broader set of indicators to focus more directly on issues of poverty. The health measure is based on nutrition and child mortality; education is measured by years of schooling and school attendance rate; while the standard of living measure is a composite of six indicators (cooking fuel, sanitation, drinking water, electricity, housing and assets). According to the UNDP report on MPI in 2019, 1.3 billion people (23.1 per cent of the world's population) were multi-dimensionally poor (UNDP 2019b). This is much higher than the 10 per cent global poverty rate suggested by the international $1.90 a day poverty rate measure.[6]

The IHDI incorporates new elements to make HDI sensitive to inequality. It takes the same indicators as the HDI index to measure health, education and living standard, and accounts for inequality by 'discounting' each dimension's average according to the level of inequality. Essentially, the IHDI and the HDI value would be equal if there were no inequality in the three dimensions of HDI; higher inequality in any of these three dimensions is reflected by greater difference between the values of HDI and IHDI. In 2018, the value of global IHDI was 20.2 per cent lower than the global HDI. Thus, the HDI value drops by a fifth (from 0.731 to 0.584) when inequality is accounted for. This drop is greatest for countries in sub-Saharan Africa (where IHDI is lower that HDI by 30.5 per cent) and less for countries in Europe and Central Asia (where IHDI is on average lower by just 11.7 per cent) (Human Development Report, UNDP 2019a, Table 3).

The GII includes measures of reproductive health (measured by maternal mortality ratio and adolescent birth rates); empowerment (measured by political participation and literacy rate); and gender disparities in labour market participation. While this indicator still leaves out important aspects of gender inequality, such as gender-based violence, women's decision-making ability, asset ownership and unpaid work, it exposes some key differences in the achievements of men and women. According to the 2019 HDR, gender-based inequality was highest in countries of sub-Saharan Africa (with GII of 0.573) followed by the Arab states (with GII of 0.531) and South Asia (with GII of 0.51), while countries in Europe and Central Asia had the lowest gender inequality (with GII of 0.276). In 2014, another indicator for measuring gender inequality, the Gender Development Index (GDI), was introduced. This metric essentially disaggregates the HDI value by gender. According to the 2018 HDR, the average HDI value for women (0.707) was 6.2 per cent lower than that for men (0.751).

In addition to introducing indicators like these, recent HDRs have also included information on a 'statistical dashboard' that focuses on the relationship between human development and five topics: quality of human development, life-course gender gap, women's empowerment, environmental sustainability and socio-economic sustainability. The HDR now provides a much deeper analysis by using these various indicators.

The Genuine Progress Indicator

Another indicator that has gained increasing attention in recent years is the Genuine Progress Indicator (GPI). The GPI attempts to broaden the conventional accounting framework and replace the GDP by adding in various aspects that are normally excluded from GDP but which contribute positively to human well-being, and subtracting those components of GDP that have an adverse impact on human well-being. It is based on the Index of Sustainable Economic Welfare (ISEW) first proposed in 1989 (Daly and Cobb 1989).

The GPI takes *consumption* of goods and services by households as the starting value (unlike GDP that accounts for the overall *production* level). It then makes adjustments to this initial figure to provide a more well-rounded picture of economic well-being. First, components of consumption that do not add to well-being, such as 'defensive' spending on medical care, insurance, and security adjustments, are subtracted. Expenditures on long-term investments, such as consumer durables and higher education are also subtracted to keep the focus on current well-being and consumption, though the value of current services provided by these investments is included. Then, an adjustment is made to account for inequality. Next, welfare enhancing components – such as benefits of household and volunteering work, gains from provision of public goods and services, and benefits from ecosystem services provided by wetlands, forests and farmlands – are added. Finally, negative effects from social costs, such as crime, unemployment, lost leisure time and family breakdown, as well as environmental costs, such as air, water and noise pollution, climate change and ozone depletion, are subtracted.

Using this methodology, the GPI has been calculated for the United States, some of its states, and at least 17 countries around the world, including Germany, Italy, the United Kingdom, Chile, China, India and Japan. The findings of all this work are noteworthy to say the least, particularly when compared with GDP. While GDP per capita has increased almost everywhere, GPI has generally either remained flat or declined in the last few decades. In the case of the United States, for example, while GDP per capita rose at an annual growth rate of 3.8 per cent from $11,672 in 1950 to $36,596 in 2004, GPI per capita grew at the rate of just 1.33 per cent. Additionally, while GDP has mostly fluctuated within a positive range for this entire period, GPI per capita growth was mostly positive between 1950 and 1980 but has either remained steady or declined since then (Talberth et al. 2007). Research by Kubiszewski et al. (2013), examining estimates of GPI for 17 countries over a 53-year period and comparing them to GDP, has similar findings. It shows that GPI per capita and GDP per capita for most countries were highly correlated during the first 20 years from the 1950s to the 1970s but, after then, the GPI per capita for most countries either levels off or declines. The study also uses the data for these 17 countries to estimate global GPI/capita and finds a similar trend, with global GDP/capita continuing to rise but global GPI flat-lining since the mid-1970s.

What are some of the key sources of this deviation between GDP and GPI? Research by Talbert and Weisdorf (2017) shows that, in the USA, the largest positive adjustments to the GPI came from increases in social capital, including unpaid work, value of leisure time and internet services. The largest deductions come from depletion of natural capital. Hence, the diverging pattern between GDP and GPI is mainly explained by increasing environmental costs, implying that the GDP growth we have been experiencing has come at a high cost of environmental degradation. Accordingly, one may infer that, if the aim is to raise GPI, policies should address environmental protection and sustainability more directly, for example, by including measures to get more energy from renewable sources, increase energy efficiency, produce more durable goods, and focus on environmental conservation. Also, shifting the focus from GDP growth to growth in sectors that do not deplete natural resources, such as the arts, culture and education, might support more *sustainable* GDP growth (Ceroni 2014). In other words, instead of a focus on notions of pro-growth and anti-growth, a more relevant approach would be to think about *growth in what sectors* and *de-growth in what sectors* would be needed to create an economy that is environmentally sustainable.

Although the GPI directly addresses some of the limitations of the GDP and points to some pertinent policy priorities, it has been subjected to criticism. First, because GPI uses monetary measures to aggregate the different aspects of well-being, there are questions about whether appropriate valuation methods are used for calculating social and environmental costs and benefits, such as loss of natural habitat or lack of leisure time to monetary values (Bagstad et al. 2014: 476). Other criticisms are that it misses out some components that are central to our well-being, such as political voice, human health, and knowledge (Brennan 2013). Also, since GPI involves estimating social and environmental costs in monetary terms and accounting for issues of inequality and defensive spending, it is much more difficult to estimate than GDP. Despite these challenges, GPI is one of the most comprehensive efforts to replace GDP and it provides a basis for improved understanding of economic and social well-being.

The Better Life Index

The Better Life Index (BLI) is another option. Developed by the Organisation for Economic Co-operation and Development (OECD), it combines several aspects of well-being into one composite index with the goal of helping governments design better policies. The OECD has identified 11 facets as being essential to well-being: housing, income and wealth, jobs (earnings, job security and unemployment), community (quality of social support network), education, quality of environment, civic engagement (involvement in democracy), health, life satisfaction, safety, and work–life balance. The OECD provides data on each of these individual indicators as well as the composite index (BLI). Interestingly, it is available through an interactive online platform that collects data from users on how much value they put on each of the 11 indicators. This data is then used to weigh the different components and create the aggregate index. This method shows which aspects of well-being are valued more in which countries and makes the index more sensitive to regional differences in prioritising different well-being goals. For example, the 2020 report from OECD shows that highest value is placed on life satisfaction in the United States, work–life balance in Australia, education in Brazil, and health in France (OECD 2020). Civic participation and community are ranked the lowest in most of these countries. The BLI also uses a broader set of indicators than both the GPI and the HDI. Also, because it is a unitless index, rather than a monetary measure, it avoids the complexities associated with converting aspects of well-being into monetary valuations. However, as of 2020, the BLI is only calculated for 37 OECD and four partner countries, meaning that it is not available for a majority of the less-developed countries, significantly limiting is scope for global comparisons.

The latest BLI report from OECD, *How's Life? 2020*, indicates that the overall quality of life in 41 countries has improved relative to 2010. In general, life expectancy has increased, people feel safer and are living in less overcrowded conditions, incomes and jobs have been on the rise, and life satisfaction levels are higher than in 2013. However, these average outcomes do not reflect the inequalities across and within countries. For example, housing affordability, relative income poverty and voter turnout have worsened in some OECD countries, and almost 40 per cent of OECD households are financially insecure. There has also been a decline in social support and a decline in time spent with friends and family, both of which impact well-being negatively. In 2020, income inequality is still as prevalent as it was in 2010, with those in top 20 per cent of the income distribution still earning five times more than people in the bottom 20 per cent. All OECD countries also face new environmental challenges, as nearly two-thirds of people in OECD countries are exposed to dangerous levels of air pollution and use more natural resources. Even though there has been a slight reduction in per capita emissions of greenhouse gases, most OECD countries have evidently not done enough to meet climate policy goals (OECD 2020).

Happy Planet Index

The Happy Planet Index (HPI) is a measure created by the New Economic Foundation (NEF) (2016) designed to measure 'sustainable well-being for all'. It combines four components – ecological footprint, inequality, well-being and life expectancy – to examine how countries use their environmental resources to achieve long and happy lives. The data is compiled by using information from three resources: Gallup World Poll data for data on well-being; UN for data on life expectancy; and Global Footprint Network for data on ecological footprints. The measure of inequality included in the index is based on how evenly distributed life expectancy and well-being are across countries. The following formula is used to calculate the HPI:

$$Happy\ Planet\ Index = \frac{Well-Being \times Life\ Expectancy \times Inequality}{Ecological\ Footprint}$$

The NEF's 2016 report on HPI, including data for 140 countries, shows that the country rankings for HPI index are quite different from that for GDP per capita or HDI. Countries in Latin America and Asia Pacific rank the highest, while wealthier countries such as the United States and Luxembourg rank quite low. For example, Costa Rica, Mexico and Colombia rank among the top three nations by HPI, while United Kingdom ranks 34th, Sweden ranks 60th, Canada ranks 85th, and United States ranks 108th out of the 140 countries included in the data. One reason for the low ranking of some of the wealthier countries is that they have large ecological footprints. The USA, for example, ranks relatively high on overall well-being and life expectancy but has one of the highest ecological footprints. Costa Rica, on the other hand, has committed to keeping its carbon footprint low: almost 99 per cent of the country's electricity comes from renewable resources, and the government has also invested robustly in public programmes on health and education.

The HPI has been criticised for weighting the ecological footprint too heavily and for ignoring other aspects of well-being related to health, happiness, and social, human and natural capital. Thus far, it also has limited uptake applicability in policy circles. Though the index has clearer implications for developed countries, it is difficult to draw guidelines for development policies from this index, since developing countries such as Bangladesh, Jamaica, Nepal, Haiti and Ethiopia rank much higher than some developed countries, such as the United States, Australia, Canada and South Korea. Despite these challenges, the HPI is simple and easily understandable and has been calculated for a large number of countries. It is also particularly useful in combining aspects of well-being with goals of environmental sustainability.

Other Indicators

Several other indicators have been used in different countries or regions, focusing on different aspects of well-being. Perhaps the most interesting, supplementing standard GNP national accounting data, are *satellite accounts*. These comprise a dashboard of indicators to measure well-being and have been used in the USA and the UK. In the former, the Bureau of Economic Analysis (BEA) publishes data on dollar denominated satellite accounts that disaggregate certain components of the GDP. The BEA's satellite accounts currently include indicators for transportation, travel and tourism, healthcare, art and cultural production, and outdoor recreation. Future extensions of this could include adding indicators on environmental costs, or household or domestic production. The UK maintains more comprehensive satellite accounts that include data on forested areas, oil and gas reserves, waste generation, greenhouse gas emissions, tourism, and domestic work.

The concept of Gross National Happiness (GNH) has also received some attention but, so far, it has been only applied in the Kingdom of Bhutan. It considers nine aspects of well-being – living standards, health, good governance, ecological diversity, resilience, time use, psychological well-being, cultural diversity and resilience, and community vitality. According to a report from the Centre for Bhutanese Studies, in 2015, 43.4 per cent of Bhutanese households were considered to be 'deeply' or 'extensively' happy (Centre for Bhutanese Studies 2016). The key strength of this measure is that it includes a broad spectrum of well-being measures and is detailed (including 148 questions, with the survey taking hours to complete). However, the index has not yet been calculated for other countries.

Another embryonic measure is the Green GDP Index, which adjusts GDP by accounting for environmental costs (Stjepanović et al. 2019). A monetary value is estimated for environmental damage as the depreciation of natural capital. National accounts produce estimates of net domestic product (NDP), which deducts the value of depreciated manufactured capital from GDP. Green GDP is obtained by subtracting the depreciation of natural capital from the NDP measure. By estimating a value for the depletion of natural resources, the green GDP provides a direct measure of environmental costs associated with economic activity.

Other notable initiatives have been taken in individual countries. In Australia, for example, there have been attempts by the government's statistical agency to measure Australia's Progress. Since 2002, it has published data on Measures of Australia's Progress (MAP), which includes data on a dashboard of indicators in the domains of society (health, education, work, crime, social cohesion, democracy and governance); economy (national income, national wealth, household economic well-being, housing and productivity); and the environment (biodiversity, land, water, oceans, atmosphere and waste). One of its MAP reports (Australian Bureau of Statistics 2012) shows that, while progress was generally being made in some aspects of health, education, work, national income and wealth, and household economic well-being, there had been regress in environmental aspects of atmosphere and biodiversity.

Meanwhile, a Canadian Index of Well-Being was launched in the aftermath of the 2008 economic crisis as an alternative to GDP to better understand the well-being of Canadians (Canadian Index of Wellbeing 2016). The indicator was created by collecting information from Canadians about what they thought were important for their well-being. The indicator includes the following key domains: education, access to healthcare, healthy environment, social programmes, responsible taxation, public safety and security, job security, employment opportunities, a living wage, balanced time use, and civic participation.

In New Zealand in 2019, the government launched a new initiative, a Well-Being Budget to re-shape the government's standard budget more towards the well-being needs of the country. A dashboard of indicators on civic engagement and governance, cultural identity, environment, health, housing, income and consumption, jobs and earnings, knowledge and skills, safety and security, social connections, subjective well-being, and time use is used to evaluate the quality of life. The government also looks at measures of financial and physical capital, human capital, natural capital and social capital to estimate sustainable and intergenerational well-being (Treasury, New Zealand 2019: 10). Based on these various measures, the 2019 budget in New Zealand focused on issues of fairness, community values and environmental protection. It allocated billions of dollars to mental health services, child poverty, and measures to tackle family violence, improve conditions of the native population, and build a sustainable, low-emissions and productive economy. It remains to be seen whether other countries could similarly re-align their budgets to focus directly on broader well-being goals.

THE COMMISSION ON THE MEASUREMENT OF ECONOMIC PERFORMANCE AND SOCIAL PROGRESS

Perhaps the most comprehensive review of the challenge to produce new and better measures of progress has emanated from France. Following the 2008 financial crisis, French President Nicolas Sarkozy created a commission, called The Commission on the Measurement of Economic Performance and Social Progress (CMEPSP), led by economists Amartya Sen, Joseph Stiglitz and Jean-Paul Fitoussi. The goal was to consider alternative metrics to better assess economic and social progress. The commission was distinctive in that it recommended a dashboard of indicators, rather than a composite index, be used to measure progress. The rationale for using multiple indicators is that this approach could give a deeper understanding of how a nation is faring on the different aspects of well-being. Since well-being is a multi-dimensional concept, trying to compress all the different components into one measure can obscure information about individual indicators. A single aggregate indicator for well-being also raises concerns about what measures to include and how to weight each measure. Using a dashboard of indicators provides flexibility in terms of measuring the different indicators in different ways. For example, well-being gains from consumption of goods could be measured in dollars while environmental costs could be measured in physical units.

The commission's report in 2009 included the following key recommendations:

- Distinguish between current well-being (including both economic and non-economic aspects of life) and sustainability (stock of capital available for future use);
- Use consumption or income levels, rather than production, as indicators of well-being, since it is possible for well-being to decline even when production is rising (for example, consider the rise in air pollution from increased manufacturing resulting in respiratory illnesses);
- Focus on household perspectives on income, consumption, and wealth levels, instead of aggregates measures of GDP;
- Include gains from non-market activities, including leisure, and develop measures of subjective well-being, such as social connections, political voice, and overall life satisfaction.

The commission defined eight dimensions of well-being, including material living standards (income, consumption and wealth), health, education, personal activities including work, political voice and governance, social connections and relationships, environment (present and future conditions), insecurity, of an economic as well as physical nature. The report discusses the importance of including both subjective and objective measures as indicators of well-being. The inclusion of subjective measures reflects concern to measure well-being by assessing how people feel about their own lives. The subjective well-being (SWB) measure, for example, is based on a survey question that asks people to rate their level of life satisfaction from 0 to 10, and then uses this data as a metric of well-being. Although this approach seems unscientific, as the responses may be influenced by survey respondents' mood at the time of the survey, empirical research shows that data on subjective well-being offers insights not available in more conventional measures of well-being such as life expectancy, incidence of diseases, and GDP (Costanza et al. 2007).

Data on subjective well-being from the World Values Survey shows that most developed countries rank among the high or medium high, but some middle-income countries such as Mexico, Colombia, Uruguay and Vietnam also rank high on subjective well-being. Less developed countries in South Asia, Africa and the former Soviet Union nations rank relatively low on the subjective well-being index (Inglehart et al. 2014). An analysis on the relationship between subjective well-being and GDP per capita shows a positive and concave relationship, indicating that, on average, well-being rises with income, especially at the initial stages, but there are diminishing returns – the marginal gains in well-being from increasing income taper off at higher income levels (Goodwin et al. 2019: 205).

CONCLUSION

While there has been growing consensus on the need for alternative indicators, no single metric has yet emerged as the best indicator of well-being. Each has strengths and weaknesses, as explained in this chapter. The use of multiple indicators on a dashboard will probably become more common. However, there is no reason why composite measures/indexes like GPI cannot themselves exist alongside, and indeed *within*, such dashboards. While there is considerable flux around economic, social and environmental measures, one thing is clear – that it is well past time to end exclusive reliance on GDP. That standard economic aggregate has a continuing role in macroeconomic models of the determinants of overall income levels, some macroeconomic policymaking and measuring market activity. However, it is not, never has been, and never should have been, an indicator of economic and social well-being.

Alternative indicators of well-being need to be central to any political economic analysis concerned with well-being and a political economic future that is more equitable and sustainable. Concurrently, political economists need to consider whether, and how, these alternative measures could change how economic arrangements function in practice. Changing the standard by which progress is measured would not directly change the nature of capitalism: capitalists could still be expected to pursue profit maximisation, but they might be required to seek their goals within different constraints. The key political economic question then is whether governments willing to adopt these alternative measures have the inclination and capacity to change the constraints. Or are they so wedded to serving the interests of capital (or competing to attract internationally mobile capital) that this cannot or will not be done? Probing questions like these would create a different (but complementary) agenda for political economists, going beyond measures of progress to issues of institutional power and practical policy implementation.

NOTES

1. The poverty gap ratio (PGR) is defined as the average income needed to get all the poor to the poverty line. The Foster–Greer–Thorbecke index is a generalised poverty measure developed by James Foster, Joel Greer and Erik Thorbecke. It accounts for inequality among the poor by putting higher weight on poverty of individuals who are further below the poverty line. See Deaton (2004), and Alkire and Santos (2013).
2. For more detailed analysis on cost–benefit analysis, some good resources include Stilwell (1999), Argyrous (2017), and Sen (2000).
3. Based on World Development Indicators data for GDP per capita values and UNDP Human Development Reports for HDI values: data is for 2018.
4. See, for example, Wilkinson and Pickett (2010) for cohesion, and Baland et al. (2007) for environmental protection.

5.   For studies exploring the relationship between economic inequality and distribution of power, see Ferreira (2003), Neckerman and Torche (2007), and Cole (2018).
6.   Based on World Development Indicators database for 2015.

REFERENCES

Ackerman, F., Kiron, D., Goodwin, N.R., Harris, J.M. and Gallagher, K. (2013) *Human Well-Being and Economic Goals, Frontier Issues in Economic Thought*, Washington, DC: Island Press.

Alexander, J.M. (2008) *Capabilities and Social Justice: The Political Philosophy of Amartya Sen and Martha Nussbaum*, Aldershot: Ashgate.

Alkire, S. and Santos, M.E. (2013) 'A Multidimensional Approach: Poverty Measurement and Beyond', *Social Indicators Research*, **112** (2), pp. 239–57.

Argyrous, G. (2017) 'Cost-Benefit Analysis as Operationalized Neoclassical Economics: From Evidence to Folklore', *Journal of Australian Political Economy*, **80**, pp. 201–11.

Australian Bureau of Statistics (2012) *Measures of Australia's Progress*, accessed 20.7.2021 at: http://base.socioeco.org/docs/measures_of_australia_s_progress_consultation_report.pdf.

Bagstad, K.J., Berik, G. and Gaddis, E.J.B. (2014) 'Methodological Developments in US state-level Genuine Progress Indicators: Towards GPI 2.0', *Ecological Indicators*, **45**, pp. 474–85.

Baland, J.M., Bardhan, B. and Bowles, S. (2007) *Inequality, Cooperation, and Environmental Sustainability*, Princeton, NJ: Princeton University Press.

Brennan, A.J. (2013) 'A Critique of the Perceived Solid Conceptual Foundations of ISEW and GPI – Irving Fisher's cognizance of human-health capital in "net psychic income"', *Ecological Economics*, **88** (April), pp. 159–66.

Canadian Index of Wellbeing (2016) *How are Canadians Really Doing? The 2016 CIW National Report*, Waterloo, ON: Canadian Index of Wellbeing and University of Waterloo.

Centre for Bhutanese Studies and GNH Research (2016) *A Compass Towards a Just and Harmonious Society: 2015 Gross National Happiness Survey Report*, accessed 19.7.2021 at: https://www.bhutanstudies.org.bt/publicationFiles/2015-Survey-Results.pdf.

Ceroni, M. (2014) 'Beyond GDP: US States Have Adopted Genuine Progress Indicators', *The Guardian*, 23 September.

Cole, W.M. (2018) 'Poor and Powerless: Economic and Political Inequality in Cross-National Perspective, 1981–2011', *International Sociology*, **33** (3), pp. 357–85.

Costanza, R., Fisher, B., Ali, S., Beer, C., Bond. L., Boumans, R., Danigelis, N.L., Dickinson, J., Elliott, C., Farley, J., Gayer, D.E., Glenn, L.M., Hudspeth, T., Mahoney, D., McCahill, L., McIntosh, B., Reed, B., Rizvi, S.A.T., Rizzo, D.M., Simpatico, T. and Snapp, R. (2007) 'Quality of Life: An Approach Integrating Opportunities, Human Needs, and Subjective Well-being', *Ecological Economics*, **61** (2–3), pp. 267–76.

Daly, H.E. and Cobb, J. (1989) *For the Common Good: Redirecting the Economy Towards Community, the Environment, and a Sustainable Future*, Boston, MA: Beacon Press.

Deaton, A. (2004) 'Measuring Poverty', Princeton Research Program in Development Studies Working Paper, accessed 21.7.2021 at: https://papers.ssrn.com/sol3/papers.cfm?abstract_id=564001.

Deb, S. (2015) 'The Human Development Index and Its Methodological Refinements', *Social Change*, **45** (1), pp. 131–6.

Ferreira, F.H.G. (2003) 'Education for the Masses? The Interaction between Wealth, Educational and Political Inequalities', *Economics of Transition*, **9** (2), pp. 533–52.

Folbre, N. (2015) 'Valuing Non-Market Work', 2015 UNDP Human Development Report Office Think Piece, accessed 21.7.2021 at: http://hdr.undp.org/sites/default/files/folbre_hdr_2015_final_0.pdf.

Fox, J. (2012) 'The Economics of Well-Being', *Harvard Business Review*, accessed 21.7.2021 at: https://hbr.org/2012/01/the-economics-of-well-being.

Ghatak, S. (2003) *Introduction to Development Economics*, 2nd edition, London: Routledge.

Goodwin, N., Harris, J., Nelson, J., Joshi Rajkarnikar, P., Roach, B. and Torras, M. (2019) *Macroeconomics in Context*, 3rd edition, London: Routledge.

Inglehart, R., Haerpfer, C., Moreno, A., Welzel, C., Kizilova, K., Diez-Medrano, J., Lagos, M., Norris, P., Ponarin, E., Puranen, B. et al. (eds) (2014) *World Values Survey: Round Six – Country-Pooled Datafile Version*, accessed 21.7.2021 at: http://www.worldvaluessurvey.org/WVSDocumentationWV6.jsp. Madrid: JD Systems Institute.

Kubiszewski, I., Costanza, R., Franco, C., Lawn, P., Talberth, J., Jackson, T. and Aylmer, C. (2013) 'Beyond GDP: Measuring and Achieving Global Genuine Progress', *Ecological Economics*, **93**, pp. 57–68.

Kuznets, S. (1934) *National Income, 1929–1932*, accessed 21.7.2021 at: https://www.nber.org/system/files/chapters/c2258/c2258.pdf.

Neckerman, K.M. and Torche, F. (2007) 'Inequality: Causes and Consequences', *Annual Review of Sociology*, **33**, pp. 335–57.

New Economic Foundation (2016) 'Happy Planet Index', accessed 21.7.2021 at: http://happyplanetindex.org/countries/.

Nussbaum, M. (2000) 'Women's Capabilities and Social Justice', *Journal of Human Development*, **1** (2), pp. 219–47.

OECD [Organisation for Economic Co-operation and Development] (2020) *How's Life? 2020: Measuring Well-Being*, Paris: OECD Publishing.

Robeyns, I. ([2011] 2016) 'The Capability Approach', *The Stanford Encyclopedia of Philosophy*, edited by Edward N. Zalta, accessed 21.7.2021 at: https://plato.stanford.edu/archives/win2016/entries/capability-approach/.

Rostow, W.W. (1960) *The Stages of Economic Growth: A Non-communist Manifesto*, Cambridge: Cambridge University Press.

Sen, A. (1995) *Inequality Reexamined*, Cambridge, MA: Harvard University Press.

Sen, A. (1999) *Development as Freedom*, Oxford: Oxford University Press.

Sen, A. (2000) 'The Discipline of Cost-Benefit Analysis', *The Journal of Legal Studies*, **29** (2), pp. 931–52.

Stanton, E.A. (2007) 'The Human Development Index: A History', Political Economy Research Institute, Working Paper Series, No. 127.

Stilwell, F. (1999) 'Cost-Benefit Analysis', in O'Hara, P.A. (ed.), *Encyclopedia of Political Economy*, London and New York: Routledge, pp. 157–62.

Stjepanović, S., Tomic, D. and Skare, M. (2019) 'Green GDP: An Analyses for Developing and Developed Countries', *Economics*, **22** (4), accessed 20.7.2021 at: https://core.ac.uk/download/pdf/295597367.pdf.

Talberth, J., Cobb, C. and Slattery, N. (2007) 'The Genuine Progress Indicator 2006: A Tool for Sustainable Development', *Redefining Progress*, accessed 21.7.2021 at: https://www.academia.edu/2130339/The_genuine_progress_indicator.

Talberth, J. and Weisdorf, M. (2017) 'Genuine Progress Indicator 2.0: Pilot Accounts for US, Maryland, and City of Baltimore 2012–2014', *Ecological Economics*, **142**, pp. 1–11.

Treasury, New Zealand (2019) 'The Wellbeing Budget', accessed 21.7.2021 at: https://www.treasury.govt.nz/sites/default/files/2019–05/b19-wellbeing-budget.pdf.

UNDP (2019a) *Human Development Report 2019, Beyond Income, Beyond Averages, Beyond Today: Inequalities in Human Development in the 21st Century*, accessed 21.7.2021 at: http://hdr.undp.org/en/content/table-3-inequality-adjusted-human-development-index-ihdi.

UNDP (2019b) *Global Multidimensional Poverty Index 2019: Illuminating Inequalities*, Oxford Poverty and Human Development Initiative, accessed 21.7.2021 at: http://hdr.undp.org/sites/default/files/mpi_2019_publication.pdf

Wilkinson, R.G. and Pickett, K. (2010) *The Spirit Level: Why Greater Equality Makes Societies Stronger*, 1st American edition, New York: Bloomsbury Press.

31. Advancing education in political economy

Frank Stilwell and Tim B. Thornton

For political economists working in universities, putting personal effort into course reform can be a frustrating experience. Concerns with teaching generally lack the *kudos* and career opportunities that result from research activities. Moreover, most economics departments teach a standard mainstream economics curriculum, with minor local variations, and are resistant to change. Trying to get curriculum reform that would allow teaching of alternative political economic perspectives in core courses is often dismissed as being impractical or undesirable. However, from a societal perspective, a strong argument can be made that teaching and the curriculum are at *least* as important as the research and publication activities into which so much effort is put.

Education in economics has enormous implications. How young adults come to understand the economy bears strongly on their subsequent attitudes, beliefs and activities. Indeed, education in economics, probably more than most academic disciplines, shapes hearts and minds. The current dominance – some might say stranglehold – that mainstream economics has in schools and universities around the world needs to be continually challenged if more critical inquiry is to flourish. Unless progress can be made in supplanting conventional economics education with critical political economic education, achieving progress in many other important areas of economic and social reform will be that much harder.

This chapter reflects on the various options and avenues through which change in economics education could occur as a result of well-targeted and sustained efforts. The dominant focus is on increasing the presence of political economy in the curriculum and fostering greater criticality. Its first section expands on these opening remarks about why reform matters. The second section considers the nature of the traditional university economics curriculum, followed by two others that review previous attempts to get more emphasis on political economy and to develop alternative teaching resources. Attention then turns to the principal strategic options for seeking future progress – both within university economics departments and beyond. Concluding the chapter are two sections that reflect on the pedagogic and strategic issues that need to be faced and the prospects for further progress. Throughout, we adopt the definitions of political economy and economics outlined in this book's introduction; reference to the 'curriculum' means the content of courses in both mainstream economics and political economy; and curricular reform refers to a shift away from the former towards the latter. Of course, within and beyond that shift are many more fine-grained questions about how teaching can be made more effective (see, for example, Earl 2002; Groenewegen 2007; Reardon 2009; Stilwell 2011a) but our primary focus here is on *what* is taught.

WHY DOES THE TEACHING OF POLITICAL ECONOMY AND ECONOMICS MATTER?

Annually, millions of people across the world undertake study of economics as part of their university degree requirements. Later in life, people in positions of power and influence – politicians, policy advisors, policy analysts and journalists, among many others – often draw on what perceptions of the economy they acquired as students. Given this, the economics curriculum represents a type of intellectual 'commanding heights', inculcating 'conventional wisdoms' about what is (and is not) possible and the means by which particular economic outcomes might be achieved. As the principal founder of the modern economics textbook notes, 'I don't care who writes a nation's laws – or crafts its advanced treatises – as long as I can write its textbooks' (Paul Samuelson, cited in Skousen 1997: 150). Whilst we may laud the original works of the great economists, they are seldom read: rather, for many generations, most students have got their understanding of economics from textbook-based curricula. The textbook market has been huge for many decades.

> At the peak of their sales, both Paul Samuelson's *Economics* and Campbell McConnell's *Economics* exceeded in a single year the lifetime sales to date of Keynes's *General Theory*. Every year, six or seven introductory textbooks achieve sales of 60,000 copies or more. The market, variously estimated at a million and a half to two million students per annum, is immense. (Lamm 1993: 104)

Nowadays, textbooks and teaching materials are increasingly online, often as open access resources, sometimes accessible free of charge. Recognising the existence of zero-marginal cost distribution, and the opportunities for shaping ideology and policy outcomes, many conservative and libertarian institutions have joined the game, presenting themselves as providers of singular and objective truths. For example, the corporate-backed Foundation for Economic Education in the United States produces open-access educational resources that draw, uncritically, on elements of neoclassical and Austrian economics to lead young, impressionable minds to Panglossian conclusions about markets and capitalism. Nuance, qualification and consideration of competing viewpoints is usually in such short supply that the material is little more than indoctrination. When society is reared on this type of poor intellectual diet, unquestioned legitimacy and authority is accorded to certain types of economic arrangements and the interests they serve.

Economists are often unaware or unconcerned about the 'social engineering' aspect of the curriculum they teach. Indeed, labouring under the common (but mistaken) belief that the standard curriculum is value-free and that teaching it is not fundamentally different to teaching physics, chemistry or maths, they may take umbrage at the suggestion. They typically see their task as steering students into 'thinking like an economist' (Mankiw 2019). Implicitly, they treat the curriculum as more or less timeless, and they teach it more or less well. Declining enrolments or expressions of students' disinterest are countered by proclaiming the curriculum's supposed virtues and/or by trying to make the content more engaging for students by using enticing pedagogical techniques, even relating the economic concepts to popular television shows. However, these adornments do not fundamentally change the faulty product.

WHAT IS CURRENTLY WRONG WITH THE TEACHING OF ECONOMICS?

For a discipline whose practitioners commonly claim academic rigour, there are fundamental logical problems embedded in orthodox economics, as previous chapters in this book have shown (see also Harcourt 1972; Mantel 1974; Mandler 2001; Fullbrook 2004; Keen and Lee 2004; Keen 2011). They include the difficulties of measuring capital and the related problems of aggregate production functions (Sraffa 1975); the impregnable circularity embedded within the concept of utility (Robinson 1978); and the impossibility of aggregating individual downward-sloping demand curves into a reliably downward-sloping market demand curve (Mantel 1974). Although the existence of theoretical weaknesses like these is not necessarily an argument against teaching the topics, concealing such weaknesses from students and not providing alternative theories is harder to justify – yet this is what often happens. As a result, students can spend years climbing an arid and difficult intellectual mountain, only (perhaps) to eventually discover that the resulting view from on high is not of the real world.

Other theoretical shortcomings include unrealistic assumptions, over-reliance on formal methods of analysis, and over-dependence on equilibrium theories rather than studying economic dynamics. The orthodox framework has inherent difficulty in incorporating history and institutions, which contributes to the blatant neglect of these central elements of economic reality. So too is the fealty to methodological individualism. Perfectly rational individuals possessing perfect information, making optimum decisions in perfectly competitive markets have, at best, only tangential relevance to a world pervaded by inequalities of power, wealth, income and opportunity. These intellectual strictures produce analyses that vary from the facile to the misleading, as some of the brighter students sooner or later come to realise.

Another deep concern relates to ethics and the value judgements that are embedded in what is studied. Treating values and ethics as not relevant to the analysis, whether explicitly stated or implicit in the teaching, is untenable (Myrdal 1970; Stretton 1999; Berry 2017). Indeed, taking such a stance is not without irony in the light of longstanding research findings that show the prevailing economics curriculum to be detrimental to students' social and ethical development. Researchers engaging students in free rider/prisoner's dilemma games, for example, have found those with a training in economics to be more aggressive, less cooperative, more pessimistic about the prospects of cooperation – and more prone to cheating – than students who had *not* studied economics (note that selection bias was controlled for in these experiments). Moreover, these characteristics that students developed through taking economics courses tended to persist long after their education had finished (Frank et al. 1993, 1996).

While the influence of studying economics on ethical development may be long-lasting, it seems that much of the specific knowledge is often not properly understood nor retained (Clarke and Mearman 2001). Within a few months of completing their studies, testing shows that students who have done an introductory economics subject at high-school or university do little better than those who had not studied economics at all (Hansen et al. 2002). This evidence is not necessarily inconsistent with the earlier claim that school or university economics education may influence the outlooks of people who attain positions of power and influence later in life. The details of particular theories may be long-since forgotten, but the broader view of the 'free market' economy as a want-satisfying mechanism – deriving from uncritical exposure to notions such as 'consumer sovereignty', 'market efficiency', and 'gains from trade' – lingers on.

Finally, and perhaps most fundamentally, there are the problems arising because the standard economics curriculum lacks pluralism (King 2012). Inculcating students into just one principal way of seeing economic issues does not systematically develop their capacities for comparative and critical inquiry. The problem could be rectified by changing the curriculum to engage with some of the other schools of political economy. Developing closer engagement with other disciplines – like history, politics, philosophy and sociology – would also help. In practice, all that tends to happen is that students are given the opportunity to take optional electives in sub-areas, such as behavioural economics and game theory, after they have done the required core courses in mainstream economic theory. The presence of this minor 'internal heterodoxy' has the appeal of adding some apparent variety to students' studies, but the 'add-ons' fall well short of engaging in structural pluralism. The general failure to make broader and more critical engagements renders the currently non-plural curriculum deficient as a means of developing the graduate knowledge, skills and attributes that employers require (O'Donnell 2007), as well as being a poor basis for a liberal education and creating an informed society.

Despite this litany of problems and failings, most university economists seem to be quite comfortable to continue with the standard curriculum, perhaps with some minor tinkering around the edges or using fancier means of presentation. This is the more remarkable because in no other discipline do students so regularly rebel against the content of their instruction (Kay 2014). The frequent and marked student dissatisfaction has sometimes led to the formation of active organisations for change.

ATTEMPTS TO REFORM THE ECONOMICS CURRICULUM

When student dissenters join forces with academics who share their dissatisfaction with the standard economics curriculum, significant change is possible. While a full historical and worldwide survey of all such attempts to create change is beyond the scope of this chapter, a brief consideration of some of the forms that dissent has taken during the last six decades may be of significant relevance and use in future struggles.

In the 1960s there were various initiatives to reform both economics and economics teaching, particularly in the USA. The Union for Radical Political Economics was formed in 1968. A handful of pluralist economics departments also emerged, such as that at the University of Massachusetts (Amherst) and the New School for Social Research in New York, joined later by other 'heterodox' departments such as the University of Missouri–Kansas City (UMKC). In the UK, the University of Cambridge became well-known for its broader approach to teaching economics and political economy in the 1960s and 1970s (Lee 2009). Initiatives of local significance also occurred in other countries. In Australia, for example, a long struggle by dissident staff and students resulted in the establishment of a separate Department of Political Economy where a pluralist curriculum was established and continues to flourish (Butler et al. 2009; Stilwell 2012).

During the 1970s it seemed that economics – and economics education – might even undergo a Kuhnian paradigm shift. The renowned institutional economist J.K. Galbraith wrote that: 'for a new and notably articulate generation of economists, a reference to neoclassical economics has become markedly pejorative ... I would judge as well as hope that the present attack will prove decisive' (Galbraith 1973: 1). However, curriculum change proved very difficult to bring about. We learnt that a wave of student dissent may not have much impact because, unless the baton is passed to incoming students, conservative forces can usually wait out the disquiet by stalling on demands for reform, sometimes combined with more nefarious responses. We found out that academic staff who 'go out on a limb' by challenging the curriculum and supporting student demands for change are vulnerable to insecurities in employment and face conservative biases in hiring and promotion processes. Such progress as was made turned out to be patchy and was often subsequently reversed.

Drawing lessons from this, advocates of heterodox economics and pluralism in economics education put more energy into developing their own organisations, nationally and internationally, during the 1980s and 1990s. The intention was to enhance the prospect of reform within the economics discipline through holding conferences, establishing new journals and newsletters, and collectively agitating for change. Some examples of this type of effort include the formation of the International Confederation of Associations for Pluralism in Economics and the creation of the *International Journal of Pluralism in Economics Education*. The process continued with the formation, both nation-based and global, of organisations such as the Association for Heterodox Economics (UK), the Society for Heterodox Economists (Australia), and the World Economics Association. There are also the *Heterodox Economics Directory* and the *Heterodox Economics Newsletter* that continue to facilitate connections and support between political economists worldwide.

Student-led organisations have also proliferated. They include the Post-Autistic Economics movement (Fullbrook 2003), the International Student Initiative for Pluralism in Economics and Rethinking Economics, operating across multiple countries. Rethinking Economics is a particularly good example of growth in an organisation seeking to achieve curricular change. Originating as a student organisation, it has expanded its membership to include academics, industry and government economists, and concerned citizens. It currently produces books, reports, festivals, webinars, newsletters and conducts research, nearly all of which is orientated to curricular reform. It has also been able to garner philanthropic funding, set up a membership council, a board of trustees, and an advisory board. The focus is genuinely global, involving over 100 groups from 41 countries. Its membership structure has a federated character, with some local groups adopting the Rethinking Economics label while others, especially those pre-existing, prefer to affiliate under the Rethinking Economics umbrella. The member organisations include other autonomous entities, such as Promoting Economic Pluralism. Active projects include curricular research, analysing economic curricula around the world; and offering a short course called *Communicating with Academics* that trains student organisers in how to more effectively push for curricular change.

DEVELOPING ALTERNATIVE RESOURCES

An alternative curriculum needs alternative teaching materials. Indeed, the two processes of seeking curricular change and developing new teaching materials are interdependent and mutually supportive. But the appropriate form of teaching materials is not self-evident. Activist movements made early initiatives in producing books of collected readings on various topics in radical political economy, which proved popular but did not displace the standard economics textbooks. One early attempt at the latter in the 1970s, Robinson and Eatwell's *An Introduction to Modern Economics*, proved difficult to use for teaching purposes (King and Millmow 2003). Another early starter, Hunt and Sherman's *Economics: An Introduction to Traditional and Progressive Views* proved more flexible and durable, subsequently going through many editions and adaptations. Others followed: Reardon, Madi and Cato's *Introducing a New Economics: Pluralist, Sustainable and Progressive* being a recent example. The Network for Pluralism in Economics provides an online textbook covering major schools of political economy and economics. We are ourselves textbook authors (Stilwell 2011; Goodwin et al. 2020). The *Heterodox Economics Directory* (2021) documents most of the books currently available and the reader is encouraged to survey the full list of options.

The variety that exists in these books reflects differences of ambition and approach that, not surprisingly, exist in any movement for reform. A political economy book for teaching purposes can seek to be an outright replacement for textbooks of the Samuelson type, aiming to facilitate profound curricular change. Most of those already mentioned are of this character. But more reformist options also exist. For example, the Economics in Context Initiative (ECI), where one of this chapter's authors has worked and has ongoing affiliations, produces textbooks and teaching modules that are designed to be amenable to reform-minded and progressively inclined mainstream economists. The implicit theory of change is that there is currently a large constituency of academic economists who are unwilling or simply unable to suddenly embrace a fully pluralist economics curriculum, so that providing them with materials that they could adopt while teaching within a quite conventional curriculum offers a plausible pathway to incremental change, hopefully laying groundwork for more comprehensive change later. ECI's 'contextual approach' provides much of the content of the standard curriculum, albeit covered in a more nuanced and qualified way, placing the economic issues in social, political, historical and ecological context. Furthermore, some political economic/heterodox content is also introduced alongside the standard content. ECI's open-access teaching modules also allow instructors to substitute one or more standard textbook chapters with a superior alternative. Some textbook chapters are also open access, allowing instructors to use them as substitutes for chapters in a traditional text. By providing these free textbook chapters and modules, instructors are very easily able 'dip their foot in the pool' of curricular change.

Another variant of a reformist approach is represented by the CORE project which, since 2013, has been creating teaching resources for an alternative introductory curriculum. CORE's approach is to incorporate a post-Walrasian economics that relaxes the neoclassical assumptions of complete contracting and endogenous preferences (see, for example, Bowles and Gintis 2000; Bowles 2005; CORE 2020a, 2020b), as well as some key ideas from game theory, behavioural economics, transaction cost economics, complexity economics and the Hayekian ideas on information. CORE understands itself as offering a new paradigm (Bowles and Carlin 2020). However, like others (Rethinking Economics 2014; Sheehan et al. 2015), we consider that CORE exhibits both change and continuities with the traditional textbook, with its continuities including a lack of plurality. Accordingly, we would classify it as only mildly reformist.

In assessing these options, our perspective derives from a view of what the curriculum should look like, which is quite different to what is contained in these sorts of reformist texts. We strongly believe in an explicitly and thoroughgoing pluralist approach (for reasons set out in this book's Chapter 28 on pluralism). However, we recognise that change is usually an iterative and evolutionary process, such that even a midly reformist approach could be a starting point for more fundamental reform – and some progress is usually better than none. There is evidently a fundamental conundrum, however, because, while any genuinely pluralist political economy course or textbook is unlikely to be acceptable to the bulk of mainstream economists because it appears 'too different', something that makes only minor improvement inevitably faces criticism from the proponents of more fundamental changes.

How best to manage this conundrum? We believe that a teacher should always seek to use the best (or least-worst) textbook possible, surveying widely and reading reviews to ascertain the best option for their purposes and seizing any opportunities to move to a better text with future iterations of the subjects they are teaching. Furthermore, a teacher should normally be able to at least flag deficiencies or problems in any text and indicate where students can access alternative viewpoints, even if such deeper interrogations might have to occur outside the formal auspices of the subject. In this regard, running a few optional tutorials or workshops, creating online appendices for particular book chapters, or simply providing an optional reading list are all worthwhile options that are generally low cost and low risk for both teacher and students. Any reading list might draw on the *World Economic Association's Textbook Commentaries Project* which has been designed to counter the problems and deficiencies of some of the dominant texts.

For textbook authors, it is important to be able to offer a spectrum of resources. Accordingly, it is helpful for some textbook authors to continue to produce resources that are knowingly 'diplomatic' and strategically aimed at that segment of the market that cannot currently countenance profound curricular change. However, it is at least as important that there is the continued production of texts that are not constrained by trying to cater to the often delicate and recalcitrant sensibilities of orthodox economists.

STRATEGIES FOR EXPANDING THE TERRITORY IN WHICH POLITICAL ECONOMY CAN BE TAUGHT

Having briefly outlined the rationale for educational reform, considered organisational initiatives and indicated some challenges relating to teaching resource materials, we need now to consider what can be useful for future efforts directed at curricular reform. What strategic options are likely to be most fruitful for extending the presence of political economy content in economics education? Consideration can usefully be given to five broad strategies:

- seeking reform within economics departments
- trying to form new departments in which political economy can be taught
- hybrid strategies that integrate the study of economics with other disciplines
- teaching political economy in other social science departments
- teaching political economy outside the school and university system.

Within, and across, these locational choices are more detailed concerns that impact on the likelihood of success, both in terms of effecting the institutional changes and in terms of achieving and sustaining good teaching and learning arrangements afterwards. These include matters such as the role of student activism, compromise, coalition building and use of the media, along with all the requisites for progressive and effective pedagogy. However, because it is the strategic choice of location that significantly conditions how these other matters play out, our analysis is structured accordingly.

Reform within Economics Departments

The *Directory of Heterodox Economics* provides a list of university departments that self-identify as heterodox. *Promoting Economic Pluralism* provides a further list of universities that self-identify as providing pluralist postgraduate degrees, some of which are based in economics departments. This is evidence that teaching some elements of heterodox economics or political economy within economics departments is feasible. Accordingly, we would not discourage anybody from seeking reform via this pathway. Indeed, we have both spent many years doing so ourselves. Moreover, it is important to recognise that economics departments will probably remain the principal focus of agitation for change because that is where most economics teaching currently occurs. Because dissent among existing economics students is a major element in the dynamics of change, where those students are located will always be a primary site of action.

Having acknowledged the importance of focusing on economics departments, however, it is equally important to recognise the barriers, frustrations and poor ratio of success thus far relative to effort expended. Aspiring reformers therefore should not presume that reform from inside economics department is always the best way, or even the only way, to make progress. Why? First, because the track record of this strategy has been lamentably poor: despite much effort, significantly pluralist economics departments represent a tiny proportion of all university economics departments worldwide, almost certainly less than 1 per cent. In general, reform by this pathway usually has a history of being slow, difficult and may, in some senses, be dangerous. By dangerous we do not mean that students and staff pushing for reform are likely to be in any physical danger, but activist students may be deterred by fear of being victimised, while academic staff may find it harder to get their employment contracts renewed, to get tenure or promotion. Another hazard is that any hard-fought gains may be quickly reversed when subsequent changes in the balance of power occur within an economics department or the university more generally. Even in benign circumstances, the heterodox or pluralist elements introduced into the curriculum may lapse – perhaps deemed to be 'too difficult to teach' – when their active proponents and teachers move on or retire.

Moreover, 'reform from within' has been made harder during the last two decades with the advent of research assessment and ranking exercises that discriminate against the research of political economists (Bouchikhi and Kimberly 2017). Given that universities usually select their academic staff appointees largely on the perceived prestige of their published research output, this makes it hard for dissident political economists to find a secure base inside economics departments.

An established literature documents these various difficulties, risks and frustrations of trying to achieve reform from within (see, for example, Butler et al. 2009; Thornton 2013; Lavoie 2015). Again, we emphasise that none of what is being said here should be misunderstood as trying to dissuade anybody from trying to achieve change. As earlier noted, there are supportive organisations and resources to which reformers now have access. Furthermore, future possibilities can be different to the past. Rather, our blunt account of previous and present difficulties is intended to be constructive, on the basis that being forewarned of potential problems is to be forearmed against them. Accordingly, we would recommend looking at existing case studies that may help reformers identify the strengths, weaknesses, opportunities and threats that may be present in their own circumstances. Looking at case studies may also be useful in helping reform minded academics and students weigh up whether a 'reform from within strategy' really is the best option to pursue in their specific institutional context. Even with an army behind you, it makes sense to carefully consider on which battle front may lie stunning and rapid success, a long trench war, or costly defeat.

Setting Up Independent Departments of Political Economy

The editorial introduction to this book made the intellectual case that political economy may be regarded as an area of knowledge that is distinct from mainstream economics even if sharing overlapping concerns. Seen in this way, political economy can be thought to be deserving of an independent institutional base. Of course, there are complexities with any social science categorisation; and there are undoubtedly fuzzy boundaries between political economy and economics (Mearman 2010, 2011, 2012). However, such features apply to *all* social science disciplines: politics versus history, anthropology versus sociology, and so on. And, ultimately, all knowledge is interconnected. So, in practice, the argument for having separate departments in universities does not depend on the existence of tidy disciplinary taxonomies: rather, it is a matter of identifying the conditions under which progress in the development and dissemination of knowledge may most fruitfully be made. On this basis, there is a strong argument for political economy to be organisationally separate from existing economics departments so that the discipline and its teaching may flourish.

Although a strategy of institutional separation may initially seem rather bold, there is 'proof of concept' for it. The Department of Political Economy at the University of Sydney is a case in point. In the mid-1970s, after years of struggle by students and a minority, dissident group of staff in the Department of Economics, the university approved the introduction of political economy courses, to be taught alongside a standard economics curriculum, allowing students to choose which they preferred. After three more decades of struggle, during which the pluralist political economy curriculum had been studied by some 15,000 students, the university authorities agreed to create a separate Department of Political Economy to formally administer the programme. It now has a staff of a dozen academics, offering both undergraduate and postgraduate courses in political economy. It was the creation of a separate department that ended decades of conflict and allowed political economy to prosper, side by side with the Department of Economics but no longer engaged in acrimonious, time-consuming conflicts.

Of course, a strategy of disciplinary differentiation and institutional independence is bound to be controversial, and like any other strategy, is not without risk. Mainstream economists, although often irritated by the presence of political economists in their departments, are usually resistant to allowing their critics independent space in which to develop. On the other side, some heterodox economists may not wish to 'vacate the current playing field' if that allows the orthodox economists to simply play on. Others fear that separate political economy departments could be even more vulnerable to future arbitrary closure. However, the Sydney experience suggests, at the very least, that this type of separation can function as a pragmatic way of responding to the unwillingness of mainstream economists to accept a principle of pluralism that includes study of bodies of knowledge deeply critical of orthodoxy. Separation, in this case at least, has produced a more desirable and sustainable outcome than would otherwise have been likely to occur. The Sydney political economists' pluralist curriculum includes introducing students to mainstream economic ideas but always in relation to alternative ways of seeing.

Not all attempts to create separate political economy departments have been positive. At both Notre Dame University in the USA and the University of Manitoba in Canada, the idea of separate departments was vigorously opposed by the political economists (and their students) who feared that it would be an interim strategy to remove them from within the economic departments and thereby weaken political economy within the university. Indeed, this is exactly what happened at Notre Dame, as the newly created department was later wound up (Bouchikhi and Kimberly 2017; Thornton 2017). Whilst this experience is relevant, it should be noted, however, that what was proposed in each case was a second department of economics rather than a department of political economy. Furthermore, the push for these changes was imposed from above, rather than coming from within the ranks of the political economists or heterodox economists themselves. Indeed, an argument can be made that the more desirable path forward may have been to negotiate for a separate department of political economy and, especially, to negotiate for it to be set up in a manner that would allow it to potentially prosper and grow.

The argument for institutional separation can even be couched, perhaps a little ironically, in mainstream economic terms as an instance of a 'Pareto improvement' because the change makes both parties better off. With separate departments, both mainstream economists and political economists can get on with the teaching and research that is important to them. It creates a more level playing field for the contest of economic ideas and creates a broader array of choices for students about their education. There must be critical mass in both camps, of course. And what to call a separate department can be a tricky issue. Some dissidents in the economics profession prefer the label 'heterodox economics' rather than political economy (in regard to this, see Stilwell 2019). However, we are unable to point to the existence of a known 'Department of Heterodox Economics'. This is probably not surprising, for at least two reasons. First, the creation of a department by this name would likely be opposed by mainstream economists who would regard it as an obvious incursion onto their 'turf'. Second, it is hard for an academic department to be defined primarily by what it is *not* – since the term 'heterodox' implies it is 'not orthodox.' There is also the question of what should happen to the name of such a department if currently heterodox ideas were to become orthodox? Should departments simply switch names at this point? To us, it seems the term 'heterodox' is better suited to contention about ideas, some of which are destined for permanent obscurity, rather than to engagement with concepts of enormous (and increasing) relevance to understanding and improving the world.

Hybrid Approaches that Integrate Study of Economics with Other Disciplines

A third approach, beyond relying on 'reform from within' or pushing for separate institutional territory, is to explore the opportunities presented by cross-disciplinary cooperation. Genuine pluralism does not just rely on coverage of multiple schools of thought within a particular discipline: it is also enhanced by some degree of interdisciplinarity. This is quite challenging for the economic mainstream because of the intellectual isolation that is baked into its basic tenets of methodological individualism, given preferences, complete contracting, and so forth (Thornton 2017). Given this, reformers can try to move the curriculum forward by structurally integrating the study of economics with other disciplines. This can take various forms, such as creating 'majors' in areas such as international development, environmental studies or globalisation, where the study of economics can be integrated with political economy and other disciplines.

Another option is the establishment of degree programmes for which different departments cooperate in teaching. Political economy can then occupy niches within the broader arrangements. Degrees in politics, philosophy and economics (PPE) are the most obvious example (Thornton 2013, 2017). Political economy as an area of knowledge has always had strong and explicit philosophical and political roots. Indeed, one could argue that political economy *is* philosophy, politics and economics. For political economists, power is not just market power, nor is it something that just structures the costs and benefits of particular choices. It is much deeper: power changes not just what we do, but also who we are, what we want and what we believe (Bartlett 1993). Recognising that the economy is a system of power (Samuels and Tool 1988) leads to an awareness that answers to economic problems nearly always raise political questions (Robinson 1981). Political economy also has a strong philosophical dimension. Indeed, it can be argued that all economics is, in the end, just a sustained form of philosophical reasoning (Fusfeld 2002). The more explicit focus on methodological issues in political economy (which is in many respects the philosophy of science as applied to economics) is a big plus here. Hugh Stretton (1999) has argued that one of the key problems in current undergraduate economics education is lack of attention to the philosophy of science; while Sheila Dow has also made the point that, if one really wants to get to the bottom of many disputes in economics, one must think methodologically and philosophically (Dow 2002). Philosophy is ultimately about rigorous and clear thinking.

Given these inherent linkages between economics, politics and philosophy, students who have some grounding in all these disciplines should be much better prepared for studying political economy than students undertaking a standard business or economics degree. The former can be expected to start specialist subjects in political economy already aware of the big debates and issues in the social sciences, enabling them to get the best use out of whatever political economy subjects are available to them.

The other advantage of PPE degrees is that it allows political economists to form linkages and networks with like-minded academics working in other departments. These linkages can lay the foundation for some degree of mobility between departments. For example, with good professional working relationships, it is sometimes possible for political economists to teach in other departments or pick up teaching and research work there. In other words, PPE degrees can function as network – and relationship-building – mechanisms for political economists and heterodox economists who might otherwise be isolated and overly dependent on the whims of their academic seniors in an economics department.

Having said all this, however, it is equally clear that PPE is no panacea. The curriculum of the economics course component in a PPE programme may simply be re-packaged mainstream economics orthodoxy. In that case, students may be quite unable to see and understand the connections between the economics and the politics and philosophy courses they take. This 'three silos' approaches to PPE degrees, unfortunately, is all too common. It is only when 'bridges' between the disciplines are explicitly built into the curriculum that the great potential of PPE degrees is reliably realised. In our view, this requires the explicit presence of political economy content in tutorials, lectures and reading. In universities with the 'three silo' type of PPE degree, the challenge is to work on building those 'bridges' more formally and extensively into the programme. In our experience, student-led PPE societies can be invaluable in the struggle for that goal (Thornton 2017).

Teaching Political Economy in Other Academic Departments

A fourth possibility is for proponents of political economy to find safe harbour in other academic departments where their approach to teaching sits more comfortably. These include departments of politics, management, industrial relations, business, history, geography, sociology and anthropology, among others. Academics in many of these disciplines commonly recognise the importance of economic factors that bear on the topics that they study. It is also commonly the case that they have little empathy for a mainstream economics approach that is variously regarded as too rigid, technical, imperialist or intellectually flawed in character. For any or all these reasons, they may regard political economists as more likely to be suitable for teaching components in their courses, or even co-designing the curricula.

Such possibilities for developing political economy education in other social sciences and humanities disciplines are many and varied. It largely depends on the relevant personnel, their awareness of each other's interests and work, levels of trust and affinity, and the institutional specificities of the university in which they work. When establishing new subjects, or new majors, we again recommend considering greater disciplinary differentiation. Specifically, if any new subjects are framed as being subjects in 'political economy' rather than 'economics', orthodox economists are significantly less likely to see them as an encroachment on to their turf (Argyrous 1996; Argyrous and Thornton 2014). Consequently, political economists may encounter less resistance in driving new subjects and majors along the often long and winding road to administrative approval.

Teaching Political Economy outside the University System

Finally, there is a strategy for progressing political economy that need not navigate any of the foregoing obstacles that exist within universities. This is to simply start teaching it through other channels where it is welcomed, appreciated and readily supported. This can be done through adult education organisations, NGOs, political parties, think tanks and trade unions. Of these options, trade unions are currently the most well-established organisational avenues for this sort of activity, especially where labour-oriented political economic analysis offers alternatives to the conventional interpretations of prevailing political economic conditions (see Stanford 2015 and Chapter 32 in this book).

Another possibility is the setting up of independent schools for the study of political economy. 'Going off the grid' in this way means offering university-level instruction, but without it being described as such or constrained by university accreditation processes. The *Exploring Economics* website offers an extensive list of such courses, many of which are free or low cost. For example, the School of Political Economy, which one of us has established and directs, was established in 2019 and offers an expanding range of both online and face-to-face teaching. Whilst still in its infancy, this 'off the grid' approach is working surprisingly well in terms of viable enrolments, effective pedagogy and a capacity to attract intellectually strong students. It is also relevant to note that, if one takes a long view of the process of educational change, it has sometimes been the case that the curricular innovation has occurred outside the university and the success of such efforts has forced the universities to play catch up (Burke 2000).

FURTHER CONSIDERATIONS

The five strategic options we have reviewed differ in terms of location – *where* we can seek to create space for the development and teaching of political economy. How a strategic decision on these options is made will necessarily vary from place to place, depending on local circumstances. It is also likely to vary over *time*, such as where a reform movement begins (as it usually does) with a focus on seeking 'reform from within' in an economics department and then, frustrated by limited success, moves on to refocus its efforts on one or more of the other options. Particularly in relation to the third and fourth options, where interdisciplinary links are crucial to progress, the question of 'where' is also inherently linked to *what*, in practice, are the relevant cognate territories. Making connections with, say, a department of anthropology could be conducive to the development of teaching on the political economy of development. For a course on the political economy of inequality, maybe a sociology department would be the preferred location. For the political economy of cities and regions, a geography department. And so on. If such shared spaces are established, pluralism may then come into the course construction. This applies even when the general structure of the curriculum is oriented around particular real-world issues or problems because, for each issue or problem, the principal competing theoretical perspectives can be considered in combination with the relevant empirical evidence, policy options and so forth. In these cases, the strategic question of *where* political economy may flourish is connected directly with the question of *what* is being studied.

There is another dimension to this 'what?' question too, relating particularly to the first strategy of trying to teach political economy within an orthodox economics department. If what is being sought is just, say, an elective on post-Keynesian economics that students can study alongside their orthodox economics core courses and electives, that strategy may have a reasonable chance of being accepted. The likelihood of success may be strengthened further if a generic sounding subject title and or subject description is used – for example, 'Capital and Growth' or 'Institutions and Markets' which avoids explicitly framing the subject as 'heterodox', 'alternative' or 'post-Keynesian'. Similarly, designing and framing a pluralist subject as a history of economic thought subject, or as a type of 'survey' subject can work. Such approaches are sometimes described as 'operating by stealth' or, to put it more diplomatically, 'taking a less combative approach' (Earl and Peng 2012). By such pragmatic means, some political economy subjects may be established amongst the suite of options in an otherwise mainstream department, and perhaps then provide the basis for further reform. Obviously, there are limits to what such pragmatism can achieve, as well as limits on how much one should compromise in describing subjects to colleagues and to potential students.

Proposing electives that mainstream economists regard as a direct challenge to their programme represents a different order of ambition and approach. For example, proposing the introduction of 'Marxist Political Economy' or 'Alternative Theories of Capitalism' is likely to meet stronger resistance within most economics departments, as is seeking to make the core economics courses explicitly and structurally pluralist. Such outcomes *can* be achieved – we have seen it done and sometimes done it ourselves, at least for a time – but the chances of success are less. Our key point in all this is that, when approaching what appear to be limits to change *in any particular domain* – or simply encountering sharply diminishing returns to one's efforts – changing track to one or more of the other four strategic options set out in this chapter may be the better path forward.

Geoffrey Hodgson's recent book *Is There a Future for Heterodox Economics?* (Hodgson 2020) is relevant in this context, especially when seen in relation to critical responses that have been offered (e.g. Lavoie 2020; Dow 2021; Chester 2021). His book raises many concerns that touch on these strategic issues, although its principal focus is on the nature of research and scholarly contributions in heterodox economics, rather than directly on teaching. It sets out a rather different array of possibilities that its author thinks require consideration. Significantly, Hodgson argues that heterodox economists may need to change *what they do*, particularly by narrowing the range of their academic work if they are to survive in the hostile environment where economic orthodoxy continues to prevail. Ultimately, he makes the case for having a more consolidated focus on a particular field, such as the institutional approach in political economy in which he is an acknowledged leader. While we have some sympathy with his call for greater unity in striving for change – or even in defending existing hard-won teaching territories – it seems both undesirable and unviable to prescribe what that focus should be in terms of a particular sub-field. Political economists inclined to Marxian analysis cannot be expected set their preferred approach aside to rally around a push for institutional or post-Keynesian economics, for example, or to concentrate their collective efforts on criticising a particular feature of orthodoxy such as the assumption of utility maximisation ('Max U'). So, while we appreciate Hodgson's significant contributions to institutional and evolutionary political economy, our understanding of what could and should be done differs in several respects. In particular, we consider that the most primary and urgent task is for political economy to 'teach its way out of trouble' by means of a pluralist curriculum. A commitment to pluralism is conducive to 'unity in diversity' (Stilwell 2021) and to celebrating and showcasing that through progressive education.

This emphasis on teaching may be seen to be going against the grain in the modern university where the managers commonly seem to give priority to research outcomes rather than teaching quality. Yet public expectations of universities continue to regard them as, first and foremost, teaching institutions. Efforts by political economy academics to push for pluralist curricula have the effect of re-focusing on the challenges of good teaching as well as providing instructors with a head start in promoting students' engagement and understanding (O'Donnell 2007, 2010). Good teaching requires clarity in *what* is being taught in the course materials and presentation; continual explanation of *why* particular issues have been selected for study; and encouragement of critical inquiry and feedback. A pluralist curriculum, although intrinsically challenging (Earl 2002), mitigates against an authoritarian pedagogy that treats students as passive, empty vessels needing to be filled (Stilwell 2012), although it offers no guarantees in this regard. Indeed, poor teaching of good content may result in levels of student engagement and understanding no higher than occurs within current mainstream economics education. Accordingly, the onus needs to be on political economy educators to make sure that the approach to teaching is conducive to the development of student interest, enthusiasm and commitment.

Finally, it is pertinent to note that there are personal investments of time and effort in all these aspects of pushing for educational change. Struggling to get a stronger foothold for political economic education may be stressful and personally costly for both academics and students, especially when facing orthodox economists who are implacably opposed to the proposed reforms and hold institutional power. Forming networks of communication and support – across universities, across countries and crossing the student–teacher divide – can be helpful in these circumstances, hopefully making the process more of an interesting adventure and less of an isolating experience. Engagement in the process of struggle can also be an important personal experience. As a former student activist, reflecting on what he learnt from active participation in the struggle to establish political economy education at the University of Sydney, put it:

> On reflection, the real learning from being in the PE [political economy] movement was about how our society works and what levers can be used to effect change and mobilise people. It was about how to force your agenda, how to keep your issue alive and not be taken out of the game in the process. In practice, that meant taking action with the ombudsman, petitioning the Senate, soliciting the support of unions and journalists, and writing in the University newspapers … (Paul Porteous, in Butler et al. 2009: 71)

Indeed, involvement in the process of pushing for change can be at least as educational as any content that students encounter in their classes.

CONCLUSION

This chapter has considered a range of strategic options by which progress in political economic education may be achieved. Its presentation of the five principal strategies for progress has sought to clarify the main options and their respective pros and cons. Which strategy is most appropriate to pursue will always depend on the specific situation and the judgements that proponents of educational reform make about what seems viable and desirable in that context. Being aware of other experiences in similar contexts can inform the choice of a broad strategy and serve as a reference point for making more finely grained judgements about how to advance the reform effort (for illustrative case studies, see Argyrous 1996; Butler et al. 2009; Thornton 2017). While we do not seek to dissuade anybody from trying to push for change from within economics departments – almost certain to remain the primary terrain of struggle – we urge consideration of greater strategic diversification because other options may be more achievable and sustainable.

Educational reforms exist synergistically alongside broader efforts at reform that include writing articles and books on political economic topics, creating and editing journals, forming and running organisations, both national and international, and using diverse media in seeking to have broader public impact. The prevailing material conditions are always important too. Educational change – especially in the territories of economics and political economy – cannot occur in a vacuum. The pursuit of progress in political economy requires developing ever better analyses for illuminating a changing world and contributing to changing it for the better. Notwithstanding its entrenched position in the academy, the 'conventional wisdom' of mainstream economics is made more vulnerable by the growing and deepening economic problems and crises in the world around us. These same problems increase the potential audience for, and interest in, an alternative political economic perspective. Seen in this broader context, advancing education in political economy is a vital ingredient in promoting and protecting our collective future.

REFERENCES

Argyrous, G. (1996) 'Teaching Political Economy at UNSW', paper presented at Political Economy Twentieth Anniversary Conference, University of Sydney.

Argyrous, G. and Thornton, T.B. (2014) 'Disciplinary differentiation and institutional independence: a viable template for a pluralist economics', *International Journal of Pluralism and Economics Education*, **5** (2), pp. 120–32.

Bartlett, R. (1993) 'Power', in Hodgson, G.M., Samuels, W.J. and Tool, M.R. (eds), *Elgar Companion to Institutional and Evolutionary Economics,* Aldershot: Edward Elgar Publishing, pp. 119–24.

Berry, M. (2017) *Morality and Power: Ethics, Economics and Public Policy*, Cheltenham, UK and Northampton, MA, USA: Edward Elgar Publishing.

Bouchikhi, H. and Kimberly, J.R. (2017) 'Paradigmatic warfare: the struggle for the soul of economics at the University of Notre Dame', *Industrial and Corporate Change*, **26** (6), pp. 1109–24.

Bowles, S. (2005) *Microeconomics: Behavior, Institutions, Evoluton*, Princeton, NJ: Princeton University Press.

Bowles, S. and Carlin, W. (2020) 'What students learn in Economics 101: time for a change', *Journal of Economic Literature*, **58** (1), pp. 176–214.

Bowles, S. and Gintis, H. (2000) 'Walrasian economics in retrospect', *Quarterly Journal of Economics*, **115** (4), pp. 1411–39.

Burke, P. (2000) *A Social History of Knowledge*, London, John Wiley and Sons.

Butler, G.J., Jones, E. and Stilwell, F. (2009) *Political Economy Now!: The Struggle for Alternative Economics at the University of Sydney*, Sydney: Darlington Press.

Clarke, P. and Mearman, A. (2001) 'Heterodoxy, educational aims and the design of economics programmes', *Economic and Social Policy*, **5** (2), pp. 1–14.

CORE (2020a) Universities using CORE, at https://www.core-econ.org/universities-using-core/.

CORE (2020b) Escaping from Imaginary Worlds, at https://www.core-econ.org/escaping-from-imaginary-worlds/.

Chester, L. (2021) 'A case of confirmation bias', *Journal of Economic Issues*, **55** (3), pp. 584–9.

Dow, G. (2021) 'Is there a future for heterodox economics?', Book Review, *Journal of Australian Political Economy*, **78**, pp. 153–7.

Dow, S.C. (2002) *Economic Methodology: An Inquiry*, Oxford: Oxford University Press.

Earl, P.E. (2002) 'The perils of pluralistic teaching and how to reduce them', *Post-Autistic Economics Review*, **11** (January).

Earl, P.E. and Peng, T.C. (2012) 'Brands of economics and the Trojan horse of pluralism', *Review of Political Economy*, **24** (3), pp. 451–67.

Frank, R.H., Gilovich, T. and Regan, D.T. (1993) 'Does studying economics inhibit cooperation?', *Journal of Economic Perspectives*, **7** (2), pp. 159–71.

Frank, R.H., Gilovich, T. and Regan, D.T. (1996) 'Do economists make bad citizens?', *Journal of Economic Perspectives*, **10** (1), pp. 187–92.

Fullbrook, E. (2003) *The Crisis in Economics: the Post-autistic Economics Movement: The First 600 Days*, London: Routledge.

Fullbrook, E. (2004) *A Guide to What's Wrong with Economics*, London: Anthem.

Fusfeld, D.R. (2002) *The Age of the Economist*, Boston, MA: Addison-Wesley.

Galbraith, J.K. (1973) 'Power and the useful economist', *American Economic Review*, **63** (1), pp. 1–11.

Goodwin, N., Roach, B., Harris, J.M., Thornton, T. and Rajkarnikar, P.J. (2020) *Essentials of Economics in Context*, New York: Routledge.

Groenewegen, J. (ed.) (2007) *Teaching Pluralism in Economics*, Cheltenham, UK and Northampton, MA, USA: Edward Elgar Publishing.

Hansen, W.L., Salemi, M.K. and Siegfried, J.J. (2002) 'Promoting economic literacy in the introductory economics course', *American Economic Review*, **92** (May), pp. 463–72.

Harcourt, G.C. (1972) *Some Cambridge Controversies in the Theory of Capital*, London: Cambridge University Press.

Heterodox Economic Directory (2021) accessed 29.7.2021 at: http://www.heterodoxnews.co/directory/.

Hodgson, G.M. (2020) *Is There a Future for Heterodox Economics? Institutions, Ideology and a Scientific Community*, Cheltenham, UK and Northampton, MA, USA: Edward Elgar Publishing.

Kay, J. (2014) 'Angry economics students are naive – and mostly right', *Financial Times*, London, 20 May, p. 1.

Keen, S. (2011) *Debunking Economics: The Naked Emperor Dethroned?*, London: Zed Books.

Keen, S. and Lee, F.S. (2004) 'The incoherent emperor: a heterodox critique of neoclassical microeconomic theory', *Review of Social Economy*, **62** (2), pp. 169–99.

King, J.E. (2012) *A Case for Pluralism in Economics*, Melbourne: Academy of the Social Sciences in Australia.

King, J. E. and A. Millmow (2003). 'Death of a revolutionary textbook', *History of Political Economy*, **35** (1), pp. 105–34.

Lamm, D.S. (1993) 'Economics and the common reader', in Colander, D. and Coates, A.W. (eds), *The Spread of Economic Ideas*, Cambridge: Cambridge University Press, pp. 95–106.

Lavoie, M. (2015) 'Should heterodox economics be taught in or outside of economics departments?', *International Journal of Pluralism and Economics Education*, **6** (2), pp. 134–50.

Lavoie, M. (2020) 'Heterodox economics as seen by Geoffrey Hodgson', *European Journal of Economics and Economic Policies: Intervention*, **17** (1), pp. 9–18.

Lee, F. S. (2009) *A History of Heterodox Economics: Challenging the Mainstream in the Twentieth Century*, London: Routledge.

Mandler, M. (2001) *Dilemmas in Economic Theory: Persisting Foundational Problems of Microeconomics*, New York: Oxford University Press.

Mankiw, N.G. (2019) *Principles of Economics*, 9th edition, Boston, MA: Cenage Publishing.

Mantel, R. (1974) 'On the characterization of aggregate excess demand', *Journal of Economic Theory*, **7**, pp. 348–53.

Mearman, A. (2010) 'What is this thing called "heterodox economics"?' Discussion Paper, Department of Economics, University of West England, Bristol.

Mearman, A. (2011) 'Who do heterodox economists think they are?', *American Journal of Economics and Sociology*, **70** (2), pp. 480–510.

Mearman, A. (2012) '"Heterodox economics" and the problems of classification', *Journal of Economic Methodology*, **19** (4), pp. 407–24.

Myrdal, G. (1970) *Objectivity in Social Research*, London: Gerald Duckworth.

O'Donnell, R. (2007) 'Teaching economic pluralism: adding value to students, economies and societies', Second International Conference for International Confederation of Associations for Pluralism in Economics, University of Utah.

O'Donnell, R. (2010) 'Economic pluralism and skill formation: adding value to students, economies, and societies', in Garnett, R., Olsen, E.K. and Starr, M. (eds), *Economic Pluralism*, New York: Routledge, pp. 262–77.

Reardon, J. (2009) *The Handbook of Pluralist Economics Education*, London: Routledge.

Rethinking Economics (2014) 'Press release: rethinking economics position on CORE curriculum', Rethinking Economics, accessed 20.7.2021 at: https://rethinkingeconomics.blogspot.com/2014/10/?m=0.

Robinson, J. (1978) *Economic Philosophy*, Harmondsworth: Penguin.

Robinson, J. (1981) *What Are the Questions? And Other Essays: Further Contributions to Modern Economics*, Armonk, NY: M.E. Sharpe.

Samuels, W.J. and Tool, M.R. (1988) *The Economy as a System of Power*, New Brunswick, NJ: Transaction Books.

Sheehan, B., Embery, J. and Morgan, J. (2015) 'Give them something to think about, don't tell them what to think: a constructive heterodox alternative to the Core Project', *Journal of Australian Political Economy*, **75**, pp. 211–31.

Skousen, M. (1997) 'The perseverance of Paul Samuelson's economics', *The Journal of Economic Perspectives*, **11** (2) pp. 137–52.

Sraffa, P. (1975) *Production of Commodities by Means of Commodities: Prelude to a Critique of Economic Theory*, Cambridge: Cambridge University Press.

Stanford, J. (2015) 'Towards an activist pedagogy in heterodox economics: the case of trade union economics training', *Journal of Australian Political Economy*, **75**, pp. 233–55.

Stilwell, F. (2011a) 'Teaching a pluralist course in economics: the University of Sydney experience', *International Journal of Pluralism and Economics Education*, **2** (1), pp. 39–56.

Stilwell, F. (2011b) *Political Economy: The Contest of Economic Ideas*, Melbourne: Oxford University Press.

Stilwell, F. (2012) 'Teaching political economy: making a difference?', *Studies in Political Economy*, **89** (Spring), pp. 147–63.

Stilwell, F. (2019) 'From economics to political economy: contradictions, challenge and change', *American Journal of Economics and Sociology*, **78** (1), pp. 35–62.

Stilwell, F. (2023) 'The future for political economy: towards unity in diversity', *Review of Political Economy*, January (forthcoming).

Stretton, H. (1999) *Economics: A New Introduction*, Sydney: UNSW Press.

Thornton, T.B. (2013) 'The possibility of a pluralist economics curriculum in Australian universities: historical forces and contemporary strategies', PhD thesis, La Trobe University, Melbourne.

Thornton, T.B. (2017) *From Economics to Political Economy: The Promise, Problems and Solutions of Pluralist Economics*, London: Routledge.

32. Progressive economics and social change movements

Jim Stanford

There is a natural synergy between progressive economists and progressive social change movements.[1] Progressive economists challenge conventional economic theories and policies, working to explain why business-dominated, market-oriented economies fail to meet human and environmental needs and to develop alternative economic models and policies that would do a better job. Progressive social movements, meanwhile, work to build stronger popular awareness of the failures and problems of modern-day capitalism, educate the public about their causes and potential solutions, and then mobilise political pressure and power to win changes that improve human and environmental conditions. The latter need the former – to make their arguments stronger and more convincing, and to help design structures and policies that could realistically solve the problems they confront. Meanwhile, progressive economists (those who care about real-world problems and conditions, at any rate, as opposed to those whose engagement is motivated only by intellectual curiosity) need social movements if they hope to see their ideas contribute to real progress. Thinking, writing and publishing will not change the world: only concrete political struggle and change can do that – whether in the electoral arena, or in broader movements and popular consciousness. So, there is an obvious common cause between the work of progressive economists and the campaigns and struggles of progressive movements fighting for similar goals.

Despite this inherent complementarity of progressive economics and progressive political movements, however, in practice it is not easy to build strong and effective ties between these two worlds. In my experience, most progressive economists (in academia and in other settings) care deeply about economic, social and environmental change, and would love for their own work to contribute to achieving those goals. And most social change activists welcome the input, knowledge, and advice that can be provided by like-minded economic experts – so long as that input is offered in a respectful, democratic manner. Nevertheless, the links between progressive economic research and activism are underdeveloped: the intellectual and personal capacities of progressive economists are rarely utilised to their fullest potential by social change movements. Progressive economists engage vigorously in the battle of ideas within academic departments, in journals and at conferences. Fewer are engaged as energetically in the real-world policy and political struggles that will determine the course of our economy and society.

Several concrete factors help to explain the limited success in bridging this gap. For progressive economists in universities, the institutional environments in which they work may limit their capacity to contribute actively to social change campaigns – the more so because of the relentless corporatisation and marketisation of universities. Too many economists (including progressive ones) are notoriously bad communicators, cloaking their discourse in jargon and often unnecessary mathematical formulations, which inhibits cooperation with grass-roots social movements that must communicate their messages accessibly and effectively. Some academic or professional economists are too quick to adopt the trappings of expertise, discounting the knowledge, experience, and perspectives of the activists they aim to advise and support – or, worse yet, offering unsolicited criticisms of movements and their leaders. These problems create needless distance between activists and heterodox economists whose expertise is genuinely valuable, but which must be offered with respect and humility.

On the social movement side of the relationship, the potential for a stronger working relationship with progressive economists may also be inhibited. Activists are naturally focused on immediate, actionable demands and opportunities, often with little time for big-picture meta-analyses and theoretical models. They may discount the contributions that professional economists could make to their theoretical understanding and strategising, preferring immediate 'facts and figures' and other easy-to-use information. They may not appreciate or respect the institutional constraints which limit what practising economists can contribute to their movements, or they may take for granted the time and resources which those responsibilities require. On rare occasions, activists may exhibit a knee-jerk 'anti-academic' bias, disparaging the knowledge and perspective of supportive economists and other experts.

While these factors may explain why progressive economists have not been as fully engaged in real-world social change movements as they could have been, they are surmountable. Indeed, throughout the history of progressive economics, there have been many examples of theorists and teachers who made outstanding contributions to social change. They have usually done so, not just by thinking great thoughts, but by connecting those thoughts to relevant political debates and supporting the efforts of grass-roots campaigners to mobilise those ideas and win change. Considering the daunting economic, social and environmental crises which face the world today, the collective body of progressive economic thought can and must be mobilised to its full potential. Achieving this goal needs appropriate effort and planning on the part of both economists and social change campaigners.

This chapter considers the nature of the challenge and what can be done. Its first section (drawing on Stanford 2008) proposes several 'best practices' that could improve and strengthen the ways in which progressive economists can participate in and support social change movements. The next section provides examples of successful connections between intellectual work and real-world social change struggles, and considers various channels of connection, including social movements; trade unions; progressive economic associations; progressive economic think tanks; political parties and governments. This is followed by a more detailed case study of one successful example of fruitful cooperation between progressive economic research and social change campaigning, embodying many of the best practices discussed earlier. Finally, the conclusion reviews the prospects for progress – at a moment in human history when the need to both critique the many failures of the existing economy and win better alternatives is perhaps more urgent than ever.

These observations inevitably reflect my personal experience as an activist, progressive economist. I trained at universities that encouraged heterodox and radical approaches to economics. I then worked professionally in various roles with great opportunities for engagement with real-world social change movements, including serving as an economist for a major trade union, working for a progressive economic think tank, and conducting popular economic literacy training in various settings. But I have also worked in universities, and hence also appreciate the challenges and constraints facing progressive economists in that milieu. This mixture of experience sparked my own thinking about practical ways to strengthen cooperation between progressive economists and social change movements.

BEST PRACTICES FOR MOBILISING PROGRESSIVE ECONOMICS (AND ECONOMISTS)

Most progressive economists care deeply about realising the changes and reforms that their research indicates would improve the human and environmental condition. Most also understand that merely expounding progressive ideas (in books, articles, and conferences) will not by itself win the policies we need – no matter how insightful or compelling their presentation. While there are numerous pragmatic and political challenges encountered in enlisting economists more fulsomely into social change movements, those challenges can be overcome (as attested by the illustrative review of successful examples provided later in this chapter). In my experience, some relatively simple strategies and practices, utilised by economists and activists alike, would support more successful engagement and cooperation.

Invest in Relationships. Cold calls from social change activists seeking immediate assistance from economists are less effective than the cultivation of ongoing relationships and partnerships. Good social movement organisers know to identify potentially sympathetic experts who can provide validation, credibility and research for their cause. Over time, maintaining a roster of intellectual allies (based in academia or other settings) is a valuable tool in any movement's arsenal. Similarly, economists who want to support progressive movements need to develop trust and credibility with their hoped-for activist partners. They cannot just 'show up' to enlighten activists with their favoured theories or strategies. Instead, they must get to know a movement, its members and leaders, making sure to understand its history and goals, and successfully complete some initial assignments. The resulting bonds of communication, trust, and goodwill will then facilitate more ambitious and ongoing participation and cooperation.

Collaborate to Identify Priorities. Progressive economists usually have their own ideas on the most important topics around which they are keen to research and mobilise. Indeed, their knowledge and perspective on economies is useful intelligence for social movements as they develop their agendas and priorities. But ultimate leadership in selecting priority issues for ongoing activism must ultimately rest with the movements attempting to build power and win change: allied economists need to follow their lead in identifying the most promising and pressing issues on which to focus their efforts. Remember, too, that successful social change movements make their own news: an issue will become important (hence sparking broad interest, among policymakers and journal editors alike) if social movements are strong enough to make it important. In that way, activist economists benefit from their connections to movements and campaigns that are effecting real-world change.

Educate Communities and Activists. One of the most important contributions heterodox economists can make to social movements is to help train their members and activists in economics (as discussed in Stanford 2015). Many activists are interested in learning more about economics but may have been deterred by the technical jargon and complexity typical of orthodox economics. Their lack of knowledge and confidence then holds them back from demanding and fighting for progressive goals, which critics claim are not 'economically viable'. Progressive economists enjoy a unique capacity to share knowledge and empower activists. Such training can occur in a range of settings: from formal educational offerings, to organised community and adult education initiatives, to online instructional resources. To fulfil this potential effectively, however, economists need to be thoughtful and respectful in how they teach. Needlessly technical or quantitative presentations are neither useful nor interesting to most non-specialist audiences. Pedagogy should focus on broad concepts and arguments that participants can wield in their real-world organising and activism, building wherever possible on the lived experience of the audiences.[2] Trying to educate activists on obscure internecine economic debates is far less useful than providing information and arguments that directly support their immediate activism. Another way that academic economists can connect their teaching with real-world activism is by supporting their own students to become more acquainted with and engaged in social justice campaigns – through term papers and research, work-study placements, and experiential learning.

Respect Mutual Constraints. Another condition for a stronger relationship between heterodox economists and social movements is a healthy understanding of the respective structures and constraints that each partner faces. Movement-based activists need to appreciate the limits typically placed on the political activity of sympathetic economists whose professional positions may require them to refrain from direct advocacy or partisan activity, or at least be careful about their statements and affiliations. That need not prevent these economists from making valuable contributions: of ideas, research, writing, verification, review, or public commentary. Indeed, in some cases, economists' effectiveness in supporting a movement may be enhanced when they maintain an arms-length institutional distance. Concurrently, social movements have their own constraints and limitations that allied economists should observe and respect. Membership-based organisations (such as movements, parties, or trade unions) are accountable to their members, and must make judgements and trade-offs accordingly – which may be frustrating for economists hoping for more undiluted or transformative programs. Movements must always judge what strategies and demands are most helpful in building their power, which may lead them to be more incremental and pragmatic than some idealistic economists would wish. Financial and political realities also constrain what movements can and cannot do, shaping both their demands and their organising strategies.

Share Resources. Professional economists can often mobilise various monetary or in-kind resources that can assist social and political movements. For those working in universities, these can include accessing funds through academic grants; providing space for meetings, classes, or offices; accessing information technology, printing, and libraries; and providing speakers and lecturers for various events. Economists in other institutional settings may be able to provide similar forms of assistance. Providing such material assistance is a tangible expression of commitment to the goals and activities of partner organisations and movements, helping to cement goodwill and two-way communication. On the other hand, progressive economists should be cautious about approaching progressive organisations and campaigns for financial or other material resources to support their own research and publishing. It is rare that progressive movements have access to discretionary resources that could legitimately be channelled to aid the work of economists; they typically operate with very scarce funds and their top priority is to use available resources to build their membership and activity. Of course, when economists perform direct work on movement-related projects or consulting they should (where appropriate) be reasonably compensated; but working economists should err on the side of generosity in these arrangements. Although they cannot usually offer payment, social and activist organisations may be able to provide access to other resources that benefit the work of their economist allies, such as access to relevant research opportunities or populations. By partnering with activist organisations with strong roots in specific communities or sectors, economists can gain unique opportunities for research, data collection and feedback.

These principles for improving cooperation between economists and social and political movements are relatively simple and straightforward. If both partners bear them in mind, while also exploring other ways to enhance goodwill and cooperation, then the success of their future joint work will be enhanced.

EXAMPLES OF EFFECTIVE POLITICAL MOBILISATION BY PROGRESSIVE ECONOMISTS

There are many notable instances in which progressive economists have successfully engaged with progressive social and political movements, fighting for and implementing progressive economic policies. This section reviews several broad categories of successful collaboration: social movement organising, trade unions, progressive economics associations, progressive economic research institutes and think tanks, and interventions in formal politics and government. The review does not purport to be comprehensive: legions of progressive economists have made important contributions to social change initiatives in innumerable ways and places, and that rich body of practice could never be fully described in a single overview. The purpose of this survey, rather, is to illustrate several different ways in which progressive economists, and their ideas, have advanced real-world economic, social and environmental progress.

Social Movements. Most social change starts with the development of popular consciousness regarding concrete economic, social, and environmental problems. As larger numbers of people express concern over these problems, and learn how they could be solved, more pressure is placed on politicians and policymakers to enact appropriate responses. That pressure may be mobilised through formal electoral channels (discussed below), or through non-parliamentary activism and advocacy. Most issues that spark progressive social movements embody some economic dimension: including understanding the economic causes of the problem, measuring its costs, and developing credible policy responses. Thus, many progressive social movements and campaigns rely on the insights and support of progressive economists.

One important area in which vital contributions have been made is the struggle for gender, racial and ethnic equality. Feminist economists have described and explained the various factors contributing to women's economic, financial and labour market inequality, including the tensions between paid and unpaid work; barriers to women's employment and financial participation and power; and the fiscal and social policies required to reduce gender inequality. Marilyn Waring highlighted the gender biases in conventional economic categories and statistics. Feminist economists such as Diane Elson, Brigitte Young and Isabella Bakker helped initiate the gender budgeting movement, which fights to evaluate fiscal and other policies of government with a gender lens, and for more gender-aware policymaking (Young et al. 2011). Economist Heidi Hartmann founded the Institute for Women's Policy Research in the USA, which has contributed abundant research and expertise to campaigns and movements fighting for gender equality. Feminists such as Marty Chen and Renana Jhabvala have linked their study of informal work to concrete struggles to improve conditions for women workers. Similarly, economists have contributed to other equality-seeking movements and campaigns – including most recently the Black Lives Matter movement and related struggles. Economists such as Lisa Cook and William Spriggs helped build campaigns to recruit black and Latino students to economics programmes, to reform curricula to include analysis of racism in university economics courses, and to fight for government policies that reduce racial economic inequality. Economist Patrick Mason, a leader of Partners for Dignity and Rights, has helped civil rights organisations develop broader proposals for economic reforms to address racial injustice in the USA (see, for example, M4BL 2021).

The environmental movement is another important progressive cause which has benefited from the participation of progressive economists. Of course, there are many varying perspectives among environmental economists – some of which are more compatible with conventional neoclassical assumptions (emphasising market signals like carbon pricing as a central policy response) than others. But many environmental economists, from varying intellectual traditions, have supported activist initiatives to raise awareness of environmental problems, and fight for appropriate policy responses. Herman Daly led environmental economics research at the World Bank, advancing arguments around the 'steady-state economy' (Daly 2014) and actively supporting numerous environmentalist campaigns and organisations. Nicholas Stern's work (2007) on the economic costs of climate change and the net benefits of reducing carbon emissions has been taken up in worldwide campaigns to support measures to reduce greenhouse gas pollution. Noted Australian economist John Quiggin has been an active advocate for environmental campaigns on many issues, including the phase-out of coal (Quiggin 2020).

Progressive economists naturally have strong views on macroeconomic policy issues too, including fiscal, monetary, labour market, and international trade policies. They express those views strongly in the standard forums of economic debate, offering suggestions to finance ministers and central bank governors. But many progressive economists have also worked hard to build active movements and campaigns to win changes in those policy areas. For example, the movement of participatory or alternative budgeting has challenged the precepts of austerity that underpin neoliberal fiscal policy, combining popular economics education (on how budgets are developed, and the true range of choice available to budget-makers) with advocacy for stronger economic and social policies. An initial experiment with this model was implemented in Puerto Alegre, Brazil, in the early 1990s under a municipal government led by Mayor Olivio Dutra (a former bank worker and union leader). Its successes in improving urban and social conditions inspired similar efforts in jurisdictions around the world (surveyed in Wilhelmy 2013) – often advised and supported by progressive economists. For example, John Loxley, a prominent development and finance economist, helped found a network of alternative budget campaigns in Canada and other countries (see Cho!ces 1998 and Serieux et al. 2021). Similarly, French economist Dominique Plihon played a central role in founding the worldwide anti-globalisation organisation ATTAC. It initially campaigned for an international financial transactions tax, and then broadened its scope to include other progressive fiscal demands. The recent expansion of interest in the economics of inequality (stimulated by writers such as Thomas Piketty, Emannuel Saez and Gabriel Zucman) has aligned naturally with advocacy movements around the world fighting for fiscal and social policies (like wealth taxes) to redistribute income and wealth; these and other economists have offered important, personal support to those campaigns. Progressive advocacy movements aimed at challenging conventional monetary and financial policies have also been strengthened by the active participation of progressive economists. For example, in recent years activist organisations in various countries have mobilised in support of policy proposals advanced by versions of 'modern monetary theory'.

Many other social movements have also benefited mightily from the passion and knowledge of progressive economists. Many economists have spoken out strongly on matters of international relations, militarism and peace. For example, the organisation Economists for Peace and

Security (founded in 1989 as Economists Against the Arms Race) has enlisted dozens of prominent economists (including numerous Nobel Prize winners) to speak out against the economic waste and risks associated with militarism, nuclear weapons and global inequality. Similarly, many progressive economists (such as Ann Pettifor and Michael Hudson) have contributed to the global movement for a 'debt jubilee' to cancel onerous international and domestic debts.

Trade Unions. Most progressive economists place emphasis in their work on issues of employment, work and income distribution, paying special attention to the status and condition of working people. For that reason, there is a natural relevance of progressive economics to the goals and activities of trade unions. Since they represent the interests of working people at the point of production (in their workplaces), unions are directly engaged in many of the processes and struggles that directly concern progressive economic theorists, including the organisation of work, struggles over wages and distribution, technological change and innovation, labour market inequality and segmentation. Some progressive economists are critical of the practices of existing trade unions and industrial relations institutions, pointing to their limited ambitions and their potential misuse as agents of control. Most would agree, however, that unions are critical to winning better economic and social outcomes under existing capitalism and are a vital element in the constellation of forces that will be needed to bring about social change.

An outstanding example of the application of progressive economic ideas within a union setting is provided by Rudolf Meidner, a PhD economist who worked for the Swedish Trade Union Confederation (*Landsorganisationen i Sverige*, or LO). In the 1950s (jointly with Gösta Rehn, another economist at the LO) he helped design what came to be known as the Rehn–Meidner model: a vision of full employment labour market regulation and economic planning which emphasised narrow wage differentials, rapid technical innovation, and export competitiveness. Implemented in part through strong corporatist governance practices under social democratic governments at the time, this approach shaped Sweden's emergence as a high-income, relatively egalitarian society. Meidner later developed and advocated for a system of gradual socialisation of capital ownership through a system of wage-earner investment funds, eventually dubbed the Meidner Plan. Under this policy, workers would be 'compensated' for their restraint in wage demands through grants of equity shares in the companies they worked for, which would ultimately lead to majority worker ownership of major Swedish businesses. The system was eventually defeated by forceful opposition from employers and sections of the ruling Social Democratic party. Nevertheless, Meidner's life work exemplifies the potential for economists to apply a grand vision of economic and social transformation within the day-to-day work of trade unions to better the lives of their members.

Other progressive economists have played vital roles advancing trade union organisation and struggles in many countries. For example, in the USA, Ron Blackwell, Thea Lee and Tom Palley worked with the American Federation of Labor and Congress of Industrial Organizations (AFL–CIO) in recent years, supporting the labour movement's campaigns against neoliberal labour, fiscal and trade policies. Economist Sam Gindin was a crucial figure in the formation and radicalisation of the Canadian Auto Workers union (now called Unifor), which split from its US affiliate (the United Auto Workers) in the 1980s, and later charted important innovations in collective bargaining and worker activism.[3] Economist Hans-Jürgen Urban is a member of the leadership team of the influential and progressive German union, IG Metall, and has advised many of their campaigns – including for shorter working hours, skills training and environmental reforms. Economist Alec Erwin played a leadership role in the National Union of Miners and other union groupings in South Africa, both before and after liberation (later serving as a minister in the post-apartheid government).

Progressive Economics Associations. Progressive economists have banded together in associations to exchange ideas, facilitate shared research, and provide platforms for heterodox approaches to economic theory and policy. Dozens of such associations exist around the world: some focused on specific streams or subject matters in progressive thought, some focused on developing networks of like-minded economists within specific countries. The *Heterodox Economics Directory* (currently hosted by the Institute for Comprehensive Analysis of the Economy at Johannes Kepler University in Linz, Austria) includes a convenient catalogue of several dozen such associations, too numerous to list here (see Kapellar and Springholz 2020).

These associations aim to achieve a stronger presence and influence for heterodox economists within academic and professional communities (as discussed in Chapter 31 in this book). But many also work to facilitate engagement by their members in social change movements and initiatives, providing progressive economics training resources and opportunities for members of social movements, and participating in real-world policy debates and campaigns. For example, the Union for Radical Political Economics in the USA sponsors a speakers' bureau to connect willing members with organisations seeking progressive economic experts; it also circulates links to connect members and students with activist campaigns and movements of relevance to left economics. Canada's Progressive Economics Forum sponsors an annual summer school for undergraduate students and others interested in progressive economic ideas, with connections to social change movements.

Global networks among heterodox associations and their members have also been nurtured. For example, the International Confederation of Associations for Pluralism in Economics (ICAPE) connects many heterodox associations, aiming to facilitate more mutual awareness and cooperation among them through exchanging information and resources, undertaking joint conferences and other initiatives. As the organisation's mission statement gently puts it: 'Achieving productive discussion and debate across schools of economic thought is not a simple matter' (ICAPE 2020). The World Economics Association has a similar mission to build connections among individual progressive economists from around the world. Aiming to be a 'truly international, inclusive, pluralist, professional association' (WEA 2020), it publishes three regular journals – including the *Real World Economics Review*, an accessible and policy-relevant bulletin that is widely read in activist communities. Finally, the International Student Initiative for Pluralism in Economics links activist student committees in universities around the world, campaigning for more relevant and pluralist economics instruction in their respective institutions. Many of these student committees have also developed strong links with local social justice movements.

Progressive Economic Research Institutes. Research institutes and think tanks produce more accessible and timely economic research and policy proposals, which may be more easily mobilised in advocacy and political campaigns than formal academic research. Some progressive think tanks are located within universities, drawing on academic staff for research input and expertise. Others have no academic affiliation, receiving funding from sources such as foundations and granting agencies, philanthropists and individual donors, and trade unions. Because of their flexibility and independence, these progressive research institutes can nurture closer relationships with social movements, trade unions and other progressive political communities. Their publications, advocacy and commentary can be integrated effectively into progressive activist movements. Many of these institutes have formal relationships with social movements of various kinds (through funding channels, advisory or directorial boards, and other shared structures), further facilitating joint research, planning, and priority-setting.

Table 32.1   *Sample of progressive economics research institutes*

Country	Name	Location	Website
Global	Institute for New Economic Thinking	New York	ineteconomics.org
	'We conduct and commission research, convene forums for exchanging ideas, develop curricula, and nurture a global community of young scholars.'		
Global	World Institute for Development Economics Research	Helsinki	wider.unu.edu
	'Sustainable and inclusive development requires transformative changes […] in the structures of economies, in the state and institutions […], and in society itself.'		
Global	International Development Economics Associates	New Delhi	www.networkideas.org
	'A pluralist network of progressive economists across the world, engaged in research, teaching and dissemination of critical analyses of economic policy and development.'		
USA	Economic Policy Institute	Washington	epi.org
	'Believes every working person deserves a good job with fair pay, affordable health care, and retirement security.'		
USA	Center for Economic & Policy Research	Washington	cepr.net
	'Promote democratic debate on the most important economic and social issues that affect people's lives.'		
USA	Political Economy Research Institute	Amherst (U. of Massachusetts)	peri.umass.edu
	'Promotes human and ecological well-being through our original research; translate what we learn into workable policy proposals that are capable of improving life on our planet.'		
USA	Institute for Policy Studies	Washington	ips-dc.org
	'Dedicated to building a more equitable, ecologically sustainable, and peaceful society. In partnership with dynamic social movements, we turn transformative policy ideas into action.'		
USA	Schwartz Center for Economic Policy Analysis	New York (New School U.)	economicpolicyresearch.org
	Economic insights for a more equitable society.'		
USA	Center for American Progress	Washington	americanprogress.org
	'America should be a land of boundless opportunity, where people can climb the ladder of economic mobility […] to protect the planet and promote peace and shared global prosperity.'		
USA	Levy Economics Institute at Bard College	Annandale-on-Hudson	levyinstitute.org
	'Encourages diversity of opinion in the examination of economic policy issues while striving to transform ideological arguments into informed debate.'		
UK	Institute for Public Policy Research	London	ippr.org
	'Promote research into (and the publication of the useful results thereof) the education of the public in the economic, social and political sciences.'		
UK	Centre for Labour & Social Studies	London	Classonline.org.uk
	'Working to ensure policy is on the side of everyday people.'		
UK	New Economics Foundation	London	neweconomics.org
	'Aims to create a new economy that works for people and within environmental limits.'		

Country	Name	Location	Website
UK	Common Wealth	London	common-wealth.co.uk
	'Focus on six systemically vital areas where democratic ownership can transform how our economy operates and for whom.'		
UK	Political Economy Research Group	London (Kingston U.)	www.kingston.ac.uk/faculties/faculty-of-business-and -social-sciences/research/perg
	'Believe that effective demand, institutions and social conflict are of fundamental importance for the understanding of economic relationships and outcomes.'		
Europe	European Trade Union Institute	Brussels	www.etui.org
	'In the service of workers' interests at European level and of the strengthening of the social dimension of the European Union.'		
Germany	Hans Böckler Foundation	Düsseldorf	boeckler.de
	'Focuses on the improvement of life chances, on social justice and fair working and living conditions.'		
France	Les Économistes Atterrés	Paris	atterres.org
	'Reopen the space of possible policies and debate alternative [...] proposals, which restrain the power of finance and organise [...] progress of European economic and social systems.'		
Austria	Institute for Comprehensive Analysis of the Economy	Linz (Johannes Kepler U.)	www.jku.at/en/institute-for-comprehensive-analysis-of -the-economy
	'Investigating the causes and consequences of the economic and financial crisis as well as its cultural and political implications.'		
Netherlands	Transnational Institute	Amsterdam	tni.org/en
	'Committed to building a just, democratic and sustainable planet; unique nexus between social movements, engaged scholars and policymakers.'		
Canada	Canadian Centre for Policy Alternatives	Ottawa	www.policyalternatives.ca
	'Independent, non-partisan research institute concerned with issues of social, economic and environmental justice.'		
Australia	Australia Institute	Canberra	australiainstitute.org.au
	'Publishes research that contributes to a more just, sustainable and peaceful society.'		
Thailand	Focus on the Global South	Bangkok	focusweb.org
	'An activist think tank [...] providing analysis and building alternatives for just social, economic and political change.'		
South Africa	Centre for Civil Society	Durban (U. KwaZulu-Natal)	ccs.ukzn.ac.za
	'Advance socio-economic and environmental justice by developing critical knowledge about, for and in dialogue with civil society through teaching, research and publishing.'		

Source: Author's compilation from organisational websites.

Table 32.1 provides a non-exhaustive but representative list of some of the more prominent progressive economic research institutes in several countries – including short excerpts from their respective mission statements.[4]

Formal Politics and Government. Many progressive economists engage directly and eagerly with political parties, electoral campaigns, and government policymaking. Indeed, efforts by progressive economists to shape the course of political history are visible throughout the history of left economic thought. Early utopian socialists, for example, such as Robert Owen and Étienne Cabet, worked to implement their visions of cooperative or intentional communities in practice, through political reforms and even establishing their own experimental communities. Marx and Engels, of course, helped found the international communist movement; they combined political activism with theoretical work throughout their careers. Subsequent socialist economists and political economists of various persuasions – such as Rosa Luxemburg and Edward Bernstein – also worked to build socialist political parties and campaign for power. In subsequent socialist revolutions, economists played key roles in experiments with economic planning, engaging in ongoing debates over development strategies, sector balances, the role of markets, and other topics. Examples include Yevgeni Preobrazhensky in the early USSR; Michał Kalecki, Oskar Lange, and Edward Lipinsky in Poland; and József Bognár in Hungary.

In the advanced capitalist economies, heterodox economists have also regularly engaged in politics and policymaking. Keynes and his colleagues helped design the post-war macroeconomic and financial order, including at the international level. Economist William Beveridge defined the main features of the post-war welfare state in the UK, and other Keynesians, such as Nicholas Kaldor, played vital roles in charting UK economic policy through the 1970s. Other left economists were active in the opposition Labour Party after Margaret Thatcher came to power, including Meghnad Desai and John Eatwell. In the USA, progressive economists such as John Kenneth Galbraith, Alvin Hansen and Wassily Leontief designed wartime planning systems and later developed post-war 'mixed economy' strategies and policies. Progressive economists were influential in post-war economic and social policy in other industrial countries, such as Gunnar Myrdal in Sweden, Jan Tinbergen in the Netherlands, and François Perroux in France.

Revolutions and national liberation in developing countries opened many opportunities for input and influence from progressive economists. For example, left economists from a rich variety of intellectual and political traditions played a critical role in the anti-apartheid struggle in South Africa, including advising the subsequent ANC government. Economists from both within South Africa (such as Vella Pillay, Vishnu Padayachee and Alan Hirsch) worked with international economists (such as Lawrence Harris, Ben Fine, John Sender and John Loxley) in formulating and debating economic policy in the post-apartheid era, in forums such as the Macroeconomic Research Group and the National Economic Forum (Freund 2013; Bond 2014; Padayachee and van Niekerk 2019). Of course, debate over the policy choices made in South Africa continues, as does the struggle over South Africa's future direction – and numerous progressive economists are active participants in those debates. Elsewhere in developing countries, prominent economists have played key roles advising and designing policy with revolutionary or progressive governments, including Jomo Kwame Sundaram, Alice Amsden, Bill Gibson and Lance Taylor.

Left-wing economic ideas – and left-wing economists – have been especially influential in Latin American debates and policymaking. The UN's Economic Commission for Latin America (CEPAL) exerted a strong intellectual influence on economic policy throughout that continent in the post-war era, projecting the analysis and policy recommendations of Raul Prebisch and other structuralist thinkers into government policy in several countries. More recently, economists have been key figures in progressive governments that came to power in several Latin American countries after the turn of the century – the so-called 'pink tide'. One government was led by a PhD economist, Rafael Correa, who was elected President of Ecuador in 2006 on a socialist platform and served for over a decade. His government undertook far-reaching health, education and redistribution measures (his successor, Lenin Moreno, tried to prosecute Correa and reversed many of his policies). Another left economist, Fander Falconi, served as Foreign Affairs Minister under Correa (and Education Minister under

Moreno). Brazilian economist Nelson Barbosa received his PhD from the heterodox New School for Social Research in New York, later serving as Minister of Finance and Minister of Planning in the Workers' Party government of Dilma Rousseff. Economist and activist Axel Kicillof served as Minister of Economy in the government of Cristina Fernández de Kirchner in Argentina, and is presently the Governor of Buenos Aires.

Modern left political parties continue to draw on the ideas, advice, and active support of progressive economists in their efforts to build popular support, contest elections, and mobilise power. For example, Bernie Sanders' insurgent campaigns for US president were advised by several progressive economists, including Robert Pollin and Stephanie Kelton. Several left economists participated in Jeremy Corbyn's policy team in the UK, including James Meadway, Mariana Mazzucato and Richard Murphy – contributing to the Labour Party's ambitious 2017 and 2019 economic platforms (advanced by then Shadow Chancellor of the Exchequer John McDonnell). Economist Francisco Louçã helped found Portugal's Left Bloc party (in 1999), which later participated in coalition governments with the larger Socialist Party. Economist Yanis Varoufakis was a key figure in the government formed by the left Greek party Syriza and served for a short time as Greece's Finance Minister in 2015 (at the height of the Euro debt crisis); he now serves as a member of parliament with the MeRA25 party.

These efforts by progressive economists of varying stripes to put their ideas into real-world political and policy practice have confronted daunting obstacles, first and foremost the vested interest of existing elites to preserve the current economic order. Moreover, it must be said that debates among these various left economists are often as fierce as their debates with orthodox thinkers. Yet, in various ways and in vastly differing circumstances, they all reflect a common goal of harnessing the power of progressive economic ideas in the service of a more equitable, humane, and sustainable future.

A CASE STUDY: PUTTING ECONOMIC IDEAS INTO ACTION

As the preceding survey has illustrated, numerous progressive economists have contributed directly to real-world movements and campaigns for progressive economic and social change. A more detailed case study can provide further insight, illustrating the importance of several of the insights and 'best practices' enunciated earlier. The case selected here is the Institute for Research on Labor and Employment (IRLE) at the University of California, Berkeley.

The IRLE is a multidisciplinary policy research centre; its publications and policy engagements reflect a strong economic bent, and many of its central figures and leaders have been economists. Economist Michael Reich was its director from 2004 to 2015, succeeded by economist Jesse Rothstein and then by economist Steven Raphael in 2020. IRLE's general mission is to 'promote better understanding of the conditions, policies, and institutions that affect the well-being of workers and their families and communities, [and] [...] inform public debate with hard evidence about inequality, the economy, and the nature of work' (IRLE 2020). The Institute (along with a sister institute at UCLA in Los Angeles) was originally founded at the end of the Second World War, with funding from the California state government. Its initial mission was to promote research and training in industrial relations, as the US economy became more acquainted with the practice of collective bargaining in the wake of Wagner Act reforms and a historic post-war increase in unionisation. Indeed, the centres were initially called the Institutes of Industrial Relations. Their names were changed in the 1990s, reflecting their broadening interests as well as the precipitous decline in US unionisation during the neoliberal era.

The UC Berkeley branch of the IRLE houses several specialised projects and sub-centres. One is the Center for Labor Research and Education (known as the Labor Center), which undertakes cooperative initiatives with regional trade unions – including union leadership and membership education, research and policy engagement. The Labor Center's close ties with the union movement have facilitated productive cooperation and engagement on the part of the broader IRLE with various labor campaigns and struggles in California, and nationally.

Like other university-based research centres, IRLE works to strengthen academic output and achievement – including sponsoring conferences, grant applications, supporting graduate students, and so on. For present purposes, however, the unique aspect of the Institute's work is its sustained and effective engagement with a range of current policy debates and labour and social justice campaigns. The collective expertise represented by the Institute's staff, affiliated academics (particularly from UC Berkeley's economics department) and students has been a powerful influence in numerous grass-roots campaigns and movements for labor and economic reforms. The issues addressed by ILRE over the years include the impact of ordinances to improve labour standards at the municipal level (Reich et al. 2014); the feasibility of policies to ensure healthcare coverage for low-wage workers (Flores and Lucia 2015); and prospects for job-creation in 'green' industries (Zabin 2020). A particular example of the Institute's influence has been its applied work on the economics of minimum wage ordinances (including at the sub-national and regional levels), which has been globally influential in shifting both economic theory and policy on this matter (see, for example, Jacobs et al. 2015). Most recently, the Institute's research on the economics of the ride-share industry (Reich 2020) has been referenced widely in campaigns to win employee status for gig workers (at platform businesses such as Uber and Lyft).

Staff and affiliates at the IRLE are committed to conducting their scholarly research to high academic standards, independent from political, labour and social justice campaigns. This approach is crucial because of regular efforts by conservative political leaders, business lobbyists, and other union opponents to discredit and defund the Institute and its centres and activities. For example, Arnold Schwarzenegger, then Governor of California, vetoed funding entirely for both the Berkeley and UCLA Institutes in the 2000s; a strong campaign by academics and community activists subsequently won back state financial support. The Institute's scholarly independence and strong public reputation help to insulate its work against these external attacks, and also enhance its value as an influential source of data, analysis and policy innovation cited by union and community campaigns around the world. IRLE affiliates participate actively in policy debates and dialogues, including as invited experts before inquiries and commissions at all levels of government. The Institute's effective work has led to requests for research on related issues from all over the USA and other countries.

While social change campaigns in the San Francisco area and other parts of the USA have benefited from the research, expertise and engagement of the IRLE, the relationships between the Institute and regional labour and social justice movements are mutually beneficial. For scholars working within the Institute, these partnerships open opportunities for access to research populations, data collection and policy engagement. This collaboration and two-way flow of information helps affiliated economists to design their future research agendas and identify relevant and timely policy topics – knowing that their work will be taken up in concrete ways by movements working to realise progressive policies.

In sum, the ongoing work of the IRLE and its affiliated academics is an encouraging example of how a group of progressive economists can effectively and respectfully develop strong, cooperative relationships with on-the-ground social movements – fighting to demand and win the policy reforms which progressive economists help to devise, and dream of realising. This productive collaboration has made a notable difference in strengthening unions and social justice organisations in California in recent years, contributing to an evident progressive shift in regional and state politics. It provides an illustration of the tremendous potential for progressive economists to contribute to real-world social change. Economists in other settings (including those outside of universities) will find their own specific ways of organising that work, but the IRLE experience shows what can be done. It reflects a successful application of core principles of mutual respect, communication, education and joint advocacy that can guide successful collaboration between progressive economists and activists in any situation.

CONCLUSION

This chapter has considered some of the challenges and pitfalls encountered in achieving stronger engagement by progressive economists in social change movements and campaigns, some best practices to keep in mind in undertaking this collaboration, and examples of ways in which progressive economists have made important contributions to progressive social and political change. This review is not comprehensive: there are innumerable other progressive economists who have devoted their ideas, their reputations, their labour, and in some cases their lives to winning real-world improvements in work, well-being, equality and sustainability. The goal here is merely to indicate the breadth and diversity of the common interest between progressive economics and social change movements – and to highlight successful examples of how that connection can be made.

After all, the historic role of progressive social change movements is to express the demands of the exploited and the oppressed, and to mobilise them into fighting for and winning a better world. Relevant, respectful academic research, analysis and expertise can help progressive movements fulfil that mission. Progressive economists – motivated by their own hopes and dreams of a better world as well as by their desire to make a personal contribution to its construction – can be important allies in that struggle. As progressive economists continue to advance the frontiers of our understanding of the failures of the existing economic order, and how it can be changed, we should keep one eye on the importance of mobilising that knowledge in the real-world campaigns and struggles that are critical to winning the change we seek.

NOTES

1. This chapter uses the terms progressive, heterodox, and left economics interchangeably, acknowledging the nuances of different meanings and applications.
2. Linking curriculum and pedagogy to the experience and existing knowledge of course participants is a core principle of popular or liberatory education, as enunciated (for example) by Horton and Freire (1990).
3. After his career in the union, Gindin later published many important political-economy writings, including with his frequent collaborator political-economist Leo Panitch (e.g. Gindin and Panitch 2013).

4.   This sample of progressive economic research centres is disproportionately composed of think tanks from industrial countries, reflecting the greater resources and hence consistent presence that research institutes in those countries can mobilise. In addition to those listed in Table 32.1, many other progressive think tanks have been established in the global South; some are surveyed by Carroll (2014). The *Heterodox Economics Directory* (Kapellar and Springholz 2020) provides a broader catalogue that includes several other progressive economic think tanks.

REFERENCES

Bond, P. (2014) *Elite Transition: From Apartheid to Neoliberalism in South Africa*, London: Pluto Press.

Carroll, W. (2014) 'Alternative Policy Groups and Transnational Counter-Hegemonic Struggle', in Y. Atasoy (ed.), *Global Economic Crisis and the Politics of Diversity*, Basingstoke: Palgrave Macmillan, pp. 259–84.

Cho!ces: A Coalition for Social Justice (1998) *Show Us the Money! The Politics and Process of Alternative Budgets*, Winnipeg: Arbeiter Ring.

Daly, H. (2014) *From Uneconomic Growth to a Steady-State Economy*, Cheltenham, UK and Northampton, MA, USA: Edward Elgar Publishing.

Flores, M.J. and Lucia, L. (2015) 'Maximizing Health Insurance Enrollment through Covered California during Work and Life Transitions', Policy Brief, Berkeley: Institute for Research on Labor and Employment.

Freund, W. (2013) 'Swimming Against the Tide: The Macro-Economic Research Group in the South African Transition 1991–94', *Review of African Political Economy*, **40** (138), pp. 519–36.

Gindin, S. and Panitch, L. (2013) *The Making of Global Capitalism: The Political Economy of American Empire*, London: Verso.

Horton, M. and Freire, P. (1990) *We Make the Road by Walking: Conversations on Education and Social Change*, Philadelphia, PA: Temple University Press.

ICAPE [International Confederation of Associations for Pluralism in Economics] (2020) 'Statement of Purpose', accessed 20.07.2021 at: https://icape.org/.

International Student Initiative for Pluralism in Economics (n.d.), accessed 20.07.2021 at: http://www.isipe.net/.

IRLE [Institute for Research on Labor and Employment] (2020) 'About IRLE', accessed 30.12.2020 at: https://irle.berkeley.edu/about/.

Jacobs, K., Perry, I.E. and MacGillvary, J. (2015) 'The High Public Cost of Low Wages', Research Brief, Berkeley: Institute for Research on Labor and Employment.

Kapellar, J. and Springholz, F. (eds) (2020) 'Heterodox Economics Directory', Linz: Institute for Comprehensive Analysis of the Economy, accessed 20.07.2021 at: http://heterodoxnews.com/directory/.

M4BL (2021) 'Economic Justice', accessed 20.07.2021 at: https://m4bl.org/policy-platforms/economic-justice/.

Padayachee, V. and van Niekerk, R. (2019) *Shadow of Liberation: Contestation and Compromise in the Economic and Social Policy of the African National Congress, 1943–1996*, Johannesburg: Wits University Press.

Quiggin, J. (2020) *Getting Off Coal: Economic and Social Policies to Manage the Phase-out of Thermal Coal in Australia*, Canberra: Australia Institute.

Reich, M. (2020) 'Pay, Passengers and Profits: Effects of Employee Status for California TNC Drivers', Working Paper #107–20, Berkeley: Institute for Research on Labor and Employment.

Reich, M., Jacobs, K. and Dietz, M. (eds) (2014) *When Mandates Work: Raising Labor Standards at the Local Level*, Berkeley: University of California Press.

Serieux, J., Chernomas, R. and Hudson, I. (2021) 'John Loxley: Radical Academic Activist', *Development and Change*, **52** (4), pp. 965–87.

Stanford, J. (2008) 'Radical Economics and Social Change Movements: Strengthening the Links between Academics and Activists', *Review of Radical Political Economics*, **40** (3), pp. 205–19.

Stanford, J. (2015) 'Toward an Activist Pedagogy in Heterodox Economics: The Case of Trade Union Economics Training', *Journal of Australian Political Economy*, **75**, pp. 11–34.

Stern, N. (2007) *The Economics of Climate Change: The Stern Review*, London: HM Treasury.

WEA [World Economics Association] (2020), accessed 20.07.2021 at: https://www.worldeconomicsa ssociation.org/.

Wilhelmy, S. (2013) 'Participatory Budgeting Worldwide: Updated Version, Study #25', Bonn: Service for Development Initiatives, accessed 20.07.2021 at: https://estudogeral.uc.pt/bitstream/10316/42267/ 1/Participatory%20Budgeting%20Worldwide.pdf.

Young, B., Bakker, I. and Elson, D. (eds) (2011) *Questioning Financial Governance from a Feminist Perspective*, Abingdon: Routledge.

Zabin, C. (2020) *Putting California on the High Road: A Jobs and Climate Action Plan for 2030*, Berkeley: Institute for Research on Labor and Employment.

Index